SAFETY SYMBOLS

SAFETY SYMBOLS	HAZARD	PRECAUTION	REMEDY
Disposal	Special disposal required	Dispose of wastes as directed by your teacher.	Ask your teacher how to dispose of laboratory materials.
Biological	Organisms that can harm humans	Avoid breathing in or skin contact with organisms. Wear dust mask or gloves. Wash hands thoroughly.	Notify your teacher if you suspect contact.
Extreme Temperature	Objects that can burn skin by being too cold or too hot	Use proper protection when handling.	Go to your teacher for first aid.
Sharp Object	Use of tools or glassware that can easily puncture or slice skin	Practice common sense behavior and follow guidelines for use of the tool.	Go to your teacher for first aid.
Fumes	Potential danger from smelling fumes	Must have good ventilation and never smell fumes directly.	Leave foul area and notify your teacher immediately.
Electrical	Possible danger from electrical shock or burn	Double-check setup with instructor. Check condition of wires and apparatus.	Do not attempt to fix electrical problems. Notify your teacher immediately.
Irritant	Substances that can irritate your skin or mucous membranes	Wear dust mask or gloves. Practice extra care when handling these materials.	Go to your teacher for first aid.
Chemical	Substances (acids and bases) that can react with and destroy tissue and other materials	Wear goggles and an apron.	Immediately flush with water and notify your teacher.
Toxic	Poisonous substance	Follow your teacher's instructions. Always wash hands thoroughly after use.	Go to your teacher for first aid.
Fire	Flammable and combustible materials may burn if exposed to an open flame or spark	Avoid flames and heat sources. Be aware of locations of fire safety equipment.	Notify your teacher immediately. Use fire safety equipment if necessary.

Eye Safety
This symbol appears when a danger to eyes exists.

Clothing Protection
This symbol appears when substances could stain or burn clothing.

Animal Safety
This symbol appears whenever live animals are studied and the safety of the animals and students must be ensured.

North Carolina
Case Studies

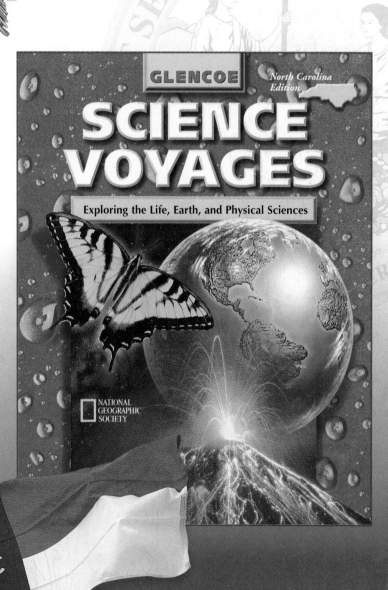

GLENCOE
North Carolina Edition

SCIENCE VOYAGES

Exploring the Life, Earth, and Physical Sciences

NATIONAL GEOGRAPHIC SOCIETY

 Glencoe McGraw-Hill

Grade 6

North Carolina

Case Studies for Grade 6

TABLE OF CONTENTS

What are the North Carolina Case Studies?   **NC3**
How to use the North Carolina Case Studies   **NC3**
The North Carolina Advisory Board   **NC3**

Competency Goal 1
The learner will build an understanding of the lithosphere.

Case Study 1   Saving the Cape Hatteras Lighthouse   **NC4**

Competency Goal 2
The learner will investigate the characteristics of matter and energy flow through an ecosystem.

Case Study 2   North Carolina's Carnivorous Plants   **NC10**
Case Study 3   Introduced Species   **NC16**

Competency Goal 3
The learner will build an understanding of the Solar System.

Case Study 4   Exploring Space from Earth   **NC21**

Competency Goal 4
The learner will investigate the characteristics of energy transfer.

Case Study 5   Nuclear Power in North Carolina   **NC26**

North Carolina Science Sites   **NC30**

What are the North Carolina Case Studies?

Welcome to Science Voyages for North Carolina. Do you like to find out what makes things work? Perhaps you just like to spend time fishing or watching birds. Whatever your interest, you will come to know that science is an exciting subject that has something for everyone. The case studies on the following pages will help you learn about science in your home state. They also will help you achieve the understanding of the standards for science that are listed in the North Carolina Standard Course of Study for Grade 6.

Science—what it is, how science is done, and the effects that scientific developments have on your life—is discussed in the articles and illustrations on the following pages. The Case Studies, and Inquiry Activities that go with them, have been selected to reinforce the Competency Goals and objectives of science for your grade level.

How to Use the North Carolina Case Studies

As you read each Case Study, notice that it is a topic about North Carolina. Notice too, at the beginning of each article, that it is correlated to the North Carolina Standard Course of Study for science. Each Case Study has one or more Inquiry Activities. These activities will help you understand each Science Competency Goal better and help you remember its importance.

At the end of each Case Study, there are references to chapters in your textbook where you will study similar concepts.

The North Carolina Advisory Board

Dr. Karen Dawkins
North Carolina
State University

Janet Doughty
H.J. MacDonald
Middle School

Bonita Long
Mount Pleasant
Middle School

Dr. Gerry Madrazo
University of North Carolina

Cherlye Moody
Duke School for Children

Rachel Russ
South View High School

Dr. Josephine Wallace
University of North Carolina

Saving the Cape Hatteras Lighthouse

COMPETENCY GOAL 1
The learner will build an understanding of the lithosphere.

Saving the Cape Hatteras Lighthouse

The lithosphere is the more rigid outer layer of Earth that includes the crust and upper mantle. The outermost layer of Earth, where soil-forming processes occur, is sometimes called the pedosphere. Serious problems can occur when beaches, soil layers, and other areas erode. In the following discussion, this problem will be explored.

A popular summer place is the Cape Hatteras National Seashore on the coast of North Carolina. This was the first national seashore park in the United States. The park is part of the Outer Banks, which is a long, narrow, curved sandbar that includes three islands. One of the islands is Hatteras Island.

At the southern tip of Hatteras Island is the most well-known lighthouse in North America—the Cape Hatteras Lighthouse. Its distinctive black-and-white, candy-cane design has made the lighthouse a popular landmark of the Carolina coastline. For many years, the tallest brick lighthouse in North America has been photographed, painted, and visited by thousands of people. Because of its historical importance to the region and the nation, the lighthouse and its buildings have been placed on the National Register of Historic Places.

A View from the Top

If you want to get a good view of the islands, visit the lighthouse and climb the 269 steps to the top. High above the beach, you can see a panoramic view of long stretches of beaches, sand dunes, marshes, and woodlands that go on for many kilometers. When you peer out over the ocean, you will see a helicopter platform rising out of the water. The platform was built on a shoal about 36 km

Figure NC1-1 This view of the Cape Hatteras Lighthouse before it was moved in 1999, shows how much the shoreline had been eroded.

Figure NC1-2 An aerial view of the Cape Hatteras Lighthouse shows the low-lying barrier island on which the lighthouse is built.

offshore. The shoal is an accumulation of shifting sand on the bottom of the ocean floor. In some places, the shoal is less than 10 m below water level at low tide. This shoal, called the Diamond Shoals, is potentially dangerous to ships. For hundreds of years, hundreds of shipwrecks have taken place at or near this location.

To protect shipping vessels, the present Cape Hatteras Lighthouse was built in 1870 and is more than 60 m high and weighs about 4700 tons. The lighthouse served as a navigational aid for sailing ships rounding the treacherous Diamond Shoals. The beacon light warned sea captains and their crews of the dangerous waters and prevented many ships from being grounded or sunk on the shoals.

Soil Erosion

The Cape Hatteras National Seashore is comprised of a series of barrier islands that are sandwiched between the Atlantic Ocean on one side and Pamlico Sound on the other side. The barrier islands, stretching for about 100 km, help protect the lowlands of eastern North Carolina from violent storms and massive waves.

However, for hundreds of years mechanical weathering and erosion have taken their toll on the islands. Fierce winds and heavy waves driven by violent storms and hurricanes have caused major erosion problems. As a result of these forces, the barrier islands have migrated westward toward Pamlico Sound. This migration occurs as storm-driven ocean waves wash completely over the islands. The water carries and deposits the sand sediments on the

Figure NC1-3 The new location (cleared area in the upper right) can be seen from the keeper's walk at the top of the lighthouse.

Pamlico side of the island. Because of this migration, barrier islands are among the most unstable landforms on Earth. Therefore, stationary buildings, such as the Cape Hatteras Lighthouse, are threatened by these conditions.

Inquiry Activity

Objective 1.03
Explain how humans can reduce the impact of erosion on Earth's pedosphere. Include the human impact on soils and sediments in coastal environments, and other developed areas.

Soil Erosion Threatens Lighthouse

When the lighthouse was built, it was situated 460 m from the shoreline. By 1919, the ocean had advanced to within 100 m of the tower. In 1997, the lighthouse was about 49 m from the eroding coastline. Erosion-control projects have been used at the lighthouse site to protect the structure. As an example, in 1969, the U.S. Navy built a series of groins (seawalls) that were placed perpendicular to the shore. The groins helped slow down the erosion. After a violent storm in the early 1980s, volunteers and citizens used sandbags, sand fences, and even synthetic seaweed to protect the lighthouse. All of these activities helped, but they did not stop the shoreline from moving closer to the lighthouse. Something more had to be done to save the lighthouse.

Objective 1.01

Why is soil erosion a serious problem? Research in the library and with other resources the physical and biological processes that form soil. Include why soil is important to humans and how long it takes soil profiles to form. What other factors besides time affect soil formation?

What can be done?

The National Park Service makes decisions on how to preserve lighthouses. So, in 1987, the National Park Service asked the National Academy of Sciences to study and provide advice on how to save the Cape Hatteras Lighthouse. Meetings were held to evaluate and develop several options for preserving the lighthouse from the invading Atlantic Ocean. Everyone agreed that the major objective was to preserve the Cape Hatteras Lighthouse so that future generations would understand and appreciate the nation's maritime heritage. However, the debate was about how to do that.

Figure NC1-4 These sea oats growing on the coastal dunes in North Carolina stabilize the dunes and reduce erosion.

Keep It Where It Is...

One local group favored keeping the lighthouse in its present location. They reported that it would cost too much to move the lighthouse and it could be damaged during the move to another site. Their recommendations included adding more sand to the beach and constructing another groin. The groin would trap a portion of the sand that is moved by the offshore current. The buildup of sand would provide a wider and more protected beach in front of the lighthouse.

Another suggestion was to use underwater groins made of elongated bags filled with concrete and positioned on heavy mats. Functioning like speed bumps, the underground groins would slow the movement of water currents, creating deposits of sand that would build up the beach and eventually cover the groins completely. Since the water passes over the groins rather than around the ends, there is no erosion to the adjacent shoreline. However, this method was never used on the barrier islands.

...Or Move It

The National Park Service and others agreed that relocation was the best option to save the lighthouse. Their plan called for moving the lighthouse about 900 m to a

Figure NC1-5 The Block Island Lighthouse in Rhode Island was successfully moved in 1993.

new site. They reported that other lighthouses have been moved successfully. As an example, moving it saved the Highland Lighthouse on Massachusetts's Cape Cod. This lighthouse was only 30 m from the edge of a cliff when it was moved about 140 m to a more secure place. If the Highland Lighthouse was not moved, experts agree that the landmark would have toppled into the ocean within three or four years. The lighthouse on Block Island, Rhode Island, shown in **Figure NC1-5,** was also moved to a new location. Structural engineers experienced in moving similar buildings indicate that the Cape Hatteras Island Lighthouse could be moved without significant risk to the structure.

Because the lighthouse would be placed further back from the beach, the structure could be preserved for a long period of time from the advancing soil and beach erosion. The group also believed that there would be a minimum of ecological damage during the move and at the new site. Relocating the lighthouse would also reinforce state and government policies of allowing the natural processes of beach erosion to continue.

After much debate, a decision was made by the National Park Service to move the lighthouse. In 1998, the National Park Service received government funding to move the Cape Hatteras Lighthouse. The lighthouse was relocated 2900 feet over a period of 23 days in the summer of 1999.

Inquiry Activity

Objective 1.02

What is a soil profile? Find an area where a hole or cut has been made into the soil, at least 1 m to 1.5 m in depth. As a class, describe the features of the soil profile and make a labeled drawing of the profile in your Science Journal. Include a description of the layers, or horizons, in the soil, the color, the texture, the amount and type of organic material; the pH, the temperature; and any soil structures.

Going Further

To learn more about the lithosphere, see:

1.01 Chapter 3, Section 1, Landforms
Chapter 4, Section 2, Igneous and Sedimentary Rock
Chapter 4, Section 3, Metamorphic Rock and the Rock Cycle
Chapter 5, Section 1, Weathering
Chapter 5, Section 2, Soil
Chapter 6, Section 1, Gravity
Chapter 6, Section 2, Glaciers
Chapter 6, Section 3, Wind
Chapter 7, Section 2, Using Land
Chapter 7, Section 3, Recycling
Chapter 8, Section 2, Seedless Plants
Chapter 9, Section 2, Plant Processes

1.02 Chapter 5, Section 2, Soil
Chapter 6, Section 3, Wind
Chapter 7, Section 2, Using Land
1.03 Chapter 1, Section 1, How Science Works
Chapter 3, Section 1, Landforms
Chapter 5, Section 2, Soil
Chapter 6, Section 1, Gravity
Chapter 6, Section 2, Glaciers
Chapter 7, Section 1, Population Impact on the Environment
Chapter 7, Section 2, Using Land
Chapter 7, Section 3, Recycling
Chapter 8, Section 1, Characteristics of Plants

North Carolina's Carnivorous Plants

COMPETENCY GOAL 2
The learner will investigate the characteristics of matter and energy flow through an ecosystem.

Most plants obtain the nutrients and the energy needed for their life processes from the soil and the sun. In the following discussion, plants that obtain some of their energy and matter in other ways will be explored.

West of Raleigh and close to Chapel Hill is the North Carolina Botanical Garden. The garden contains a collection of plants that reflect the vegetation of the various regions of North Carolina. Near the visitor's center is a notable collection of the carnivorous plants found within the state.

A Pattern for Survival

Several carnivorous plants grow in North Carolina. Venus's-flytraps, pitcher plants, sundews, butterworts, and bladderworts can be found in the sandy, boggy soil in coastal areas. This soil is low in nitrogen and the carnivorous nature of these plants is an adaptation to the nutrient-poor soils in which they grow. To obtain enough nutrients, especially nitrogen, these plants

Figure NC2-1 Shown here is the extensive pitcher plant display at the North Carolina Botanical Garden in Chapel Hill.

have evolved the ability to extract nutrients from the flesh of other organisms. The adaptations for this ability include sticky, flypaper-like surfaces, spring-like trap-doors, and pitfalls leading to vats filled with digestive enzymes. The trapping mechanisms of these plants are either passive or active. Passive traps involve no movement to trap their prey; active traps move.

Pitcher Plants

Pitcher plants get their name from the shape of their leaves. Like a pitcher, the leaves are bowl-shaped at the bottom and narrow at the top. Glands on the outside of the green leaf secrete nectar, a sweet-tasting liquid that attracts many kinds of insects. The end of the leaf forms a hood that curves over the plant's mouth providing shade and keeping rainwater from filling the leaf.

Figure NC2-3 There are six different varieties of pitcher plants that live in North Carolina. This example is the *Sarracenia leucophylla* variety.

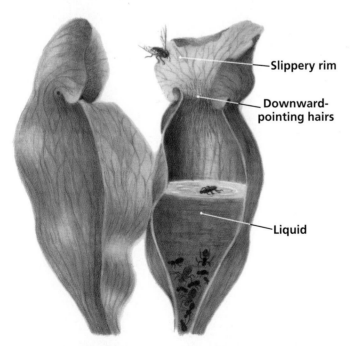

Figure NC2-2 The slippery outer rim and the downward-pointing hairs trap the insects in the pitcher plant. The liquid contains digestive enzymes that break down the insects.

Slippery rim

Downward-pointing hairs

Liquid

The underside of the hood is covered with hairs that point downward. An insect clings to these hairs as it moves down the leaf to get more nectar. At the mouth, the hairs stop and a waxy substance makes the walls of the leaf slippery. The insect slides down into the bowl-shaped bottom where digestive enzymes have collected. In some species, the digestive enzymes are strong and in others, they consist mostly of water. Bacteria that live on the insects help break them down.

Of the nine known, native, North American species of pitcher plants, six are found in North Carolina. The odor of decaying insects in pitcher plants is foul to humans but attracts other insects that feed on dead organisms.

Objective 2.03

Explain how the activity of the pitcher plant and an insect is an example of a predator-prey relationship.

Trigger hairs

Venus's-flytraps

The Venus's-flytrap lives within a 200-kilometer radius of Wilmington, North Carolina. It is found in bogs, or savannas and traps ants, beetles, spiders, and flies. It has sticky leaves at the end of its broad, flat, green stalk. The active trap is a specialized leaf blade with oval halves that are hinged along the middle. Trigger hairs on the inside of each leaf half cause the trap to close. The edge of the trap has a row of long stiff spines. Its upper surface is bright-red to pale-green in color and has glands that produce digestive enzymes.

When an insect gets between the two halves of the trap and touches any two of six trigger hairs, the halves silently snap shut in less than one second. The insect

Figure NC2-4 The Venus's-flytrap has sticky leaves. When an insect lands on the leaves, trigger hairs cause the hinged leaves to close. This traps the insect.

Figure NC2-5 This Venus's-flytrap is the variety *Dionaea muscipula.*

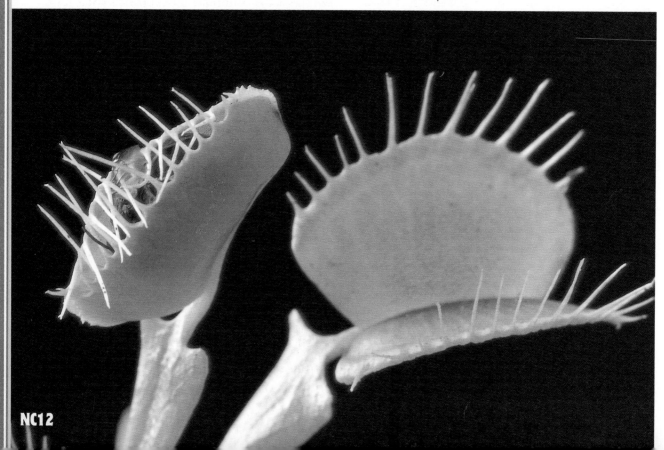

Figure NC2-6 The sundew attracts insects with a scent and then traps them with a sticky substance on the leaves.

struggles for an hour or so as the tiny area fills with enzymes that digest the insect. The trap absorbs the liquid food and reopens in three days to two weeks. A trap wears out after one to four insects are consumed, and then the whole leaf turns black and dies. The plant continues to grow new leaves with fresh traps.

Sundews

Sundews are beautiful, carnivorous plants that are often difficult to see because larger plants obscure them. At least five species grow in North Carolina. The roundleaf sundew covers about 9 centimeters and has a pink or white flower. Tiny, red tentacles cover each of its green leaves. A gland at the end of each tentacle produces a sticky substance that glistens in the sun and looks like dew. This is how the plant gets its name.

The sundew's deceptive appearance and attractive smell draw flies and other insects to its leaves. When an insect lands on a leaf, it becomes trapped in the sticky liquid. The more the insect struggles, the more liquid is given off by the gland at the tip of each tentacle. When the prey is trapped, the plant curls over its entire leaf in order to produce digestive enzymes. The leaf stays curled over for four or five days as the plant digests the insect. The leaf then unfolds to catch another insect.

Inquiry Activity

Objective 2.04
What might be the consequences for carnivorous plants if they were deprived of their insect-food supply? Give reasons for your answer.

Figure NC2-7 The horned bladderwort, *Utricularia cornuta*, is one of the many carnivorous plants that live in North Carolina.

Figure NC2-8 This butterwort, *Pinguicula sp.*, is found in the Croation National Forest in North Carolina.

Bladderworts

Bladderworts are tiny plants that usually live in water. Part of the plant is a long, thin stalk with a small flower on top that grows above the surface of the water. Underneath the water surface, the plant looks like tree roots with tiny sacs or bladders. The sacs trap insects that provide nourishment for the whole plant.

While waiting to catch an insect, the sac is flat. When a water insect brushes the hairs around the opening of the sac, the sides of the sac quickly expand. Water rushing into the sac carries the insect with it. Most bladderworts digest small insects within 30 minutes and large insects within two hours.

Butterworts

Butterworts, also called bog violets, live in warm, marshy areas and produce flowers that look like violets. Their leaves are small and fleshy with edges that curl toward the center. The leaves are covered with a musty-smelling substance that feels greasy, or buttery, and attracts insects.

Butterworts, as shown in **Figure NC2-8,** trap tiny insects such as gnats and small ants. When the insect becomes trapped on the greasy surface of the leaves, digestive juices come out of specialized leaf cells and the leaves start to curl. It takes a butterwort about one day to close completely and another day to digest the insect.

Protecting Carnivorous Plants

Sundews and butterworts are plentiful in North Carolina but Venus's-flytraps, pitcher plants, and some bladderworts are either endangered or threatened species. Poaching is one reason for the scarcity of Venus's-flytraps. Another reason is the control of fires. Without periodic fires, shrubs and hardwoods take over the savanna regions. When the dominant plants are woody, fires seldom occur. As a result, the savanna disappears along with nonwoody plants. Caterpillars and moths damage the flowers and leaves of some carnivorous plants such as pitcher plants.

Development is the worst enemy of carnivorous plants. By draining swamplands, development has caused the loss of habitats of many carnivorous plants. This, along with poaching, may cause all carnivorous plants to become endangered.

Inquiry Activity

Objective 2.04
Find out what laws in North Carolina protect the carnivorous plants described here. What are the consequences for poaching these plants? Put together an informative brochure on a particular carnivorous plant in North Carolina. Include information about laws that protect plants in North Carolina.

Going Further

To learn more about matter and energy flow through an ecosystem, see:

2.01 Chapter 7, Section 2, Using Land
Chapter 8, Section 1, Characteristics of Plants
Chapter 8, Section 2, Seedless Plants
Chapter 8, Section 3, Seed Plants
Chapter 9, Section 1, Photosynthesis and Respiration
2.02 Chapter 7, Section 2, Using Land
Chapter 8, Section 1, Characteristics of Plants
Chapter 10, Section 3, Matter and Energy
Chapter 11, Section 2, Unity of Life
2.03 Chapter 7, Section 1, Population Impact on the Environment
Chapter 7, Section 2, Using Land

Chapter 9, Section 1, Photosynthesis and Respiration
Chapter 9, Section 2, Plant Processes
Chapter 10, Section 1, The Living and Nonliving Environment
Chapter 10, Section 2, Interactions Among Living Organisms
Chapter 10, Section 3, Matter and Energy
Chapter 11, Section 1, Diversity of Life
Chapter 11, Section 2, Unity of Life
Chapter 16, Section 2, Why do things fall?
2.04 Chapter 7, Section 1, Population Impact on the Environment
Chapter 10, Section 3, Matter and Energy

Introduced Species

COMPETENCY GOAL 2
The learner will investigate the characteristics of matter and energy flow through an ecosystem.

When settlers flocked to North Carolina in the 1600s, they were greeted by the songs of bluebirds. These tiny songbirds were once common throughout the eastern United States, heralding the approach of spring with cheerful warbles. By the 1960s, however, bird watchers began to notice a drop in bluebird numbers. Why? Other bird species, such as the European starlings and house sparrows, were competing with bluebirds for nesting sites. Bluebirds, starlings, and sparrows all nest in cavities—old woodpecker holes, fence posts, and bird boxes. When a sparrow comes across a bluebird nest, it will toss out the pale blue eggs and claim the nest for its own.

A Long Way from Home

Unlike bluebirds, starlings and sparrows are not native to North Carolina. They are introduced species that were brought to America from Europe. Introduced species are plants and animals that have been transported from their native ecosystems to new ecosystems.

The introduction of a new species can occur in several ways. Animals, for instance, sometimes migrate to new areas. Plant seeds may be carried by wind or water to new habitats. People, however,

Figure NC2-9 Building bluebird boxes provides nesting sites for the Eastern bluebird.

Figure NC2-10 European starlings (A) and house sparrows (B), are both species that were introduced into North America from Europe.

A

B

usually play the largest role in transporting species from one place to another. The introduction may be accidental, as when tiny insects hitchhike across borders in crates of fruit. Or the introduction can be intentional. In the 1800s, 16 house sparrows and 100 European starlings were released in New York City. These two small groups of birds are the ancestors of the millions of sparrows and starlings that live in North Carolina and other parts of the United States. Introduced species such as starlings and sparrows can cause serious problems when they interact with the plants, animals, and humans that already live within the ecosystem.

Upsetting Native Interaction

In an ecosystem, a delicate balance is maintained among the various native species. These native species depend upon the ecosystem for resources such as food, water, sunlight, soil, and space. In normal conditions, there are enough resources for all the native species, but the natural balance can be upset when a new species is introduced. The new arrival may consume plants that other species need for food. If there is no natural predator to keep them in check, the newcomers could multiply quickly until they overran the area. Or, the introduced species could be the predator, eliminating a previously existing population.

This is what is currently happening to the Fraser fir, a native tree of the southern Appalachian Mountains. Fraser firs in the Great Smoky Mountains National Park in North Carolina and Tennessee are being destroyed by an invasion of the balsam wooly aphid, a sap-sucking insect from Europe. The death of the trees, in turn, is causing a decrease in the population of the already-rare Fraser fir moss spider. The moss spider is a tiny tarantula that makes its home in moss on boulders and logs. As

Figure NC2-11 The balsam wooly aphid, an insect introduced from Europe, can infest and destroy trees.

Kudzu

Animals are not the only type of introduced species that can harm an ecosystem. Nonnative plants can cause problems, too. Kudzu, a vine native to Asia, is a good example of a destructive, introduced plant. Kudzu was brought into the United States from Asia in 1876. In the 1930s, with encouragement from the government, farmers began planting kudzu as ground cover to help prevent soil erosion and to provide food for cattle. But, everyone got more than they bargained for.

With abundant rain and sunshine, kudzu vines can grow at the almost-unbelievable rate of up to one foot a day. It didn't take long for kudzu to spread over the landscape like a thick, green blanket, as shown in **Figure NC2-12.** Today, kudzu has spread over millions of acres throughout the south, devastating native habitats. The vines climb high into tree branches, damaging the trees by breaking off small limbs and keeping sunlight from reaching the leaves by blanketing the tree.

the fir trees die, the forest canopy opens to sunlight and the moss dries out, destroying the spider's habitat. In this way, the loss of one native species in an ecosystem can have dire effects on other native species.

Trying to Enforce Limits

The problem of introduced species has become more critical since rapid transportation has made the world a global village. Jet planes carry passengers around the world to faraway lands in short amounts of time. When these travelers return home, they often bring with them (intentionally or unintentionally) nonnative organisms. For this reason, many countries have laws against the introduction of species that are known to be invasive. The United States, for example, has a list of more than 100 plants and animals that are not allowed into the country. Passengers and their baggage are inspected

Inquiry Activity

Objective 2.03

Identify limiting factors that impact populations. Longleaf pines, the state tree of North Carolina, once covered an estimated 10 million acres throughout the state. By the late 1800s, however, longleaf pine forests had been largely destroyed. Research and write about the factors that led to the decline of the longleaf pine. What are forest managers doing to bring back this native species?

when they enter at the border to make sure there aren't any undesirable or illegal hitch-hikers aboard.

Scientific Solutions

Scientists, too, are working to control the spread of introduced species. At the North Carolina State University in Raleigh, researchers are developing a strategy to combat kudzu. Kudzu has no natural enemies in the United States, so scientists are importing Asian caterpillars called soybean loopers to eat the plants. To ensure that the caterpillars don't become a menace, scientists are injecting the caterpillars with the eggs of stingless wasps. The eggs serve two purposes. First, they cause the caterpillars to eat nearly twice as much kudzu as they normally would. Second, the eggs will eventually hatch and destroy the caterpillars before they can reproduce and multiply. The kudzu strategy is currently being tested in both North and South Carolina.

Inquiry Activity

Objective 2.04
Make a list of some plants and animals in your area. Interview a local forest manager or wildlife specialist to find out which of the listed species are native to North Carolina. Are any of these species threatened? If so, why?

Figure NC2-12 Kudzu, or *Pueraria lobata*, was introduced from Asia to stabilize eroding slopes. Kudzu grows so rapidly it can overwhelm native plants and even buildings.

Individual Efforts

You don't have to be a scientist or a government official to help ease the problem of introduced species. Anyone can make a difference. In 1973, Jack Finch of Bailey, North Carolina, started *Homes for Bluebirds,* an organization dedicated to building and distributing special bird boxes for bluebirds. The boxes have small entrances to keep starlings out. Unlike bluebirds, starlings and sparrows favor bird boxes with perches, so the boxes are built without perches. These features help ensure that bluebird competitors won't take over the new nesting sites. To date, *Homes for Bluebirds* has distributed more than 60 000 bluebird boxes across the United States. As a result, bluebirds have made a comeback and are no longer considered a threatened species in North Carolina.

Figure NC2-13 The Soybean looper caterpillar has been imported to eat kudzu in an attempt to control the plant.

Inquiry Activity

Objective 2.03
Find out what it would take for your class to participate in *Homes for Bluebirds.*

Going Further

To learn more about matter and energy flow through an ecosystem, see:

2.01 Chapter 7, Section 2, Using Land
Chapter 8, Section 1, Characteristics of Plants
Chapter 8, Section 2, Seedless Plants
Chapter 8, Section 3, Seed Plants
Chapter 9, Section 1, Photosynthesis and Respiration
2.02 Chapter 7, Section 2, Using Land
Chapter 8, Section 1, Characteristics of Plants
Chapter 10, Section 3, Matter and Energy
Chapter 11, Section 2, Unity of Life
2.03 Chapter 7, Section 1, Population Impact on the Environment
Chapter 7, Section 2, Using Land
Chapter 9, Section 1, Photosynthesis and Respiration
Chapter 9, Section 2, Plant Processes

Chapter 10, Section 1, The Living and Nonliving Environment
Chapter 10, Section 2, Interactions Among Living Organisms
Chapter 10, Section 3, Matter and Energy
Chapter 11, Section 1, Diversity of Life
Chapter 11, Section 2, Unity of Life
Chapter 16, Section 2, Why do things fall?
2.04 Chapter 7, Section 1, Population Impact on the Environment
Chapter 10, Section 3, Matter and Energy

Exploring Space from Earth

COMPETENCY GOAL 3
The learner will build an understanding of the Solar System.

When we think of space exploration, we often imagine shiny spacecrafts drifting through the blackness of outer space. But, some of the most exciting new discoveries about the universe are taking place here on Earth. High atop the isolated peaks of the Andes in South America, scientists are using high-tech telescopes to get amazingly clear views of distant planets and stars—better views, even, than those obtained by most spacecrafts. Researchers at the University of North Carolina in Chapel Hill are among the many groups involved in this exciting new trend. The university is planning to build a 28 million-dollar telescope on top of a 2700-m peak in the Andes.

Why would these and other scientists build their telescopes in such remote parts of South America?

Star Light, Star Bright

Few people live in the Andes, therefore big cities are not located in these rugged mountains. That's one reason why astronomers—scientists who study stars and planets—are building telescopes in these isolated mountains. City lights cause a glow in the sky called light pollution.

Figure NC3-1 The high, isolated peaks of the Andes in South America are good places to build telescopes.

Figure NC3-2 Cerro Pachon, Chile is the proposed site of the new telescope.

Light pollution makes the sky glow bright enough that dim stars and distant galaxies can't be seen. Galaxies are large groups of stars, gas, and dust held together by gravity. The galaxy that we live in is called the Milky Way. From the Andes, astronomers can get a clear view of the Milky Way Galaxy and other objects in space without the dimming effects of light pollution.

High and Dry

The weather in the Andes is often clear and dry. That's another reason why scientists are building telescopes in this area—they need clear skies to view space. In addition, the height of the mountain peaks reduces the distorting effects of air. Air moves almost constantly because of changes in temperature, pressure, and other factors. This movement dims and distorts the light from stars. Because the amount of air in the atmosphere decreases with height, astronomers like to build telescopes on mountaintops—less air means less distortion of star images.

Southern Views

There's one more reason why astronomers are studying space from the Andes—they want to explore new territory. Most big telescopes have been built in the northern hemisphere. That's the part of Earth that lies north of the equator, the imaginary line that circles Earth exactly halfway between the north and south poles. The Andes lie in the southern hemisphere. Astronomers want to observe space from this hemisphere. Just as you can see different views of your neighborhood from different parts of your house, astronomers can see different views of space from different hemispheres of Earth.

In North Carolina, which is in the northern hemisphere, they can only see the Milky Way Galaxy for a few hours each night during the summer. But, in the Andes, astronomers can observe the Milky Way all night long through most seasons.

Bigger and Better?

Location is an important factor when it comes to building telescopes. Technology, however, is just as important. Astronomers are excited about the new telescopes in the Andes because these telescopes use advanced technology that enables them to see farther into the universe than ever before. The Very Large Telescope (VLT), for instance, will be completed in 2002 using a system of four 8-m telescopes combined with several smaller telescopes. This will give the overall system the power of a telescope with a 16-m mirror. To date, the largest telescope mirror is 10 m wide. The VLT is being built in the Atacama Desert of South America by a group of eight European nations. Total cost of the project will be $564 million. In 1998, the first of the four large telescopes was constructed and tested. The images were amazingly clear—when the system is complete, astronomers predict they'll be able to view objects as small and as distant as an astronaut walking on the moon.

Figure NC3-3 This diagram shows a scale drawing of the proposed telescope at Cerro Pachon, Chile.

14.5 m

12.5 m

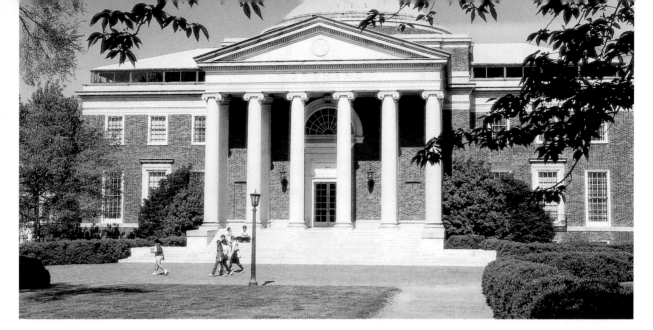

Figure NC3-4 Students and teachers can participate in the SOLAR project at the Morehead Observatory in Chapel Hill, North Carolina. (See page NC25.)

Tracking Patterns in Space

Before construction of the VLT, the Blanco telescope in Cerro Tololo was the most powerful stargazing tool in the southern hemisphere. Built by a group of North and South American countries, this telescope has a powerful 4-m mirror. In 1998, U.S. astronomers working at Cerro Tololo observed, for the first time, the birth of a new solar system. Using the Blanco telescope, astronomers have also found evidence that the universe is expanding at a much faster rate than was previously thought.

Inquiry Activity

Objective 3.01
Find out more about the Blanco telescope, which is located at Cerro Tololo. Using this telescope, astronomers observed the formation of a new solar system. Have these observations changed views of our own solar system? Explain.

Within sight of Cerro Tololo, a group of seven countries that includes the United States is building an 8.1-m telescope as part of Project Gemini. Located on Cerro Pachon, which means "peaceful mountain," the telescope will be linked by computer to a matching telescope in Hawaii. Project Gemini should be up and running by 2001. But, the most important new project, from the point of view of a student in North Carolina, is called SOAR.

SOAR

SOAR stands for Southern Observatory for Astrophysical Research. The four partners in this project are the government of Brazil, the National Optical Astronomy Observatory, Michigan State University, and the University of North Carolina at Chapel Hill. Scheduled for completion in 2001, SOAR will be located at Cerro Pachon. A major goal of SOAR is to build the first high-resolution telescope in the southern hemisphere. This means that the telescope will enable viewers to see objects that are too close together for the naked eye—and for most other telescopes—to distinguish. In addition, the 4-m, lightweight telescope will use a new system that allows large instruments such as cameras to be switched in minutes. On other large telescopes, these instruments can take more than a day to switch. If the telescope isn't set up with the correct instruments, some events, such as fast-exploding stars, can be missed. Thus, the SOAR telescope will help scientists study a wider range of astronomical events.

Inquiry Activity

Objective 3.06
Many items developed for astronauts in space are now used by people on Earth. These items are called spin-offs. Research and write about spin-offs that are now in use in daily life.

SOLAR

The SOAR telescope has another unique feature that makes it stand out from most telescopes—it can be controlled by computer from North Carolina and other locations. Using computer monitors, college students in Chapel Hill will be able to see through the lens of the telescope located thousands of kilometers away in the Andes.

Students in North Carolina's public schools will also participate in SOAR through a program called Students Online As Researchers (SOLAR). In spring 1998, 18 teachers from across the state of North Carolina were trained on a telescope at Morehead Observatory in Chapel Hill as part of the SOLAR project. Eventually, the students of these and other trained teachers will operate the actual SOAR telescope from remote computers. Time on the telescope will be limited, but even a brief view of space promises to be exciting. Imagine—with a click of a computer mouse, students in North Carolina will soon be able to point one of the most powerful telescopes in the world toward the spectacular rings of Saturn or the red, rocky surface of Mars.

Inquiry Activity

Objective 3.05
Telescopes are just one form of technology used to explore space. Make a table listing other types of technology used to study space. Find out how your school can participate in SOLAR.

Going Further

To learn more about the Solar System, see:

3.01 Chapter 13, Section 2, The Solar System
3.02 Chapter 2, Section 2, SI Units
Chapter 13, Section 1, Earth's Place in Space
Chapter 13, Section 2, The Solar System
Chapter 16, Section 2, Why do things fall?
3.03 Chapter 13, Section 1, Earth's Place in Space
Chapter 16, Section 2, Why do things fall?
3.04 Chapter 9, Section 2, Plant Processes

Chapter 13, Section 1, Earth's Place in Space
3.05 Chapter 12, Section 1, Radiation from Space
Chapter 12, Section 2, Early Space Missions
Chapter 12, Section 3, Recent and Future Space Missions
Chapter 13, Section 2, The Solar System
Chapter 16, Section 3, How do things move?
3.06 Chapter 3, Section 3, Maps

Nuclear Power in North Carolina

COMPETENCY GOAL 4
The learner will investigate the characteristics of energy transfer.

Energy can be transferred in different ways, including radiation from the sun, convection, and conduction. In the following discussion you will explore how energy inside the atom is transferred into useable electricity.

North Carolina has three operating nuclear power plants: the McGuire Nuclear Station, the Brunswick Nuclear Plant, and the Shearon Harris Nuclear Power Plant. The locations of the three power plants are shown in **Figure NC4-1.**

Pros and Cons of Nuclear Power

Nuclear power plants produce electricity efficiently. A pellet of uranium dioxide, about the size of a half-inch piece of chalk, produces the amount of power equivalent to three fourths of a ton of coal. There are other reasons for optimism about the use of nuclear power. Costs are competitive with coal, which is considered to be relatively inexpensive. Uranium is abundant. Plutonium, a by-product of commercial nuclear plant operation, can also be used as a fuel. The amount of waste produced is the least of any major energy production process. But, nuclear power plants are expensive to build and can pose a threat to the environment if they are not properly maintained.

Inquiry Activity

Objective 4.01
Describe three examples of energy transfer that you can observe in your daily activities that involves radiation, conduction, and convection.

Figure NC4-1 The map shows the locations of the three operating nuclear power plants in North Carolina.

Figure NC4-2 Uranium-238 and Uranium-235 are two isotopes of uranium. Both have 92 protons. When the nucleus of Uranium-235 is split, a large amount of energy is released.

Uranium-238

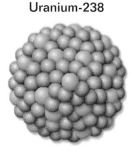

92 protons
146 neutrons

Uranium-235

92 protons
143 neutrons

Nuclear Fission

Uranium-235 is the isotope of uranium that is used in nuclear reactors. This isotope is used because when its nucleus is hit by a neutron, the atom can split in two and release a lot of energy as heat. This splitting is called nuclear fission.

Commercial nuclear power generation involves containing and controlling the fission reactions so the heat can be used to make steam that will turn a turbine to generate electricity. A controlled nuclear fission reaction occurs inside a nuclear reactor.

The Nuclear Power Process

During nuclear fission, neutrons are released. These neutrons cause the fission of other uranium nuclei, causing a chain reaction. A moderator, in control rods, absorbs some of these neutrons. This keeps the chain reaction controlled. Control rods regulate the rate of reaction. When control rods are withdrawn, the chain reaction begins, releasing large amounts of energy that are transferred into heat. When control rods are inserted, they absorb some of the neutrons, slowing the reaction and the release of heat.

Figure NC4-3 The McGuire Nuclear Power Plant is located northwest of Charlotte on Lake Norman.

Figure NC4-4 This diagram shows how a nuclear reactor transfers the energy produced by nuclear fission into electricity.

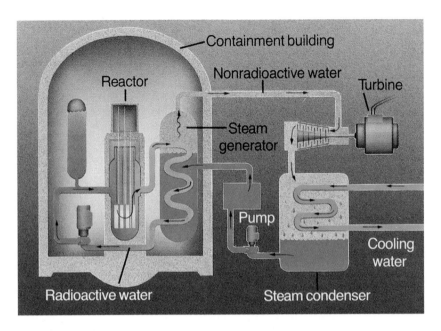

Containment building

Reactor

Nonradioactive water

Turbine

Steam generator

Pump

Cooling water

Radioactive water

Steam condenser

Cycling Water for Cooling

The heat produced during the fission process turns water into steam that is used to drive turbines to generate electricity. The steam then moves into a condenser where water flowing through cooling pipes causes the steam to condense back into water. This condensate goes back to the reactor to start the cycle, or process, over again.

All electric plants that make steam need water to cool the steam and prevent the reactor from overheating. In the process of cooling, the water in the cooling pipes gets hot and has to be pumped through a cooling tower or a pond.

The Brunswick Nuclear Plant draws water for its cooling system from the Cape Fear River via an intake canal. Cooling water from the plant is carried by a discharge canal to the Atlantic Ocean. This water is neither contaminated nor radioactive. The Shearon Harris Nuclear Power Plant gets rid of excess heat through a 158-meter cooling tower. Water lost through evaporation is drawn from Lake Harris. The McGuire Nuclear Station uses water from Lake Norman.

Figure NC4-5 The Shearon Harris Nuclear Power Plant uses water from Lake Harris to cool the reactor.

Inquiry Activity

Objective 4.04
Describe how the energy released from the nuclear fission is used to generate electricity. Include a diagram that shows the processes involved.

Power Plant Safety

The 1979 accident at Three Mile Island near Harrisburg, Pennsylvania, and the 1986 accident at Chernobyl in Russia remind us that nuclear safety requires constant monitoring and regulating. The discharge of thermal energy into surrounding bodies of water can cause thermal pollution and disrupt the ecosystem near a nuclear power plant. Cracks in the reactor or failure of the cooling system can result in the release of radioactive materials and pose a threat to health and the environment. Another environmental concern is the disposal of spent fuel, which will stay highly radioactive for thousands of years.

Nuclear Waste Policy Act

The Nuclear Waste Policy Act of 1982 and 1987 amendments mandated that the U.S. Department of Energy (DOE) begin accepting used nuclear fuel from nuclear power plants by January 31, 1998. However, the DOE has not yet met its obligation to store used fuel. Electricity customers are financing this program through charges in their electric bill. Until the DOE finds a suitable site for spent fuel storage, each utility has to find ways to store its own used fuel.

Inquiry Activity

Objective 4.06
Does nuclear fission follow the law of conservation of energy? Explain.

Going Further

To learn more about energy transfer, see:

4.01 Chapter 15, Section 1, Energy and How It Changes
Chapter 15, Section 2, Temperature and Thermal Energy

4.02 Chapter 15, Section 2, Temperature and Thermal Energy

4.03 Chapter 12, Section 1, Radiation from Space
Chapter 17, Section 1, What are waves?
Chapter 17, Section 2, Wave Properties
Chapter 17, Section 3, Behavior of Waves

4.04 Chapter 14, Section 1, Structure of Matter
Chapter 14, Section 2, Elements

Chapter 15, Section 1, Energy and How it Changes
Chapter 15, Section 3, Chemical Energy

4.05 Chapter 14, Section 1, Structure of Matter
Chapter 17, Section 2, Wave Properties
Chapter 17, Section 3, Behavior of Waves
Chapter 18, Section 1, Properties of Light

4.06 Chapter 14, Section 1, Structure of Matter
Chapter 15, Section 1, Energy and How It Changes

North Carolina Science Sites

Where to see and do science in North Carolina

(1) **Aurora Fossil Museum,** Aurora
Geological history exhibit of the coastal region

(2) **Catawba Science Center,** Hickory
Mountain stream and hands-on displays of light and sound

(3) **City of Rocky Mount Children's Museum,** Rocky Mount
Live local animals, displays of marshlands and forests, and a planetarium

(4) **Discovery Place,** Charlotte
Planetarium, aquarium, space station, recreated rain forest, and human body exhibits.

(5) **Duke Power State Park Energy Emporium,** Huntersville
Interactive exhibits on different forms of energy production

(6) **Imagination Station,** Wilson
Interactive displays on electricity, magnetism, simple machines, and communications

(7) **Long Branch Environmental Education Center,** Leicester
Passive solar energy displays, organic farming and composting

(8) **Mattamuskeet National Wildlife Refuge,** Swan Quarter
Migrating birds and pine forests in last stages of succession

(9) **Morehead Planetarium,** Chapel Hill
Large-scale model of the solar system and planetarium shows

(10) **Natural Science Center,** Greensboro
Meteorology, paleontology, geology, and health

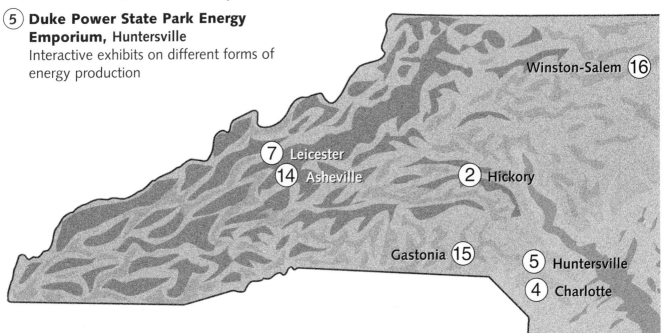

⑪ **North Carolina Aquarium,** Fort Fisher
Marine animal displays range from sharks to eels

⑫ **North Carolina Museum of Life and Science,** Durham
Space technology and an interactive nature center

⑬ **North Carolina State University Arboretum,** Raleigh
More than 5000 plants from around the world on an 8-acre park

⑭ **Pack Place—Education, Arts & Science Center,** Asheville
Colburn Gem & Mineral Museum and The Health Adventure

⑮ **Shiele Museum of Natural History and Planetarium,** Gastonia
Planetarium shows, natural minerals, fossils, flora and fauna

⑯ **Sciworks,** Winston-Salem
Interactive environmental exhibits

⑰ **Wright Brothers National Memorial,** Kill Devil Hills
Details the history flight and gliders of Orville and Wilbur Wright

⑱ **Pea Island National Wildlife Refuge,** Manteo
5880-acre refuge with observation decks for watching several hundred species of different native and migrating birds

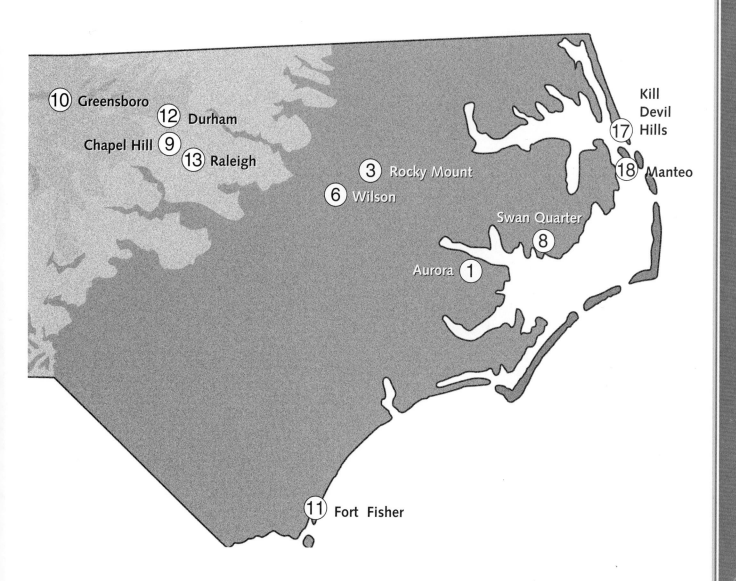

North Carolina
The Tar Heel State

State Bird: Cardinal

State Flower: Dogwood

**State Tree:
Longleaf Pine**

PHOTO AND ART CREDITS: NC4 Billy E. Barnes; **NC5** Robert Llewellyn/Picturesque; **NC6** Mike Booher; **NC7** Carl Galie/Picturesque; **NC8** Alice Jacobs; **NC10** Rob Gardner/North Carolina Botanical Garden; **NC11** Jeff Lepore/Photo Researchers; **NC12** Michel Viard/Peter Arnold, Inc.; **NC13** Ed Reschke/Peter Arnold, Inc.; **NC14** (l)Jeff Lepore/Photo Researchers, (r)Ed Reschke/Peter Arnold, Inc.; **NC16** Michael Ederegger/Peter Arnold, Inc.; **NC17** (l)Stephen Dalton/Photo Researchers, (r)Sam Fried/Photo Researchers; **NC18** Hans Pfletschinger/Peter Arnold, Inc.; **NC19** Gilbert Grant/Photo Researchers; **NC20** Norm Thomas/Photo Researchers; **NC21** Francois Gohier/Photo Researchers; **NC22, NC23** courtesy of SOAR; **NC24** Billy E. Barnes; **NC27** Kelly Culpepper/TRANSPARENCIES, Inc.; **NC28** McIntyre Photography, Inc./Picturesque.

P/N G86316.11

GLENCOE

North Carolina Edition

SCIENCE VOYAGES

Exploring the Life, Earth, and Physical Sciences

NATIONAL GEOGRAPHIC SOCIETY

Glencoe McGraw-Hill

New York, New York   Columbus, Ohio   Woodland Hills, California   Peoria, Illinois

A Glencoe Program

North Carolina Edition

Glencoe Science Voyages

North Carolina Student Edition
North Carolina Teacher Wraparound Edition
North Carolina Resource Book
Assessment
 Chapter Review
 North Carolina Standard Course of Study
  Practice Questions
 Performance Assessment
 Assessment—Chapter and Unit Tests
 ExamView Test Bank Software
 Performance Assessment in the Science
  Classroom
 Alternate Assessment in the Science Classroom
Study Guide for Content Mastery, SE and TE
Chapter Overview Study Guide, SE and TE
Reinforcement
Enrichment
Critical Thinking/Problem Solving
Multicultural Connections

Activity Worksheets
Laboratory Manual, SE and TE
Science Inquiry Activities, SE and TE
Home Involvement
Teaching Transparencies
Section Focus Transparencies
Science Integration Transparencies
Spanish Resources
North Carolina Lesson Plans
Lab and Safety Skills in the Science Classroom
Cooperative Learning in the Science Classroom
Exploring Environmental Issues
MindJogger Videoquizzes and Teacher Guide
English/Spanish Audiocassettes
Interactive Lesson Planner CD-ROM
Interactive CD-ROM
Internet Site
Using the Internet in the Science Classroom

THE PRINCETON REVIEW

The "Test-Taking Tip" and "Test Practice" features in this book were written by The Princeton Review, the nation's leader in test preparation. Through its association with McGraw-Hill, The Princeton Review offers the best way to help students excel on standardized assessments.

The Princeton Review is not affiliated with Princeton University or Educational Testing Service.

Glencoe/McGraw-Hill

A Division of The McGraw-Hill Companies

Send all inquiries to:
Glencoe/McGraw-Hill
8787 Orion Place
Columbus, OH 43240

ISBN 0-02-828631-6
Printed in the United States of America.
2 3 4 5 6 7 8 9 10 027/046 06 05 04 03 02 01 00

Series Authors

Alton Biggs
Biology Instructor
Allen High School
Allen, Texas

John Eric Burns
Science Teacher
Ramona Jr. High School
Chino, California

Lucy Daniel, Ph.D.
Teacher, Consultant
Rutherford County Schools
Rutherfordton, North Carolina

Cathy Ezrailson
Science Department Head
Oak Ridge High School
Conroe, Texas

Ralph Feather, Jr., Ph.D.
Science Department Chair
Derry Area School District
Derry, Pennsylvania

Patricia Horton
Math and Science Teacher
Summit Intermediate School
Etiwanda, California

Thomas McCarthy, Ph.D.
Science Department Chair
St. Edwards School
Vero Beach, Florida

Ed Ortleb
Science Consultant
St. Louis Public Schools
St. Louis, Missouri

Susan Leach Snyder
Science Department Chair
Jones Middle School
Upper Arlington, Ohio

Eric Werwa, Ph.D.
Department of Physics and Astronomy
Otterbein College
Westerville, Ohio

National Geographic Society
Educational Division
Washington D.C.

Contributing Authors

Al Janulaw
Science Teacher
Creekside Middle School
Rohnert Park, California

Gerry Madrazo, Ph.D.
Mathematics and Science Education
   Network
University of North Carolina
Chapel Hill, North Carolina

Series Consultants

Chemistry

Douglas Martin, Ph.D.
Chemistry Department
Sonoma State University
Rohnert Park, California

Cheryl Wistrom, Ph.D.
Associate Professor of
    Chemistry
Saint Joseph's College
Rensselaer, Indiana

Earth Science

Tomasz K. Baumiller, Ph.D.
Museum of Paleontology
University of Michigan
Ann Arbor, Michigan

Maureen Allen
Science Resource Specialist
Irvine Unified School District
Laguna Hills, California

Connie Sutton, Ph.D.
Department of Geoscience
Indiana University
Indiana, Pennsylvania

Physics

Thomas Barrett, Ph.D.
Department of Physics
The Ohio State University
Columbus, Ohio

David Haase, Ph.D.
Professor of Physics
North Carolina State
    University
North Carolina

Life Science

William Ausich, Ph.D.
Department of Geological
    Sciences
The Ohio State University
Columbus, Ohio

Dennis Stockdale
Asheville High School
Asheville, North Carolina

Daniel Zeigler, Ph.D.
Director
Bacillus Genetic Stock Center
The Ohio State University
Columbus, Ohio

Reading

Nancy Farnan, Ph.D.
School of Teacher Education
San Diego State University
San Diego, California

Gary Kroesch
Mount Carmel High School
San Diego, California

Safety

Mark Vinciguerra
Lab Safety Instructor
Department of Physics
The Ohio State University
Columbus, Ohio

Curriculum

Tom Custer, Ph.D.
Maryland State Department of
    Education
Challenge/Reconstructed
    Schools
Baltimore, Maryland

Series Reviewers

Jhina Alvarado
Potrero Hill Middle School
for the Arts
San Francisco, California

Richard Cheeseman
Bert Lynn Middle School
Torrance, California

Linda Cook
Rider High School
Wichita Falls, Texas

John B. Davis
Niagara-Wheatfield
Central School
Sanborn, New York

Shirley Ann DeFilippo
Timothy Edwards
Middle School
South Windsor, Connecticut

Janet Doughty
H J McDonald Middle School
New Bern, North Carolina

Jason Druten
Jefferson Middle School
Torrance, California

Lin Harp
Magellan Middle School
Raleigh, North Carolina

Doris Holland
West Cary Middle School
Raleigh, North Carolina

Deborah Huffine
Noblesville Intermediate
School
Noblesville, Indiana

Paul Osborne
DeValls Bluff High School
DeValls Bluff, Arkansas

Erik Resnick
Robert E. Peary Middle School
Gardena, California

Robert Sirbu
Lowell Junior High School
Oakland, California

Michael Tally
Wake County
Public Schools
Raleigh, North Carolina

Cindy Williamson
Whiteville City Schools
Whiteville, North Carolina

Maurice Yaggi
Middlebrook School
Wilton, Connecticut

Donna York
Anchorage School District
Anchorage, Alaska

Activity Testers

Clayton Millage
Science Teacher
Lynden Middle School
Lynden, Washington

Science Kit and Boreal Laboratories
Tonawanda, New York

Contents in Brief

UNIT 1 The Nature of Science   2

Chapter 1   The Nature of Science 4
Chapter 2   Measurement 28

UNIT 2 Earth Materials and Resources   58

Chapter 3   Views of Earth. 60
Chapter 4   Earth Materials 90
Chapter 5   Weathering and Soil. 122
Chapter 6   Erosional Forces. 148
Chapter 7   Our Impact on Land. 180

UNIT 3 The Web of Life   210

Chapter 8   Plants. 212
Chapter 9   Plant Processes 242
Chapter 10   Life and the Environment. 266
Chapter 11   Diversity and Adaptations 294

UNIT 4 Exploring Space   324

Chapter 12   Exploring Space. 326
Chapter 13   The Solar System and Beyond 354

UNIT 5 Interactions in the Physical World   382

Chapter 14   Matter 384
Chapter 15   Energy 412
Chapter 16   Motion and Forces 444
Chapter 17   Waves 474
Chapter 18   Light, Mirrors, and Lenses 500

Contents

UNIT 1   The Nature of Science   2

Chapter 1   The Nature of Science   4

1-1	How Science Works	6
	Activity 1-1 Design Your Own Experiment: Model an Archaeological Dig	12
1-2	Scientific Problem Solving	14
	Activity 1-2 Advertising Inferences	22
	Science & Society NATIONAL GEOGRAPHIC	23

Chapter 2   Measurement   28

2-1	Description and Measurement	30
	Science & Society NATIONAL GEOGRAPHIC	36
2-2	SI Units	37
	Activity 2-1 Scale Drawing	42
2-3	Communicating Data	43
	Activity 2-2 Design Your Own Experiment: Pace Yourself	48
	FIELD GUIDE to Laboratory Equipment	50

Contents

UNIT 2   **Earth Materials and Resources**   **58**

Chapter 3   Views of Earth   **60**

3-1   Landforms 62
3-2   Viewpoints 70
3-3   Maps 74
   Activity 3-1 Design Your Own Experiment:
     Modeling Earth 82
   History of Science NATIONAL GEOGRAPHIC 84
   Activity 3-2 Making a Topographic Map 85

Chapter 4   Earth Materials   **90**

4-1   Minerals—Earth's Jewels 92
   Reading & Writing in Science NATIONAL GEOGRAPHIC . . 102
4-2   Igneous and Sedimentary Rocks 103
   Activity 4-1 Design Your Own Experiment:
   Cool Crystals vs. Hot Crystals 110
4-3   Metamorphic Rocks and the Rock Cycle 112
   Activity 4-2 Gneiss Rice 117

Chapter 5   Weathering and Soil   **122**

5-1   Weathering 124
   Activity 5-1 Design Your Own Experiment:
     Weathering Chalk 130
5-2   Soil 132
   Activity 5-2 Soil Characteristics 142
   How it Works NATIONAL GEOGRAPHIC 143

Contents

Chapter 6 Erosional Forces   148

6-1 Gravity 150
6-2 Glaciers................................ 158
     Activity 6-1 Glacial Grooving.............. 165
     Reading & Writing in Science NATIONAL GEOGRAPHIC .. 166
6-3 Wind 167
     Activity 6-2 Design Your Own Experiment:
       Blowing in the Wind 174

Chapter 7 Our Impact on Land   180

7-1 Population Impact on the Environment 182
     Activity 7-1 A Crowded Encounter......... 186
7-2 Using Land 188
7-3 Recycling 197
     Activity 7-2 A Model Landfill 200
     Science & Society NATIONAL GEOGRAPHIC 201
     FIELD GUIDE to Waste Management...... 202

Contents

UNIT 3 The Web of Life   210

Chapter 8 Plants   212

8-1 Characteristics of Plants 214
8-2 Seedless Plants 220
     Activity 8-1 Comparing Seedless Plants 226
     How **it** Works NATIONAL GEOGRAPHIC 227
8-3 Seed Plants 228
     Activity 8-2 Comparing Monocots
     and Dicots 237

Chapter 9 Plant Processes   242

9-1 Photosynthesis and Respiration 244
     Activity 9-1 Stomata in Leaves 253
9-2 Plant Responses 254
     How **it** Works NATIONAL GEOGRAPHIC 259
     Activity 9-2 Design Your Own Experiment:
     Plant Tropisms 260

Chapter 10   Life and the Environment   266

10-1   The Living and Nonliving Environments....   268

Activity 10-1 Soil Composition   273

10-2   Interactions Among Living Organisms......   274

Activity 10-2 Design Your Own Experiment: Identifying a Limiting Factor...........   280

10-3   Matter and Energy   282

Reading & Writing in Science ☐ NATIONAL GEOGRAPHIC ..   289

Chapter 11   Diversity and Adaptations   294

11-1   Diversity of Life   296

Reading & Writing in Science ☐ NATIONAL GEOGRAPHIC ..   302

11-2   Unity of Life   303

Activity 11-1 Design Your Own Experiment: Simulating Selection   312

11-3   History of Life.........................   314

Activity 11-2 Dinosaur Size   319

Contents

UNIT 4   Exploring Space   **324**

Chapter 12   Exploring Space   **326**

12-1   Radiation from Space 328

Activity 12-1 Telescopes 334

How **it** Works   NATIONAL GEOGRAPHIC 335

12-2   Early Space Missions 336

Activity 12-2 On the Internet:
    Star Sightings 342

12-3   Recent and Future Space Missions 344

Chapter 13   **The Solar System and Beyond**   **354**

13-1   Earth's Place in Space 356

Activity 13-1 Moon Phases 361

13-2   The Solar System 362

Reading **&** Writing in Science   NATIONAL GEOGRAPHIC . . 369

Activity 13-2 Design Your Own Experiment:
    Space Colony 370

13-3   Stars and Galaxies 372

Contents

UNIT 5 — Interactions in the Physical World 382

Chapter 14 — Matter 384

14-1 Structure of Matter 386
14-2 Elements. 394
    Activity 14-1 Elements and the
       Periodic Table. 399
    History **of** Science NATIONAL GEOGRAPHIC 400
14-3 Compounds and Mixtures 401
    Activity 14-2 Mystery Mixture. 406

Chapter 15 — Energy 412

15-1 Energy Changes 414
    Activity 15-1 Where's the energy?. 422
15-2 Temperature and Thermal Energy. 423
    Activity 15-2 Can you observe a
       temperature change?. 432
15-3 Chemical Energy. 434
    Science **&** Society NATIONAL GEOGRAPHIC 439

Chapter 16 — Motion and Forces 444

16-1 How does speed change? 446
    Activity 16-1 Time Trials 451
16-2 Why do things fall? 452
16-3 How do things move? 458
    Science **&** Society NATIONAL GEOGRAPHIC 467
    Activity 16-2 On the Internet:
       Making a Paper Airplane. 468

Contents

Chapter 17 **Waves**   **474**

17-1   What are waves?.   476
17-2   Wave Properties   481
         Activity 17-1 Waves on a Spring   485
17-3   Wave Behavior   486
         Science & Math NATIONAL GEOGRAPHIC   493
         Activity 17-2 On the Internet:
                Doing the Wave   494

Chapter 18 **Light, Mirrors, and Lenses**   **500**

18-1   Properties of Light   502
18-2   Reflection and Mirrors.   509
         Activity 18-1 Reflection from
                a Plane Mirror   515
18-3   Refraction and Lenses   516
         Activity 18-2 Image Formation by
                a Convex Lens   520
18-4   Microscopes, Telescopes, and Cameras.   522
         Science & Math NATIONAL GEOGRAPHIC   527

Contents

Appendices   532

Appendix A   Safety in the Science Classroom 533
Appendix B   SI/Metric to English Conversions 534
Appendix C   SI Units of Measurement 535
Appendix D   Care and Use of a Microscope 536
Appendix E   Diversity of Life: Classification of
                          Living Organisms 537
Appendix F   Minerals 541
Appendix G   Rocks. 543
Appendix H   Topographic Map Symbols 544
Appendix I   Weather Map Symbols 545
Appendix J   Star Charts 546

Science Skill Handbook   548

Technology Skill Handbook   568

Skill Activities   577

Glossary   596

Spanish Glossary   607

Index   622

Science & Society

Radar 23
Global Positioning System 36
Using Plants to Reduce Pollution 201
Development of the Periodic Table 400
Hot-Vent Inhabitants 439
Building In Safety 467

Science & Math

Graphing Waves 493
Scientific Notation 527

History of Science

Mapmaking 84

How it Works

Compost 143
Preservation in Peat Bogs 227
Carnivorous Plants 259
Seeing in 3-D 335

Reading & Writing in Science

Navajo Sand Painting 102
Music of the Dust Bowl 166
Never Cry Wolf 289
Using Field Guides 302
Barbary 369

Activities

1-1 Design Your Own Experiment: Model an Archaeological Dig. 12

1-2 Advertising Inferences. 22

2-1 Scale Drawing 42

2-2 Design Your Own Experiment: Pace Yourself 48

3-1 Design Your Own Experiment: Modeling Earth 82

3-2 Making a Topographic Map. 85

4-1 Design Your Own Experiment: Cool Crystals vs. Hot Crystals. 110

4-2 Gneiss Rice. 117

5-1 Design Your Own Experiment: Weathering Chalk 130

5-2 Soil Characteristics 142

6-1 Glacial Grooving. 165

6-2 Design Your Own Experiment: Blowing in the Wind 174

7-1 A Crowded Encounter 186

7-2 A Model Landfill. 200

8-1 Comparing Seedless Plants . . 226

8-2 Comparing Monocots and Dicots 237

9-1 Stomata in Leaves. 253

9-2 Design Your Own Experiment: Plant Tropisms. 260

Activities

10-1 Soil Composition 273

10-2 Design Your Own Experiment:
Identifying a Limiting
Factor 280

11-1 Design Your Own Experiment:
Simulating Selection 312

11-2 Dinosaur Size 319

12-1 Telescopes 334

12-2 On the Internet:
Star Sightings 342

13-1 Moon Phases 361

13-2 Design Your Own Experiment:
Space Colony 370

14-1 Elements and the
Periodic Table 399

14-2 Mystery Mixture 406

15-1 Where's the energy? 422

15-2 Can you observe a
temperature change? 432

16-1 Time Trials 451

16-2 On the Internet:
Making a Paper Airplane . . . 468

17-1 Waves on a Spring 485

17-2 On the Internet:
Doing the Wave 494

18-1 Reflection from a
Plane Mirror 515

18-2 Image Formation by a
Convex Lens 520

Mini Lab

2 Measuring Accurately 32

3 Interpreting Latitude and
 Longitude 71

4 Classifying Minerals 97

5 Comparing Components
 of Soil 134

6 Observing Mass Movements . . . 155

7 Modeling Runoff 194

8 Measuring Water Absorption
 by a Moss 221

 Observing Water Moving
 in a Plant 229

9 Observing Plant Use of
 Carbon Dioxide 247

 Demonstrating Respiration
 in Yeast 250

10 Observing Symbiosis 278

11 Identifying Adaptions
 of Fish 300

12 Modeling Gravity 346

13 Observing Distance and Size . . . 359

14 Making a Model 390

15 Classifying Types of Energy . . . 420

16 Inferring Free Fall 456

 Measuring Friction 459

17 Comparing Sounds 479

18 Viewing Colors Through
 Color Filters 506

 Forming an Image
 with a Lens 518

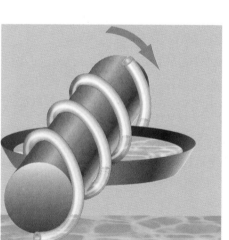

1 Observing and Inferring...... 20

2 Measuring Volume 39

3 Profiling the United States 64

4 Modeling How Fossils Form
   Rocks 108

5 Observing the Formation
   of Rust 128

6 Observing How Soil Is Held
   in Place 170

7 Classify Your Trash
   for One Day 191

10 Modeling the Water Cycle 286

11 Modeling a Fossil........... 308

12 Comparing the Effects of
   Light Pollution 340

13 Modeling Constellations...... 373

14 Inferring Atomic Structure.... 392

15 Comparing Energy
   Content 430

17 Observing How Light
   Refracts 487

Explore Activities

1 Model an Excavation   5

2 Measuring Length   29

3 Describe Landforms   61

4 Observe a Rock   91

5 Observe Weathering   123

6 Observe Movement
   of Sediments   149

7 Draw a Population
   Growth Model   181

8 Infer Which Plant Parts
   Are Edible   213

9 Observe Plants   243

10 Measure Space   267

11 Identify Organisms   295

12 Observe White Light   327

13 Estimate Grains of Rice   355

14 Observe Matter   385

15 Observe Energy   413

16 The Marble Skateboard
   Model   445

17 Observe Wave Behavior   475

18 Observe Light Bending   501

Problem Solving

1 Flex Your Brain.   16

2 Communicate with Art
   and Words.   44

3 Interpreting a Topographic
   Map   79

7 The Effects of Trash Disposal. . .   193

8 Cause and Effect in Nature . . .   218

9 Predicting Plant Responses . . .   256

10 Changes in Antarctic
   Food Webs.   285

11 Comparing Protein
   Sequences   309

12 Interpreting Telescope Data . . .   331

13 Determining Distances
   in Space   364

14 Drinking Water from
   Salt Water   403

15 Chemical Energy
   in Action   436

16 Illustrating Force   460

17 Scattering Light.   490

18 Radio Telescopes   525

4 Identifying Mineral Origin. . . .   98

5 Interpret Crop Data.   136

6 Deserts.   169

Skill Builders

Classifying: 236, 288, 438

Communicating: 196, 526

Comparing and Contrasting: 11, 258, 405, 492

Concept Mapping: 69, 141, 157, 225, 311, 341, 480

Developing Multimedia Presentations: 368

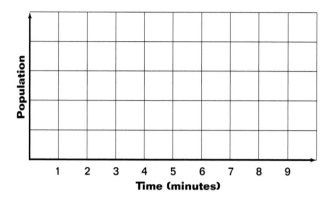

Observing and Inferring: 129, 252, 272, 279, 301, 393, 457, 508

Predicting: 519

Recognizing Cause and Effect: 164, 318, 466

Separating and Controlling Variables: 21

Sequencing: 109, 173, 333

Using Numbers: 35, 431 450

Forming a Hypothesis: 219, 514

Forming Operational Definitions: 41

Inferring: 360

Interpreting Data: 398

Interpreting Scientific Illustrations: 73, 484

Making and Using Graphs: 47, 185, 349, 421

Making and Using Tables: 101, 199

Making Models: 81, 377

Observing: 116

Skill Activities

Chapter 1 Separating and Controlling Variables 578
Chapter 2 Using Numbers 579
Chapter 3 Making Models 580
Chapter 4 Interpreting Tables 581
Chapter 5 Observing and Inferring 582
Chapter 6 Concept Mapping 583
Chapter 7 Communicating 584
Chapter 8 Classifying 585
Chapter 9 Observing and Inferring 586
Chapter 10 Predicting 587
Chapter 11 Recognizing Cause and Effect 588
Chapter 12 Making and Using Graphs 589
Chapter 13 Inferring 590
Chapter 14 Observing and Inferring 591
Chapter 15 Using Numbers 592
Chapter 16 Using Numbers 593
Chapter 17 Interpreting Scientific Illustrations 594
Chapter 18 Communicating 595

The Nature of Science

What's Happening Here?

A girl dangles her fingers in the cool, clear waters of Minnesota's Lake Itasca (below), source of the mighty Mississippi River. Does she realize that the water she touches will pass by great cities of America's heartland and form the borders of ten states? Hundreds of miles south of the lake, the river loses speed as it enters the Gulf of Mexico, drops its sediment, and creates a bird-foot delta (left) as its grand finale. Like the girl on the lake, we don't see what lies beyond our immediate surroundings. Science can help us explore the unknown and discover patterns that organize and guide our curiosity. Today, with the help of scientific tools such as the infrared survey camera that captured this image of the delta, we can see farther and more clearly into the world beyond our senses.

*inter*NET CONNECTION

Explore the Glencoe Science Web Site at **www.glencoe.com/sec/ science/nc** to find out more about topics found in this unit.

The Nature of Science

Chapter Preview

Section 1-1
How Science Works

Section 1-2
Scientific Problem Solving

Skills Preview

Skill Builders
- Compare and Contrast
- Separate and Control Variables

Activities
- Model
- Observe and Infer

MiniLabs
- Observe and Infer

Reading Check ✓

As you read about the nature of science, think about the role of fact and opinion in this field. Is there a place for opinion in science? Why or why not?

Explore Activity

The scientist in the photograph is excavating, or digging up, the remains of an ancient, elephant-like mammal called a mastodon in South Dakota. Excavations to unearth bones or other evidence of past life are often slow processes that involve a lot of careful work. Care must be taken so that the remains are not broken or destroyed as they are removed from the soil. Try your hand at excavating an oatmeal cookie without destroying the treasures within.

Model an Excavation

CAUTION: *Never eat or drink in the science lab and never use lab glassware as food or drink containers.*

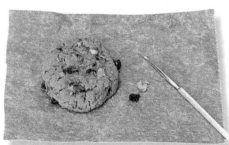

1. Obtain an oatmeal cookie with raisins and walnuts from your teacher.

2. Place the cookie on a piece of waxed paper.

3. Use a biology probe to carefully remove the raisins and walnuts from the cookie without damaging either.

4. Wash your hands with soap and water when you have finished.

5. Give all pieces of the excavated cookie to your teacher for disposal.

Science Journal

In your Science Journal, write a paragraph that explains how probing the cookie might be similar to removing bones, tools, or other evidence of ancient life from Earth's crust.

How Science Works

Groundbreaking News!

It was Friday morning and the students in Ms. Garcia's science lab were anxiously waiting for class to start. Unlike most days in science class at York Middle School, this class would be a field trip to the north end of the school. Students were eager to observe work that would result in the long-awaited gymnasium. The students in group 4— Ben, Emily, Maria, and Juan— peered out the windows. They saw bulldozers and other construction equipment much like the one shown in **Figure 1-1** pull up to the school. With pencils and notebooks in hand, the interested students hiked out to the site. They watched as massive shovels moved hundreds of kilograms of dirt from one spot to another.

Buried Treasure?

All of a sudden, the power-shovel operator stopped the giant scoop in midair. He looked curiously into the hole he was making as he climbed from his seat high above the ground. He called some of the other workers over. They all stared into the pit. One of the workers motioned for Ms. Garcia and her students to come a little closer. Everyone was surprised at what they saw. A piece of broken pottery was sticking out from the loose soil.

What **You'll Learn**

► Archaeology is the study of the cultural remains of ancient people
► Science is a process of understanding the world
► Technology is the use of scientific knowledge

Vocabulary
science
technology

Why **It's Important**

► Science and technology are important parts of your everyday world.

Figure 1-1 Construction efforts sometimes unearth prehistoric sites.

Science in Action

One worker suggested that the pottery might be only one of thousands of pieces of trash that were buried long before the school was built. Another worker, however, wasn't so sure. He thought that the pottery could perhaps be an ancient piece of art, such as the one shown in **Figure 1-2A.** Nonetheless, a decision was made to stop the excavation, at least for the moment.

Back in the classroom, the students talked excitedly about the find. This, they all agreed, was real science. **Science,** they knew, is the process of trying to understand the world.

Calling in the Experts

While not wanting to dampen their enthusiasm, Ms. Garcia reminded the students that the piece of pottery might be something that was thrown out only decades ago. To be sure, however, the school's principal called an archaeologist at the local college. An *archaeologist,* such as the two shown in **Figure 1-2B,** is a scientist who studies the cultural remains of ancient peoples. Cultural remains might be tools, weapons, rock drawings, buildings, or pottery, such as that found at the school. Dr. Lum, the students were told, would be at the school on Monday to examine the pottery.

Ms. Garcia suggested that her students go to the library to research more about the history of their area. Ben and the others in his group quickly began their research. Maria thought that it would be a good idea to take notes on their findings. That way, they could compare what they found with what Dr. Lum told them on Monday. The others in the group agreed and put their science notebooks into their backpacks before heading to the library.

Figure 1-2

A Archaeologists study pottery and other items found at sites to learn more about ancient peoples.

B Archaeologists work in the field to gather data.

Researching the Past

Once at the library, Juan used an encyclopedia to begin his research. He found out that archaeology is a branch of science that studies the tools and other cultural remains of humans. There are two major branches of archaeology, as shown in **Figure 1-3.** One branch focuses on groups of people who lived before history was written. The other branch studies civilizations that developed since people began writing things down. To his surprise, Juan also discovered that archaeology covers a time span of more than 3 million years. About 3.5 million years ago, he read, our first ancestors appeared on Earth. ✔

The other students took turns finding out about the history of their area. Ben found out that many scientists hypothesize that the first people came to North America from Asia about 12 000 years ago. Over thousands of years, these people migrated to different parts of the country. Emily and Maria discovered that the area around their city was settled about 2000 years ago. After locating a few more sources, the students took notes on all the information they had gathered. Emily suggested that they also should write down any questions they had about the pottery or the science of archaeology. Juan, Ben, and Maria agreed and each wrote down a few questions. The group left the library anxious to hear how its findings would compare with what Dr. Lum would have to say on Monday.

Reading Check ✔

What is archaeology?

Figure 1-3

A One branch of archaeology studies the cultural remains of people who lived before history was written.

Dr. Lum's Visit

Dr. Lum arrived a few minutes before nine o'clock. The students could hardly contain their excitement. When the bell rang, Emily's hand shot up. She was hoping to be the first to ask the scientist about the pottery. But, before calling on her, Dr. Lum explained that she wanted to give the students a little background information and then she would answer questions.

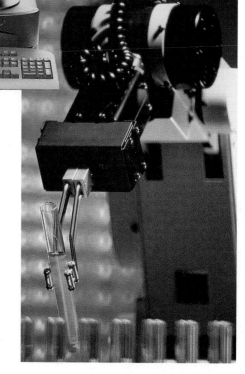

Figure 1-4
Computers and robots are two examples of technology. **Name at least three other forms of technology.**

Dr. Lum began by saying that it is important to preserve prehistoric sites and remains for present and future generations. She also said that many archaeological sites, like the one on the school grounds, are found by accident. More scientific work would have to be done before construction on the site could continue. Several kinds of technology would be used to study the area, such as computers and cameras. **Technology** is the use of knowledge gained through science to make products or tools people can use. **Figure 1-4** shows some common types of technology.

Dr. Lum explained that a radar survey would be conducted to help study the find at the school. This type of technology, Dr. Lum explained, helps scientists "see" what's beneath the ground without disturbing the site. Experts from other fields of science probably would be called upon to help evaluate the site. For instance, geologists, scientists who study Earth processes, might be contacted to help with soil studies.

B Archaeologists also study civilizations that have developed since people began recording history. **The two branches of archaeology cover a time span of how many years?**

Working Together

Dr. Lum ended her talk by suggesting that the students go back to the site with her. There, she would examine what had been found. She also would try to answer any questions the students might have about the find.

Maria and Emily led the group of curious students back toward the north end of the school yard. Dr. Lum used her hand lens to examine the piece of pottery carefully. After a few minutes, she announced that she was sure the pottery was old and that an archaeological dig, or excavation of the site, was in order. The students asked if they could participate in the dig. Dr. Lum said she would welcome all the help they could give.

Digging In

Weeks passed before the radar surveys were complete. The students in Ms. Garcia's class spent most of their time learning about how an archaeological excavation is done. Maria reported to the class that the holes and ditches being dug around the site would help determine the size of the site. She also added that it was important that the site be disturbed as little as possible. By keeping the site intact, much of the history of the site could be retold.

Finally, the day came when the students could participate in the dig. Each was given a small hand shovel, a soft paintbrush, and a pair of gardening gloves, such as those shown in **Figure 1-5.** Each student was paired with an amateur archaeologist. All of those involved were instructed to work slowly and carefully in order to excavate this important piece of their city's past.

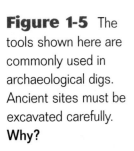

interNET
CONNECTION

Visit the Glencoe Science Web Site at **www. glencoe.com/sec/ science/nc** for more information about archaeology.

Figure 1-5 The tools shown here are commonly used in archaeological digs. Ancient sites must be excavated carefully. **Why?**

Clues to the Past

Many pieces of pottery, along with some tools, were found at the site. Before the artifacts were removed from the soil, college students working with Dr. Lum took pictures or made drawings of the pieces. These were used to make maps showing the exact location of each artifact before it was excavated. The maps also would be used to show differences in the site both vertically and horizontally.

Lab Work

Each piece was given a number that described its location and its orientation in the soil. After the artifacts were registered and cataloged, they were removed from the site. Dr. Lum told the students that she would take the finds back to her lab. There, they would be cleaned, studied, and stored, as shown in **Figure 1-6.**

Dr. Lum explained that chemical analyses of the pottery and tools would be used to determine the exact age of each piece. Based on her knowledge of the area, Dr. Lum thought that the site was at least several thousand years old.

Figure 1-6 After artifacts are excavated, they're cleaned and tagged for further study.

Section Assessment

1. What is archaeology?
2. Describe some common forms of technology.
3. Why do scientists conduct radar surveys of archaeological sites?
4. **Think Critically:** Why are maps of prehistoric sites often made before removing the artifacts?
5. **Skill Builder**
   Comparing and Contrasting
   Compare and contrast science and technology. If you need help, refer to Comparing and Contrasting in the **Skill Handbook** on page 556.

Using Computers

Word Processing Use some local reference books to find out about the prehistoric history of your state or the area around your town. Write a creative yet factual story based on what you find. If you need help, refer to page 568.

Model an Archaeological Dig

Possible Materials

- Small stones and pebbles
- Craft sticks
- Bits of black tissue paper
- Toothpicks
- Sand
- Small plastic, interlocking building blocks
- Small paintbrushes
- Plastic shovels
- Large plastic dishwashing tub or clear storage box
- Ruler, pencil, and paper

Have you ever put together a model airplane? If so, your model was a small version of a large object. Scientists often use models to study objects that are too large or too small to observe directly. In this activity, your group will construct a model of a prehistoric site. You'll cover the site with sand and give it to another group to unearth. As amateur archaeologists, each of you will attempt to reconstruct the site based on what you find.

Recognize the Problem

What can be learned from an archaeological excavation?

Form a Hypothesis

Think about some of the things you use every day. Based on your basic needs, make a hypothesis as to what you might find at a prehistoric site once inhabited by humans.

Goals

- **Make a model** of a prehistoric site.
- **Design an experiment** to show how the prehistoric site might be excavated.
- **Make a map** of the site you construct.

Safety Precautions

Test Your Hypothesis

Plan

1. Based on the basic needs generated by your group, **make a model** of an ancient site where people once lived. You might want to include a hearth used for cooking, a trash pit, some sort of shelter, a protective wall, a burial site, a water source, and some tools.

2. **Decide** which of the possible materials listed would be best for each item you include in your site. Remember that others will be trying to determine what is contained at your site.

3. How will you cover your site so that other groups can **excavate** the artifacts?

4. Using the ruler, **determine** a way to make a map of your site.

Do

1. Make sure your teacher approves your plan before you proceed. Make any suggested changes in your plan before you start.

2. **Make the model** in the plastic dish-washing tub or storage box.

3. **Make a map** of your site.

4. **Exchange** your model with another group. Carefully **excavate** the site your group is given using the brushes and shovels.

5. **Make a map** that shows where you found each item in the model you are excavating.

6. While doing the experiment, **record** your observations in your Science Journal.

Analyze Your Data

1. Were any of the items in the site similar to the items you use or see around your community every day? Were any of the items unfamiliar? **Explain.**

2. Why did you make maps of your site and the site you excavated?

3. Did any of the excavating tools damage or disturb the site?

4. **Write** a report explaining what you found and what it might have been used for.

Draw Conclusions

1. How did your map of the site you excavated **compare** with that produced by the group that made the site?

2. Radar surveys that penetrate the ground are often conducted over possible archaeological sites. Why?

1•2 Scientific Problem Solving

What You'll Learn

► Scientific methods include several steps that are taken to try to solve a problem
► Many scientific experiments test variables
► A control can be used to make comparisons during an experiment

Vocabulary
scientific methods
observation
inference
hypothesis
independent variable
dependent variable
constant
control

Why It's Important

► Scientific methods can help you solve problems.

Scientific Methods

Several steps were taken to solve the pottery problem at York Middle School. When the pottery was found, a decision was made to stop construction. One adult guessed that the pottery was fairly old. An expert was called to verify the guess made about the pottery. Based on prior knowledge and further testing, it was concluded that the pottery was from a prehistoric culture.

Step-by-step procedures of scientific problem solving are called **scientific methods.** Any scientific method involves several steps. These steps can vary from situation to situation and aren't necessarily done in a specific order. The basic steps in a commonly used scientific method are shown in **Figure 1-7.** Let's take a look at each step in turn.

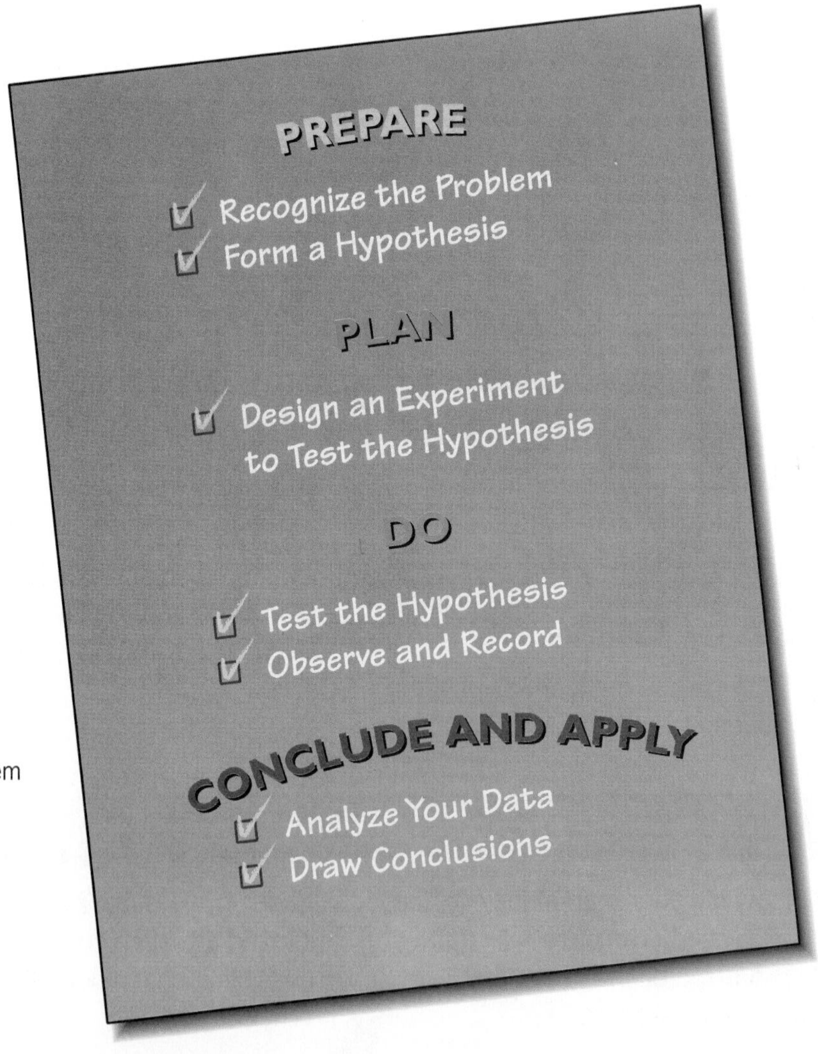

PREPARE
☑ Recognize the Problem
☑ Form a Hypothesis

PLAN
☑ Design an Experiment to Test the Hypothesis

DO
☑ Test the Hypothesis
☑ Observe and Record

CONCLUDE AND APPLY
☑ Analyze Your Data
☑ Draw Conclusions

Figure 1-7 This illustration shows one way to solve a problem or find an answer to a question. **What are scientific methods used for?**

Figure 1-8 Gathering information in the library or on the Internet can make your problem-solving tasks easier. **Besides books and computers, what other resources can you use to help you gather information?**

Recognize the Problem

Ben thought about all the science he had learned over the past few months. He was eager to find out more about the world around him. What can I explore, he thought to himself as he looked around his bedroom. It was then that Ben noticed that the plant on his window sill was droopy. He quickly watered the wilting plant. Later in the day, Ben observed that the droopy plant had perked up. He concluded that he should remember to water the plant on a regular basis. So, every day after school, he watered the plant in his room.

After a few weeks, Ben noticed that the leaves on his plant had turned yellow and brown. He knew from science class that plants need water, so why was this plant not doing well? He talked to his teacher about the plant. She suggested that Ben use what he learned in science class to solve his problem. She pointed out that this problem might make a good project for the upcoming science fair.

Ben has already completed the first step in a scientific approach to solving a problem—he recognizes a problem. A scientific problem is simply a question you don't know the answer to. In order to solve his problem, Ben must do research about his plant. Using reference materials such as those shown in **Figure 1-8,** Ben identified his plant as a fig. In his Science Journal, he drew a picture of a plant and listed some facts about it. ✔

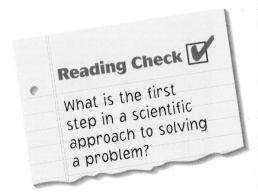

Reading Check ✔

What is the first step in a scientific approach to solving a problem?

Flex Your Brain

If you are faced with a scientific problem like Ben's, you can use the *Flex Your Brain* activity on the next page to help you solve the problem. *Flex Your Brain* is a way to keep your thinking on track when you are investigating a topic or a problem. It helps you explore what you already know and can lead you to new conclusions and awareness about a topic. Lastly, *Flex Your Brain* encourages you to review and talk about the steps you took. Communicating the results of your research is an important part of doing science. Scientists share their results so that other scientists can analyze the results or conduct new tests based on previously learned knowledge. Scientists may communicate by writing papers for science journals, speaking before large groups, or talking with other scientists directly. **Figure 1-9** shows some scientists sharing lab results. To learn more about communicating and other science skills, refer to the **Skill Handbook** at the back of this book.

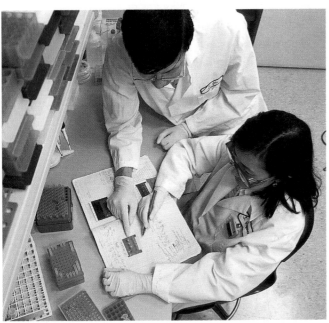

Figure 1-9 These scientists are sharing the results of an experiment with one another.

Problem Solving

Flex Your Brain

Solving problems requires a plan. This plan may be a simple thing that you do in your head, or it may be something more complicated that you actually write down. Use the *Flex Your Brain* activity on the next page to help you organize a plan for solving a problem. You may want to learn more about plants or about archaeological digs. Record your results in your Science Journal. The photograph on the right shows a Science Journal entry. You can use your Science Journal to record observations, express ideas, and draw sketches. Your Science Journal helps you practice communicating your thoughts and ideas, which you can then share with your classmates.

Think Critically: Why does *Flex Your Brain* ask you to share what you learned?

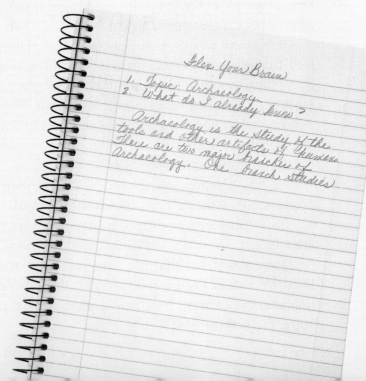

Flex Your Brain

1 Topic: _____

2 ❓ **What do I already know?**
1. _____
2. _____
3. _____
4. _____
5. _____

3 **Q:** Ask a question
_____

4 **A:** Guess an answer
_____

5 **How sure am I? (circle one)**

Not sure				Very sure
1	2	3	4	5

6 ❓ **How can I find out?**
1. _____
2. _____
3. _____
4. _____
5. _____

7 **EXPLORE**

8 **Do I think differently?** → yes no

9 ❓ **What do I know now?**
1. _____
2. _____
3. _____
4. _____
5. _____

10 **SHARE**
1. _____
2. _____
3. _____

1 Fill in the topic.

2 Jot down what you already know about the topic.

3 Using what you already know (step 2), form a question about the topic. Are you unsure about one of the items you listed? Do you want to know more? Do you want to know what, how, or why? Write down your question.

4 Guess an answer to your question. In the next few steps, you will be exploring the reasonableness of your answer. Write down your guess.

5 Circle the number in the box that matches how sure you are of your answer in step 4. This is your chance to rate your confidence in what you've done so far and, later, to see how your level of sureness affects your thinking.

6 How can you find out more about your topic? You might want to read a book, ask an expert, or do an experiment. Write down ways you can find out more.

7 Make a plan to explore your answer. Use the resources you listed in step 6. Then, carry out your plan.

8 Now that you've explored, go back to your answer in step 4. Would you answer differently?

9 Considering what you learned in your exploration, answer your question again, adding new things you've learned. You may completely change your answer.

10 It's important to be able to talk about thinking. Choose three people to tell about how you arrived at your response in every step. For example, don't just read what you wrote down in step 2. Try to share how you thought of those things.

Observe and Infer

Before Ben could communicate his results, he had to plan and carry out his experiment. First, he made and recorded careful observations about his plant. **Observations** can be bits of information you gather with your senses. Most scientific observations are made with your eyes and ears. But, you also can observe with your senses of touch, taste, and smell. Ben observed that many of the leaves had fallen off his plant. The stem, in places, was peeling. Ben also noticed that some white, powdery, smelly stuff was covering the soil in the pot. He stuck his finger into the soil. It was very wet.

Observations like Ben's often lead to inferences. An **inference** is a conclusion about an observation. Ben inferred that he was perhaps watering his plant too often. Can you make any other inferences about why Ben's plant wasn't thriving?

LIFE SCIENCE

INTEGRATION

Conserving Water

Deserts are regions of Earth that receive less than 25 cm of precipitation annually. Most of the plants in these natural habitats are cacti. Cacti have thin leaves called spines. Research how the spines and the roots of the cacti help these plants survive in desert areas.

Form a Hypothesis

After a problem has been identified, a scientist may make a hypothesis. A **hypothesis** is a statement that can be tested. Hypotheses are based on observations, research, and prior knowledge of a problem. **Table 1-1** compares and contrasts hypotheses with two other scientific statements—scientific theories and scientific laws. Ben decided to use his inference about watering too often as his hypothesis. His hypothesis was: Fig plants grow best when they are watered only once a week.

Table 1-1

Scientific Statements		
Hypothesis	**Theory**	**Law**
A hypothesis is a statement that can be tested. Hypotheses that are supported by repeated tests are used to form theories.	A theory is an explanation supported by results obtained from repeated experiments. Theories attempt to explain why something happens.	A scientific law describes the behavior of something in nature. Generally, laws predict or describe what will happen in a given situation but don't explain why. **What is the difference between a scientific theory and a scientific law?**

Figure 1-10 The amount of water added to the plants is the variable in this experiment.

A At the beginning of the experiment, similar sized plants received the same amount of sunlight and were planted in the same type of soil. The plant on the right received no water at all. It was the control.

Test Your Hypothesis

In order to test his hypothesis, Ben will carry out an experiment using three plants. An experiment, as you probably already know, is a series of carefully planned steps used to test a hypothesis. In any experiment, it's important to keep everything the same except for the item or variable you are testing so that you'll know which variable caused the results. The one factor that you change in an experiment is called the **independent variable.**

In Ben's proposed experiment, the independent variable will be the number of times he waters each plant in a week. He will then observe how well each plant grows based on the amount of water the plants receive. The growth of the plants is the dependent variable in Ben's experiment. A **dependent variable** is the factor being measured in an experiment. **Figure 1-10** shows an experiment that tests the effects of water on plants.

B Three weeks later, by controlling other factors and changing only one variable—how frequently the plant was watered—the results of the experiment clearly show the effect of water on plants.

Plan the Experiment

In order to truly test only one variable at a time, scientists often use constants. **Constants** are factors in an experiment that stay the same. In his experiment, Ben will use the same size plants, which will be potted with the same kinds and amounts of soil. His teacher pointed out that Ben also must put his plants into identical containers. Other constants in Ben's experiment will be the amount of water he'll use to water each plant and the amount of light each plant will get.

Some experiments also have a control. A **control** is a standard used for comparison. Ben knows that all plants, even cacti, need water. He's just not sure how often a fig plant needs to be watered. His control might be a plant that receives no water during the experiment.

*inter*NET
CONNECTION

Visit the Glencoe Science Web Site at **www. glencoe.com/sec/ science/nc** for more information about doing scientific experiments.

MiniLab

Observing and Inferring

Procedure

1. Look at the illustration in **Figure 1-11**. It is part of a larger illustration.
2. Record in your Science Journal everything you can observe about the illustration.
3. Use your list of observations to make inferences about what might be happening in the illustration.

Analysis

1. What do you think is happening in the illustration?
2. Compare your inference with the entire illustration on the Reviewing Main Ideas page under Section 1-2. How close was your inference to the illustration?

Figure 1-11 Study this illustration. Then do the MiniLab above to practice observing and inferring—two important science skills.

Do the Experiment

Ben gathered all the materials he would need to test his experiment. Before he starts, Ben knows from Ms. Garcia's labs that he must write down a plan to follow. In his Science Journal, he wrote that he would use three different plants. One (Plant A) would not be watered. This would be his control. A second plant (Plant B) would get watered every day during the week. The third plant (Plant C) would get watered only once a week. His experiment would last one month.

Ben then made a table in which to record his observations. He listed each plant and the number of times it was to get watered. Ben made room in the table for his measurements. He also made a plan to record his observations, which would include the height of each plant, the color of its leaves, and the number of leaves it dropped, if any. To learn more about observing, study **Figure 1-11** and do the MiniLab on this page.

Analyze Your Data

Data are collected during any scientific study. Some data are numeric values such as the length of an object or the temperature of a liquid. Other data include observations that use adjectives and phrases such as *faster than, smaller, not as well as,* and *greener.* An experimenter must record and study the data collected before he or she can draw conclusions about an experiment.

By the end of the month, Ben observed that the few leaves still left on the plant that received no water were brown and shriveled. It had lost most of its leaves. The plant that was watered every day had a few leaves left on its branches, but these leaves didn't look too healthy. Some white, smelly stuff covered the soil. Ben noticed that the plant that was watered once a week had grown the tallest. Many healthy green and white leaves hung from its branches.

Draw Conclusions

Figure 1-12

A These students are preparing for their school's science fair.

After studying his data, Ben was ready to draw some conclusions. A conclusion is a statement based on what has been observed. Ben concluded that not watering a plant caused the leaves to dry out and die. Watering a plant too much also caused the leaves to die. Watering the plant once a week seemed to be the best schedule for a fig plant.

Ben told his teacher about his results. She reminded him that in order to make sure his conclusions were valid, he should repeat his experiment. Ben agreed and did the same experiment again. Based on the results of his second experiment, Ben was able to conclude confidently that watering a plant once a week made it grow well in the temperature and light conditions he used. His hypothesis was supported, and he entered his project in his school's science fair, much like the students shown in **Figure 1-12.**

Plant Height Observations

Week	Plant A	Plant B	Plant C
1	10.5 cm	10.3 cm	10.8 cm
2	10.7 cm	11.2 cm	12.6 cm
3	10.9 cm	12.0 cm	14.6 cm
4	11.1 cm	12.4 cm	15.5 cm

B This table shows the results of an experiment similar to Ben's.

Section Assessment

1. Name the steps followed in a commonly used scientific method.

2. How are observations different from inferences?

3. Why should experiments be repeated more than once?

4. **Think Critically:** Why is it important to test only one variable at a time?

5. 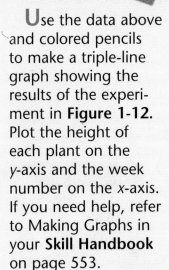 **Skill Builder**
   Separating and Controlling Variables Separating and controlling variables is an important part of conducting an experiment. Do the **Chapter 1 Skill Activity** on page 578 to practice this science skill.

Using Math

Use the data above and colored pencils to make a triple-line graph showing the results of the experiment in **Figure 1-12.** Plot the height of each plant on the *y*-axis and the week number on the *x*-axis. If you need help, refer to Making Graphs in your **Skill Handbook** on page 553.

Materials

- Magazine advertisements
- Paper (one sheet)
- Colored pencils or markers

Advertising Inferences

Imagine you're flipping through your favorite magazine and you see an ad showing a skateboard with wings. Would you infer that the skateboard could fly? In this activity, you'll use advertisements to practice the science skills of observing and inferring. Do the products really do what the ads lead you to infer?

What You'll Investigate

What observations and inferences can you make from advertisements?

Goals

- **Make inferences** based on observations.
- **Recognize** the limits of observations.

Procedure

1. **Select** three ads from those supplied by your teacher. In your Science Journal, **make a table** like the one shown below.

2. For each ad, **list** your observations. For example, you may **observe** that there are athletic people pictured in a soda ad.

3. What inferences does the advertiser want you to make from the ad? **Make inferences** that relate your observations to the product that the ad is selling. The soda ad, for example, may lead you to infer that if you drink that soda, you will be athletic.

4. **Share** your inferences and advertisements with others in your class.

Conclude and Apply

1. **Compare** and **contrast** your classmates' inferences with your own. Are there other explanations for the things you observed in the ads?

2. **Create** your own ad to sell a product. Think about what people will observe in the ad and what you want them to infer from it.

3. Have a classmate make inferences about your ad. What did your classmate infer about the ad you created? Is this what you wanted the classmate to infer? **Explain.**

Ad Data		
	Observation	Inference
Ad 1		
Ad 2		
Ad 3		

interNET CONNECTION

Visit the Glencoe Science Web Site at **www.glencoe.com/sec/science/nc** for more information about the uses of GPR. How is GPR used in environmental cleanups or in efforts to locate abandoned mines?

Radar

Radar is an electronic system used to locate and identify distant objects. Police officers (top left) use radar to detect drivers who go over the speed limit. Meteorologists use radar to keep tabs on weather systems (bottom left). Air-traffic controllers rely on radar for tracking airplanes. People who fish use radar to locate schools of fish.

How Radar Works

The term *radar* stands for **RA**dio **D**etecting **A**nd **R**anging system. A radar system is made of several parts. The transmitter generates electromagnetic waves, which are produced by the motion of electrically charged particles. Light, radio waves, and microwaves are all examples of electromagnetic waves. In a radar system, these waves leave the transmitter through one or more antennae. When the waves encounter an object, the radio waves scatter. These scattered waves, often called echoes, are received by other antennae in the radar system. An amplifier increases the signals of these echoes. A computer then processes the signals and displays them on a screen. The distance to the target object, its altitude or depth, and the object's position relative to the radar source also can be displayed on the screen.

Ground Penetrating Radar

A type of radar called ground penetrating radar (GPR) can be used to explore archaeological sites. The system can be used to identify important underground features before a site is excavated. This step helps scientists decide which parts of the site are safe to explore and which should be avoided to prevent damaging the site. Computers process the data gathered by radar and use the information to create three-dimensional maps of the site.

Radar Development in World War II

Even before the United States entered World War II, the first Army radar was patented in May of 1937. By 1941, early warning radars could detect an approaching plane, though not its altitude or size. Radar was one of the most important communication developments of World War II.

For a **preview** of this chapter, study this Reviewing Main Ideas before you read the chapter. After you have studied this chapter, you can use the Reviewing Main Ideas to **review** the chapter.

The Glencoe MindJogger, Audiocassettes, and CD-ROM provide additional opportunities for review.

Section

1-1 HOW SCIENCE WORKS

Science is a process of understanding the world around you. **Technology** is the use of the knowledge gained through scientific thinking and problem solving. Archaeologists, scientists who study the artifacts of ancient people, use both science and technology in their work. Many archaeological sites and the artifacts they contain are found by accident. The excavation of an archaeological find is done slowly and carefully so that the artifacts and the site itself are not damaged or destroyed. Artifacts such as tools and pottery can be dated using chemical analyses. During an archaeological dig, maps are often made to show the location of each artifact with respect to the site. *Describe the two branches of archaeology.*

Section

1-2 SCIENTIFIC PROBLEM SOLVING

Scientific methods are step-by-step approaches to solving problems. Steps that can be used in scientific problem solving include identifying the problem, forming and testing a **hypothesis,** analyzing the results of the test, and drawing conclusions. Many scientific experiments involve two variables, or factors, that change. An **independent variable** is a factor that the experimenter changes. The **dependent variable** is the factor that changes as a result of the independent variable. **Constants** are factors in an experiment that don't change. A **control,** when one is included, is a standard used for comparison. *Why should you test only one variable at a time?*

Career
CONNECTION

Amanda Shaw, International Science Fair Contestant

Amanda Shaw is an example of how young people can become involved in science. Her science fair project studied the effects of carbon dioxide and plants on global warming. After winning first place in a regional competition, Amanda went on to compete against hundreds of other young scientists at the International Science and Engineering Fair (ISEF). Many scientists first become interested in environmental issues by participating in science fair projects. *What does it take to make a good science fair project?*

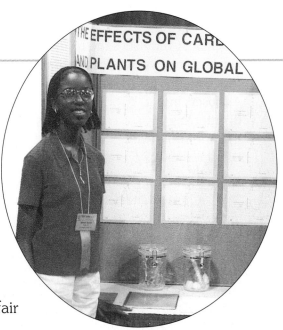

Chapter 1 Assessment

Using Vocabulary

a. constant
b. control
c. dependent variable
d. hypothesis
e. independent variable
f. inference
g. observation
h. science
i. scientific methods
j. technology

Each phrase below describes a science term from the list. Write the term that matches the phrase describing it.

1. variable changed by the person doing the experiment
2. a statement that can be tested
3. step-by-step approach to solving problems
4. information you gather with your senses
5. the process of understanding the world around you

Checking Concepts

Choose the word or phrase that best answers the question.

6. A scientist publishes the results of her experiments. Which science skill is she practicing?
   A) observing
   B) inferring
   C) communicating
   D) hypothesizing

7. What technology helps archaeologists to "see" a buried site before they begin excavating it?
   A) mapmaking
   B) digging
   C) radar
   D) experimenting

8. What is the first step in a commonly used scientific method?
   A) forming a hypothesis
   B) recognizing a problem
   C) drawing conclusions
   D) analyzing data

9. Why do scientists make maps of archaeological sites?
   A) to photograph artifacts
   B) to calculate the exact age of artifacts
   C) to record where the artifacts were found
   D) to discover artifacts

10. What is a standard used for comparison in an experiment called?
    A) a constant
    B) an independent variable
    C) a dependent variable
    D) a control

11. What is a conclusion based on an observation?
    A) a control
    B) a hypothesis
    C) an inference
    D) a variable

12. What is a series of carefully planned steps used to test a hypothesis?
    A) a constant
    B) an observation
    C) an experiment
    D) a conclusion

13. Why should an experiment be repeated?
    A) to form a hypothesis
    B) to reduce the chance of error
    C) to change controls
    D) to identify the problem

14. What should an experimenter do after analyzing test results?
    A) identify the problem
    B) draw conclusions
    C) carry out the experiment
    D) form a hypothesis

15. A computer is an example of which of the following?
    A) an experiment
    B) a control
    C) an excavation
    D) technology

Thinking Critically

16. An archaeologist finds a site that contains many different layers of artifacts. What might she conclude about the people who lived at the site?
17. Is every scientific problem solved using the same steps? Explain.
18. Explain why the following statement is false. Scientists do all their work in laboratories.
19. Describe how you might test which laundry soap cleans the best. Be sure to include variables, constants, and a control.
20. Why is it important to accurately record and measure data during an experiment?

Developing Skills

If you need help, refer to the Skill Handbook.

21. **Concept Map:** Use the following terms to complete the concept map of a commonly used scientific method shown on this page: *analyze data, form a hypothesis, design an experiment to test the hypothesis,* and *observe and record.*

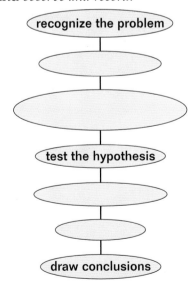

22. **Separating and Controlling Variables:** Give an example of how Ben controlled variables in his fig plant experiment.

THE PRINCETON REVIEW

Test-Taking Tip

Don't Guess When answering questions about a topic, do not guess. Always return to the original material to reread and get the details from there.

Test Practice

Use these questions to test your Science Proficiency.

1. Min observed that a plant in a shady corner of her bedroom was not growing as well as a plant on the windowsill. She guessed that plants need sunlight to grow and decided to conduct an experiment to test her hypothesis. She put one plant in the cool dark basement of her house and another in the warm bright kitchen. What is wrong with Min's experiment?
   A) She did not form a hypothesis.
   B) She did not control variables.
   C) She did not carry out the experiment.
   D) She did not identify the problem.

2. You see a flock of geese flying south and think that the geese must be migrating to a warmer climate for the winter. Which of the following **BEST** describes how you reached this explanation?
   A) You made an observation, then an inference.
   B) You made an inference, then an observation.
   C) You made an inference, then a conclusion.
   D) You made a conclusion, then a hypothesis.

Chapter Preview

Section 2-1
Description and Measurement

Section 2-2
SI Units

Section 2-3
Communicating Data

Skills Preview

Skill Builders
- Use Numbers
- Make a Graph

Activities
- Make a Model
- Design an Experiment

MiniLabs
- Measure in SI

Reading Check

Look up words that begin with the prefixes listed in **Table 2-2.** Explain why the words have these prefixes.

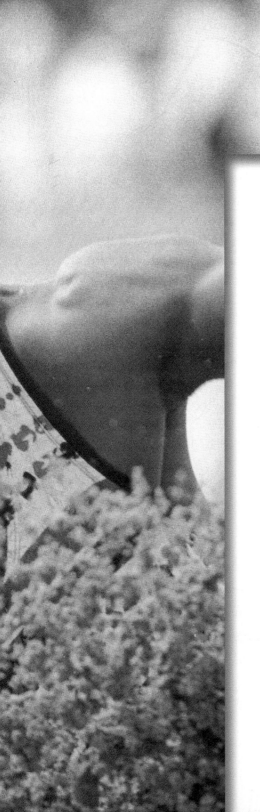

Explore Activity

Carl Lewis goes the distance in both the long jump shown here and in other Olympic events. He won a total of nine gold medals at the Olympic Games in 1984, 1988, 1992, and 1996. Four of his gold medals are in the long jump. His winning jump at the 1996 Olympics was a distance of 8.5 m. Carl Lewis and other athletes depend on accurate and precise measurement in competitions. A fraction of a centimeter can separate the gold and silver medalists in the long jump.

Measuring Length

1. Horses are measured in a unit called *hands*. One hand is about 10 cm. Measure several items using the width of your own hand as *1 hand.*

2. About how many hands long is your arm from shoulder to fingertip? How wide is this book?

3. Now, measure two other objects in the classroom using your hand.

Science Journal

Why switch from hands to meters and centimeters as units of length?

2·1 Description and Measurement

What You'll Learn

▶ Different methods of measurement
▶ How exact a measurement is

Vocabulary
measurement
estimation

Why It's Important

▶ Measurement helps you communicate information and ideas.

CHEMISTRY INTEGRATION

Descriptions of Matter
A description of matter that does not involve measurement is qualitative. For example, water is composed of hydrogen and oxygen. A quantitative description uses measurement. For example, one water molecule is composed of one oxygen atom and two hydrogen atoms. Give a qualitative and quantitative description of your hand.

Measurement

If someone asked you to describe what you are wearing today, what would you say? You'd probably start by describing colors and styles. Then, you might mention sizes: size 7 shoes, size 13 shirt. Every day, you are surrounded by numbers. **Measurement** is a way to describe the world with numbers. It answers questions such as how much, how long, or how far. Measurement can describe the amount of milk in a carton, the cost of a new compact disc, or the distance between your home and your school. It also can describe the volume of water in the oceans, the mass of an atom, or how fast a penguin's heart pumps blood.

Figure 2-1 shows a fossilized *Knightia* fish. This fossil is about 50 million years old. An average *Knightia* was about 10 cm long. About 60 percent of the fish in the Green River shale quarries, from which this fossil comes, are *Knightia*. Scientists use these measurements to describe and understand fossils. Information described with numbers, such as length and age, is a measurement.

Figure 2-1 This *Knightia* fossil fish is from the Green River shale formation in western Wyoming. **Does this photo show the actual size of the fossil? Explain.**

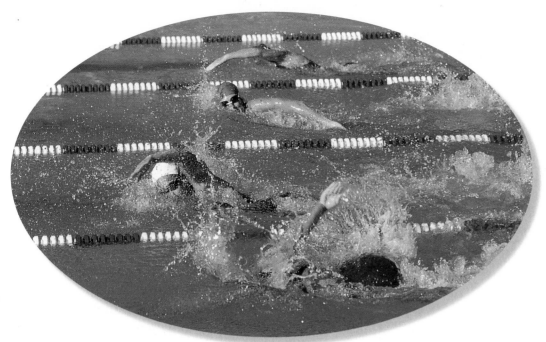

Figure 2-2 Accurate measurement of distance and time is important for competitive sports such as swimming. **Would a clock that only measured in minutes be accurate enough for this race?**

Measurement also can describe events such as the one shown in **Figure 2-2.** In the 1968 summer Olympics, swimmer Debbie Meyer of the United States came in first in the women's 200-m freestyle. She swam the race in 130.5 s. Claudia Poli of Costa Rica won first place in 1996. She swam the 200 meters in 118.16 s. In this example, measurement conveys information about the year of the race, the length, the finishing order, and the time. Information about who competed and in what sport are not measurements but are needed to describe the event completely.

Figure 2-3 This student is about 1.5 m tall. **Estimate the size of the tree in the photo.**

Estimation

You have probably used a ruler, meterstick, or tape measure to find an object's length. What happens when you want to describe a tree's height but you can't measure it with a meterstick? You can use your knowledge about the height of a familiar object to estimate the height of the tree.

Estimation can help you make a rough measurement of an object by guessing. Estimation is based on experience, as shown in **Figure 2-3.** It is useful when you are in a hurry and exact data are not required. Estimation is a valuable skill that improves with experience, practice, and understanding.

Mini Lab

Measuring Accurately

Procedure

Use the equipment in your classroom to practice measuring. You can use a graduated cylinder to measure water volume, a balance to measure the mass of a small object, a meterstick to measure the door, and a clock to measure pulse rate. For hints on making measurements, use the **Field Guide to Laboratory Equipment** at the end of this chapter.

Analysis

1. What measurements could you easily make at home?
2. What limitations does each piece of equipment have?
3. Before standardized instruments were widely available, a scientist might have used a pulse or the swing of a pendulum to measure time. What are some of the limitations of these measures?

Using Estimation

You can compare an object whose length you do not know with familiar objects to estimate its length. When you estimate, you often use the word *about*. One meter is about the height of a doorknob above the floor. One centimeter is about the width of the tip of your smallest finger. One millimeter is about the thickness of a dime. To estimate your height, would you use meters, centimeters, or millimeters? What unit would you use to estimate the size of the point of your pencil?

Estimation also is used to check that an answer is reasonable. Suppose you calculate your friend's running speed as 47 m/s. You are familiar with how long a second is and how long a meter is. Can you picture your friend running a 50-m dash in 1 s? Estimation tells you that 47 m/s is too high a speed, and you should check your work.

Figure 2-4 Precision depends on the tool used.

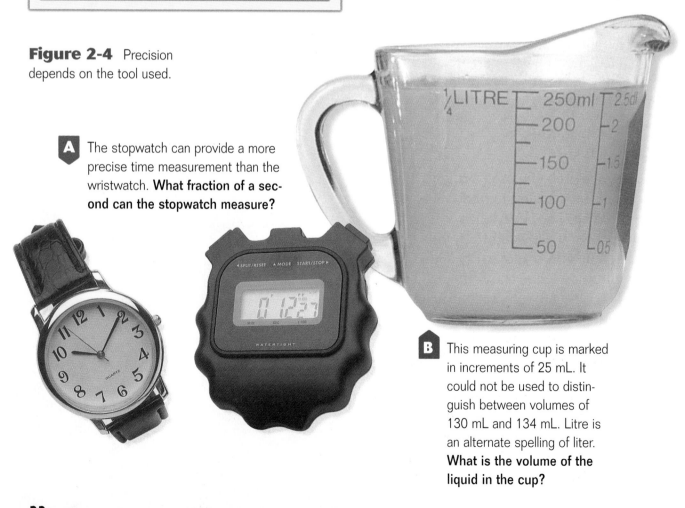

A The stopwatch can provide a more precise time measurement than the wristwatch. **What fraction of a second can the stopwatch measure?**

B This measuring cup is marked in increments of 25 mL. It could not be used to distinguish between volumes of 130 mL and 134 mL. Litre is an alternate spelling of liter. **What is the volume of the liquid in the cup?**

Figure 2-5 Shooting baskets illustrates accuracy and precision.

A When your shots hit all over, they are not accurate or precise.

B When your shots consistently hit a point well to the left of the basket, they are precise but not accurate.

C When your shots are consistently in the basket, they are precise and accurate.

Precision and Accuracy

Precision describes how carefully you make your measurement. The precision of the tool used determines the precision of the measurement, as shown in **Figure 2-4.** If you measure the width of this book with a ruler marked to millimeters, you can determine the precise width of the book only to the nearest millimeter. A precise measurement can be reproduced. For example, if you measure your desk to be precisely 85 cm high, the person next to you will also measure 85 cm.

Look at an almanac that lists Olympic winners of the past. Winning measurements for some events are given with more precision over time. Times from the 1896 Olympics might be given to the nearest second. Times for later Olympics are given to the nearest tenth of a second, then the nearest hundredth of a second. This is an example of how improved tools make more precise measurements.

Accuracy compares a measurement to the real value. A clock that does not work well could give precise measurements that are inaccurate. **Figure 2-5** illustrates the difference between precision and accuracy. ☑

Reading Check ☑
What is accuracy?

Figure 2-6 This laboratory scale can measure to the nearest hundredth of a gram. **What is the mass of the object rounded to the nearest tenth of a gram?**

Rounding a Measure

Sometimes, you have more precision than you need, as shown in **Figure 2-6.** Not all measurements must be made with instruments that measure with great precision. For example, you could measure the length of the sidewalk outside your school to the nearest millimeter. However, you would probably need to know the length only to the nearest meter or tenth of a meter. If your teacher told you the length was 135.841 m, you could round the distance to 135.8 m or 136 m. To round a given value, follow these steps.

1. Look at the digit to the right of the place being rounded.

    • The digit remains the same if the digit to the right is 0, 1, 2, 3, or 4.

    • Round up if the digit to the right is 5, 6, 7, 8, or 9.

2. The remaining digits to the right of the rounding place are eliminated from the rounded answer.

Using Math

Rounding

Example Problem

Refer to the periodic table inside the back cover of this book. The atomic mass of lithium is 6.941 atomic mass units. The atomic mass of neon is 20.180 atomic mass units. You decide that you need to know these values only to the nearest unit to solve a problem. What are the rounded values?

Problem-Solving Steps

1. What number is to the right of the ones place? lithium: 9 neon: 1
2. Do you round the ones place up or down? lithium: up; neon: down
3. **Solution:** lithium: 6.941 rounds to 7 atomic mass units
              neon: 20.180 rounds to 20 atomic mass units

Practice Problem

What are the rounded atomic masses to the nearest tenth of a unit?

Strategy Hint: To round to a certain place, remember to ignore all the numbers more than one place to the right. For example, to round 31 498.89 to the nearest thousand, look at the 4 and round down. Ignore the 8s and 9s that follow the 4.

Precision and Number of Digits

Suppose you want to divide a 2-L bottle of soda equally among seven people. You find $2 \div 7$ on your calculator: 0.285 714 285 7. Will you measure exactly 0.285 714 285 7 L of soda for each person? (Even this number is inexact. Your calculator rounds or cuts off the answer when its display is out of room.) In this case, you need to know that each person gets about 0.3 L. You don't have to copy every digit that appears on your calculator.

A good way to determine the number of digits in the answer when you multiply or divide is to look at the number of digits in each piece of information. In this case, 2 L has one digit and seven people has one digit. The answer should probably have only one or two digits.

Suppose you measure a folder to be 0.008 m thick. You place it on a desk that is 1 m off the ground. Is the top of the folder exactly 1.008 m off the ground? Probably not. The desk might be 1.05 m, or 0.937 m, or any other measure that rounds to 1 m. Because you know the height of the desk only to the ones digit and the height of the folder to the thousandths digit, trying to add them exactly does not make sense. If you round to the ones, the least precise digit in the problem, you get 1 m as the height.

*inter*NET
CONNECTION

Visit the Glencoe Science Web Site at **www.glencoe.com/ sec/science/nc** for more information about measurement.

Section Assessment

1. Estimate the distance between your desk and your teacher's desk. Explain the method you used.

2. Measure the height of your desk to the nearest half-centimeter.

3. Sarah measured her father's garden. It is 11.72 m long. Round the measure to the nearest tenth of a meter.

4. **Think Critically:** You are given two metric rulers, one marked in half-centimeters and one marked in millimeters. Which would be most helpful in measuring small items such as the width of a wire?

5.  **Skill Builder**
   Using Numbers Numbers are used to make measurements. Do the **Chapter 2 Skill Activity** on page 579 to use numbers to describe familiar objects.

Science **Journal**
In your Science Journal, describe your backpack. Include one set of qualities that have no measurements, such as color and texture, and one set of measurements, such as width and mass.

Science & Society

Global Positioning System

In the early days of flight, pilots flew relatively close to the ground and navigated by landmarks and natural features such as rivers and mountains. In darkness or bad weather, pilots were out of luck. The invention of radar made it possible to navigate without seeing the ground. Today, pilots can determine their position with even greater precision using the Global Positioning System (GPS). The GPS can determine the position, speed, and direction of movement of a pilot or any other person using the system anywhere on Earth.

How GPS Works

Twenty-four GPS satellites orbit in a circular path 20 200 km above Earth. The satellites, powered by solar cells (see inset), send signals to receivers on Earth. Each receiver measures the distance between itself and every satellite within range. Three satellite readings are enough for people using a GPS receiver to determine their position on Earth's surface. To ensure accuracy, receivers use information from four satellites. The woman at right holds an antenna that is receiving position data from the GPS satellite system.

The GPS measures the time it takes for the receiver to communicate with each satellite. This measurement is used to calculate latitude, longitude, and elevation. If the receiver is moving, its velocity also can be determined. Receivers at ground-based stations with fixed positions are used to check accuracy and to make corrections for errors.

A variety of GPS receiving units are available, with different levels of precision. Small receivers, used by boaters and hikers, are precise to within a few hundred meters. GPS receivers used for making topographic maps and construction layouts measure position to within several centimeters, while those used for measuring difficult terrain such as mountains and rivers can measure accurately to within less than 1 cm.

interNET CONNECTION

To research how scientists use GPS to help them in their studies, visit the Glencoe Science Web Site at **www.glencoe. com/sec/science/nc.**

SI Units

The International System

Can you imagine how confusing it would be if scientists in every country used different measuring systems? Sharing data and ideas would be complicated. To avoid confusion, scientists need a common language. The International System of Units, or **SI,** was established in 1960 as the general system for measurement. It was designed to provide a worldwide standard of physical measurement for science, industry, and commerce. SI uses units such as meter, cubic meter, kilogram, and kelvin, as shown in **Table 2-1.**

The SI units are related by multiples of ten. A unit, such as the meter, can be converted to a smaller or larger unit by multiplying by a power of 10. The new unit is renamed by adding a prefix, shown in **Table 2-2.** For example, one millionth of a meter is one *micro*meter. One thousand grams is one *kilo*gram.

To convert between units, multiply by the appropriate power of ten. For example, to rewrite a kilogram measurement as a gram measurement, multiply by 1000.

What You'll Learn

► SI is the international system of measurement
► The SI units of length, volume, mass, temperature, time, and rate

Vocabulary

SI	kilogram
meter	Kelvin
mass	rate

Why It's Important

► The SI system is used throughout the world.

Table 2-1

SI Units		
Quantity	**Unit**	**Symbol**
length	meter	m
volume	cubic meter	m^3
mass	kilogram	kg
temperature	kelvin	K
time	second	s

Table 2-2

Prefixes Used with SI Units	
Prefix	**Multiplier**
tera-	1 000 000 000 000
giga-	1 000 000 000
mega-	1 000 000
kilo-	1000
hecto-	100
deca-	10
[unit]	1
deci-	0.1
centi-	0.01
milli-	0.001
micro-	0.000 001
nano-	0.000 000 001

Using Math

Using Unit Analysis

Example Problem
Rafael measured his classroom to be 468 cm long. Find the length in meters.

Problem-Solving Steps
1. Write the number you want to convert. 468 cm
2. Determine what unit you want the answer to be in. meters
3. Write the number of centimeters in a meter as a fraction. In this case, there are 100 cm in 1 m.

   Use $\dfrac{100\ cm}{1\ m}$ or $\dfrac{1\ m}{100\ cm}$.

4. Write the expression, including the units. Check that the units cancel correctly so the answer will be in meters.

5. **Solution:** $468\ cm \times \dfrac{1\ m}{100\ cm} = 4.68\ m$

Practice Problem
How many milliseconds are in 23.6 s?

Strategy Hint: Check that the units cancel appropriately before making calculations. For example, if your expression for speed will produce an answer in square meters, you can see that you have made an error before doing any calculations.

Figure 2-7 The actual size of these red blood cells is about 15 micrometers across. **How many meters is this?**

Length

Length is defined as the distance between two points. Length can describe the distance from Earth to Mars or the distance across a cell under a microscope, as shown in **Figure 2-7.** In your science lab, you will usually measure length with a metric ruler or meterstick.

The **meter** (m) is the SI unit of length. One meter is about the length of a baseball bat. The size of a room would be measured in meters.

Smaller objects can be measured in centimeters (cm) or millimeters (mm). The length of your textbook or pencil would be measured in centimeters. Millimeters might be used to measure the width of the letters on this page. To measure the length of small things such as blood cells, bacteria, or viruses, scientists use micrometers (millionths of a meter) and nanometers (billionths of a meter).

Sometimes scientists need to measure long distances, such as the distance a migrating bird travels. To measure such lengths they use kilometers. Kilometers may be most familiar to you as the measure of a race or the distance traveled in a car, as shown in **Figure 2-8.**

Volume

The amount of space an object occupies is its volume. The cubic meter (m^3), shown in **Figure 2-9,** is the SI unit of volume. You can measure smaller volumes with the cubic centimeter (cm^3 or cc). To find the volume of a square or rectangular object, such as a brick or your textbook, measure its length, width, and height, and multiply them. What is the volume of a compact disc case?

You are probably familiar with a 2-liter bottle. A liter is a measurement of liquid volume. A cube 10 cm on a side (1000 cm^3) holds one liter of water. A cube 1 cm on a side (1 cm^3) holds one milliliter of water.

Figure 2-8 Long distances are measured in kilometers. This sign warns drivers in Australia about animals crossing the road. **About how many kilometers is the distance between your home and your school?**

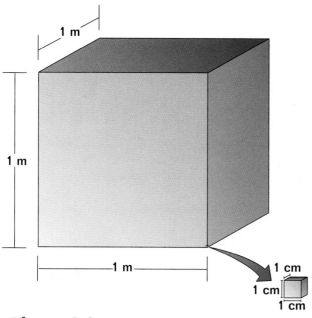

Figure 2-9 A cubic meter equals the volume of a cube 1 meter by 1 meter by 1 meter. **How many cubic centimeters are in a cubic meter?**

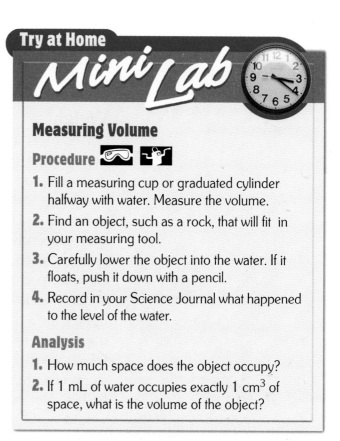

Try at Home
Mini Lab

Measuring Volume

Procedure

1. Fill a measuring cup or graduated cylinder halfway with water. Measure the volume.
2. Find an object, such as a rock, that will fit in your measuring tool.
3. Carefully lower the object into the water. If it floats, push it down with a pencil.
4. Record in your Science Journal what happened to the level of the water.

Analysis

1. How much space does the object occupy?
2. If 1 mL of water occupies exactly 1 cm^3 of space, what is the volume of the object?

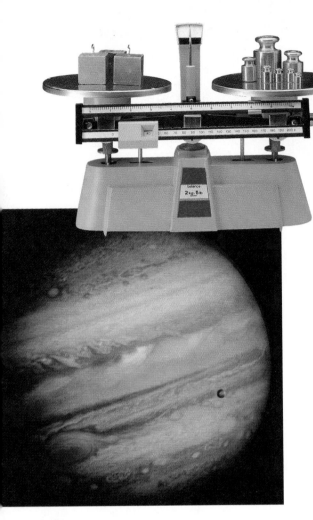

Figure 2-10 Mass is not the same as weight.

A A pan balance compares an unknown mass to known masses.

Mass

The **mass** of an object measures the amount of matter in the object. The **kilogram** (kg) is the SI unit for mass. One liter of water has a mass of about 1 kg. Smaller masses are measured in grams (g). One gram is about the mass of a large paper clip. You can measure mass with a pan balance, shown in **Figure 2-10A.** The pan balance compares an object to a known mass. It is balanced when the masses on both sides are equal.

Why use the word *mass* instead of weight? Weight and mass are not the same. Mass depends on the amount of matter in an object. Mass never changes, as shown in **Figure 2-10B.** When you ride in an elevator or on the space shuttle, your mass stays the same.

B Jupiter has a mass of 1.90×10^{27} kg. It does not make sense to talk about the weight of Jupiter because it is not on the surface of Earth or another planet.

Weight

Weight is a measurement of force. It depends on gravity, which can change depending on where the object is located. A spring scale, shown in **Figure 2-11,** measures weight. The reading on the scale depends on the force pulling the spring. When you start riding up in an elevator, you feel heavier for a moment. When the elevator starts down, you feel lighter for a moment. If you were standing in the elevator on a bathroom scale, which uses a spring, you would see a slight change in your weight. But, if you had a pan balance in the elevator, it would not suddenly tip. The masses in the pans would not change, and it would remain balanced. ☑

Figure 2-11 A spring scale measures an object's weight by how much it stretches a spring. **What is the weight of the rock?**

Reading Check ☑

What does weight measure?

Temperature

The physical property of temperature is used to measure how hot or cold an object is. You may know about the Fahrenheit or Celsius temperature scale on a thermometer. Temperature is measured in SI with the **Kelvin** scale. A 1 K difference in temperature is the same as a 1°C difference in temperature, as shown in **Figure 2-12.** However, the two scales start at different points. Zero degrees Celsius is the freezing point of water at sea level. Water boils at 100°C. Zero kelvin is the coldest temperature possible in nature.

Time and Rates

Time is the interval between two events. The SI unit of time is the second (s). Time is sometimes measured in hours (h). Though this is not an SI unit, it is easier to use when you discuss long periods.

A **rate** is a ratio of two measurements with different units. One rate you are familiar with is speed, the distance traveled in a given time. Speeds are often measured in kilometers per hour (km/h).

Rates are combinations of SI units. Rates are most often seen with units of time, but any measures with different units can be combined in a rate. Other rates might be

$$\frac{grains}{liter}, \frac{insects}{square\ meter}, or \frac{°C}{hour}.$$

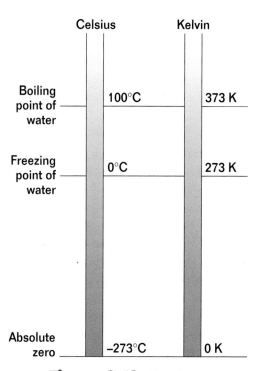

Figure 2-12 The Kelvin scale starts at 0 K.

PHYSICS
◄ INTEGRATION

Section Assessment

1. What property of an object does the cubic meter measure?

2. How would you change a measure in centimeters to kilometers?

3. **Think Critically:** You are given a small metal cube and told to find its mass. What tool(s) will you need, and how will you use the tool(s) to determine its mass?

4. **Skill Builder**
   Forming Operational Definitions
   Give an operational definition of a spring scale. If you need help, refer to Forming Operational Definitions in the **Skill Handbook** on page 558.

Using Math

A block of wood is 0.2 m by 0.1 m by 0.5 m. Find its dimensions in centimeters. Use these to find its volume in cubic centimeters.

Scale Drawing

Materials

- Graph paper (1 cm)
- Pencil
- Metric ruler
- Meterstick

A scale drawing is used to represent something that is too large or too small to be drawn at its actual size. Blueprints for a house are a good example of a scale drawing.

What You'll Investigate

How can you represent your classroom accurately in a scale drawing?

Goals

- **Measure** using SI.
- **Make** a data table.
- **Calculate** new measurements.
- **Draw** an accurate scale drawing.

Procedure

1. Use your meterstick to **measure** the length and width of your classroom. Note the locations and sizes of doors and windows.

2. **Record** the lengths of each item in a data table.

3. Use a scale of 2 cm = 1 m to calculate the lengths to be used in the drawing. **Record** them in your data table.

4. **Draw** the floor plan. Include the scale.

Conclude and Apply

1. How did you **calculate** the lengths to be used on your drawing?

2. What would your scale drawing look like if you choose a different scale?

3. Sketch your room at home, estimating the distances. **Compare** this to your scale drawing of the classroom. When would you use each type of illustration?

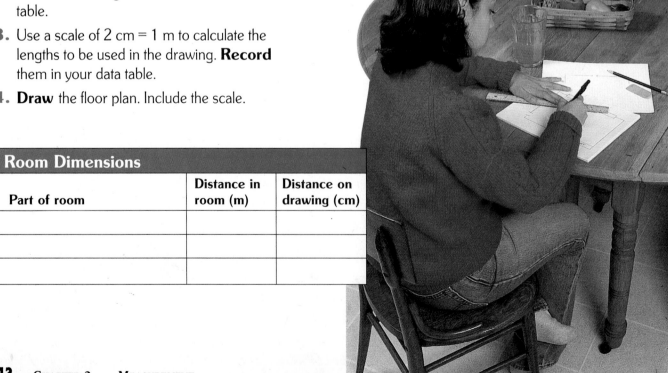

Room Dimensions		
Part of room	Distance in room (m)	Distance on drawing (cm)

Communicating Data

Scientific Illustrations

Most science books include some pictures. Photographs and drawings illustrate the ideas in the book. They also can give new information. For example, a drawing of an airplane engine can show how all the parts fit together.

Photographs

A photograph can show an object exactly as it is. A movie can show how an object moves. A movie can be slowed down or speeded up to show interesting features, as shown in **Figure 2-13.** In your schoolwork, you might use photographs in a report. For example, you could show the different types of trees in your neighborhood for a report on ecology.

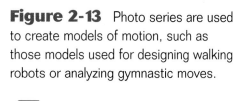

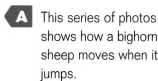

Figure 2-13 Photo series are used to create models of motion, such as those models used for designing walking robots or analyzing gymnastic moves.

A This series of photos shows how a bighorn sheep moves when it jumps.

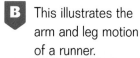

B This illustrates the arm and leg motion of a runner.

What You'll Learn

► How to use pictures and tables to give information
► How to identify and use three types of graphs
► How to distinguish the correct use of each type of graph

Vocabulary

table	bar graph
graph	circle graph
line graph	

Why It's Important

► Illustrations, tables, and graphs help communicate data.

*inter*NET CONNECTION

Visit the Glencoe Science Web Site at **www.glencoe.com/ sec/science/nc** for more information about scientific illustration.

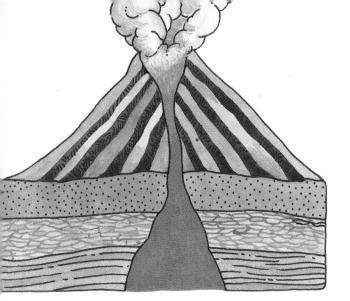

Figure 2-14 This drawing shows the layers of rock around a volcano. It also shows the volcano's interior.

Drawings

Sometimes a photograph is not the best kind of illustration to use. For example, a canyon cut through red rock reveals many rock layers. If the layers are all shades of red, a drawing can show where the line between two layers lies. The drawing can show important things, like the size of each layer, and can leave out unimportant details, like the patterns of dust on the rock.

In your studies, you might use a drawing of the Earth-moon-sun system to explain an eclipse. A drawing also can show things we can't photograph. We do not have photographs of our solar system from far away, but from drawings you know what it looks like. You also will make quick sketches to help model problems. For example, you could sketch the outline of two continents to show how they might have fit together.

A drawing can show hidden things. Geologists can use a drawing to show the inside of a volcano, as in **Figure 2-14.** Architects use drawings to show what the inside of a building will look like. Biologists use drawings to show where the nerves in your arm are found. ☑

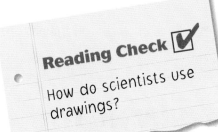

Reading Check ☑

How do scientists use drawings?

Problem Solving

Communicate with Art and Words

Imagine you are an engineer. You have a clever idea for improving a machine. Or, you are a botanist with a new idea about a plant's structure. How do you explain your idea?

To explain your ideas, you must communicate them clearly. One way is with a picture. How hard is it to describe something using only words?

Use a ruler and pencil to sketch a simple design, such as a triangle inside a square. Write a description that would explain how to make the design without actually seeing it. For example, it might start: "Draw a square 3 cm on a side. Mark a point 1 cm to the right of the lower-left corner . . ."

Trade your description with another student and try to draw the design based on the directions. Compare your design with the original.

Think Critically: Explain how this exercise relates to the problem of describing a new invention for people who cannot see it.

Tables and Graphs

Scientists and mathematicians need an organized way to collect and display data. A **table** displays information in rows and columns so that it is easier to read and understand, as seen in **Figure 2-15.** The data in the table could be presented in a paragraph, but it would be harder to pick out the facts or make comparisons.

A graph can show the relationships between the data. A **graph** is used to collect, organize, and summarize data in a visual way. A graph can display one set of data or more. Three common types of graphs are line graphs, bar graphs, and circle graphs.

Line Graph

The table in **Figure 2-15** has two variables, type of animal and speed. A variable is something that can change, or vary. A **line graph** is used to show the relationship between two variables. An example is shown in **Figure 2-16.** Both variables must be numbers. Age and height will work, but age and favorite sport will not. One variable is shown on the bottom line, or axis, of the graph. The other variable is placed along the vertical axis. A line shows the relationship between the two variables.

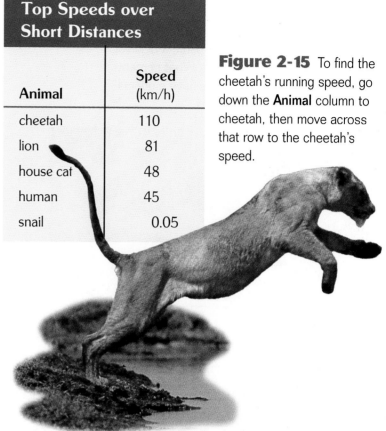

Top Speeds over Short Distances	
Animal	Speed (km/h)
cheetah	110
lion	81
house cat	48
human	45
snail	0.05

Figure 2-15 To find the cheetah's running speed, go down the **Animal** column to cheetah, then move across that row to the cheetah's speed.

The normal October temperature in San Francisco is 16°C.

Figure 2-16 The line graph has a horizontal axis and a vertical axis. This graph shows that Minneapolis and Asheville reach the same summer temperature, but Minneapolis has a much greater variation in temperature. The normal temperature in San Francisco peaks later than the temperature in the other two cities. It also has less variation.

Average Normal Temperature

San Francisco, California

Asheville, North Carolina

Minneapolis, Minnesota

(Temperature (°C) vs. Month graph)

Figure 2-17

A This bar graph has categories on the horizontal axis and numbers on the vertical axis. You can see that about 53 percent of junior high schools have modems. **What percentage of senior high schools have modems?**

B The bar graph below has numbers on both axes. Bar graphs can be horizontal or vertical. They can display any numerical data, not just percents. **Based on the bar graph, how did the percentage of homes with computers change between 1991 and 1997?**

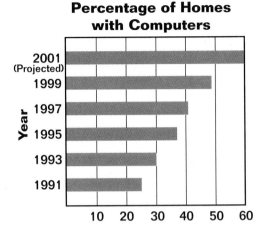

Percentage of Homes with Computers

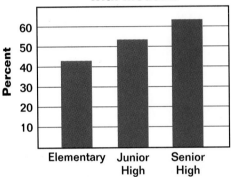

Percentage of Schools with Modems

Figure 2-18 This graph uses a circle divided into sections. All the sections together equal 100 percent. **What category has the greatest number of endangered species?**

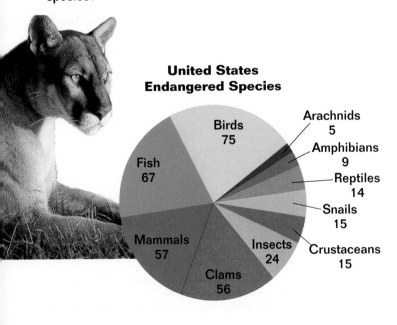

United States Endangered Species

Birds 75
Arachnids 5
Amphibians 9
Reptiles 14
Snails 15
Crustaceans 15
Insects 24
Clams 56
Mammals 57
Fish 67

Bar Graph

A **bar graph** uses bars to show the relationships between variables. A bar graph is similar to a line graph. One variable is divided into parts. It can be numbers, such as the time of day, or a category, such as an animal. The second variable must be a number. The bars show the size of the second variable. For example, if you made a graph of the running speed data, the bar for the lion would represent 81 km/h. Examples of bar graphs are shown in **Figure 2-17**.

Circle Graph

Suppose you want to show how many people in your class play soccer. A **circle graph** shows the parts of a whole. The circle represents the whole. The sections of the circle represent the parts of the whole, as shown in **Figure 2-18**.

To make a circle graph, find the percent for each part. Multiply the percent by 360° to find the angle measure of that part. For example, there are 337 endangered species in **Figure 2-18** and 57 are mammals. Mammals account for 17 percent of endangered species. Multiply 360° by 0.17. A 62° section represents the mammals.

Misleading Graphs

When using or making graphs to display data, be careful. The scale of a graph can be misleading. The way you mark the scale on a graph can create the wrong impression, as seen in **Figure 2-19A.**

A broken scale is used for small but significant changes. Examples include a climate warming by 0.01°C a year or the finishing times for the top runners in a marathon, as shown in **Figure 2-19B.**

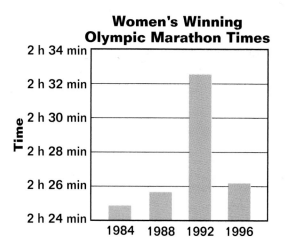

Women's Winning Olympic Marathon Times

Figure 2-19 An axis that does not start at zero can be misleading. However, it is sometimes necessary.

A The vacation-time graph uses a broken vertical axis (not starting at zero) to make it appear that vacation time has doubled since 1996. The actual increase is about 15 percent.

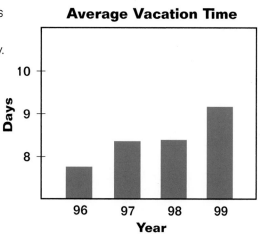

Average Vacation Time

B The difference between the winning times is small. Without the broken axis, all the bars would appear to be the same height because the vertical axis would be divided into hours.

Section Assessment

1. Suppose your class surveys the students in your school about their favorite after-school activities. What type of graph would you use to display your data? Explain your choice.

2. Explain how to use **Figure 2-19B** to find the running time of the 1988 women's Olympic marathon winner.

3. **Think Critically:** How are line, bar, and circle graphs the same? How are they different?

4. **Skill Builder**
   Making and Using Graphs Graph the amount of time you spent reading each day for the past week. What type of graph will you use? If you need help, refer to Making and Using Graphs in the **Skill Handbook** on page 553.

Using Computers

Spreadsheet Use a spreadsheet table to display the total mass of a 500-kg elevator as passengers of 50 kg each are added. If you need help, refer to page 574.

Pace Yourself

In a track meet, you run a distance. The distance you are to run has been precisely measured. Officials watch the start to be sure all of the runners begin the race at the same time. The finish line is carefully observed so the timer is stopped at the moment you cross the line. The officials measure your time as precisely as possible. The runner with the shortest time to cover that distance wins. The results are then communicated using tables or other data displays.

Possible Materials

- Meterstick
- Stopwatch
  *watch with a second hand

  *Alternate Materials

Recognize the Problem

Measure running speed for each person in your group and display these data.

Form a Hypothesis

Think about the information you have learned about precision, measurement, and graphing. In your group, make a hypothesis about a technique that will provide you with the most precise measurement of each person's walking and running pace.

Goals

- **Design an experiment** that allows you to accurately measure speed for each member of your group.
- **Display data** in a table and a graph.

Safety Precautions

- Work in an area where it is safe to run.
- Participate only if you are physically able to exercise safely.

Test Your Hypothesis

Plan

1. As a group, decide what materials you will need.

2. How far will you walk? How far will you run? How will you **measure** that distance? How precise can you be?

3. How will you **measure** time? How precise can you be?

4. List the steps and materials you will use to **test your hypothesis.** Be specific. Will you repeat any part of your test?

5. Before you begin, **create a data table.** Your group must decide on its design. Be sure to leave room to record the results for each person's walking and running time. If more than one trial is to be run for each measurement, include room for the additional data.

Do

1. Make sure that your teacher approves your plan and data table before you begin.

2. **Carry out the experiment** as planned and approved.

3. Be sure to **record your data** in the data table as you proceed with the measurements.

Analyze Your Data

1. **Graph** your data. What type of graph would be best?

2. Are your data table and graph easy to understand? Explain.

3. How do you know that your measurements are precise?

Draw Conclusions

1. How is it possible for different members of a group to find different times while **measuring** the same event?

2. What tools would help you collect more precise **data?**

3. What other data displays could you use? What are the advantages and disadvantages of each?

FIELD GUIDE to Laboratory Equipment

FIELD ACTIVITY

Look around your science classroom. Use this field guide to identify the pieces of equipment available in your classroom or in a laboratory. Practice using the equipment provided by your teacher.

Scientists make observations, form hypotheses, plan and do experiments, collect and analyze their data, and draw conclusions. You will do activities in which you also will use scientific methods while you study science. The quality of the information that you gather during the activities will depend upon correct use of laboratory equipment.

Each set of instructions will tell you what materials and equipment you will need to do the activity. Some of the items will be found around your classroom or at home. Others will be the same types of equipment used by scientists in laboratories and out in the field. Safety symbols guide you in how to use them safely. To find out more about safety symbols, refer to the chart inside the front cover of this book.

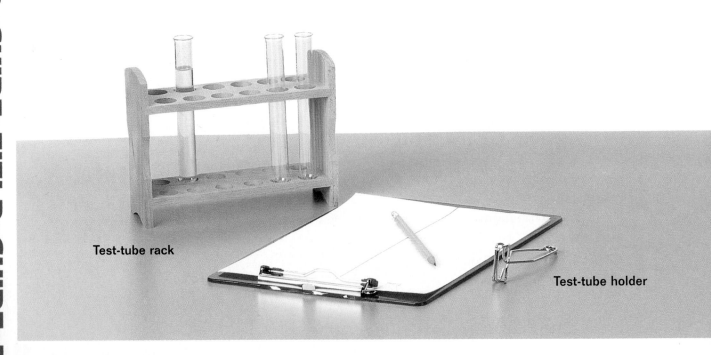

Test-tube rack

Test-tube holder

Laboratory Safety

In the science classroom or laboratory, you are responsible for your own safety and for the safety of your teacher and your classmates. To prevent accidents, be sure to use the following steps.

- Do not perform an activity without your teacher's permission.
- Tie back long hair. Do not wear loose, dangling clothing or jewelry that could catch fire or get caught in something.
- Read through the entire activity before you begin. If you do not understand any part of it, ask your teacher for help.
- Look at the safety symbols. Always wear your goggles, apron, and gloves whenever you are told. Read the safety precautions at the beginning of the procedure.
- Never taste any of the substances you use or make in an activity.
- Immediately report any accident, injury, or damaged equipment to your teacher.

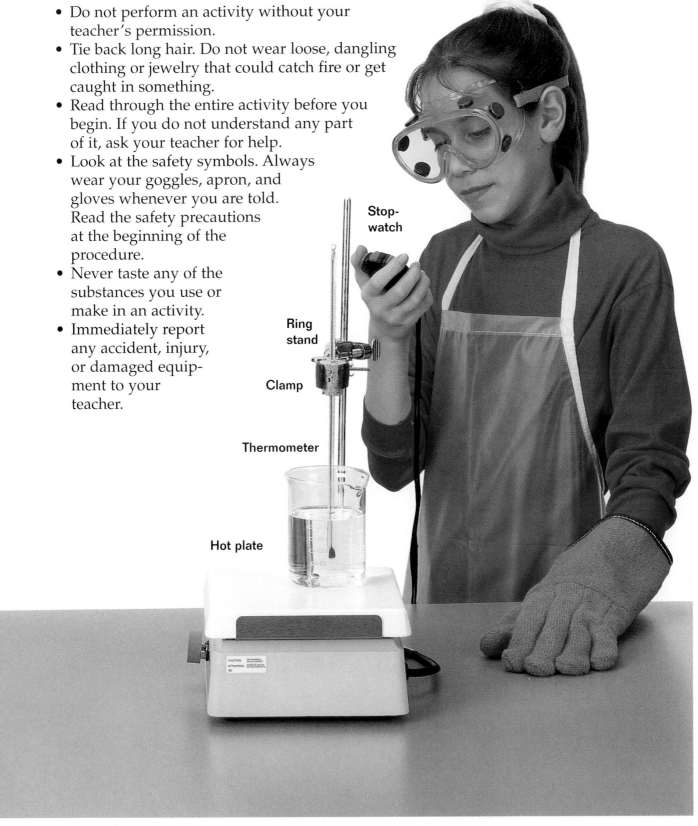

Stop-watch

Ring stand

Clamp

Thermometer

Hot plate

Guide to Labware

Many of your activities will tell you to use the laboratory glassware below. Identify which of the pieces would be most useful for measuring. Explain.

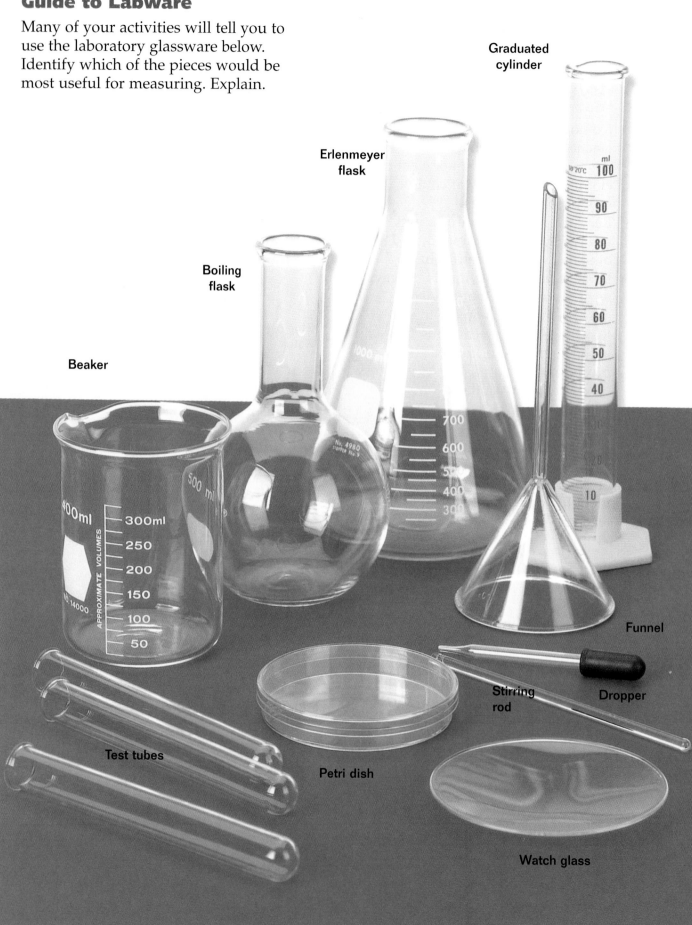

Graduated cylinder

Erlenmeyer flask

Boiling flask

Beaker

Funnel

Stirring rod

Dropper

Test tubes

Petri dish

Watch glass

How to Take Good Measurements

To be sure that your measurements are accurate and precise, laboratory instruments must be used correctly.

Measuring Length

- Never measure from the end of a meterstick (or metric ruler). Place the meterstick next to the object and read the metric scale at each end of the object. Subtract your readings to find the length of the object.
- A meterstick should be read while you are looking straight at the mark. You will have to look directly in front or overhead, not at an angle.

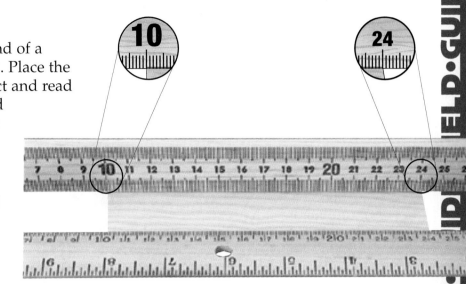

Measuring Liquid Volume and Temperature

- The meniscus is the curve at the top of a liquid. It can curve downward or upward. Look straight at the meniscus when you make your measurement, not above or below.
- A graduated cylinder is used to measure liquid volume. It is often marked in 1-mL segments. To get an accurate measurement, you should read the marking at the bottom of the meniscus.
- Thermometers use liquid volume to measure temperature. The curve of the meniscus will vary due to the type of liquid in the thermometer.

Measuring Mass

- Place the item to be measured in the pan.
- Slide the rider with the largest mass along the balance arm until the pointer drops below zero. Back that rider off one notch.
- Repeat the process with the other two riders. The pointer will swing an equal distance above and below the zero point when the mass of the object is balanced. You do not have to wait for the pointer to stop moving.
- Add the values of the masses on each beam to find the object's mass.

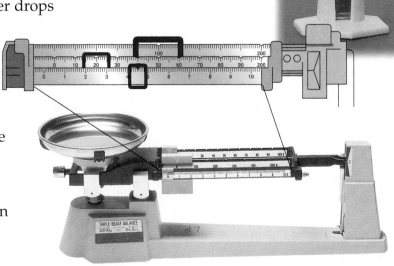

For a **preview** of this chapter, study this Reviewing Main Ideas before you read the chapter. After you have studied this chapter, you can use the Reviewing Main Ideas to **review** the chapter.

The Glencoe MindJogger, Audiocassettes, and CD-ROM provide additional opportunities for review.

Section 2-1 MEASUREMENT

Measurement is a way to describe the world. Measurements such as length, volume, mass, temperature, and rates are used to describe objects and events. *Name three quantities that could be used to describe your pen.*

ESTIMATION, ACCURACY, AND PRECISION

Estimation is used to make an educated guess at a measurement. It also is used when determining which point on a ruler or other scale is closest to the correct value. Accuracy describes how close a measurement is to the true value. Precision describes the exactness of a measurement. A mass of 55 kg is known to the nearest kilogram. A mass of 55.040 kg is known to the nearest thousandth of a kilogram. *If the digital readout on a scale is 48.049 g, what is the mass to the nearest tenth of a gram?*

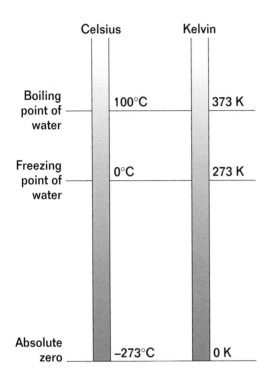

Celsius   Kelvin

Boiling point of water — 100°C   373 K

Freezing point of water — 0°C   273 K

Absolute zero — −273°C   0 K

2-2 SI UNITS

The international system of measurement is called **SI.** It is used throughout the world for communicating data in trade, commerce, and science. *Why do scientists need to use the same measurement system?*

The SI unit of length is the **meter.** Volume, the amount of space an object occupies, can be measured in cubic meters. The **mass** of an object is measured in **kilograms.** Temperature can be measured on different scales. The SI unit of temperature is the **Kelvin.** *What units would you use to describe the speed of a paper airplane?*

2-3 COMMUNICATING DATA

Tables, illustrations, and **graphs** can present data more clearly than explaining everything in words. They help scientists collect, organize, summarize, and display data in a way that is easy to use and understand. *Why is the graph shown here a better choice for the data than a circle graph?*

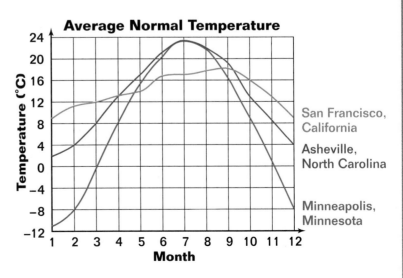

Average Normal Temperature

Temperature (°C) vs. Month

San Francisco, California

Asheville, North Carolina

Minneapolis, Minnesota

Chapter 2 Assessment

Using Vocabulary

a. bar graph
b. circle graph
c. estimation
d. graph
e. Kelvin
f. kilogram
g. line graph
h. mass
i. measurement
j. meter
k. rate
l. SI
m. table

Each phrase below describes a science term from the list. Write the term that matches the phrase describing it.

1. the SI unit for length
2. a description with numbers
3. a method of making a rough measurement
4. the amount of matter in an object
5. a graph that shows parts of a whole

Checking Concepts

Choose the word or phrase that best answers the question.

6. The measurement 25.81 g is precise to the nearest what?
   A) gram
   B) kilogram
   C) tenth of a gram
   D) hundredth of a gram

7. What is the SI unit of mass?
   A) kilometer
   B) meter
   C) liter
   D) kilogram

8. What would you use to measure the length of an object?
   A) graduated cylinder
   B) balance
   C) meterstick
   D) spring scale

9. The cubic meter is the SI unit of what?
   A) volume
   B) weight
   C) mass
   D) distance

10. Which of the following can improve with practice?
    A) length
    B) estimation
    C) precision
    D) mass

11. Thermometers measure temperature with what scale?
    A) volume
    B) mass
    C) Celsius
    D) mercury

12. Which is used to organize data?
    A) table
    B) rate
    C) precision
    D) graduated cylinder

13. To show the number of wins for each football team in your district, use which of the following?
    A) circle graph
    B) line graph
    C) bar graph
    D) SI

14. What organizes data in rows and columns?
    A) bar graph
    B) circle graph
    C) line graph
    D) table

15. To show 25 percent on a circle graph, the section must measure what angle?
    A) 25 degrees
    B) 90 degrees
    C) 180 degrees
    D) 360 degrees

Thinking Critically

16. How would you estimate the volume your backpack could hold?
17. Why do scientists in the United States use SI rather than the English system (feet, pounds, pints, etc.) of measurement?
18. List the following lengths in order from smallest to largest: 1 m, 1 mm, 10 km, 100 mm.
19. When would you use a line graph? Can you use a bar graph for the same purpose?
20. This chapter has treated color as a quality that is not measured. However, computer artists can specify a color by using numbers to describe the amount of each

color of ink to be used at each point in a picture. Why do you think this method of describing color was invented?

Developing Skills

If you need help, refer to the Skill Handbook.

21. **Measuring in SI:** Make a fist. Use a centimeter ruler to measure the height, width, and depth of your fist.

22. **Comparing and Contrasting:** How are volume, length, and mass similar? How are they different? What units are used to measure each?

23. **Making and Using Graphs:** The table gives the area of several bodies of water. Make a bar graph of the data.

Areas of Bodies of Water	
Body of Water	**Area (km²)**
Currituck Sound (North Carolina)	301
Pocomoke Sound (Maryland/Virginia)	286
Chincoteague Bay (Maryland/Virginia)	272
Core Sound (North Carolina)	229

24. **Interpreting Scientific Illustrations:** What does the figure show? How has it been simplified?

25. **Forming Operational Definitions:** Give an operational definition of a pan balance.

Test-Taking Tip

Survey the Surroundings Find out what the conditions will be for taking the test. Will the test be timed? Will you be allowed a break? Know these things in advance so that you can practice taking tests under the same conditions.

Test Practice

Use these questions to test your Science Proficiency.

1. Estimate the percentage of hydrogen in the human body.

Elements in the Human Body

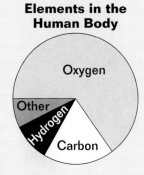

A) 50 percent
B) 25 percent
C) 10 percent
D) 1 percent

2. What are commonly used units for SI?
A) meter, cubic meter, kilogram, second
B) length, volume, mass, time
C) kilo, deci, centi, milli
D) inch, mile, foot, pound

2

Earth
Materials &
Resources

What's Happening Here?

Buried in Earth's crust are great riches. To obtain them, people launch massive operations, such as this gravel quarry on the island of Oahu, Hawaii (left). What makes these resources worth such a tremendous effort? In this unit, you will learn about some of the 4000 minerals found on Earth and why they are valuable. Though we call only certain minerals precious—such as diamonds and gold—all minerals are precious because their supply is limited. In the case of some minerals, rather than mining them until they run out, we can use them again and again. For example, we mine the mineral ore bauxite for its aluminum content and make soda cans from the aluminum. Now, instead of burying the used cans in a landfill, we can recycle them. Crushed and packed soda cans in Kailua-Kona, Hawaii (below), are ready to be shipped to a processing plant where they will be made into new cans.

interNET CONNECTION

Explore the Glencoe Science Web Site at **www.glencoe. com/sec/science/nc** to find out more about topics found in this unit.

Views of Earth

Chapter Preview

Section 3-1
Landforms
Section 3-2
Viewpoints
Section 3-3
Maps

Skills Preview

Skill Builders

- Map Concepts
- Measure in SI

Activities

- Compare and Contrast
- Interpret Data

MiniLabs

- Interpret Scientific Illustrations
- Make a Model

Reading Check

Locate a legend, myth, or folktale from another culture that explains the creation of mountains, plains, or other landforms. Share it with the class.

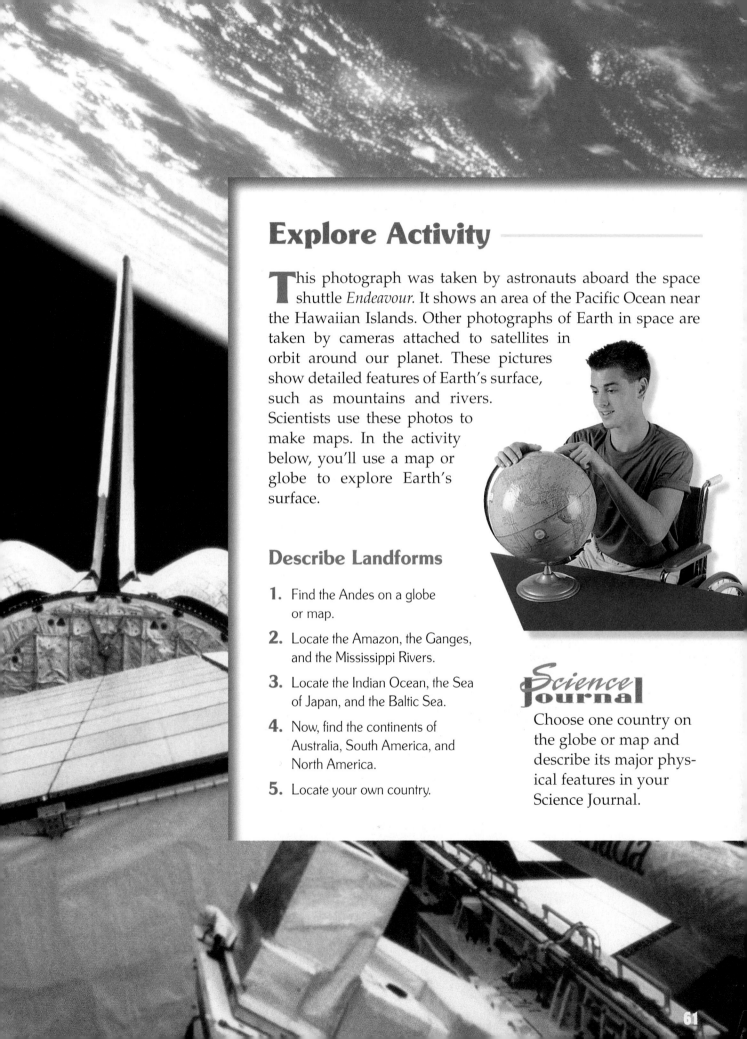

Explore Activity

This photograph was taken by astronauts aboard the space shuttle *Endeavour*. It shows an area of the Pacific Ocean near the Hawaiian Islands. Other photographs of Earth in space are taken by cameras attached to satellites in orbit around our planet. These pictures show detailed features of Earth's surface, such as mountains and rivers. Scientists use these photos to make maps. In the activity below, you'll use a map or globe to explore Earth's surface.

Describe Landforms

1. Find the Andes on a globe or map.

2. Locate the Amazon, the Ganges, and the Mississippi Rivers.

3. Locate the Indian Ocean, the Sea of Japan, and the Baltic Sea.

4. Now, find the continents of Australia, South America, and North America.

5. Locate your own country.

Science Journal

Choose one country on the globe or map and describe its major physical features in your Science Journal.

3·1 Landforms

What You'll Learn

▶ Differences between plains and plateaus
▶ Describe folded, upwarped, fault-block, and volcanic mountains

Vocabulary
plain
plateau
folded mountain
upwarped mountain
fault-block mountain
volcanic mountain

Why It's Important

▶ You'll learn how the land around you formed.

Plains

A lot of interesting landforms can be seen around the world. A landform is a feature that makes up the shape of the land on Earth's surface. **Figure 3-1** shows the three basic types of landforms: plains, plateaus, and mountains.

We all know what mountains are. In our minds, we can see tall peaks reaching toward the sky. But what do you think of when you hear the word *plains?* You might think of endless flat fields of wheat or grass. That would be correct, because many plains are used to grow crops. **Plains** are large, flat areas. Most plains are found in the interior regions of continents. Those found near the ocean are called coastal plains. Together, interior plains and coastal plains make up one-half of all the land in the United States.

Coastal Plains

Coastal plains are broad areas along the ocean's shore. They are often called lowlands because of their low elevations. Elevation refers to distance above or below sea level. As you might guess, sea level has zero elevation. The Atlantic Coastal Plain is a good example of this type of landform.

Mountains

Interior plains

Plateau

Coastal plains

Figure 3-1 Three basic types of landforms are plains, plateaus, and mountains.

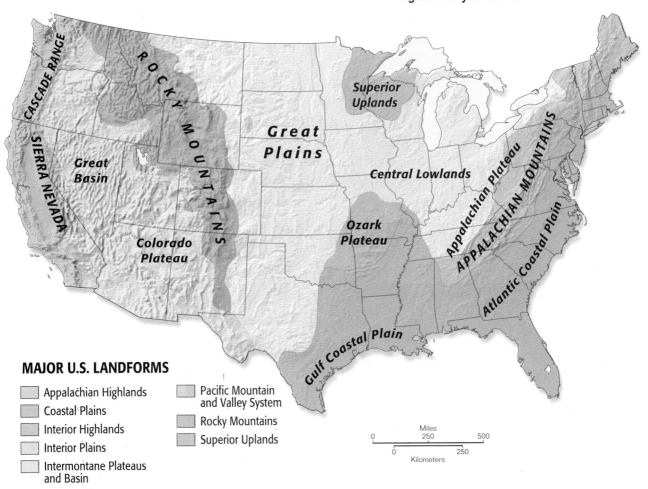

Figure 3-2 The plains, plateaus, and mountains of the United States are divided into eight major regions. **Based upon the information in this map, describe the region that you live in.**

MAJOR U.S. LANDFORMS

- Appalachian Highlands
- Coastal Plains
- Interior Highlands
- Interior Plains
- Intermontane Plateaus and Basin
- Pacific Mountain and Valley System
- Rocky Mountains
- Superior Uplands

Miles
0   250   500

0   250
Kilometers

It stretches along the east coast of the United States. This area has low rolling hills, swamps, and marshes. A marsh is grassy wetland, usually flooded with water.

If you hiked along the Atlantic Coastal Plain, you would know it isn't perfectly flat. Many low hills and valleys have been carved by rivers. What do you suppose caused the Atlantic Coastal Plain to form? It actually began forming under water about 70 million years ago from sediments made of marine organisms that fell to the ancient ocean floor. When sea level dropped, the plain was exposed.

Another example of this landform is the Gulf Coastal Plain shown in **Figure 3-2.** It includes the lowlands in the southern United States that surround the Gulf of Mexico. Much of this plain was formed from sediments deposited by the Mississippi River as it entered the Gulf of Mexico.

Using Math

The elevation of Denver, Colorado, is about 1624.5 m above sea level. The elevation of New Orleans, Louisiana, is 1626 m lower than Denver's. Find the elevation of New Orleans.

Interior Plains

A large part of the center of the United States is called the interior plains. The interior plains of the United States are also shown in **Figure 3-2.** They stretch from the Appalachian Mountains in the east, to the Rocky Mountains in the west, to the Gulf Coastal Plain in the south. They include the rolling hills of the Great Lakes area and the Central Lowlands around the Missouri and Mississippi Rivers.

A large part of the interior plains is known as the Great Plains. They lie between the Mississippi lowlands and the Rocky Mountains. The Great Plains are flat, grassy, dry areas with few trees. They are called high plains because of their elevation. They range from 350 m above sea level at their eastern border to 1500 m above sea level at their western boundary. The Great Plains are covered with nearly horizontal layers of loose materials eroded from the Rocky Mountains. Streams deposited these sediments over the last 28 million years.

Try at Home

Mini Lab

Profiling the United States

Procedure

1. Place the bottom edge of a piece of paper across the middle of **Figure 3-2,** extending from the west coast to the east coast.

2. Mark where different landforms are located along this edge.

3. Use a map of the United States and the descriptions of the landforms in Section 3-1 to help you draw a profile, or side view, of the United States. Use steep, jagged lines to represent mountains. Low, flat lines can represent plains.

Analysis

1. Describe how your profile changed shape as you moved from west to east.

2. Describe how the shape of your profile would be different if you moved from north to south.

Plateaus

If you would like to explore some higher regions, you might be interested in going to the second basic type of landform—a plateau. **Plateaus** (pla TOHZ) are flat,

raised areas of land. They are areas made up of nearly horizontal rocks that have been uplifted by forces within Earth. Plateaus are different from plains in that they rise steeply from the land around them. An example of a plateau in the United States is the Colorado Plateau, which lies just west of the Rocky Mountains. The Colorado River, as shown in **Figure 3-3,** has cut deeply into the rock layers of the plateau, forming the Grand Canyon. Because the Colorado Plateau is located in what is now a dry region, only a few rivers have developed on its surface. If you hiked around on this plateau, you would see a desert landscape.

Mountains

Plains and plateaus are mostly flat. If you want to see a steep rock face, you must go to the third basic type of landform—a mountain. Mountains rise high above the surrounding land, often showing a spectacular view from the top. The world's highest mountain peak is Mount Everest in the Himalayas. It is more than 8800 m above sea level. By contrast, mountain peaks in the United States reach just over 6000 m. Mountains vary greatly in size and in how they are formed. The four main types of mountains are folded, upwarped, fault-block, and volcanic. ☑

Reading Check ☑

What are the four main types of mountains?

Figure 3-3 Rivers cut deep into the Colorado Plateau, as shown by the Colorado River near Moab, Utah. **How are plateaus different from plains?**

Figure 3-4 Folded mountains form when rock layers are squeezed from opposite sides. **When did the Appalachian Mountains form?**

Folded Mountains

PHYSICS
INTEGRATION ➤

The first mountains we will investigate are folded mountains. If you travel through a road cut in the Appalachian Mountains, you'll see rock layers that are folded like the ones in **Figure 3-4.** Folded rock layers look like a rug that has been pushed up against a wall. What do you think caused this to happen?

Tremendous forces inside Earth force horizontal rock layers together. When rock layers are squeezed from opposite sides, they buckle and fold into **folded mountains.** The Appalachian Mountains are folded mountains that formed 250 to 350 million years ago. They are some of the oldest and longest mountain ranges in North America, stretching from Newfoundland, Canada, all the way south to Alabama. At one time, the Appalachians were higher than the Rocky Mountains. Weathering and erosion have worn them down to less than 2000 m above sea level.

Figure 3-5
The southern Rocky Mountains are upwarped mountains that formed when crust was pushed up by forces inside Earth.

Upwarped Mountains

The southern Rocky Mountains in Colorado and New Mexico, the Black Hills in South Dakota, and the Adirondack Mountains in New York are upwarped mountains. **Figure 3-5** shows a mountain range in Colorado. What do you notice about the shape of the mountains? The sharp peaks and ridges are characteristic of upwarped mountains. **Upwarped mountains** are formed when crust is pushed up by forces inside Earth. Over time, the soil and other materials on top of Earth's crust erode, leaving the rock underneath exposed. These rocks then erode to form peaks and ridges.

Figure 3-6 Fault-block mountains such as the Grand Tetons are formed when faults occur. Some rock blocks move up, while others move down. **What types of peaks are characteristic of these mountains?**

Fault-Block Mountains

The Grand Teton Mountains of Wyoming, shown in **Figure 3-6,** and the Sierra Nevada in California formed in yet another way. **Fault-block mountains** are made of huge, tilted blocks of rocks that are separated from surrounding rock by faults. A fault is a large crack in rocks along which there is movement. As **Figure 3-6** shows, when these mountains formed, one block was tilted and pushed up. The other block was pushed down. If you ever go to the Tetons or to the Sierra Nevada, you'll see the sharp, jagged peaks that are characteristic of fault-block mountains.

Volcanic Mountains

Mount St. Helens in Washington and Mauna Loa in Hawaii are two of many volcanic mountains in the United States. **Volcanic mountains** like the one shown in **Figure 3-7** begin to form when molten material reaches the surface through a

weak area of the crust. The materials pile up, one layer on top of another, until a cone-shaped structure forms. The Hawaiian Islands are huge volcanoes that sit on the ocean floor. Only their peaks stick out above the water.

Plains, plateaus, and mountains offer different kinds of landforms to explore. They range from low coastal plains and high desert plateaus to mountain ranges thousands of meters high.

Figure 3-7
The volcanic mountains of Hawaii are made of molten material that oozed from Earth's crust and formed cone-shaped structures.

Section Assessment

1. Describe the eight major landform regions in the United States.

2. What causes some mountains to be folded and others to be upwarped?

3. **Think Critically:** If you wanted to know whether a particular mountain was formed by a fault, what would you look for?

4. **Skill Builder**
   Concept Mapping Make an events-chain concept map to explain how upwarped mountains form. If you need help, refer to Concept Mapping in the **Skill Handbook** on page 550.

Using Computers

Spreadsheet Design a spreadsheet that compares the origin and features of folded, upwarped, fault-block, and volcanic mountains. Label the columns and rows. Explain an advantage of using a spreadsheet to compare different types of mountains. If you need help, refer to page 574.

Viewpoints

Latitude and Longitude

To explore landforms, you'll want to learn how to find locations on Earth. If you wanted to go to the Hawaiian Islands, how would you describe their location? You might say that they are located in the Pacific Ocean. That's correct, but there is a more exact way to locate places on Earth—lines of latitude and longitude. These lines form an imaginary grid system that shows exactly where places on Earth are located.

Latitude

Look at **Figure 3-8.** The **equator** is an imaginary line that circles Earth exactly halfway between the north and south poles. The equator separates Earth into two equal halves, called the northern hemisphere and the southern hemisphere. The lines running parallel to the equator are called lines of latitude, or parallels. **Latitude** is the distance in degrees either north or south of the equator. Because parallel lines do not intersect, lines of latitude do not intersect.

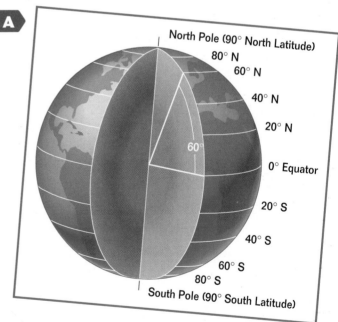

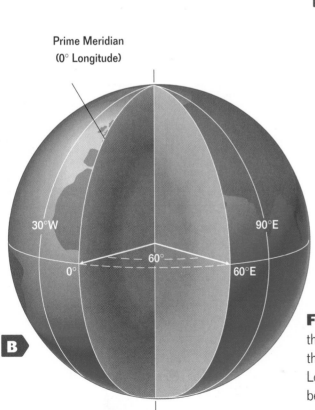

Figure 3-8 Latitude is the measurement of the imaginary angle created between the equator, the center of Earth, and a location on Earth (A). Longitude is the measurement of the angle created between the prime meridian, the center of Earth, and a location on Earth (B).

The equator is numbered 0° latitude. The poles are each numbered 90°. Therefore, latitude is measured from 0° at the equator to 90° at the poles. Locations north of the equator are referred to by degrees north latitude. Locations south of the equator are referred to by degrees south latitude.

Longitude

Latitude lines are used for locations north and south of the equator, but what about locations in east and west directions? These vertical lines, seen in **Figure 3-8B,** have two names—meridians and lines of longitude. Just as the equator is used as a reference point for north/south grid lines, there's a reference point for east/west grid lines—the **prime meridian.** This imaginary line represents 0° longitude. In 1884, astronomers decided the prime meridian should go through the Greenwich (GREN itch) Observatory near London, England.

Longitude refers to distances in degrees east or west of the prime meridian. Points west of the prime meridian have west longitude measured from 0° to 180°, while points east of the prime meridian have east longitude, also measured from 0° to 180°.

The prime meridian does not circle Earth as the equator does. Rather, it runs from the north pole through Greenwich, England, to the south pole. The line of longitude on the opposite side of Earth from the prime meridian is the 180° meridian. East lines of longitude meet west lines of longitude at the 180° meridian.

Using latitude and longitude, you can locate Hawaii more accurately, as shown in **Figure 3-9.** Hawaii is located at 20° north latitude and about 155° west longitude, or 20°N, 155°W. Note that latitude comes first when the latitude and longitude of a particular location are given.

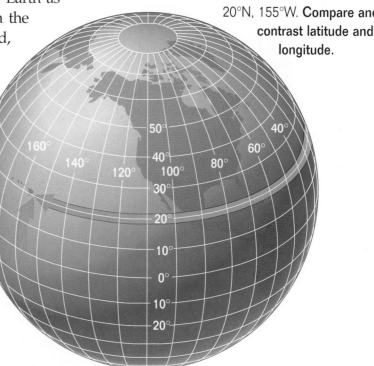

Figure 3-9 The large island of Hawaii is located at about 20°N, 155°W. **Compare and contrast latitude and longitude.**

Earth Time

What time is it right now? That depends on where you are on Earth. Time is measured by tracking Earth's movement in relation to the sun. Earth rotates once every 24 hours. When one half of Earth is facing the sun, the other half is facing away from it. For the half facing the sunlight, it is day. For the half in darkness, it is night.

Time Zones

How can you know what time it is at different places on Earth? Earth is divided into time zones. Because Earth takes 24 hours to rotate, it is divided into 24 time zones, each one hour different. Each time zone is 15 degrees wide on a globe or map. The United States has six different time zones. Look at **Figure 3-10.** Because Earth is rotating, the eastern United States starts a new day while the western part of the country is still in darkness. ✔

As you can see in **Figure 3-11,** time zones do not strictly follow lines of longitude. Time zone boundaries have been adjusted in local areas. For example, if a city were split by a time zone boundary, the results could be confusing. In such a situation, the time zone boundary is moved outside of the city.

Calendar Dates

One day ends and the next day begins at midnight. If it is 11:59 P.M. Tuesday, two minutes later it is 12:01 A.M. Wednesday. The calendar moves forward to the next day in each time zone at midnight.

You gain or lose time each time you travel through a time zone. If you travel far enough, you gain or lose a whole day. The **International Date Line** is the transition line for calendar days. If you were traveling west across the International Date Line, located at the 180° meridian, you would move your calendar forward one day. If you were traveling east, you would move your calendar back one day.

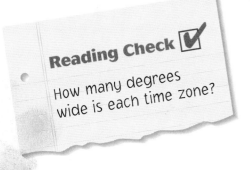

Reading Check

How many degrees wide is each time zone?

Figure 3-10 There are six time zones in the United States.

A Atlanta, Georgia, lies in the eastern time zone. Students there would be on their way to school at 7:00 A.M.

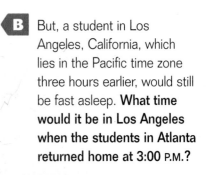

B But, a student in Los Angeles, California, which lies in the Pacific time zone three hours earlier, would still be fast asleep. **What time would it be in Los Angeles when the students in Atlanta returned home at 3:00 P.M.?**

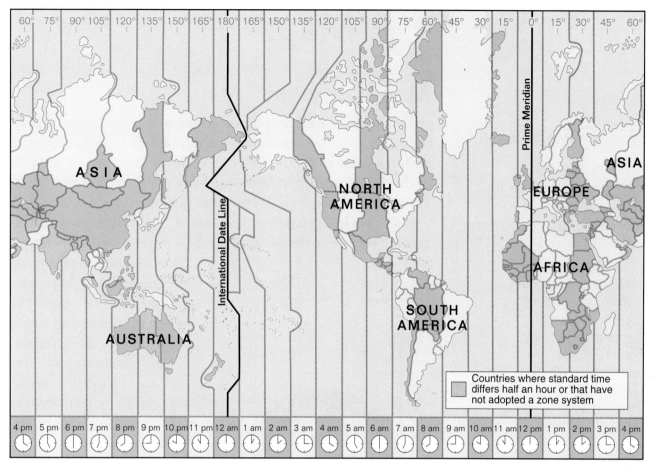

Figure 3-11 Lines of longitude roughly determine the locations of time zone boundaries. These boundaries are adjusted locally to avoid splitting cities and other political subdivisions (such as counties) into different time zones.

Section Assessment

1. How do lines of latitude and longitude help us find locations on Earth?

2. What are the latitude and longitude of New Orleans?

3. **Think Critically:** How could you leave home on Monday to go sailing, sail for an hour on Sunday, and return home on Monday?

4. 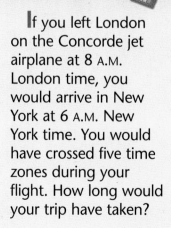 **Skill Builder**
   Interpreting Scientific Illustrations
   Use a world map to find the approximate latitude and longitude of the following locations: Sri Lanka; Tokyo, Japan; and the Falkland Islands. If you need help, refer to Interpreting Scientific Illustrations in the **Skill Handbook** on page 562.

Using Math

If you left London on the Concorde jet airplane at 8 A.M. London time, you would arrive in New York at 6 A.M. New York time. You would have crossed five time zones during your flight. How long would your trip have taken?

Map Projections

Think of the different types of maps you have seen. There are road maps, weather maps, and maps that show physical features such as mountains and valleys. They are all models of Earth's surface. But because Earth's surface is curved, it is not easy to show on a flat piece of paper.

Maps are made using projections. A map projection is made when points and lines on a globe's surface are transferred onto paper, as shown in **Figure 3-12.** Map projections can be made in several different ways. But, all types of projections distort either the shapes of landmasses or their areas. Antarctica, for instance, might look smaller or larger than it really is.

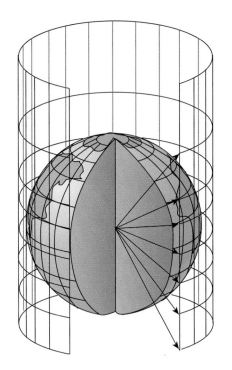

Figure 3-12 Because Earth's surface is curved, all types of map projections distort either the shapes of landmasses or their areas.

 A In a Mercator projection, lines of longitude are drawn parallel to each other. **What does this do to areas near the poles?**

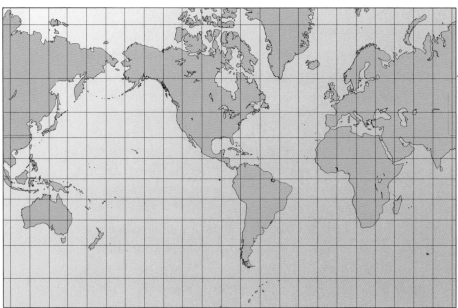

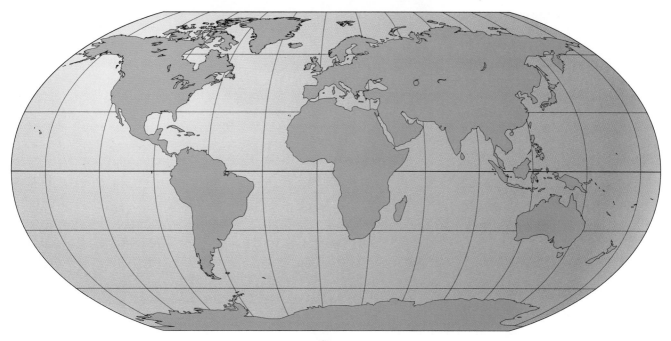

B A Robinson projection shows less distortion near the poles than a Mercator projection.

Mercator Projection

A **Mercator projection** has correct shapes of continents, but their areas are distorted. Lines of longitude are projected onto the map parallel to each other. As you learned earlier, only latitude lines are parallel. Longitude lines meet at the poles. When longitude lines are projected as parallel, areas near the poles appear bigger than they should. Look at Greenland in the Mercator projection in **Figure 3-12A.** It appears to be larger than South America. Greenland is actually much smaller than South America. Mercator projections are mainly used on ships.

Robinson Projection

A **Robinson projection** has accurate continent shapes and shows accurate land areas. As shown in **Figure 3-12B,** lines of latitude remain parallel, and lines of longitude are curved as they would be on a globe. This results in more correct continent shapes.

Conic Projection

A third type of projection is a conic projection. You use this type of projection, shown in **Figure 3-12C,** whenever you look at a road map or a weather map. **Conic projections** are used to produce maps of small areas. They are made by projecting points and lines from a globe onto a cone.

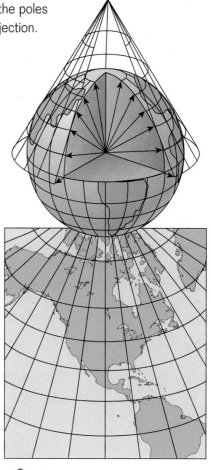

C A conic projection is accurate for small areas of Earth. **What could you use this type of map for?**

Figure 3-13 A topographic map shows changes in the elevation of Earth's surface.

A Wizard Island is a volcanic cinder-cone that forms an island in Crater Lake, Oregon.

B Different points of elevation are projected onto paper.

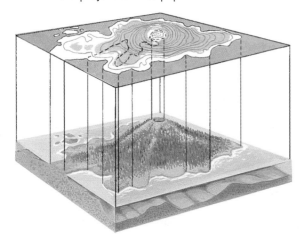

C The points of elevation are connected to form a topographic map of the island. **What do contour intervals tell us about elevation?**

Topographic Maps

If you wanted to go hiking, a conic map projection would get you to the mountain. Next, you would need a detailed map showing the hills and valleys of that specific area. A **topographic map** shows the changes in elevation of Earth's surface. With a topographic map, you could tell how steep the mountain trail is. It would also show natural features such as mountains, hills, plains, lakes, and rivers, and cultural features such as roads, cities, dams, and other structures built by people.

Contour Lines

Before starting your hike up the mountain, you would look at the contour lines on your topographic map to see the trail's changes in elevation. A **contour line** is a line on a map that connects points of equal elevation. Elevation refers to the distance of a location above or below sea level. The difference in elevation between two side-by-side contour lines is called the **contour interval.** If the contour interval were 10 m, then when you walked between those two lines on the trail, you would have climbed or walked down 10 m.

As **Figure 3-13C** shows, the elevation of the contour interval can vary. For mountains, the contour lines might be close and the contour interval might be as great as 100 m. This would tell you that the land is steep because there is a large change in elevation between lines. However, if there isn't a great change in elevation and the contour lines are far apart, your map might have a contour interval of 5 m. **Table 3-1** gives additional tips for examining contour lines.

Index Contours

Some contour lines, called index contours, are marked with their elevation. If the contour interval is 5 m, you can tell the elevation of other lines around the index contour. You would add or subtract 5 m from the elevation shown on the index contour.

*inter*NET
CONNECTION

Visit the Glencoe Science Web Site at **www. glencoe.com/sec/ science/nc** for more information about maps.

Table 3-1

Contour Rules

Here are some rules to remember when examining contour lines.

1. **Contour lines close around hills and basins or depressions.** To decide whether you're looking at a hill or basin, you can read the elevation numbers or look for hachures. Hachures are short lines at right angles to the contour line that are used to show depressions. These lines point toward lower elevations. See **Figure 3-14.**

2. **Contour lines never cross.** If they did, it would mean that the spot where they cross would have two different elevations.

3. **Contour lines form Vs that point upstream whenever they cross streams.** This is because streams flow in depressions that are beneath the elevation of the surrounding land surface. When the contour lines follow the depression, they appear as Vs pointing upstream on the map.

Map Scale

Another thing you would want to know before you set out on your hike is, "How far is it to the top of the mountain?" Because maps are small models of Earth's surface, distances and sizes of things on a map are proportional to the real thing on Earth. This is done by using scale distances.

The **map scale** is the relationship between the distances on the map and actual distances on Earth's surface. Scale is often represented as a ratio. For example, a topographic map of the Grand Canyon may have a scale that reads "1:80 000." This means that one unit on the map represents 80 000 units on land. If the unit you wanted to use was a centimeter, then 1 cm on the map would equal 80 000 cm on land. The unit of distance may be in feet or millimeters or any other measure of distance. However, the units of measure on each side of the ratio must always be the same. A map scale may also be in the form of a small bar that is divided into units. The units are scaled down to match real distances on Earth.

Map Legend

Topographic maps and most other maps have a legend. A **map legend** explains what the symbols used on the map mean. Some frequently used symbols for topographic maps are shown in **Figure 3-14.**

Three-Dimensional Maps

Topographic maps are two-dimensional models used to study features on Earth's surface. To unravel Earth's complex structure, however, scientists need to know what Earth looks like inside. With computers, topographic maps are digitized to get a three-dimensional or 3-D view of features such as rock beds or river systems. Digitizing is a process by which points are located on a coordinate grid.

Map Uses

As you have learned, there are many different ways to view Earth. The map you choose to use will depend upon your need. For instance, if you wanted to determine New Zealand's location relative to Canada, you would probably examine a Mercator projection. In your search, you would use lines of latitude and longitude, and a map scale. If you

Reading Check

What is a map scale?

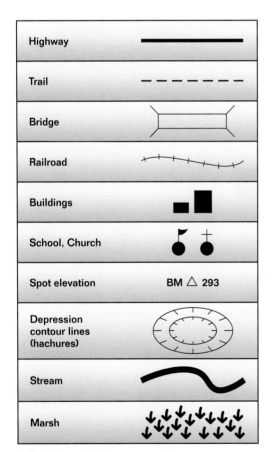

Highway	
Trail	
Bridge	
Railroad	
Buildings	
School, Church	
Spot elevation	BM △ 293
Depression contour lines (hachures)	
Stream	
Marsh	

Figure 3-14 Here are some typical symbols used on topographic maps.

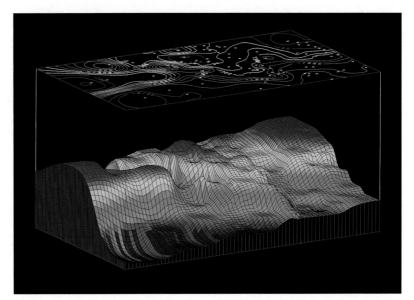

Figure 3-15 This computer-generated map shows a river system in Montana. **How does this map differ from a topographic map?**

wanted to travel across the country, you would rely on a conic projection. You would also use a map legend to help you locate features along your trip. And, if you wanted to scale the highest peak in your county, you would take along a topographic map.

As **Figure 3-15** shows, mapmaking, also called cartography, has experienced a technological revolution in the past few decades. Remote sensing and computers have changed the way maps are made. Read on to learn more about remote sensing.

Problem Solving

Interpreting a Topographic Map

The map at right is a topographic map of an area in California. One sunny day, two hikers started from the point marked with the + on the map. One hiker climbed the peak of Cedar Mountain, while the other climbed the peak of Orr Mountain.

Both traveled at the same rate on flat or gentle slopes. Their climbs slowed as the ground grew steeper. Study the map, then answer the questions below.

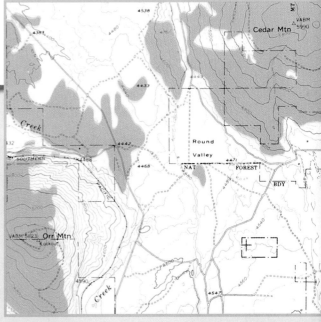

1 cm = 1.3 km

Solve the Problem

1. Which peak is higher?

2. Which hiker had the steeper climb? Explain using contour lines.

3. Name three items found in a map legend that the hiker heading for Orr Mountain crossed before reaching his or her goal.

Think Critically

1. If each hiker could choose any route to his or her destination, which one do you think reached his or her goal first? Explain.

2. Once at the top, could the hiker on Cedar Mountain see the hiker on Orr Mountain? Why or why not?

Remote Sensing

Scientists use remote-sensing techniques to collect much of the data used for making maps. **Remote sensing** is a way of collecting information about Earth from a distance. Satellites and sonar are two remote-sensing devices.

Topex-Poseidon Satellite

The Topex-Poseidon Satellite (*Topex* stands for "topographic experiment") uses radar to compute the distance to the ocean's surface. Radar waves are high-frequency radio signals that are beamed from the satellite to the ocean. As **Figure 3-16** illustrates, a receiving device then picks up the returning echo as it bounces off the water. The distance to the water's surface is calculated using the radar speed and the time it takes for the signal to be reflected. Using satellite-to-sea measurements, computers can draw maps of ocean features.

Global Positioning System

The Global Positioning System, or GPS, is a satellite-based, radio-navigation system that allows users to determine their exact position anywhere on Earth. Twenty-four satellites orbit 20 200 km above the planet. Each satellite sends an accurate position and time signal. The satellites are arranged in their orbits so that signals from at least six can be picked up at any given moment by someone using a GPS receiver. By processing the signals coming from multiple satellites, the receiver calculates the user's exact location. GPS technology is a valuable navigational tool. It is also used to create detailed maps and to track wildlife.

Sea Beam

Sonar refers to the use of sound waves to detect ocean-bottom features. First, a sound wave is sent from a ship toward the ocean floor. A receiving device then picks up the returning echo when it bounces off the bottom. Shipboard computers measure the distance to the bottom using the speed of sound in water and the time it takes for the sound to be reflected.

*inter*NET
CONNECTION

Visit the Glencoe Science Web Site at **www. glencoe.com/sec/ science/nc** to find out more about the Global Positioning System.

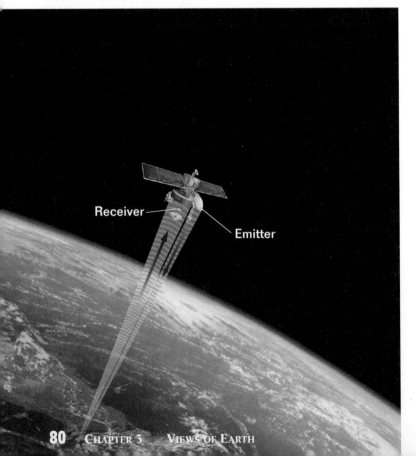

Figure 3-16 Using high-frequency radio waves, the Topex-Poseidon Satellite can map ocean floor features.

Receiver

Emitter

Using a technology called Sea Beam, scientists make accurate maps of the ocean floor. A ship equipped with Sea Beam, shown in **Figure 3-17,** has more than a dozen sonar devices, each aimed at different parts of the sea. Computers assemble these sonar data into detailed, continuous maps of the ocean floor.

Figure 3-17 This underwater formation was mapped using data from Sea Beam.

Section Assessment

1. Why does Greenland appear to be larger on a Mercator projection than it does on a Robinson projection?

2. Why can't contour lines ever cross?

3. Name two remote-sensing devices.

4. **Think Critically:** Suppose you have a topographic map with a contour interval of 50 m. According to the map scale, 1 cm on the map equals 1 km. The distance between points A and B on the map is 8 cm. Four contour lines lie between them. How far apart are the points, and what is the change in elevation?

5. 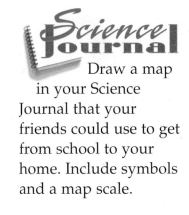 **Skill Builder**
   Making Models Architects use detailed maps called scale drawings to help them plan their work. Do the **Chapter 3 Skill Activity** on page 580 to make a scale drawing of your classroom.

Science Journal Draw a map in your Science Journal that your friends could use to get from school to your home. Include symbols and a map scale.

Modeling Earth

Possible Materials

- Fine-point, transparency marker
- Blank transparency
- Overhead projector
- Sheet of white paper
- Pencil
- Tape
- Corrugated cardboard sheets
  * foam board sheets
- Scissors
- Glue
- Metric ruler

  * *Alternate Materials*

Have you ever built a model plane, train, or car? Modeling is more than just fun. Models are used to help engineers and designers build actual planes, trains, and cars. A topographic map is a two-dimensional model—on flat paper. How can you build a three-dimensional model of a landform?

Recognize the Problem

How can a 3-D model be made of an area shown on a topographic map?

Form a Hypothesis

Based on the drawing below, state a hypothesis about how you can make a large model of Blackberry Hill, such that its base is the length of a piece of notebook paper.

Goals

- **Design and make a 3-D model** that shows the relationship between topographic maps and landforms.

- **Interpret** data from your model.

Safety Precautions

Be careful while working near the overhead projector light. It can get hot. While using scissors, be careful not to cut yourself.

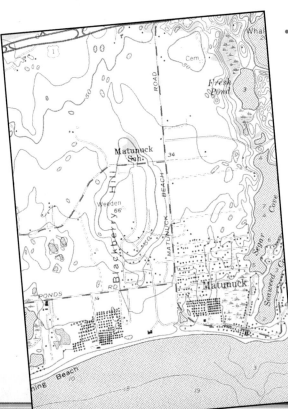

Test Your Hypothesis

Plan

1. With your partner, **design** a way that you can make an enlarged **copy** of the topographical features of Blackberry Hill using a transparency marker, overhead projector, pencil, sheet of white paper, and tape. **Write down** the steps you will take.

2. **Explain** how you can use the contour lines on your white paper as patterns for making the different layers of your model.

3. **Describe** a way to make your 3-D model using stacked sheets of cardboard or foam board.

Do

1. Make sure your teacher approves your plan before you proceed.

2. Read over your entire plan to make sure that all steps are in a logical order.

3. **Build** your model as planned.

4. While the activity is going on, **record** observations in your Science Journal.

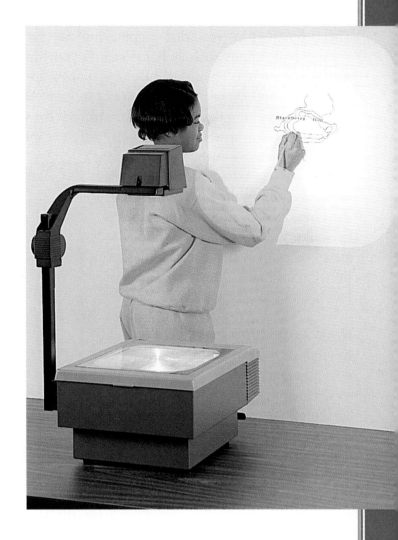

Analyze Your Data

1. **Compare** your model with other students' models. How are they similar? How are they different?

2. **Determine** the horizontal scale of your model.

Draw Conclusions

1. **Infer** what the height of each sheet in your model represents.

2. **Describe** the most difficult part of making your model.

Mapmaking

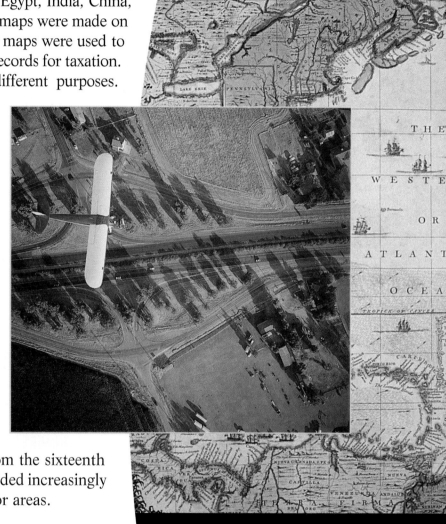

Ancient Maps

The beginnings of recorded mapmaking can be traced to ancient civilizations such as Babylonia, Egypt, India, China, and Mesopotamia. The oldest surviving maps were made on clay tablets and mosaic tile. Those early maps were used to mark property boundaries and to keep records for taxation. Other early cultures used maps for different purposes. Marshall Islanders in the Pacific made navigation charts. In Mexico, people mapped roads. In the sixth century B.C., the Greeks used information gathered by military and sailing expeditions to map bodies of water and landmasses. But, Greek maps drawn on paper or parchment have disappeared.

Map Improvements

By the thirteenth century, advances in mathematics led to more accurate measurements. Mapmakers, called cartographers, used these measurements and their observations of physical features to create more detailed maps. The development of the printing press and engraving techniques made maps more widely available. From the sixteenth to nineteenth centuries, explorers provided increasingly accurate maps of coastlines and interior areas.

View from Above

Aerial photography (inset) revolutionized mapmaking through photogrammetry—making measurements from photographs. Today, photographs from space satellites give cartographers even greater details of Earth. In addition, modern cartographers use computers to make and update maps. When they enter data on a computer, the computer draws the map. Digital map data can be used in many ways. For instance, computer programs in cars can inform drivers where they are and how to reach their destinations.

Science JOURNAL

Pretend you have hidden a treasure. In your Science Journal, draw a map that would lead a friend to the treasure.

Making a Topographic Map

Materials

- Plastic model landform
- Water tinted with food coloring
- Transparency
- Clear, plastic storage box with lid
- Beaker
- Metric ruler
- Tape
- Transparency marker

Have you ever wondered how topographic maps are made? Today, radar and remote-sensing devices aboard satellites collect data, and computers and graphic systems make the maps. In the past, surveyors and aerial photographers collected data. Then, maps were hand drawn by cartographers, or mapmakers. In this activity, you can try your hand at cartography.

What You'll Investigate

How is a topographic map made?

Goals

- **Make** a topographic map.
- **Compare and contrast** contour intervals.

Procedure

1. Using the ruler and the transparency marker, make marks up the side of the storage box 2 cm apart.

2. **Secure** the transparency to the outside of the box lid with tape.

3. Place the plastic model in the box. The bottom of the box will be zero elevation.

4. Using the beaker, **pour** water into the box to a height of 2 cm. Place the lid on the box.

5. Use the transparency marker to **trace** the top of the water line on the transparency.

6. Using the scale 2 cm = 10 m, **mark** the elevation on the line.

7. Remove the lid and **add** water until a depth of 4 cm is reached.

8. **Map** this level on the storage box lid and **record** the elevation.

9. Repeat the process of **adding** water and **tracing** until you have the hill **mapped.**

10. **Transfer** the tracing of the hill onto a sheet of white paper.

Conclude and Apply

1. What is the contour interval of this topographic map?

2. How does the distance between contour lines on the map show the steepness of the slope on the landform model?

3. **Determine** the total elevation of the hill.

4. How was elevation represented on your map?

5. How are elevations shown on topographic maps?

6. Must all topographic maps have a 0-m elevation contour line? **Explain.**

7. **Compare** the contour interval of an area of high relief with one of low relief on a topographic map.

For a **preview** of this chapter, study this Reviewing Main Ideas before you read the chapter. After you have studied this chapter, you can use the Reviewing Main Ideas to **review** the chapter.

GLENCOE TECHNOLOGY

The Glencoe MindJogger, Audiocassettes, and CD-ROM provide additional opportunities for review.

Section

3-1 LANDFORMS

The three main types of landforms are plains, plateaus, and mountains. **Plains** are large, flat areas. **Plateaus** are relatively flat, raised areas of land made up of nearly horizontal rocks that have been uplifted by forces within Earth. **Mountains** rise high above the surrounding land. They vary greatly in size and how they are formed. *Which type of mountain is shown here?*

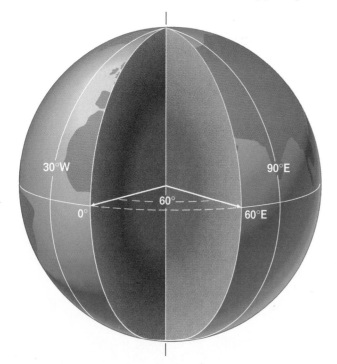

Section

3-2 VIEWPOINTS

Latitude and **longitude** form an imaginary grid system that enables points on Earth to be located exactly. **Latitude** is the distance in degrees north or south of the equator. Lines of latitude are parallel to the equator. **Longitude** is the distance in degrees east or west of the prime meridian. The prime meridian runs through Greenwich, England. *What line of longitude is located on the side of Earth opposite to the prime meridian?*

Reading Check ✓

Locate three or four words that are not on the vocabulary list but were unfamiliar to you before you read this chapter. Define these words.

Section
3-3 MAPS

Topographic maps show the changes in elevation of Earth's surface. **Mercator, Robinson,** and **conic projections** are made by transferring points and lines on a globe's surface onto paper. *Why are all map projections distorted in either the shapes of landmasses or the areas of landmasses?*

REMOTE SENSING

Remote Sensing is a way of collecting information about Earth from a distance. Satellites and sonar are two remote-sensing devices. Using sonar, for instance, scientists can make detailed maps of the ocean floor. Other remote-sensing devices are used to navigate or track wildlife. *What is the Global Positioning System?*

Chapter 3 Assessment

Using Vocabulary

a. conic projection
b. contour interval
c. contour line
d. equator
e. fault-block mountain
f. folded mountain
g. International Date Line
h. latitude
i. longitude
j. map legend
k. map scale
l. Mercator projection
m. plain
n. plateau
o. prime meridian
p. remote sensing
q. Robinson projection
r. topographic map
s. upwarped mountain
t. volcanic mountain

For each set of terms below, choose the one term that does not belong and explain why it does not belong.

1. contour interval, contour line, conic projection
2. map scale, latitude, longitude
3. upwarped mountain, equator, volcanic mountain
4. plain, plateau, prime meridian
5. Mercator projection, Robinson projection, remote sensing

Checking Concepts

Choose the word or phrase that best answers the question.

6. What makes up about 50 percent of all land areas in the United States?
   A) plateaus   C) mountains
   B) plains   D) volcanoes

7. Where is the north pole located?
   A) 0°N   C) 50°N
   B) 180°N   D) 90°N

8. What kind of mountains are the Hawaiian Islands?
   A) fault-block   C) upwarped
   B) volcanic   D) folded

9. What do we call lines parallel to the equator?
   A) lines of latitude   C) lines of longitude
   B) prime meridians   D) contour lines

10. How many degrees apart are the 24 time zones?
    A) 10   C) 15
    B) 34   D) 25

11. Which type of map is distorted at the poles?
    A) conic   C) Robinson
    B) topographic   D) Mercator

12. Which type of map shows changes in elevation at Earth's surface?
    A) conic   C) Robinson
    B) topographic   D) Mercator

13. What is measured with respect to sea level?
    A) contour interval   C) conic projection
    B) elevation   D) sonar

14. What marks are used to show depressions on topographic maps?
    A) degrees   C) hachures
    B) scales   D) legends

15. Which major U.S. landform includes the Grand Canyon?
    A) Great Plains
    B) Colorado Plateau
    C) Gulf Coastal Plain
    D) Appalachian Mountains

Thinking Critically

16. How would a topographic map of the Atlantic Coastal Plain differ from a topographic map of the Rocky Mountains?

17. If you left Korea early Wednesday morning and flew to Hawaii, on what day of the week would you arrive?

18. If you were flying directly south from the north pole and reached 70° north latitude, how many more degrees of latitude would be left to pass over before reaching the south pole?

19. Using a map, arrange these cities in order from the city with the earliest time to that with the latest time on a given day: Anchorage, Alaska; San Francisco, California; Bangor, Maine; Columbus, Ohio; Houston, Texas.

20. What does a map scale of 1:50 000 mean?

Developing Skills

*If you need help, refer to the **Skill Handbook.***

21. **Measuring in SI:** What is the area in square kilometers of the topographic map in the Problem Solving feature in Section 3-3?

22. **Comparing and Contrasting:** Compare and contrast Mercator, Robinson, and conic map projections.

23. **Concept Mapping:** Make a network tree concept map that explains how topographic maps are used. Use the following terms: *topographic maps, mountains, rivers, natural features, contour lines, changes in elevation, equal elevation, hills,* and *plains.*

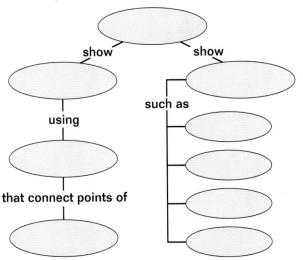

THE PRINCETON REVIEW

Test-Taking Tip

Stock Up on Supplies Be sure to supply yourself with the test-taking essentials: number two pencils, pens, erasers, a ruler, and a pencil sharpener. If the room doesn't have a pencil sharpener, a broken pencil can be a problem.

Test Practice

Use these questions to test your Science Proficiency.

1. The Adirondack Mountains are upwarped mountains. Today, the rock material that was once present on the tops of these mountains is gone. Why?
   A) The rock material was pushed inside Earth.
   B) Sharp peaks and ridges formed over the rock material.
   C) The rock material became magma.
   D) The rock material was eroded.

2. Ships use sonar to detect and map ocean-bottom features. Which of the following events occurs first in the map-making process?
   A) Computers transform sonar data into detailed maps.
   B) A sound wave is sent from the ship to the ocean floor.
   C) Computers calculate the distance from the ship to the ocean floor.
   D) A receiving device picks up the echo of sonar bouncing off the ocean floor.

Earth Materials

Chapter Preview

Section 4-1
Minerals—Earth's Jewels

Section 4-2
Igneous and Sedimentary Rocks

Section 4-3
Metamorphic Rocks and the Rock Cycle

Skills Preview

Skill Builders
- Use a CD-ROM
- Sequence

MiniLabs
- Classify
- Infer

Activities
- Observe
- Hypothesize

Reading Check ✔

List the chapter vocabulary terms in a column. Beside each one, write what you think the word means. As you read, revise your definitions as necessary.

Explore Activity

You're at the top! You and a friend have been climbing Zane's Bluff. Now, after all the hard work of the climb, you are treated to a great view. You also take time to get a closer look at the rock you've been climbing. First, you notice that it sparkles in the sun because of the silvery specks that are stuck in the rock. Looking closer, you also see clear, glassy pieces and gray, irregular chunks. What is the rock made of, and how did it get here?

Observe a Rock

1. Obtain a sparkling rock from your teacher. You also will need a hand lens.

2. Observe the rock with the hand lens. Your job is to observe and record as many of the features of the rock as you can.

3. Return the rock to your teacher.

4. Try to describe your rock so that other students could pick your rock out of the group of rocks.

Science Journal

In your Science Journal, describe and draw how the parts of the rock fit together to form the rock. Be sure to label your drawing.

Minerals—Earth's Jewels

What You'll Learn

► The difference between a mineral and a rock
► Properties that are used to identify minerals

Vocabulary
mineral
rock
crystal
gem
ore

Why It's Important

► Minerals and rocks are valuable to humans.

What is a mineral?

Get ready! You're going on an expedition to find minerals (MIHN uh rools). Where will you look? Do you think you'll have to crawl into a cave or brave the depths of a mine? Well, put away your flashlight and hard hat. You can find minerals right in your own home—in the salt shaker on your table and in the "lead" of your pencil. The metal pots and pans, glassware, and dishes in your kitchen are products made from minerals. Minerals, as shown in **Figure 4-1,** are everywhere around you.

What is a mineral? A **mineral** is an inorganic solid material found in nature. Inorganic substances are things that usually are not formed by plants or animals. A mineral must always have the same general chemical makeup. Tiny particles called atoms are the basic chemical building blocks of minerals. The atoms in a mineral are arranged in an orderly pattern. And, the atoms in any given mineral are always arranged in the same way. Minerals are also the basic building blocks for all rocks. A **rock,** like the granite or basalt used in the Explore Activity, is usually made of two or more minerals. More than 4000 different minerals have been identified. Each mineral has characteristics you can use to identify it.

Figure 4-1 You use minerals every day without realizing it. Minerals are used to make many common objects.

A Quartz is melted to form glass.

B The mineral gypsum is used to make drywall, a building material.

How do minerals form?

On your rock-climbing adventure, you started asking questions about how minerals and rocks form. Minerals can form in several ways. One way is from melted rock called magma. As magma cools, atoms combine in orderly patterns to form minerals in the cooling rock. These minerals can form on Earth's surface or deep inside Earth.

Minerals also form when solutions evaporate. As water leaves a solution, minerals are left behind. This is how the salt you put on your popcorn formed. Another way minerals form is also from solution. If a solution is extremely rich in minerals, the minerals may crystallize out of the liquid without evaporation. A solution can hold only so much of the dissolved mineral. If more minerals are added, some will separate out as solid materials.

Sometimes, you can tell how a mineral formed by how it looks. If the mineral grains fit together like a puzzle, they may have cooled from magma. If you see layers of different minerals, the minerals could have formed under directed pressure or through evaporation. The beautiful crystals you see in **Figure 4-2** grew from a solution rich in dissolved minerals. To figure out how a mineral forms, you have to think about its texture. Texture is the size of the mineral grain or crystal, whether it is made up of layers, and how the crystals or mineral grains fit together. Next, you will learn ways to identify different minerals. Identifying minerals is fun and also helps you figure out how they formed.

Figure 4-2
These fluorite crystals formed from a solution rich in dissolved minerals.

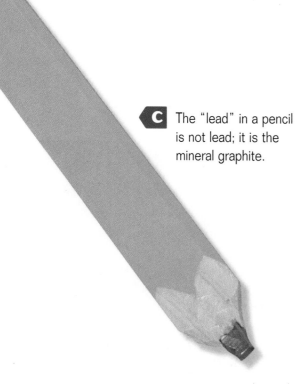

C The "lead" in a pencil is not lead; it is the mineral graphite.

D These whistles are made from iron ores such as hematite or magnetite.

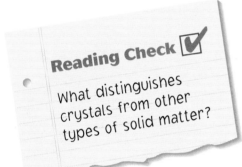

Figure 4-3
This beautiful amethyst has large crystals. Amethyst is a variety of the mineral quartz.

Reading Check ☑

What distinguishes crystals from other types of solid matter?

Properties of Minerals

Perched on your rocky outlook, you notice another person on a ledge some distance away. Is it someone you know? She's wearing a yellow shirt and has her long, dark hair in braids, just like a friend you saw this morning. You're only sure it's your friend when she turns, and you recognize her smile. You've identified your friend by physical properties that set her apart from other people—her clothing, hair color and style, and facial features. Each mineral, too, has a set of physical properties that you can use to identify it. No fancy equipment is needed. Most common minerals can be identified with items you have around the house and can carry in your pocket, like a penny and a nail. Now, let's take a look at the properties that will help you identify minerals.

Crystals

All minerals have an orderly pattern of atoms. The atoms that make up the mineral are arranged in a repeating pattern. Solid materials that have such a pattern of atoms are called **crystals.** Some mineral samples, such as the amethyst pictured in **Figure 4-3**, have beautiful crystals. Crystals have smooth surfaces, sharp edges, and points. Some crystals look like tiny cubes. In **Figure 4-4,** the magnified view of table salt reveals that each grain is a little cube. These cubes are crystals of the mineral halite. ☑

Magnification: 50 ×

Figure 4-4 Common table salt is the mineral halite. Halite crystals are tiny cubes.

Figure 4-5 Cleavage is one of the most useful properties of minerals. Some minerals have one or more directions of cleavage. If minerals do not break in a regular way, they have what is called fracture.

A Mica has one cleavage direction and can be peeled off in sheets.

B Calcite has three directions of cleavage.

Cleavage and Fracture

Another clue to a mineral's identity is the way it breaks. Minerals that split into pieces with smooth, regular surfaces that reflect light are said to have *cleavage* (KLEE vihj). The mineral mica in **Figure 4-5A** shows cleavage by splitting into thin sheets. Splitting one of these minerals along a cleavage surface is something like peeling off a piece of presliced cheese. Cleavage is caused by weaknesses within the arrangement of atoms that make up the mineral.

Not all minerals have cleavage. Some break into pieces with jagged or rough edges. Instead of neat slices, these pieces are shaped more like hunks of cheese torn from an unsliced block. Materials that break this way, such as quartz, have what is called *fracture* (FRAK chur). **Figure 4-5C** shows the jagged fracture of native copper.

C Native copper has a jagged fracture.

Color

The reddish-gold color of a new penny shows that it's made of copper. The bright yellow color of sulfur is a valuable clue to its identity. Sometimes a mineral's color can help you figure out what it is. But, color also can fool you. The common mineral pyrite (PI rite) has a shiny, gold color similar to real gold—close enough to disappoint many prospectors during the California Gold Rush in the 1800s. Because of this, pyrite is also called fool's gold.

Streak and Luster

A test called the streak test will help identify a mineral, even if it looks a lot like a different mineral. Scratching a mineral sample across an unglazed, white

D The smooth, curved fracture of obsidian also is observed in the mineral quartz.

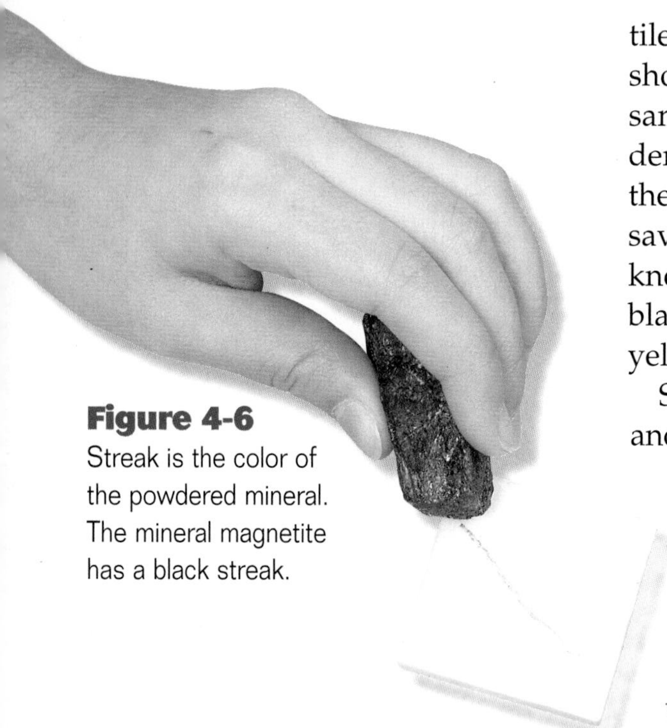

tile, called a streak plate, produces a streak of color, as shown in **Figure 4-6.** The streak is not necessarily the same color as the mineral itself. This streak of powdered mineral is more useful for identification than the mineral's color. Gold prospectors could have saved themselves a lot of heartache if they had known about the streak test. Pyrite makes a greenish-black or brownish-black streak, while gold makes a yellow streak.

Shiny? Dull? Pearly? Words like these describe another property of minerals called luster. Luster describes how light reflects from a mineral's surface. If it shines like a metal, the mineral has metallic (muh TAL lihk) luster. Nonmetallic minerals can be described as having pearly, glassy, dull, or earthy luster, as shown in **Figure 4-7.** Using color, streak, and luster helps identify minerals. What other properties can be used?

Figure 4-6
Streak is the color of the powdered mineral. The mineral magnetite has a black streak.

Hardness

As you investigate different minerals, you'll find that some are harder than others. Some minerals, like talc, are so soft that they can be scratched with a fingernail. Others, like diamond, are so hard that they can be used to cut almost anything else.

In 1822, an Austrian geologist named Friedrich Mohs also noticed this property. He developed a way to classify minerals by their hardness. The Mohs scale, as shown in **Table 4-1,** classifies minerals from 1 (softest) to 10 (hardest). You can determine hardness by trying to scratch one mineral with

Galena

Talc

Figure 4-7 Luster describes how a mineral reflects light. Galena has a metallic luster. Talc has a nonmetallic, pearly luster.

Table 4-1

Mineral Hardness			
Mohs scale		Hardness of common objects	
	softest		
Talc	1		
Gypsum	2	fingernail (2.5)	
Calcite	3	copper penny (3.5)	
Fluorite	4	iron nail (4.5)	
Apatite	5	glass (5.5)	
Feldspar	6	steel file (6.5)	
Quartz	7	streak plate (7)	
Topaz	8		
Corundum	9		
Diamond	10		
	hardest		

another to see which is harder. For example, fluorite (4 on the Mohs scale) will scratch calcite (3 on the scale), but fluorite will not scratch apatite (5 on the scale). You can also use a homemade mineral identification kit: a penny, a nail, and a glass plate with smooth edges. You just find out what scratches what. Is the mineral hard enough to scratch a penny? Will it scratch glass?

Other Properties

Some minerals have other unusual properties that can help identify them. Magnetism occurs in a few minerals, such as magnetite. The mineral calcite has two other unusual properties. It will fizz when it comes into contact with an acid like vinegar. And, if you look through a clear calcite crystal, you will see a double image. Although, because of safety concerns, you should not try it, taste can be used by scientists to identify some minerals. Halite, also called rock salt, has a salty taste. Combinations of all of these properties are used to identify minerals. Learn to use them, and you can be a mineral detective.

Classifying Minerals

Procedure

1. Place samples of quartz, calcite, hornblende, and magnetite in separate sealable, plastic bags and dip each in a pile of iron filings. Record which mineral(s) attract the filings.

2. Place each sample in a small beaker about half full of vinegar and record what happens.

3. Rinse off all samples with water.

Analysis

1. Describe how each mineral reacted to the tests in steps 1 and 2.

2. Describe, in a data table, the other physical properties of the four minerals.

Common Minerals

In the chapter opener, the rocks you scrambled up on your climb were made of minerals. But only a few of the more than 4000 minerals make up most rocks. Some of the most common minerals found in rocks are quartz, feldspar, mica, calcite, gypsum, hornblende, augite, and hematite. Most rocks on Earth are made up of these common minerals. Other minerals, such as diamonds and emeralds, are rare.

Gems

Which would you rather win, a diamond ring or a quartz ring? A diamond ring would be more valuable. Why? The diamond in a ring is a kind of mineral called a gem. **Gems** are minerals that are rare and can be cut and polished, giving them a beautiful appearance, as shown in **Figure 4-8.** This makes them ideal for jewelry. Not all diamonds are gems. To be gem quality, a mineral must be clear with no blemishes or cracks. It also must have a beautiful luster or color. Few minerals meet these standards. That's why the ones that do are rare and valuable.

*inter*NET
CONNECTION

Visit the Glencoe Science Web Site at **www. glencoe.com/sec/ science/nc** for more information about gems.

Problem Solving

Identifying Mineral Origin

At a neighbor's yard sale, you find a dusty old box filled with mineral samples. The neighbor, a former science teacher, says she'll sell you the whole thing for ten dollars. Then, she gives you a challenge. If you can come back in a week with the samples organized by the way they formed, she'll give your money back. You rush home to start your detective work.

Think about the characteristics of mineral crystals that are formed from magma and minerals that crystallize out of solution. Refer to **Figure 4-2** for help.

Think Critically

1. How will you identify and separate the samples by how they formed? What steps will you follow?

2. Determine the characteristics that you will look for in each group.

Gypsum

Biotite Mica

The Making of a Gem

Have you ever wondered why gems are so rare? One reason is that special conditions are needed to produce them. Take diamonds, for instance. Scientists make artificial diamonds in laboratories. To produce a diamond, which is a form of the element carbon, extremely high pressures are needed. These pressures are so great that they are not similar to pressures that exist anywhere in Earth's crust. Therefore, scientists suggest that diamonds form deep in Earth's mantle. To bring a diamond close enough to Earth's surface to find it and mine it takes a special kind of volcanic eruption. This type of eruption forces magma from the mantle toward the surface of Earth at high speeds, bringing diamonds right along with it. This type of magma is called kimberlite magma. **Figure 4-9** shows a kimberlite rock in Western Australia that is mined for diamonds.

Figure 4-8 Gems such as these are rare and beautiful.

Ores

A mineral is called an **ore** if it contains something that is useful and sold for a profit. Many of the metals that we use come from ores. For example, the iron used to make steel comes from the mineral hematite, lead for batteries is produced from galena, and the magnesium used in vitamins comes from dolomite. Ores of these useful metals must be extracted from Earth, which is called mining. A copper mine is shown in **Figure 4-10.**

Figure 4-9 This mine in Western Australia is mining an ore known as kimberlite, which contains diamonds.

Figure 4-10 To be profitable, ores must be found in large deposits or rich veins. Mining is expensive. Copper ore is obtained from this mine in Montana.

Figure 4-11
This smelter heats and melts copper ore. **Why is smelting necessary to process copper ore?**

Ore Processing

Once an ore has been mined, it must be processed to extract the desired mineral or element. **Figure 4-11** shows a copper smelting plant that melts the ore and then separates and removes most of the unwanted materials. After this smelting process, copper can be refined, which means that it is made pure, and processed into many materials that you use every day. Examples of useful copper products include sheet metal products, electrical wiring in cars and homes, and just about anything electronic. Some examples of copper products are shown in **Figure 4-12.**

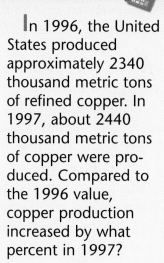

Figure 4-12 Many metal objects you use everyday are made with copper. **What other metals are used to produce everyday objects?**

Now you have a better understanding of minerals and their uses. Can you name five things in your classroom that come from minerals? You will find that you use lots of minerals every day. Next, you will look at rocks, which are Earth materials that are made up of combinations of minerals.

Section Assessment

1. Explain the difference between a mineral and a rock. Name five common rock-forming minerals.

2. List five properties that are used to identify minerals.

3. Where in Earth are diamonds formed? What condition is necessary in order for them to form?

4. **Think Critically:** Would you want to live close to a working gold mine? Explain your answer.

5. **Skill Builder**
   Making and Using Tables To see examples of how the physical properties of minerals can be organized in a table, do the **Chapter 4 Skill Activity** on page 581.

Using Math

In 1996, the United States produced approximately 2340 thousand metric tons of refined copper. In 1997, about 2440 thousand metric tons of copper were produced. Compared to the 1996 value, copper production increased by what percent in 1997?

Navajo Sand Painting

Keeping Your Balance

According to the traditional tales of the Navajo people of the southwestern United States, the universe is a delicate balance of good and evil. Illness is a sign of imbalance. To restore balance, Navajo medicine men, or singers, conduct healing ceremonies for a patient that can last from one to nine days. The ceremonies include the traditional Chants, or Ways, of the Navajo, as well as prayers, legends, medicinal herbs, sweat baths, and sand paintings like the one at right. As a legend is retold, the patient identifies with the hero of the story. This helps to restore harmony and help the patient.

Sand Paintings

Ceremonial sand paintings consist of five sacred colors: white, yellow, black, blue, and red. According to legend, the symbols used in the sand paintings were a gift to the Navajo from their holy ancestors.

We will not give you this picture;
Men are not as good as we;
They might quarrel over the picture and tear it
and that would bring misfortune.
The black cloud would not come again,
and the rain would not fall;
the corn would not grow.
But you may paint it on the ground,
with the colors of the earth.

To create sand paintings, Navajo artists and medicine men grind the sand from local mudstone, charcoal, and sandstone rocks. Facing east, the patient sits on the completed sand painting, gaining strength from the spirits. Symbolically, the illness leaves the patient and enters the sand painting, which is carefully erased. The sand is then collected and carried away, taking the illness with it.

Sand paintings are examples of using Earth materials to satisfy a spiritual need. The Navajo people use minerals and rocks to produce the colored sand they must use in their traditional ceremonies.

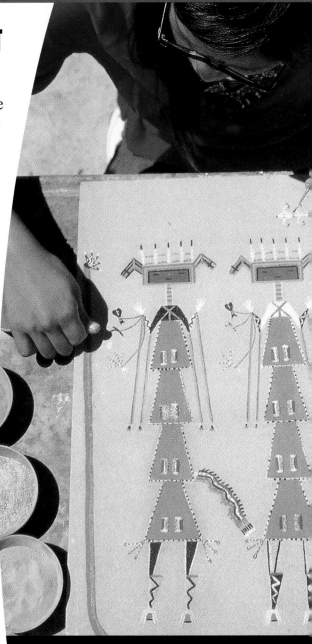

Science
JOURNAL ▶

In your Science Journal, make a list of the properties of sand that would allow you to make a picture. Obtain a shoe box lid and some sand. Try making some simple geometric shapes with the sand. Describe how you poured the sand to make straight lines and curves.

Igneous and Sedimentary Rocks

Earth's Fire

A rocky cliff, a jagged mountain peak, a huge boulder—they all look solid and permanent. Rocks seem as if they've always been here and always will be. But, things are constantly changing on Earth. New rocks form, and old rocks crack and wear away. These and other processes produce three main kinds of rocks—igneous, sedimentary, and metamorphic.

If you could travel into the interior of Earth, you would find that the deeper you go, the higher the temperature and the greater the pressure. Deep inside Earth, it is hot enough to melt rock, as seen in **Figure 4-13. Igneous** (IHG nee us) **rocks** are produced when melted rock, or magma, from inside Earth cools. Igneous rocks can cool and harden on or under Earth's surface. When magma cools, it makes either an extrusive (ehk STREW sihv) igneous rock or an intrusive (ihn TREW sihv) igneous rock.

What You'll Learn

▶ How extrusive and intrusive igneous rocks are different
▶ How different types of sedimentary rocks form

Vocabulary
igneous rock
extrusive
intrusive
sedimentary rock

Why It's Important

▶ Rocks form the land all around you.

Figure 4-13 Mount Etna in Italy is an active volcano. Both molten and solid rock were thrown 200 meters into the air during an October 1998 eruption.

Rocks from Lava

Extrusive igneous rocks form when magma cools on Earth's surface. Magma that reaches Earth's surface is called lava. Lava cools quickly, before large mineral crystals have time to form. That's why extrusive igneous rocks usually have a smooth, sometimes glassy appearance. Like the basalt in **Figure 4-14A,** they have few or no visible crystals.

Extrusive igneous rocks can form in two ways. In one way, volcanoes erupt and shoot out lava and ash. Also, large cracks in Earth's crust, called fissures (FIHSH urs), can open up. When they do, the lava oozes out onto the ground or in water. Oozing lava from a fissure or a volcano is called a lava flow. When a lava flow is exposed to air or water, it cools quickly. This rapid cooling produces mineral grains that are small. At the fastest cooling rates, no grains form at all. In Hawaii, lava flows are so common that you can observe one almost every day. ☑

Reading Check ☑

What is a fissure?

VISUALIZING
Igneous Rocks

Figure 4-14 Intrusive igneous rocks form when melted rock (magma) cools inside Earth. Extrusive igneous rocks form when lava cools at Earth's surface.

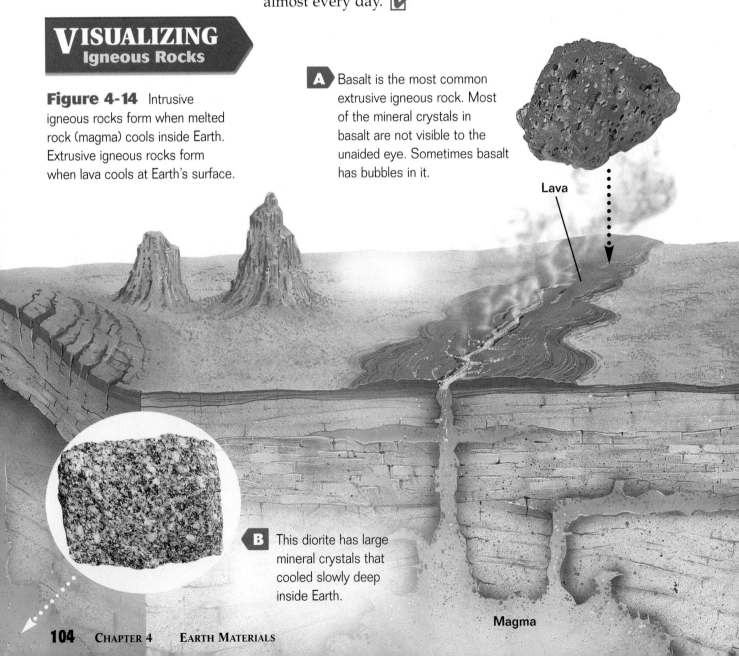

A Basalt is the most common extrusive igneous rock. Most of the mineral crystals in basalt are not visible to the unaided eye. Sometimes basalt has bubbles in it.

Lava

B This diorite has large mineral crystals that cooled slowly deep inside Earth.

Magma

Rocks from Magma

What about magma that doesn't reach the surface? Can it form rocks, too? Yes, **intrusive** igneous rocks are produced when magma cools below the surface of Earth, as shown in **Figure 4-14.**

Intrusive igneous rocks form when a huge glob of magma from inside Earth rises toward the surface, but never erupts onto the surface. It's similar to a helium balloon that is let loose in a gym and gets stuck on the ceiling. It doesn't make it outside—just to the ceiling. This hot mass of rock sits under the surface and cools slowly over thousands of years until it is solid. The cooling is so slow that the minerals in the magma have time to form large crystals. The size of the mineral crystals is the main difference between intrusive and extrusive igneous rocks. Intrusive igneous rocks have large crystals that are easy to see. Extrusive igneous rocks do not have large crystals that you can see easily.

Lava

C This intrusive rock is granite. Like diorite, it cooled slowly inside Earth, forming large mineral crystals.

Magma

D The extrusive rock rhyolite has a similar composition to granite, but, the magma it formed from cooled quickly. It has few visible mineral crystals.

Sedimentary Rocks

The second major group of rocks is called sedimentary (sed uh MENT uh ree) rocks. **Sedimentary rocks** are made when pieces of other rocks, plant and animal matter, or dissolved minerals collect to form rock layers, as shown in **Figure 4-15.** These pieces of rock and other materials are called sediments (SED uh munts). Rivers, ocean waves, mudslides, and glaciers can carry sediments. Sediments can also be carried by the wind. When the sediments are dropped, or deposited, by wind, ice, gravity, or water, they collect in layers. After the sediments are deposited, they begin the long process of becoming rock. Most sedimentary rocks take thousands to millions of years to form. The changes that form sedimentary rocks are always happening in our world, as shown in **Figure 4-16.** ✓

Reading Check ✓

How are sediments carried from one place to another?

Detrital Rocks

When most people talk about sedimentary rocks, they are usually thinking about rocks like sandstone, which is a detrital rock (DEH trih tuhl). Detrital rocks are made of grains of minerals or other rocks that are moved and deposited by water, ice, gravity, or wind into layers. These layers are then cemented together by other minerals and squeezed or compacted into rock by the weight of sediments on top of them.

VISUALIZING **Sedimentary Rocks**

Figure 4-15 All of these sedimentary rocks are exposed at Cathedral Rocks in Arizona. The different layers are types of sedimentary rocks. **Why do sedimentary rocks form in layers?**

A Conglomerate is made up of large pebbles cemented together.

B Sandstone is made up of sand grains cemented together.

Detrital sedimentary rocks are identified by the size of the grains that make up the rock. Rocks made of the smallest, clay-sized grains are called shale. Silt-sized grains, which are slightly larger than clay, make up siltstone. Sandstone is made of sand-sized grains. Sand is larger than silt. Pebbles are larger still. Pebbles mixed and cemented together with other sediments make up rocks called conglomerates (kun GLAHM ruts).

Chemical Rocks

Some sedimentary rocks form when seawater, loaded with dissolved minerals, evaporates. Chemical sedimentary rock can also form when mineral-rich water from geysers or hot springs evaporates. As the water evaporates, layers of minerals are left behind. If you've ever sat in the sun after swimming in the ocean, you may have noticed salt crystals on your skin. The seawater on your skin evaporated, leaving behind deposits of halite. The halite had been dissolved in the water. Something similar happens to form chemical rocks.

Figure 4-16 Waves deposit and move sand around on this beach in California. **How else are sediments carried and deposited?**

C Siltstone is made up of grains that are smaller than sand grains.

D Shale is made of the smallest grains, clay.

Mini Lab

Modeling How Fossils Form Rocks

Procedure

1. Fill a small aluminum pie pan with an assortment of broken macaroni. These represent different kinds of fossils.
2. Mix three tablespoons of white glue into half a cup of water. Pour this solution over the macaroni and set it aside to dry.
3. When your fossil rock sample has set, pop it out of the pan and compare it with a real fossil limestone sample.

Analysis

1. Explain why you used the glue solution and what this represents in nature.
2. Using whole macaroni samples as a guide, match the macaroni pieces in your "rock" to the intact macaroni fossils. Then draw and label them in your Science Journal.

Biochemical Rocks

Would it surprise you to know that the chalk your teacher is using on the chalkboard may also be a rock? The coal that is used as a fuel to produce electricity is also a sedimentary rock.

Chalk and coal are examples of the group of sedimentary rocks called biochemical rocks. Biochemical rocks form over millions of years. Living matter dies, piles up, and then is compressed into rock. If the rock is produced from layers of plants piled on top of one another, it is called coal. Biochemical sedimentary rocks also can form in the oceans and are most often classified as limestone. Many different kinds of limestone exist. Chalk is a kind of limestone made from the fossils of millions of tiny animals and algae, as shown in **Figure 4-17B.** A fossil is the remains or trace of a once-living plant or animal. A dinosaur bone and footprint are both fossils.

A This coral reef is located in New Guinea. The framework of the reef is limestone.

Figure 4-17 There are a great variety of biochemical sedimentary rocks.

Camarasaurus **skull**

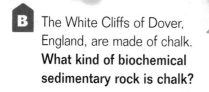

B The White Cliffs of Dover, England, are made of chalk. **What kind of biochemical sedimentary rock is chalk?**

C Fossils like these in Dinosaur National Monument in Utah are found in limestone or in sandstones or siltstones.

Section Assessment

1. Describe the different ways that extrusive and intrusive igneous rocks form.

2. Infer why igneous rocks that solidify underground cool so slowly.

3. Diagram how each of the three kinds of sedimentary rocks forms. List one example of each kind of rock: detrital, chemical, and biochemical.

4. **Think Critically:** If someone handed you a sample of an igneous rock and asked you if it was extrusive or intrusive, what would you look for first? Explain.

5.  **Skill Builder**

   Sequencing Describe one possible sequence of events that explains how coal is formed. If you need help, refer to Sequencing in the **Skill Handbook** on page 550.

Science Journal
Research a national park or monument that has had volcanic activity. Read about the park and the features that you'd like to see. Then describe the features in your Science Journal.

Cool Crystals vs. Hot Crystals

Possible Materials

- 3-quart saucepan
- Measuring cup
- Large wooden spoon
- Stove or hot plate
- Pint jars or glasses (2)
- Paper clips (2)
- Pencils (2)
- Cotton string (3-cm) (2)
- White, granulated sugar (3 cups)
- Refrigerator
- Igneous rocks (4)

Two types of igneous rocks can look different, even though they are made of the same minerals. Extrusive rocks have an even texture with few or no visible crystals, while intrusive rocks have large, beautiful crystals. How does this happen?

Recognize the Problem

How can different-sized crystals form from a solution?

Form a Hypothesis

Based on your observations, the goals of this experiment, and the possible materials, form a hypothesis about how you think the rate of cooling affects the different sizes of crystals that can be formed.

Goals

- **Design an experiment** that compares crystal growth in a solution by using different methods of cooling.
- **Write** a general rule about crystal size in igneous rocks based on your observations in this experiment.

Safety Precautions

Never eat or taste anything from a lab, even if you are confident that you know what it is.
CAUTION: *Use care when handling hot objects and liquids.*

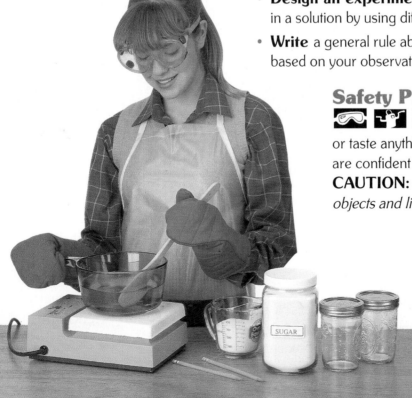

Test Your Hypothesis

Plan

1. As a group, agree upon and write out your hypothesis.

2. As a group, **list** the steps that you will take to test your hypothesis. Be specific, describing exactly how you are going to make different sizes of crystals. If you have questions about how to mix the solution, check with your teacher.

3. **List** all of the materials that you will need to complete your experiment.

4. Before you begin, make a data table or graph that will allow you to compare the size of the crystals that form in each solution.

5. **Read** over your entire experiment to make sure that all the steps are in logical order.

6. Be sure to double-check your list of materials and method for creating sizes of crystals.

7. Will you repeat any part of the experiment more than once to allow for human error?

8. Is your data table ready to handle the amount of data that you want to collect?

Do

1. Make sure your teacher approves your plan before you proceed.

2. Carry out the lab as planned and approved.

3. Record your observations in the data table as you complete each test.

Analyze Your Data

1. **Compare** the sizes of crystals that formed at different rates.

2. Using your data table, **conclude** how this information could help you to classify igneous rocks.

Draw Conclusions

1. **Identify** four igneous rock samples as either intrusive or extrusive.

2. How could an igneous rock contain some large and some small crystals?

Metamorphic Rocks and the Rock Cycle

What You'll Learn

▶ The conditions needed for metamorphic rocks to form
▶ How all rocks are tied together in the rock cycle

Vocabulary
metamorphic rock
foliated
non-foliated
rock cycle

Why It's Important

▶ Metamorphic rocks and the rock cycle show that Earth is a constantly changing planet.

New Rocks from Old Rocks

When you wake up in the morning, does the land around you look different from the way it did the day before? Usually not. But, even if you can't detect it, Earth is constantly changing. Layers of sediment are piling up in the bottoms of lakes, landmasses are moving, and rocks are disappearing below Earth's surface. Some of these changes cause sedimentary and igneous rocks to be heated and squeezed, as shown in **Figure 4-18.** In the process, new rocks form.

Figure 4-18 These mountains in the Swiss Alps were formed under great pressures and temperatures. The rocks were squeezed into these spectacular shapes.

Metamorphic Rocks

Do you recycle your plastic milk jugs? After the jugs are collected, sorted, and cleaned, they are heated and squeezed into pellets. The pellets later can be made into useful new products. Did you know that rocks get recycled, too? New rocks that form when existing rocks are heated or squeezed are called **metamorphic** (met uh MOR fihk) **rocks.** The word *metamorphic* means "change of form." This describes well how some rocks take on a whole new look when under great temperatures and pressures, as shown in **Figure 4-19.** Minerals in metamorphic rocks are re-formed and realigned too, as shown in **Figure 4-20.** ☑

Reading Check ☑

How do metamorphic rocks change in form?

Figure 4-19 This rock formation from the state of Washington has been folded and deformed under high pressures and temperatures deep within Earth.

Figure 4-20 This metamorphic rock has minerals that were squeezed, causing them to line up because of pressure placed on them.

Magnification: 30 ✕

Types of "Changed" Rocks

New metamorphic rocks can form from any existing type of rock—igneous, sedimentary, or metamorphic. Metamorphic rocks are divided into two texture groups: foliated (FOH lee ay tud) and non-foliated, as shown in **Figure 4-21. Foliated** rocks have bands of minerals. These minerals have been heated and squeezed into parallel layers. Many foliated metamorphic rocks have bands of different-colored minerals. Slate, gneiss (NISE), phyllite (FIHL ite), and schist (SHIST) are all examples of foliated rocks. **Non-foliated** metamorphic rocks do not have distinct layers or bands. These rocks, such as quartzite, marble, and soapstone, usually are more even in color than foliated rocks.

Try Activity 4-2 to better understand how metamorphic rock textures are made.

Figure 4-21 There are many different types of metamorphic rocks. **What force could cause the parallel layers in foliated rocks?**

A This carved figure is soapstone, a non-foliated metamorphic rock.

E Gneiss is a foliated metamorphic rock.

B This schist is a foliated metamorphic rock.

C This statue from a fountain in Italy is made of marble, a non-foliated metamorphic rock.

D The roof and siding on this house are made of slate, a foliated metamorphic rock.

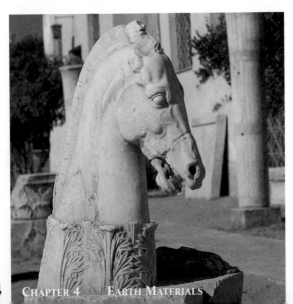

The Rock Cycle

Rocks are constantly changing from one type to another. If you wanted to describe the process to someone, how would you do it? Would you use words or pictures? Scientists have created a diagram called the **rock cycle** to show the process. It shows how different kinds of rock are related to one another and how rocks change from one type to another. Each rock is on a continuing journey through the rock cycle, as shown in **Figure 4-22.**

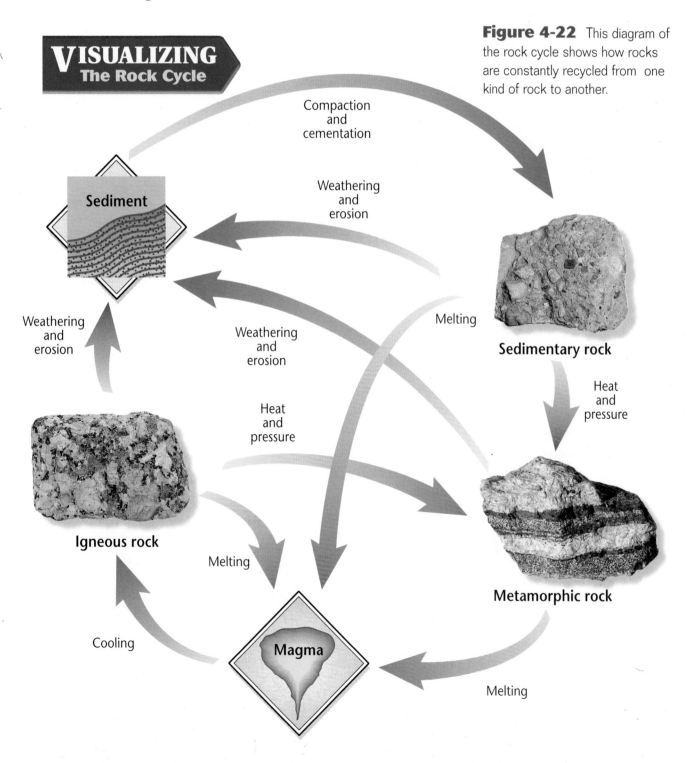

VISUALIZING
The Rock Cycle

Figure 4-22 This diagram of the rock cycle shows how rocks are constantly recycled from one kind of rock to another.

Compaction and cementation

Weathering and erosion

Sediment

Weathering and erosion

Weathering and erosion

Heat and pressure

Melting

Sedimentary rock

Heat and pressure

Igneous rock

Melting

Metamorphic rock

Cooling

Magma

Melting

The Journey of a Rock

Pick any point on the diagram of the rock cycle in **Figure 4-22,** and you will see how a rock in that part of the cycle could become any other kind of rock. Let's start with a blob of lava that oozes to the surface and cools, as shown in **Figure 4-23.** It forms an igneous rock. If that rock happens to fall into the ocean, the water will wear off small pieces. These pieces of rock are now called sediment and will be washed along the shore. In time, this sediment is piled up and cemented together. It becomes a sedimentary rock. If this sedimentary rock is buried deeply, pressure and heat inside Earth may change it into a metamorphic rock. In this way, all rocks on Earth are changed over millions and millions of years. This process is happening right now.

Figure 4-23 This lava in Hawaii is flowing into the ocean and cooling rapidly, causing steam to form.

Section Assessment

1. Identify two factors that combine to produce metamorphic rocks.

2. Name examples of foliated and non-foliated rocks. Explain the difference between the two types of metamorphic rocks.

3. High temperatures and pressures can produce both metamorphic and igneous rocks. Explain the difference between these two rock types.

4. **Think Critically:** Trace the journey of a granite through the rock cycle. Explain how this rock could be changed from an igneous rock to a sedimentary and then to a metamorphic rock.

5. **Skill Builder**
   Observing Describe a part of the rock cycle you can observe occurring around you or that you see on television news. If you need help, refer to Observing and Inferring in the **Skill Handbook** on page 556.

Using Computers

Spreadsheet Using a spreadsheet program, create a data table to list and compare the properties of different rocks and minerals that you have studied in this chapter. If you need help, refer to page 574.

Gneiss Rice

Materials

- Rolling pin
- Lump of modeling clay
- Uncooked rice (wild rice, if available) ($\frac{1}{2}$ cup)
- Granite sample
- Gneiss sample

You know that metamorphic rocks are often layered. But did you realize that individual mineral grains can change in orientation? This means that the grains can line up in certain directions. You'll experiment with rice grains in clay to see how foliation is produced.

What You'll Investigate

You will model conditions that cause an igneous rock texture to change into a metamorphic rock texture.

Goals

- **Investigate** ways rocks are changed.
- **Model** a metamorphic rock texture.

Procedure 🔧 🥽 CAUTION: *Don't eat anything from the experiment.*

1. **Sketch** the granite specimen in your Science Journal.

2. **Pour** the rice onto the table. **Roll** the ball of clay in the rice. Some of the rice will stick to the outside of the ball. **Knead** the ball until the rice is spread out fairly evenly. Roll and knead the ball again, and repeat until your clay sample has lots of "minerals" distributed throughout it.

3. Using the rolling pin, **roll** the clay so that it is about 0.5 cm thick. Don't roll it too hard. The grains of rice should be pointing in different directions. Draw a picture of the clay in your Science Journal.

4. Take the edge of the clay closest to you and **fold** it toward the edge farthest from you. **Roll** the clay in the direction you folded it. Fold and roll the clay in the same direction several more times. Flatten the lump to 0.5 cm thickness again. Draw what you observe in your "rock" and in the gneiss sample in your Science Journal.

Conclude and Apply

1. What features did the granite and the first lump of clay have in common?

2. What force caused the positions of rice grains in the lump of clay to change? How is this process similar to and also different from what happens in nature?

For a **preview** of this chapter, study this Reviewing Main Ideas before you read the chapter. After you have studied this chapter, you can use the Reviewing Main Ideas to **review** the chapter.

The Glencoe MindJogger, Audiocassettes, and CD-ROM provide additional opportunities for review.

Section 4-1 MINERALS

All **minerals** occur naturally, are inorganic solids, and have an orderly pattern of atoms and definite chemical makeup. *List four properties that can be used to help identify a mineral.*

Section 4-2 IGNEOUS ROCKS

Intrusive igneous rocks form below Earth's surface and have large mineral crystals. **Extrusive** igneous rocks form above Earth's surface and have small or no mineral crystals. The differences in crystal sizes result from the differences in the cooling rates. *Why don't rocks formed by volcanic activity have large mineral crystals?*

Reading Check ☑

Suggest one or two additional illustrations for this chapter and explain why they would be valuable.

SEDIMENTARY ROCKS

Sedimentary rocks can form from grains of other rocks, organic material, and minerals that evaporate or crystallize out of solution. *How could the grains in a sedimentary rock like sandstone be moved and then deposited?*

Section 4-3 METAMORPHIC ROCKS

Earth processes change the form of Earth materials, forming **metamorphic rocks.** The texture and mineral composition of a rock can be altered during metamorphism. *What causes the changes that produce this type of rock?*

THE ROCK CYCLE

Rocks form and change because of processes in the **rock cycle.** *Explain or draw the route through the rock cycle that granite could take, from an igneous rock to a metamorphic rock, to ending up as a sandstone.*

Chapter 4 Assessment

Using Vocabulary

a. crystal
b. extrusive
c. foliated
d. gem
e. igneous rock
f. intrusive
g. metamorphic rock
h. mineral
i. non-foliated
j. ore
k. rock
l. rock cycle
m. sedimentary rock

Explain the difference between each pair of Vocabulary words.

1. crystal; gem
2. foliated; non-foliated
3. intrusive; extrusive
4. rock; ore
5. metamorphic rock; sedimentary rock

Checking Concepts

Choose the word or phrase that best answers the question.

6. Which of the following describe what rocks are usually composed of?
   A) pieces
   B) minerals
   C) fossil fuels
   D) foliations

7. When do metamorphic rocks form?
   A) when layers of sediment are deposited
   B) when lava solidifies in seawater
   C) when particles of rock break off at Earth's surface
   D) when heat and pressure change rocks

8. How can sedimentary rocks be classified?
   A) foliated or non-foliated
   B) biochemical, chemical, or detrital
   C) extrusive or intrusive
   D) gems or ores

9. What kind of rock do volcanic eruptions produce?
   A) sedimentary
   B) banded
   C) old
   D) extrusive

10. Which of the following must be true of all minerals?
    A) They must be organic.
    B) They must be glassy.
    C) They must be gems.
    D) They must be naturally occurring.

11. Which of the following describes grains in igneous rocks that form slowly from magma below Earth's surface?
    A) no grains
    B) visible grains
    C) sedimentary grains
    D) foliated grains

12. How do sedimentary rocks form?
    A) They are deposited on Earth's surface.
    B) They form from magma.
    C) They are squeezed into foliated layers.
    D) They form deep in Earth's crust.

13. Which of these is **NOT** a physical property of a mineral?
    A) cleavage
    B) organic
    C) fracture
    D) hardness

14. Which is true of all minerals?
    A) They have an orderly arrangement of atoms.
    B) They have a glassy luster.
    C) They have a conchoidal fracture.
    D) They have a hardness greater than a penny.

15. All detrital rocks form under which of the following conditions?
    A) from grains of preexisting rocks and minerals
    B) on the ocean floor
    C) under water
    D) from pieces of sedimentary rock

Thinking Critically

16. Is a sugar crystal a mineral? Why or why not?

17. Metal deposits in Antarctica are not considered to be ores. List some reasons for this.

18. How could pieces of gneiss, granite, and basalt all be found in one conglomerate?

19. Would you expect to find a well-preserved dinosaur bone in a metamorphic rock like schist? Explain.

20. Explain how the mineral quartz could be in an igneous rock and in a sedimentary rock.

Developing Skills

If you need help, refer to the **Skill Handbook.**

21. **Observing and Inferring:** You are hiking in the mountains and as you cross a shallow stream, you spy an unusual rock. When you pick it up, you notice it is full of fossil shells. Your friend asks you what it is. What do you say and why?

22. **Interpreting Scientific Illustrations:** Observe the pictures below and determine whether each is a sedimentary, igneous, or metamorphic rock.

Test-Taking Tip

Dress Comfortably Loose, layered clothing is best. Whatever the temperature, you're prepared. Important test scores do not take climate into consideration.

Test Practice

Use these questions to test your Science Proficiency.

1. Which of the following helps distinguish basic rock types you have studied?
   A) Igneous rocks form above the surface of Earth, while metamorphic rocks form below.
   B) Both sedimentary rocks and metamorphic rocks are layered, but metamorphic rock layering is foliated.
   C) Igneous rocks form below the surface of Earth, while sedimentary rocks form at Earth's surface.
   D) Like sedimentary rocks, metamorphic rocks form at low temperatures and pressures.

2. Which of the following is **NOT** a necessary condition for a rock to be an ore?
   A) The rock must contain a useful element or mineral.
   B) The rock must contain gold.
   C) The rock must contain a material that is reasonably concentrated.
   D) The rock must be able to be mined at a profit.

3. Which of the following is **NOT** a necessary condition for an object to be a mineral?
   A) It was found in nature.
   B) It has an orderly pattern of atoms.
   C) It formed from the cooling of magma.
   D) It has a definite chemical make up.

Weathering and Soil

Chapter Preview

Section 5-1
Weathering
Section 5-2
Soil

Skills Preview

Skill Builders
- Recognize Cause and Effect
- Map Concepts

Activities
- Hypothesize
- Interpret Data

MiniLabs
- Observe
- Compare and Contrast

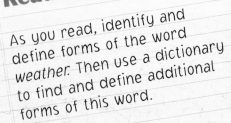

Reading Check ✓

As you read, identify and define forms of the word *weather.* Then use a dictionary to find and define additional forms of this word.

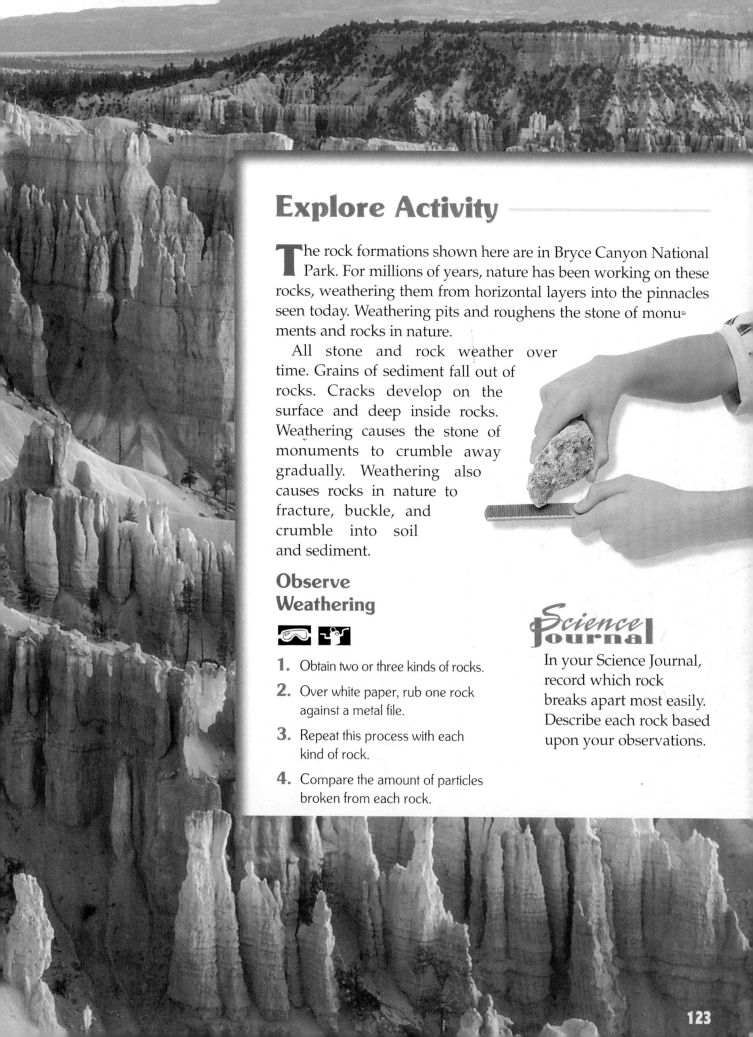

Explore Activity

The rock formations shown here are in Bryce Canyon National Park. For millions of years, nature has been working on these rocks, weathering them from horizontal layers into the pinnacles seen today. Weathering pits and roughens the stone of monuments and rocks in nature.

All stone and rock weather over time. Grains of sediment fall out of rocks. Cracks develop on the surface and deep inside rocks. Weathering causes the stone of monuments to crumble away gradually. Weathering also causes rocks in nature to fracture, buckle, and crumble into soil and sediment.

Observe Weathering

1. Obtain two or three kinds of rocks.
2. Over white paper, rub one rock against a metal file.
3. Repeat this process with each kind of rock.
4. Compare the amount of particles broken from each rock.

Science Journal

In your Science Journal, record which rock breaks apart most easily. Describe each rock based upon your observations.

5·1 Weathering

Evidence of Weathering

The next time you take a walk or a drive, notice the sand and grit along the sidewalk and curb. Much of the gritty sediment you see comes from small particles that break loose from concrete curbs and from rocks exposed to the natural elements. These sediments are evidence that weathering is taking place.

Weathering is the process that breaks down rocks into smaller and smaller fragments. Conditions and processes in the environment cause the weathering of rock and concrete. Rocks break down into small pieces called sediment. These sediments also can form soil. Soil formation is dependent upon the process of weathering.

Over millions of years, the process of weathering has helped change Earth's surface. It continues today. **Figure 5-1** illustrates how weathering wears down mountains to hills. Weathering makes it difficult to read the writing on tombstones and slowly breaks down statues. Weathering also can cause potholes in streets. The two types of weathering are mechanical and chemical. They work together to break down rock.

What You'll Learn

▶ The difference between mechanical weathering and chemical weathering
▶ The effects of climate on weathering

Vocabulary
weathering
mechanical weathering
ice wedging
chemical weathering
oxidation
climate

Why It's Important

▶ Weathering causes rocks to crumble and landforms to change shape over time.

Figure 5-1 Over long periods of time, weathering helps change sharp, jagged mountains into smooth, rolling mountains and hills.

A The Grand Tetons in Wyoming (A) have not been exposed to agents of weathering as long as the mountains of Mount Washington Valley, New Hampshire, (B) have been.

Figure 5-2 Pavements such as driveways and sidewalks can be broken up by tree roots.

A As trees grow, their roots spread throughout the soil.

B As roots grow under a sidewalk, their increased size forces the concrete to crack.

C Over time, the sidewalk buckles and breaks apart.

Mechanical Weathering

Mechanical weathering breaks apart rocks without changing their chemical composition. Each fragment and particle weathered away by a mechanical process keeps the same characteristics as the original rock. Mechanical weathering can be caused by growing plants, expanding ice, mineral crystal growth, lightning, and expansion and contraction when an area heats and cools. These physical processes produce enough force to break rocks into smaller pieces. ✓

Plants

Plant roots grow into cracks of rocks where they find water and nutrients. As roots grow, they wedge rocks apart. If you've skated on a sidewalk and tripped over a crack near a tree, you have experienced the results of mechanical weathering. The sidewalk near the tree in **Figure 5-2C** shows signs of weathering. How could cracks in rocks occur in the same way? **Figure 5-3** might give you some ideas.

Reading Check

What is mechanical weathering?

Lichen also cause mechanical weathering. Parts of lichen expand and shrink with the amount of available water. This is similar to the process of ice wedging described below.

Ice Wedging

The mechanical weathering process known as **ice wedging** is illustrated in **Figure 5-4.** In cold areas, low temperatures freeze water. Warmer temperatures thaw the ice. Ice wedging is noticeable in the mountains. It is one factor that wears down sharp mountain peaks to rounded hills—a process pictured in **Figure 5-1.** This cycle of freezing and thawing not only breaks up rocks but also breaks up roads and highways. When water enters cracks in road pavement and freezes, it forces the pavement apart. This can cause potholes to form in roads. Weathering by both roots and ice wedging rapidly can reduce rocks to smaller pieces. Breaking up rocks through mechanical weathering exposes a greater surface area to additional weathering. As the amount of surface area increases, the rate of weathering increases.

Figure 5-3 Tree roots cause mechanical weathering of rocks as shown by this tree in Glacier National Park, Montana.

Figure 5-4 When water freezes in cracks of rocks, it expands. Pressure builds and breaks apart the rock. As the ice thaws and then the water refreezes, this process occurs again.

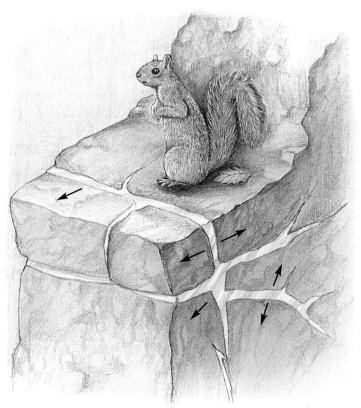

Chemical Weathering

The second type of weathering occurs when water, air, and other substances react with the minerals in rocks. This type of weathering is called **chemical weathering** because the chemical composition of the rock changes. Let's see how chemical weathering happens.

CHEMISTRY
◄ INTEGRATION

Water

Water is an important agent of chemical weathering. When the hydrogen and oxygen atoms in water react with the chemicals in some rocks, new substances form. These substances are much different from those of the original rock.

Acids

Naturally formed acids can weather rocks chemically. When water mixes with carbon dioxide from the air, a weak acid, called carbonic acid, forms. Carbonic acid is the same weak acid that makes soft drinks fizzy. Carbonic acid reacts with minerals such as calcite, the main mineral in limestone. The product of this reaction then dissolves and can be carried away with the acid. Over thousands of years, carbonic acid has weathered so much limestone that caves have formed, such as the one shown in **Figure 5-5.**

Figure 5-5 Lehman Cave in Great Basin National Park, Nevada, is a product of chemical weathering. **How did water help form this cave?**

Chemical weathering also occurs when carbonic acid comes in contact with granite rock. Over a long time, the mineral feldspar in granite is broken down into the clay mineral kaolinite. Kaolinite clay makes up most of the material in some soils. Clay is an end product of weathering.

Some roots and decaying plants give off acids that can dissolve minerals in rock. Removing these minerals weakens the rock. Eventually, the rock will break into smaller pieces. The next time you find a moss-covered rock, peel back the moss and look at the small pits underneath. Acids from the rootlike structures of the moss caused the pits.

CHEMISTRY
INTEGRATION

Cave Beauty
Some cave formations are made of calcite. The chemical formula for calcite, a common rock-forming mineral, is $CaCO_3$.
Use the periodic table in the back of the book to identify the elements in this formula.

Try at Home

Mini Lab

Observing the Formation of Rust

Procedure

1. Place some steel wool in a glass dish with 1 cm of water.
2. Observe for several days.

Analysis

1. What changes occurred?
2. What caused the changes?
3. How are these changes related to weathering?

Oxygen

Oxygen helps cause chemical weathering. You've seen rusty swing sets and cars. Rust is caused by oxidation. **Oxidation** (ahk sih DAY shun) occurs when a material such as iron is exposed to oxygen and water. When rocks containing iron are exposed to water and the oxygen in the air, the iron in the rock rusts and turns reddish, as seen in **Figure 5-6**.

Climate and Weathering

Mechanical and chemical weathering occur everywhere. However, climate affects the rate and type of weathering. **Climate** is the pattern of weather that occurs in a particular area over many years. In cold climates, where freezing and thawing are frequent, mechanical weathering breaks down rocks rapidly through the process of ice wedging.

Chemical weathering is more rapid in warm, wet climates. Thus, chemical weathering occurs quickly in tropical areas such as the Amazon River region of South America. Lack of moisture in deserts and low temperatures in polar regions slow down chemical weathering. How weathering affects rock depends on the type of rock, as illustrated in **Figure 5-7**.

Mechanical and chemical weathering work together. For example, when rocks break apart because of mechanical weathering, more surface area is exposed, and the rate of chemical weathering increases.

Figure 5-6 These rocks in Utah have been chemically weathered. **What caused them to be a reddish color?**

Figure 5-7 These old tombstones are about the same age, but they have weathered differently. The type of rock also influences how fast a surface weathers. **Why?**

Now you can understand how weathering affects roads, buildings, streets, cemeteries, sidewalks, rocks, caves, and mountains. When weathering breaks down rocks, it contributes to the rock cycle by making sediment that can form sedimentary rocks. Weathering also begins the process of breaking down rock into soil. These steps are discussed in the next section.

Section Assessment

1. What is the difference between mechanical and chemical weathering?

2. How is mechanical weathering affected by climate?

3. **Think Critically:** How can water be a factor in both mechanical and chemical weathering?

4. **Skill Builder**
   Observing and Inferring Do the **Chapter 5 Skill Activity** on page 582 to learn more about mechanical weathering.

Using Computers

Spreadsheet Make a spreadsheet that identifies examples of weathering that you see around your neighborhood and school and classifies each example as the result of mechanical weathering, chemical weathering, or both. If you need help, refer to page 574.

Weathering Chalk

Possible Materials

- Equal-sized pieces of chalk (6)
- Small beakers or clear plastic cups (2)
- Metric ruler
- Water
- White vinegar (100 mL)
- Hot plate
- Graduated cylinder (250 mL)

Chalk is a type of limestone made of the shells of tiny organisms. When you write your name on the chalkboard or draw a picture on the driveway with a piece of chalk, what happens to the chalk? It is mechanically weathered. This experiment will help you understand how chalk can be chemically weathered.

Recognize the Problem

How can chalk be chemically weathered? What variables affect the rate of chemical weathering?

Form a Hypothesis

How do you think acidity, surface area, and temperature affect the rate of chemical weathering of chalk? What happens to chalk in water or acid (vinegar)? How will the size of the chalk pieces affect the rate of weathering? What will happen if you heat the acid? **Make hypotheses** to support your ideas.

Goals

- **Design** experiments to compare the effects of acidity, surface area, and temperature on the rate of chemical weathering of chalk.
- **Describe** factors that affect chemical weathering.

Safety Precautions

Wear safety goggles when pouring acids.

CAUTION: *If mixing liquids, always add acid to water.* Be careful when using a hot plate and heated solutions.

Test Your Hypothesis

Plan

1. **Develop** hypotheses about the effects of acidity, surface area, and temperature on the rate of chemical weathering.

2. Decide how to test your first hypothesis. **List** the steps needed to test the hypothesis.

3. Repeat step 2 for your other two hypotheses.

4. **Design** data tables in your Science Journal. Make one for acidity, one for surface area, and one for temperature.

5. **Identify** what remains constant in your experiment and what varies. Each test should have only one variable. Have you allowed for a control in each experiment?

6. **Summarize** your data in a graph. Decide from reading the **Skill Handbook** which type of graph to use.

Do

1. Make sure your teacher approves your plan before you start the experiment.

2. Carry out the three experiments as planned.

3. While the experiments are going on, **write** your observations and **complete** the data tables in your Science Journal.

Analyze Your Data

1. **Analyze** your graph to find out which substance—water or acid—weathered the chalk more quickly. Was your hypothesis supported by your data?

2. **Infer** from your data obtained in the surface-area experiment whether the amount of surface area makes a difference in the rate of chemical weathering. Explain why this occurs.

Draw Conclusions

1. **Explain** how the chalk was chemically weathered.

2. How does heat affect the rate of chemical weathering?

3. What does this imply about weathering in the tropics?

5·2 Soil

What You'll Learn

► How soil develops from rock
► How to describe soil by comparing the A, B, and C soil horizons
► How environmental conditions affect the development of soils
► Ways to reduce soil erosion

Vocabulary

soil   horizon
humus   litter
soil profile   leaching

Why It's Important

► Some regions of Earth are more fertile than others because soil forms in different ways.

Formation of Soil

How often have you been told "Take off those dirty shoes before you come into this house"? Ever since you were a child, you've had experience with what many people call dirt, which is actually soil. Soil is found in lots of places: empty lots, farm fields, gardens, and forests.

What is soil and where does it come from? The surface of Earth is covered by a layer of rock and mineral fragments produced by weathering. As you learned in Section 5-1, weathering gradually breaks rocks into smaller and smaller fragments. But, these fragments are not soil until plants and animals live in them. Plants and animals add organic matter such as leaves, twigs, and dead worms and insects to the rock fragments. Then, soil begins to develop. **Soil** is a mixture of weathered rock, organic matter, mineral fragments, water, and air. **Figure 5-8** illustrates the process of soil development. Soil is a material that supports vegetation. Climate, types of rock, slope, amount of moisture, and length of time rock has been weathering affect the formation of soil.

VISUALIZING Soil Development

Figure 5-8 Soil is constantly developing from rock.

A Rock at the surface begins to fracture and break down.

B As rock weathers into smaller fragments, plants begin to grow in the weathered rock.

Composition of Soil

Soil may contain small rodents, insects, worms, algae, fungi, bacteria, and decaying organic matter. As soil develops, organic material, such as plants, decays until the original form of the matter has disappeared. The material turns into dark-colored matter called **humus** (HYEW mus). Humus serves as a source of nutrients for plants, providing nitrogen, phosphorus, potassium, and sulfur. Humus also promotes good soil structure and helps soil hold water. As worms, insects, and rodents burrow throughout soil, they mix the humus with the fragments of rock. In good-quality surface soil, about half of the volume is humus and half is broken-down rock.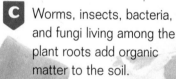

Soil can take thousands of years to form and can range in thickness from 60 m in some areas to just a few centimeters in others. A fertile soil is one that supplies nutrients for plant growth. Soils that develop near rivers often are fertile. Other soils, such as those that develop on steep slopes, may be poor in nutrients and have low fertility.

Soils have small spaces in them. These spaces fill with air or water. In swampy areas, water may fill these spaces year-round. In other areas, soil may fill up with water after rains or during floods.

Reading Check

Why is humus important?

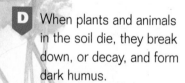

C Worms, insects, bacteria, and fungi living among the plant roots add organic matter to the soil.

D When plants and animals in the soil die, they break down, or decay, and form dark humus.

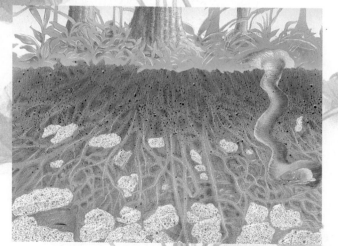

Mini Lab

Comparing Components of Soil

Procedure

1. Collect a sample of soil.
2. Observe it closely with a magnifying glass or a microscope.

Analysis

1. Describe the different particles found in your sample. Did you find any remains of once-living organisms?
2. Compare and contrast your sample with those other students have collected. How are the samples the same? How are they different?

Soil Profile

You may have seen layers of soil if you've ever dug a deep hole or driven by a steep slope such as a road cut where the soil and rock are exposed. You might have observed that plants grow in the top layer of soil. The top layer of soil is darker than the soil layers below it. These different layers of soil make up what is called a **soil profile.** Each layer in the soil profile is called a **horizon.** There are generally three horizons. They are labeled A, B, and C, as in the diagram in **Figure 5-9.**

Figure 5-9 Under this meadow is soil with a specific profile.

A The soil profile of this meadow has three main horizons.

B The horizons in this soil profile reflect the climatic conditions under which it formed. The A horizon contains humus and small grains of rocks. The dark color reflects the organic material it contains. The B horizon contains minerals that have been dissolved and moved from the A horizon plus some clay. The C horizon consists mainly of original rock that has not been changed and that has no organic material.

The photo in **Figure 5-10** shows soil horizons in an eroded hillside. You might also see soil profiles in streambeds, at construction sites, or even in your own garden.

Horizon A

The A horizon is the top layer of soil. In a forest or unplowed area, it may be covered with litter. **Litter** is composed of leaves, twigs, and other organic material that changes to humus when it is exposed to decomposing organisms. Litter helps prevent erosion and hold water. The A horizon is also known as topsoil. Topsoil has more humus and smaller rock and mineral particles than the other layers in a soil profile. A scoop of topsoil will show dark-colored soil, grains of rocks and minerals, decayed leaves, plant roots, insects, and worms. The A horizon is the key to successful plant growth and development.

Figure 5-10 Each soil horizon is unique due to the amount of mineral and organic material. **In which direction are minerals moved?**

Horizon B

The layer below the A horizon is the B horizon. It contrasts sharply with the A horizon. Because litter does not add to this horizon, it is lighter in color than the A horizon and contains less humus. The B horizon also contains elements washed down from the A horizon by the process of leaching.

Leaching is the removal of minerals that have been dissolved in water. The process of leaching resembles making coffee in a drip coffeemaker. In a coffeemaker, water drips into ground coffee. In the soil, water seeps into the A horizon. In a coffeemaker, the water absorbs the flavor and color from the coffee and flows down into a coffeepot. In the soil, the water reacts with humus to form an acid. This acid dissolves some of the elements from the minerals in the A horizon and carries them into the B horizon. Some leaching also occurs in the B horizon and moves minerals into the C horizon.

Horizon C

The C horizon is below the B horizon. It is the bottom of the soil profile and consists mostly of partially weathered parent rock. Leaching from the B horizon also may provide other minerals. What would you find if you dug all the way to the bottom of the C horizon? As you might have guessed, there would be solid rock. This is the rock that gave rise to the soil horizons above it.

In many places on Earth, the land is covered by material that was deposited by glaciers. This unsorted mass of ground-up rock, broken rock, and boulders has filled in the low spots in many places, creating, for example, the flat landscapes of the Midwest. The soils that developed on this glacial material are extremely fertile. The rich soils are an important part of the Midwest's agricultural industry. How does this soil profile differ from the one described above? If you were to dig down through the C horizon, you would find solid bedrock as before, but it would not be the rock that the soil formed from. What is the material that formed this soil profile?

Problem Solving

Interpret Crop Data

Good soil is necessary for crop production. Fertilizers and good farming practices help improve soil quality. Today's increasing world population requires that more food be produced to curb starvation. The chart below shows how world agricultural yield and population increased from 1950 to 1996.

Think Critically: Analyze the chart. Is the increase in agricultural production keeping up with human population growth? What do you think is the reason?

Food and Population Data

Time Span	Percent increase in world agricultural production	Average percent growth rate in population
1960s	3.0	1.95
1970s	2.4	1.83
1980s	2.2	1.78
1990–1996	1.6	1.61

Types of Soil

The texture of soil depends on the amounts of sand, silt, and clay that are in it. In turn, the texture of soil affects how water runs through it. That is not all you'll discover from examining soil profiles.

If you examine a soil profile in one place, it will not look exactly like a soil profile from another location. Different locations affect the way a profile looks. Deserts are dry. Prairies are semidry. The temperate zone profile represents a soil from an area with a moderate amount of rain and moderate temperatures. Crops like the wheat in **Figure 5-11** grow well in temperate zone soils.

Soil Types Reflect Climate

The thickness of the soil horizons and the soil composition of the profiles also depend on a number of conditions, including climate. Examples of three soil profiles from different climates are shown in **Figure 5-12.**

Chemical weathering is much slower in areas where there is little rainfall, and soils in desert climates contain little organic material. The soil horizons in drier areas also are thinner than soil horizons in wetter climates. The amount of precipitation affects how much leaching of minerals occurs in the soil. Soils that have been leached are light in color. Some can be almost white.

Time also affects soil development, changing the characteristics of soil. If the weathering of the rock has been going on for a short time, the parent rock of the soil determines the soil characteristics. As the weathering continues for a longer time, the soil resembles the parent rock less and less.

*inter***NET**
CONNECTION

Visit the Glencoe Science Web Site at **www. glencoe.com/sec/ science/nc** for more information about soil and climate.

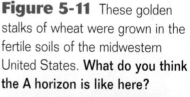

Figure 5-11 These golden stalks of wheat were grown in the fertile soils of the midwestern United States. **What do you think the A horizon is like here?**

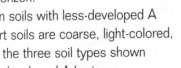

Slope also affects soil profiles. On steep slopes, soil horizons are often poorly developed. In bottomlands, where there is a lot of water, soils are often thick, dark, and full of organic material. A south-facing slope receives more sunlight and consequently has different soil development than a north-facing slope. The amount of humus in the soil also affects soil profiles. In the United States, nine groups of soils are recognized, as well as many subgroups. The map in **Figure 5-13** shows the nine main soil groups.

Soil—An Important Resource

Soil is important. Many of the things we take for granted—food, paper, and cotton—have a direct connection to the soil. Vegetables, grains, and cotton come from plants. Livestock such as cattle and pigs feed on grasses. Paper comes from

VISUALIZING
Soil Profiles

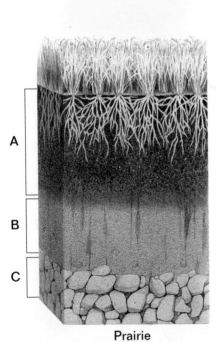

Prairie

Temperate

Desert

Figure 5-12 Prairie soils are brown and fertile with thick grass roots that fill the deep A horizon. Temperate soils are loose, brown soils with less-developed A horizons than prairie soils. Desert soils are coarse, light-colored, and contain a lot of minerals. Of the three soil types shown here, desert soils have the least-developed A horizon.

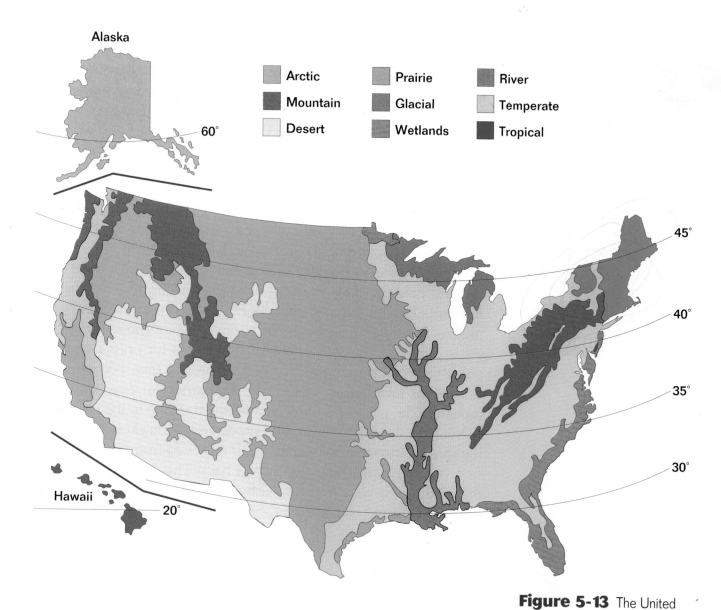

Figure 5-13 The United States has nine different soil types. They vary in color, depth of horizons, soil moisture, texture, and fertility.

trees. Plants, grasses, and trees all grow in soil. Without soil, we cannot grow food, raise livestock, or produce paper or other products we need.

When vegetation is removed from soil, the soil is exposed to the direct action of rain and wind. Rain and wind can erode the topsoil and carry it away, destroying the soil's structure. Also, without plants, soil development slows and sometimes stops because humus is no longer being produced.

Plowing and Soil Loss

Every year, the population of Earth increases by nearly 95 million people. More people means a need for more food. Farmers plow more fields to raise more food for the increasing population. This increases the use of our soil resources.

It is difficult to manage soils effectively. Plowing soil mechanically turns and loosens the soil, improving it for crops. However, plowing soil removes the plant cover that

Figure 5-14 With some farming practices, soil loss can occur.

Figure 5-15 Soil in tropical rain forests weathers quickly when trees are cut down. **What type of weathering is occurring here?**

holds soil particles in place, leaving soils open to wind and water erosion. Wind is harmful when the soil is dry. Sometimes, as shown in **Figure 5-14,** the wind blows soil from a newly plowed field. Soil erosion in many places occurs at a much faster rate than the natural processes of weathering can replace it. Under these conditions, soil is a nonrenewable resource because lost soil cannot be replaced in a short amount of time.

Soil Erosion in the Tropics

Soil loss is severe in the tropics. Tropical rains running down steep slopes quickly erode soil. Each year, thousands of square kilometers of tropical rain forest are cleared for farming and grazing. Soils in tropical rain forests appear rich in nutrients but are almost infertile below the first few centimeters. **Figure 5-15** shows what happens when the rain forest is removed. The soil is useful to farmers for only a few years before the nutrients are gone. The soil then becomes useless for farming or for grazing. Farmers clear new land, repeating the process and increasing the damage to the soil.

Near the deserts of the world, sheep and cattle eat much of the grass. When natural vegetation is removed from land that receives little rain, plants don't grow back. This leads to a loss of soil through wind erosion. Groundwater evaporates. The dry, unprotected surface can be blown away. The desert spreads. Desert formation happens on every continent.

B Harsh results of deforestation can be seen in the Tobago Rain Forest in the Caribbean.

A In the Cuyabeno Wildlife Reserve in Ecuador, portions of the rain forest have been cut down for use in settlements.

Farmers Work to Minimize Soil Loss

All over the world, farmers take steps to slow down soil erosion. They plant shelter belts of trees to break the force of the wind. They cover bare soils with decaying plants to hold soil particles in place. In dry areas, instead of plowing under the natural vegetation to plant crops, farmers graze animals on the vegetation. Proper grazing management can keep plants in place and reduce soil erosion.

Steep slopes, prone to erosion, can be taken out of cultivation or terraced. In the tropics, planting trees to block the force of rain falling on open ground reduces erosion. On gentle slopes, plowing along the natural contours of the land or planting crops in strips helps reduce water erosion. In strip cropping, a crop that covers the ground is alternated with a crop such as corn that leaves a considerable amount of land exposed. In recent years, many farmers have begun to practice no-till farming. Normally, farmers till or plow their fields three or more times a year. In no-till farming, seen in **Figure 5-16,** plant stalks are left in the field. At the next planting, farmers seed crops without destroying these stalks and without plowing the soil. No-till farming provides cover for the soil all year-round and reduces erosion.

Figure 5-16 In no-till farming, the soil is not plowed before planting. **How does this conserve soil?**

Section Assessment

1. How do organisms help soils develop?
2. Why do soil profiles contain layers or horizons?
3. Why does horizon B contain minerals from horizon A?
4. **Think Critically:** Why is the soil profile in a rain forest different from one in a desert?

5. **Skill Builder**
   Concept Mapping Make an events chain map that explains how soil develops. Use the following terms and phrases: *soil is formed, humus develops, rock is weathered, plants grow, worms and insects move in,* and *humus mixes with weathered rock.* If you need help, refer to Concept Mapping in the **Skill Handbook** on page 550.

Using Math

Soil texture depends on the percentages of three different types of particles: clay, silt, and sand. The best texture for growing most crops is a mixture of at least two of these. If a 400-g sand sample has 150 g of clay, 200 g of silt, and 50 g of sand, what is the percentage of each type of particle?

Soil Characteristics

Materials

- Soil sample
- Cheesecloth squares
- Sand
- Graduated cylinder (100 mL)
- Gravel
- Plastic coffee-can lids (3)
- Clay
- Rubber bands (3)
- Water
- Beakers (250 mL) (3)
- Watch
- Large polystyrene or plastic cups (3)
- Pie pans
- Hand lens
- Scissors
- Thumbtack

There are thousands of soils around the world. In your area, you've probably noticed that there are a number of different soils. Collect samples of soil to compare from around your neighborhood and from designated areas of your school grounds.

What You'll Investigate

What are the characteristics of soils?

Goals

- Analyze permeability of different soils.

Procedure

1. **Spread** your soil sample in a pie pan.

2. **Describe** the color of the soil and **examine** the soil with a hand lens. Describe the different particles.

3. **Rub** a small amount of soil between your fingers. **Describe** how it feels. Also, press the soil sample together. Does it stick together? Wet the sample and try this again. Record all your observations.

4. **Test** the soil for how water moves through it. **Label** the three cups A, B, and C. Using a thumbtack, punch ten holes in and around the bottom of each cup.

5. **Cover** the area of holes with a square of cheesecloth and **secure** with a rubber band.

6. To hold the cups over the beakers, **cut** the three coffee-can lids so that the cups will just fit inside the hole (see photo). **Place** a cup and lid over each beaker.

7. Fill cup A halfway with dry sand and cup B with clay. Fill cup C halfway with a mixture of equal parts of sand, gravel, and clay.

8. Use the graduated cylinder to pour 100 mL of water into each cup. **Record** the time when the water is first poured into each cup and when the water first drips from each cup.

9. Allow the water to drip for 25 minutes, then **measure and record** the amount of water in each beaker.

Conclude and Apply

1. How does the addition of gravel and sand affect the permeability of clay?

2. **Describe** three characteristics of soil. Which characteristics affect permeability?

3. Use your observations to **explain** which soil sample would be best for growing plants.

Compost

A composter allows you to recycle food wastes, grass clippings, and other organic materials and turn them into something useful. By composting, people can reduce the amount of garbage to be picked up, save precious landfill space, and make a soil conditioner at the same time.

THE COMPOST PROCESS

1

Composting begins when plant materials such as grass clippings, organic garbage, and weeds are piled up, usually layered with soil or manure, and allowed to decay. At left, a compost heap has been prepared.

2 55°C 131°F

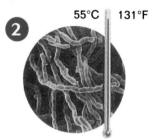

The activity of bacteria heats the interior of the compost heap. Fungi and actinomycetes (in circle), a form of bacteria, break down tough debris, enabling bacteria to decompose it more quickly.

3

Invertebrates (animals without backbones) such as insect larvae and worms eat decaying vegetation. Their droppings are added to the mix. As these organisms tunnel, they create more surface area for fungi and bacteria to work on.

4

The completed compost is a rich, crumbly, dark, soil-like substance used to fertilize soil and improve its structure. Compost also can be used as mulch on the soil surface to help retain soil moisture and prevent the growth of weeds.

Think Critically

1. How does compost help plants?
2. Why does food waste decompose better in a compost pile than in a landfill?

For a **preview** of this chapter, study this Reviewing Main Ideas before you read the chapter. After you have studied this chapter, you can use the Reviewing Main Ideas to **review** the chapter.

The Glencoe MindJogger, Audiocassettes, and CD-ROM provide additional opportunities for review.

Section 5-1 MECHANICAL WEATHERING

Mechanical weathering breaks apart rocks without changing their chemical composition. Water, by expanding and contracting through freeze-and-thaw cycles, is a major agent of mechanical weathering. Plant and tree roots also weather rocks. Mechanical weathering is not limited to rocks. Roads and sidewalks also are affected by freeze-and-thaw cycles or growing roots. *Compare and contrast the different agents of mechanical weathering.*

CHEMICAL WEATHERING

Chemical weathering changes the mineral composition of rocks. Water that is acidic may dissolve rock or simply dissolve certain minerals within a rock. Exposure to oxygen causes some rocks to turn red, or rust. Some plants even cause chemical weathering by secreting acids. *Describe how water can become an agent of chemical weathering.*

A

B

C

Reading Check ✓

After reviewing the illustrations on soil development, describe the steps in your own words. Be sure to number the steps.

Section 5-2 SOIL

Soil develops when rock is weathered and organic matter is added. Soil has **horizons** that differ in their color and composition. Climate, parent rock, slope, amount of **humus,** and time affect the development of soil and give soil its characteristics. *Explain why some soils take more time to develop than others.*

Career
CONNECTION

Susan Colclazer, Naturalist A naturalist is a person who studies the life sciences in the field more than in a laboratory. Many types of scientists are interested in Bryce Canyon. Naturalists, geologists, archaeologists, sociologists, and botanists have made studies there, as well. Make a list of things these types of scientists might study in the canyon, and tell how their findings would add to the overall picture of the canyon's history.

Chapter 5 Assessment

Using Vocabulary

a. chemical weathering
b. climate
c. horizon
d. humus
e. ice wedging
f. leaching
g. litter
h. mechanical weathering
i. oxidation
j. soil
k. soil profile
l. weathering

The sentences below include italicized terms that have been used incorrectly. Change the incorrect terms so that the sentence reads correctly. Underline your change.

1. When rocks break down without changing in chemical composition, *oxidation* occurs.
2. *Mechanical weathering* results in a change in a rock's composition.
3. *Desert* formation occurs when weathered rock and organic matter are mixed together.
4. *Litter* is composed of decayed organic matter.
5. The A, B, and C layers of a soil make up the soil *horizon*.

Checking Concepts

Choose the word or phrase that best answers the question.

6. What is caused when plants produce acids?
   A) desert formation
   B) overgrazing
   C) mechanical weathering
   D) chemical weathering
7. What happens to water that allows freezing and thawing to weather rocks?
   A) contracts
   B) gets more dense
   C) expands
   D) percolates

8. What occurs when roots force rocks apart?
   A) mechanical weathering
   B) leaching
   C) ice wedging
   D) chemical weathering
9. What reacts with iron to form rust?
   A) oxygen
   B) carbon dioxide
   C) feldspar
   D) paint
10. What can result when poor farming practices occur in areas that receive little rain?
    A) ice wedging
    B) oxidation
    C) leaching
    D) desert formation
11. In what region is chemical weathering most rapid?
    A) cold, dry
    B) cold, moist
    C) warm, moist
    D) warm, dry
12. What is a mixture of weathered rock and organic matter called?
    A) soil
    B) limestone
    C) carbon dioxide
    D) clay
13. What is another term for decayed organic matter?
    A) leaching
    B) humus
    C) soil
    D) sediment
14. In what horizon is humus found almost exclusively?
    A) A horizon
    B) B horizon
    C) C horizon
    D) D horizon
15. What does no-till farming help prevent?
    A) leaching
    B) crop rotation
    C) overgrazing
    D) soil erosion

Thinking Critically

16. Which type of weathering, mechanical or chemical, would you expect to have more effect in a desert region? Explain.
17. Plants cause mechanical weathering. Explain how animals also can be considered agents of mechanical weathering.
18. Why is soil so important?
19. Why is it difficult to replace lost topsoil?

20. Explain how chemical weathering can form a cavern.

Developing Skills

If you need help, refer to the **Skill Handbook**.

21. Sequencing: Do a sequence chart of soil development.

22. Concept Mapping: Complete the events chain concept map that shows two ways in which acids can cause chemical weathering.

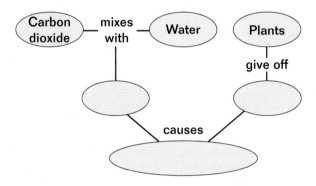

23. Using Variables, Constants, and Controls: Juan Carlos wanted to know if planting grass on a slope would prevent soil from being washed away. To find out, he put the same amount and kind of soil in two identical pans. In one of the pans, he planted grass. To create equal slopes for his test, he placed identical wooden wedges under one end of each pan. He was careful to pour the same amount of water at the same rate over the soil in the two pans. What is Juan's control? What factors in his activity are constants? What is the variable he is testing?

24. Classifying: Classify the following events as either chemical or mechanical weathering. Rocks that contain iron rust. Freezing and thawing of water cause cracks to form in the street. Acids from mosses leave small pits in rocks. Roots of trees break rocks apart. Water seeping through cracks in limestone dissolves away some of the rock.

Test-Taking Tip

Wear a Watch   If you are taking a timed test, you should pace yourself. Do not spend too much time on any one question, but don't spend time staring at the clock. When the test begins, place your watch on the desk and check it after each section of the test.

Test Practice

Use these questions to test your Science Proficiency.

1. The curb along a street is crumbling and a big weed is growing from one of the cracks. Which of the following is an inference and not an observation?
A) Tiny pieces of concrete are found along the base of the curb.
B) Plant roots are located among the cracks in the curb.
C) Mechanical and chemical weathering are causing the curb to crumble.
D) The curb has cracks of varying lengths and widths.

2. Soils have several horizons. Which of the following **BEST** describes the B horizon?
A) It is made of humus, small rocks, and mineral particles.
B) It is mostly partly weathered bedrock.
C) It is full of organisms like insects and worms.
D) It is light in color and contains soil materials leached from the A horizon.

CHAPTER

6

Erosional Forces

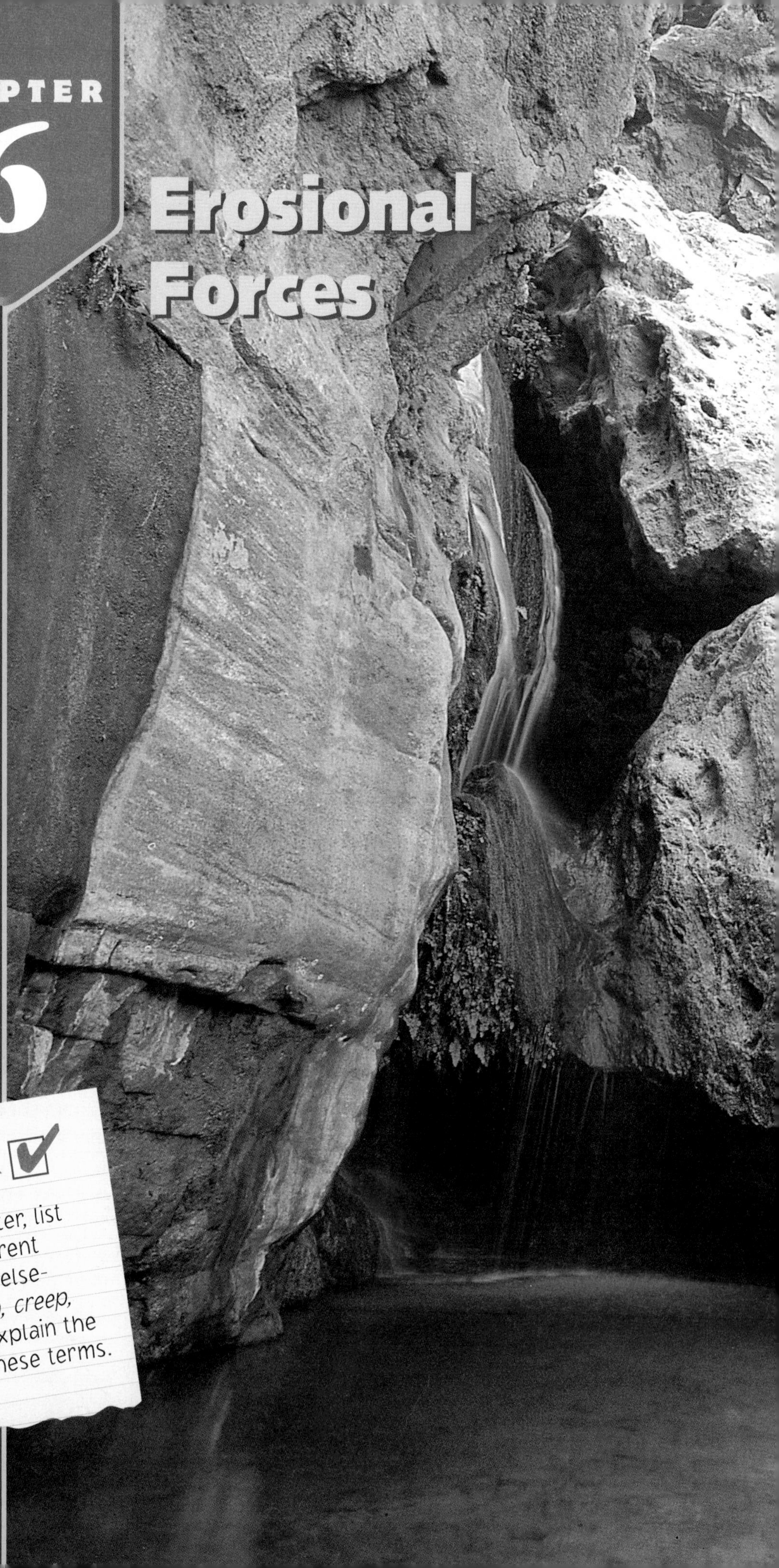

Chapter Preview

Section 6-1
Gravity

Section 6-2
Glaciers

Section 6-3
Wind

Skills Preview

Skill Builders

- Compare and Contrast
- Sequence

Activities

- Design an Experiment
- Analyze Data

MiniLabs

- Observe
- Infer

Reading Check

As you read this chapter, list words that have different meanings when used elsewhere, such as *slump, creep, till,* and *deposition*. Explain the other meanings of these terms.

Explore Activity

The forces of nature are strong enough to wear the jagged peaks of young mountains into the rolling, smooth tops of older mountain ranges. Weathering breaks down rocks into smaller particles. Then forces of nature move these particles and deposit them elsewhere. One of these forces, water, has eroded the canyon to the left in Grand Canyon National Park. Erosional forces constantly change the surface of Earth, making changes in our landscape.

Observe Movement of Sediments

1. Place a small pile of a sand and gravel mixture in one end of a large shoe box lid.

2. Move the pile to the other end of the lid without touching the particles with your hands.

3. Try to move the mixture in a number of different ways.

Science Journal

In your Science Journal, describe the methods you used. Explain how your methods compare with forces of nature that move sediment.

6·1 Gravity

Erosion and Deposition

Have you ever been by a river just after a heavy rain? The water may look as muddy as the water in **Figure 6-1**. A river looks muddy when there is a lot of sediment and soil in it. Some of the soil comes from along the riverbank itself. In the upper left part of the photograph, you can see where the bank is being eroded at the curve in the river. The rest of the sediment in the photograph is carried to the river from more distant sources.

Muddy water is a product of erosion. **Erosion** is a process that wears away surface materials and moves them from one place to another. The major causes of erosion are gravity, glaciers, wind, and water. The first three will be discussed in this chapter. Another kind of erosion is shown in **Figure 6-2**.

What You'll Learn

▶ The differences between erosion and deposition
▶ The similarities and differences of slumps, creep, rockslides, and mudflows
▶ Why building on steep slopes is a questionable practice

Vocabulary
erosion
deposition
mass movement
slump
creep

Why It's Important

▶ Landforms change because of erosion, deposition, and mass movements.

Figure 6-1 The muddy look of some rivers comes from the load of sediment carried by water.

As you investigate the agents of erosion, you will notice that they have several things in common. Gravity, glaciers, wind, and water all wear away materials and carry them off. But, these agents erode materials only when they have enough energy of motion to do work. For example, air can't erode sediments when the air is still. But, once air begins moving and develops into wind, it carries dust, soil, and even rock along with it.

All agents of erosion deposit the sediments they are carrying when their erosion energy decreases. This dropping of sediments is called **deposition.** Deposition is the final stage of an erosional process. Sediments and rocks are deposited. The surface of Earth is changed. But, next year or a million years from now, those sediments may be eroded again.

Erosion and Deposition by Gravity

Gravity is the force of attraction that exists between all objects. Because Earth has great mass, other objects are attracted to Earth. This makes gravity a force of erosion and deposition. Gravity causes loose materials to move down a slope.

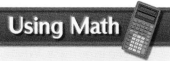

Using Math

Two rocks fall off a cliff at the same time. One rock weighs 10 N, and the other rock weighs 30 N. They both reach the ground at the same time. Explain why this happened.

Figure 6-2
This hill has been eroded. **What was the agent of erosion?**

Figure 6-3 Slumps occur when material slips downslope as one large mass. **What might have caused this slump to happen?**

When gravity alone causes materials to move downslope, this type of erosion is called **mass movement.** Some mass movements are slow. You hardly notice that they're happening. Others, however, happen quickly.

Slump

A **slump** is a mass movement that happens when loose materials or rock layers slip down a slope. In a slump, strong rock or sediment lies over weaker materials. The underlying material weakens even more and can no longer support the rock and sediment above. The soil and rock slip downslope in one large mass.

Sometimes, a slump happens when water enters the upper layer on a slope but cannot flow through the lower layers. Water and mud build up. The upper layer of sediments slips along the mud and slides downslope. As shown in **Figure 6-3,** a curved scar is left where the slumped materials originally rested. Slumps happen most often after earthquakes or heavy, continuing rains.

Figure 6-4 Perhaps you can find evidence of soil creep around your home or school. Look for tilted retaining walls and fences and even sod that has stretched apart.

A Several years of creeping downslope can cause objects such as trees and fence posts to lean.

B Below the surface, as the ground freezes, expanding ice in the soil pushes up fine-grained sediment particles. Then, when the soil thaws, the sediment falls downslope, often less than 1 mm at a time.

Creep

On your next drive, look along the roadway for slopes where trees, utility poles, and fence posts lean downhill. Leaning poles show another mass movement called creep. **Creep** gets its name from the way sediments slowly inch their way down a hill. As **Figure 6-4** illustrates, creep is common in areas of freezing and thawing.

Rockslides

"Falling Rock" signs warn of another type of mass movement called a rockslide. Rockslides happen when large blocks of rock break loose from a steep slope and start tumbling. As they fall, these rocks crash into other rocks and knock them loose. More and more rocks break loose and tumble to the bottom.

Rockslides are fast and can be destructive in populated mountain areas. They commonly occur in mountainous areas or where there are steep cliffs, as shown in **Figure 6-5.** Rockslides happen most often after heavy rains or during earthquakes, but they can happen on any rocky slope at any time without warning.

The fall of a single, large rock down a steep slope can cause serious damage to structures at the bottom. During the winter, when ice freezes and thaws in the cracks of the rocks, pieces

Figure 6-5 Piles of broken rock at the bottom of a cliff, such as these rockfalls in southwestern Montana, tell you that rockslides have occurred and are likely to happen again.

Figure 6-6 In the Alps, a rock fell from the cliff above and struck this apartment building. **Why did this happen?**

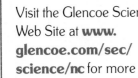
of the rock fracture. In the spring, the pieces of rock break loose and fall down the mountainside. Rockfalls like the one in **Figure 6-6** often occur in mountainous areas.

Mudflows

Imagine traveling along a mountain road during a rainstorm. Suddenly a wall of mud, the thickness of chocolate pudding, slides down a slope and threatens to cover your car. You've been caught in a mudflow, a thick mixture of sediments and water flowing down a slope. The mudflow in **Figure 6-7** caused a lot of destruction.

Mudflows usually occur in normally dry areas where there are thick layers of dry sediments. When heavy rains fall in these areas, water mixes with sediments and becomes thick and pasty. Gravity causes this mass to slide downhill. When a mudflow finally reaches the bottom of a slope, it loses its energy of motion and deposits all the sediments and other things it has been carrying. These deposits usually form a mass that spreads out in a fan shape. Why might mudflows cause more damage than flood-waters?

Mudflows, rockslides, creep, and slump are similar in some ways. They are most likely to occur on steep slopes. They all depend on gravity to make them happen. And, no matter what type of mass movement, they occur more often after a heavy rain. The water adds mass and makes the area slippery where different layers of sediment meet.

Erosion-Prone Land

Some people like to live in houses and apartments on the sides of hills and mountains. But, when you consider gravity as an agent of erosion, do you think steep slopes are safe places to live?

Building on Steep Slopes

When people build homes on steep slopes, they must constantly battle natu-rally occurring erosion. Sometimes, when they build, people make a slope steeper or remove vegetation. This speeds up the ero-sion process and creates additional prob-lems. Some steep slopes are prone to slumps because of weak sediment layers underneath.

Making Steep Slopes Safe

People can have a beautiful view and reduce erosion on steep slopes. One of the best ways is to plant vegetation. Plant roots may not seem strong, but they do hold soil in place. Plants also absorb large amounts of water. A person living on a steep slope might also build terraces or walls to reduce erosion.

Figure 6-7 A mudflow, such as this one in Seattle, Washington, has enough energy to move almost anything in its path. **How do mudflows differ from slumps, creep, and rockslides?**

Observing Mass Movements

Procedure

1. Put a mixture of dry sand and gravel in a pan. Use these sediments to model how mass movements of sediments occur.

2. After you have modeled slumps and rockslides with dry sediment, add small amounts of water to different parts of your landforms to model mudflows, slumps, and rockslides.

Analysis

1. What factors must be present for mass move-ments to occur?

2. In what ways are the three mass movements similar? Different?

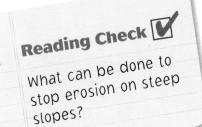

interNET
CONNECTION

Visit the Glencoe Science Web Site at **www. glencoe.com/sec/ science/nc** for more information about agriculture in developing countries.

Terraces are broad, steplike cuts made into the side of a slope, as shown in **Figure 6-8.** When water flows into a terrace, it slows down and loses its energy. Terracing slows soil erosion. Walls made of concrete or railroad ties can also reduce erosion by keeping soil and rocks from sliding downhill. However, preventing mass movements on a slope is difficult because rain or earthquakes can cause the upper layers of rock to slip over the lower layers. Not even planting bushes and trees could save the houses in **Figure 6-9.** ☑️

People who live in areas with erosion problems spend a lot of time and money trying to preserve their land. Sometimes, they're successful in slowing down erosion, but they can never eliminate it and the danger of mass movement. Eventually, gravity wins. Sediments move from place to place, constantly making slopes less steep and changing the shape of the land.

Figure 6-8 These terraces in Java help conserve soil so vegetables can grow. **How do terraces keep soil from eroding away?**

Figure 6-9 Heavy rains caused by El Niño resulted in this landslide in California. **What type of mass movement occurred here?**

Section Assessment

1. Define *erosion* and name the agents that cause it.
2. How does erosion change the surface of Earth?
3. What characteristics do all types of mass movements have in common?
4. If creep has occurred in an area, what evidence would you see?
5. **Think Critically:** When people build houses and roads, they often pile up dirt or cut into the sides of hills. Predict how these activities affect sediments on a slope.

6. **Skill Builder**

   Concept Mapping Learn more about erosional forces by doing the **Chapter 6 Skill Activity** on page 583.

Using Computers

Spreadsheets Pretend that you live along a beach where the water is 500 m from your front door. Each year, slumping causes about 1.5 m of your beach to cave into the water. Design a spreadsheet that will predict how much property will be left each year for ten years. Use the labels "Years" and "Meters Left." Type a formula that will compute the amount of land left the second year. If you need help, refer to page 574.

Glaciers

Continental and Valley Glaciers

What **You'll Learn**

► How glaciers move
► Glacial erosion
► Similarities and differences between till and outwash

Vocabulary
glacier
plucking
till
moraine

Why **It's Important**

► Erosion and deposition by glaciers are responsible for creating many landforms on Earth.

Does it snow where you live? In some areas of the world, it is so cold that snow remains on the ground year-round. When snow doesn't melt, it begins piling up. As it accumulates, the weight of the snow becomes great enough to compress its bottom layers into ice. Eventually, the snow can pile so high that the pressure on the ice on the bottom causes partial melting. The ice becomes putty-like. The whole mass begins to slide on this putty-like layer, and it moves downhill. This moving mass of ice and snow is a **glacier.**

Glaciers are agents of erosion. As glaciers pass over land, they erode it, changing its features. Glaciers then carry eroded material along and deposit it somewhere else. Glacial erosion and deposition change large areas of Earth. There are two types of glaciers: continental glaciers and valley glaciers.

Continental Glaciers

Continental glaciers are huge masses of ice and snow. In the past, continental glaciers covered up to 28 percent of Earth. **Figure 6-10** shows how much of North America was covered

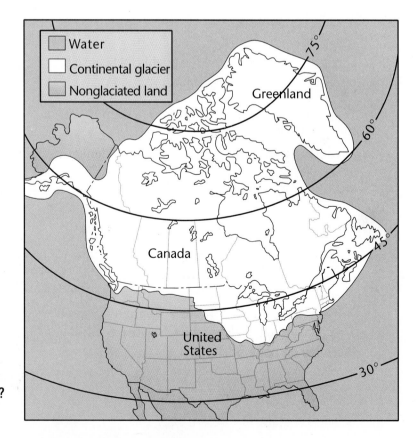

Figure 6-10 This map shows how far the continental glaciers spread in North America about 20 000 years ago. **Was your location covered? If so, what evidence of glaciers does your area show?**

A Today, a continental glacier covers Antarctica.

B Glaciers, like this one in Tibet, form between mountain peaks that lie above the snowline, where snow lasts all year.

during the last ice age. Scientists call the periods when glaciers covered much of Earth *ice ages*. The most recent ice age began over a period of 2 to 3 million years ago. During the time when much of North America was covered by ice, the average air temperature on Earth was about 5°C lower than it is today. Then, about 20 000 years ago, the ice sheets began to melt. Today, glaciers like the one in **Figure 6-11A** cover only ten percent of Earth, mostly near the poles in Antarctica and Greenland. Continental glaciers are so thick that they can almost bury mountain ranges on the land they cover. Glaciers make it impossible to see most of the land features in Antarctica.

Valley Glaciers

Valley glaciers occur even in today's warmer global climate. In the high mountains where the average temperature is low enough to prevent snow from melting during the summer, valley glaciers grow and creep along. **Figure 6-11B** shows a valley glacier in Tibet.

How is it possible that something as fragile as snow or ice can become an agent of erosion that pushes aside trees, drags along rocks, and erodes the surface of Earth?

Glacial Erosion

As they move over land, glaciers are like bulldozers, pushing loose materials they encounter. Eroded sediments pile up along its sides, as seen in **Figure 6-12A,** are pushed in front of a glacier, or are carried underneath it. Glaciers also weather and erode rock and soil that isn't loose. When glacial ice melts, water flows into cracks in rocks. Later, the water refreezes in these cracks, expands, and fractures the rock into pieces. These rock pieces are then lifted out by the glacial ice sheet. This process, called **plucking,** results in boulders, gravel, and sand being added to the bottom and sides of a glacier.

As a glacier moves forward, plucked rock fragments and sand at its base scrape the soil and bedrock, eroding even more material than ice alone could. When bedrock is gouged deeply by dragged rock fragments, marks such as those in **Figure 6-12B** are left behind. These marks, called grooves, are

Figure 6-12 The diagram and photos show landforms characteristic of glacial erosion.

Arête

Valley glaciers

A No agent of erosion is more powerful than an advancing glacier.

B When glaciers melt, striations or grooves may be found on the rocks beneath. These glacial grooves on Kelley's Island, Ohio, are 10 m wide and 5 m deep.

Moraine

deep, long, parallel scars on rocks. Less-deep marks are called striations (stri AY shuns). These marks indicate the direction the glacier moved.

Evidence of Valley Glaciers

If you visit the mountains, you can see if valley glaciers ever existed there. You might look for striations, then search for evidence of plucking. Glacial plucking often occurs near the top of a mountain where a glacier is in contact with a wall of rock. Valley glaciers erode bowl-shaped basins, called cirques (SURKS), in the sides of the mountains. A cirque is shown in **Figure 6-12C.** If two or more glaciers erode a mountain summit from several directions, a ridge, called an arête (ah RET), or sharpened peak, called a horn, forms. The photo in **Figure 6-12D** shows a mountain horn.

Mountain
horn

U-shaped valley

Cirque

C This cirque, a bowl-shaped basin, was formed by erosion at the start of a valley glacier.

D A horn is a sharpened peak formed by glacial action in three or more cirques.

Valley glaciers flow down mountain slopes and along valleys, eroding as they go. Valleys that have been eroded by glaciers have a different shape from those eroded by streams. Stream-eroded valleys are normally V-shaped. Glacially eroded valleys are U-shaped because a glacier plucks and scrapes soil and rock from the sides as well as from the bottom. A U-shaped valley is illustrated in **Figure 6-12.**

Glacial Deposition

When glaciers begin to melt, they no longer have enough energy to carry much sediment. The sediment drops, or is deposited, on the land.

Figure 6-13 Till has been deposited by the Tasman Glacier in New Zealand.

Till

When the glacier slows down, a jumble of boulders, sand, clay, and silt drops from its base. This mixture of different-sized sediments is called **till. Figure 6-13** shows the unlayered appearance of till. Till deposits can cover huge areas of land. During the last ice age, continental glaciers in the northern United States dropped enough till to completely fill valleys and make these areas appear flat. Till areas include the wide swath of wheat land running northwestward from Iowa to northern Montana; some farmland in parts of Ohio, Indiana, and Illinois; and the rocky pastures of New England. ☑

Till is also deposited in front of a glacier when it stops moving forward. Unlike the till that drops from a glacier's base, this second type of deposit doesn't cover a wide area. Because it's made of the rocks and soil that the glacier has been pushing along, it looks like a big ridge of material left behind by a bulldozer. Such a ridge is called a **moraine. Figure 6-14** shows moraines that were deposited at the end and along the sides of the glacier. A moraine that was deposited at the end of a glacier is shown in **Figure 6-15** and is called a terminal moraine.

Reading Check ☑

What is till?

Outwash

When more snow melts than is accumulated, the glacier starts to melt and retreat. Material deposited by the meltwater from a glacier is called outwash. Outwash is shown in **Figure 6-15.** The meltwater carries sediments and deposits them in layers much as a river does. Heavier sediments drop first so the bigger pieces of rock are deposited closer to the glacier. The outwash from a glacier can also form into a fan-shaped deposit when the stream of meltwater drops sand and gravel in front of the glacier.

Another type of outwash deposit looks like a long, winding ridge. This deposit forms beneath a melting glacier when meltwater forms a river within the ice. This river carries sand and gravel and deposits them within its channel. When the glacier melts, a winding ridge of sand and gravel, called an esker (ES kur), is left behind. An esker is shown in **Figure 6-15.** Meltwater also forms outwash plains of deposited materials in front of a retreating glacier.

Figure 6-14 The Athabaska Glacier in Jasper National Park in Alberta, Canada, is surrounded by many glacial features. **Which ones do you see?**

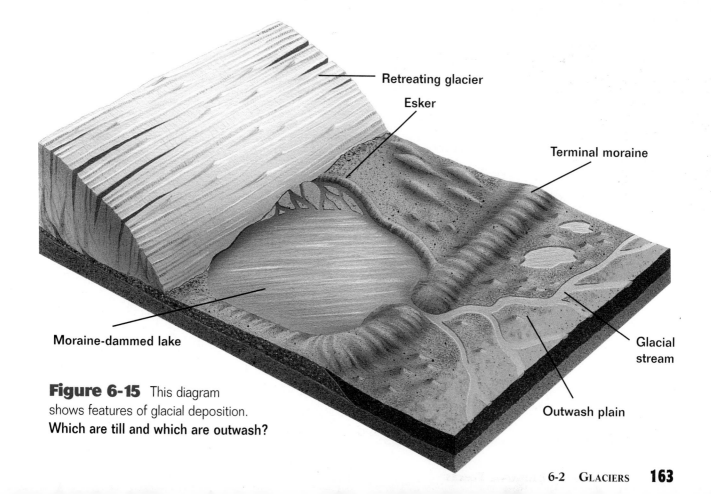

Retreating glacier

Esker

Terminal moraine

Glacial stream

Outwash plain

Moraine-dammed lake

Figure 6-15 This diagram shows features of glacial deposition. **Which are till and which are outwash?**

B This V-shaped valley, cut by the Yellowstone River in what is now Yellowstone National Park, looks different from the U-shaped valley.

Figure 6-16

A This U-shaped valley in Gates of the Arctic National Park in Alaska was carved by a glacier.

Glaciers from the last ice age changed the surface of Earth. Glaciers eroded mountaintops and dug out valleys like the U-shaped one in **Figure 6-16A.** Water erosion forms V-shaped valleys like the one in **Figure 6-16B.** Glaciers also deposited sediments over vast areas of North America and Europe. Today, glaciers in the polar regions and in mountains continue to change the surface features of Earth.

Section Assessment

1. How does a glacier cause erosion?

2. Explain how till and outwash are different.

3. How do moraines form?

4. **Think Critically:** Rivers and lakes that receive water from glacial meltwater often appear milky blue in color. Explain why this occurs.

5. **Skill Builder**
   Recognizing Cause and Effect Since 1900, the Alps have lost 50 percent of their ice caps, and New Zealand's glaciers have shrunk by 26 percent. Describe what you think is causing glaciers to melt around the world. Describe what you think the effects of melting have been. If you need help, refer to Recognizing Cause and Effect in the **Skill Handbook** on page 557.

Science Journal

An erratic is a rock fragment deposited by a glacier. Erratic comes from the Latin word *errare* meaning "to wander." Research how glaciers erode and deposit erratics. In your Science Journal, write a poem about the "life" of an erratic.

Glacial Grooving

Throughout the world's mountainous regions, there are 200 000 valley glaciers moving in response to local freezing and thawing conditions, as well as gravity.

What You'll Investigate

What happens when a valley glacier moves? How is the land affected?

Goals

- **Observe** glacial deposits.
- **Compare** stream and glacial valleys.

Procedure

1. Set up the large tray as shown. Place the books under one end of the tray to give it a slope.

2. Cut a narrow channel, like a river, through the sand. **Measure** and **record** its width and depth. **Draw** a sketch that includes these measurements.

3. Position the overhead light source to shine on the channel as shown.

4. Force the ice block into the river channel at the upper end of the stream table.

Materials

- Sand
- Large plastic or metal tray
  stream table
- Ice block containing sand, clay, and gravel
- Books (2−3)
  wood block
- Metric ruler
- Overhead light source with reflector

Alternate Materials

5. Gently push the "glacier" along the river channel until it's halfway between the top and bottom of the stream table and is positioned directly under the light.

6. Turn on the light and allow the ice to melt. **Record** what happens. Does the meltwater change the original channel?

7. **Record** the width and depth of the glacial channel. **Draw** a sketch of the channel and include these measurements.

Conclude and Apply

1. **Explain** how you can determine the direction a glacier traveled from the location of deposits.

2. **Explain** how you can determine the direction of glacial movement from sediments deposited by meltwater.

3. How do valley glaciers affect the surface over which they move?

Glacier Data			
Sample Data	Width	Depth	Observations
Original channel	6 cm	3 cm	stream channel looked V-shaped
Glacier channel			
Meltwater channel			

Music of the Dust Bowl

Blowing in the Wind

In the 1930s, a severe drought struck Texas, Oklahoma, Colorado, Kansas, and New Mexico. Years of overgrazing and overfarming had stripped vast expanses of the land of protective grass. With nothing to hold the parched soil, it blew away, forming towering clouds of dust (right) that traveled hundreds of miles. This dry region of the United States became known as the Dust Bowl.

Songs for the People

Woody Guthrie (inset) wrote and sang folk songs about the hardships faced by the people of the Dust Bowl. His song "The Great Dust Storm" describes a region where, according to Guthrie, "the dust flows and the farmer owes."

The storm took place at sundown
It lasted through the night.
When we looked out next morning
We saw a terrible sight.
We saw outside our window
Where wheat fields they had grown,
Was now a rippling ocean
Of dust the wind had blown.
It covered up our fences,
It covered up our barns,
It covered up our tractors
In this wild and dusty storm. ©

Guthrie's songs also tell of courage and humor. His lyrics in "Dust Pneumonia Blues" describe a girl so unused to water that she faints in the rain. Her boyfriend throws a bucket of dirt on her to revive her.

Science
JOURNAL

Research details of Woody Guthrie's life. In your Science Journal, compare his life with the lyrics of his songs. How did his experiences influence his lyrics? Write a song or poem that reflects an event that you or someone you know has experienced.

Wind

Wind Erosion

When air moves, it can pick up loose material and transport it to other places. Air differs from other erosional forces because it usually cannot pick up heavy sediments. But, unlike rivers and glaciers that move in channels and through valleys, wind can carry and deposit sediments over large areas. Sometimes wind carries dust from fields or volcanoes high into the atmosphere and deposits it far away.

Deflation and Abrasion

Wind erodes Earth's surface by deflation and abrasion. When wind erodes by **deflation,** it blows across loose sediment, removing small particles such as clay, silt, and sand. The heavier, coarser material is left behind. **Figure 6-17** illustrates deflation. When these windblown sediments strike rock, the surface gets scraped and worn away. This type of erosion is called **abrasion.** Both deflation and abrasion happen to all land surfaces but occur mostly in deserts, beaches, and plowed fields. In these areas, there are fewer plants to hold the sediments. When winds blow over them, there is nothing to hold them down.

What **You'll Learn**

► How wind causes deflation and abrasion
► How loess and dunes form

Vocabulary
deflation
abrasion
loess

Why **It's Important**

► Wind erosion and deposition help change the landscape.

Figure 6-17 Deflation produces airborne sediments and leaves behind what is called desert pavement.

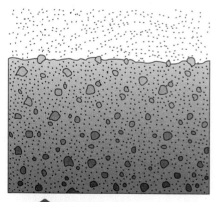

A As deflation begins, wind blows away silt and sand.

C After finer particles are blown away, the larger pebbles and rocks left behind form a pavement that prevents further deflation.

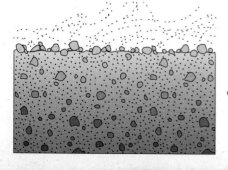

B Deflation continues to remove finer particles. Deflation lowers the surface.

Figure 6-18 Wind erosion can be just like sandblasting.

A When modern archaeologists discovered the Sphinx, it was buried up to its neck in sand. The head shows how abrasive Egypt's desert winds can be.

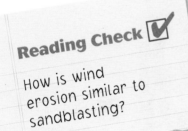

B This worker is using abrasion to clean and smooth a limestone waterfall.

Abrasion works similar to sandblasting that a crew of restoration workers might do. These workers use machines that spray a mixture of sand and water against a building. The blast of sand wears away dirt from stone, concrete, or brick walls. It also polishes the building walls by breaking away small pieces and leaving an even, smooth finish.

Wind acts like a sandblasting machine rolling and blowing sand grains along. These sand grains strike rocks and break off small fragments. The rocks become pitted or worn down. **Figure 6-18** shows how machine and wind abrasion are similar. ✔

Sandstorms

Even when the wind blows strongly, it seldom bounces sand grains higher than one-half meter from the ground. Sand grains are too heavy for wind to lift high in the air. However, sandstorms do occur. When the wind blows forcefully in the sandy parts of deserts, sand grains bounce along and hit other sand grains, causing more and more grains to rise into the air. These wind-blown sand grains form a low cloud, just above the ground. Most sandstorms occur in deserts and sometimes on beaches and in dry riverbeds.

Dust Storms

When soil is moist, it stays packed on the ground. But, when the soil dries out, it can be eroded by wind. Because soil particles weigh less than sand, wind can pick them up and blow

Reading Check

How is wind erosion similar to sandblasting?

them high into the atmosphere. But, because silt and clay particles are small and closely packed, a faster wind is needed to lift these fine particles of soil than is needed to lift grains of sand. Once the wind does lift them, it can hold these particles and carry them long distances. In the 1930s, silt and dust picked up in Kansas fell in New England and in the North Atlantic Ocean. Today, dust blown from the Sahara can be traced as far as the West Indies.

Dust storms play an important part in soil erosion. Where the land is dry, dust storms can cover hundreds of miles. The storms blow topsoil from open fields, overgrazed areas, and places where vegetation has disappeared. A dust storm is shown in **Figure 6-19.**

Figure 6-19 During the 1930s, the southern part of the Great Plains of the United States was known as the Dust Bowl because dust storms swept away the soil. Dust storms still occur around the world in places such as Mongolia, in western India, in northern Africa, and in the United States.

Problem Solving

Deserts

Precipitation, like rainfall and snowfall, and temperature help determine whether or not a region is a desert. Some deserts have such low amounts of precipitation that evaporation from the soil and plants is actually greater than the amount of precipitation. When this happens, plants must get their moisture from underground sources near their deep roots. Deserts also receive a varying amount of precipitation from year to year.

The temperature of deserts can vary a great deal, also. All deserts are not hot. Some deserts in mountain valleys can be quite cold. Because deserts absorb and give up their heat quickly, they can be much warmer during the day than at night.

The graph on the right shows how the amount of precipitation and temperature compare for different kinds of ecological communities (biomes). Study the graph to answer the questions.

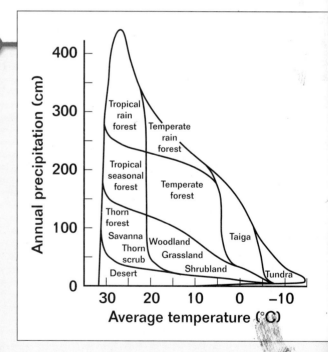

Think Critically: Of all the ecological communities shown in the graph, which shows the greatest range of average temperature? What is the greatest annual precipitation an ecological community can receive and still be classified as a desert? In which ecological community do you live?

Figure 6-20 This marram grass was planted to limit the erosion of sand dunes in Cornwall, England. **How does grass slow erosion?**

Reducing Wind Erosion

As you've learned, wind erosion is most common where plants do not exist to protect the soil. One of the best ways to slow or stop wind erosion is to plant vegetation.

Windbreaks

People in many countries plant vegetation to reduce wind erosion. For centuries, farmers have planted trees along their fields that act as windbreaks and prevent soil erosion. As the wind hits the trees, its energy of motion is reduced and no longer has the energy to lift particles.

In one study, a thin belt of cottonwood trees reduced the effect of a 25 km/h wind to about 66 percent of its normal speed. Tree belts also trap snow and hold it on land, adding to the moisture of the soil, which helps prevent further erosion.

Roots

Along many steep slopes, seacoasts, and deserts, vegetation is planted to help reduce erosion. Plants with fibrous root systems, such as grasses, are the best to stop wind erosion. Grass roots are shallow and slender. They also have many fibers. They twist and turn between particles in the soil and hold the soil in place.

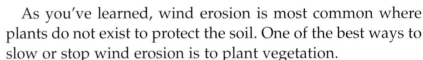

Try at Home

Mini Lab

Observing How Soil Is Held in Place

Procedure

1. Obtain a piece of sod (a chunk of soil about 5 cm thick with grass growing from it).
2. Carefully remove the soil from the sod roots by hand. Examine the roots with a magnifying glass or hand lens.

Analysis

1. Draw several of these roots in your Science Journal.
2. What characteristics of grass roots help hold soil in place and thus help reduce erosion?

Planting vegetation is a good way to reduce the effects of deflation and abrasion. But, if the wind is strong and the soil is dry, nothing can stop it completely. **Figure 6-20** shows a project to stop wind erosion.

Deposition by Wind

Sediments blown away by wind are eventually deposited. These windblown deposits develop into several types of landforms.

Loess

Some large deposits of wind-blown sediments are found near the Mississippi River. These wind deposits of fine-grained sediments are known as **loess** (LUSS). Strong winds that blew across glacial outwash areas carried the sediments and deposited them. The sediments settled on hilltops and in valleys. Once there, the particles were packed together, creating a thick, unlayered yellow-brown–colored deposit.

Loess is as fine as talcum powder. Many farmlands of the midwestern United States are on the fertile soils that have developed from loess deposits. The loess pictured in **Figure 6-21** was deposited by winds that blew across the outwash plains of retreating glaciers.

Dunes

What happens when wind blows sediments against an obstacle such as a rock or a clump of vegetation? The sediments settle behind the obstacle. More and more sediments build up, and eventually a dune is formed. A dune is a mound of sand drifted by the wind.

Sand dunes move as wind erodes them and deposits the sand downwind of the dune. On Cape Cod, Massachusetts, and along the Gulf of California, the coast of Oregon, and the eastern shore of Lake Michigan, you can see beach sand dunes. Sand dunes build up where there is sand and prevailing winds or sea breezes that blow daily.

To understand how a dune forms, think of the sand at the back of a beach. That sand is dry because the ocean and lake waves do not reach these areas. The wind blows this dry sand farther inland until something such as a rock or a fence slows the wind. The wind sweeps around or over the rock. Like a river, air drops sediment when its energy decreases.

Figure 6-21 Scott's Bluff, near Scott's Bluff, Nebraska, is composed partially of windblown loess.

LIFE SCIENCE
INTEGRATION

Plant Roots
Red clover has a taproot system consisting of one main root that grows directly downward. Sea oats have a fibrous root system that branches out in all directions. Infer which type of plant would be better to plant along coastal sand dunes to prevent wind erosion. Explain your answer.

Figure 6-22 Dunes are the most common wind deposits. Sand dunes form in deserts and beaches where sand is abundant. They are constantly changing and moving as wind erodes them. **What is the wind direction in this photo?**

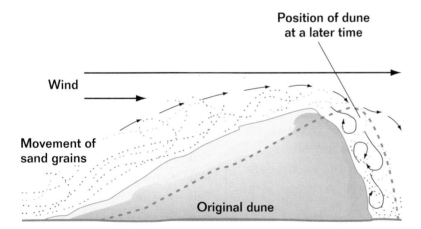

Figure 6-23 As wind blows the sand, the grains jump, roll, and slide up the gentler slope of the dune, accumulate at the top, then slide down the steeper slope on the side away from the wind.

Sand starts to build up behind the rock. As the sand continues to build up, the mound of sand becomes an obstacle itself and traps even more sand. If the wind blows long enough, the mound of sand will become a sand dune, as shown in **Figure 6-22.**

Sand will continue to build up and form a dune until the sand runs out or the obstruction is removed. Some sand dunes may grow to 50 m to 180 m high, but most are much lower.

Dune Movement

A sand dune has two sides. The side facing the wind has a gentler slope. The side away from the wind is steeper. Examining the shape of a dune tells you the direction from which the wind usually blows.

Unless sand dunes are planted with grasses, most dunes don't stay still. They move away or migrate from the direction of the wind. This process is shown in **Figure 6-23.** Some dunes are known as traveling dunes because they move across desert areas as they lose sand on one side and build it up on the other.

Dune Shape

The shape of a dune can also tell you the wind direction. The most commonly known dune shape is a crescent-shaped dune. The open end of a crescent-shaped dune points downwind. When viewed from above, the points are directed downwind. This type of dune forms on hard surfaces where the sand supply is limited. They often occur as single dunes. **Figure 6-24** shows several dune shapes.

When dunes and loess form, the landscape is changed. Wind, like gravity, running water, and glaciers, shapes the land as it erodes sediments. But, the new landforms created by these agents of erosion are themselves being eroded. Erosion and deposition are part of a cycle of change that constantly shapes and reshapes the land.

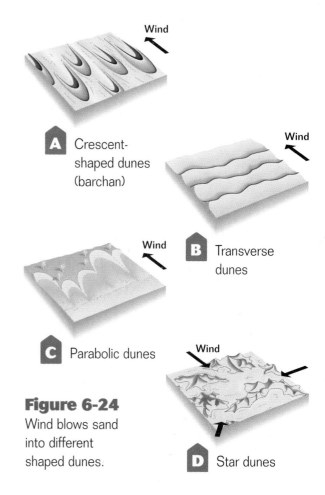

A Crescent-shaped dunes (barchan)

B Transverse dunes

C Parabolic dunes

Figure 6-24
Wind blows sand into different shaped dunes.

D Star dunes

Section Assessment

1. Compare and contrast abrasion and deflation. How do they affect the surface of Earth?

2. Explain the differences between dust storms and sandstorms. Describe how the energy of motion affects the deposition of sand and dust by these storms.

3. **Think Critically:** You notice that snow is piling up behind a fence outside your apartment building. Why?

4. **Skill Builder**

   Sequencing Sequence the following events that describe how a sand dune forms. If you need help, refer to Sequencing in the **Skill Handbook** on page 550.

   a. Grains collect to form a mound.

   b. Wind blows sand grains until they hit an obstacle.

   c. Wind blows over an area and causes deflation.

   d. Vegetation grows on the dune.

Using Math

Between 1972 and 1992, the Sahara Desert in northern Africa increased by nearly 700 km^2 in Mali and the Sudan. Calculate the average number of square kilometers the desert increased each year between 1972 and 1992. At this rate, predict how much additional desert that area will have by 2002.

Blowing in the Wind

Possible Materials

- Flat pans (4)
- Fine sand (400 mL)
- Gravel (400 mL)
- Hair dryer
- Sprinkling can
- Water
- Cardboard sheets (28 cm × 35 cm) (4)
- Tape
- Mixing bowl
- Metric ruler

Have you ever played a sport outside and suddenly had the wind blow dust into your eyes? What did you do? Turn your back? Cover your eyes? How does wind pick up sediment? Why does wind pick up some sediments and leave others on the ground?

Recognize the Problem

What factors affect wind erosion? Do both sediment moisture and speed of wind affect the rate of wind erosion?

Form a Hypothesis

How does the amount of moisture in the sediment affect the ability of wind to erode the sediments? Does the speed of the wind limit the size of sediments it can transport? Form a hypothesis about how sediment moisture affects wind erosion. Form another hypothesis about how wind speed affects the size of the sediment the wind can transport.

Goals

- **Observe** the effects of soil moisture and wind speed on wind erosion.
- **Design** and carry out experiments that test the effects of soil moisture and wind speed on wind erosion.

Safety Precautions

Wear your safety goggles at all times when using the hair dryer on sediments.

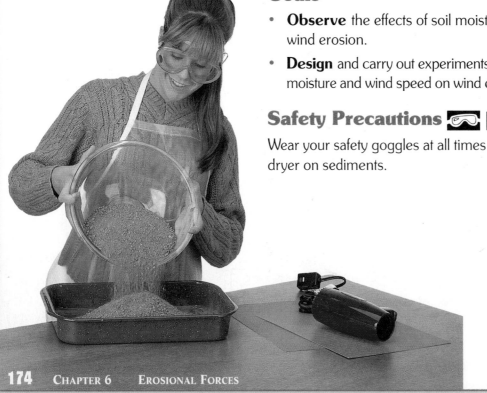

Test Your Hypothesis

Plan

1. As a group, agree upon and write out your hypothesis statements.

2. List the steps needed to test your first hypothesis. Plan specific steps and vary only one factor at a time. Then, list the steps needed to test your second hypothesis. Test only one factor at a time.

3. Mix the sediments in the pans. Plan how you will fold cardboard sheets and attach them to the pans to keep sediments contained.

4. Design data tables in your Science Journal. Use them as your group collects data.

Do

1. Make sure your teacher approves your plan before you proceed.

2. Carry out the experiments as planned.

3. During the experiments, record observations that you make and complete the data tables in your Science Journal.

Analyze Your Data

1. **Compare** your results with those of other groups.

2. **Graph** the relationship that exists between the speed of the wind and the size of the sediments it transports.

Draw Conclusions

1. How does the energy of motion explain the results of your experiment?

2. **Explain** the relationship between the sediment moisture and the amount of sediment eroded.

3. Based on your graph, **explain** the relationship between wind speed and sediment size.

For a **preview** of this chapter, study this Reviewing Main Ideas before you read the chapter. After you have studied this chapter, you can use the Reviewing Main Ideas to **review** the chapter.

The Glencoe MindJogger, Audiocassettes, and CD-ROM provide additional opportunities for review.

Section 6-1 GRAVITY

Erosion is the process that wears down and transports sediments. **Deposition** occurs when an agent of erosion loses its energy of motion and can no longer carry its load. **Slump, creep,** rockslides, and mudflows are all mass movements related to gravity. *What characteristics do slump and creep have in common?*

EROSION-PRONE LAND

Vegetation, terraces, and retaining walls can reduce erosion on slopes. Removing vegetation from and building on steep slopes increases erosion. The roots that help hold the soil together and the plants that block wind and rain on the surface are no longer there to do their job. *What do you think happened in this picture?*

Reading Check ✓

Choose a section of this chapter and rewrite the main headings as questions. Then, answer each question.

Section
6-2 GLACIERS

Glaciers are powerful agents of erosion. **Plucking** adds rock and soil to a glacier's sides and bottom as water freezes and thaws and breaks off pieces of surrounding rocks. Glaciers deposit two kinds of material, **till** (sediments dropped directly from glacial ice and snow) and outwash (debris deposited by its meltwater). *Which of these two sediments is a jumbled pile of rocks?*

Section
6-3 WIND

Deflation occurs when wind erodes only fine-grained sediments, leaving coarse sediments behind. The pitting and polishing of rocks and sediments by windblown sediments is called **abrasion**. Wind deposits include loess and dunes. **Loess** consists of fine-grained particles that are tightly packed. Dunes form when windblown sediments pile up behind an obstacle. *What determines how far dust and sand are blown by the wind?*

Chapter 6 Assessment

Using Vocabulary

a. abrasion
b. creep
c. deflation
d. deposition
e. erosion
f. glacier
g. loess
h. mass movement
i. moraine
j. plucking
k. slump
l. till

Explain the difference in the terms given below. Then, explain how the terms are related.

1. abrasion, plucking
2. creep, mass movement
3. deflation, loess
4. erosion, slump
5. glacier, till

Checking Concepts

Choose the word or phrase that best answers the question.

6. Which of the following is the slowest type of mass movement?
   A) abrasion   C) slump
   B) creep   D) mudflow

7. The best vegetation to plant to reduce erosion has what kind of root system?
   A) taproot system
   B) striated root system
   C) fibrous root system
   D) sheet root system

8. What does a valley glacier create at the point where it starts?
   A) esker   C) till
   B) moraine   D) cirque

9. What happens when glacial erosion occurs?
   A) Eskers form.
   B) Landforms such as arêtes and grooves are formed.
   C) Moraines are deposited.
   D) The climate gets warmer.

10. What term describes a mass of snow and ice in motion?
    A) loess deposit   C) outwash
    B) glacier   D) abrasion

11. What shape do glacier-created valleys have?
    A) V shaped   C) U shaped
    B) L shaped   D) S shaped

12. Which term is an example of a structure created by deposition?
    A) cirque   C) striation
    B) abrasion   D) dune

13. Which characteristic is common to all agents of erosion?
    A) They carry sediments when they have enough energy of motion.
    B) They are most likely to erode when sediments are moist.
    C) They create deposits called dunes.
    D) They erode large sediments before they erode small ones.

14. What type of wind erosion leaves pebbles and boulders behind?
    A) deflation   C) abrasion
    B) loess   D) sandblasting

15. What is a ridge formed by deposition of till called?
    A) striation   C) cirque
    B) esker   D) moraine

Thinking Critically

16. How can striations give information about the direction a glacier moved?

17. How effective would a retaining wall made of fine wire mesh be against erosion?

18. Sand dunes often migrate. What can be done to prevent the migration of beach dunes?

19. Scientists have found evidence of movement of ice within a glacier. Explain how this could occur. (HINT: Recall

how putty-like ice forms at the base of a glacier.)

20. The front end of a valley glacier is at a lower elevation than the tail end. How does this explain melting at its front end while snow is still accumulating at its tail end?

Developing Skills

If you need help, refer to the **Skill Handbook.**

21. **Making Tables:** Make a table to contrast continental and valley glaciers.

22. **Designing an Experiment:** Explain how to test the effect of glacial thickness on a glacier's ability to erode.

23. **Sequencing:** Copy and complete the events chain to show how a sand dune forms. Use the terms *sand rolls, migrating, wind blows, sand accumulates, dune, dry sand, obstruction traps,* and *stabilized.*

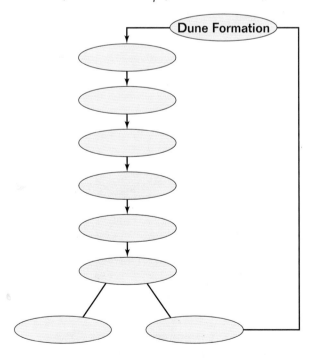

24. **Hypothesizing:** Hypothesize why the materials of loess deposits were transported farther than those of sand dune deposits.

THE
PRINCETON
REVIEW

Test-Taking Tip

Ignore Everyone While you take a test, pay no attention to anyone else in the room. Don't worry if your friends finish a test before you do. If someone tries to talk to you during a test, don't answer. You run the risk of the teacher thinking you were cheating—even if you weren't.

Test Practice

1. A glacier doesn't develop overnight. Several things must happen before a glacier forms. Of the choices below, which occurs first?
   A) Snow falls in an area. It doesn't melt but instead begins piling up.
   B) The mass of snow and ice moves downhill.
   C) The bottom of the snow layer is compressed into layers of ice.
   D) The bottom of the snow layer partially melts and becomes putty-like.

2. All of the following can be classified as erosional features of a glacier except one. Which one doesn't fit?
   A) striations   C) cirque
   B) U-shaped valley   D) till

3. Wind can be a strong erosional force. What determines the amount of erosion that wind can cause in a particular region?
   A) the size of the sediments
   B) the amount of cloud cover
   C) the number of sand dunes
   D) the amount of loess

Chapter Preview

Section 7-1
Population Impact on the Environment

Section 7-2
Using Land

Section 7-3
Recycling

Skills Preview

Skill Builders
- Use a Graph
- Communicate

Activities
- Design an Experiment
- Make a Model

MiniLabs
- Classify
- Make a Model

Reading Check ✔

As you read this chapter, choose two illustrations and explain the purpose of each. Describe other types of illustrations that could replace the two that you choose.

Explore Activity

Have you ever considered the impact that each of us has on the land? Each person on Earth competes for space and resources. Each one generates trash; consumes products made in factories; uses natural resources such as water, soil, and energy; and creates pollution. Do you think our impact on land is significant?

Draw a Population Growth Model

1. Use a piece of paper and a pencil to draw a square that is 10 cm on each side. This represents 1 km^2 of Earth's land surface.

2. In 1965, the average number of people for every square kilometer of land was 21. Draw 21 small circles inside your square to represent this.

3. In 1990, the average was 35. Add 14 circles to illustrate this increase.

4. In 2025, there will be an estimated 52 people per km^2. Add circles to represent the average number of people per square kilometer of land in 2025.

5. Prepare a bar graph that shows population density for each year discussed above.

Science Journal

In your Science Journal, explain whether or not human population is increasing more rapidly as time goes on. How do you think population growth affects the environment?

7·1 Population Impact on the Environment

What You'll Learn

► How to interpret data from a graph that shows human population growth
► Reasons for Earth's rapid increase in human population
► Several ways each person in an industrialized nation affects the environment

Vocabulary

carrying capacity
population
population explosion

Why It's Important

► Humans directly impact the environment. The more humans there are, the greater the impact.

The Human Population Explosion

At one time, people thought of Earth as a world with unlimited resources. They thought the planet could provide them with whatever materials they needed. Earth seemed to have an endless supply of metals, fossil fuels, and rich soils. Today, we know this isn't true. Earth has a carrying capacity. The **carrying capacity** is the maximum number of individuals of a particular species that the planet will support. Thus, Earth's resources are limited. Unless we treat those resources with care, they will disappear.

Many years ago, few people lived on Earth. Fewer resources were used and less waste was produced than today. But, in the last 200 years, the number of people on Earth has increased at an extremely rapid rate. The increase in the world population has changed the way we must view our world and how we care for it for future generations, like the babies in **Figure 7-1.**

Figure 7-1 The human population is growing at an increasingly rapid rate. **Why does Earth have a carrying capacity?**

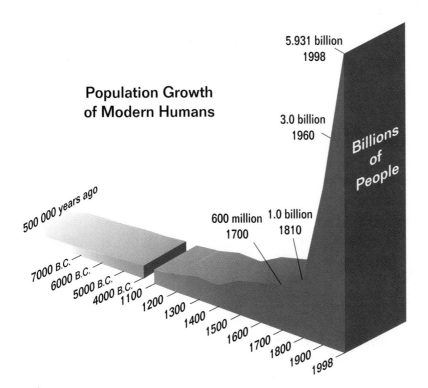

**Population Growth
of Modern Humans**

5.931 billion
1998

3.0 billion
1960

Billions
of
People

500 000 years ago

600 million
1700

1.0 billion
1810

7000 B.C.
6000 B.C.
5000 B.C.
4000 B.C.
1100
1200
1300
1400
1500
1600
1700
1800
1900
1998

Figure 7-2 The human species, *Homo sapiens*, may have appeared about 500 000 years ago. Our population numbers remained relatively steady until about 200 years ago. **Why have we experienced such a sharp increase in growth rate since about 1800?**

Human Population

A **population** is the total number of individuals of a particular species in a particular area. The area can be small or large. For example, we can talk about the human population of one particular community, such as Los Angeles, or about the human population of the entire planet.

Have you ever wondered how many people live on Earth? The global population in 1998 was 5.9 billion. Each day, the number of humans increases by approximately 215 000. Earth is now experiencing a **population explosion.** The word *explosion* is used because the rate at which the population is growing has increased rapidly in recent history. ☑

Our Increasing Population

Look at **Figure 7-2.** You can see that it took hundreds of thousands of years for Earth's population to reach 1 billion people. After that, the population increased much faster. Population has increased so rapidly in recent years because the death rate has been slowed by modern medicine, and we have better sanitation and better nutrition. This means that more people are living longer. Also, the number of births has increased because more people survive to the age at which they can have children.

The population explosion has seriously affected the environment. Scientists predict even greater changes as more people use Earth's limited resources. The population is predicted to be about 11 billion by 2100—nearly twice what it is now.

Reading Check ☑

Why is the increasing number of humans on Earth called a population explosion?

LIFE SCIENCE

INTEGRATION

Carrying Capacity
One of the things that affects carrying capacity is food. When a region does not have enough food, animals either migrate or starve. Infer what other factors determine the carrying capacity of a particular region for a species.

The population density of a region is the average number of people per unit of area. Find the population density of Pennsylvania, which has a population of about 12 million people and an area of about 117 000 km².

We need to be aware of the effect such a large human population will have on our environment. We need to ask ourselves whether we have enough natural resources to support such a large population.

How People Affect the Environment

By the time you're 75 years old, you will have produced enough garbage to equal the mass of six African elephants (43 000 kg). You will have consumed enough water to fill 100 000 bathtubs (26 million L). If you live in the United States, you will have used five times as much energy as an average person living elsewhere in the world.

Our Daily Activities

In your daily activities, you use electricity, some of which is generated by the burning of fuels. The environment changes when fuels are mined and again, later, when they are burned. The water that you use must be made as clean as possible before being returned to the environment. You eat food, which takes land to grow. Much of the food you eat is grown using chemical substances, such as pesticides and herbicides, to kill insects and weeds. These chemicals can get into water supplies and threaten the health of living things if they become too concentrated. How else do you and other people affect the environment?

Many of the products you buy are packaged in plastic and paper. Plastic is made from oil. The process of refining oil produces pollutants. Producing paper requires cutting down trees, using gasoline to transport them to a paper mill, and producing pollutants in the process of transforming the trees into paper.

Figure 7-3 shows some items that may require these activities to produce them.

We change the land when we remove resources from it, and we further impact the environment when we shape those resources into usable products. Then, once we've produced and consumed products, we must dispose of them. Look at **Figure 7-4.** Unnecessary packaging is only one of the problems associated with waste disposal.

Figure 7-3 Every day, you use many of Earth's resources. **What resources were consumed to produce the items shown in this photograph?**

The Future

As the population continues to grow, more demands will be made on the environment. Traffic-choked highways, overflowing garbage dumps, shrinking forests, and vanishing wildlife are common. What can we do? People are the problem, but we also are the solution. As you learn more about how we affect the environment, you'll discover what you can do to help make the future world one that everyone can live in and enjoy. An important step that we can take is to think carefully about our use of natural resources. If everyone learns to conserve resources, we can make a positive impact on the environment.

Figure 7-4 This toy car is overpackaged. Because of consumer demands, many products now come in environmentally friendly packages.

Section Assessment

1. Using **Figure 7-2,** estimate how many years it took for the *Homo sapiens* population to reach 1 billion. How long did it take to triple to 3 billion?

2. Why is human population increasing so rapidly?

3. **Think Critically:** In nonindustrial nations, individuals have less negative impact on the environment than citizens in industrialized nations. In your Science Journal, explain why you think this is so.

4. **Skill Builder**
   Making and Using Graphs Use **Figure 7-2** to answer the questions below. If you need help, refer to Making and Using Graphs in the **Skill Handbook** on page 553.

   a. Early humanlike ancestors existed more than 4 million years ago. Why does the graph indicate that it should extend back only 500 000 years?

   b. How would the slope of the graph change if, in the near future, the growth rate were cut in half?

Using Math

Make a line graph of the data shown below. Plot years on the *x*-axis and population on the *y*-axis. Use your completed graph to infer the population of humans in the year 2040.

Human Population in Billions

1998	2010	2025
5.931	6.849	7.923

A Crowded Encounter

Materials

- Many small objects, such as dried beans, popcorn, or paper clips
- Beaker (250 mL)
- Clock or watch

Think about the effects of our rapidly increasing human population. One of these is overcrowding. Every second, five people are born, and two people die. The result is a net increase of three people every second, or 180 people every minute.

What You'll Investigate

Goals

- **Make a model** of human population growth over a ten-minute time period.
- **Observe** the effects of a population increase on a limited space.
- Record, graph, and interpret population data.

Safety Precautions

Never eat or taste anything from a lab, even if you are confident that you know what it is.

Procedure

1. Use the empty beaker to represent the space left on Earth that is unoccupied by humans at the moment you begin.

2. Let each of your small objects represent five people.

3. **Design** a table with two columns. One column will show the time (1 to 10 minutes), and the other column will show the population at the designated time.

4. **Begin timing** your first minute. At the end of one minute, place the appropriate number of small items in your beaker. **Record** the data in your table. Continue for each minute of time.

5. After completing your table, **make a graph** that shows the time in minutes on the horizontal axis and the population on the vertical axis.

Conclude and Apply

1. At the end of ten minutes, what is the net increase in human population?

2. **Compare and contrast** the graph you just made with the graph shown in **Figure 7-2**. How do you account for the differences?

3. Today, approximately 5.9 billion people inhabit Earth. That number will double in about 40 years. Assuming the rate remains unchanged, **predict** what the population will be 80 years from now.

4. Suggest ways in which the net increase in human population affects Earth's limited resources.

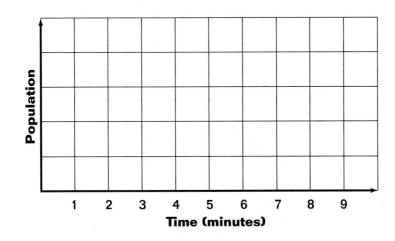

7.2 Using Land

What You'll Learn

▶ Ways that we use land
▶ Environmental problems created because of land use
▶ Things you can do to help protect the environment

Vocabulary
landfill
hazardous waste
conservation
composting

Why It's Important

▶ Land is a resource that we need to use responsibly.

Land Usage

You may not think of land as a natural resource. Yet, it is as important to people as oil, clean air, and clean water. Through agriculture, logging, garbage disposal, and urban development, we use land—and sometimes abuse it.

Farming

Earth's total land area is 149 million km². We use about 16 million km² as farmland. Even so, about 20 percent of the people living in the world are hungry. Millions starve and die each year. To fight this problem, some farmers work to increase the productivity of croplands by using higher-yield seeds and chemical fertilizers. Herbicides and pesticides also are used to reduce weeds, insects, and other pests that can damage crops.

Other farmers rely on organic farming techniques to lessen the environmental impact of chemicals on the land and to increase yield. **Figure 7-5** shows an organic farm in China that has been farmed for many centuries.

Figure 7-5 Organic farming techniques can rebuild topsoil rather than deplete it. Organic farmers use natural fertilizers, crop rotation, and biological pest controls to help their crops thrive.

Figure 7-6 Farmers reduce erosion with contour plowing, as shown on this farm in Washington State. Erosion is reduced because the path of plowing follows the shape of the land. **How can contour plowing control the direction that water flows in a farm field?**

Whenever vegetation is removed from an area, such as on construction sites, mining sites, or tilled farmland, the soil can erode easily. With plants gone, nothing prevents the soil from being carried away by running water and wind. Several centimeters of topsoil may be lost in one year. In some places, it can take more than 1000 years for new topsoil to develop and replace eroded topsoil. Some farmers practice no-till farming, which reduces erosion because land is not loosened by plowing. **Figure 7-6** shows another way farmers work to reduce erosion.

Grazing Livestock

Land also is used for grazing livestock. Animals such as cattle eat vegetation and then often are used as food for humans. In the United States, the majority of land used for grazing is unsuitable for crops. However, about 20 percent of the total cropland in our country is used to grow feed for livestock, such as the corn shown in **Figure 7-7.**

A square kilometer of vegetable crops can feed many more people than a square kilometer used to raise livestock. Some people argue that a more efficient use of the land would be to grow crops directly for human consumption, rather than for livestock. For many, however, meat and dairy products are an important part of their diet. They also argue that livestock have ecological benefits that justify livestock production.

Figure 7-7 Corn, as shown on this farm in Lancaster, Pennsylvania, is used for human food, for livestock feed, and for industrial products such as ceramics, textiles, ethanol, and paint. About half the corn grain raised in the United States is fed to livestock.

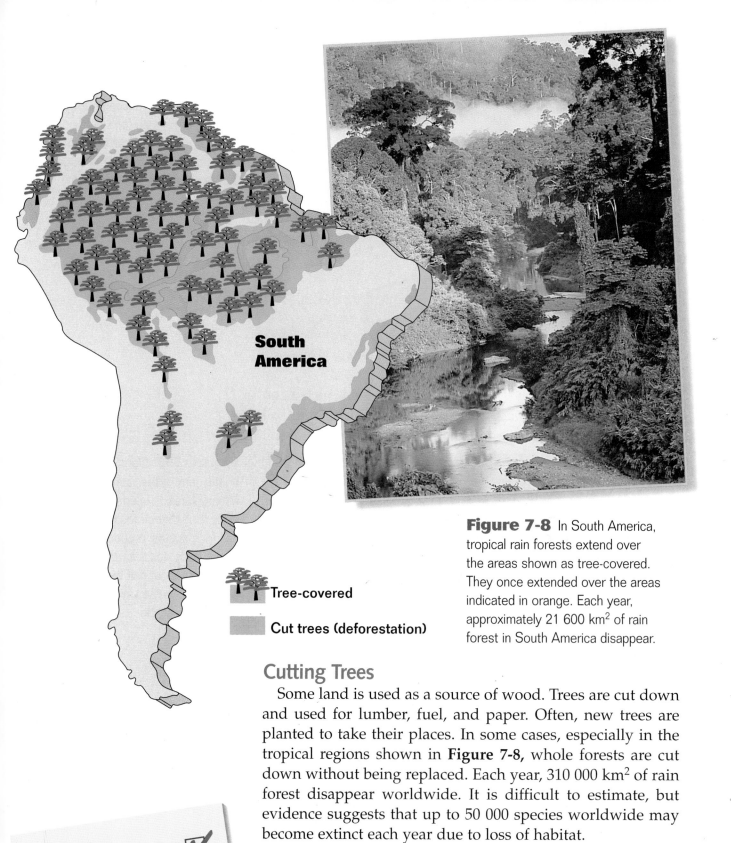

Figure 7-8 In South America, tropical rain forests extend over the areas shown as tree-covered. They once extended over the areas indicated in orange. Each year, approximately 21 600 km² of rain forest in South America disappear.

Tree-covered

Cut trees (deforestation)

Cutting Trees

Some land is used as a source of wood. Trees are cut down and used for lumber, fuel, and paper. Often, new trees are planted to take their places. In some cases, especially in the tropical regions shown in **Figure 7-8,** whole forests are cut down without being replaced. Each year, 310 000 km² of rain forest disappear worldwide. It is difficult to estimate, but evidence suggests that up to 50 000 species worldwide may become extinct each year due to loss of habitat.

Organisms living outside of the tropics also suffer because of the lost vegetation. Plants remove carbon dioxide from the air when they photosynthesize. The process of photosynthesis also produces oxygen that organisms need to breathe. Therefore, reduced vegetation may result in higher levels of carbon dioxide in the atmosphere. Carbon dioxide is a gas that may contribute to a rise in temperatures on Earth. ☑

Reading Check ☑

How do plants remove carbon dioxide from the air?

Landfills

Land also is used when we dispose of the products we consume. About 60 percent of our garbage goes into landfills. A **landfill** is an area where waste is deposited. In a *sanitary landfill,* such as the one illustrated in **Figure 7-9,** each day's deposit is covered with dirt. The dirt prevents the deposit from blowing away and reduces the odor produced by the decaying waste. Sanitary landfills also are designed to prevent liquid wastes from draining into the soil and groundwater below. A sanitary landfill is lined with plastic, concrete, or clay-rich soils that trap the liquid waste.

Sanitary landfills greatly reduce the chance that pollutants will leak into the surrounding soil and groundwater. However, some may still find their way into the environment.

Another problem is that we're filling up our landfills and running out of acceptable areas to build new ones. Many materials placed into landfills decompose slowly.

Hazardous Wastes

Some of the wastes we put into landfills are dangerous to organisms. Poisonous, cancer-causing, or radioactive wastes are called **hazardous wastes.** Hazardous wastes are put into landfills by everyone—industries and individuals alike. We contribute to this problem when we throw away insect sprays, batteries, drain cleaners, bleaches, medicines, and paints.

It may seem that when we throw something in the garbage can, even if it's hazardous, it's gone and we don't need to be concerned with it anymore. Unfortunately, our garbage does not disappear. It can remain in a landfill for hundreds of years. In the case of radioactive waste, it

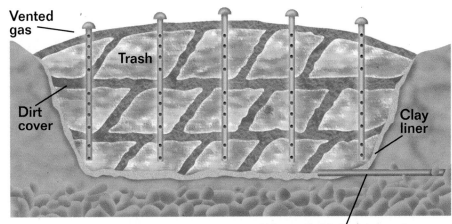

Figure 7-9 The vast majority of our garbage is deposited in landfills. **What are some problems associated with landfill disposal?**

Try at Home

Mini Lab

Classifying Your Trash for One Day

Procedure

1. Prepare a table for yourself with the following column headings: *Paper, Plastic, Glass, Metal, Food Waste.*
2. During the day, record everything you throw out in the appropriate column.
3. At the end of the day, determine the number of trash items in each column.

Analysis

1. Rank each column by number from the least trash items (number 5) to the most trash items (number 1).
2. Compare your rankings with those of others in your household.
3. Compare your daily activities with others to account for differences in the tables.
4. What activities can you change to decrease the amount of trash you produce?

may remain harmful for thousands of years, creating problems for many future generations. Fortunately, industries and individuals are becoming more aware of the problems associated with landfills and are disposing of their wastes in a more responsible manner. You can help by disposing of hazardous wastes you generate at home at special hazardous waste-collection sites. Contact your local government to find out about dates, times, and locations of collections in your area. You can learn more about disposing wastes in the **Field Guide to Waste Management** at the end of this chapter.

Phytoremediation

Earlier, you learned that hazardous substances sometimes contaminate soil. These contaminants may come from nearby industries, residential areas, or landfills. Water contaminated from such a source can filter into the ground and leave behind the toxic substances within soil. Did you know that plants are sometimes used to help fix this problem? Methods of phytoremediation (*phyto* means "plant"; *remediation* means "to fix, or remedy a problem") are being studied to help decontaminate soil.

Extracting Metals

Certain varieties of plants can help remove metals from soil. When soil becomes too concentrated with metallic elements, human health may be at risk. Plant roots can absorb certain metals such as copper, nickel, and zinc. **Figure 7-10** shows how metals are absorbed from the soil and taken into plant tissue. Plants that become concentrated with metals from soil must eventually be harvested and either composted to obtain and recycle the metals or incinerated. If incineration is used to dispose of the plants, the ash residue must be handled carefully and disposed of at a hazardous waste site.

Figure 7-10 Metals such as copper can be removed from soil and incorporated into the tissues of plants. **How does this process illustrate the law of conservation of matter?**

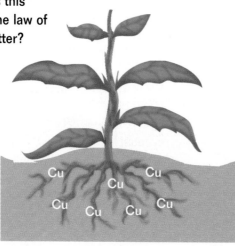
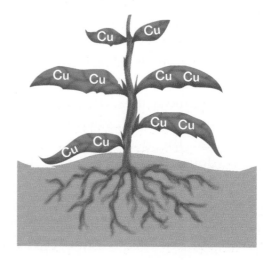

Breaking Down Organic Contaminants

Organic contaminants are hazardous wastes that contain carbon, hydrogen, and other elements such as oxygen, nitrogen, or chlorine. Some common examples of hazardous wastes are gasoline, oil, and solvents. Enzymes are chemical substances that can speed chemical reactions. Some enzymes that can break down organic pollutants are found in plant tissue. Similar to metals extraction, this type of cleanup occurs at the root of the plant. The enzyme is released by the root and causes the organic pollutant in the soil to break down into harmless substances, some of which are useful to the plant and promote its growth.

CHEMISTRY
◄ INTEGRATION

Human-Built Structures

Concrete and asphalt are quickly replacing grass and woodlands in our communities. The impact on the environment, particularly in urban and suburban areas, is easy to observe. Asphalt and concrete absorb solar radiation. The atmosphere is then heated by conduction and convection, which causes the air temperature to rise. You may have observed this if you've ever traveled from a rural area to the city and noticed a rise in temperature.

Problem Solving

The Effects of Trash Disposal

In the early days of the United States, the population was sparse and few people considered the impact of their actions on the environment. They threw their trash into rivers, buried it, or burned it. Today, we must consider the consequences of our methods of trash disposal. The graph at right shows how we deposit our waste.

Think Critically: More than half of the states in our country are running out of landfill space. New landfills will have to be made, but most people have a NIMBY attitude. NIMBY means "Not In My BackYard." People don't want to live near a landfill. What percent of our trash presently goes into landfills? If we reduce the amount of trash in landfills, what alternatives do we have for disposal? How could these

alternatives influence the environment? List the pros and cons for each alternative you think of in your Science Journal.

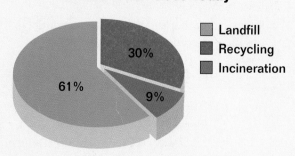

Where Trash Goes Today

- Landfill
- Recycling
- Incineration

61%
30%
9%

Figure 7-11 Some cities are working to preserve green space within city limits, such as this area in Portland, Oregon. **How does more green space in the city improve the environment?**

Mini Lab

Modeling Runoff

Procedure

1. Divide into groups of four or five.
2. Obtain two buckets of water for each group from your teacher.
3. With your teacher present, carefully take your buckets outside.
4. Find a paved area and a grassy area on your school grounds.
5. Pour one bucket of water on the paved area and observe how the water flows on the pavement.
6. Repeat step 5 for the grassy area.

Analysis

1. Describe how the water flowed over each area.
2. Infer what properties of the pavement and the grassy area control how the water flows over each.

Paving over the land prevents water from easily soaking into the soil. Instead, it runs off into sewers or streams. During heavy rainstorms in paved areas, sewer pipes can overflow or become clogged with debris. This causes increased runoff of rainwater directly into streams, and increases the risk of flooding in urban and suburban areas.

A stream's discharge increases when more water enters its channel. Stream discharge is the volume of water flowing past a point per unit of time. For example, the Mississippi River discharges an average of about 19 000 m³ of water into the Gulf of Mexico every second. This is a large volume of moving water, but the Mississippi is a major river. Many thousands more cubic meters flow per second when the Mississippi is flooding. If discharge increases too rapidly, as happens in urban areas from time to time, a stream can flow over its banks and flood a populated area. This happened to the Mississippi and Missouri Rivers and their tributaries during the summer of 1993.

Increased runoff also influences groundwater. Some of the water that does not soak into the soil evaporates. This reduces the amount of water in groundwater aquifers. Many communities rely on groundwater for drinking water. But covering more and more land with roads, sidewalks, and parking lots prevents the water from reaching aquifers.

Some cities are actively preserving more space that cannot be paved over. This type of activity, shown in **Figure 7-11,** beautifies the urban environment, increases the area into which water can soak, and provides more space for recreation.

Natural Preserves

Not all land on Earth is being utilized to produce usable materials or for storing waste. Look at **Figure 7-12.** Some land remains mostly uninhabited by people. National forest lands, grasslands, and parks in the United States are protected from many of the problems that you've read about in this section. In many countries throughout the world, land is set aside as natural preserves. As the world population continues to rise, the strain on our environment is likely to increase. Preserving some land in its natural state should continue to benefit future generations.

Conserving Resources

In the United States and other industrialized countries, people have a throwaway lifestyle. When we are done with something, we throw it away. This means more products must be produced to replace what we've thrown away, more land is used, and landfills overflow. You can help by conserving resources. **Conservation** is the careful use of resources to reduce damage to the environment.

Reduce, Reuse, Recycle

The United States makes up only five percent of the world's human population, yet it consumes 25 percent of the world's natural resources. Each of us can reduce our consumption of materials in simple ways, such as using both sides of notebook paper or carrying lunch to school in a non-disposable container. Ways to conserve resources include reducing our use of materials and reusing and recycling materials. Reusing an item means finding another use for it instead of throwing it away. You can reuse old clothes by giving them to someone else or by cutting them into rags. The rags can be used in place of paper towels for cleaning jobs around your home.

Figure 7-12 Many countries set aside land as natural preserves. **How do these natural preserves benefit humans and other living things?**

Using Math

Assume 17 fewer trees are cut down when 1000 kg of paper are recycled. Calculate the number of trees conserved per year if 150 000 kg of paper are recycled each month.

Reusing plastic and paper bags is another way to reduce waste. Some grocery stores even pay a few cents when you return and reuse paper grocery bags.

Outdoors, there are things you can do, too. If you cut grass or rake leaves, you can compost these items instead of putting them into the trash. **Composting** means piling yard wastes where they can gradually decompose. The decomposed matter can be used as fertilizer in gardens or flower beds. Some cities no longer pick up yard waste to take to landfills. In these places, composting is common. If everyone in the United States composted, it would reduce the trash put into landfills by 20 percent.

The Population Outlook

The human population explosion already has had devastating effects on the environment and the organisms that inhabit Earth. It's unlikely that the population will begin to decline in the near future. To compensate, we must use our resources wisely. Conserving resources by reducing, reusing, and recycling is an important way that you can make a difference.

Section Assessment

1. In your Science Journal, list six ways that people use land.

2. Discuss environmental problems that are sometimes created by agriculture, mining, and trash disposal.

3. How can phytoremediation positively impact the environment?

4. **Think Critically:** Choose one of the following items, and list three ways it can be reused: an empty milk carton, vegetable scraps, used notebook paper, or an old automobile tire. Be sure your uses are environmentally friendly.

5. **Skill Builder**
   Communicating Do the **Chapter 7 Skill Activity** on page 584 to find out ways in which an environmental problem can be communicated.

Using Computers

Word Processing
Suppose that a new landfill is needed in your community. Where do you think it should be located? Now, suppose that you want to convince people that you've selected the best place for the landfill. Use your word-processing skills to write a letter to the editor of the local newspaper, listing reasons in favor of your choice. If you need help, refer to page 568.

Recycling

Recyclable Objects

Did you know that any object is **recyclable** if it can be processed and then used again? Look at **Figure 7-13.** Glass and aluminum are two of the many things that can be recycled.

Paper makes up about 40 percent of the mass of our trash. If it is recycled, landfill space and trees are conserved. Also, the production of recycled paper takes 58 percent less water and generates 74 percent fewer air pollutants than the production of brand-new paper made from trees.

How much energy do you think is saved when you recycle one aluminum can? Answer: enough energy to keep a TV running for about three hours. Twenty aluminum cans can be recycled with the energy that is needed to produce a single brand-new can from aluminum ore.

What You'll Learn

► The advantages of recycling
► The advantages and disadvantages of required recycling

Vocabulary
recyclable

Why It's Important

► Recycling helps conserve resources and reduces solid waste.

VISUALIZING
Recycling

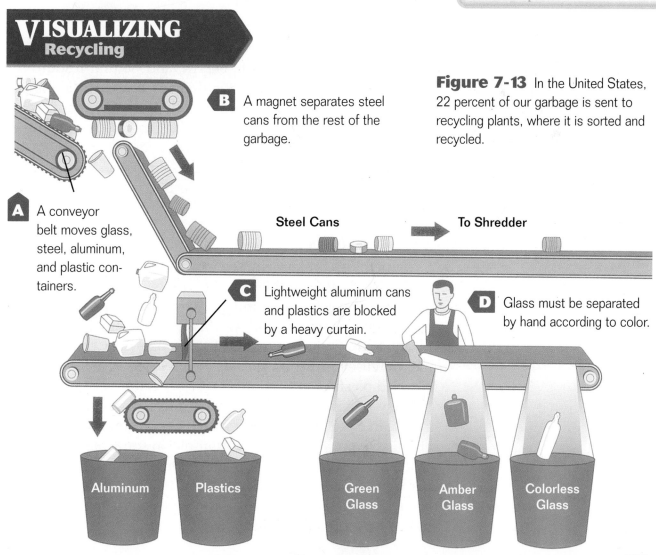

B A magnet separates steel cans from the rest of the garbage.

Figure 7-13 In the United States, 22 percent of our garbage is sent to recycling plants, where it is sorted and recycled.

A A conveyor belt moves glass, steel, aluminum, and plastic containers.

Steel Cans → **To Shredder**

C Lightweight aluminum cans and plastics are blocked by a heavy curtain.

D Glass must be separated by hand according to color.

Aluminum Plastics Green Glass Amber Glass Colorless Glass

Figure 7-14 Recycling saves landfill space, energy, and natural resources. Many community volunteers adopt sections of a highway. They pick up trash and recycle the salvageable part.

Everyone agrees that recycling is good for the environment. It saves landfill space, energy, and natural resources. Recycling also helps reduce the damage caused by mining, cutting trees, and manufacturing. Did you know that if you recycle, you will reduce the trash you generate in your lifetime by 60 percent? If you don't recycle, you'll generate trash equal to at least 600 times your mass. No one argues that recycling is not a good thing. The question is should recycling be required?

Required Recycling

Many things are thrown away because some people aren't in the habit of recycling. In the United States, much less garbage is recycled than in countries with mandatory recycling, such as Japan and Germany. Mandatory recycling means that people are required to recycle. This creates new jobs in reuse industries, such as the production of items from recycled plastics.

Many states already have some form of recycling laws. People in these states comply with the laws because they benefit directly in some way. For example, in some places people who recycle pay lower trash-collection fees. In other places, garbage is not collected if it contains items that should have been recycled. **Figure 7-14** shows typical containers used to help people organize their recyclable objects.

In some states, a refundable deposit is made on all beverage containers. This means paying extra money at the store for a drink. You get your money back if you return the container to the store for recycling. Some people suggest that if we had a national container law, we could save enough energy to light up a large city for four years. ☑

Voluntary Recycling

Today, many people already recycle voluntarily because their cities provide curbside collection or convenient drop-off facilities. In this case, people have the freedom to decide whether or not to recycle, without government intervention.

Some people argue that the cost of recycling outweighs the benefits. Recycling requires money to pay for workers, trucks, and buildings. Also, some workers, such as miners and manufacturers who make brand-new containers, might lose their jobs.

Another problem is what to do with all of the recyclable items. Recycling businesses must make a profit, or they can't exist. The only way to make a profit in recycling is to sell the recycled material, so there must be a market for the material. Whether voluntary or mandatory, recycling conserves resources. In addition to saving landfill space, recycling also protects our environment by minimizing our need to extract raw materials from Earth.

Reading Check ☑

In what ways have states encouraged people to participate in recycling?

*inter*NET
CONNECTION

Visit the Glencoe Science Web Site at **www.glencoe.com/ sec/science/nc** to learn more about conservation. Make a list of conservation tips for individuals.

Section Assessment

1. List at least four advantages of recycling.

2. What are the advantages and disadvantages of mandatory recycling?

3. **Think Critically:** Spend a day at home keeping track of what you throw away and what you recycle. Record these items in your Science Journal. Did you throw away anything that could have been recycled?

4.  **Skill Builder**
   Making and Using Tables As you will see in the **Field Guide to Waste Management** at the end of this chapter, plastics must be carefully sorted before they can be reprocessed into new usable items. Do the Activity in the field guide to find out how to organize your recyclable plastic items. If you need help, refer to Making and Using Tables in the **Skill Handbook** on page 552.

Science Journal
In your Science Journal, write a letter to your local chamber of commerce suggesting ways to encourage businesses to recycle.

A Model Landfill

Materials

- Bottles (2L) (2)
- Soil
- Thermometer
- Plastic wrap
- Graph paper
- Rubber band
- Trash (including fruit and vegetable scraps, a plastic item, a metal item, a foam cup, and notebook paper or newsprint)

When garbage is put into landfills, it is covered under other trash and soil and isn't exposed to sunlight and other things that help decomposition. When examined by a researcher, one landfill was found to contain grass clippings that were still green and bread that had not molded.

What You'll Investigate

At what rates do different materials decompose in a landfill?

Goals

- **Make a model** of a sanitary landfill.
- **Compare and contrast** the decomposition of different materials in a landfill.

Safety Precautions

CAUTION: *Be especially careful not to expose your skin or eyes to garbage items.*

Procedure

1. **Cut** off the tops of two 2-L bottles.
2. **Add** soil to each bottle until it is half filled.
3. On graph paper, **trace** the outline of all the garbage items that you will place into each bottle. **Label** each outline and keep the tracings.
4. **Place** the items, one at a time, in each bottle. Completely **cover** each item with soil.
5. **Add** water to your landfill until the soil is slightly moist. **Place** a thermometer in each bottle and seal the bottle with the plastic wrap

and a rubber band. **Store** one bottle in a cold place and put the other on a shelf.

6. **Check** the temperature of your landfill on the shelf each day for two weeks. **Record** the temperatures in a data table that you design.

7. After two weeks, **remove** all of the items from the soil in both bottles. Trace the outlines of each on a new sheet of graph paper. **Compare** the sizes of the items with their original sizes.

8. **Wash** your hands thoroughly after cleaning up your lab space. Be sure to dispose of each item properly as instructed by your teacher.

Conclude and Apply

1. Most decomposition in a landfill is due to the activity of microorganisms. The organisms can live only under certain temperature and moisture conditions. **Explain** how the decomposition rates would have differed if the soil had been completely dry.

2. **Compare** your results with the results from the bottle that was stored at a cold temperature. **Explain** the differences you observe.

3. Why do some items decompose more rapidly than others?

4. What problems are created in landfills by plastics?

Using Plants to Reduce Pollution

Pollution-Absorbing Plants

Plants are helping clean up hazardous chemicals in soil and water. By taking in pollutants through their roots, some plants can make hazardous substances less harmful to humans and other organisms. These helpful plants include poplar trees, mustard (left), and fescue grass (below).

Fescue to the Rescue

High concentrations of the metal selenium (suh LEE nee uhm) are harmful to the environment. In central California, soil became contaminated when irrigation water containing selenium flowed through fields. Farmers in the area planted fescue grass and Indian mustard to absorb selenium from the contaminated irrigation water. Researchers have found that mustard and fescue are able to convert selenium metal into a gas that is eventually given off by the plants. Scientists suggest that the gas is many times less harmful to the environment than concentrated levels of selenium in soils.

Advantages of Using Plants

Using plants to control or eliminate certain types of pollution is becoming increasingly popular. Cost is one reason. It is often less expensive to use plants than other methods of reducing pollutants. Plants clean up contaminated soil or water on the site, so there is no expense of digging up soil or removing water. Plants also can make an area more attractive. Finally, few, if any, people object to using plants to reverse the negative effects of pollution.

inteNET CONNECTION

To find information about the Environmental Protection Agency's Citizen's Guide to Phytoremediation, visit the Glencoe Science Web Site at **www.glencoe.com/ sec/science/nc.**

FIELD GUIDE *to Waste Management*

FIELD *ACTIVITY*

The type of plastic contained in a recyclable item is indicated by a coded number placed on the item. Arrange collection centers at your school for plastic to be recycled. Name your collection activity and advertise it with posters. Operate the collection of recyclable plastics for one week. Use the Plastics Code System Table in this field guide to organize the plastic products by code number so they can be recycled. Arrange to have your plastics taken to a recycling center. Make a bar graph that shows how many pieces of each type of plastic you collected. In your Science Journal, list examples of products that can be made from the collected plastics.

Managing waste properly can reduce the use of resources and prevent pollution. People can do three things to cut down on waste production and reduce harm to the environment. They can follow the three Rs of waste management: reduce, reuse, and recycle. For example, a 450-g family-size box of cereal uses a lot less cardboard than 18 single-serving boxes that each contain 25 g of cereal. Finding another function for used items such as wrapping gifts with old magazines or newspapers greatly reduces waste. And, you can use many products every day that are recyclable. You can also help complete the cycle by purchasing items that are made from recycled materials.

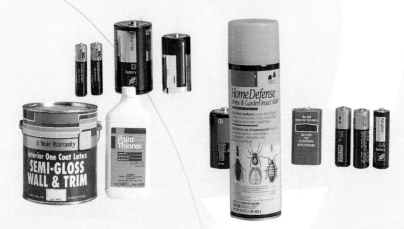

Household Hazardous Wastes

- Household Hazardous Wastes (HHWs) are products containing chemicals that can cause injury or are harmful if used, stored, or disposed of improperly. Some of these products include household and car batteries, bleach and household cleaners, paint, paint thinner, old motor oil, old gasoline, herbicides and pesticides.
- These chemicals pose a threat to people (especially children, firefighters, and refuse workers) and to our environment.

- HHWs have caution words, skull and crossbones, or special handling directions.
- Some communities provide information to help people dispose of HHWs properly.
- Follow these steps to reduce HHWs:
  1. Whenever possible, buy nontoxic alternatives to hazardous products.
  2. If you buy a hazardous product, buy only what you need to do the job.
  3. Before you put leftover products on the shelf, try to find someone who can use them.

Plastics

- Plastics are among the most difficult products to recycle. Most plastics are composed of complex molecules that tend not to break down easily.
- Many different types of plastics exist, and they often cannot be recycled together.
- **Table 7-1** below lists the codes used to identify specific types of plastics used in products. This helps people sort common plastic items for proper recycling.
- Plastic beverage containers are recycled into insulation, carpet yarn, strapping, and packing material.

Table 7-1

The Plastics Code System			
Code	Material	% of Containers	Reclaimed For
1 PET	Polyethylene terephthalate	7	Carpet, food packaging, fiberfill, fibers, and auto parts
2 HDPE	High-density polyethylene	31	Drainage pipes, drums, traffic cones, plastic lumber, and combs
3 V	Vinyl chloride	5	Pipes, hoses, mud flaps, and tile
4 LDPE	Low-density polyethylene	33	Mixed with HDPE to produce cases, recycling bins, and garbage bags
5 PP	Polypropylene	9	Household and janitorial products
6 PS	Polystyrene	11	Insulation and food trays
7 Other	All others and mixed	4	Storage containers, lumber, and animal-pen floors

Glass

- Glass is often separated by color into green, brown, or colorless types before recycling.
- Most glass bottles are recyclable, but some glassware is not because it is too thin. For example, broken or burned-out lightbulbs cannot be recycled.
- New products made from recycled glass include beverage containers.

Metals

- A variety of metals are recyclable, such as aluminum beverage cans and steel used in a variety of canned goods.
- Aluminum is processed to make lawn chairs, siding, cookware, or new beverage cans.
- Even precious metals such as silver, gold, and platinum used in laboratories or in jewelry, for example, are recyclable.

Paper

- Plain white paper, newspaper, magazines, and telephone books are common paper goods that can be recycled. New products made from these items include newsprint, cardboard, egg cartons, and building materials.
- Not all glossy and colored papers are recyclable at all recycling centers.

- As for any recycled material, you should check with your neighborhood recycling center for specific instructions about properly sorting your paper goods.

Yard Waste

- Grass clippings, leaves, sticks, and other yard wastes can be placed in bags and taken to your local recycling center. Some communities provide for the collection of yard wastes from your home after you gather them together.
- Another approach is to practice your own mulching. Rake your leaves and then place them on a garden plot to compost over the winter. This will enrich the soil in your garden when you're ready to plant in the spring.
- Some communities shred sticks and leaves to make mulch. Whatever the approach, recycling yard waste reduces the amount of material we send to landfills.

For a **preview** of this chapter, study this Reviewing Main Ideas before you read the chapter. After you have studied this chapter, you can use the Reviewing Main Ideas to **review** the chapter.

GLENCOE TECHNOLOGY

The Glencoe MindJogger, Audiocassettes, and CD-ROM provide additional opportunities for review.

Section
7-1 POPULATION IMPACT ON THE ENVIRONMENT

The rapid increase in human **population** in recent years is due to an increase in the birthrate, advances in medicine, better sanitation, and better nutrition. *How does an increase in the number of humans affect Earth's carrying capacity for other organisms?*

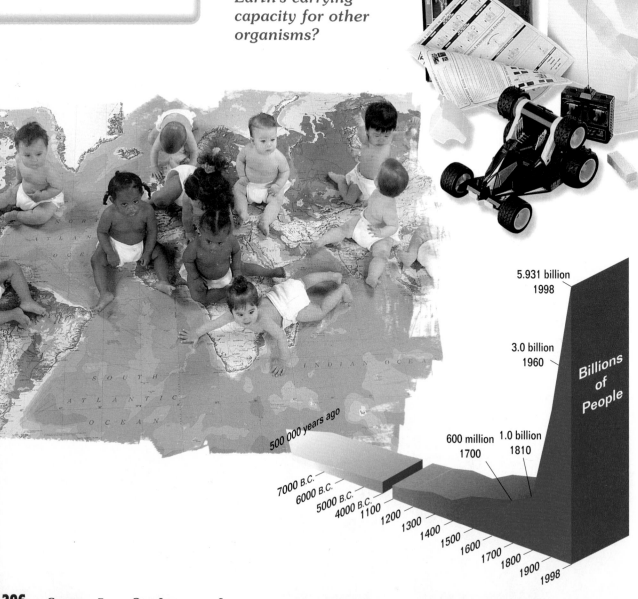

500 000 years ago

7000 B.C.
6000 B.C.
5000 B.C.
4000 B.C.
1100
1200
1300
1400
1500
1600
1700
1800
1900
1998

600 million
1700

1.0 billion
1810

3.0 billion
1960

5.931 billion
1998

Billions of People

Reading Check ☑

List at least two facts and two opinions related to population growth or related to recycling.

Section 7-2 USING LAND

Land is used for farming, grazing livestock, lumber, and mining coal and mineral ores. We also build structures and **landfills** on land. Land becomes polluted by **hazardous wastes** thrown away by industries and individuals. Fertilizers and pesticides pollute groundwater and soil. *What happens to soil quality and atmospheric carbon dioxide when trees are cut down?*

Section 7-3 RECYCLING

Recycling, reducing, and reusing materials are important ways we can conserve natural resources. Recycling saves energy and much-needed space in landfills. Some parts of the world have mandatory recycling, while other parts have voluntary programs. *Why do some people oppose having mandatory recycling programs?*

Chapter 7 Assessment

Using Vocabulary

a. carrying capacity
b. composting
c. conservation
d. hazardous waste
e. landfill
f. population
g. population explosion
h. recyclable

Which vocabulary word describes the phrase or process given below?

1. total number of individuals of a particular species in an area
2. careful use of resources
3. area lined with plastic, concrete, or clay where garbage is dumped
4. items that can be processed and used again
5. maximum number of individuals of a particular type that the planet will support

Checking Concepts

Choose the word or phrase that best answers the question.

6. Where is most of the trash in the United States disposed of?
   A) recycling centers
   B) landfills
   C) hazardous waste sites
   D) old mine shafts

7. Between 1960 and 1998, world population increased by how many billions of people?
   A) 5.9   C) 1.0
   B) 3.2   D) 2.9

8. What percent of Earth's resources does the United States use?
   A) 5   C) 25
   B) 10   D) 50

9. About what percent of U.S. cropland is used to grow feed for livestock?
   A) 100   C) 50
   B) 1   D) 20

10. What do we call an object that can be processed in some way so that it can be used again?
    A) trash   C) disposable
    B) recyclable   D) hazardous

11. What is about 40 percent of the mass of our trash made up of?
    A) glass   C) yard waste
    B) aluminum   D) paper

12. In which type of facility do humans cover trash with soil?
    A) recycling center   C) sanitary landfill
    B) surface mine   D) coal mine

13. By what order of magnitude are people starving each year?
    A) the hundreds   C) the millions
    B) the thousands   D) the billions

14. Organisms living outside the tropics suffer when rain forests are cut down. This is because fewer trees are available to produce which?
    A) carbon dioxide   C) water
    B) methane   D) oxygen

15. Which of the following is an example of a hazardous waste?
    A) piece of glass   C) steel can
    B) plastic jug   D) can of paint

Thinking Critically

16. How would reducing the packaging of consumer products impact our disposal of solid wastes?

17. Renewable resources are those resources that can be replenished by nature in the foreseeable future. Nonrenewable resources cannot be replenished. Which kind of resource is oxygen? Explain.

18. Although land is farmable in many developing countries, hunger is a major problem in many of these places. Give some reasons why this might be so.

19. Forests in Germany are dying due to acid rain. What effects might this loss of trees have on the environment?

20. Describe how you could encourage your neighbors to recycle their aluminum cans.

Developing Skills

If you need help, refer to the **Skill Handbook.**

21. **Making and Using Graphs**: In a population of snails, each snail produces two offspring each month. Each offspring also produces two offspring. Using the graph below, determine how many new snails would be produced during the fifth month if the initial population were only two snails.

22. **Interpreting Scientific Illustrations:** Why does the curve of the line graph below change its slope over time? Suppose half of the snails died after six months. Draw a new graph to illustrate the effect.

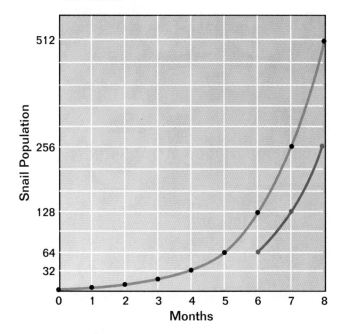

THE PRINCETON REVIEW

Test-Taking Tip

Don't Be Afraid to Ask for Help Ask for advice on things you don't understand. If you're practicing for a test and find yourself stuck, unable to understand why you got a question wrong, or unable to do it in the first place, ask for help.

Test Practice

Use these questions to test your Science Proficiency.

1. In some areas of the world, when rain forests are destroyed for lumber, a few fast-growing species of trees are planted in their place. Why is this a problem?
   A) The trees won't grow as quickly as the original rain forest trees.
   B) The tree farm won't produce oxygen.
   C) The roots of the new trees won't hold the soil.
   D) The biodiversity is decreased.

2. In 1946, there were 2.4 billion people on Earth. In 1998, there were 5.9 billion people. By how much did world population increase in 52 years?
   A) 226 percent
   B) 41 percent
   C) 146 percent
   D) 69 percent

3. Which of the following must be true for a recycling center to be profitable?
   A) The center must recycle glass.
   B) Mandatory recycling is enforced.
   C) Glossy and colored paper are recycled.
   D) There is a market for the recycled items.

The Web of Life

What's Happening Here?

Indian paintbrush and aster flowers splash vivid color above a grassy meadow in the Tatoosh Range of Mount Rainier National Park in Washington state (left). Good soil and abundant water support the meadow's lush growth. In contrast, the poor soil and extreme conditions on the distant mountain slopes support a few hardy plants. Support for plants also may come from animals. Flying from flower to flower, a honeybee (below) picks up pollen on its hairy legs. Each time it visits a flower, the honeybee may leave some pollen behind. This process, called pollination, must take place before a plant can produce seeds that grow into new plants. In this unit you will learn how all life on Earth is connected, how living things are adapted to their particular settings, and how plants and other producers play an essential role in the web of life.

interNET CONNECTION

Explore the Glencoe Science Web Site at **www.glencoe com/sec/science/nc** to find out more about topics in this unit.

Chapter Preview

Section 8-1
Characteristics of Plants

Section 8-2
Seedless Plants

Section 8-3
Seed Plants

Skills Preview

Skill Builders
- Hypothesize
- Map Concepts

Activities
- Predict
- Compare and Contrast

MiniLabs
- Measure in SI
- Observe and Infer

Reading Check ✓

As you read, list terms that describe parts of both plants and people, such as *vascular tissue, cuticle,* and *epidermis.* Define the terms as they relate to plants and to people.

Explore Activity

Plants are all around—in parks and gardens, by streams and on rocks, in houses, and even on dinner plates. Do you eat salads? Salads are made up of edible plants. What plants would you choose for a salad? Do you know what plant parts you would be eating? In the following activity, find out which plant parts are edible. Then, in the chapter, learn about plant life.

Infer Which Plant Parts Are Edible

1. Make a list of five foods that you might eat during a typical day.

2. Decide whether the foods contain any plant parts.

3. Infer what plant parts were used to make your five foods.

Science Journal

Plants provide many nutrients. List the nutrients from a package of dried fruit in your Science Journal. As a class, compare the nutrients in the dried fruits each student selected.

What You'll Learn

▶ The characteristics of plants
▶ What plant adaptations make it possible for plants to survive on land
▶ Similarities and differences between vascular and nonvascular plants

Vocabulary
cellulose
cuticle
vascular plant
nonvascular plant

Why It's Important

▶ Plants produce food and oxygen for most organisms on Earth. Without plants, there would be no life.

What is a plant?

Do you enjoy walking along nature trails in parks like the one shown in **Figure 8-1?** Maybe you've taken off your shoes and walked barefoot on soft, cool grass. Perhaps you've climbed a tree to see what your world looks like from high in its branches. In every instance, members of the plant kingdom surrounded you.

Now look at **Figure 8-2.** These organisms, mosses and liverworts, have characteristics that identify them as plants, too. What do they have in common with grasses, trees, and ferns? What makes a plant a plant?

Characteristics of Plants

All plants are made of eukaryotic cells that have cell walls. Cell walls provide structure and protection for plant cells. Many plant cells contain the green pigment chlorophyll. Plants range in size from microscopic water ferns to giant sequoia trees that are sometimes more than 100 m in height. They have roots or rootlike structures that hold them in the ground or onto something. Plants have successfully adapted to nearly every environment on Earth. Some grow in frigid, ice-bound polar regions and others grow in hot, dry deserts. Many plants must live in or near water.

About 285 000 plant species have been discovered and identified. Scientists think many more are still to be found, mainly in tropical rain forests. If you were to make a list of all

Figure 8-1 All plants are many celled and nearly all contain chlorophyll. Grasses, trees, and ferns all are members of Kingdom Plantae.

Figure 8-2 Plants include liverworts (A) and mosses (B).

the plants you could name, you probably would include vegetables, fruits, and field crops like wheat, rice, or corn. These plants are important food sources to humans and other consumers. Without plants, most life on Earth as we know it would not be possible.

Origin and Evolution of Plants

Where did the first plants come from? Like all life, early plants probably came from the sea, evolving from plantlike protists. What evidence is there that this is true? Both plants and green algae, a type of protist, have the same types of chlorophyll and carotenoids (KER uh tuh noydz) in their cells. Carotenoids are red, yellow, or orange pigments found in some plants and in all cyanobacteria.

Fossil Record

One way to understand the evolution of plants is to look at the fossil record. Unfortunately, plants usually decay before they form fossils. The oldest fossil plants are from the Silurian period and are about 420 million years old. Fossils of early plants are similar to the plantlike protists. Fossils of *Rhynia major*, illustrated in **Figure 8-3,** represent the earliest land plants. Scientists hypothesize that these kinds of plants evolved into some plants that exist today.

Cone-bearing plants, such as pines, probably evolved from a group of plants that grew about 350 million years ago. Fossils of these plants have been dated to the Paleozoic era, 300 million years ago. Flowering plants did not exist until the Cretaceous period, about 120 million years ago. The exact origin of flowering plants is not known.

Using Math

Fossil evidence shows that the first land plants lived about 420 million years ago. If Earth is 4.6 billion years old, what percent of Earth's age was Earth without land plants?

Figure 8-3 Fossils of *Rhynia major*, an extinct, small land plant, show that it had underground stems but no true roots or leaves.

Adaptations to Land

Imagine life for a one-celled green alga, a protist, floating in a shallow pool. The water in the pool surrounds and supports it. The alga can make its own food through the process of photosynthesis. Materials enter and leave the cell through the cell membrane and cell wall. The alga has everything it needs to survive.

Now, imagine a summer drought. The pool begins to dry up. Soon, the alga is on damp mud and is no longer supported by the pool's water, as shown in **Figure 8-4.** It won't starve because it still can make its own food. As long as the soil stays damp, the alga can move materials in and out through the cell membrane and cell wall. But, what will happen if the drought continues, and the soil becomes drier and drier? The alga will continue to lose water because water diffuses through the cell membrane and cell wall from where there is more water to where there is less water. Without water in its environment, the alga will dry up and die.

Protection and Support

What adaptations would make it possible for plants to survive on land? Losing water is a major problem for plants. What would help a plant conserve water? Plant cells have cell membranes, but they also have rigid cell walls outside the membrane. Cell walls contain **cellulose** (SEL yuh lohs), an organic compound made up of long chains of glucose molecules. Some woody plants, such as oaks and pines, are as much as 50 percent cellulose. Cell walls provide structure and support and help reduce water loss.

Figure 8-4 Algae must have water to survive.

A Each green alga produces its own food and moves materials in and out through the cell membrane and cell wall. **By what process do algae make food?**

B If a pond completely dries up, the algae in it will die.

Figure 8-5 A waxy cuticle is an adaptation that enables plants to survive on land.

A Rain beads up on the leaves of some plants because of the cuticle. This reduces the amount of moisture on plant surfaces.

B A waxy cuticle prevents moisture loss from this prickly pear cactus. **Why is this important for a cactus?**

C Waxy cuticles are often found on flowers such as this orchid.

Covering the stems, leaves, and flowers of some land plants is a cuticle. The **cuticle** (KYEWT ih kul) is a waxy, protective layer secreted by the cell walls. It slows down the evaporation of water from a plant. After it rains, go outside and see how raindrops bead up on some plant surfaces, as illustrated in **Figure 8-5A.** Removing water from plant surfaces is important because too much moisture on a plant may affect cell functions. Too much surface moisture also may lead to fungal diseases. The cuticle is an adaptation that enabled plants to live on land. ✓

Life on land meant that plant cells could not depend on water to support them or to move substances from one cell to the next. Support came with the evolution of stems and substances that strengthen the cell walls. Eventually, plants developed tissues that distribute materials.

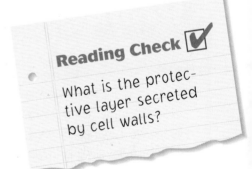

Reading Check

What is the protective layer secreted by cell walls?

Reproduction

The move to land by plants not only meant changes to reduce water loss and increase support, but it also meant a change in plant reproduction. Plants evolved from organisms that reproduced in water. They completely depended on water for reproduction and survival. Some plants still require water to reproduce, but others do not. The development of cones and flowers that produce seeds allowed these plants to survive on land.

Life on Land

Life on land has some advantages for plants. There is more sunlight and carbon dioxide for plants on land than in water. Plants use sunlight and carbon dioxide for the food-making process, photosynthesis. During photosynthesis, plants give off oxygen. As more and more plants adapted to life on land, the amount of oxygen in Earth's atmosphere increased. This paved the way for the evolution of organisms that depend on oxygen. In some cases, it meant that some organisms evolved together. For example, some flowering plants provided animals with food, and the animals pollinated the plant's flowers.

Classification of Plants

Today, the plant kingdom is classified into major groups called divisions, as illustrated in **Figure 8-6.** A division is the same as a phylum in other kingdoms, as listed in Appendix E of this book. A less formal way to group plants is as vascular or nonvascular plants. **Vascular plants** have tissues that make up the organ system that carries water, nutrients, and other substances throughout the plant. **Nonvascular plants** have no vascular tissue and use other ways to move water and substances.

interNET CONNECTION

Visit the Glencoe Science Web Site at **www.glencoe.com/sec/science/nc** for more information about plants that are sources of medicines. In your Science Journal, list five medicines that come from plants.

Problem Solving

Cause and Effect in Nature

People in all cultures have used and still use plants as medicine. Some Native American cultures used willow bark to cure headaches. Heart problems were treated with foxglove in England and sea onions in Egypt. In Peru, the bark of the cinchona tree was used to treat malaria. Scientists have found that many native cures are medically sound. Willow bark contains salicylates, the main ingredient in aspirin. Foxglove, as seen in the photo to the right, is still the main source of digitalis, a drug prescribed for heart problems. Cinchona bark contains quinine, an anti-malarial drug.

Think Critically: Predict how the destruction of the rain forests might affect research for new drugs from plants.

Figure 8-6 The diversity of Kingdom Plantae is represented by a branching tree, composed of different divisions. All of these plant groups are related but have differences that separate them. **What differences can you detect among the plant divisions in this illustration?**

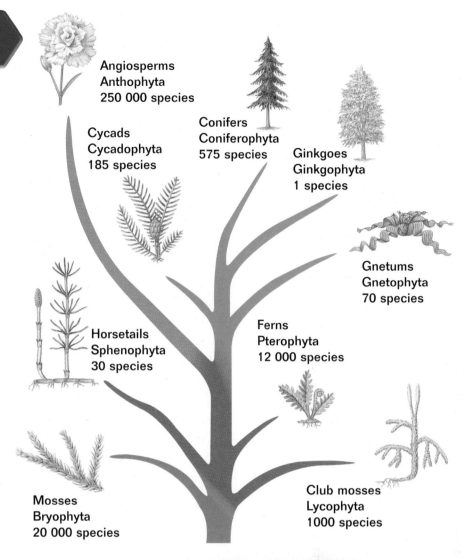

Angiosperms
Anthophyta
250 000 species

Cycads
Cycadophyta
185 species

Conifers
Coniferophyta
575 species

Ginkgoes
Ginkgophyta
1 species

Gnetums
Gnetophyta
70 species

Horsetails
Sphenophyta
30 species

Ferns
Pterophyta
12 000 species

Mosses
Bryophyta
20 000 species

Club mosses
Lycophyta
1000 species

Section Assessment

1. List the characteristics of plants.

2. Compare vascular and nonvascular plants.

3. Name three adaptations that allow plants to survive on land.

4. **Think Critically:** If you left a board lying on the grass for a few days, what would happen to the grass underneath the board? Why?

5. **Skill Builder**
   Forming a Hypothesis From what you have learned about adaptations necessary for life on land, make a hypothesis as to what types of adaptations land plants might have if they had to survive submerged in water. If you need help, refer to Forming a Hypothesis in the **Skill Handbook** on page 558.

Science Journal
The oldest surviving plant species is *Ginkgo biloba*. Research the history of this species, then write about it in your Science Journal.

8·2 Seedless Plants

Seedless Nonvascular Plants

If you were asked to name the parts of a plant, you probably would list roots, stems, leaves, and perhaps flowers. You also may know that many plants grow from seeds. But, did you know that some plants do not have all of these parts? **Figure 8-7** shows some common types of nonvascular plants.

Liverworts and Mosses (Bryophytes)

The bryophytes (BRI uh fites)—liverworts and mosses—are small, nonvascular plants that are usually just a few cells thick and only 2 cm to 5 cm in height. They have stalks that look like stems and leafy green growths. The threadlike roots of bryophytes are called **rhizoids.** Water is absorbed and distributed directly through their cell walls. Bryophytes grow in damp environments such as the forest floor, the edges of ponds and streams, and near the ocean. Bryophytes usually reproduce by spores because they do not have flowers to produce seeds.

Liverworts get their name because to some people, one type looks like a liver. It is a rootless plant that has a flattened, leaflike body. Liverworts usually have one-celled rhizoids. In the ninth century, liverworts were thought to be useful in treating diseases of the liver. The ending, -*wort*, means "herb," so the word *liverwort* means "herb for the liver." Of approximately 20 000 species of nonvascular plants, most are classified as mosses. Have you ever seen mosses growing on tree trunks, rocks, or the ground in damp or humid areas? Mosses have green, leaflike

What **You'll Learn**

▶ Characteristics of seedless nonvascular plants and seedless vascular plants

▶ The importance of some non-vascular and vascular plants

Vocabulary
rhizoid
pioneer species

Why **It's Important**

▶ Seedless plants are often the first to grow in damaged or disturbed environments.

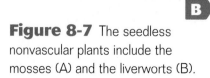

A

B

Figure 8-7 The seedless nonvascular plants include the mosses (A) and the liverworts (B).

Figure 8-8 Mosses are often among the first organisms to live in a new environment, such as this lava field. **Where do the mosses come from?**

growths in a spiral around a stalk. Their threadlike rhizoids are only a few cells in length.

The Importance of Bryophytes

Mosses and liverworts are important in the ecology of many areas. Although mosses require moist conditions to grow and reproduce, many of them can withstand long, dry periods. Often, they are among the first plants to grow in new environments, such as lava fields as shown in **Figure 8-8,** or disturbed environments, such as forests destroyed by fire.

When a volcano erupts, lava covers the land and destroys the plants living there. After the lava cools, spores of mosses and liverworts are carried by the wind to the new rocks. The spores will grow into plants if enough water is available and other growing conditions are right. Organisms that are the first to grow in new or disturbed areas like these are called **pioneer species.** As pioneer plants grow and die, decaying plant material builds up. This, along with the breakdown of rocks, begins the formation of soil. Pioneer plants change environmental conditions so that other plants can grow.

EARTH SCIENCE
INTEGRATION

Soil Formation
Soil is a mixture of weathered rock and decaying organic matter (plant and animal). Infer what roles pioneer species such as lichens, mosses, and liverworts play in building soil.

Mini Lab

Measuring Water Absorption by a Moss

Procedure

1. Place a few teaspoons of *Sphagnum* moss on a piece of cheesecloth. Twist the cheesecloth to form a ball and tie it securely.
2. Weigh the ball.
3. Put 200 mL of water in a container and add the ball.
4. Predict how much water the ball will absorb.
5. Wait 15 minutes. Remove the ball and drain the excess water back into the container.

Analysis

1. Weigh the ball and measure the amount of water left in the container.
2. In your Science Journal, calculate how much water the *Sphagnum* moss absorbed.

Seedless Vascular Plants

The plants in **Figure 8-9** are like mosses because they are seedless plants that reproduce by spores. They are different from mosses because they have vascular tissue. The vascular tissue in the seedless vascular plants is made up of long, tubelike cells. These cells carry water, minerals, and nutrients to cells throughout the plant. Why is having cells like these an advantage to a plant? Remember that bryophytes are only a few cells thick. Each cell absorbs water directly from its environment. As a result, these plants cannot grow large. Vascular plants, on the other hand, can grow bigger and thicker because the vascular tissue distributes water and nutrients. ✔

Types of Seedless Vascular Plants

Seedless vascular plants include the ground pines, spike mosses, horsetails, and ferns. Today, there are about 1000 species of ground pines, spike mosses, and horsetails. Ferns are more abundant, with at least 12 000 species known. Many species of seedless vascular plants are known only from fossils. They flourished during the warm, moist Paleozoic era. Fossil records show that some horsetails grew 15 m tall, unlike modern species that only grow 1 m to 2 m tall.

Reading Check ✔

What makes up the vascular tissue in seedless vascular plants?

Figure 8-9 The seedless vascular plants include ground pines, spike mosses, horsetails, and ferns. **Why can these plants grow taller than mosses and liverworts?**

Ferns

Horsetails

Spike moss

Ground pine

Figure 8-10 Club mosses such as ground pines (A) and spike mosses (B) produce spores at the end of stems in tiny, conelike structures. Photographers once used the dry, flammable spores of club mosses as flash powder. It burned rapidly and produced the light to take photographs.

Ground Pines and Spike Mosses

The photographs in **Figure 8-10** show ground pines and spike mosses. Both groups of plants are often called club mosses. They are seedless vascular plants with needlelike leaves. Spores are produced at the end of the stems in structures that look like tiny pine cones. Ground pines are found from arctic regions to the tropics, but never in large numbers. In some areas, they are endangered because they have been overcollected to make wreaths and other decorations.

Spike mosses resemble ground pines. One species of spike moss, the resurrection plant, is adapted to desert conditions. When water is scarce, the plant curls up and seems dead. When water becomes available, the resurrection plant unfurls its green leaves and begins making food again. The plant can repeat this process whenever necessary.

Horsetails

Horsetails have a stem structure unique among the vascular plants. Their stems are jointed and have a hollow center surrounded by a ring of vascular tissue. At each joint, leaves grow around the stem. In **Figure 8-11,** you can see these joints easily. If you pull on a horsetail stem, it will pop apart in sections. Like the club mosses, spores from horsetails are produced in a conelike structure at the tips of some stems.

Figure 8-11 The spores of horsetails are found in conelike structures on the tips of some stems.

Figure 8-12 Most ferns produce spores in special structures on the leaves, but the spores of the cinnamon fern are on a separate stalk.

interNET
CONNECTION

Visit the Glencoe Science Web Site at **www.glencoe.com/ sec/science/nc** for more information about which ferns are native to your state. In your Science Journal, list three of these ferns and describe their environments.

EARTH SCIENCE
INTEGRATION ➤

The stems of the horsetails contain silica, a gritty substance found in sand. For centuries, horsetails have been used for polishing objects, sharpening tools, and scouring cooking utensils. Another common name for horsetails is scouring rush.

Ferns

Ferns belong to the largest group of seedless vascular plants. Ferns, like those in **Figure 8-12,** have stems, leaves, and roots. They also have characteristics of both nonvascular and vascular plants. Like the bryophytes, ferns produce spores, and they have vascular tissue like vascular plants. Today, thousands of species of ferns grow on Earth, but once there were many more. From clues left in rock layers, scientists know that during the Carboniferous period of the Paleozoic era, much of Earth was tropical. Steamy swamps covered large areas, as illustrated in **Figure 8-13.** The tallest plants were species of ferns. The ancient ferns grew as tall as 25 m—much taller than any fern species alive today. The tallest, modern tree ferns are about 3 m to 5 m in height.

Formation of Fuel

When ferns and other plants of the Carboniferous period died, many of them became submerged in water and mud before they could decompose. This plant material built up, became compacted and compressed, and eventually turned into coal. This process took millions of years.

Today, a similar process is taking place in bogs. A bog is a poorly drained area of land that contains decaying plants. The decay process is slow because waterlogged soils do not

contain oxygen. The plants in bogs are mostly seedless plants like mosses and ferns. Peat, the remains of peat mosses, is mined from bogs in some countries for a low-cost fuel. Scientists hypothesize that over time, if additional layers of soil bury, compact, and compress the peat, it will become coal.

Figure 8-13 Many more species of club mosses, horsetails, and ferns grew in carboniferous swamp forests than are alive today.

Section Assessment

1. Compare and contrast the mosses and ferns.

2. What do fossil records tell us about seedless plants?

3. Under what conditions would you expect to find pioneer plants?

4. **Think Critically:** List ways seedless plants affect your life each day. (HINT: Where do electricity and heat for homes come from?)

5. **Skill Builder**
   Concept Mapping Make a concept map showing how seedless nonvascular and seedless vascular plants are related. Include these terms in the concept map: *plant kingdom, bryophytes, seedless nonvascular plants, seedless vascular plants, ferns, ground pines, horsetails, liverworts, mosses,* and *spike mosses.* If you need help, refer to Concept Mapping in the **Skill Handbook** on page 550.

Using Math

There are approximately 8000 species of liverworts and 9000 species of mosses. Estimate what fraction of bryophytes are mosses.

Comparing Seedless Plants

Materials

One living example of each of these plants:
- Moss
- Liverwort
- Club moss
- Horsetail
- Fern
  - *detailed photographs of the above plant types*
  - *Alternate Material*

Liverworts, mosses, ferns, horsetails, and club mosses have at least one common characteristic—they reproduce by spores. But, do they have other things in common? In this activity, discover their similarities and differences.

What You'll Investigate

How are seedless plants alike and how are they different?

Goals

- **Observe** types of seedless plants.
- **Compare and contrast** seedless plants.

Procedure

1. Copy the Plant Observations table into your Science Journal.
2. Examine each plant and fill in the table using the following guidelines:
   Color—green or not green
   Growth—mostly flat and low or mostly upright
   Root Type—small and fiberlike or rootlike
   Leaf Form—needlelike, scalelike, or leaflike

Conclude and Apply

1. **Observe and infer** what characteristics seedless plants have in common.
2. **Hypothesize** about the differences in growth.
3. **Compare and contrast** the seedless plants.

Plant Observations				
Plant	**Color**	**Growth**	**Root Type**	**Leaf Form**
Moss				
Liverwort				
Club moss				
Horsetail				
Fern				

Preservation in Peat Bogs

A bog is a wetland, characterized by wet, spongy, poorly drained ground. It typically contains a thin layer of living plants overlying a thick layer of partially decomposed plant material called peat. One of the major types of peat is moss peat. It is formed mostly from *Sphagnum* moss. Peat bogs are acidic, low in minerals, and lack oxygen. These conditions provide a unique environment. When some types of organisms become trapped and buried in a peat bog, they do not decay. In Europe and North America, the well-preserved bodies of humans and other animals have been found in peat bogs.

STEP BY STEP

1 Mosses and other wetland plants grow on the surface of a bog.

2 Over time, a layer of partially decayed plant matter accumulates. Eventually, this becomes a thick layer of peat.

3 A substance in the cell walls of *Sphagnum* moss reacts with, and ties up, certain nutrients. These nutrients are essential for the survival of decay-causing bacteria. Without these nutrients, the bacteria cannot live in a bog.

4 When an animal is buried in a bog, its soft tissues, such as skin and internal organs, are not destroyed by decay. But, the animal's bones are dissolved away because of the acidic environment.

5 The skin of animals buried in a peat bog undergoes a sort of tanning process. Human skin becomes leatherlike and coffee colored, as seen in the photograph below.

Think Critically

1. What kinds of information might scientists gain by studying bog-preserved ancient humans?

2. Another type of peat is fuel peat. What property of peat do you think makes it usable as a fuel?

Career CONNECTION

Archaeologists have found hundreds of preserved animals in peat bogs. An archaeologist studies ancient peoples, their remains, and their culture. Pretend you are an archaeologist. Imagine what it must be like for archaeologists to discover human remains.

8·3 Seed Plants

What is a seed plant?

Have you ever eaten vegetables like the ones shown in **Figure 8-14?** All of these foods come from seed plants. What fruits and vegetables have you eaten today? If you had an apple, a peanut butter and jelly sandwich, or a glass of orange juice for lunch, you ate foods that came from seed plants.

Nearly all the plants you are familiar with are seed plants. Seed plants have roots, stems, leaves, and vascular tissue and produce seeds. A seed usually contains an embryo and stored food. The stored food is the source of energy for growth of the embryo into a plant. More than 250 000 species of seed plants are known in the world today. Seed plants are generally classified into two major groups: the gymnosperms and the angiosperms.

What **You'll Learn**

▶ The characteristics of seed plants
▶ The structures and functions of roots, stems, and leaves
▶ The main characteristics of gymnosperms and angiosperms and their importance
▶ Similarities and differences of monocots and dicots

Vocabulary

xylem	gymnosperm
phloem	angiosperm
cambium	monocot
stomata	dicot
guard cell	

Why **It's Important**

▶ Understanding seed plants will help you appreciate how much you depend on them.

Figure 8-14 The products of plants, like these being sold at a market in Ecuador, provide food for humans. **How are plants an important part of the world's food supply?**

Figure 8-15 The vascular tissue of some seed plants includes xylem, phloem, and cambium. **Which of these tissues transports food throughout the plant?**

A Phloem transports dissolved sugar throughout the plant.

B Cambium produces xylem and phloem as the plant grows.

C Xylem transports water and dissolved substances throughout the plant.

Vascular Tissue

Three tissues usually make up the vascular system in a seed plant. **Xylem** (ZI lum) tissue transports water and dissolved substances from the roots throughout the plant. **Phloem** (FLOH em) tissue moves food up from where it is made to other parts of the plant where it is used or stored. In some plants, a cambium is between xylem and phloem, as shown in **Figure 8-15. Cambium** (KAM bee um) is a tissue that produces new xylem and phloem cells. These three tissues completely circle some stems and roots. Groups of vascular tissue called vascular bundles are found in other plants.

Stems

Did you know that the trunk of a tree is really its stem? Stems are usually above ground and support the branches, leaves, and flowers. Some stems, such as potatoes and onions, are underground. The stem allows movement of materials between leaves and roots. Some stems store food. Sugarcane has an aboveground stem that stores large quantities of food. Stems of cacti are adapted to carry on photosynthesis and make food for the rest of the plant.

MiniLab

Observing Water Moving in a Plant

Procedure

1. Into a clear container, about 10 cm tall and 4 cm in diameter, pour water to a depth of 1.5 cm. Add 15 drops of red food coloring to the water.
2. Put the root end of a whole green onion in the colored water in the container. Do not cut the onion in any way.
3. Let the onion stand overnight.
4. The next day, examine the outside of the onion. Peel off the layers of leaves and examine them.

Analysis

1. In your Science Journal, compare the appearance of the onion before and after it was in the colored water.
2. Describe the location of red color inside the onion.
3. Infer how the red color inside the onion might be related to vascular tissue.

Figure 8-16 The root system of a dandelion is longer than the plant is tall. When you pull up a dandelion, you often pull off the top portion of the plant. The root quickly produces new leaves, and another dandelion grows.

Plant stems are either herbaceous (hur BAY shus) or woody. Herbaceous stems usually are soft and green, like the stems of peppers, corn, and tulips. Oak, birch, and other trees and shrubs have hard, rigid, woody stems.

Roots

Imagine a large tree growing alone on top of a hill. What is the largest part? Maybe you said the trunk or the branches. Did you consider the roots? The root systems of most plants are as large or larger than the aboveground stems and leaves, like the dandelion in **Figure 8-16.**

Roots are important to plants. Water and other substances enter a plant through its roots. Roots have vascular tissue to move water and dissolved substances from the ground up through the stems to the leaves. Roots also anchor plants. If they didn't, plants could be blown away by wind or washed away by water. Each root system must support the plant parts that are above the ground—the stem, branches, and leaves of a tree, for example. Sometimes, part or all of roots are above ground, too.

Roots may store food. When you eat carrots or beets, you eat roots that contain stored food. Root tissues also may perform special functions such as absorbing oxygen that is used in the process of respiration.

Leaves

Have you ever rested in the shade of a tree's leaves on a hot, summer day? Leaves are the organs of the plant that usually trap light and make food through the process of photosynthesis. Leaves come in many shapes, sizes, and colors.

Using Math

The roots of some cacti are shallow but grow horizontally as much as 15 m in all directions from the stem. How much soil surface area do these roots cover?

Leaf Structure

Look at the structure of a typical leaf shown in **Figure 8-17.** The epidermis is a thin layer of cells that covers and protects both the upper and lower surfaces of a leaf. A waxy cuticle that protects and reduces water loss covers the epidermis of many leaves. A feature of most leaves is stomata. **Stomata** are small pores in the leaf surfaces that allow carbon dioxide, water, and oxygen to enter and leave a leaf. The stomata are surrounded by **guard cells** that open and close the pores. The cuticle, stomata, and guard cells all are adaptations that help plants survive on land. ☑

Reading Check ☑

What is the role of stomata in a leaf?

Leaf Cells

A typical leaf is made of different layers of cells. Covering the upper and lower surfaces of a leaf is the epidermis. Just below the upper epidermis is the palisade layer. It consists of closely packed, long, narrow cells that usually contain many chloroplasts. Most of the food produced by plants is made in the palisade cells. Between the palisade layer and the lower epidermis is the spongy layer. It is a layer of loosely arranged cells separated by air spaces. In a leaf, xylem and phloem are in the spongy layer.

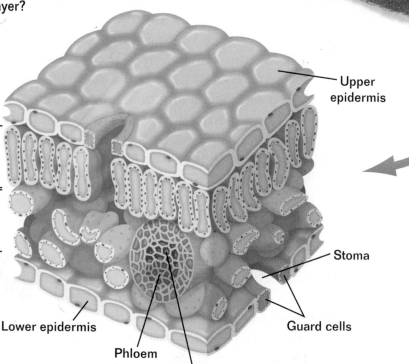

Figure 8-17 The structure of a typical leaf is adapted for photosynthesis. **Why do cells in the palisade layer have more chloroplasts than cells in the spongy layer?**

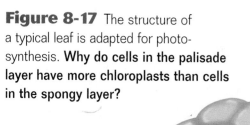

Palisade layer

Spongy layer

Upper epidermis

Stoma

Lower epidermis

Guard cells

Phloem

Xylem

A Conifers are the largest, most diverse division of the gymnosperms. Most conifers are evergreen plants, such as this blue spruce.

Figure 8-18 The gymnosperms include conifers (A), cycads (B), ginkgoes (C), and gnetophytes (D).

B About 100 species of cycads exist today. Only one genus grows naturally in the United States. This sago palm comes from Java, an island in Indonesia.

EXAMPLES OF
Gymnosperms

- Pine
- Hemlock
- Spruce
- Sago Palm
- Ginkgo
- Joint Fir

Gymnosperms

The oldest trees alive today are gymnosperms (JIHM nuh spurmz). A bristlecone pine tree in the White Mountains of eastern California is estimated to be 4900 years old. **Gymnosperms** are vascular plants that produce seeds on the surface of the female reproductive structure. The word *gymnosperm* comes from the Greek language and means "naked seed." Seeds of gymnosperms are not protected by a fruit. Gymnosperms do not produce flowers. Leaves of most gymnosperms are needlelike or scalelike. Gymnosperms are often called evergreens because most keep their leaves for more than one year.

Four divisions of plants—conifers, cycads, ginkgoes, and gnetophytes—are classified as gymnosperms. **Figure 8-18** shows examples of the four divisions. You are probably most familiar with the division Coniferophyta, the conifers. Pines, firs, spruces, redwoods, and junipers belong to this division. It contains the greatest number of gymnosperm species. All conifers produce two types of cones, the male and female reproductive structures. These are usually on the same plant. Seeds develop on the female cone.

D The 70 species of gnetophytes are classified into three genera. More than half of the species, such as this joint fir, are in one genus, another genus has just one species, and the rest of the species are in the third genus.

C Today, the ginkgoes are represented by only one living species. Ginkgoes lose their leaves in the fall. **How is this different from most gymnosperms?**

Angiosperms

When people are asked to name a plant, most people name an angiosperm (AN jee uh spurm). Angiosperms are familiar plants no matter where you live. They grow in parks, fields, forests, jungles, deserts, freshwater, salt water, cracks of sidewalks, or dangling from wires or other plants. One species of orchid even grows underground. Angiosperms make up the plant division Anthophyta. More than eighty-five percent of plant species known today belong to this division.

An **angiosperm** is a vascular plant that flowers and has a fruit that contains seeds. The fruit develops from a part or parts of one or more flowers. The flowers of angiosperms vary in size, shape, and color. Duckweed, an aquatic plant, has a flower that is only 0.1 mm long. A plant in Indonesia has a flower that is nearly 1 m in diameter and can weigh 9 kg. Nearly every color can be found in some flower, although some people would not include black. Multi-colored flowers are common. Some plants have flowers that are not easily recognized as flowers, such as those found on oak and birch trees.

EXAMPLES OF
Angiosperms

- **Grasses and grains**
- **Cacti**
- **Palms**
- **Garden flowers**
- **Vegetables**
- **Fruits**
- **Nuts**
  (except pine nuts)
- **Leafy trees**
  (except ginkgoes)

Figure 8-19 By observing a monocot and a dicot, their plant characteristics can be determined.

Monocots

A Monocots, such as these lilies, have flower parts in multiples of three. If you had cereal for breakfast, you ate part of a monocot. Corn, rice, oats, and wheat are monocots.

Seed   **Seedling**

B In monocots, vascular tissues are arranged as bundles scattered throughout the stem. Monocot leaves are usually more narrow than long. The vascular bundles show up as parallel veins in leaves.

Monocots and Dicots

The two classes of angiosperms are the monocots and the dicots. The terms *monocot* and *dicot* are shortened forms of the words *monocotyledon* and *dicotyledon*. The prefix *mono* means "one," and *di* means "two." A cotyledon is a seed leaf inside a seed. Therefore, **monocots** have one seed leaf inside their seeds and **dicots** have two. **Figure 8-19** compares the characteristics of monocots and dicots.

Importance of Seed Plants

Imagine that your class is having a picnic in the park. You cover the wooden picnic table with a red-checked, cotton tablecloth and pass out paper cups and plates. Your lunch includes hot dogs, potato chips, and apple cider. Perhaps you collect leaves or flowers for a science project. Later, you clean up and put leftovers in paper bags.

Now, let's imagine this scene if there were no seed plants on Earth. There would be no wooden picnic table and no

Dicots

C Dicots, such as the hibiscus, have flower parts in multiples of four or five. Oaks, maples, and many other trees are dicots. Most vegetables and fruits are dicots, as are many garden flowers.

D In dicot stems, vascular bundles occur in rings. These bundles of rings are the annual rings in woody stems. The vascular bundles are the network of veins in dicot leaves.

Seed   Seedling

pulp to make paper products such as cups, plates, and bags. The hot dog came from the meat of animals that eat only plants. Bread for buns, apples for cider, and potatoes for chips all come from plants. The tablecloth is made from cotton, a plant. Without seed plants, there would be no picnic.

Uses of Gymnosperms and Angiosperms

Conifers are the most economically important gymnosperms. Most of the wood used for construction, as in **Figure 8-20,** and for paper production, comes from conifers such as pines and spruces. Resin, a waxy substance secreted by conifers, is used to make chemicals found in soap, paint, varnish, and some medicines.

Figure 8-20 The wood from conifers, such as pines, is commonly used in construction. Resin is used to make household products.

Figure 8-21 Cotton is a flowering plant that yields long fibers that can be woven into a wide variety of fabrics. **What chemical compound makes up these fibers?**

The most common plants on Earth are the angiosperms. They are important to all life because they form the basis for the diets of most animals. Grains such as barley and wheat and legumes such as peas and lentils were among the first plants ever grown by humans. Angiosperms also are the source of many of the fibers used in clothing. Cotton fibers, as seen in **Figure 8-21,** grow from the outer surface of cotton-seeds. The fibers of the flax plant are processed and woven into linen fabrics. The production of medicines, rubber, oils, perfumes, pesticides, and some industrial chemicals uses substances found in angiosperms.

Section Assessment

1. What are the characteristics of a seed plant?

2. Compare and contrast the characteristics of gymnosperms and angiosperms.

3. You are looking at a flower with five petals, five sepals, one pistil, and ten stamens. Is it from a monocot or dicot plant?

4. **Think Critically:** The cuticle and epidermis of leaves are transparent. If they were not transparent, what might be the result?

5. **Skill Builder**
   Classifying Conifers have needlelike or scalelike leaves. Do the **Chapter 8 Skill Activity** on page 585 to learn how to use this characteristic to classify conifers.

Using Computers

Word Processing Use a word-processing program to outline the structures and functions that are associated with roots, stems, and leaves. If you need help, refer to page 568.

Comparing Monocots and Dicots

Materials
- Monocot and dicot flowers
- Monocot and dicot seeds
- Scalpel
- Forceps
- Iodine solution

You have read that monocots and dicots are similar because they are both groups of flowering plants. However, you also have learned that these two groups are different. Try this activity to compare and contrast monocots and dicots.

What You'll Investigate

How do the characteristics of monocots and dicots compare?

Goals

- **Observe** similarities and differences between monocots and dicots.
- **Classify** plants as monocots or dicots based on flower characteristics.
- **Infer** what type of food is stored in seeds.

Procedure

1. Copy the Plant Data table in your Science Journal.
2. **Observe** the leaves on the stem of each flower. In your Science Journal, describe the monocot and the dicot leaves.

3. **Examine** the monocot and the dicot flower. For each flower, remove and count the sepals and petals. Enter these numbers on the table.
4. Inside each flower, you should see a pistil(s) and several stamens. **Count** each type and enter these numbers as "Other Observations."
5. **Examine** the two seeds. **Cut** the seeds lengthwise, **observe** each half, and **identify** the embryo and cotyledon(s).
6. Place a drop of iodine on different parts of the seed. A blue-black color indicates the presence of starch. **CAUTION:** *Iodine is poisonous. It will stain and can burn your skin.*

Conclude and Apply

1. **Compare** the numbers of sepals and petals of monocot and dicot flowers.
2. What characteristics are the same for monocot and dicot flowers?
3. Distinguish between a monocot and a dicot seed.
4. What type of food is stored in monocot and in dicot seeds?

Plant Data				
	Number of Sepals	**Number of Petals**	**Number of Cotyledons**	**Other Observations**
Monocot				
Dicot				

For a **preview** of this chapter, study this Reviewing Main Ideas before you read the chapter. After you have studied this chapter, you can use the Reviewing Main Ideas to **review** the chapter.

The Glencoe MindJogger, Audiocassettes, and CD-ROM provide additional opportunities for review.

Section
8-1 CHARACTERISTICS OF PLANTS

Plants are made up of eukaryotic cells. They usually have some form of leaves, stems, and roots. Plants vary greatly in size and shape. Most plants are adapted to live on land. As plants evolved from aquatic to land forms, changes in structure and function occurred. The changes included how they reproduced, supported themselves, and moved substances from one part of the plant to another. The plant kingdom is classified into groups called divisions. *What are some plant adaptations for living on land?*

Section
8-2 SEEDLESS PLANTS

Seedless plants include **nonvascular** and **vascular** types. Bryophytes—mosses and liverworts—are seedless **nonvascular plants.** They have no true leaves, stems, roots, or vascular tissues and live in moist environments. For bryophytes, reproduction usually is by spores. Bryophytes may be considered **pioneer species** because they are some of the first plants to grow in new or disturbed environments. They change the environment so that other plant species may grow there. Club mosses, horsetails, and ferns are seedless **vascular plants.** They have vascular tissues, a pipeline that moves substances throughout the plant. Like bryophytes, these plants may reproduce by spores. When ancient forms of these plants died, they underwent a process that, over time, resulted in the formation of coal. *How are bryophytes and ferns alike?*

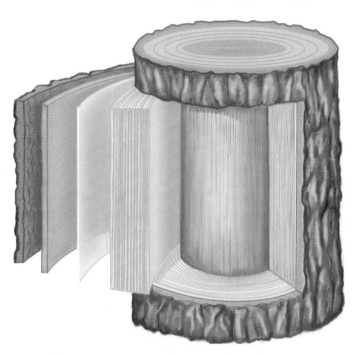

Reading Check ✓

Choose a topic in this chapter that interests you. Look it up in a reference book, an encyclopedia or on a CD. Think of a way to share what you learn.

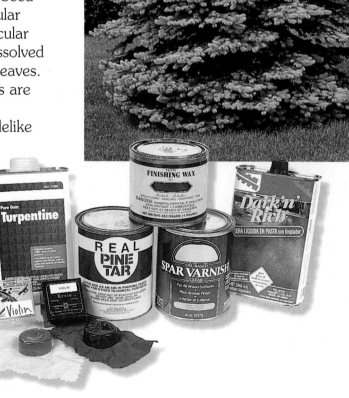

Section 8-3 SEED PLANTS

Seed plants are what most people think of when they hear the word *plants.* These plants have adapted to survive in nearly every environment on Earth. Seed plants produce seeds and have vascular tissue, stems, roots, and leaves. Vascular tissues transport food, water, and dissolved substances in the roots, stems, and leaves. The two major groups of seed plants are gymnosperms and angiosperms. **Gymnosperms** generally have needlelike leaves and some type of cone. **Angiosperms** are plants that flower and are classified as **monocots** or **dicots.** Seed plants provide food, shelter, clothing, and many other products. *What structures are common to all seed plants?*

Chapter 8 Assessment

Using Vocabulary

a. angiosperm
b. cambium
c. cellulose
d. cuticle
e. dicot
f. guard cell
g. gymnosperm
h. monocot
i. nonvascular plant
j. phloem
k. pioneer species
l. rhizoid
m. stomata
n. vascular plant
o. xylem

Explain the differences between the terms in each of the following sets.

1. xylem, phloem, cambium
2. angiosperm, dicot, monocot
3. guard cell, stomata
4. cuticle, cellulose
5. vascular plant, gymnosperm

Checking Concepts

Choose the word or phrase that best answers the question.

6. Which of the following is a seedless, vascular plant?
   A) moss   C) horsetail
   B) liverwort   D) pine

7. What are the small openings in the surface of a leaf surrounded by guard cells?
   A) stomata   C) rhizoids
   B) cuticles   D) angiosperms

8. What is the plant structure that anchors the plant?
   A) stem   C) roots
   B) leaves   D) guard cell

9. What kind of plants have structures that move water and other substances?
   A) vascular   C) nonvascular
   B) protist   D) moneran

10. What division has plants that are only a few cells thick?
    A) Anthophyta   C) Pterophyta
    B) Cycadophyta   D) Bryophyta

11. Where is new xylem and phloem produced?
    A) guard cells   C) stomata
    B) cambium   D) cuticle

12. Which of the following is NOT part of an angiosperm?
    A) flowers   C) cones
    B) seeds   D) fruit

13. In what part of a leaf does most photosynthesis happen?
    A) epidermis   C) stomata
    B) cuticle   D) palisade layer

14. Which of these is an advantage to life on land for plants?
    A) more direct sunlight
    B) less carbon dioxide
    C) greater space to grow
    D) less competition for food

15. What do ferns NOT have?
    A) fronds   C) spores
    B) rhizoids   D) vascular tissue

Thinking Critically

16. What might happen if a land plant's waxy cuticle were destroyed?

17. Well-preserved human remains have been found in peat bogs. Explain why this occurs.

18. Plants called succulents store large amounts of water in their leaves, stems, and roots. In what environments would you expect to find succulents growing naturally?

19. Explain why mosses are usually found on moist areas.

20. How do pioneer species change environments so that other plants may grow there?

Developing Skills

If you need help, refer to the **Skill Handbook.**

21. **Concept Mapping:** Complete this map for the seedless plants of the plant kingdom.

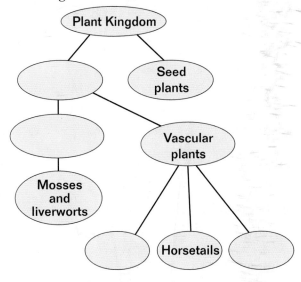

22. **Interpreting Data:** What do the data in this table tell you about where gas exchange occurs in each plant leaf?

Stomata (per mm²)		
	Upper Surface	**Lower Surface**
Pine	50	71
Bean	40	281
Fir	0	228
Tomato	12	13

23. **Making and Using Graphs:** Make two circle graphs using the table in question 22.

24. **Interpreting Scientific Illustrations:** Using **Figure 8-19,** compare and contrast the *number of seed leaves, bundle arrangement in the stem, veins in leaves*, and *number of flower parts* for monocots and dicots.

THE PRINCETON REVIEW

Test-Taking Tip

You Are Smarter Than You Think
Nothing on the science tests that you will take this year is so difficult that you can't understand it. You can learn to master any of it. Be confident and just keep practicing your test-taking skills.

Test Practice

Use these questions to test your Science Proficiency.

1. What does the cuticle found on the surface of many plant cells help to do?
   A) increase the carbon dioxide released
   B) change the method of reproduction
   C) reduce water loss for the plant
   D) keep the surface area as small as possible

2. What is one explanation for why bryophytes grow just a few centimeters tall?
   A) They lack reproductive structures.
   B) Their rhizoids are not real roots.
   C) Many creatures trample them on the forest floor.
   D) They do not have vascular tissues.

3. What is one feature that gymnosperms and flowering plants have in common?
   A) reproduce naturally from seeds
   B) have leaves that stay on the plant for more than one year
   C) produce the same types of fruit
   D) are nonvascular plants

Plant Processes

Chapter Preview

Section 9-1
Photosynthesis and Respiration

Section 9-2
Plant Responses

Skills Preview

Skill Builders
- Compare and Contrast
- Observe and Infer

Activities
- Predict
- Design an Experiment

MiniLabs
- Observe and Infer
- Measure in SI

Reading Check ✔

Before you read the chapter, make a list of all the vocabulary words. Next to each word, write what you think it means. Then, as you read, change your definitions if necessary.

Explore Activity

P lants are similar to other living things. They are made of cells, reproduce, make and use substances, and need water. If someone forgot to water the petunias shown in the photograph, what do you think would happen? From your own experience, you probably know they would wilt. Do the following activity to discover the relationship between plants and water. Find out how water goes in and out of a plant. In this chapter, you will learn about other plant processes.

Observe Plants

1. Obtain a resealable plastic bag and a small potted plant from your teacher.

2. Place the potted plant in the plastic bag.

3. Seal the bag and place it in a sunny window.

4. Look at the plant at the same time every day for a few days.

Science Journal

In your Science Journal, describe what happens in the bag. If enough water is lost by a plant and not replaced, predict what will happen to the plant.

9·1 Photosynthesis and Respiration

What You'll Learn

▶ How plants take in and give off gases
▶ Why photosynthesis and respiration are important
▶ Why photosynthesis and respiration are related

Vocabulary
stomata
transpiration
photosynthesis
respiration

Why It's Important

▶ Understanding photosynthesis and respiration in plants will help you understand their importance to life on Earth.

Gas Exchange in Plants

When you breathe, you take in and release mixtures of gases. You inhale air, a mixture of nitrogen, oxygen, carbon dioxide, and other gases. The mixture of gases that you exhale is mostly nitrogen, carbon dioxide, and water vapor. Gas exchange is one of the ways living cells obtain raw materials and get rid of waste products. For most organisms, carbon dioxide and water vapor are waste products of cell processes.

In plants, water and carbon dioxide are two of the raw materials needed for survival. Plant roots or rootlike structures absorb most of the water and it moves up through the plant to where it is needed. Water leaves a plant as water vapor. It may leave cells by diffusion and then be released through openings called **stomata** (sing., *stoma*). Stomata are on the surface(s) of a leaf or leaflike structure.

Stomata

How does carbon dioxide enter a leaf? Each stoma is surrounded by two guard cells that control the size of the opening. Water moves into and out of guard cells by osmosis. As water moves into guard cells, they swell and change shape,

Figure 9-1 Stomata open when guard cells absorb water (A). They close when water is lost (B). **Would a build-up of salt in the soil around a plant make the stomata open or close?**

Magnification: 300×

Magnification: 300×

Stoma
Guard cell

A

B

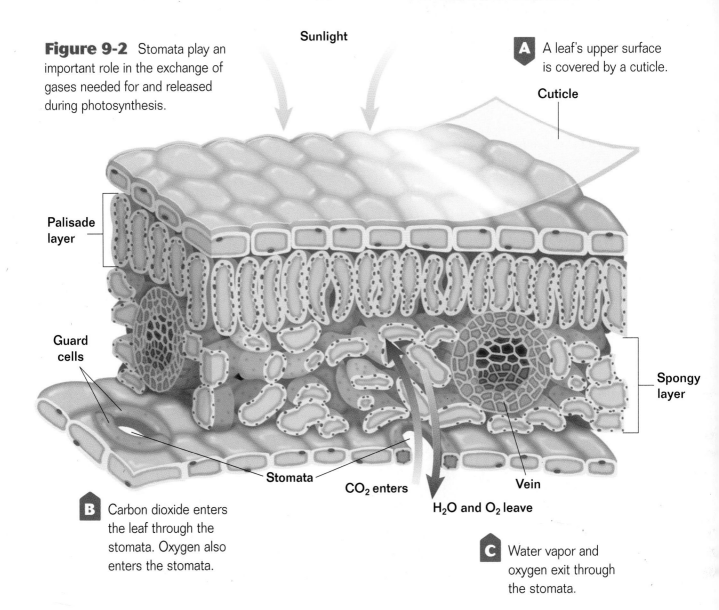

Figure 9-2 Stomata play an important role in the exchange of gases needed for and released during photosynthesis.

Sunlight

A A leaf's upper surface is covered by a cuticle.

Cuticle

Palisade layer

Guard cells

Spongy layer

Stomata

CO_2 enters

H₂O and O₂ leave

Vein

B Carbon dioxide enters the leaf through the stomata. Oxygen also enters the stomata.

C Water vapor and oxygen exit through the stomata.

resulting in a stoma. Carbon dioxide enters the leaf through the stoma and water vapor may escape during this process. When guard cells lose water, they deflate and change shape again. This action closes the stoma. **Figure 9-1** shows open and closed stomata.

Light, water, and carbon dioxide all affect the opening and closing of stomata. Stomata usually are open during the day and closed at night. Less carbon dioxide enters and less water vapor escapes from the leaf when stomata are closed. Because leaves usually have more stomata on the lower surface, more carbon dioxide reaches the spaces around the spongy layer, as shown in **Figure 9-2.** Water vapor also is found in the air spaces of the spongy layer.

If you did the Explore Activity for this chapter, you saw that water vapor condensed on the inside of the plastic bag. Loss of water vapor through stomata of a leaf is called **transpiration.** Far more water is lost by transpiration than is used during the food-making process of photosynthesis.

Using Math

A corn plant transpires about 15 L of water per week. How much water will it transpire in a 100-day growing season?

Figure 9-3 Light and chlorophyll are both essential parts of photosynthesis.

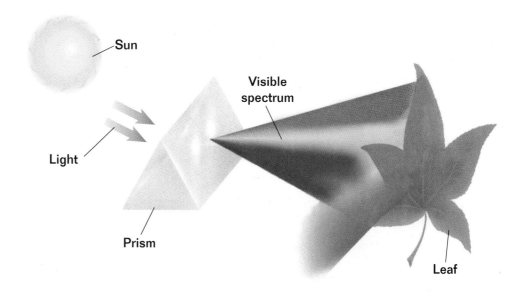

Sun

Visible spectrum

Light

Prism

Leaf

A As light from the sun passes through a prism, it separates into the colors of the visible spectrum. When light strikes a green leaf, most of the colors are absorbed. Green is reflected by the leaf and is seen by the viewer.

B Leaves of some trees, such as those on this sweet gum, change color in the autumn.

Spring

Summer

Fall

Reading Check ✔

What happens in the fall to the chlorophyll in some leaves?

Photosynthesis

Why aren't all the leaves of the trees in **Figure 9-3B** green? If you live in a place that has changing seasons, you may see trees in the fall like in the photograph on the far right. In some places, many trees and bushes change color as the days get shorter and the weather grows colder. Leaves may change from green to red, brown, yellow, or orange. Some plants may even have leaves of different colors at the same time. These colors are the result of pigments in leaves. A pigment is a substance that reflects a particular part of the visible spectrum and absorbs the rest. In the spring and summer, there is so much green pigment chlorophyll in most leaves that it hides all other pigments. In the fall, chlorophyll breaks down and the other pigments become visible. ✔

As shown in **Figure 9-3A,** light from the sun contains all colors. When you see a green leaf, orange carrot, or red rose, you are seeing the reflected color. In plant cells, pigments absorb the other colors and trap light energy.

The Food-Making Process

Chlorophyll is a pigment in plants that traps light energy. Plants use this energy to make food. **Photosynthesis,** illustrated in **Figure 9-4,** is the process in which plants use light energy to produce food.

What do plants use besides light to make food? Carbon dioxide and water are the raw materials for photosynthesis. Some of the light energy trapped in the chlorophyll is used to split water molecules. Light energy is then used to join hydrogen from the water to carbon dioxide molecules. The new molecule formed is a simple sugar called glucose. The chemical bonds of glucose contain the energy a plant uses for growth and maintenance.

Mini Lab

Observing Plant Use of Carbon Dioxide

Procedure

1. Pour 5 mL of tap water into a clean test tube.
2. Add 10 drops carbonated water and 20 drops of bromothymol blue indicator to the tap water. Place the test tube in a holder.
3. Write the color of the solution in your Science Journal.
4. Repeat steps 1 and 2. Then, add a sprig of *Elodea* to this test tube.
5. Write the color of this test tube's solution in your Science Journal.
6. Place the two test tubes in sunlight for 30 minutes. Observe the test tubes every five minutes. If using artificial lights, increase the time to one hour.

Analysis

1. In your Science Journal, describe and compare the two test tubes of solution before and after the 15 minutes.
2. What gas did you add to the solution?
3. Relate your observations to photosynthesis.

VISUALIZING
Photosynthesis

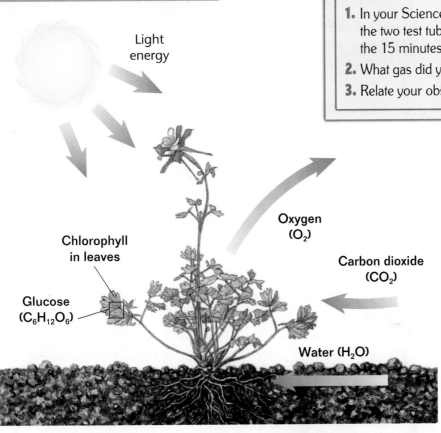

Light energy

Oxygen (O_2)

Carbon dioxide (CO_2)

Chlorophyll in leaves

Glucose ($C_6H_{12}O_6$)

Water (H_2O)

Figure 9-4 During photosynthesis, carbon dioxide from the air, water from the soil, and light energy react to form glucose and oxygen.

Photosynthesis is illustrated in the following equation:

$$6CO_2 + 6H_2O + \text{light energy} \longrightarrow C_6H_{12}O_6 + 6O_2$$

carbon dioxide   water   chlorophyll   glucose   oxygen

A plant needs six molecules of carbon dioxide (CO_2) and six molecules of water (H_2O) to make one molecule of glucose ($C_6H_{12}O_6$). Six molecules of oxygen gas (O_2) are also produced during photosynthesis. Light energy is used in photosynthesis, then stored in the chemical bonds that hold the glucose molecule together.

What happens to the products of photosynthesis? Most of the oxygen from photosynthesis is released through stomata. But some of it is used to break down food molecules and release the energy stored in the chemical bonds of the food molecules. This energy is used for all of the plant's life processes such as growth and reproduction. Glucose is the main form of food for plant cells. A plant usually produces more glucose than it can use. Excess glucose is stored in plants as other sugars and starches. When you eat beets, carrots, potatoes, or onions, you are eating stored food. Glucose is also the basis of a plant's structure. The cellulose in plant cell walls is made from glucose.

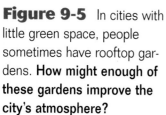

*inter*NET
CONNECTION

Besides glucose, what other sugars do plants produce? Visit the Glencoe Science Web Site at **www.glencoe. com/sec/science/nc** for more information about plant sugars.

Figure 9-5 In cities with little green space, people sometimes have rooftop gardens. **How might enough of these gardens improve the city's atmosphere?**

Importance of Photosynthesis

Why is photosynthesis important to living things? First, photosynthesis is food production. Organisms that carry on photosynthesis provide food for nearly all the other organisms on Earth. Second, photosynthetic organisms, like the plants in **Figure 9-5,** use carbon dioxide and release oxygen. This removes carbon dioxide from the atmosphere and replaces the oxygen most organisms, including humans, need to stay alive. As much as 90 percent of the oxygen entering our atmosphere today is a result of photosynthesis.

In most algae and photosynthetic bacteria, photosynthesis occurs in every cell. However, in green plants, only cells with chloroplasts carry on photosynthesis.

Respiration

Look at the photographs in **Figure 9-6.** Do these organisms have anything in common? Both of these organisms are similar in that they break down food to release energy.

Photosynthesis and Earth's Air

Earth's atmosphere had no oxygen before the evolution of organisms that carry on photosynthesis. In the last 2 billion years, the relative amount of oxygen in Earth's atmosphere has increased more than 50 times. What might happen if photosynthesis suddenly stopped?

Figure 9-6 Respiration, the release of energy from food, occurs in all living cells. You may know that animals such as the cheetah respire, but so do all plants such as the oak tree.

MiniLab

Demonstrating Respiration in Yeast

Procedure

1. Pour 10 mL of bromothymol blue into a clean test tube.
2. Add 20 drops of yeast suspension and 10 drops of sugar solution.

Analysis

1. Record in your Science Journal any color change observed after five minutes, ten minutes, and 15 minutes.
2. What caused the color change you observed?
3. Compare the results of this MiniLab with those from the one earlier in the chapter.

Respiration is a series of chemical reactions by which all organisms break down food to release energy. The breakdown of food may or may not require oxygen. For organisms that are only one prokaryotic cell—a cell without a nucleus or other organelles—respiration takes place in the cytoplasm of the cell. For organisms made of one or more eukaryotic cells—cells that have a nucleus and other organelles—respiration involves organelles called mitochondria (sing., *mitochodrion*), as shown in **Figure 9-7.** Respiration that uses oxygen to chemically break down food is called aerobic respiration. The overall chemical equation for aerobic respiration is as follows.

$$C_6H_{12}O_6 \; + \; 6O_2 \longrightarrow 6CO_2 \; + \; 6H_2O \; + \; energy$$

glucose   oxygen   carbon   water
                                dioxide

Is the equation for aerobic respiration familiar? How does it relate to the chemical equation for photosynthesis? If you look closely, you can see that aerobic respiration is the reverse of photosynthesis. Photosynthesis combines carbon dioxide and water by using light energy. The end products are glucose (food) and oxygen. During photosynthesis, energy is stored in food. Photosynthesis occurs only in cells that contain chlorophyll, such as those in the leaves of plants. Aerobic respiration

Table 9-1

Comparing Photosynthesis and Aerobic Respiration				
	Energy	Raw materials	End products	Where
Photosynthesis	stored	water and carbon dioxide, plus energy	glucose, oxygen	cells with chlorophyll
Aerobic respiration	released	glucose, oxygen	water and carbon dioxide, plus energy	all eukaryotic cells

combines oxygen and food to release the energy in the chemical bonds of the food. The end products of aerobic respiration are energy, carbon dioxide, and water. Aerobic respiration occurs in cells with mitochondria. It provides the energy needed by the cell and the entire organism. **Table 9-1** compares the processes of photosynthesis and aerobic respiration.

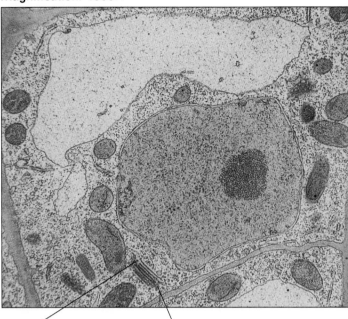

VISUALIZING
Respiration

Figure 9-7 Respiration takes place in the mitochondria of eukaryotic cells.

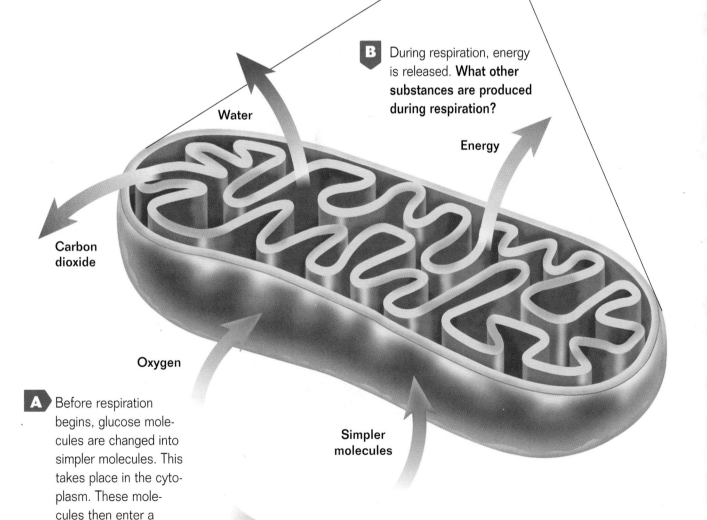

B During respiration, energy is released. **What other substances are produced during respiration?**

Water

Energy

Carbon dioxide

Oxygen

Simpler molecules

A Before respiration begins, glucose molecules are changed into simpler molecules. This takes place in the cytoplasm. These molecules then enter a mitochondrion, where they react with oxygen.

Glucose

Importance of Respiration

If food, like the items in **Figure 9-8**, contains energy, why do cells carry out the process of respiration? The energy in food molecules is in a form that cannot be used by cells. During respiration, the food energy is changed into a form all cells can use. This energy drives the life processes used by almost all organisms on Earth. Even the process of photosynthesis uses some of this energy. Aerobic respiration returns carbon dioxide to the atmosphere, where it may again be used by photosynthetic organisms.

Figure 9-8 Humans and other animals depend on the glucose produced by plants during photosynthesis. Animals use the glucose to produce energy through respiration.

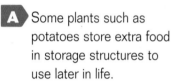
A Some plants such as potatoes store extra food in storage structures to use later in life.

B Wheat and rice are important sources of food for much of the world's population.

Section Assessment

1. Explain how carbon dioxide and water vapor are exchanged by a leaf.

2. Why are photosynthesis and respiration important?

3. What must happen to food molecules before respiration begins?

4. **Think Critically:** Humidity is water vapor in the air. How do plants contribute to humidity?

5. **Skill Builder**
   Observing and Inferring To learn how observation is a good scientific tool, do the **Chapter 9 Skill Activity** on page 586.

Using Math

How many carbon dioxide molecules (CO_2) result from the aerobic respiration of one glucose molecule ($C_6H_{12}O_6$)? Refer to the equation in the section about respiration.

Stomata in Leaves

One of the interesting things about leaves is how stomata open and close to allow gases into and out of a leaf. Stomata are usually invisible without the use of a microscope. Try this activity to see some stomata for yourself.

What You'll Investigate

Where are stomata in lettuce leaves?

Goals

- **Describe** guard cells and stomata.
- **Infer** the conditions that make them open and close.

Procedure

1. Copy the Stomata Data table into your Science Journal.

2. From a head of lettuce, tear off a piece of an outer, crisp, green leaf.

3. Bend the piece of leaf in half to remove the epidermis, the transparent tissue that covers a leaf. Carefully use a pair of forceps to peel off some of the epidermis. Prepare a wet mount of this tissue.

4. Examine your wet mount slide under low and high power on the microscope. Using **Figure 9-2** as a guide, draw and label this tissue in your Science Journal.

5. Count the total number of stomata in your field of view and then count the number of open stomata. Enter these numbers in the data table.

6. Make a second slide of the lettuce leaf epidermis. This time, place a few drops of salt solution on the leaf instead of water.

7. Repeat steps 4 and 5 with the second wet mount of tissue.

Materials

- Lettuce in dish of water
- Coverslip
- Microscope
- Microscope slide
- Salt solution
- Forceps

8. Using the following equation, calculate the percent of open stomata.

(number of stomata open ÷ total number of stomata) × 100 = percent open

Stomata Data		
	Wet mount	**Salt solution mount**
Total number of stomata		
Number of open stomata		
Percent open		

Conclude and Apply

1. How are guard cells different from the other cells of the leaf epidermis?

2. **Infer** why fewer stomata were open in the salt solution mount.

3. Which slide preparation had a greater percent of open stomata?

4. What can you **infer** about the function of stomata in a leaf?

9·2 Plant Responses

What are plant responses?

What You'll Learn

▶ The relationship between stimuli and tropisms in plants
▶ Differences between long-day and short-day plants
▶ How plant hormones and responses are related

Vocabulary
tropism
auxin
photoperiodism
long-day plant
short-day plant
day-neutral plant

Why It's Important

▶ You will be a better gardener if you understand how plants respond to certain stimuli.

It's dark. You're alone in a room watching a horror film on television. Suddenly, the telephone near you rings. You jump, and your heart begins to beat faster. Did you know that you've just responded to a stimulus? A stimulus is anything in the environment that causes a change in the behavior of an organism. The organism's change in behavior is called a response. A stimulus may come from outside or inside the organism. The ringing telephone is an example of an outside stimulus. It caused you to jump, a response. Inside stimuli include chemical reactions and hormones. Hormones are substances made by cells for use somewhere else in the organism. Your beating heart is a response to inside stimuli. All living organisms, including plants, respond to stimuli. Plants respond to outside and inside stimuli. The response of a plant to an outside stimulus is a **tropism.** A tropism may be seen as movement or a change in growth. Tropisms can be positive or negative. For example, plants might grow toward or away from a stimulus.

Tropisms

Touch is one stimulus that results in a change in a plant's behavior. The pea plants in **Figure 9-9** show a response to touch. The response to touch is thigmotropism, from the Greek

Figure 9-9
The pea plant's tendrils respond to touch by coiling around things. The response to touch is called *thigmotropism.*

Figure 9-10 Plants also show phototropism. This plant is obviously growing toward the light, an example of positive phototropism. **What do you think would happen if the plant were turned halfway around?**

word *thigma*, meaning "touch." Plants also respond to the stimuli of light, gravity, temperature, and amount of water.

Did you ever see a plant leaning toward a window? Light is an important stimulus to plants. When a plant responds to sunlight, the cells on the side of the plant opposite the light get longer than those facing the light. This causes the plant to bend toward the light. The response of a plant to light is called phototropism. A plant growing toward light is called a positive phototropism, as shown in **Figure 9-10.**

The response of an organism to gravity is called gravitropism. The downward growth of plant roots is a positive gravitropism. A stem growing upward is a negative gravitropism.

Plant Hormones

When you visit a supermarket or fruit stand, have you ever noticed that oranges are all about the same size and color? In nature, orange trees flower and produce fruit over a period of time. How do growers get fruits to respond so that most of it is ripe when it reaches the market? One way that growers do this is by using plant hormones.

Auxin and Ethylene

Plant hormones are chemical substances that affect growth. An **auxin** is a type of plant hormone. One of the ways auxin affects plants is that it causes plant stems and leaves to exhibit positive phototropism. When light shines on a plant from one side, the auxin moves to the shaded side of the stem. The auxin causes cells on the shaded side of the stem to increase in length. This causes the stem to curve toward the light.

*inter*NET
CONNECTION

Auxin and ethylene are just two of the hormones found in plants. Visit the Glencoe Science Web Site at **www.glencoe. com/sec/science/nc** for more information about other plant hormones.

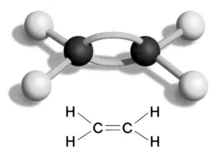

Figure 9-11 Ethylene, C_2H_4, is the plant hormone responsible for fruit ripening, such as these grapes.

Many plants produce the hormone ethylene, a chemical of carbon and hydrogen, as illustrated in **Figure 9-11.** Ethylene causes different plant responses. One response is that it causes fruit to ripen.

Today, fruit growers and shippers use this knowledge to get ripe fruit to market. Fruits such as oranges, grapes, and bananas are picked when they are still green. Green fruit is easier to handle because it does not bruise like ripe fruit does. During shipping, green fruit is exposed to ethylene gas. When the fruit arrives at the store, most of it has ripened.

Problem Solving

Predicting Plant Responses

Jason and his family returned from their two-week vacation and found that several potted plants on the patio were on their sides. After unpacking the car, Jason began to set up the potted plants. To his surprise, the plants looked like they were growing sideways. Later that day, Jason's grandmother telephoned. Jason told her about the plants. She told him not to worry because the plants would soon start to grow upright again.

Solve the Problem

1. Explain why the plants grew as they did.

2. What hormone may have played a part in this plant response?

Think Critically: Predict what Jason might find if he removed a plant's pot and looked at its roots. Explain.

Photoperiods

Sunflowers bloom in the summer, and cherry trees flower in the spring. Some plant species produce flowers at specific times during the year. **Photoperiodism** is a plant's response to the number of hours of daylight and darkness it receives daily.

Earth makes one revolution around the sun every year. As it moves in its orbit about the sun, Earth also rotates. One rotation takes 24 hours. Because Earth is tilted about 23.5° from a line perpendicular to its orbit, the hours of daylight and darkness vary with the seasons. You may have noticed that the sun sets later in summer than in winter. These changes in lengths of daylight and darkness affect plant growth.

Most plants require a specific length of darkness to begin the flowering process. Generally, plants that require less than ten to 12 hours of darkness are called **long-day plants.** You may be familiar with long-day plants such as spinach, lettuce, and beets. Those plants that need 12 or more hours of darkness are called **short-day plants.** Some short-day plants are poinsettias, strawberries, and ragweed. **Figure 9-12** shows both long-day plants and short-day plants. ☑

EARTH SCIENCE
◄**INTEGRATION**

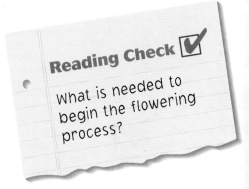

Reading Check ☑

What is needed to begin the flowering process?

Figure 9-12 Long-day plants such as zinnias (A) and short-day plants such as primroses (B) flower in response to specific periods of darkness.

Other plants like the marigolds shown in **Figure 9-13** are day-neutral. **Day-neutral plants** have no specific photoperiod, and the flowering process can begin within a range of hours of darkness.

In nature, photoperiodism is one factor that affects where flowering plants can grow and produce fruit. Even if the proper temperature and other growing conditions for a plant are in a particular environment, the plant will not flower and produce fruit without the correct photoperiod. Sometimes, the photoperiod of a plant has a narrow range. For example, some soybeans will flower with 14.5 hours of daylight but will not flower with only 14 hours of daylight. Farmers must choose the variety of soybeans with a photoperiod that matches the hours of daylight where they plant their crop.

Today, greenhouse growers can provide any length of artificial daylight or darkness. This means that all types of flowers are available year-round. You can buy short-day plants during the summer and long-day plants during the winter.

Figure 9-13 Day-neutral plants, as seen in this garden, produce flowers all summer long.

Section Assessment

1. Describe the difference between a response and a tropism.

2. Compare photoperiodism and phototropism.

3. Some red raspberries produce fruit in late spring, then again in the fall. What term describes their photoperiod?

4. **Think Critically:** What is the relationship between plant hormones and tropisms?

5.  **Skill Builder**
   Comparing and Contrasting Different plant parts exhibit positive and negative tropisms. Compare and contrast the responses of roots, stems, and leaves to light. If you need help, refer to Comparing and Contrasting in the **Skill Handbook** on page 556.

Science Journal
For three years, a farmer in Costa Rica grew healthy strawberry plants. But, each year he was disappointed because the plants never produced any fruit. In your Science Journal, explain why this happened.

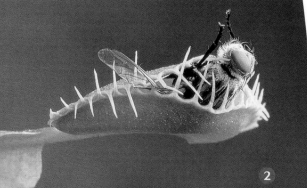

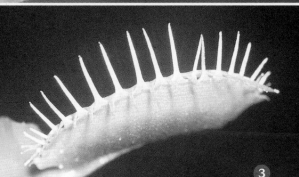

Carnivorous Plants

Carnivorous plants grow in soils that lack or are low in certain nutrients, particularly nitrogen. Over time, these plants have evolved ways to secure the nutrients they need. A Venus's-flytrap is one kind of carnivorous plant. It is currently on the list of endangered species. The ones available in stores are grown in nurseries because collecting Venus's-flytraps in the wild is illegal.

EATING HABITS OF A VENUS'S-FLYTRAP

1 The leaves form a hinged trap. Each half of the trap has three trigger hairs (see arrow) in a triangular arrangement.

2 When an insect or other small animal touches two of these hairs in quick succession, it causes a series of reactions that snap the trap shut within 0.4 s.

3 Stiff hairs along the outer edges of the leaf interlock, preventing the animal's escape.

4 Glands on the leaf secrete enzymes that help digest the prey. The glands are stimulated as the prey struggles to get free.

5 Digestion takes about ten days. During this time, the plant absorbs the digested nutrients. The leaf opens again when digestion and absorption are complete. The insect remains are then blown away.

Think Critically

1. Insects and other small animals provide carnivorous plants with nitrogen compounds. From what other sources do these plants get nutrients?

2. A pitcher plant is another carnivorous plant. Look again at the name of this plant. How do you think this plant traps its prey?

Career CONNECTION

Knowing about soils is important when growing Venus's-flytraps or any plants. Soil science is called agronomy. An agronomist studies the biological, chemical, and physical components and properties of soil. Research this career, and then make a list of jobs that require a degree in agronomy or knowledge of soil science.

Plant Tropisms

Possible Materials

- Petri dish
- Tape
- String
- Corn seeds
- Bean seeds
- Paper towels
- Water

Have you ever seen a Venus's-flytrap's leaves close around an insect? Its movement was a response to a stimulus. In this case, the stimulus was the movement of the insect against sensitive, hairlike structures on the leaves. Tropisms are specific plant responses to stimuli outside of the plant. They can be positive or negative. What stimuli will cause responses by plants?

Recognize the Problem

How do plants respond to stimuli?

Form a Hypothesis

Based on your knowledge of tropisms, state a hypothesis about how the plant will respond to a stimulus.

Goals

- **Design** an experiment that tests the effects of a variable.
- **Observe** and analyze a plant response to a stimulus.

Safety Precautions

Some kinds of seeds are poisonous. Do not put any seed in your mouth.

Test Your Hypothesis

Plan

1. As a group, agree upon and write out a hypothesis statement.

2. As a group, **list** the steps needed to test your hypothesis. Be specific, describing exactly what you will do at each step. **List** your materials.

3. It is important to keep the seeds moist during the experiment. **Devise a method** to keep your seeds moist.

4. **Read** over your entire experiment to make sure that all your steps are in a logical order.

5. **Identify** any constants, variables, and controls of the experiment.

6. Is it necessary to run any tests more than one time?

7. If you need a data table, design one in your Science Journal so that it is ready to use as your group collects data.

8. Will the data be summarized in a graph? If yes, what kind of graph would be most useful?

Do

1. Make sure your teacher approves your plan before you proceed.

2. Carry out the experiment as planned.

3. While you are conducting the experiment, write down any observations that you make and complete the data table in your Science Journal.

Analyze Your Data

1. **Compare** your results with those of other groups.

2. **Identify** how the plants responded to the stimulus.

Draw Conclusions

1. What name would you give to the response you observed?

2. **Classify** the responses as positive or negative.

3. Infer why many plant growers sprout seeds under artificial light from lamps that are placed just a short distance above the soil.

Chapter 9 Reviewing Main Ideas

For a **preview** of this chapter, study this Reviewing Main Ideas before you read the chapter. After you have studied this chapter, you can use the Reviewing Main Ideas to **review** the chapter.

GLENCOE TECHNOLOGY

The Glencoe MindJogger, Audiocassettes, and CD-ROM provide additional opportunities for review.

Section 9-1 PHOTOSYNTHESIS AND RESPIRATION

Gases like carbon dioxide and water vapor enter and leave a plant through openings called **stomata.** Stomata are usually found in the epidermis covering a leaf. Two guard cells surround each stoma. Water diffusing into and out of the guard cells causes stomata to open and close. *What role do stomata play in transpiration?*

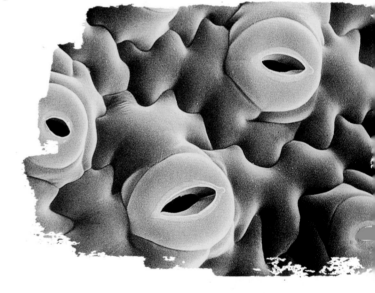

PHOTOSYNTHESIS

In plants, food is produced during the process of **photosynthesis.** Photosynthesis takes place in the chloroplasts of plant cells. Light energy is trapped by chlorophyll, the green pigment in chloroplasts. This energy is used to produce glucose and oxygen from carbon dioxide and water. The energy is stored in the chemical bonds of glucose. Photosynthesis provides the food for most organisms on Earth. *Why are plants called producers?*

Reading Check ✓

What approach to read-
ing is most helpful to
you? Is it asking your-
self questions, outlining,
or something else?
Share your approach
with another student.

RESPIRATION

All organisms use **respiration** to release the energy stored in food molecules. The process begins in the cytoplasm of cells. First, food molecules are broken down into simpler forms. In prokaryotic cells, the process continues in the cytoplasm and some energy is released. Eukaryotic cells generally use oxygen to complete respiration. The release of energy occurs in the mitochondria. Carbon dioxide and water vapor are also products of respiration in eukaryotic cells. *What are the three products of respiration for most eukaryotic cells?*

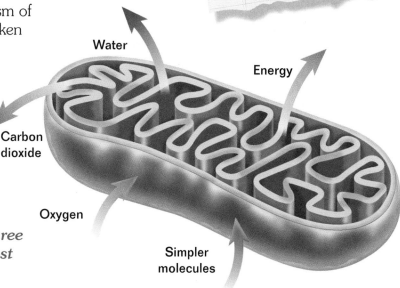

Water

Energy

Carbon
dioxide

Oxygen

Simpler
molecules

Glucose

Section 9-2 PLANT RESPONSES

Plants respond to stimuli. The response may be a movement, change in growth, or the beginning of some process, such as flowering. A stimulus from outside the plant is called a **tropism.** Outside stimuli include such things as light, gravity, and touch. The lengths of daylight and darkness each day may affect flowering times of plants. Hormones are stimuli from inside plants. These chemicals affect plants in many ways. **Auxin** and ethylene are two plant hormones.*What things may act as outside stimuli for plants?*

Chapter 9 Assessment

Using Vocabulary

a. auxin
b. day-neutral plant
c. long-day plant
d. photoperiodism
e. photosynthesis
f. respiration
g. short-day plant
h. stomata
i. transpiration
j. tropism

Match each phrase with the correct term from the list of Vocabulary words.

1. a plant hormone
2. using light to make glucose and oxygen
3. loss of water through stomata
4. plant that requires long nights to flower
5. releases energy from food

Checking Concepts

Choose the word or phrase that best answers the question.

6. What enters a plant when stomata open?
   A) sugar
   B) water
   C) carbon dioxide
   D) light

7. Which of these is a product of respiration?
   A) CO_2
   B) O_2
   C) C_2H_4
   D) H_2

8. Water, carbon dioxide, and energy are all products of what plant process?
   A) cell division
   B) photosynthesis
   C) growth
   D) respiration

9. What type of plant needs short nights to flower?
   A) day-neutral
   B) short-day
   C) long-day
   D) nonvascular

10. What do you call such things as light, touch, and gravity that cause plant responses?
    A) tropisms
    B) growth behaviors
    C) responses
    D) stimuli

11. What is a plant's response to gravity called?
    A) phototropism
    B) gravitropism
    C) thigmotropism
    D) hydrotropism

12. What are plant substances that affect plant growth called?
    A) tropisms
    B) glucose
    C) germination
    D) hormones

13. Leaves change colors because what substance breaks down?
    A) hormone
    B) carotenoid
    C) chlorophyll
    D) cytoplasm

14. What is a function of stomata?
    A) photosynthesis
    B) to guard the interior cells
    C) to allow sugar to escape
    D) to permit the release of oxygen

15. What are the products of photosynthesis?
    A) glucose and oxygen
    B) carbon dioxide and water
    C) chlorophyll and glucose
    D) carbon dioxide and oxygen

Thinking Critically

16. Growers of bananas pick green bananas, then treat them with ethylene during shipping. Why?

17. Identify each response as a positive or negative tropism.
    a. stem grows up
    b. roots grow down
    c. plant grows toward light
    d. a vine grows around a pole

18. Scientists who study sedimentary rocks and fossils suggest that oxygen did not occur on Earth until plantlike protists appeared. Why?

19. Explain why crab apple trees bloom in the spring but not in the summer.

20. Why do day-neutral and long-day plants grow best in countries near the equator?

Developing Skills

If you need help, refer to the **Skill Handbook.**

21. **Hypothesizing:** Make a hypothesis about when guard cells open and close in desert plants.

22. **Designing an Experiment to Test a Hypothesis:** Design an experiment to test your hypothesis from question 21.

23. **Observing and Inferring:** Based on your knowledge of plants, infer how the number and location of stomata differ in land and water plants.

24. **Classifying:** Make a chart that classifies these plants according to their photoperiod: flower year-round—corn, dandelion, tomato; flower in the spring, fall, or winter—chrysanthemum, rice, poinsettia; flower in summer—spinach, lettuce, petunias.

25. **Comparing and Contrasting:** Compare and contrast the action of auxin and the action of ethylene on a plant.

26. **Concept Mapping:** Complete the following concept map using the terms and plants in question 24.

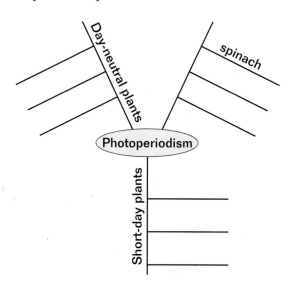

THE
PRINCETON
REVIEW

Test-Taking Tip

You Are Smarter Than You Think
Nothing on the science tests you will take this year is too difficult for you to understand. You can learn to master any of it. Be self-confident, and just keep practicing.

Test Practice

Use these questions to test your Science Proficiency.

1. What diffuses into and out of guard cells, causing them to open and close?
   A) carbon dioxide
   B) ethylene
   C) water
   D) glucose

2. What does respiration provide for every cell?
   A) energy
   B) food
   C) oxygen
   D) water

3. What is a plant's change in behavior to an outside stimulus called?
   A) hormone
   B) tropism
   C) transpiration
   D) reactant

4. What term is used for a plant's response to the number of hours of daylight and darkness it receives daily?
   A) gravitropism
   B) thigmotropism
   C) transpiration
   D) photoperiodism

Life and the Environment

Chapter Preview

Section 10-1
The Living and Nonliving Environments

Section 10-2
Interactions Among Living Organisms

Section 10-3
Matter and Energy

Skills Preview

Skill Builders
- Classify

Activities
- Graph

MiniLabs
- Infer

Reading Check ✔

Define several terms that begin with the prefix *a* (meaning "without"), such as *abiotic*.

Explore Activity

Mountain goats rely on winter winds to uncover food plants buried beneath the snow. Surefooted and strong, they scale high cliffs to get their next meal. A mountain goat's range consists of high terrain where few other animals dare to tread. This reduces competition from different organisms for food. How does the number of related organisms in an area affect each individual? You share your science classroom with other students. How much space is available to each student?

Measure Space

1. Use a meterstick to measure the length and width of the classroom.

2. Multiply the length times the width to find the area of the room in square meters.

3. Count the number of individuals in your class. Divide the number of square meters in the classroom by the number of individuals.

Science Journal

In your Science Journal, record how much space each person has. Determine the amount of space each person would have if the number of individuals in your class doubled. Predict how having that amount of space would affect you and your classmates.

The Living and Nonliving Environment

What You'll Learn

▶ How to identify biotic and abiotic factors in an ecosystem
▶ The characteristics of populations
▶ The levels of biological organization

Vocabulary
biosphere
ecology
abiotic factor
biotic factor
population
community
ecosystem

Why It's Important

▶ Abiotic and biotic factors work together to form your ecosystem.

The Biosphere

Think of all the organisms on Earth. Millions of species exist. Where do all these organisms live? Living things can be found 11 000 m below the surface of the ocean and on tops of mountains 9000 m high. The part of Earth that supports organisms is known as the **biosphere** (BI uh sfihr). The biosphere seems huge, but it is actually only a small portion of Earth. The biosphere includes the topmost portion of Earth's crust, all the waters that cover Earth's surface, and the surrounding atmosphere. Overall though, the thickness could be compared to the thickness of the skin of an apple.

Within the biosphere, many different environments can be found. For example, red-tailed hawks are found in environments where tall trees live near open grassland. The hawks nest high in the trees and soar over the land in search of rodents and rabbits to eat. In environments with plenty of moisture, such as the banks of streams, willow trees provide food and shelter for birds, mammals, and insects. All organisms interact

Figure 10-1 The biosphere is the region of Earth that contains all living organisms. An ecologist is a scientist who studies relationships among organisms and between organisms and the physical features of the biosphere.

with the environment. The science of **ecology** is the study of the interactions that take place among organisms and between organisms and the physical features of the environment. Ecologists, such as the one in **Figure 10-1,** are the scientists who study interactions between organisms and the environment.

Abiotic Factors

A forest environment is made up of trees, birds, insects, and other living things that depend on one another for food and shelter. But, these organisms also depend on factors that surround them such as soil, sunlight, water, temperature, and air. These factors—the nonliving, physical features of the environment—are called **abiotic factors.** Abiotic—*a* meaning "not" and *biotic* meaning "living"—factors have effects on living things and often determine the organisms that are able to live in a certain environment. Some abiotic factors are shown in **Figure 10-2.**

Figure 10-2 Abiotic factors help determine which species can survive in an area.

A **Soil**
Soil consists of minerals mixed with decaying, dead organisms. It contains both living and nonliving components.

B **Light**
Seasonal events, such as flowering in plants or migration of birds, are often triggered by a change in the number of hours of daylight.

C **Water**
Many organisms live in water, such as this lake in Pennsylvania, rather than air.

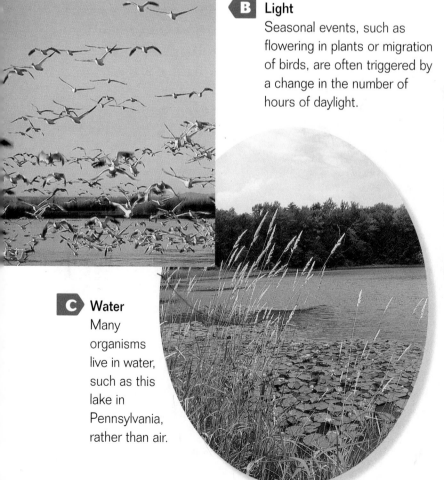

D **Temperature**
Temperatures change with daily and seasonal cycles. Desert-dwelling rattlesnakes, like this sidewinder in the Colorado desert, are active only in the cool, early morning hours. During the hottest part of the day, they rest in the shade.

Water

Water is an important abiotic factor. The bodies of most organisms are 50 to 95 percent water. Water is an important part of cytoplasm and the fluid that surrounds cells. Respiration, photosynthesis, digestion, and other important life processes can take place only in the presence of water.

Soil

The type of soil in a particular location helps determine which plants and other organisms live in that location. Most soil is a combination of sand, clay, and humus. Soil type is determined by the relative amounts of sand, clay, and humus in the soil. Humus is the decayed remains of dead organisms. The greater the humus content, the more fertile the soil.

Light and Temperature

The abiotic factors of light and temperature also impact the environment. Through the process of photosynthesis, the radiant energy of sunlight is transformed into chemical energy that drives virtually all of life's processes. The availability of sunlight is a major factor in determining where green plants and other photosynthetic organisms live, as shown in **Figure 10-3.** Sunlight does not penetrate far into deep water. Most green algae benefit from living near the surface. In a similar situation, because little sunlight reaches the shady darkness of the forest floor, plant growth there is limited.

Figure 10-3 Many wildflowers that live on the forest floor, such as these padres shooting stars and Johnny jump-ups, produce seeds early in the spring. At this time, they receive the maximum amount of sunlight. When the leaves are fully out on the trees, they receive little direct sun.

Biotic Factors

Abiotic factors do not provide everything an organism needs for survival. Mushrooms would not be able to grow without the decaying bodies of other organisms to feed on. Honeybees could not survive without pollen from flowers. Some species of owls and woodpeckers prefer to nest in the hollow trunks of dead trees. Organisms depend on other organisms for food, shelter, protection, or reproduction. Living or once-living organisms in the environment are called **biotic factors.** ✔

Levels of Biological Organization

The living world is highly organized. Atoms are arranged into molecules, which are in turn organized into cells. Cells form tissues, tissues form organs, and organs form systems. Similarly, the biotic and abiotic factors studied by ecologists can be arranged into layers of organization, as shown in **Figure 10-4.**

Reading Check ✔

What are the living organisms in the environment called?

Figure 10-4 The living world is organized into several levels.

Organism
An organism is a single individual from a population.

Population
A population is all of the individuals of one species that live and reproduce in the same area at the same time.

Community
A community is made up of populations of different species that interact in some way.

Ecosystem
An ecosystem consists of communities and the abiotic factors that affect them.

Biosphere
The biosphere is the highest level of biological organization. It is made up of all the ecosystems on Earth.

Figure 10-5 This coral reef is an example of an ecosystem. It is made up of hundreds of populations of organisms, as well as ocean water, sunlight, and other abiotic factors.

Populations

Individual organisms of the same species that live in the same place and can produce young form a **population.** Members of several populations on a coral reef are seen in **Figure 10-5.** Members of populations of organisms compete with each other for food, water, mates, and space. The resources of the environment and how the organisms use these resources determine how large a population can be.

Communities

Most populations of organisms do not live alone. They live and interact with populations of other organisms. Groups of populations that interact with each other in a given area form a **community.** Populations of organisms in a community depend on each other for food and shelter and for other needs.

Ecosystem

An **ecosystem** is made up of a biotic community and the abiotic factors that affect it. The rest of this chapter will discuss in more detail the kinds of interactions that take place between abiotic and biotic factors in an ecosystem.

Section Assessment

1. What is the difference between an abiotic factor and a biotic factor? Give at least five examples of each.

2. What is the difference between a population and a community? A community and an ecosystem?

3. **Think Critically:** Could oxygen in the atmosphere be considered an abiotic factor? Why or why not? What about carbon dioxide?

4. **Skill Builder**
   Observing and Inferring Each person lives in a population as part of a community. Describe your population and community. If you need help, refer to Observing and Inferring in the **Skill Handbook** on page 556.

Using Computers

Spreadsheet Obtain two months of temperature and rainfall data from your local newspaper or the Internet. Enter the data in a spreadsheet and then average the totals for temperature and the totals for rainfall. What kind of climate do you think you have based on your calculations? If you need help, refer to page 574.

Soil Composition

Soil is more than minerals mixed with the decaying bodies of dead organisms. It contains other biotic and abiotic factors.

What You'll Investigate

What are the components of soil?

Goals

- **Determine** what factors are present in soil.

Materials

- Small paper cups containing freshly dug soil (3)
- Newspaper
- Beaker of water
- Hand lens
- Jar with lid
- Scale

Procedure

1. **Obtain** 3 cups of soil from your teacher. **Record** the source of your sample in your Science Journal.

2. **Pour** one of your samples onto the newspaper. **Sort** through the objects in the soil. Try to separate abiotic and biotic items. Use a hand lens to help identify the items. **Describe** your observations in your Science Journal.

3. Carefully place the second sample in the jar, disturbing it as little as possible. Quickly fill the jar with water and screw the lid on tightly. Without moving the jar, **observe** its contents for several minutes. **Record** your observations in your Science Journal.

4. **Weigh** the third sample. **Record** the weight in your Science Journal. Leave the sample undisturbed for several days, then weigh it again. **Record** the second weight in your Science Journal.

Conclude and Apply

1. Can you **infer** the presence of any organisms? Explain.

2. **Describe** the abiotic factors in your sample. What biotic factors did you **observe?**

3. Did you **record** any change in the soil weight over time? If so, why?

10·2 Interactions Among Living Organisms

What You'll Learn

▶ The characteristics of populations

▶ The types of relationships that occur among populations in a community

▶ The habitat and niche of a species in a community

Vocabulary
population density
limiting factor
carrying capacity
symbiosis
habitat
niche

Why It's Important

▶ You must directly or indirectly interact with other organisms to survive.

Characteristics of Populations

As shown in **Figure 10-6,** populations can be described by their characteristics. These include the size of the population, spacing (how the organisms are arranged in a given area), and density (how many individuals there are in a specific area). Suppose you spent several months observing a population of field mice living in a pasture. You would probably observe changes in the size of the population. Older mice die, baby mice are born, some are eaten by predators, and some mice wander away to new homes. The size of a population— the number of individual organisms it contains—is always changing, although some populations change more rapidly than others. In contrast to a mouse population, the number of pine trees in a forest changes fairly slowly, but a forest fire could quickly reduce the population of pine trees in the forest.

Figure 10-6 Populations have several characteristics that define them.

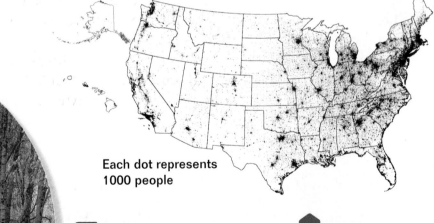

Each dot represents 1000 people

A Spacing
A characteristic of populations is spacing. In some populations, such as the oak trees of an oak-hickory forest, individuals are spaced fairly evenly throughout the area.

B Density
Human population density is higher in and around cities than in rural areas. **Which part of the United States has the highest population density?**

Population Density

At the beginning of this chapter, when you figured out how much space is available to each student in your classroom, you were measuring another population characteristic. The size of a population that occupies an area of limited size is called **population density.** The more individuals there are in a given amount of space, as seen in **Figure 10-7,** the more dense the population. For example, if 100 mice live in an area of a square kilometer, the population density is 100 mice per km².

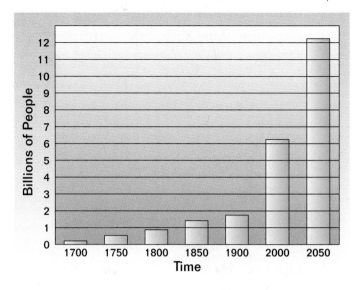

Figure 10-7 The size of the human population is increasing at a rate of about 1.6 percent per year. At the present time, it is about 6 billion. In 2050, the population will be about 12 billion.

Limiting Factors

Populations cannot continue to grow larger and larger forever. In any ecosystem, there are limits to the amount of food, water, living space, mates, nesting sites, and other resources available. A **limiting factor** is any biotic or abiotic factor that restricts the number of individuals in a population. A limiting factor can also indirectly affect other populations in the community. For example, a drought might restrict the growth of seed-producing plants in a forest clearing. Fewer plants means that food may become a limiting factor for a mouse population that feeds on the seeds. Food also may become a limiting factor for hawks and owls that feed on the mice, as well as for the deer in **Figure 10-8.** ☑

Competition is the struggle among organisms to obtain the resources they need to survive and reproduce. As population density increases, so does competition among individuals.

Reading Check ☑

What is a limiting factor?

Figure 10-8 In many parts of the United States, deer populations, such as this one in northern Wisconsin, have become large enough to exceed the environment's ability to produce adequate food. Individuals starve or, weakened from lack of food, fall victim to disease.

Carrying Capacity

Suppose a population of robins continues to increase in size, year after year. At some point, food, nesting space, or other resources become so scarce that some individuals may not be able to survive or reproduce. When this happens, the environment has reached its carrying capacity, as seen in **Figure 10-9. Carrying capacity** is the largest number of individuals an environment can support and maintain for a long period of time. If a population begins to exceed the environment's carrying capacity, some individuals will be left without adequate resources. They may die or be forced to move elsewhere.

Biotic Potential

What would happen if there were no limiting factors? A population living in an environment that supplies more than enough resources for survival will continue to grow. The maximum rate at which a population increases when there is plenty of food, water, ideal weather, and no disease or enemies is its biotic potential. However, most populations never reach their biotic potential, or do so for only a short period of time. Eventually, the carrying capacity of the environment is reached and the population stops increasing.

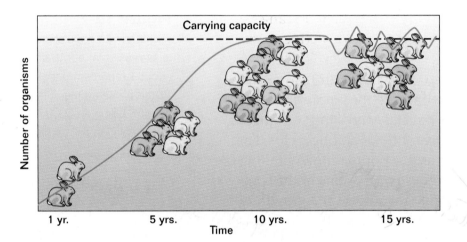

Figure 10-9 This graph shows how the size of a population increases until it reaches the carrying capacity of its environment. At first, growth is fairly slow. It speeds up as the number of adults capable of reproduction increases. Once the population reaches carrying capacity, its size remains fairly stable.
Why don't most populations achieve their biotic potential?

Interactions in Communities

Populations are regulated not only by the supply of food, water, and sunlight, but also by the actions of other populations. The most obvious way one population can limit another is by predation (prih DAY shun). One organism feeds on another. Owls and hawks are predators that feed on mice. Mice are their prey. Predators are biotic factors that limit the size of prey populations. Because predators are more likely to capture old, ill, or young prey, predation also helps maintain the health of a prey population. Predators leave the strongest individuals to reproduce. **Figure 10-10** shows how some predators work together to hunt their food.

Figure 10-10 Hyenas work together to hunt their food. This is called cooperation and helps all members of their population survive.

Symbiosis

Many types of relationships exist between organisms in ecosystems. Many species of organisms in nature have close, complex relationships in order to survive. When two or more species live close together, their relationship is called a symbiotic relationship. **Symbiosis** (sihm bee OH sus) is any close relationship between two or more different species.

Using Math

Calculating Population Growth

Example Problem: Estimates show the total human population will be about 6 billion in the year 2000. This number is thought to increase by 1.6 percent each year. What will the population be in the year 2005?

Problem-Solving Steps

1. What is known? Current population is 6 000 000 000. Yearly increase is 1.6%.
2. What is unknown? The population in 2001, 2002, 2003, 2004, and 2005.
3. **Solution:** Calculate the population increase for one year. Then, repeat the process four more times using the answer you came up with as a starting point.

6 000 000 000	6 000 000 000
$\times$ 0.016	+ 96 000 000
36 000 000 000	6 096 000 000 people in 2001
60 000 000 000	
96 000 000 more people	

The estimated population in the year 2005 is 6 495 607 732 people.

Practice Problem

An endangered species of fish currently has a population of 136 individuals. If the population increases by two percent every year, how many individuals will there be in three years?
Strategy Hint: When calculating percentages, remember to move your decimal two spaces to the left (0.02).

Mini Lab

Observing Symbiosis

Procedure

1. Carefully wash then examine the roots of a legume plant and a nonlegume plant.
2. Examine a prepared microscope slide of the bacteria that live in the roots of legumes.

Analysis

1. What differences do you observe in the roots of the two plants?
2. The bacteria help legumes thrive in poor soil. What type of symbiotic relationship is this? Explain.

Not all relationships benefit one organism at the expense of another as in predation. Symbiotic relationships can be identified by the type of interaction between organisms, as shown in **Figure 10-11.** Many types of symbiotic relationships occur between organisms. These are usually described by how each organism in the relationship is affected by the relationship.

A symbiotic relationship that benefits both species is called mutualism. An example of mutualism is the lichen. Each lichen species is made up of a fungus and an alga or cyanobacterium. The fungus provides a protected living space, and the alga or bacterium provides the fungus with food.

B Tropical orchids grow on the trunks of trees. The tree provides the orchid with a sunlit living space high in the forest canopy. This relationship is an example of commensalism because the orchid benefits from the relationship without harming or helping the tree.

Figure 10-11 Many examples of symbiotic relationships occur in nature.

A The partnership between the desert yucca plant and the yucca moth is an example of mutualism. Both species benefit from the relationship. The yucca depends on the moth to pollinate its flowers. The moth depends on the yucca for a protected place to lay its eggs and a source of food for its larvae.

C Tapeworms are parasites that feed inside the intestines of some mammals. This one was found inside a cat.

In shallow tropical seas, brightly colored anemone fish find protection from predators by swimming among the stinging tentacles of sea anemones. The presence of the fish does not affect the anemone in a harmful or beneficial way. Commensalism is a symbiotic relationship that benefits one partner but does not harm or help the other.

Parasitism is a symbiotic relationship that benefits the parasite and does definite harm to the parasite's host. Many parasites live on or in the body of the host, absorbing nutrients from the host's body fluids. Tapeworms live as parasites in the intestines of mammals. Mistletoe is a parasitic plant that penetrates tree branches with its roots.

Habitats and Niches

In a community, every species plays a particular role. Each also has a particular place to live. The physical location where an organism lives is called its **habitat.** The habitat of an earthworm is soil. The role of an organism in the ecosystem is called its **niche.** The niche of an earthworm is shown in **Figure 10-12.** What a species eats, how it gets its food, and how it interacts with other organisms are all parts of its niche. An earthworm takes soil into its body to obtain nutrients. The soil that leaves the worm enriches the soil. The movement of the worm through soil also loosens it and aerates it, creating a better environment for plant growth.

Figure 10-12 Each organism in an ecosystem uses and affects its environment in particular ways. **What role does the earthworm play in the environment?**

EARTH SCIENCE ◄ **INTEGRATION**

Section Assessment

1. Describe how limiting factors can affect the organisms in a population.

2. Describe the difference between a habitat and a niche.

3. **Think Critically:** A parasite can obtain food only from its host. Most parasites weaken but do not kill their hosts. Why?

4. **Skill Builder**
   Predicting There are methods used to determine the size of a population without counting each organism. Do the **Chapter 10 Skill Activity** on page 587 to learn how to infer population size.

Using Math

In a 12 m² area of weeds, 46 dandelion plants, 212 grass plants, and 14 bindweed plants are growing. What is the population density per square meter of each species?

Identifying a Limiting Factor

Organisms depend on many biotic and abiotic factors in their environment to survive. When these factors are limited or are not available, it can affect an organism's survival. By experimenting with some of these limiting factors, you will see how organisms depend on all parts of their environment.

Recognize the Problem

How do abiotic factors such as light, water, and temperature affect the germination of seeds?

Form a Hypothesis

Based on what you have learned about limiting factors, make a hypothesis about how one specific abiotic factor may affect the germination of a bean seed. Be sure to consider factors that you can change easily.

Goals

- **Observe** the effects of an abiotic factor on the germination and growth of bean seedlings.

- **Design** an experiment that demonstrates whether or not a specific abiotic factor limits the germination of bean seeds.

Safety Precautions

Wash hands after handling soil and seeds.

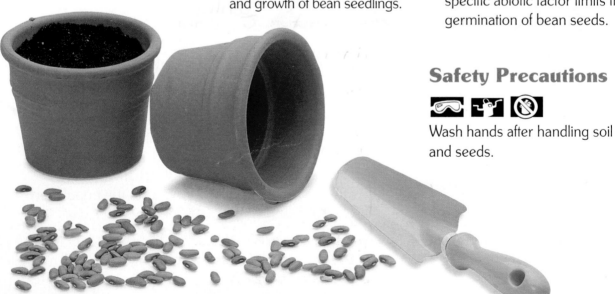

Test Your Hypothesis

Plan

1. As a group, agree upon and write out a hypothesis statement.

2. Decide on a way to test your group's hypothesis. Keep available materials in mind as you plan your procedure. **List** your materials.

3. **Prepare** a data table in your Science Journal.

4. Remember to **test** only one variable at a time and use suitable controls.

5. **Read** over your entire experiment to make sure that all steps are in logical order.

6. **Identify** any constants, variables, and controls in your experiment.

7. Be sure the factor you test is measurable.

Do

1. Make sure your teacher has approved your plan before you proceed.

2. Carry out the experiment as planned.

3. While the experiment is going on, write down any observations that you make and complete the data table in your Science Journal.

Analyze Your Data

1. **Compare** your results with those of other groups.

2. **Infer** how the abiotic factor you tested affected the germination of bean seeds.

3. **Graph** your results in a bar graph that compares the number of bean seeds that germinated in the experimental container with the number of seeds that germinated in the control container.

Draw Conclusions

1. **Identify** which factor had the greatest effect on the seeds.

2. **Determine** whether you could substitute one factor for another and still grow the seeds.

Matter and Energy

What You'll Learn

► How energy flows through ecosystems
► The cycling of matter in the biosphere

Vocabulary
food chain
food web
ecological pyramid
water cycle
nitrogen cycle

Why It's Important

► You depend on the recycling of matter and energy to survive.

Energy Flow Through Ecosystems

As you can see, life on Earth is not simply a collection of living organisms. Even organisms that seem to spend most of their time alone interact with other members of their species. They also interact with other organisms. Most of the interactions between members of different species are feeding relationships. They involve the transfer of energy from one organism to another. Energy moves through an ecosystem in the form of food. Producers are organisms that capture energy from the sun. They use the sun's energy for photosynthesis to produce chemical bonds in carbohydrates. Consumers are organisms that

Figure 10-13 In any community, energy flows from producers to consumers. Follow several food chains in the pond ecosystem shown here.

B The second link of a food chain is usually an herbivore, an organism that feeds only on producers. Here, snails and small aquatic crustaceans are feeding on the algae and pond plants.

A The first link in any food chain is a producer. In this pond ecosystem, the producers are phytoplankton, algae, and a variety of plants—both aquatic and those on the shore.

C The third link of a food chain is a carnivore, an animal that feeds on other animals. Some of the carnivores in this pond are bluegill, turtles, and frogs.

obtain energy when they feed on producers or other consumers. The transfer of energy does not end there. When organisms die, other organisms called decomposers obtain energy when they break down the bodies of the dead organisms. This movement of energy through a community can be drawn as food chains, and food webs.

Food Chains and Food Webs

A **food chain** is a simple way of showing how energy in the form of food passes from one organism to another. The pond community pictured in **Figure 10-13** shows examples of several aquatic food chains. When drawing a food chain, arrows between organisms indicate the direction of energy transfer. An example of a pond food chain would be as follows.

phytoplankton ➤ insects ➤ bluegill ➤ bass

Food chains usually have three or four links. Most have no more than five links. This is due to the decrease in energy available at each link. The amount of energy left by the fifth link is only a small portion of the total amount of energy available at the first link. This is because at each transfer of energy, a portion of the energy is lost as heat due to the activities of the organisms as they search for food and mates.

D The fourth link of a food chain is a top carnivore, which feeds on other carnivores. Examples of these consumers in this pond are large fish such as crappies and bass.

E When an organism dies in any ecosystem, bacteria and fungi, which are decomposers, feed on the dead organism, breaking down the remains of the organism.

CHEMISTRY
INTEGRATION

Making Food
Certain bacteria obtain their energy through a process called chemosynthesis. In chemosynthesis, the bacteria produce food and oxygen using chemical compounds. Where do you think these bacteria are found?

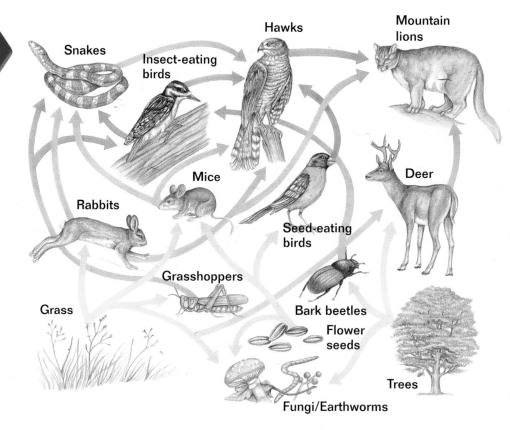

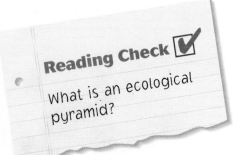

VISUALIZING Food Webs

Figure 10-14 A food web includes many food chains. It provides a more accurate model of the complex feeding relationships in a community than a single food chain does.

Snakes

Insect-eating birds

Hawks

Mountain lions

Rabbits

Mice

Deer

Seed-eating birds

Grass

Grasshoppers

Bark beetles

Flower seeds

Trees

Fungi/Earthworms

Single food chains are too simple to describe the many interactions among organisms in an ecosystem. Many food chains exist in any ecosystem. A **food web** is a series of overlapping food chains, as seen in **Figure 10-14.** This concept provides a more complete model of the way energy moves through a community. Food webs are also more accurate models because they show the many organisms that feed on more than one level in an ecosystem.

Ecological Pyramids

Almost all the energy used in the biosphere comes from the sun. Producers capture and transform only a small part of the energy that reaches Earth's surface. When an herbivore eats a plant, some of the energy in the plant is passed on to the herbivore. However, most of it is given off into the atmosphere as heat. The same thing happens when a carnivore eats an herbivore. This transfer of energy can be modeled by an **ecological pyramid.** The bottom of an ecological pyramid represents the producers of an ecosystem. The rest of the levels represent successive organisms in the food chain.

Reading Check ☑

What is an ecological pyramid?

Energy Pyramid

The flow of energy from grass to the hawk in **Figure 10-15** can be illustrated by an energy pyramid. An energy pyramid compares the energy available at each level of the food chain in an ecosystem. Just as most food chains have three or four links, a pyramid of energy usually has three or four levels. Only about ten percent of the energy available at each level of the pyramid is available to the next level. By the time the top level is reached, the amount of energy is greatly reduced.

The Cycles of Matter

The energy available at each link in the food chain is constantly renewed by sunlight. But, what about the physical matter that makes up the bodies of living organisms? The laws of conservation of mass and energy state that matter on Earth is never lost or gained. It is used over and over again. In other words, it is recycled. The carbon atoms present in your body right now have been on Earth since the planet formed billions of years ago.

Figure 10-15

An energy pyramid illustrates that energy decreases at each successive feeding step. **Why aren't there more levels in an energy pyramid?**

Problem Solving

Changes in Antarctic Food Webs

The food chain in the ice-cold Antarctic Ocean is based on phytoplankton—microscopic algae that float near the water's surface. The algae are eaten by tiny shrimp-like krill, which are consumed by baleen whales, squid, and fish. The fish and squid are eaten by toothed whales, seals, and penguins. In the past, humans have hunted baleen whales. Now with laws against it, there is hope that the population of baleen whales will increase. How will an increase in the whale population affect this food web? Which organisms compete for the same source of food?

Think Critically

1. Populations of seals, penguins, and krill-eating fish increased in size as populations of baleen whales declined. Why?

2. What might happen if the number of baleen whales increases, but the amount of krill does not?

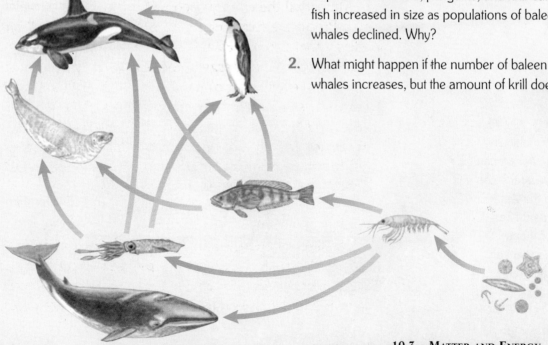

Mini Lab

Modeling the Water Cycle

Procedure 🥽

1. With a marker, make a line halfway up on a plastic cup. Fill the cup to the mark with water.
2. Cover the top with plastic wrap and secure it with a rubber band or tape.
3. Put the cup in direct sunlight. Observe the cup for three days. Record your observations.
4. Remove the plastic wrap and observe it for a week.

Analysis

1. What parts of the water cycle did you observe in this activity?
2. What happened to the water level in the cup when the plastic wrap was removed?

They have been recycled untold billions of times. Many important materials that make up your body cycle through ecosystems. Some of these materials are water, carbon, and nitrogen.

The Water Cycle

Water molecules on Earth are on a constant journey, rising into the atmosphere, falling to land or the ocean as rain or snow, and flowing into rivers and oceans. The **water cycle** involves the processes of evaporation, condensation, and precipitation.

When energy, such as heat, is added to a liquid, its molecules begin to move faster. The more energy the molecules absorb, the faster they move, until they are moving so fast they break free and rise into the atmosphere. The liquid evaporates, or changes from a liquid to a gas. The heat of the sun causes water on the surface of Earth to evaporate and rise into the atmosphere as water vapor.

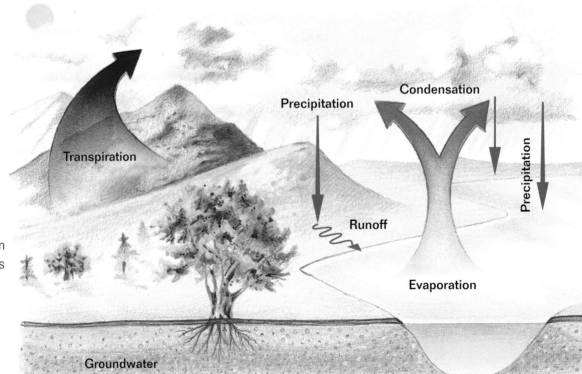

Figure 10-16
A water molecule that falls as rain can follow several paths through the water cycle. **Identify as many of these paths as you can in this diagram.**

VISUALIZING
The Carbon Cycle

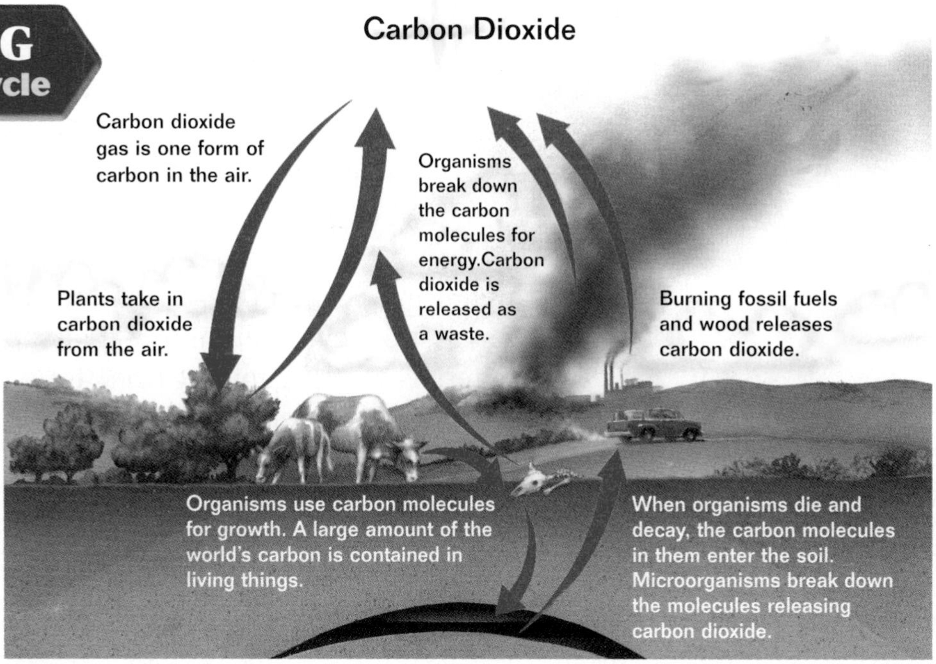

Figure 10-17 Carbon is cycled between the atmosphere and living organisms. **Why is the carbon cycle important?**

Carbon dioxide gas is one form of carbon in the air.

Organisms break down the carbon molecules for energy. Carbon dioxide is released as a waste.

Plants take in carbon dioxide from the air.

Burning fossil fuels and wood releases carbon dioxide.

Organisms use carbon molecules for growth. A large amount of the world's carbon is contained in living things.

When organisms die and decay, the carbon molecules in them enter the soil. Microorganisms break down the molecules releasing carbon dioxide.

As the water vapor rises, it encounters colder and colder air temperatures. As the molecules of water vapor become colder, they slow down. Eventually, the water vapor changes back into tiny droplets of water. It condenses, or changes from a gas to a liquid. These water droplets clump together to form clouds. When the droplets become large and heavy enough, they fall back to Earth as rain, or precipitation. This process is illustrated in **Figure 10-16.**

The Carbon Cycle

What do you have in common with all organisms? You all contain carbon. Earth's atmosphere contains about 0.03 percent carbon in the form of a gas called carbon dioxide. The movement of the element carbon through Earth's ecosystem is called the carbon cycle.

The carbon cycle begins with plants. During photosynthesis, plants remove carbon from the air and use it along with sunlight and water to make carbohydrates. These carbohydrates are used by other organisms and then returned to the atmosphere through cellular respiration, combustion, and erosion. See **Figure 10-17.** Once the carbon is returned to the atmosphere, the cycle begins again.

The Nitrogen Cycle

Nitrogen is an important element that is used by organisms to make proteins. Even though nitrogen gas makes up 78 percent of the atmosphere, most living organisms cannot use nitrogen in this form. It has to be combined with other elements through a process that is called nitrogen fixation.

*inter*NET
CONNECTION

Visit the Glencoe Science Web Site at **www.glencoe.com/ sec/science/nc** for more information about food chains and food webs.

You can see in **Figure 10-18** how nitrogen is changed into usable compounds by bacteria associated with certain plants. A small amount is changed into nitrogen compounds by lightning. The transfer of nitrogen from the atmosphere to plants and back to the atmosphere or directly into plants again is the **nitrogen cycle.**

Phosphorus, sulfur, and other elements needed by living organisms also are used and returned to the environment. Just as we recycle aluminum, glass, and paper products, the materials that organisms need to live are recycled continuously in the biosphere.

Figure 10-18 Nitrogen can be cycled from bacteria on plant roots to plants, then to animals, and directly back to plants again as a result of decomposition.

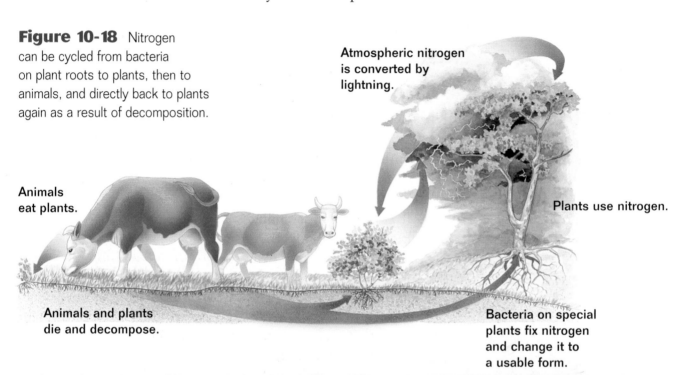

Atmospheric nitrogen is converted by lightning.

Plants use nitrogen.

Animals eat plants.

Animals and plants die and decompose.

Bacteria on special plants fix nitrogen and change it to a usable form.

Section Assessment

1. What is the difference between a food chain and a food web?

2. How does the cycling of matter affect a food chain?

3. **Think Critically:** Use your knowledge of food chains and the energy pyramid to explain why fewer lions than gazelles live on the African plains.

4.  **Skill Builder**
   Classifying Look at the food web pictured in **Figure 10-14.** Classify each organism pictured as a producer, an herbivore, a carnivore, or a decomposer. If you need help, refer to Classifying in the **Skill Handbook** on page 549.

Science Journal
In your Science Journal, compare the water cycle, carbon cycle, and nitrogen cycle. Use this information to discuss the processes that are involved in each cycle and how each cycle is important to living organisms.

Science JOURNAL

Never Cry Wolf was made into a movie based on the book. In your Science Journal, explain how books and movies like **Never Cry Wolf** can be used to persuade or to change a person's attitude toward a subject.

Never Cry Wolf
by Farley Mowat

In the book *Never Cry Wolf*, Canadian biologist Farley Mowat details his yearlong expedition learning about wolves and surviving on the frozen tundra of northern Canada. When Mowat set up camp in a remote wilderness area, he didn't know he would end up eating mice to prove a point. Mowat was hired by the Canadian Wildlife Service to investigate and live among the wolves to help solve the country's growing "*Canis lupus* problem." Hunters were reporting that packs of bloodthirsty wolves were slaughtering caribou by the thousands and contributing to their extinction.

Mowat's Discovery

This action-packed book is more than just an adventure story. It's also the report of a stunning scientific discovery. Instead of fierce killers, Mowat found wolves to be gentle, skillful providers and devoted protectors of their young. Mowat challenged the idea that wolves were causing the decline in the caribou population. He showed that his wolf population fed almost exclusively on mice during the warmer summer months when the mouse population skyrocketed. To prove that a large mammal could survive on mice, he ate them himself. Following the publication of *Never Cry Wolf*, Mowat's conclusions about the habits and behaviors of wolves were criticized by people clinging to the old image of wolves as vicious killers.

Filled with beautiful images of animals in their natural setting, *Never Cry Wolf* describes one person's struggle to preserve a vanishing species. Mowat's heroic efforts to document never-before-seen behaviors in wild wolves focused international attention on wolves, which are threatened with extinction in North America and elsewhere. In 1983, Mowat's groundbreaking book was made into an entertaining movie.

For a **preview** of this chapter, study this Reviewing Main Ideas before you read the chapter. After you have studied this chapter, you can use the Reviewing Main Ideas to **review** the chapter.

The Glencoe MindJogger, Audiocassettes, and CD-ROM provide additional opportunities for review.

Section 10-1 THE LIVING AND NONLIVING ENVIRONMENT

The region of Earth in which all organisms live is the **biosphere.** The nonliving features of the environment are **abiotic factors,** and the organisms in the environment are **biotic factors. Populations** and **communities** make up an **ecosystem. Ecology** is the study of interactions among organisms and their environment. *How does the relationship between an organism, a population, and a community affect an ecosystem?*

Section 10-2 INTERACTIONS AMONG LIVING ORGANISMS

A **population** can be described by characteristics that include size, spacing, and density. Any biotic or abiotic factor that limits the number of individuals in a population is a **limiting factor.** A close relationship between two or more species is a symbiotic relationship. The place where an organism lives is its **habitat,** and its role in the environment is its **niche.** *How could two similar species of birds live in the same area and nest in the same tree without occupying the same niche?*

Reading Check ✓

Translate the information in Figure 10-14 into a diagram. Clearly show the relationships among the links in a food chain.

^{Section}
10-3 MATTER AND ENERGY

Food chains and **food webs** are models that describe the feeding relationships in a community. An **energy pyramid** describes the flow of energy through a community. Energy is distributed at each level of the food chain but is replenished by the sun. Matter is never lost or gained but is recycled. *If the rabbits, birds, mice, beetles, and deer were removed from the food web shown in this figure, which organisms would be affected and how?*

Career
CONNECTION

Isidro Bosh, Aquatic Biologist

As an aquatic biologist, Isidro Bosh studies ocean invertebrates such as sea urchins, sea slugs, and sponges. He is interested in how these animals live in tough environmental conditions, such as cold polar oceans and the dark deep sea with its high pressure. He has explored the oceans in everything from huge research vessels to small, inflatable rafts. He also has explored tropical coral reefs and giant kelp forests. *Why is it important to study how animals adapt to tough environments?*

Chapter 10 Assessment

Using Vocabulary

a. abiotic factor	**j.** food web
b. biosphere	**k.** habitat
c. biotic factor	**l.** limiting factor
d. carrying capacity	**m.** niche
e. community	**n.** nitrogen cycle
f. ecological pyramid	**o.** population
g. ecology	**p.** population density
h. ecosystem	**q.** symbiosis
i. food chain	**r.** water cycle

Match each phrase with the correct term from the list of Vocabulary words.

1. any living thing in the environment
2. number of individuals of a species living in the same place at the same time
3. all the populations in an ecosystem
4. series of overlapping food chains
5. where an organism lives in an ecosystem

Checking Concepts

Choose the word or phrase that best answers the question.

6. Which of the following is a biotic factor?
   A) animals
   B) air
   C) sunlight
   D) soil

7. What are coral reefs and oak-hickory forests examples of?
   A) niches
   B) habitats
   C) populations
   D) ecosystems

8. What is made up of all populations in an area?
   A) niche
   B) habitat
   C) community
   D) ecosystem

9. What does the number of individuals in a population occupying an area of a specific size describe?
   A) clumping
   B) size
   C) spacing
   D) density

10. Which of the following is an example of an herbivore?
    A) wolf
    B) moss
    C) tree
    D) rabbit

11. Which level of the food chain has the most energy?
    A) omnivores
    B) herbivores
    C) decomposers
    D) producers

12. What is a relationship in which one organism is helped and the other is harmed?
    A) mutualism
    B) parasitism
    C) commensalism
    D) symbiosis

13. Which of the following is NOT cycled in the biosphere?
    A) nitrogen
    B) soil
    C) water
    D) carbon

14. Which of the following is a model that shows how energy is lost as it flows through an ecosystem?
    A) pyramid of biomass
    B) pyramid of numbers
    C) pyramid of energy
    D) niche

15. What does returning wolves to Yellowstone National Park add to the food web?
    A) producer
    B) herbivore
    C) top carnivore
    D) decomposer

Thinking Critically

16. What would be the advantage to a human or other omnivore of eating a diet of organisms that are lower rather than higher on the food chain?

17. Why are viruses considered parasites?

18. What does carrying capacity have to do with whether or not a population reaches its biotic potential?

19. Why are decomposers vital to the cycling of matter in an ecosystem?

20. Describe your own habitat and niche.

Developing Skills

If you need help, refer to the **Skill Handbook**.

21. **Classifying:** Classify each event in the water cycle as the result of either evaporation or condensation.

    A) A puddle disappears after a rainstorm.

    B) Rain falls.

    C) A lake becomes shallower.

    D) Clouds form.

22. **Making and Using Graphs:** Use the following data to graph the population density of a deer population over the years. Plot the number of deer on the *y*-axis and years on the *x*-axis. Propose a hypothesis to explain what might have happened to cause the changes in the size of the population.

Arizona Deer Population	
Year	Deer per 400 hectares
1905	5.7
1915	35.7
1920	142.9
1925	85.7
1935	25.7

23. **Observing and Inferring:** A home aquarium contains water, an air pump, a light, algae, a goldfish, and algae-eating snails. What are the abiotic factors in this environment? Which of these items would be considered a population? A community?

24. **Concept Mapping:** Use the following information to draw a food web of organisms living in a goldenrod field. *Goldenrod sap is eaten by aphids, goldenrod nectar is eaten by bees, goldenrod pollen is eaten by beetles, goldenrod leaves are eaten by beetles, stinkbugs eat beetles, spiders eat aphids, assassin bugs eat bees.*

THE PRINCETON REVIEW

Test-Taking Tip

Skip Around, If You Can Just because the questions are in order doesn't mean you have to answer them that way. You may want to skip over hard questions and come back to them later. Answer all the easier questions first to guarantee you more points toward your score.

Test Practice

Use these questions to test your Science Proficiency.

1. According to the table, at which point are there more deer than available food?
    A) 1
    B) 2
    C) 3
    D) 4

2. In the water cycle, how is water returned to the atmosphere?
    A) evaporation
    B) condensation
    C) precipitation
    D) fixation

3. What are the food relationships among all organisms in the same environment called?
    A) food chain
    B) ecological pyramid
    C) food web
    D) energy pyramid

4. In an energy pyramid, which level has the most available energy?
    A) first
    B) second
    C) third
    D) fourth

Chapter Preview

Section 11-1
Diversity of Life
Section 11-2
Unity of Life
Section 11-3
History of Life

Skills Preview

Skill Builders

- Map Concepts
- Recognize Cause and Effect

Activities

- Design an Experiment
- Make a Model

MiniLabs

- Observe and Infer
- Compare and Contrast

Reading Check ✓

After reading a section, summarize its main ideas in one sentence and list three or four important details from this section.

Explore Activity

Walking through your grandmother's garden, you come across the scene shown in this photograph. At first, you see nothing unusual. Then, your grandmother whispers, "Look at that amazing spider! Can you see it?" This spider is a female goldenrod spider. It blends into its surroundings. The yellow color makes it almost invisible on the center of a sunflower. Goldenrod spiders are found from southern Canada through North America. Goldenrod spiders are just one of the many species that are hidden among the plants of North America. In this chapter, many different types of living things will be examined.

Identify Organisms

1. Obtain a card with a category of living organisms written on it from your teacher.

2. Look at the card. How many different types of organisms can you name or describe that fit this category?

3. In your Science Journal, list as many different examples of organisms in your category as you can.

Science Journal

Find a picture of one of the living things you listed in your Science Journal. Observe the traits of this living thing. What traits help it survive in its environment?

11·1 Diversity of Life

Life's Endless Variety

What You'll Learn

► Why some environments have high biodiversity
► How organisms are adapted to their environments

Vocabulary
biodiversity
adaptation

Why It's Important

► Learning the connection between environments and the organisms that live there will help you make better decisions about Earth's resources.

Earth is filled with an enormous number of different living things. Life can be found almost everywhere on Earth—in the air, on water, on land, underground, and in the soil. Why do you think so many different forms of life exist on Earth?

How many different types of animals and plants did you name in the Explore Activity? Perhaps you named people, dogs, cats, birds, squirrels, bees, and other familiar organisms in your environment. No matter how many kinds of living things you named, they will be only a small portion of the many organisms known.

How do scientists keep track of all these organisms? All living things on the planet can be classified into major categories called kingdoms. Within these kingdoms, approximately 1.4 million different organisms have been identified and named. Scientists estimate that many more millions of different organisms are yet to be discovered. Some scientists estimate that the total of all life on Earth may be somewhere between 3 million and 10 million different organisms. The graph in **Figure 11-1** shows that plants, insects, and other animals show the most numbers of organisms that we know. Are you surprised to learn that insects represent more than half of all known organisms?

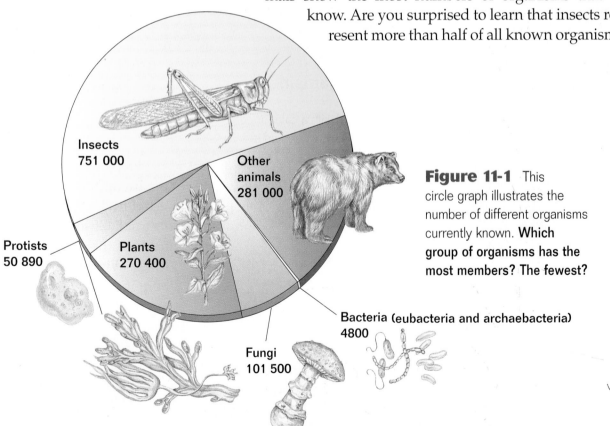

Insects
751 000

Other animals
281 000

Protists
50 890

Plants
270 400

Fungi
101 500

Bacteria (eubacteria and archaebacteria)
4800

Figure 11-1 This circle graph illustrates the number of different organisms currently known. **Which group of organisms has the most members? The fewest?**

Figure 11-2 The tropical rain forest (A) has a plentiful supply of food, water, and shelter. Therefore, it is home to many different animals and plants, including the blue-crowned motmot (B) and the eyelash viper (C).

Rain Forest Diversity

You're now in the tropical rain forest, staring at all of the amazing plants and animals. The forest is thick with vines, mosses, orchids, and trees, trees, trees. Insects buzz all around. Brightly colored birds fly from branch to branch. Other animals feed and rest in the treetops.

Tropical rain forests are full of life. These environments have a high number of species. Biological diversity or **biodiversity** (bi oh duh VUR suh tee) is the measure of the number of different species in an area. Tropical rain forests have more different types of living things than any other places on Earth. They have a high biodiversity. ☑

Why do tropical rain forests have such high biodiversity? To answer this question, think about an environment that contains fewer species, such as a desert. In the desert, temperatures are high and not much rain falls. Some deserts have little plant life. What kinds of animals might be able to survive in this environment? Where would they live? What would they eat?

In tropical areas of the world, temperatures remain warm and steady all year, and rainfall is high. These conditions are perfect for the growth of tropical plants. In the rain forest, you might find more than 200 different kinds of plants growing in an area the size of a football field. Living among these plants are many insects, birds, mammals, reptiles, and amphibians such as the ones shown in **Figure 11-2.** These animals use the plants for food and shelter. You can see that tropical environments have high biodiversity because food, water, and shelter are plentiful.

Reading Check ☑

What is biodiversity?

Figure 11-3 Plants and animals show a variety of adaptations for survival. **What evidence of adaptations do you see in this caladium plant (A) and snowy owl (B)?**

A

B

Diversity and Adaptation

From the snake in the rain forest, to a deep-sea fish, to a lizard in the desert, Earth is filled with living things that seem to fit into their environments. Their colors, shapes, sizes, and behaviors suit them to live in their surroundings. Any body shape, body process, or behavior that helps an organism survive in its environment and carry out its life processes is called an **adaptation.**

As you can see in **Figure 11-3,** species of organisms have different adaptations that help them survive. Some adaptations include physical features, such as the body shape and color of a snowy owl or a waxy cuticle on leaves that prevents water loss. These features cause the owl to blend into its environment and hide it from predators. Some animals that have coloration that helps them blend into the environment also may have behaviors that help protect them. The bobwhite quail and viper remain absolutely still in times of danger. As a result, these animals are not easily seen by their predators.

Adapting to the Environment

How do you think an organism living in the frozen Arctic would be different from one that lives in the rain forest or the desert? Why would it have different adaptations? An organism's environment includes all of the living things in its surroundings. It also includes the nonliving things such as water, sunlight, and soil. For example, kangaroo rats live in the deserts where there is little water. On hot days, they remain in their burrows where the air is moist. Kangaroo rats also have body adaptations that prevent water loss. They get all the water they need from dry, but fatty seeds. These mammals neither sweat nor pant as other animals do to keep cool, and their kidneys are adapted so that they rid their bodies of waste with little loss of water. These are all adaptations the kangaroo rat has to its particular surroundings. Some organisms such as the duck in **Figure 11-4** can move to find a suitable environment.

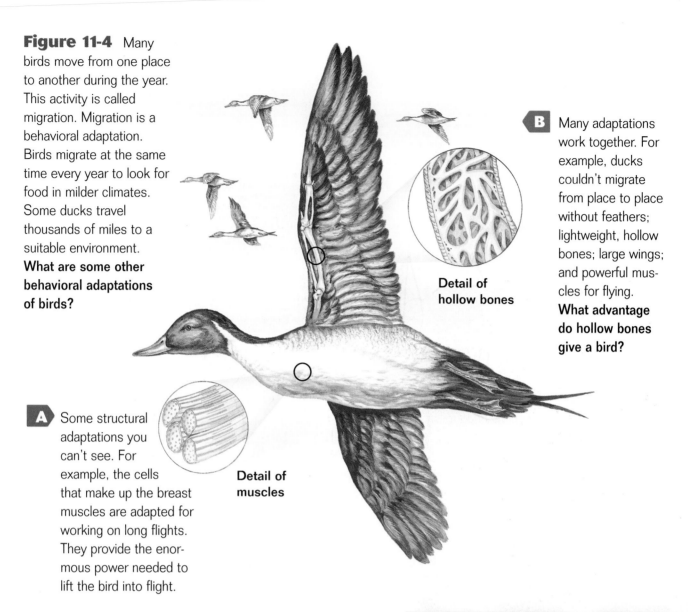

Figure 11-4 Many birds move from one place to another during the year. This activity is called migration. Migration is a behavioral adaptation. Birds migrate at the same time every year to look for food in milder climates. Some ducks travel thousands of miles to a suitable environment. **What are some other behavioral adaptations of birds?**

B Many adaptations work together. For example, ducks couldn't migrate from place to place without feathers; lightweight, hollow bones; large wings; and powerful muscles for flying. **What advantage do hollow bones give a bird?**

Detail of hollow bones

A Some structural adaptations you can't see. For example, the cells that make up the breast muscles are adapted for working on long flights. They provide the enormous power needed to lift the bird into flight.

Detail of muscles

Figure 11-5 shows a close-up view of an adaptation of a cactus plant. Cacti live in desert environments where water is in short supply. Thick, waxy coatings on the stems of cactus plants help prevent the cactus from drying up. This is an adaptation for conserving water.

Animals in the Arctic

In the Arctic, the ground is covered with snow and ice for months. For several weeks each winter, the sun never even rises above the horizon. Large areas of ice melt with the arrival of spring and summer, but the ground never thaws. Animals that live here are adapted for this harsh, cold climate of the Arctic.

Figure 11-5 A waxy outer layer and sharp spines are protective adaptations for cacti and many other plants.

Mini Lab

Identifying Adaptations of Fish

Procedure

1. Obtain a set of four adaptation cards from your teacher.
2. Look at the cards. On a sheet of paper, draw a picture of a fish that matches the features given to you.
3. On a separate sheet of paper, draw the type of environment your fish could survive in.

Analysis

1. Describe the adaptations of your fish.
2. Explain how the adaptations of your fish make it well suited to its environment.

The thick, white hair of the polar bear, shown in **Figure 11-6,** not only helps it blend into its icy, snowy surroundings, it also protects it against the cold. Its hair is both hollow and transparent. The air inside the hair helps the bears float in the ice water and provides insulation against the cold air. Such hair acts as a greenhouse. It allows the limited heat from the sunlight to pass through the hair, where it is taken in by the polar bear's black skin and trapped by its fur. Polar bears also have hair on the bottoms of their feet for added warmth.

Sea otters and seals have fur so thick that the cold arctic water never even touches their skin. As seen in **Figure 11-7,** musk oxen have hair on the neck, chest, and rump that may be 0.6 m to 1 m long. This long hair protects them against the cold temperatures of the arctic winter, in addition to protecting them against the mosquitoes that are abundant in the Arctic in the summer.

Figure 11-6 Polar bears are efficient swimmers. They have been spotted more than 100 km from the closest land. **How can polar bears survive in such cold water?**

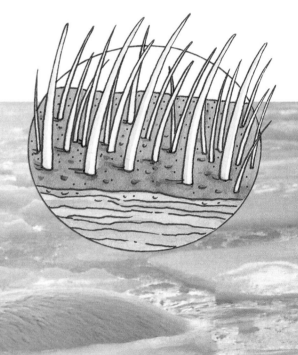

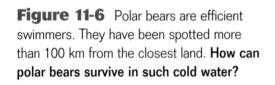

Figure 11-7 Musk oxen are named for the musk glands located under their eyes. When attacked, they rub the gland on their legs. This releases an unpleasant odor that discourages many enemies from approaching.

*inter***NET**
C O N N E C T I O N

Visit the Glencoe Science Web Site at **www.glencoe.com/ sec/science/nc** for more information about polar bears.

Organisms are adapted for the environments they live in. What is your environment? Can you name some adaptations of native plants and animals in your area that help them to survive and carry out their life processes? In the next section, you will learn how organisms have changed through time.

Section Assessment

1. Define the term *biodiversity*.
2. Explain why tropical rain forests have high biodiversity.
3. What are adaptations? Give an example of one.
4. **Think Critically:** What adaptations would an animal living in a desert need to survive?
5. **Skill Builder**
   Observing and Inferring Think of an organism, not a pet, that is familiar to you. Make a list of its traits. Next to each trait, describe how it helps the organism survive in its environment. If you need help, refer to Observing and Inferring in the **Skill Handbook** on page 556.

Using Math

Scientists have identified and named approximately 1 032 000 different species of animals. If 751 000 of these are insects, what percentage do insects make up in the total animal population? Show all of your work.

Using Field Guides

A bird with a red head and black wings (right) lands on a tree. It hammers into the bark with its beak. You're pretty sure it's a woodpecker, but what kind?

One place to find out is a field guide, such as the *National Geographic Society Field Guide to the Birds of North America*. Field guides are handbooks that help identify living things, from mushrooms to mammals. They contain descriptions and photographs or illustrations, as well as information about where organisms live. Field guides are useful tools for making sense of the often-bewildering diversity of life on Earth.

Some field guides are organized around easily identifiable characteristics, such as shape or color. A field guide to flowers might group yellow flowers in one section, red in another, and so on. Other guides group together species that may look different but belong to the same scientific family.

Using field guides is a bit like detective work. You follow clues, gradually narrowing your search until you can finally answer the question: "What *is* that?"

Red-headed Woodpecker
(*Melanerpes erythrocephalus*)

Description: L 9¼" (24 cm) Entire head, neck, and throat are bright red in adults, contrasting with blue-black back and snowy-white underparts. Juvenile is brownish; acquires red head during gradual winter molt. Look for distinctive white inner wing patches and white rump.
Call: A loud *queark*.
Habitat: Inhabits open woods, farmlands, bottomlands, parks, backyards. Forages on tree trunks and on the ground for insects, berries, acorns; occasionally seen catching flies.
Nesting: Bores nest holes in dead trees, fence posts, telephone poles.
Range: The Red-headed Woodpecker has become rare in the northeast, partly due to habitat loss and competition for nest holes. Somewhat more numerous in the rest of their range. In map above, orange shows year-round range, green the breeding range.

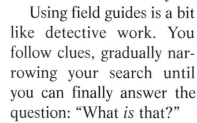

Science
JOURNAL

Spend 15 minutes observing nature. Describe five plants or animals you see. Make sketches and note colors, shapes, and sizes. Then, using field guides, try to identify the organisms on your list. If you have a beetle on your list, good luck —there are nearly 300 000 different kinds!

Unity of Life

Why are they like that?

You probably would never confuse an eagle with a hummingbird. Both have wings, beaks, feathers, and other familiar features of birds, but they are different in size, shape, and where they live. On the other hand, you might have trouble recognizing different kinds of birds unless you were an experienced bird-watcher. Many groups of birds look alike. Why are some groups more similar than others? How do new types form? Through the study of living and once-living organisms, scientists try to find the answers.

Organisms are adapted to the environments in which they live. How do these adaptations happen? Individual organisms are not identical to each other, even if they belong to the same group, as illustrated in **Figure 11-8.** In every group, variations, or differences, occur in the traits of that group.

What **You'll Learn**

► How species change and new species form through natural selection
► About the evidence that supports the idea that organisms change through time

Vocabulary
natural selection
common ancestor
fossil

Why **It's Important**

► Knowing how organisms are adapted to their environment may explain the features of the environment itself.

A Mallard duck

B Wood duck

Figure 11-8 Only an experienced bird-watcher may be able to recognize all three types of birds as ducks, especially if they are in flight.

C Northern pintail duck

Adaptation Through Natural Selection

In a population of gray squirrels, for example, individuals may have slightly different colors of fur. Most will have brown-gray fur color. A few will have dark fur, and some will have light fur.

Now, imagine this same population of squirrels in an environment that changed. Suppose the environment changed so that squirrels with dark fur are better able to survive than squirrels with a lighter fur color because predators are not able to see squirrels with darker fur as easily. Dark squirrels would be better off in this environment. They would be more likely to survive and have offspring, as shown in **Figure 11-9.** This process, in which organisms with characteristics best suited for the environment survive, reproduce, and pass these traits to their offspring, is called **natural selection.**

Now, think about the process of natural selection happening over many, many years. With each generation, more and more dark squirrels will survive and pass their coat color on to their offspring. Squirrels with lighter fur don't survive and so produce fewer offspring. The population changes. Every generation, the population consists of more dark squirrels than the one before it. This process of natural selection is the main way changes happen in a population.

VISUALIZING
Natural Selection

Figure 11-9 A population of squirrels can change through natural selection.

A In all species, individual organisms within a population have differences, or variations.

B In this population, some squirrels may be alert and hide more quickly when predators come near.

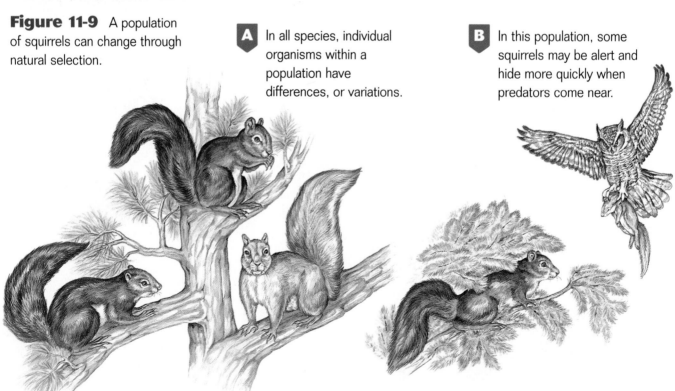

Natural selection can explain why polar bears are white, why some other bears are brown, and why some insects that live in the leaves of a tree are green. Think of how the snowy owl came to look the way it does. Individuals with traits most favorable for a specific environment survive and pass on these traits to their offspring. Natural selection, therefore, means that organisms with traits best suited to their environments are more likely to survive. The four general principles involved in natural selection are listed in **Table 11-1.**

Table 11-1

Principles of Natural Selection

1. Organisms produce more offspring than can survive.

2. Variations are found among individuals of a group of organisms.

3. Some variations make it possible for members of a population to survive and reproduce more successfully.

4. Over time, offspring of individuals with helpful variations make up more and more of a population.

C Organisms that survive reproduce and pass on their traits.

D There is still variation, but the population has a higher percentage of individuals with beneficial variations.

The Origin of New Species

If you've ever watched nature programs showing lions and tigers in the wild, you've seen the animals hunting, washing themselves, and caring for their young. You may have seen these same behaviors in a house cat. Maybe you've also noticed that all types of cats—lions, tigers, bobcats, and others—have similar features. How did the various species of cats form, and why do they share so many features?

Scientists define a species as a group of organisms that look alike and reproduce fertile offspring. One way a new species can form is if a large population of organisms becomes separated into smaller populations. They no longer breed with others of their kind. A barrier, such as a mountain range or river, can cause this separation. **Figure 11-10** shows an example. ☑

Reading Check ☑

What is a species?

A New Species Develops

Let's look at a population of lizards. Suppose a river divides the whole population into two smaller populations. Lizards in one group can no longer mate with lizards in the other groups. They can mate only among themselves. Over time, each small population will adapt to its own environment. Because each environment is a little bit different, each small population will develop different adaptations. Over time, the populations may become so different from each other that offspring couldn't be produced even if the lizards could again mate with one another. Each small population of lizards has become a new species. Because the different species of lizards

Figure 11-10 One way new species form is for a population to be separated. **What other factors could contribute to forming new species?**

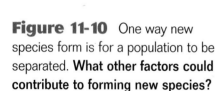

A The members of this population of lizards all look alike and are able to interbreed.

in this example all arose from one population, we can say that they share a **common ancestor** (AN ses tur). Each of the new lizard species now has its own specific traits. But, all the species share some traits that they inherited from their common ancestor.

Evidence for Change over Time

It is not always possible to see everything you'd like to study. Objects may be too tiny or too far away for you to see. Processes may happen too quickly or too slowly for us to observe. That's the problem with natural selection. It occurs in all species, but it usually occurs so slowly that it's not possible to see the process in action. How can scientists be sure that species have changed over time? They rely on several types of evidence. They compare physical traits of species that are similar. They study the DNA and proteins of species for clues to how closely they are related. They look at fossils. Now, you can take a closer look at each of these types.

CHEMISTRY
INTEGRATION

DNA
The DNA molecule is made up of five common elements: hydrogen, oxygen, carbon, nitrogen, and phosphorus. These elements are combined in different chemical groups and arranged in two chains. These chains twist around each other in a double spiral, like a twisted ladder. What words do the letters "DNA" represent?

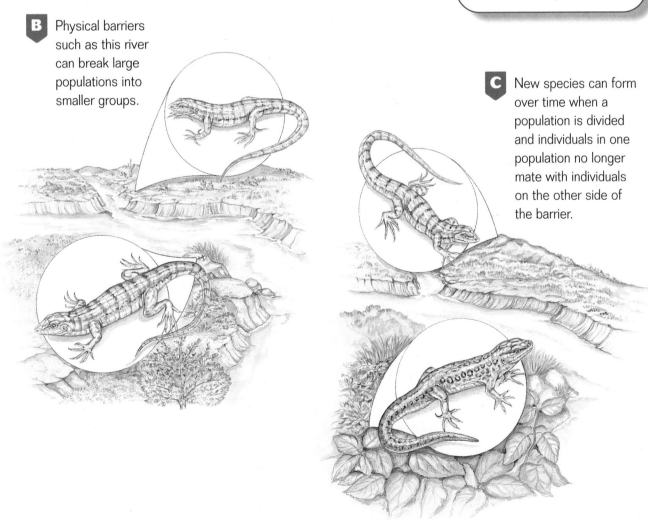

B Physical barriers such as this river can break large populations into smaller groups.

C New species can form over time when a population is divided and individuals in one population no longer mate with individuals on the other side of the barrier.

Mini Lab

Modeling a Fossil

Procedure

1. A mold fossil is formed when an organism leaves an impression in clay or mud. When the mold is later filled in, a cast fossil can be formed.

2. To make a model of a fossil, pour plaster of paris into the milk container until it is half full.

3. When the plaster begins to thicken, use a small paintbrush and vegetable oil to coat some small objects and press them into the plaster.

4. After the plaster has hardened, remove the objects. You have now made a mold.

5. Next, paint the entire layer of hard plaster with a generous coating of vegetable oil. Pour another layer of colored plaster to fill in the mold.

6. After the plaster hardens, tear away the milk container. Use a butter knife or putty knife to carefully pry apart the two layers of plaster. The colored layer shows your cast.

Analysis

Which fossil showed the most details of the objects you used, the mold or the cast?

Fossils Show Change over Time

Although dinosaurs have been extinct for millions of years, they come to life in the movies. Do you think those giant, roaring creatures on screen are anything like real dinosaurs were? How do scientists and the movie producers know how dinosaurs looked and acted? Scientists have learned a lot about the ancient reptiles by studying their fossils. **Fossils** are the remains or traces of ancient life.

Fossils give scientists the most direct evidence that species change over time. For example, fossils of trilobites (TRI luh bites) show that change occurred in their structure over time, as illustrated in **Figure 11-11.** Trilobites are extinct relatives of animals you know today such as lobsters, crabs, and insects. Early trilobites had generalized body structures with few segments. Fossils of later trilobites show many differences in shape. Through the study of fossils, scientists have shown that trilobites changed over time.

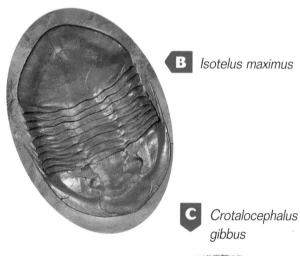

B *Isotelus maximus*

A *Modocia typicales*

C *Crotalocephalus gibbus*

Figure 11-11 Trilobites changed over time. *Modocia typicales* (A) lived around 500 million years ago. *Isotelus maximus* existed about 450 million years ago, and *Crotalocephalus gibbus* (C) were on Earth around 400 million years ago.

Figure 11-12 Timber wolves and dogs such as this Alaskan husky are closely related. **What physical similarities can you see between these two animals?**

DNA Shows Relationships

Appearances can trick you. Some species such as the wolf and dog in **Figure 11-12** look a lot alike and are closely related. Scientists need something besides physical appearance to help them find out how closely related species are. DNA determines the traits of organisms. The more similar the DNAs of two species are, the more closely they are related. For example, in comparing the DNA of modern breeds of dogs, wolves, and foxes, the gray wolf was found to be the closest relative of the domestic dog.

Problem Solving

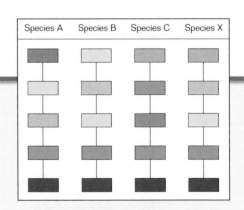

Comparing Protein Sequences

DNA can be used to show how organisms are related. Scientists also use other chemicals found in living things to show how closely related two species are. One type of chemical they study is protein. Proteins perform a variety of jobs in living things. Some are used in the building of living material, such as bones, muscles, and skin. Others help living things grow, digest foods, and fight diseases. Scientists can learn about the relationships between species by studying the structure of proteins. Each protein is made of building blocks put together in a specific order. In closely related species, similar proteins have a similar order of building blocks. In species that are more distantly related, the same proteins have different arrangements of building blocks.

The illustration shows the structure of a type of protein used in digestion found in three unknown bird species (Species A, Species B, and Species C) and in a known bird species (Species X). The colored blocks represent the building blocks of the digestive protein. Compare the structure of the proteins in all four species.

Think Critically: Which bird species (A, B, C) do you think is most closely related to Species X? Why did you reach your decision?

Anatomy and Ancestry

If you were a biologist studying the many species of cichlid (SIH klud) fish in Africa's Lake Victoria, you would see differences in the jaws and teeth of these fish. You also would see differences in their color. Some of these differences are shown in **Figure 11-13.** Some species have small mouths and sharp teeth for eating insects. Others have mouths adapted for scraping algae. Still others are adapted for eating the scales of other fish. However, despite the differences, all 170 species of cichlids in the lake have many more things in common.

Scientists compare similarities and differences in the body structures of all living things. This gives them clues to how species may have changed over time. After comparing the

Figure 11-13 All the fish below are ciclids. The differences in the head shapes of these fish allow them to eat different things and feed in different ways. Two species may feed on insects but do so in different ways.

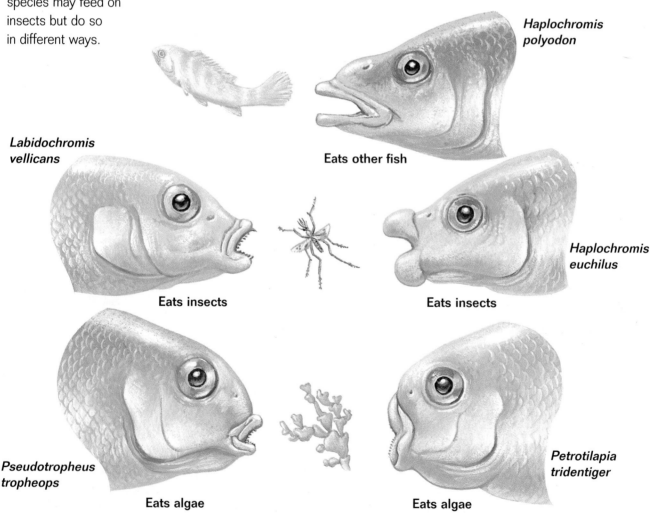

Haplochromis
polyodon

Eats other fish

Labidochromis
vellicans

Eats insects

Haplochromis
euchilus

Eats insects

Pseudotropheus
tropheops

Eats algae

Petrotilapia
tridentiger

Eats algae

anatomy of many species, scientists conclude that all species may have come from a common ancestor.

Another example of similarities in anatomy between two organisms is seen in **Figure 11-14.** Do you see these similarities? If you said yes, then you made the type of observation that scientists use to find relationships among organisms. Scientists view these similarities as evidence that two populations of organisms developed from a common ancestor.

Figure 11-14

Archaeopteryx (A) has many similarities to *Ornitholestes* (B), a small dinosaur. *Archaeopteryx* is considered a close relative of the ancestor of modern birds. **What do the similarities between these two organisms tell you about the probable ancestor of *Archaeopteryx*?**

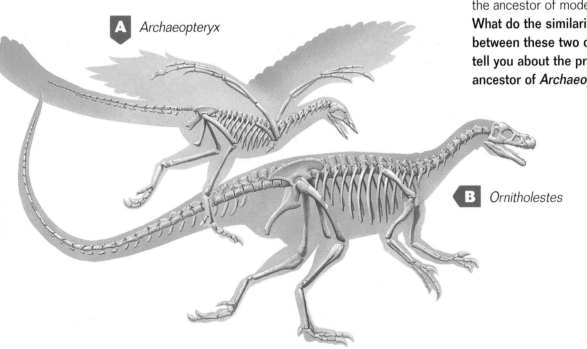

A *Archaeopteryx*

B *Ornitholestes*

Section Assessment

1. Explain natural selection. What are the four general principles involved in natural selection?

2. Briefly describe how natural selection plays a role in how species adapt to the environment.

3. What is a common ancestor?

4. **Think Critically:** Explain how fossils can show that species change over time.

5. **Skill Builder**
   Concept Mapping Make an events chain concept map that describes how camouflage adaptations may arise in a population of birds. If you need help, refer to Concept Mapping in the **Skill Handbook** on page 550.

Science Journal
Some scientists hypothesize that dinosaurs and birds are closely related. Imagine you are a scientist who wants to examine this hypothesis. In your Science Journal, describe methods you would use to investigate the relationship between dinosaurs and birds.

Design Your Own Experiment

Activity 11•1

Simulating Selection

Natural selection causes a population to change. In this activity, you will design an experiment to discover how camouflage adaptations—those adaptations that allow organisms to blend into the environment—happen through natural selection.

Possible Materials

- Bag of small-sized jelly beans in assorted colors (approximately 100 beans)
- Meterstick
- Paper
- Pencil
- Green rug or another solid-colored rug
- Watch with second hand

Recognize the Problem

How does natural selection work?

Form a Hypothesis

Any body shape, structure, or coloration of an organism that helps it blend in with its surroundings is a camouflage adaptation. Make a hypothesis about how natural selection can explain camouflage adaptations.

Goals

- **Model** natural selection in a population of insects.
- **Explain** how natural selection produces camouflage adaptations.

Safety Precautions

Do not eat any jelly beans used in this activity.

Test Your Hypothesis

Plan

1. With a partner, **discuss** the process of natural selection. How does natural selection cause species to change?

2. In this activity, one student will play the role of the bird that eats insects (jelly beans) that live in grass. With your partner, think about how you can model natural selection.

3. With your partner, **make a list** of the different steps you might take to model natural selection.

4. You might start the experiment with a particular insect population. How many insects (jelly beans) will be in your starting population? How will you show variation in your starting population?

5. Think about how many generations of insects you will use in the experiment.

6. What data will you collect? Will you need a data table for this experiment? If so, **design a table** in your Science Journal for recording data.

7. Decide what happens to individual organisms if they have favorable variations for a particular environment? What happens if an organism has unfavorable variations? Think about these questions when designing your experiment.

8. **Review** your list of steps to make sure that the experiment makes sense and that all of the steps are in logical order.

Do

1. Make sure that your teacher approves your plan before you proceed.

2. Carry out the experiment as planned.

3. While doing the experiment, **record** your observations and **complete** your data table in your Science Journal.

Analyze Your Data

1. **Observe** which types of insects the bird in your experiment was able to locate most quickly. Why?

Draw Conclusions

1. Did your population of insects change over time? **Explain** your answer.

2. How can your experiment be used to **explain** camouflage adaptations in organisms?

11·3 History of Life

A Trip Through Geologic Time

Have you ever seen a movie or read a book about time travel? What if you could travel back in time into Earth's past? What kinds of interesting plants and animals would you see? Time travel will always be science fiction rather than science fact. But, in a way, scientists can travel back through time by studying fossils. Fossils are evidence of ancient life. Fossils help scientists form a picture of the past. They provide a history for life on Earth. Let's go along on the journey through Earth's history.

The Fossil Record

Earth's rocky crust is a vast graveyard that contains the fossil remains of species that have lived throughout Earth's history. Large fossils are carefully removed from the ground as shown in **Figure 11-15.** All of the fossils that scientists have recovered from the ground make up the **fossil record.** The fossil record for life on Earth is a rich one. Fossils from almost every major group of plants and animals are part of the fossil record.

However, the fossil record doesn't show a complete history. Not every species is represented in the fossil record. It is much more common for an organism to decay without ever becoming a fossil.

What You'll Learn

▶ The importance of the fossil record
▶ About the geologic time scale
▶ The possible causes of mass extinctions

Vocabulary
fossil record
geologic time scale
mass extinction

Why It's Important

▶ The history of life on Earth helps explain how species have changed over time.

Figure 11-15 These men (A) are carefully uncovering a *Hadrosaur* fossil at an excavation site on a Navajo reservation. Fossils give scientists information that can be used to make models of dinosaurs, such as this *Hadrosaur* (B).

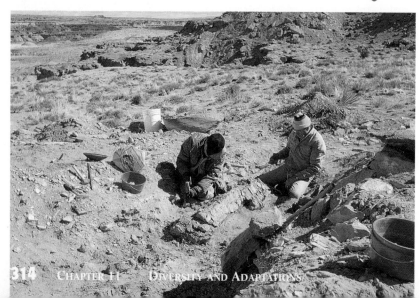

Geologic Time Scale

By studying the fossil record, scientists have put together a sort of diary for life on Earth called the **geologic time scale.** The geologic time scale helps scientists keep track of when a species appeared on Earth or when it disappeared from Earth.

You can see the geologic time scale in **Table 11-2.** As you can see, the geologic time scale is divided into four large periods of time called eras, and each era is subdivided into periods. The beginning or end of each time period marks an important event in Earth's history, such as the appearance or disappearance of a group of organisms. The fossil record of life on Earth gives scientists strong evidence that life has changed over time. ☑

Reading Check ☑

How many eras are included in the geologic time scale?

Table 11-2

Geologic Time Scale				
Era	**Period**	**Million years ago**	**Major evolutionary events**	**Representative organisms**
Cenozoic	Quaternary	1.6	First humans	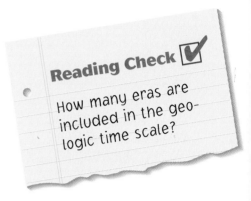
Cenozoic	Tertiary	66.4		
Mesozoic	Cretaceous	146	Large dinosaurs First flowering plants	
Mesozoic	Jurassic	208	First birds First mammals	
Mesozoic	Triassic	245		
Paleozoic	Permian	290	First conifer trees; first reptiles and insects	
Paleozoic	Pennsylvanian	323		
Paleozoic	Mississippian	362	First amphibians and land plants; first bony fish	
Paleozoic	Devonian	408		
Paleozoic	Silurian	439	First fish with jaws	
Paleozoic	Ordovician	510	First vertebrates, armored fish without jaws	
Paleozoic	Cambrian	540	Simple invertebrates	
	Precambrian		First fossilized animals and plants; protozoa, sponges, coral and algae	
		4000	First fossil bacteria	

Compsognathus, a meat eater, was one of the smallest dinosaurs at 60 cm long. *Sauropods* were the biggest dinosaurs at 40 m long. How many times longer was a *Sauropod* than a *Compsognathus*?

Extinction of Species

Why don't you see dinosaurs at the zoo? These large reptiles ruled Earth for more than 100 million years, but they're all gone now. Among the dinosaurs were the largest land animals, such as the plant-eating *Brachiosaurus* and the meat-eating *Tyrannosaurus rex*. Yet, despite the great success and long history of the dinosaurs, all of them became extinct about 66 million years ago. So did many other land and sea animals.

Scientists aren't surprised that dinosaurs are now extinct. That's because about 99 percent of all species that have ever existed are now extinct. Usually, extinction is a natural event. Earth's environments are constantly changing. When a species can't adapt to changes in its environment, it becomes extinct.

Figure 11-16 The second-largest mass extinction event in Earth's history occurred 66 million years ago at the end of the Cretaceous period. One half of all living things—including many dinosaurs—became extinct around this time.

Mass Extinctions

The extinction event that killed the dinosaurs around 66 million years ago was a mass extinction. A **mass extinction** is a large-scale disappearance of many species within a short time.

The extinction of the dinosaurs was not the only mass extinction event in Earth's history. Other large extinctions have occurred. The most severe mass extinction happened about 245 million years ago. Scientists estimate that nearly 96 percent of all animal species became extinct at this time. Most were animals without backbones, such as clams, jellyfish, sponges, and trilobites. Most fish and land species survived.

What causes mass extinctions? Scientists are not sure about the exact causes of all the mass extinctions. One idea that has been hypothesized for the extinction of the dinosaurs is that large asteroids slammed into Earth. According to this hypothesis, the collision sent huge clouds of dust into the atmosphere. Over time, the clouds blocked out sunlight. The result would have been a cooling of the environment. Over a brief period of time, species of dinosaurs and other organisms probably would not have been able to adapt quickly enough to survive.

*inter*NET
CONNECTION

Visit the Glencoe Science Web Site at **www.glencoe.com/ sec/science/nc** for more information about dinosaurs and extinctions.

Loss of Biodiversity

Mass extinctions are not just a part of the past. Extinctions also have been occurring within the last few thousand years. For instance, large mammals such as mammoths and mastodons, shown in **Figure 11-17,** disappeared from North America about the time the first humans appeared here.

Today, scientists are discovering that human activity is rapidly causing more species to become extinct. Humans use large areas of land for many reasons. Some of these uses are changing or limiting the habitat for many organisms. The tropical rain forests, where biodiversity is high, are in the greatest danger from changes from humans. Many rain forest species have not yet been discovered or named. If these species are lost, people may lose possible sources of food or new medicines.

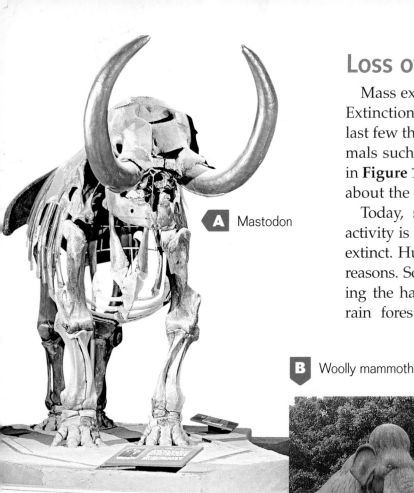

A Mastodon

B Woolly mammoth

Figure 11-17 Many organisms, such as the mastodon and the mammoth, disappeared from Earth for reasons not completely understood.

Section Assessment

1. What is the fossil record?
2. What is the geologic time scale?
3. What is a mass extinction? Give an example.
4. **Think Critically:** How might the extinction of a single plant species from a forest affect other organisms that live there?
5. 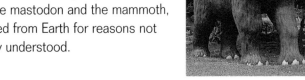 **Skill Builder**
   Recognizing Cause and Effect Have you ever wondered why something happened? Do the **Chapter 11 Skill Activity** on page 588 to look for possible cause-and-effect relationships.

Using Math

The Precambrian era represents about 4.1 billion years of Earth's 4.6-billion-year history. What percent of the total does this represent?

Activity 11·2

Dinosaur Size

Fossils can be used to estimate the size of a dinosaur. The models made from fossil observations also can be used to estimate dinosaur size.

What You'll Investigate

How can you estimate the mass of a dinosaur?

Goals

- **Estimate** the mass of a dinosaur using a model.

Procedure

1. **Make a data table** in your Science Journal. Include type of dinosaur, its scale, and volume of water displaced in your table.

2. Obtain a plastic dinosaur model. Fill in your data table. A good scale to use is a 1:40 scale, meaning that each dimension of the model—length, width, and height—is 1/40 of the dinosaur's actual size.

3. Almost **fill** the pail with water. Carefully place the pail in the utility pan. Fill the pail to the brim, taking care not to let any water spill over into the utility pan. **CAUTION:** *Clean up water spills immediately.*

4. **Submerge** the dinosaur model in the water, allowing the water to flow out of the pail and into the utility pan.

5. Carefully remove the pail from the utility pan.

6. Pour the water from the utility pan into a graduated cylinder. The volume of the water displaced is equal to the volume of the dinosaur model.

7. **Record** your measurement in your data table.

8. To find the mass of the actual dinosaur in grams, multiply the volume of the model by the cube of the scale. If the scale is 1:40 and the model has a volume of 10 mL, you would multiply 10×40^3 ($10 \times 40 \times 40 \times 40$). To find the mass in kilograms, divide by 1000.

Materials

- Plastic dinosaur model
- Plastic graduated cylinder
- Marking pen
- Calculator
- Water
- Small pail
- Utility pan

Conclude and Apply

1. Assuming that the density of a live dinosaur is similar to that of water, **estimate** the mass of your dinosaur in kilograms.

2. Male Indian elephants have a mass of about 5500 kg. What can you **infer** about the approximate size of some dinosaurs?

For a **preview** of this chapter, study this Reviewing Main Ideas before you read the chapter. After you have studied this chapter, you can use the Reviewing Main Ideas to **review** the chapter.

The Glencoe MindJogger, Audiocassettes, and CD-ROM provide additional opportunities for review.

Section

11-1 BIODIVERSITY

Biodiversity is the measure of the number of different species in an area. This term is used to describe the variety of plants, animals, and other species. Biodiversity changes and is dependent upon the environment. *Why do tropical rain forests have high biodiversity?*

ADAPTATION

An **adaptation** is any structure or behavior that helps a species survive in its environment. Some adaptations involve physical features, such as body shape and color. Others involve behaviors such as animals being able to migrate. *What are some adaptations of fish?*

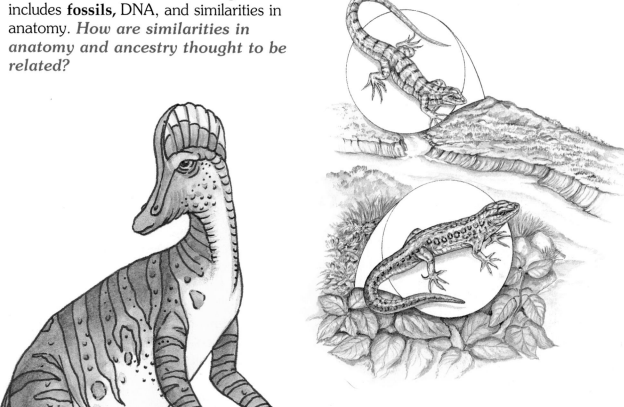

Reading Check ✓

Predict an adaptation that animals living in urban areas might develop over the next century.

Section
11-2 NATURAL SELECTION

Natural selection is a process in which organisms with characteristics best suited for the environment survive, reproduce, and pass these traits to their offspring. Such a process cannot be directly observed. Evidence for this change over time includes **fossils,** DNA, and similarities in anatomy. *How are similarities in anatomy and ancestry thought to be related?*

Section
11-3 GEOLOGIC TIME SCALE

The **geologic time scale** shows when species appeared and disappeared during Earth's history. The geologic time scale is divided into four large intervals of time called eras, and each era is subdivided into periods. *When were the dinosaurs the dominant land animals on Earth?*

Chapter 11 Assessment

Using Vocabulary

a. adaptation
b. biodiversity
c. common ancestor
d. fossil
e. fossil record
f. geologic time scale
g. mass extinction
h. natural selection

Match each phrase with the correct term from the list of Vocabulary words.

1. traces or remains of ancient life
2. numbers of different species in an area
3. mechanism for species' change over time
4. dolphin's flipper or a bird's wing
5. diary of life on Earth

Checking Concepts

Choose the word or phrase that best answers the question.

6. What is the disappearance of many species in a short time called?
   A) natural selection
   B) adaptation
   C) fossil
   D) mass extinction

7. What is the hollow hair on a polar bear an example of?
   A) fossil formation
   B) an adaptation
   C) biodiversity
   D) mass extinction

8. What are dinosaur bones examples of?
   A) species
   B) adaptations
   C) fossils
   D) biodiversity

9. Which of the following can form new species when split into smaller groups?
   A) fossils
   B) adaptations
   C) populations
   D) biodiversity

10. Species adapt to the environment through the processes of mutation and which of the following?
    A) natural selection
    B) biodiversity
    C) mass extinction
    D) fossil formation

11. Which of the following rabbits will best survive in the Arctic during winter?
    A) a brown rabbit
    B) a black rabbit
    C) a white rabbit
    D) a black-and-white rabbit

12. What is the most direct evidence that species change over time?
    A) similar anatomies
    B) DNA
    C) fossils
    D) mass extinctions

13. About what percent of all species that have ever existed are now extinct?
    A) 25 percent   C) 75 percent
    B) 50 percent   D) 99 percent

14. Which of the following organisms adapted to their environment?
    A) ones that are extinct
    B) ones that are not reproducing
    C) ones that are surviving and reproducing
    D) those that formed fossils

15. Which of the following terms describes any body shape, body process, or behavior that helps an organism survive in its environment?
    A) biodiversity
    B) extinction
    C) mass extinction
    D) adaptation

Thinking Critically

16. Which of the following variations would be most beneficial to a bird living in a wetland: webbed feet, clawed feet, feet with toes for gripping branches? Explain.

17. If a scientist had DNA samples from four organisms, how could he find out which organisms were related?

18. What types of adaptations would be beneficial to an organism living in the desert?

19. Use the idea of natural selection to explain why polar bears are white and why some other bears are brown.

20. Horseshoe crabs are an example of an organism that has changed very little through time. What factors might have kept these organisms from changing?

Developing Skills

If you need help, refer to the Skill Handbook.

21. Observing and Inferring: Look at the graph below. Scientists hypothesize that millions more microscopic species exist than we now know. Why do you think the number of microscopic species known to science is so low?

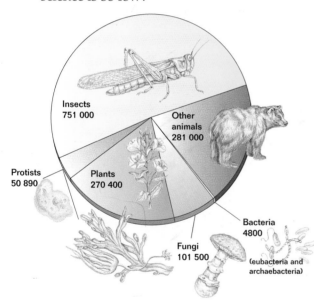

Insects 751 000

Other animals 281 000

Protists 50 890

Plants 270 400

Bacteria 4800

Fungi 101 500

(eubacteria and archaebacteria)

22. Recognizing Cause and Effect: A new predator is introduced into a population of rabbits. Rabbits with longer back legs have an advantage because they can run faster. Using the concept of natural selection, explain what might happen to the rabbit population over time.

23. Interpreting Illustrations: Study the geologic time scale on page 315. Make a table that lists when the following groups of organisms appeared on Earth: amphibians, fish, land plants, mammals, reptiles, birds, and simple animals.

THE PRINCETON REVIEW

Test-Taking Tip

Don't Be Afraid to Ask for Help Ask for advice on things you don't understand. If you're practicing for a test and you find yourself stuck, unable to understand why you got a question wrong, or unable to do it in the first place, ask for help.

Test Practice

Use these questions to test your Science Proficiency.

1. Why do tropical rain forests have a large number of animal species?
   A) Temperatures remain warm and steady all year and rainfall is high.
   B) Temperatures fluctuate greatly and rainfall is high.
   C) Temperatures remain warm all year and rainfall is low.
   D) Temperatures remain cool and steady all year and rainfall is high.

2. Fossils enable scientists to study how species have changed over time. Which of the following statements about the fossil record is true?
   A) The fossil record shows a complete history of Earth.
   B) A fossil represents every species on Earth.
   C) It is more common for an organism to decay without ever becoming a fossil.
   D) Fossils from almost every major group of plants and animals are part of the fossil record.

UNIT 4

Exploring Space

What's Happening Here?

Much of the light you see twinkling in the night sky bears witness to a distant past. How so? If you peered at one of those stars through a powerful telescope, you would discover not how the star appears today but how it appeared millions of years ago. Likewise, if people on a distant planet were to aim a telescope at you, they would see Earth as it existed in the age of the dinosaurs! Outer space is so vast that light traveling at 300 000 kilometers a second takes millions of years to span the distance from a distant star to Earth. To grasp the subject of astronomy, you must expand your notion of distance to the unfathomable. In this unit, you will learn how the lure of this vastness has triggered a new age of exploration. En route into deep space, the *Voyager* probes launched in 1977 photographed Jupiter's Great Red Spot (left), a massive storm in the planet's outer gases. In 1996, this astronaut (inset) tested a minirocket backpack by flying solo above the space shuttle *Discovery*.

inter**NET** CONNECTION

Explore the Glencoe Science Web Site at **www.glencoe.com/sec/science/nc** to find out more about topics found in this unit.

Exploring Space

Chapter Preview

Section 12-1
Radiation from
Space

Section 12-2
Early Space
Missions

Section 12-3
Recent and Future
Space Missions

Skills Preview

Skill Builders
- Sequence
- Map Concepts

MiniLabs
- Analyze Data
- Infer

Activities
- Draw Conclusions

Reading Check ✔

As you read this chapter about space, write four or five questions that are answered in each section.

Explore Activity

The first space exploration didn't occur in a spaceship or a satellite. Instead, it was done by a person simply looking upward, studying countless points of shimmering light. Over time, people devised more and more accurate ways to study the moon, the planets, and the stars. We can learn a lot about a star's temperature, size, and composition, for instance, by studying its light. In this activity, you'll observe some of the colors that make up visible light, which is one form of radiation emitted by stars.

Observe White Light

1. Cover the end of a flashlight with green cellophane paper.

2. Cover another flashlight with blue cellophane and a third with red cellophane.

3. In a darkened room, experiment with the three lights by shining different combinations of two lights on the same spot on a sheet of white paper.

Science **Journal**

Observe all colors shining on the same spot on the paper and infer what is happening. Record your observations and inferences in your Science Journal.

12•1 Radiation from Space

What You'll Learn

▶ The electromagnetic spectrum
▶ The differences between refracting and reflecting telescopes
▶ The differences between optical and radio telescopes

Vocabulary

electromagnetic spectrum
refracting telescope
reflecting telescope
observatory
radio telescope

Why It's Important

▶ You'll learn about the tools and methods used to study space.

Electromagnetic Waves

On a crisp, autumn evening, you take a break from your homework to gaze out the window at the many stars that fill the night sky. Looking up at the stars, it's easy to imagine future spaceships venturing through space and large space stations circling above Earth, where people work and live. But, when you look into the night sky, what you're really seeing is the distant past, not the future.

Light from the Past

When you look at a star, you see light that left the star many years ago. The light that you see travels fast. Still, the distances across space are so great that it takes years for the light to reach Earth—sometimes millions of years.

The light and other energy leaving a star are forms of radiation. Recall that radiation is energy that's transmitted from one place to another by electromagnetic waves. Because of the electric and magnetic properties of this radiation, it's called electromagnetic radiation. Electromagnetic waves carry energy through empty space as well as through matter.

Figure 12-1 The electromagnetic spectrum ranges from gamma rays with wavelengths of less than 0.000 000 000 01 m to radio waves more than 100 000 m long. **What happens to frequency (the number of waves that pass a point per second) as wavelength shortens?**

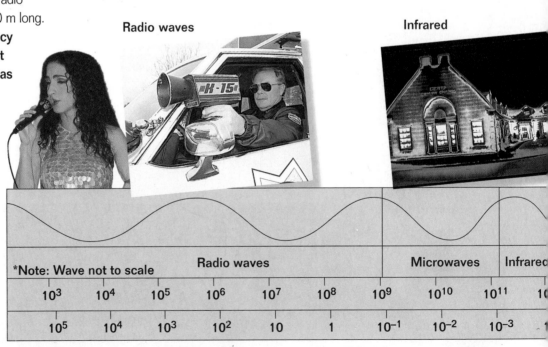

Radio waves

Infrared

*Note: Wave not to scale

	Radio waves					Microwaves		Infrared
10^3	10^4	10^5	10^6	10^7	10^8	10^9	10^{10}	10^{11}
10^5	10^4	10^3	10^2	10	1	10^{-1}	10^{-2}	10^{-3}

Electromagnetic Radiation

Sound waves, a type of mechanical wave, can't travel through empty space. How do we hear the voices of the astronauts while they're in space? When they speak into a microphone, the sound is converted into electromagnetic waves called radio waves. The radio waves travel through space and through our atmosphere. They are then converted back into sound by electronic equipment and audio speakers.

Radio waves and visible light from the sun are just two types of electromagnetic radiation. The other types include gamma rays, X rays, ultraviolet waves, infrared waves, and microwaves. **Figure 12-1** shows these forms of electromagnetic radiation arranged according to their wavelengths. This arrangement of electromagnetic radiation is called the **electromagnetic spectrum.**

Although the various electromagnetic waves differ in their wavelengths, they all travel at the speed of 300 000 km/s in a vacuum. You're probably more familiar with this speed as the "speed of light." Visible light and other forms of electromagnetic radiation travel at this incredible speed, but the universe is so large that it takes millions of years for the light from some stars to reach Earth.

Once electromagnetic radiation from stars and other objects reaches Earth, we can use it to learn about the source of the electromagnetic radiation. What tools and methods do scientists use to discover what lies beyond our planet? One tool for observing electromagnetic radiation from distant sources is a telescope.

PHYSICS
INTEGRATION

Bending Light
Pass a beam of white light through a prism. Note that different colors of light are bent, forming a spectrum. Infer how the white light and prism form a spectrum with violet on one end and red on the other.

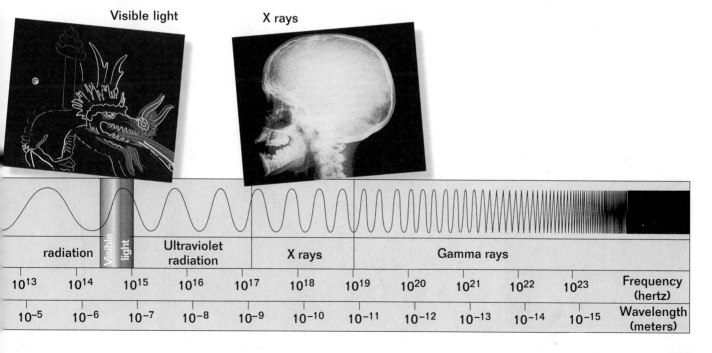

Visible light   X rays

radiation	Visible light	Ultraviolet radiation	X rays	Gamma rays	

| 10^{13} | 10^{14} | 10^{15} | 10^{16} | 10^{17} | 10^{18} | 10^{19} | 10^{20} | 10^{21} | 10^{22} | 10^{23} | Frequency (hertz) |
| 10^{-5} | 10^{-6} | 10^{-7} | 10^{-8} | 10^{-9} | 10^{-10} | 10^{-11} | 10^{-12} | 10^{-13} | 10^{-14} | 10^{-15} | Wavelength (meters) |

Optical Telescopes

Optical telescopes produce magnified images of objects. Light is collected by an objective lens or mirror, which then forms an image at the focal point of the telescope. The eyepiece lens then magnifies the image. The two types of optical telescopes are shown in **Figure 12-2.**

In a **refracting telescope,** the light from an object passes through a double convex objective lens and is bent to form an image on the focal point. The image is then magnified by the eyepiece.

A **reflecting telescope** uses a mirror as an objective to focus light from the object being viewed. Light passes through the open end of a reflecting telescope and strikes a concave mirror at its base. The light is then reflected to the focal point to form an image. A smaller mirror is often used to reflect the light into the eyepiece lens so the magnified image can be viewed.

Using Optical Telescopes

Most optical telescopes used by professional astronomers are housed in buildings called **observatories.** Observatories often have a dome-shaped roof that opens up to let in light. However, not all telescopes are in observatories.

Figure 12-2 These diagrams show how each type of optical telescope collects light and forms an image.

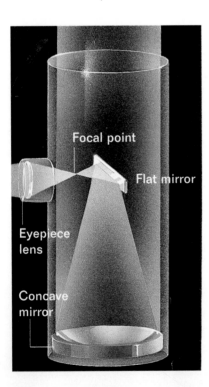

A In a refracting telescope, a double convex lens focuses light to form an image at the focal point.

B In a reflecting telescope, a concave mirror focuses light to form an image at the focal point.

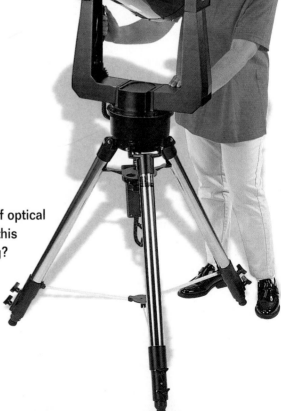

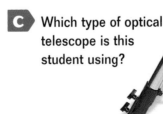

C Which type of optical telescope is this student using?

The *Hubble Space Telescope,* shown in **Figure 12-3,** was launched in 1990 by the space shuttle *Discovery.* Earth's atmosphere absorbs and distorts some of the energy received from space. Because *Hubble* didn't have to view space through our atmosphere, it should have produced clear images. However, when the largest mirror of this reflecting telescope was shaped, there was a mistake. Images obtained by the telescope were not as clear as expected. In December 1993, a team of astronauts repaired *Hubble's* telescope mirror and other equipment. Now, the clear images obtained by *Hubble Space Telescope* are changing scientists' ideas about space.

Figure 12-3 The *Hubble Space Telescope* was released from the cargo bay of the space shuttle *Discovery* on April 25, 1990. It's now orbiting Earth, sending back images and data about distant space objects.

Problem Solving

Interpreting Telescope Data

The magnifying power *(Mp)* of a telescope is determined by the focal lengths of the telescope's objective lens and eyepiece. Once built, you cannot easily change the objective lens, but you can easily change the eyepiece. That's why telescopes are often sold with three or four eyepieces—each with a different focal length. The magnifying power of a telescope is equal to the focal length of its objective lens divided by the focal length of its eyepiece.

Telescopes also have light-gathering power (LGP). Generally, the larger the diameter (aperture) of a telescope's objective, the more light the telescope can gather. Therefore, a telescope with an objective aperture of 125 mm will gather more light than a telescope with an objective aperture of 75 mm.

The following table lists the characteristics of two telescopes. Study the data about each telescope and interpret which has the greater magnifying power and which has the greater light-gathering power.

Telescope Data			
Tele-scope	Aperture	Objective Focal Length	Eyepiece Focal Length
1	75 mm	1200 mm	9 mm, 12 mm
2	125 mm	900 mm	9 mm, 12 mm

Think Critically: Which telescope would you want to use to observe stars? Which telescope would you want to use to observe craters on the moon? Explain your selections.

Active Optics

Since the early 1600s, when the Italian scientist Galileo Galilei first turned a telescope toward the stars, people have been searching for better ways to study what lies beyond our atmosphere, such as the twin Keck telescopes shown in **Figure 12-4.** Today, the largest reflector has a segmented mirror 10 m wide. The most recent innovations in optical telescopes involve active and adaptive optics. With active optics, a computer is used to compensate for changes in temperature, mirror distortions, and bad viewing conditions. Even more ambitious is adaptive optics, which uses a laser to probe the atmosphere and relay information to a computer about air turbulence. The computer then adjusts the telescope's mirror thousands of times per second, thus reducing the effects of atmospheric turbulence. ☑

Reading Check ☑

How big is the mirror on the largest reflector?

Figure 12-4 The twin Keck telescopes on Mauna Kea in Hawaii can be used together, more than doubling the resolving power. Each individual telescope has an objective mirror 10 m in diameter. To cope with the difficulty of building such a large mirror, this telescope design used several smaller mirrors positioned to work as one. **Although the Keck telescopes are much larger than the *Hubble Space Telescope*, the *Hubble* is able to achieve better resolution. Why?**

Radio Telescopes

As you know, stars and other objects radiate energy throughout the electromagnetic spectrum. A **radio telescope,** such as the one shown in **Figure 12-5,** is used to study radio waves traveling through space. Unlike visible light, radio waves pass freely through Earth's atmosphere. Because of this, radio telescopes are useful 24 hours a day under most weather conditions.

Radio waves reaching Earth's surface strike the large, curved dish of a radio telescope. This dish reflects the waves to a focal point where a receiver is located. The information allows scientists to detect objects in space, to map the universe, and to search for intelligent life on other planets.

In the remainder of this chapter, you'll learn about the instruments that travel into space and send back information that telescopes on Earth's surface cannot obtain.

Figure 12-5 This radio telescope is used to study radio waves traveling through space.

Section Assessment

1. What is the difference between radio telescopes and optical telescopes?

2. The frequency of electromagnetic radiation is the number of waves that pass a point in a specific amount of time. If red light has a longer wavelength than blue light, which would have a greater frequency?

3. **Think Critically:** It takes light from the closest star to Earth (other than the sun) about four years to reach us. If there were intelligent life on a planet circling that star, how long would it take for us to send them a radio transmission and for us to receive their reply?

4. **Skill Builder**
   Sequencing Sequence these electromagnetic waves from longest wavelength to shortest wavelength: *gamma rays, visible light, X rays, radio waves, infrared waves, ultraviolet waves,* and *microwaves.* If you need help, refer to Sequencing in the **Skill Handbook** on page 550.

Using Math

The magnifying power (*Mp*) of a telescope is determined by dividing the focal length of the objective lens (FL_{obj}) by the focal length of the eyepiece (FL_{eye}) using the following equation.

$$Mp = \frac{FL_{obj}}{FL_{eye}}$$

If $FL_{obj} = 1200$ mm and $FL_{eye} = 6$ mm, what is the telescope's magnifying power?

Telescopes

Materials

- Candle
- White cardboard
  (50 cm × 60 cm)
- Flashlight
- Hand lens
- Large glass of water
- Concave mirror
- Plane mirror
- Masking tape
- Convex mirror
- Empty paper-towel tube

You have learned that optical telescopes use lenses and mirrors as objectives to collect light from an object. They use eyepiece lenses to magnify images of that object. Try this activity to see how the paths of light differ in reflecting and refracting telescopes.

What You'll Investigate

In what way are paths of light affected by the lenses and mirrors in refracting and reflecting telescopes?

Goals

- **Observe** how different mirrors and lenses affect light and the appearance of objects.

Procedure

1. **Observe** your reflection in plane, convex, and concave mirrors.

2. Hold an object in front of each of the mirrors. **Compare** the size and position of the images.

3. **Darken** the room and hold the convex mirror in front of you at a 45° angle, slanting downward. Direct the flashlight toward the mirror. **Note** the size and position of the reflected light.

4. Repeat step 3 using a plane mirror. **Draw** a diagram to show what happens to the beam of light.

5. **Tape** the paper-towel tube to the flashlight so that the beam of light will pass through the tube. Direct the light into a glass of water, first directly from above, then from an angle 45° to the water's surface. **Observe** the direction of the light rays when viewed from the side of the glass.

6. **Light** a candle and set it some distance from the vertically held cardboard screen. **CAUTION:** *Keep hair and clothing away from the flame.* Using the hand lens as a convex lens, move it between the candle and the screen until you have the best possible image.

7. **Move** the lens closer to the candle. Note what happens to the size of the image. Move the cardboard until the image is in focus.

Conclude and Apply

1. How did you **determine** the position of the focal point of the hand lens in step 6? What does this tell you about the position of the light rays?

2. **Compare and contrast** the effect the three types of mirrors had on your reflection.

3. **Compare and contrast** the path of light in refracting and reflecting telescopes.

4. What is the purpose of the concave mirror in a reflecting telescope?

Seeing in 3-D

Why do humans have two eyes? One reason is that the second eye lets us see more of the world. It increases our field of view. Many animals have eyes set on opposite sides of their heads, so each eye sees a separate half of the world. But, human eyes are set closer together. They see almost the same scene but from a slightly different angle. Look at the student in front of you, first through only your right eye then only your left eye. You'll notice that each eye sees a slightly different view. But, your brain puts the two different views together, giving you the ability to figure out which object is closer to you and which is farther away. You see in three dimensions (3-D).

In the figure on the left, notice how the green block appears to the left of the yellow cylinder when seen by the left eye but to the right when seen by the right eye. Your brain interprets these two images, and you know that the yellow cylinder is in front of the green block.

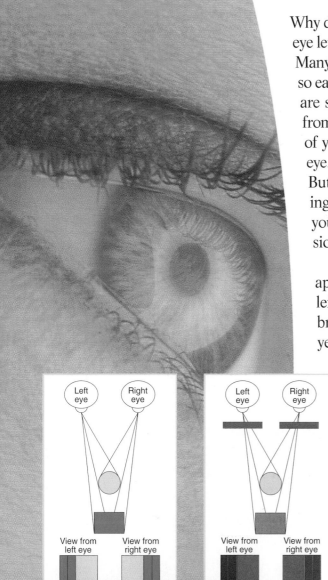

Movies and Television

How can you have a 3-D experience at the movies or on a TV? A camera with two lenses a few inches apart records the images on film or videotape. But, one lens has a red filter in front of it and the other a blue, as shown in the figure on the right. So, the image recorded by one lens is in shades of red, while the one recorded by the other lens is in shades of blue. The viewer watches the film through 3-D glasses that have the same color filters. Because the red filter allows only red light through it, only the image meant for that eye passes through that filter. The filters send the images meant for the right eye only to the right eye and the images meant for the left only to the left. The brain does the rest of the work. It combines the two colors, giving different shades of gray and interprets the slightly different images so that you can tell which object is in front and which is behind.

Career
CONNECTION

Research how 3-D technology is being used in the latest computer animation software. Find out how the 3-D images used in computer animations are made.

What You'll Learn

► How to compare and contrast natural and artificial satellites
► The differences between artificial satellites and space probes
► The history of the race to the moon

Vocabulary

satellite
orbit
space probe
Project Mercury
Project Gemini
Project Apollo

Why It's Important

► Learning about space exploration will help you better understand the vastness of space.

The First Steps into Space

If you had your choice of watching your favorite sports team on television or from the stadium, which would you prefer? You would probably want to be as close as possible to the game so you wouldn't miss any of the action. Scientists feel the same way about space. Even though telescopes have taught them a great deal about the moon and planets, they want to learn more by actually going to those places or by sending spacecraft where they can't go.

Satellites

Space exploration began in 1957 when the former Soviet Union used a rocket to send *Sputnik I* into space. It was the first artificial satellite. A **satellite** is any object that revolves around another object. When an object enters space, it travels in a straight line unless a force such as gravity deflects it. When Earth's gravity pulls on a satellite, it falls toward Earth. The result of the satellite traveling forward while at the same time falling toward Earth is a curved path, called an **orbit**, around Earth. This is shown in **Figure 12-6.**

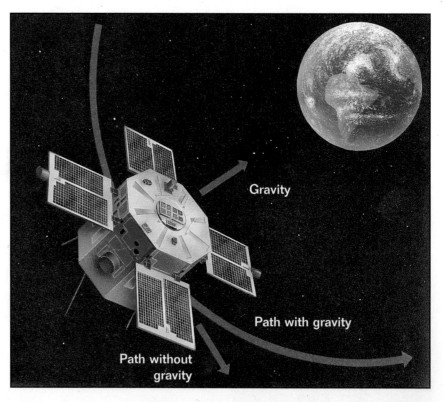

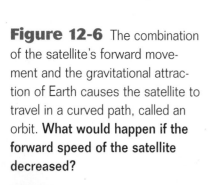

Figure 12-6 The combination of the satellite's forward movement and the gravitational attraction of Earth causes the satellite to travel in a curved path, called an orbit. **What would happen if the forward speed of the satellite decreased?**

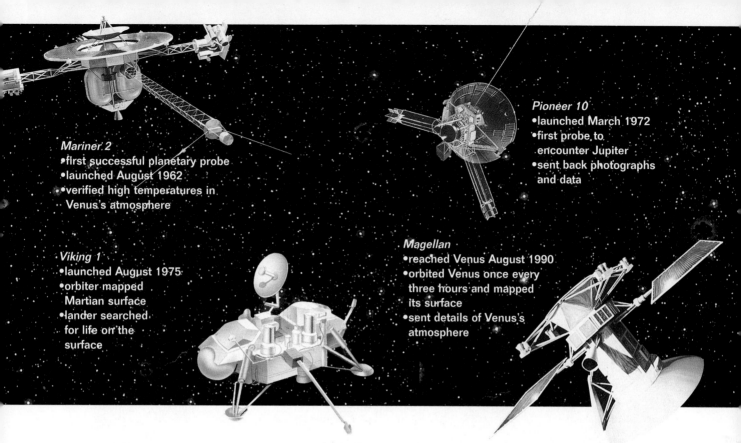

Mariner 2
- first successful planetary probe
- launched August 1962
- verified high temperatures in Venus's atmosphere

Pioneer 10
- launched March 1972
- first probe to encounter Jupiter
- sent back photographs and data

Viking 1
- launched August 1975
- orbiter mapped Martian surface
- lander searched for life on the surface

Magellan
- reached Venus August 1990
- orbited Venus once every three hours and mapped its surface
- sent details of Venus's atmosphere

Satellite Uses

The moon is a natural satellite of Earth. It completes one orbit every month. *Sputnik I* orbited Earth for 57 days before gravity pulled it back into the atmosphere, where it burned up. *Sputnik I* was an experiment to show that artificial satellites could be made. Today, thousands of artificial satellites orbit Earth.

Present-day communication satellites transmit radio and television programs to locations around the world. Other satellites gather scientific data that can't be obtained from Earth, and weather satellites constantly monitor Earth's global weather patterns.

Space Probes

Not all objects carried into space by rockets become satellites. Rockets also can be used to send instruments into space. A **space probe** is an instrument that gathers information and sends it back to Earth. Unlike satellites that orbit Earth, space probes travel far into the solar system. Some have even traveled out of the solar system. Space probes, like many satellites, carry cameras and other data-gathering equipment, as well as radio transmitters and receivers that allow them to communicate with scientists on Earth. **Figure 12-7** shows some of the early space probes launched by NASA (National Aeronautics and Space Administration).

Figure 12-7 Some early U.S. space probes and their missions provided much useful data.

Using Math

Suppose a spacecraft is launched at a speed of 40 200 km per hour. Express this speed in kilometers per second.

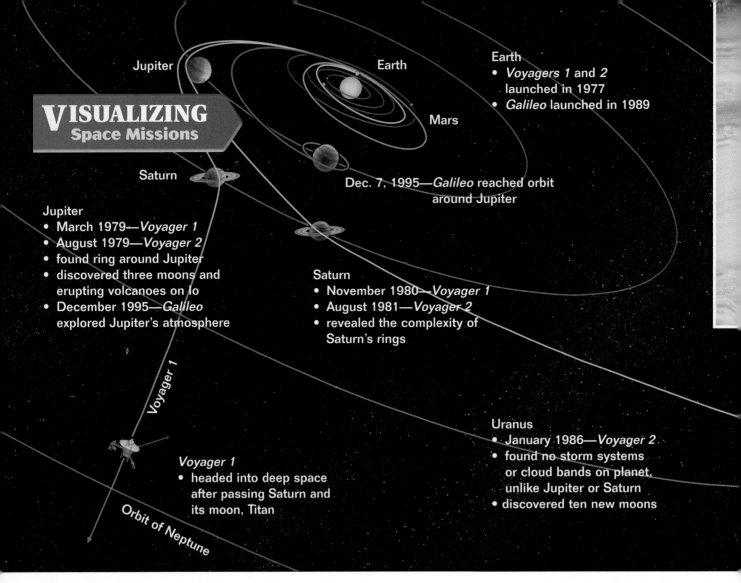

Jupiter

Earth

Earth
- *Voyagers 1* and *2* launched in 1977
- *Galileo* launched in 1989

Mars

Saturn

Dec. 7, 1995—*Galileo* reached orbit around Jupiter

Jupiter
- March 1979—*Voyager 1*
- August 1979—*Voyager 2*
- found ring around Jupiter
- discovered three moons and erupting volcanoes on Io
- December 1995—*Galileo* explored Jupiter's atmosphere

Saturn
- November 1980—*Voyager 1*
- August 1981—*Voyager 2*
- revealed the complexity of Saturn's rings

Voyager 1

Voyager 1
- headed into deep space after passing Saturn and its moon, Titan

Uranus
- January 1986—*Voyager 2*
- found no storm systems or cloud bands on planet, unlike Jupiter or Saturn
- discovered ten new moons

Orbit of Neptune

Figure 12-8 The *Voyager* and *Galileo* spacecraft helped make many major discoveries.

You've probably heard of the space probes *Voyager 1* and *Voyager 2*. These two probes were launched in 1977 and are now heading toward deep space. *Voyager 1* flew past Jupiter and Saturn. *Voyager 2* flew past Jupiter, Saturn, Uranus, and Neptune. **Figure 12-8** describes some of what we've learned from the *Voyager* probes. Now, these probes are exploring beyond our solar system as part of the Voyager Interstellar Mission. Scientists expect these probes to continue to transmit data to Earth for at least 20 more years.

The fate of a probe is never certain, and not all probes are successful. In 1993, *Mars Observer* was only days away from entering orbit around Mars when it was lost. The problem was most likely a critical failure in the propulsion system.

Galileo, launched in 1989, reached Jupiter in 1995. In July 1995, *Galileo* released a smaller probe that began a five-month approach to Jupiter. The small probe took a parachute ride through Jupiter's violent atmosphere in December 1995.

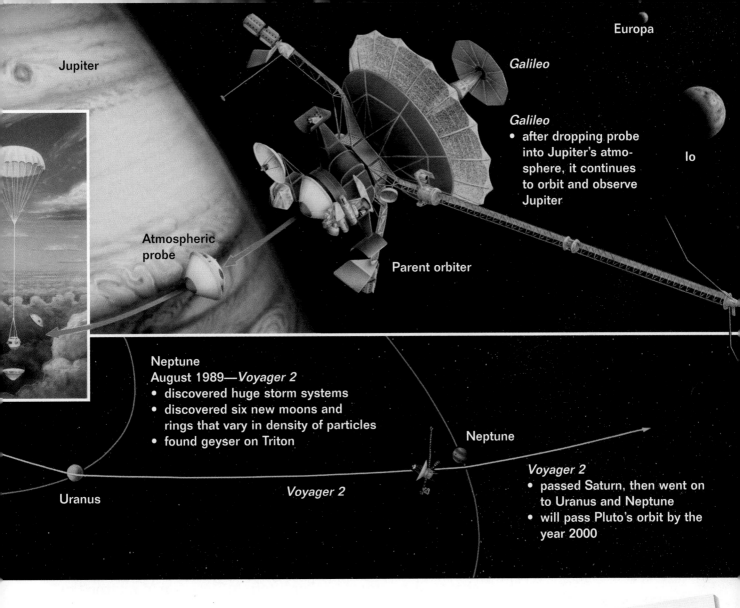

Jupiter

Europa

Galileo

Galileo
• after dropping probe into Jupiter's atmosphere, it continues to orbit and observe Jupiter

Io

Atmospheric probe

Parent orbiter

Neptune
August 1989—*Voyager 2*
• discovered huge storm systems
• discovered six new moons and rings that vary in density of particles
• found geyser on Triton

Neptune

Voyager 2
• passed Saturn, then went on to Uranus and Neptune
• will pass Pluto's orbit by the year 2000

Voyager 2

Uranus

Before being crushed by the atmospheric pressure, it transmitted information about Jupiter's composition, temperature, and pressure to the ship orbiting above. *Galileo* studied Jupiter's moons, rings, and magnetic fields and then relayed this information back to scientists who were eagerly waiting for it on Earth. ☑

Galileo

Recent studies of Jupiter's moon Europa by *Galileo* indicate that an ocean of water or ice may exist under the outer layer of ice that covers Europa's cracked surface. The cracks in the surface may be caused by geologic activity that heats the ocean underneath the surface. Sunlight penetrates these cracks, further heating the ocean and setting the stage for the possible existence of life on Europa. *Galileo* studied Europa through 1999. More advanced probes will be needed to determine whether molecular life actually does exist on this icy moon.

Reading Check ☑

What did the *Galileo* space probe study?

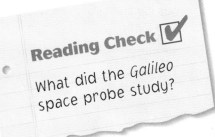

LIFE SCIENCE
◀ **INTEGRATION**

Comparing the Effects of Light Pollution

Procedure

1. Obtain a cardboard tube from an empty roll of paper towels.

2. Select a night when clear skies are predicted. Go outside about two hours after sunset and look through the cardboard tube at a specific constellation decided upon ahead of time.

3. Count the number of stars you are able to see without moving the observing tube. Repeat this three times.

4. Determine the average number of observable stars at your location.

Analysis

1. Compare and contrast the number of stars visible from other students' homes.

2. Explain the cause and effect of differences in your observations.

The Race to the Moon

Throughout the world, people were shocked when they turned on their radios and television sets in 1957 and heard the radio transmissions from *Sputnik I* as it orbited over their heads. All that *Sputnik I* transmitted was a sort of beeping sound, but people quickly realized that putting a human into space wasn't far off.

In 1961, the Soviet cosmonaut Yuri A. Gagarin became the first human in space. He orbited Earth and then returned safely. Soon, President John F. Kennedy called for the United States to place people on the moon and return them to Earth by the end of that decade. The "race for space" had begun.

The U.S. program to reach the moon began with **Project Mercury.** The goals of Project Mercury were to orbit a piloted spacecraft around Earth and to bring it safely back. The program provided data and experience in the basics of space flight. On May 5, 1961, Alan B. Shepard became the first U.S. citizen in space. In 1962, *Mercury* astronaut John Glenn became the first U.S. citizen to orbit Earth. **Figure 12-9** shows Glenn preparing for liftoff. In 1998, Glenn returned to space aboard the space shuttle *Discovery*. You'll learn more about space shuttles in the next section.

Project Gemini

Project Gemini was the next step in reaching the moon. Teams of two astronauts in the same *Gemini* spacecraft orbited Earth. One *Gemini* team met and connected with another spacecraft in orbit—a skill that would be needed on a voyage to the moon.

Along with the *Mercury* and *Gemini* programs, a series of robotic probes was sent to the moon. *Ranger* proved we could get spacecraft to the moon. *Surveyor* landed gently on the moon's surface, indicating that the moon's surface could support spacecraft and humans. The mission of *Lunar Orbiter* was to take pictures of the moon's surface to help determine the best landing sites on the moon.

Figure 12-9 John Glenn was the first U.S. astronaut to orbit Earth.

Project Apollo

The final stage of the U.S. program to reach the moon was **Project Apollo.** On July 20, 1969, *Apollo* 11 landed on the lunar surface. Neil Armstrong was the first human to set foot on the moon. His first words as he stepped onto its surface were, "That's one small step for man, one giant leap for mankind." Edwin Aldrin, the second of the three *Apollo* 11 astronauts, joined Armstrong on the moon, and they explored its surface for two hours. Michael Collins remained in the Command Module orbiting the moon, where Armstrong and Aldrin returned before beginning the journey home. A total of six lunar landings brought back more than 2000 samples of moon rock and soil for study before the program ended in 1972. **Figure 12-10** shows astronauts on the moon.

During the past three decades, most missions in space have been carried out by individual countries, often competing to be the first or the best. Today, there is much more cooperation among countries of the world to work together and share what each has learned. Projects are now being planned for cooperative missions to Mars and elsewhere. As you read the next section, you'll see how the U.S. program has progressed since the days of Project Apollo, and where it may be going in the future.

Figure 12-10 The Lunar Rover Vehicle was first used during the *Apollo 15* mission. Riding in the moon buggy, *Apollo 15, 16,* and *17* astronauts explored large areas of the lunar surface.

Section Assessment

1. Currently, no human-made objects are orbiting Neptune, yet Neptune has eight satellites. Explain.

2. *Galileo* was considered a space probe as it traveled to Jupiter. Once there, however, it became an artificial satellite. Explain.

3. **Think Critically:** Is Earth a satellite of any other body in space? Explain your answer.

4. **Skill Builder**
   Concept Mapping Make an events-chain concept map that lists the events in the U.S. space program to place people on the moon. If you need help, refer to Concept Mapping in the **Skill Handbook** on page 550.

Using Computers

Spreadsheet Use the spreadsheet feature on your computer to generate a table of recent successful satellites and space probes launched by the United States. Include a description of the craft, the date launched, and the mission. If you need help, refer to page 574.

Activity 12•2

Star Sightings

For thousands of years, humans have used the stars to learn about the planet we live on. From star sightings, you can map the change of seasons, navigate the oceans, and even determine the size of Earth.

Polaris, or the North Star, has occupied an important place in human history. The location of Polaris is not affected by Earth's rotation. At any given observation point, it always appears at the same angle above the horizon. At Earth's north pole, Polaris appears directly overhead. At the equator, it is just above the northern horizon. Polaris provides a standard from which other locations can be measured. Such star sightings can be made using the astrolabe, an instrument used to measure the height of a star above the horizon.

Recognize the Problem

How can you determine the size of Earth?

Form a Hypothesis

Think about what you have learned about sightings of Polaris. How does this tell you that Earth is round? Knowing that Earth is round, **form a hypothesis** about whether you can estimate the circumference of Earth based on star sightings.

Goals

- **Record** your sightings of Polaris.
- **Share** the data with other students to **calculate** the circumference of Earth.

Safety Precautions

Do not use the astrolabe during the daytime to observe the sun.

Data Sources

Go to the Glencoe Science Web Site at **www.glencoe. com/sec/science/nc** to obtain instructions on how to make an astrolabe, for more information about the location of Polaris, and for data from other students.

Test Your Hypothesis

Plan

1. Obtain an astrolabe or **construct** one using the instructions posted on the Glencoe Science Web Site.

2. **Design** a data table in your Science Journal similar to the one below.

3. Decide as a group how you will make your observations. Does it take more than one person to make each observation? When will it be easiest to see Polaris?

Do

1. Make sure your teacher approves your plan before you proceed.

2. Carry out your observations.

3. **Record** your observations in your data table.

4. **Average** your readings and post them in the table provided on the Glencoe Science Web Site.

Analyze Your Data

1. **Research** the names of cities that are at approximately the same longitude as your hometown. **Gather** astrolabe readings at the Glencoe Science Web Site from students in one of those cities.

2. **Compare** your astrolabe readings. **Subtract** the smaller reading from the larger one.

3. Determine the distance between your star sighting location and the other city.

4. To calculate the circumference of Earth, use the following relationship.

$$\text{Circumference} = \frac{(360°)(\text{distance between locations})}{\text{difference between readings}}$$

Draw Conclusions

1. How does the circumference of Earth that you calculated compare with the accepted value of 40 079 km?

2. What are some possible sources of error in this method of determining the size of Earth? What improvements would you suggest?

Polaris Observations		
Your location:		
Date	Time	Astrolabe Reading
Average astrolabe reading:		

12·3 Recent and Future Space Missions

What You'll Learn

▶ The benefits of the space shuttle

▶ The usefulness of orbital space stations

▶ Future space missions

Vocabulary

space shuttle
space station

Why It's Important

▶ Many exciting things are planned for the future of space exploration.

The Space Shuttle

Imagine spending millions of dollars to build a machine, sending it off into space, and watching its 3000 metric tons of metal and other materials burn up after only a few minutes of work. That's exactly what NASA did for many years. The early rockets lifted a small capsule holding the astronauts into orbit. Sections of the rocket separated from the rest of the rocket body and burned as they reentered the atmosphere.

A Reusable Spacecraft

NASA administrators, like many others, realized that it would be less expensive and less wasteful to reuse resources. The reusable spacecraft that transports astronauts, satellites, and other materials to and from space is the **space shuttle.** The space shuttle is shown in **Figure 12-11.**

At launch, the space shuttle stands on end and is connected to an external liquid-fuel tank and two solid-fuel booster rockets. When the shuttle reaches an altitude of about 45 km, the emptied solid-fuel booster rockets drop off and parachute back to Earth. They are recovered and used again. The larger, external liquid-fuel tank eventually separates and falls back to Earth, but it isn't recovered.

Once the space shuttle reaches space, it begins to orbit Earth. There, astronauts perform many different tasks. The cargo bay can carry a self-contained laboratory, where astronauts conduct scientific experiments and determine the effects of space flight on the human body. On missions in which the cargo bay isn't used as a laboratory, the shuttle can launch, repair, and retrieve satellites.

To retrieve a satellite, a large mechanical arm in the cargo bay is extended. An astronaut inside the shuttle moves the arm by remote control. The arm grabs the satellite and pulls it back into the cargo bay. The doors are closed, and it is then returned to Earth.

Figure 12-11 The space shuttle is designed to make many trips into space.

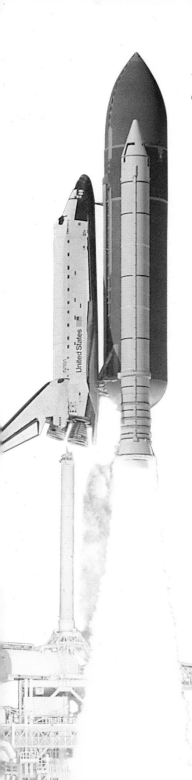

Similarly, the mechanical arm can be used to lift a satellite or probe out of the cargo bay and place it into space. In some cases, a defective satellite can be pulled in by the mechanical arm, repaired while in the cargo bay, and then placed into space once more.

After each mission is completed, the space shuttle glides back to Earth and lands like an airplane. A large landing field is needed because the gliding speed of the shuttle is 335 km/hr.

Space Stations

Astronauts can spend only a short time in space in the space shuttle. Its living area is small, and the crew needs more room to live, exercise, and work. A **space station** has living quarters, work and exercise areas, and all the equipment and support systems needed for humans to live and work in space.

The United States had such a station in the past. The space station *Skylab* was launched in 1973. Crews of astronauts spent up to 84 days in it performing experiments and collecting data on the effects that living in space had on humans. In 1979, the abandoned *Skylab* fell out of orbit and burned up as it entered Earth's atmosphere.

Mini Lab

Modeling Gravity

Procedure

1. Locate a stereo record album and turntable you can use for this activity.
2. Fold 8-cm-wide strips of construction paper in half, then unfold them.
3. Wrap the strips along the fold around the circumference of the record so there is a 4-cm wall around the outside edge of the disc.
4. Securely tape the rest underneath the record.
5. Place the record on a turntable and place three marbles at its center.
6. Switch on the turntable.

Analysis

1. What did you observe about the movements of the marbles?
2. Hypothesize how what you've observed could be useful for simulating the effects of gravity on a space station.

Crews from the former Soviet Union have spent the most time in space aboard the space station *Mir*. Cosmonaut Dr. Valery Polyakov returned to Earth after 438 days in space studying the long-term effects of weightlessness.

Cooperation in Space

In 1995, the United States and Russia began an era of cooperation and trust in exploring space. Early in the year, Dr. Norman Thagard was launched into orbit aboard the Russian *Soyuz* spacecraft, along with two Russian cosmonaut crewmates. Dr. Thagard was the first U.S. astronaut launched into space by a Russian booster and the first American resident of the Russian space station *Mir*.

In June 1995, Russian cosmonauts rode into orbit aboard the space shuttle *Atlantis*, America's 100th crewed launch. The mission of *Atlantis* involved, among other studies, a rendezvous and docking with space station *Mir*. The cooperation that existed on this mission continued through

Figure 12-12 The proposed International Space Station is scheduled for completion in 2003.

eight more space shuttle-*Mir* docking missions. Each was an important step toward building and operating the International Space Station.

The International Space Station

The International Space Station (ISS) will be a permanent laboratory designed to use in long-term research. Diverse topics will be studied, such as researching the growth of protein crystals. This project will help scientists determine protein structure and function. This could enhance work on drug design and the treatment of diseases.

The space station will draw on the resources of more than 16 nations. Various nations will build units for the space station, which will then be transported into space aboard the space shuttle and Russian launch rockets. The station will be constructed in space. **Figure 12-12** shows what the completed station will look like. ☑

NASA is planning the space station program in three phases. Phase One, now concluded, involved the space shuttle-*Mir* docking missions. Phase Two began in 1998 with the launch of the Russian-built Functional Cargo Block, and will end with the delivery of a U.S. laboratory aboard the space shuttle. During Phase Two, a crew of three people will be delivered to the space station. This is expected to occur by January 2000.

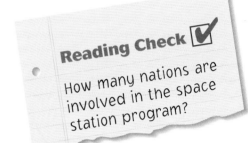

Reading Check ☑

How many nations are involved in the space station program?

Figure 12-13 Using the space shuttle, scientists have already performed extensive experiments in the weightlessness of space.

Living in Space

The project will continue with Phase Three when the Japanese Experiment Module, the European Columbus Orbiting Facility, and another Russian lab will be delivered.

The U.S. hopes to deliver its Habitation module in 2003, although this date may be delayed. This will end Phase Three and make the International Space Station fully operational and ready for its permanent six- or seven-person crew. A total of 45 separate launches are required to take all components of ISS into space. NASA plans for crews of astronauts to stay on board the station for several months at a time. As shown in **Figure 20-13,** NASA has already conducted numerous tests to prepare astronauts for extended space missions. One day, the station could be a construction site for ships that will go to the moon and Mars.

Exploring Mars

Two of the most successful missions in recent years were the 1996 launchings of the Mars *Global Surveyor* and Mars *Pathfinder*. *Surveyor* orbited Mars, taking high-quality photos of the planet's surface. *Pathfinder* descended to the Martian surface, using rockets and a parachute system to slow its descent. Large balloons were used to absorb the shock of landing. *Pathfinder* carried technology to study the surface of the planet, including a remote-controlled robot rover called *Sojourner.* Using information gathered by the rover and photographs taken by *Surveyor*, scientists determined that areas of the planet's surface were once covered with water during Mars's distant past.

Exploring the Moon

Does water exist in the craters of the moon's poles? This is one question NASA intends to explore with data gathered from the *Lunar Prospector* spacecraft. Launched in 1998, the *Lunar Prospector's* one-year mission was to orbit the moon, taking photographs of the moon's surface for mapping purposes. Early data obtained from the spacecraft indicate that hydrogen is present in the rocks of the moon's poles. Hydrogen is one of the elements found in water. Scientists now theorize that ice on the floors of the moon's polar craters may be the source of this hydrogen.

Cassini

In October 1997, NASA launched the space probe *Cassini.* Destination: Saturn. *Cassini* will not reach its goal until 2004. At that time, the space probe will explore Saturn and surrounding areas for four years. One part of its mission is to deliver the European Space Agency's *Huygens* probe to Saturn's largest moon, Titan, as shown in **Figure 12-14.** Some scientists theorize that Titan's atmosphere may be similar to the atmosphere of early Earth.

Figure 12-14 *Cassini* will reach Saturn in 2004.

Section Assessment

1. What is the main advantage of the space shuttle?
2. Why were the space shuttle-*Mir* docking missions so important?
3. Describe Phase Three of the International Space Station program.
4. Recent space missions have been characterized by a spirit of cooperation. How does this compare and contrast with early space missions?
5. **Think Critically:** Why is the space shuttle more versatile than earlier spacecraft?
6.  **Skill Builder**
   Making and Using Graphs *Lunar Prospector* was placed in lunar orbit to photograph the moon's surface. Do the **Chapter 12 Skill Activity** on page 589 to learn more about satellites placed in orbit around Earth.

Science Journal Suppose you're in charge of assembling a crew for a new space station. Select 50 people you want for the station. Remember, you will need people to do a variety of jobs, such as farming, maintenance, scientific experimentation, and so on. In your Science Journal, explain whom you would select and why.

For a **preview** of this chapter, study this Reviewing Main Ideas before you read the chapter. After you have studied this chapter, you can use the Reviewing Main Ideas to **review** the chapter.

The Glencoe MindJogger, Audiocassettes, and CD-ROM provide additional opportunities for review.

Section

12-1 RADIATION FROM SPACE

Electromagnetic waves are arranged in the electromagnetic spectrum according to their wavelengths. Optical telescopes produce magnified images of objects. A **refracting telescope** bends light to form an image. A **reflecting telescope** uses mirrors to focus light to produce an image. **Radio telescopes** collect and record radio waves given off by some space objects. *Why can radio telescopes be used during the day or night and in all types of weather?*

Section

12-2 EARLY SPACE MISSIONS

A **satellite** is an object that revolves around another object. The moons of planets are natural satellites. Artificial satellites are those made by people. An artificial satellite collects data as it **orbits** a planet. A **space probe** travels into the solar system, gathers data, and sends the information back to Earth. Some space probes become artificial satellites of the planet or other object they are sent to study. *Why can the Galileo spacecraft be referred to both as a probe and as an artificial satellite of Jupiter?*

Reading Check ✓

Review the space missions discussed in the chapter. Then, create a timeline that shows these discoveries in chronological order.

Section
12-3 RECENT AND FUTURE SPACE MISSIONS

The **space shuttle** is a reusable spacecraft that carries astronauts, satellites, and other equipment to and from space. **Space stations,** such as *Mir* and *Skylab,* provide the opportunity to conduct research not possible on Earth. The International Space Station will be constructed in Earth orbit with the cooperation of 16 different nations. Completion of the ISS should occur in the year 2003, if all goes as planned. *What advantage does the space shuttle have over other launch vehicles?*

Chapter 12 Assessment

Using Vocabulary

a. electromagnetic spectrum
b. observatory
c. orbit
d. Project Apollo
e. Project Gemini
f. Project Mercury
g. radio telescope
h. reflecting telescope
i. refracting telescope
j. satellite
k. space probe
l. space shuttle
m. space station

The sentences below include italicized terms that have been used incorrectly. Change the incorrect terms so that the sentences read correctly. Underline your change.

1. A *reflecting telescope* uses lenses to bend light toward a focal point.
2. A *space probe* is an object that revolves around another object.
3. *Project Apollo* was the first piloted U.S. space program.
4. A *space station* carries people and tools to and from space.
5. In an *observatory*, electromagnetic waves are arranged according to their wavelengths.

Checking Concepts

Choose the word or phrase that best answers the question.

6. Which spacecraft has sent back images of Venus?
   A) *Voyager*   C) *Apollo 11*
   B) *Viking*   D) *Magellan*

7. Which telescope uses mirrors to collect light?
   A) radio   C) refracting
   B) electromagnetic D) reflecting

8. *Sputnik I* was the first what?
   A) telescope   C) observatory
   B) artificial satellite D) U.S. space probe

9. Which telescope can be used during day or night and during bad weather?
   A) radio   C) refracting
   B) electromagnetic D) reflecting

10. When fully operational, the International Space Station will be crewed by up to how many people?
    A) 3   C) 15
    B) 7   D) 50

11. Which space mission had the goal to put a spacecraft in orbit and bring it back safely?
    A) Project Mercury C) Project Gemini
    B) Project Apollo   D) *Viking I*

12. The space shuttle reuses which of the following?
    A) liquid-fuel tanks C) booster engines
    B) *Gemini* rockets D) *Saturn* rockets

13. What does the space shuttle use to place a satellite into space?
    A) liquid-fuel tank C) mechanical arm
    B) booster rocket   D) cargo bay

14. What was *Skylab?*
    A) space probe   C) space shuttle
    B) space station D) optical telescope

15. Which of the following is a natural satellite of Earth?
    A) *Skylab*   C) the sun
    B) the space shuttle D) the moon

Thinking Critically

16. How would a moon-based telescope have advantages over the Earth-based telescopes being used today?

17. Would a space probe to the sun's surface be useful? Explain.

18. Which would you choose—space missions with people aboard or robotic space probes? Why?

19. Suppose two astronauts were outside the space shuttle, orbiting Earth. The audio speaker in the helmet of one astronaut quits working. The other astronaut is 1 m away, so she shouts a message to him. Can he hear her? Explain.

20. No space probes have visited the planet Pluto. Nevertheless, probes have crossed Pluto's orbit. How?

Developing Skills

If you need help, refer to the **Skill Handbook**.

21. Measuring in SI: Explain whether or not the following pieces of equipment could be used aboard the space shuttle as it orbits Earth: a balance, a meterstick, and a thermometer.

22. Making and Using Tables: Copy the table below. Use information in the chapter as well as news articles and other resources to complete your table.

U.S. Space Probes

Probe	Launch Date	Destinations	Planets or Objects Visited
Vikings 1 & 2			
Galileo			
Lunar Prospector			
Mars Pathfinder & Sojourner			

23. Classifying: Classify the following as a satellite or a space probe: *Cassini*, *Sputnik I*, *Hubble Space Telescope*, *space shuttle*, and *Voyager 2*.

THE PRINCETON REVIEW

Test-Taking Tip

Best Times If your test is going to be timed, then practice under timed conditions. Try timing yourself on specific sections to see if you can improve your overall speed while maintaining accuracy.

Test Practice

Use these questions to test your Science Proficiency.

1. Large telescopes are usually reflectors. Which of the following statements **BEST** explains why this is true?
   A) Reflecting telescopes are easier to use and carry around.
   B) Reflecting telescopes have greater magnifying power.
   C) Reflecting telescopes are less expensive to build and maintain.
   D) In reflecting telescopes, the objective mirror can be supported from beneath and, therefore, can be made larger.

2. The *Lunar Prospector* was classified as a space probe when launched but is now classified as a satellite. What does this illustrate about this spacecraft's flight?
   A) The *Lunar Prospector* is in orbit around Earth.
   B) The *Lunar Prospector* was a space probe on its flight to the moon and became a satellite when it went into orbit around the moon.
   C) The *Lunar Prospector* is moving out of our solar system.
   D) The *Lunar Prospector* was launched from Earth, went into orbit around the moon, and landed on the moon.

CHAPTER

13

The Solar System and Beyond

Chapter Preview

Section 13-1
Earth's Place in Space

Section 13-2
The Solar System

Section 13-3
Stars and Galaxies

Skills Preview

Skill Builders
- Infer
- Develop a Multimedia Presentation

Activities
- Infer
- Classify

MiniLabs
- Observe
- Model

Reading Check ✔

As you read about the phases of the moon and other topics in this chapter, write down unfamiliar words. Define them as you read.

spacelab

·e esa

Explore Activity

Here's a view of Earth taken from space by astronauts on the *Space Lab* orbiter. Do you ever gaze at the night sky? What do you see? On a clear night, it seems like the sky is full of sparkling points of lights. You can see dozens, no, hundreds, of these sparkles. Just how many stars are there?

Estimate Grains of Rice

1. Divide a sheet of black construction paper into two-inch squares. Draw the lines with white crayon or chalk so that they show up clearly.

2. Spill a teaspoonful of rice onto the black paper.

3. Count the number of grains of rice in one square. Repeat this step with a different square. Add the number of grains of rice in the two squares, then divide this number by 2 to calculate the average number of grains of rice in the two squares.

4. Multiply this number by the total number of squares on the paper. This will give you an estimate of the total grains of rice on the paper.

Science Journal

How might scientists use this same method to count the number of stars in the sky? In your Science Journal, describe the process scientists might use.

Earth's Place in Space

What You'll Learn

▶ How seasons are caused by the tilt of Earth's axis
▶ What causes the phases of the moon

Vocabulary
rotation
revolution
eclipse

Why It's Important

▶ The movement of Earth causes night and day.

Earth Moves

You wake up, stretch and yawn, then glance out your window to see the first rays of dawn peeking over the houses. By lunch, the sun is high in the sky. As you sit down to dinner that evening, the sun appears to sink below the horizon. It might seem like the sun moves across the sky. But, it is Earth that is really moving.

Earth's Rotation

Earth spins in space like a dog chasing its tail—but not as fast! Our planet spins around an imaginary line called an axis. **Figure 13-1** shows this imaginary axis.

The spinning of Earth on its axis is called Earth's **rotation** (roh TAY shun). Earth rotates once every 24 hours. In the morning, as Earth rotates, the sun comes into view. In the afternoon, Earth continues to rotate, and the sun appears to move across the sky. In the evening, the sun seems to go down because the place where you are on Earth has rotated away from the sun.

You can see how this works by standing and facing the chalkboard. Pretend you are Earth and the chalkboard is the sun. Now, turn around slowly in a counterclockwise direction. The chalkboard moves across your vision, then disappears. You rotate until finally you see the chalkboard again. The chalkboard didn't move—you did. When you rotated, you were like Earth, spinning in space so that different parts of the planet face the sun at different times. This movement of Earth, not the movement of the sun, causes night and day.

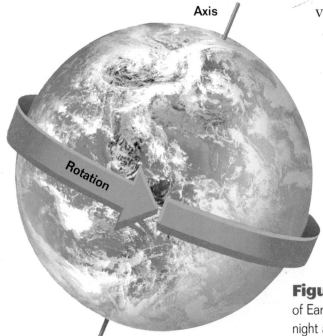

Axis

Rotation

Figure 13-1 The rotation of Earth on its axis causes night and day.

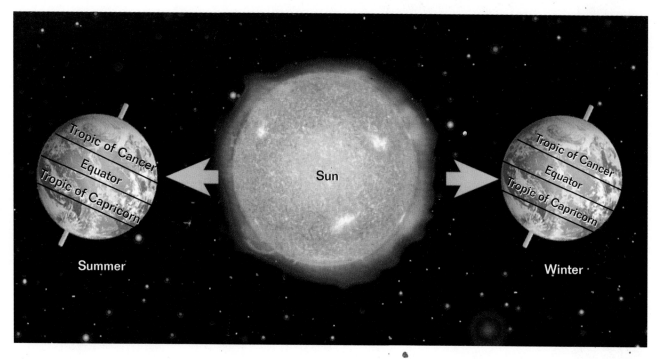

Figure 13-2 In the northern hemisphere on June 21 or 22, the sun's rays directly strike the Tropic of Cancer. On December 21 or 22, the sun's direct rays strike the Tropic of Capricorn. **When it's summer in the northern hemisphere, what season is it in the southern hemisphere?**

Earth's Revolution

You know that Earth rotates in space. It also moves in other ways. Like an athlete running around a track, Earth moves around the sun in a regular, curved path. This path is called an orbit. The movement of Earth around the sun is known as Earth's **revolution** (rev uh LEW shun). A year on Earth is the time it takes for Earth to revolve around the sun once. How many revolutions old are you?

Seasons

Who doesn't love summer? The days are long and warm. It's a great time to go swimming, ride a bike, or read a book just for fun. Why can't we have summer all year round? Blame it on Earth's axis. The axis, that imaginary line that our planet spins around, is not straight up and down. It is tilted at an angle. It's because of this tilt that there are seasons in many areas on Earth. Why?

Look at **Figure 13-2.** The part of Earth that is tilted toward the sun receives more direct sunlight and more energy from the sun than the part of Earth that is tilted away from the sun. When the part of Earth that you live on is tilted away from the sun, you have winter. When the part of Earth that you live on is tilted toward the sun, you have summer. ☑

Reading Check ☑

What causes seasons?

Waxing crescent

New moon

First quarter

Movements of the Moon

Imagine a dog running in circles around an athlete who is jogging on a track. That's how you can picture the moon moving around Earth. As Earth revolves around the sun, the moon revolves around Earth. The moon revolves around Earth once every 27.3 days. But, as you have probably noticed, the moon does not always look the same from Earth. Sometimes, it looks like a big, glowing disk. Other times, it's a thin sliver.

Waxing gibbous

Moon Phases

How many different moon shapes have you seen? Round shapes? Half-circle shapes? The moon looks different at different times of the month, but it doesn't really change. What does change is the way the moon appears from Earth. We call these changes moon phases. **Figure 13-3** shows the different phases of the moon.

Full moon

Light from the Sun

The moon phase you see on any given night depends on the positions of the moon, the sun, and Earth in space. Wait a minute. How can we see the different phases of the moon? Is someone shining a giant flashlight up there? No, the moon receives light from the sun, just as Earth does. And, just as half of Earth experiences day while the other half experiences night, one half of the moon is lit by the sun while the other half is dark. As the moon revolves around Earth, we see different parts of the side of the moon that is facing the sun. This makes the moon appear to change shape.

Waning gibbous

Figure 13-3 The moon is said to be waxing when it seems to be getting larger night by night. It is said to be waning when it seems to be getting smaller.

Third quarter

Waning crescent

Eclipses

Have you ever tried to watch TV with someone standing between you and the screen? You can't see a thing! The light from the screen can't reach your eyes because someone is blocking it. Sometimes, the moon is like that person standing in front of the TV. It moves between the sun and Earth in a position that blocks sunlight from reaching Earth. The moon's shadow travels across parts of Earth. This event, shown in **Figure 13-4,** is called an **eclipse** (ih KLIHPS). Because it is an eclipse of the sun, it is known as a solar eclipse. The moon is much smaller than the sun, so not everywhere on Earth is in the moon's shadow. Sunlight is completely blocked only in the small area of Earth where the moon's shadow falls. In that area, the eclipse is said to be a total solar eclipse.

Lunar Eclipse

Sometimes, Earth can be like a person standing in front of the TV. It gets between the sun and the moon, blocking sunlight from reaching the moon. When Earth's shadow falls on the moon, we have an eclipse of the moon, which is called a lunar eclipse. **Figure 13-5** shows a lunar eclipse.

Mini Lab

Observing Distance and Size

Procedure

1. Place a basketball on a table at the front of the classroom. Then, stand at the back of the room.
2. Extend your arm, close one eye, and try to block the ball from sight with your thumb.
3. Slowly move your thumb closer to you until it completely blocks the ball.
4. Repeat the experiment using a golf ball.

Analysis

1. In your Science Journal, describe what you observed. When did your thumb block your view of the basketball? When did your thumb block your view of the golf ball?
2. A small object can sometimes block a larger object from view. Explain how this relates to the moon, the sun, and Earth during a solar eclipse.

Figure 13-4 The photo below shows a solar eclipse. Only a small area of Earth ever experiences a total solar eclipse. **Why?**

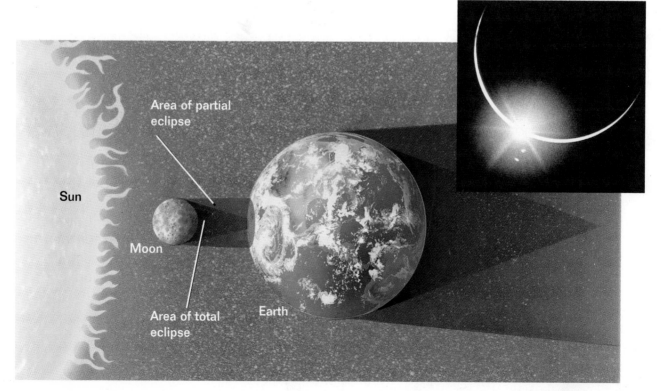

Area of partial eclipse

Sun

Moon

Area of total eclipse

Earth

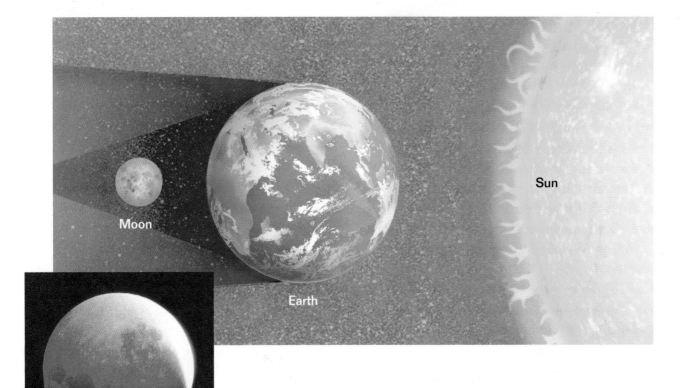

Moon

Earth

Sun

Figure 13-5 During a lunar eclipse, Earth moves between the sun and the moon.

Our Neighbors in Space

In this section, you've learned about what causes day and night and the seasons. You've also learned about the moon, Earth's nearest neighbor in space. Next, you'll look at our other neighbors in space—the planets that make up our solar system.

Section Assessment

1. Explain the difference between Earth's revolution and its rotation.

2. Draw a picture showing the positions of the sun, the moon, and Earth during a solar eclipse.

3. **Think Critically:** Seasons are caused by the tilt of Earth's axis. What do you think seasons would be like if Earth's axis were not tilted?

4. **Skill Builder**

   Inferring The surfaces of Earth's moon and other objects in space are covered with impact craters. Do the **Chapter 13 Skill Activity** on page 590 to infer the ages of impact craters.

Using Math

Light travels 300 000 km per second. There are 60 s in a minute. If it takes eight minutes for the sun's light to reach us, how far is the sun from Earth?

Activity 13·1

Moon Phases

The moon is our nearest neighbor in space. But, the sun, which is much farther away, affects how we see the moon from Earth. In this activity, you'll observe how the positions of the sun, the moon, and Earth cause the different phases of the moon.

Materials

- Drawing paper (several sheets)
- Softball
- Flashlight
- Scissors

What You'll Investigate

How do the positions of the sun, the moon, and Earth affect the phases of the moon?

Goals

- **Observe** moon phases.
- **Record** and **label** phases of the moon.
- **Infer** how the positions of the sun, the moon, and Earth affect phases of the moon.

Procedure

1. **Turn on** the flashlight and darken other lights in the room. **Select** a member of your group to hold the flashlight. This person will be the "sun." **Select** another member of your group to hold up the softball so that the light shines directly on the ball. The softball will be the "moon" in your experiment.

2. The remaining members of your group should sit between the sun and the moon.

3. **Observe** how light shines on the moon. **Draw** the moon, being careful to **shade** in its dark portion.

4. The student who is holding the "moon" should begin to **walk** in a slow circle around the group, stopping at least seven times at different spots. Each time the "moon" stops, **observe** the moon, **draw** the moon, and **shade** in its dark portion.

Conclude and Apply

1. **Compare** and **contrast** your drawings with those of other students. **Discuss** similarities and differences in the drawings.

2. In your own words, **explain** how the positions of the sun, the moon, and Earth affect the phase of the moon we see on Earth.

3. **Compare** your drawings with **Figure 13-3**. Which phase is the moon in for each drawing? **Label** each drawing with the correct moon phase.

Distances in Space

Imagine that you are an astronaut living far in the future, doing research on a space station near the edge of our solar system. You've been working hard for a long time. You need a vacation. Where will you go? How about a tour of the solar system? The **solar system,** shown in **Figure 13-6,** is made up of the nine planets and numerous other objects that orbit the sun. How long do you think it would take you to cross the solar system?

Measuring Space

Distances in space are hard to imagine because space is so vast. Let's get back down to Earth for a minute. Suppose you had to measure your pencil, the hallway outside your classroom, and the distance from your home to school. Would you

What You'll Learn

▶ About distances in space
▶ About the objects in our solar system

Vocabulary
solar system
astronomical unit

Why It's Important

▶ You'll learn more about how the planets, including Earth, were formed.

VISUALIZING
The Solar System

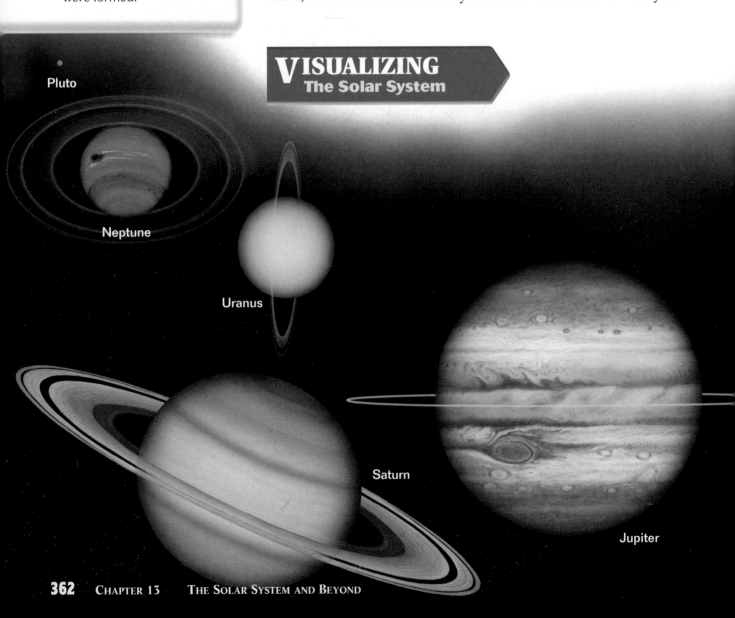

Pluto

Neptune

Uranus

Saturn

Jupiter

use the same units for each measurement? Probably not. You'd probably measure your pencil in centimeters. You'd probably use something bigger to measure the length of the hallway, such as meters. You might measure the trip from your home to school in kilometers. We use larger units to measure longer distances. Imagine trying to measure the trip from your home to school in centimeters. If you didn't lose count, you'd end up with a very large number!

Astronomical Unit

Kilometers are fine for measuring long distances on Earth. But, we need even bigger units to measure vast distances in space. One such measure is the **astronomical** (as truh NAHM ih kul) **unit.** An astronomical unit equals 150 million km, which is the average distance from Earth to the sun. It is abbreviated *AU.* If something is 3 AU away from Earth, it means that the object is three times as far away as Earth is from the sun.

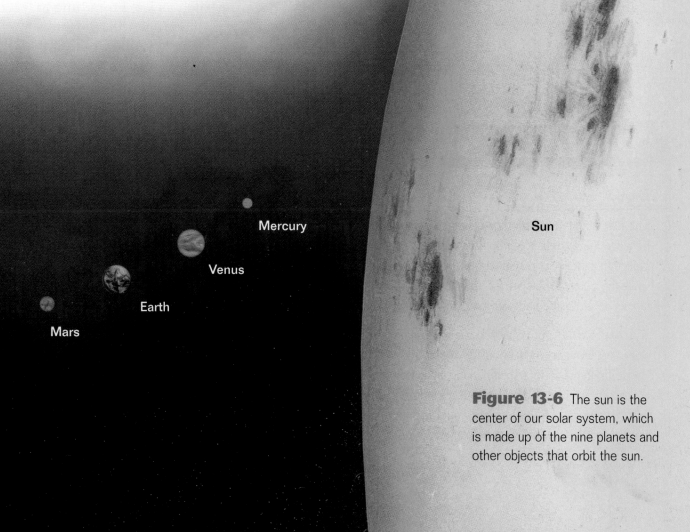

Mercury

Venus

Earth

Mars

Sun

Figure 13-6 The sun is the center of our solar system, which is made up of the nine planets and other objects that orbit the sun.

Figure 13-7 The tails of comets point away from the sun, pushed by solar wind. Solar wind is a stream of charged particles from the sun.

A Tour of the Solar System

Now you know how far you have to travel to tour the solar system, starting from your space station on the outer edge of the solar system. Strap yourself into your spacecraft. It's time to begin your journey. What will you see first as you enter the solar system?

Comets

What's this in **Figure 13-7?** A giant, dirty snowball? No, it's a comet—the first thing you see on your trip. Comets are made up of dust and frozen gases such as ice. From time to time, they swing close to the sun. When they do, the sun's radiation vaporizes some of the material. Gas and dust spurt from the comet, forming bright tails.

interNET
CONNECTION

Visit the Glencoe Science Web Site at **www. glencoe.com/sec/ science/nc** for more information about comets.

Problem Solving

Determining Distances in Space

The following table shows the distances in AU between the planets in our solar system and the sun. Notice that the inner planets are fairly close together, while the outer planets are far apart. Study the distances carefully, then answer the questions below.

Think Critically: Which planets do you think scientists know the most about? Explain your answer. Based on the distances shown in the table, how would you go about making a scale model of the solar system? What unit of measurement would you use to show the distances between the planets? What scale would you use to show size?

Solar System Data	
Planet	**Average Distance from Sun**
Mercury	0.39 AU
Venus	0.72 AU
Earth	1 AU
Mars	1.5 AU
Jupiter	5 AU
Saturn	9.5 AU
Uranus	19 AU
Neptune	30 AU
Pluto	39 AU

Outer Planets

Moving past the comets, you come to the outer planets. The outer planets are Pluto, Neptune, Uranus, Saturn, and Jupiter. Let's hope you aren't looking for places to stop and rest. Trying to stand on most of these planets would be like trying to stand on a cloud. That's because all of the outer planets except Pluto are huge balls of gas. Each may have a solid core, but none of them has a solid surface. The gas giants have lots of moons, which orbit the planets just like our own moon orbits Earth. They have outer rings made of dust and ice. In fact, the only outer planet that doesn't have rings is Pluto. Pluto isn't a gas giant. What does it look like? You'll soon find out.

Pluto

The first planet that you come to on your tour is Pluto, a small, rocky planet with a frozen crust. Pluto, the last planet discovered by scientists, is normally farthest from the sun. It is the smallest planet in the solar system and the one we know the least about. Pluto, shown in **Figure 13-8A,** has no ring system. Its one moon, Charon, is more than half the size of the planet itself.

Neptune

Neptune is the next stop in your space travel. Neptune, shown in **Figure 13-8B,** is the eighth planet from the sun most of the time. Sometimes, Pluto's orbit crosses inside Neptune's orbit during part of its voyage around the sun. When that happens, Neptune is the ninth planet from the sun. Neptune is the first of the big, gas planets with rings around it. Neptune's atmosphere includes a gas called methane. Methane gives the planet a blue-green color.

Uranus

After Neptune, you come to the seventh planet from the sun, Uranus. Uranus needs a careful look because of the interesting way it spins on its axis.

The axis of most planets, including Earth, is tilted just a little, somewhat like the hands of a clock when they are at 1 and 7. Uranus is shown in **Figure 13-8C.**

Figure 13-8 The outer planets include Pluto, Neptune, and Uranus. Pluto is so small and far away that this is the best image current technology can produce.

 Pluto

B Neptune

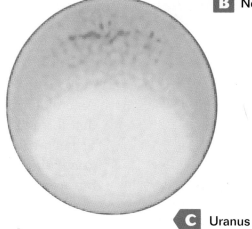

C Uranus

Figure 13-9 Saturn and Jupiter are gas giants. **In your Science Journal, list one unique characteristic of each of these planets.**

A Saturn

B
Jupiter

Reading Check ✓

What are asteroids?

Uranus has an axis that is tilted almost even with the plane of its orbit, as if the hands of the clock were at 3 and 9.

Saturn

You might think that Uranus was unusual. Wait until you see Saturn, the sixth planet from the sun! You'll be dazzled by its rings, shown in **Figure 13-9A.** Saturn's several broad rings are made up of thousands of smaller rings, which are made up of pieces of ice and rock. Some of these pieces are like specks of dust. Others are many meters across.

Jupiter

If you're looking for excitement, you'll find it on Jupiter, the largest planet in the solar system and the fifth from the sun. Watch out for a huge, red whirlwind rotating slowly around the middle of the planet. That's the Great Red Spot, a giant storm on Jupiter's surface. Jupiter, shown in **Figure 13-9B,** has 16 moons. Some are larger than Pluto! One of Jupiter's moons, Io, is more volcanically active than anyplace else in the solar system.

Asteroid Belt

Look out for asteroids! On the next part of your trip, you must make your way through the asteroid belt that lies between Jupiter and the next planet, Mars. Asteroids are pieces of rock made of minerals similar to those that formed the planets. In fact, asteroids might have become planets if it weren't for that big giant, Jupiter. Jupiter's huge gravitational force probably kept any planets from forming in the area of the asteroid belt. ✓

Inner Planets

After traveling dozens of astronomical units, you finally reach the inner planets. These planets are solid and rocky. How do we know that? As with all the planets, much of what we know about planets comes from spacecraft that send data back to Earth to help us learn more about space. Look at **Figure 13-10A.** This photograph was taken by a spacecraft.

Mars

Hey! Has someone else been here? You see signs of earlier visits to Mars, the first of the inner planets. Tiny robot explorers have been left behind. But, it wasn't a person who left them here. The roving robots were left by spacecraft sent from Earth to explore Mars's surface. If you stay long enough and look around, you may notice that Mars, shown in **Figure 13-10A,** has seasons and polar ice caps. There are signs that the planet once had liquid water. You'll also notice that the planet looks red. That's because the rocks on its surface contain iron oxide, which is what makes rust look red.

Earth

Home sweet home! You've finally reached Earth, the third planet from the sun. You didn't realize how unusual your home planet was until you saw the other planets. Earth's surface temperatures allow water to exist as a solid, a liquid, and a gas. Also, Earth's atmosphere works like a screen to keep ultraviolet (ul truh VI uh lut) rays from reaching the planet's surface. Ultraviolet rays are harmful rays from the sun. Because of Earth's atmosphere, life can thrive on the planet. You would like to linger on Earth, shown in **Figure 13-10B,** but you have two more planets to explore.

Venus

Maybe you should have stayed on Earth. You won't be able to see much at your next stop, shown in **Figure 13-10C.** Venus, the second-closest planet to the sun, is hard to see because its surface is surrounded by thick clouds. Venus's clouds trap the energy that reaches the planet's surface from the sun. That energy causes surface temperatures on the planet to hover around 470°C. That's hot enough to melt lead, and far too hot for you. You're on to your next stop.

Figure 13-10 Mars, Earth, and Venus are inner planets.

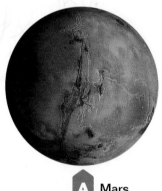

A Mars

B Earth

C Venus

Figure 13-11
Mercury is the closest planet to the sun. Like our moon, its surface is scarred by meteorites.

Mercury

The last planet that you visit, the one that is closest to the sun, is Mercury. Mercury, shown in **Figure 13-11,** is the second-smallest planet. Its surface is heavily scarred by craters made by meteorites. Meteorites come from meteors, which are chunks of rock that fall from the sky when asteroids break up. Because of Mercury's small size and low gravitational pull, most gases that could form an atmosphere escape into space. The thin atmosphere and the closeness of this planet to the sun cause Mercury to have great extremes in temperature. Its surface temperature can reach 450°C during the day and drop to −170°C at night.

Section Assessment

1. List the nine planets in order from the sun, beginning with the planet closest to the sun.

2. In general, how are the outer planets different from the inner planets? How are they alike?

3. **Think Critically:** We use larger units of measure for increasingly larger distances. How do you think scientists handle increasingly smaller distances, such as the distances between molecules?

4. **Skill Builder**
   Developing Multimedia Presentations Use your knowledge of the solar system to develop a multimedia presentation of the solar system. You may want to begin by drawing a poster that includes the sun, the planets, the asteroid belt, and comets. If you need help, refer to Developing Multimedia Presentations in the **Technology Skill Handbook** on page 572.

Using Computers

Spreadsheet Using the table in the Problem Solving on page 364, make a spreadsheet showing the distances of the planets from the sun. Calculate the distances using a scale of 10 cm = 1 AU. If you need help, refer to page 574.

Barbary
by Vonda N. McIntyre

…But the stars were fantastic. Barbary thought she must be able to see a hundred times as many as on earth, even in the country where sky-glow and smog did not hide them. They spanned the universe, all colors, shining with a steady, cold, remote light. She wanted to write down what they looked like, but every phrase she could think of sounded silly and inadequate.

Barbary is hoping to find a home for herself—and her mysterious stowaway—on the space station *Einstein.* (See NASA's concept of a possible moon station at left.) On the way, Barbary learns from Jeanne Velory, the astronaut who is taking command of the station, that an alien ship is moving into the solar system. Some people think it may be abandoned. Others aren't so sure.

The alien vessel is approaching on a path above the plane of the solar system. *Einstein,* circling Earth in a long orbit, is the ideal spot from which to observe, and hopefully contact, the mysterious ship.

Barbary explores the research station with her new sister, Heather. She learns how to "sly," or move gracefully in zero gravity, how to pilot a space raft, and how to do her homework with a helpful computer. Along the way, she also learns to trust others and her own abilities.

Then, without warning, Barbary finds herself using all her newfound skills to save her friends and discover the truth about the alien vessel and its inhabitants.

The construction of the International Space Station is paving the way for cooperation in space exploration. Sixteen nations, including the United States, are working together in this effort. Construction in Earth's orbit began in 1998, and the space station is scheduled for completion in 2004. The space station will provide a laboratory for researching and developing new technologies in industrial materials, communications, medicine, and much more.

Science JOURNAL

In your Science Journal, describe what you think life would be like at a remote outpost in space. What life-support systems would you need? How would you deal with weightlessness? What would you miss most about Earth?

Space Colony

Possible Materials

- Drawing paper
- Markers
- Books about the planets

Have you ever seen a movie or read a book about astronauts from Earth living in space colonies on other planets? Some of these make-believe space colonies look awfully strange! So far, we haven't built a space colony on another planet. But, if we did, what do you think it would look like?

Recognize the Problem

How would conditions on a planet affect the type of space colony that might be built there?

Form a Hypothesis

Research a planet. Review conditions on the surface of the planet. Make a hypothesis about the things that would have to be included in a space colony to allow humans to survive on the planet.

Goals

- **Infer** what a space colony might look like on another planet.
- **Classify** planetary surface conditions.
- **Draw** a space colony for a planet.

Test Your Hypothesis

Plan

1. **Select** a planet and **study** its surface conditions.

2. **Classify** the surface conditions in the following ways.

   a. solid or gas

   b. hot, cold, or changing temperatures

   c. heavy atmosphere or no atmosphere

   d. bright or dim sunlight

   e. special conditions unlike other planets

3. **List** the things that humans need to survive. For example, humans need air to breathe. Does your planet have air that humans can breathe, or would your space colony have to provide the air?

4. **Make a table** for the planet showing its surface conditions and the features the space colony would have to have so that humans could survive on the planet.

5. **Discuss** your decisions as a group to make sure they make sense.

Do

1. Make sure your teacher approves your plan and your data table before you proceed.

2. **Draw** a picture of the space colony. **Draw** another picture showing the inside of the space colony. **Label** the parts of the space colony and explain how they help humans to survive.

3. Present your drawing to the class. **Explain** the reasoning behind it.

Analyze Your Data

1. **Compare and contrast** your space colony with those of other students who researched the same planet you did. How are they alike? How are they different?

2. Would you change your space colony after seeing other groups' drawings? If so, what changes would you make?

Draw Conclusions

1. What was the most interesting thing you learned about the planet you studied?

2. Was your planet a good choice for a space colony? **Explain** your answer.

Stars and Galaxies

Stars

Every night, a whole new world opens to us. The stars come out. The fact is, stars are always in the sky. We just can't see them during the day because the sun's light is brighter than starlight. The sun is a star, too. It is the closest star to Earth. We can't see it at night because as Earth rotates, our part of Earth is facing away from it.

Constellations

Ursa Major, Orion, Taurus. Do these names sound familiar? They are **constellations** (kahn stuh LAY shunz), or groups of stars that form patterns in the sky. **Figure 13-12** shows some constellations.

Constellations are named after animals, objects, and people—real or imaginary. We still use many names that early Greek astronomers gave the constellations. But, throughout history, different groups of people have seen different things in the constellations. In early England, people thought the Big Dipper, found in the constellation Ursa Major, looked like a plow. Native Americans saw it as a giant bear. To the Chinese, it looked like a governmental official and his helpers moving on a cloud. What does the Big Dipper look like to you?

What **You'll Learn**

▶ How a star is born
▶ About the galaxies that make up our universe

Vocabulary
constellation
galaxy
light-year

Why **It's Important**

▶ Understanding the vastness of the universe helps us understand Earth's place in space.

Figure 13-12 Find the Big Dipper in the constellation Ursa Major. **Why do you think people call it the Big Dipper?**

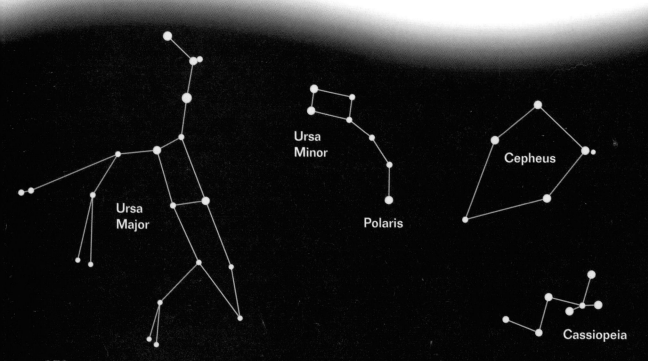

Ursa Major

Ursa Minor

Polaris

Cepheus

Cassiopeia

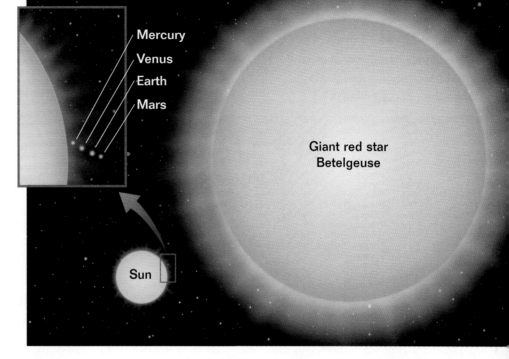

Figure 13-13 Although our sun is large compared to the inner planets, it looks small next to the giant star Betelgeuse.

Mercury
Venus
Earth
Mars

Giant red star
Betelgeuse

Sun

Starry Colors

When you glance at the sky on a clear night, the stars look like tiny pinpoints of light. It's hard to tell one from another, but stars come in different sizes and colors.

The larger a star is, the cooler it tends to be. How do you measure a star's temperature? You can't go there with a big thermometer. But, you can use a star's color as a clue to its temperature. Red stars are the coolest. Yellow stars are of medium temperature. Bluish-white stars are the hottest. Our sun is a yellow, medium-sized star. The giant red star called Betelgeuse (BEE tul joos) is much bigger than the sun. Look at **Figure 13-13**. If this huge star were in the same place as our sun, it would swallow Mercury, Venus, Earth, and Mars.

The Lives of Stars

You've grown up and changed a lot since you were born. You've gone through several stages in your life, and you'll go through many more. Stars go through stages in their lives, just as people do.

Scientists theorize that stars begin their lives as huge clouds of gas and dust. The force of gravity causes the dust and gases to move closer together. When this happens, temperatures within the cloud begin to rise. A star is formed when this cloud gets so dense and hot that it starts producing energy.

Figure 13-14 The life of a star depends greatly on its mass. **What happens to supergiants when their cores collapse?**

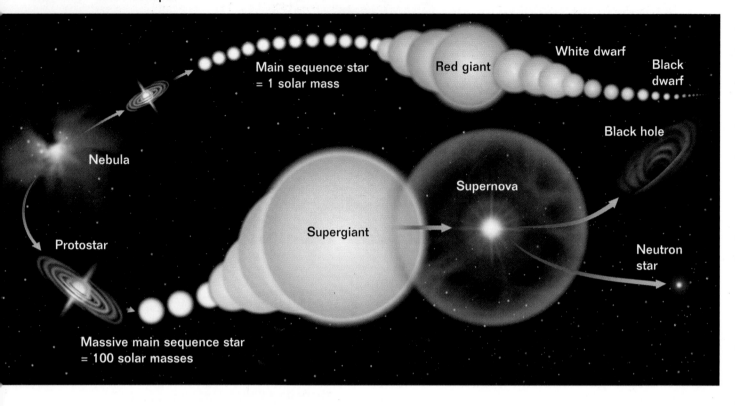

The stages a star goes through in its life depend on the star's size. When a medium-sized star like our sun uses up some of the gases in its center, it expands to become a giant. Our sun will become a giant in about 5 billion years. When the remaining gases are used up, our sun will contract to become a black dwarf. **Figure 13-14** illustrates the lives of stars.

Supergiants

When a huge star begins to use up the gases in its core, it becomes a supergiant. Over time, the core of a supergiant collapses. Then, the outer part of the star explodes and gets very bright. This event, shown in **Figure 13-15,** is called a supernova. For a few brief days, the supernova might shine more brightly than a whole galaxy. The dust and gases released by this explosion may eventually form other stars.

Meanwhile, the core of the supergiant is still around. It is now called a neutron star. If the core is massive enough, it may rapidly become a black hole. Black holes are so dense that light shone into them would disappear.

PHYSICS
INTEGRATION ►

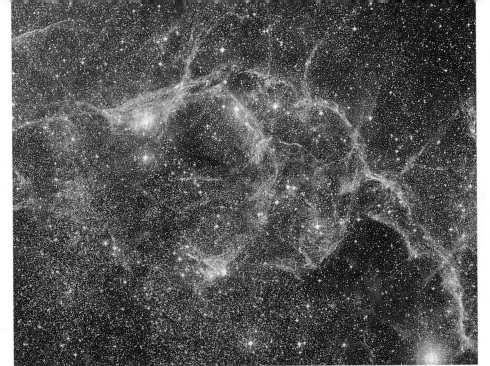

Figure 13-15 This photo shows the remains of the Vela supernova, located trillions of kilometers from Earth.

Galaxies

What do you see when you look at the night sky? If you live in a city, you may not see much. The glare from city lights makes it hard to see the stars. If you go to a dark place, far from the lights of towns and cities, you can see much more. In a dark area, with a powerful telescope, you might see dim clusters of stars grouped together. These clusters are galaxies (GAL uk seez). A **galaxy** is a group of stars, gas, and dust held together by gravity. **Figure 13-16** shows two differently shaped galaxies.

*inter***NET**
CONNECTION

Explore the Glencoe Science Web Site at **www.glencoe.com/ sec/science/nc** for more information about telescopes.

Figure 13-16 Elliptical galaxies are shaped like footballs or spheres. Irregular galaxies have irregular shapes. **Which of the galaxies shown here is an irregular galaxy?**

Types of Galaxies

You know planets and stars differ from one another. Galaxies come in different shapes and sizes, too. The three major types of galaxies are elliptical, spiral, and irregular. Elliptical galaxies may be the most common. They're shaped like huge footballs or spheres. Spiral galaxies have arms radiating outward from their center. Irregular galaxies are just that—irregular. They come in all sorts of different shapes and can't be classified easily. Irregular galaxies are usually smaller and less common than other galaxies.

The Milky Way Galaxy

Which type of galaxy do you live in? Look at **Figure 13-17.** We live in the Milky Way Galaxy, a spiral galaxy. There are about 200 billion stars in the Milky Way Galaxy, including our sun. Just as Earth revolves around the sun, stars revolve around the centers of galaxies. Our sun revolves around the Milky Way Galaxy about once every 240 million years.

A View from Within

We can see part of the Milky Way Galaxy as a band of light across the sky. But, we can't see the whole Milky Way Galaxy. Why not? Think about it. When you're sitting in your classroom, can you see the whole school? No, you are inside the school and can see only parts of it. Our view of the Milky Way Galaxy from Earth is like the view of your school from a classroom. We can see only parts of our galaxy because we are inside it. ☑

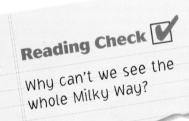

PHYSICS
INTEGRATION

Galaxies in Motion
The Milky Way belongs to a cluster of galaxies called the Local Group. Scientists have determined that galaxies outside of the Local Group are moving away from us. Based on this, what can you infer about the size of the universe?

Reading Check ☑

Why can't we see the whole Milky Way?

Figure 13-17 The Milky Way Galaxy has spiral arms made up of dust and gas. Its inner region is an area of densely packed stars.

Light-Years

Do you remember what you learned earlier about astronomical units or AU? Distances between the planets are measured in AU. But, to measure distances between galaxies, we need an even bigger unit of measure. Scientists use light-years to measure distances between galaxies. A **light-year** is the distance light travels in a year—about 9.5 trillion km. Light travels so fast it could go around Earth seven times in one second.

Have you ever wished that you could travel back in time? In a way, that's what you're doing when you look at a galaxy. The galaxy might be millions of light-years away. So, the light that you see started on its journey long ago. You are seeing the galaxy as it was millions of years ago.

The Universe

Each galaxy probably has as many stars as the Milky Way Galaxy. Some may have more. And, there may be as many as 100 billion galaxies. All these galaxies, with all their countless stars, make up the universe. Look at **Figure 13-18.** In this great vastness of revolving solar systems, exploding supernovas, and star-filled galaxies is one small planet called Earth. If you think about how huge the universe is, Earth seems like a speck of dust. Yet, as far as we know, it's the only place where life exists.

Figure 13-18 Stars are forming in the Orion Nebula.

Section Assessment

1. What is a constellation? Name three constellations.
2. Describe the life of a medium-sized star such as the sun.
3. **Think Critically:** Some stars may no longer be in existence, but we still see them in the night sky. Why?
4. **Skill Builder**
   Making Models The Milky Way Galaxy is 100 000 light-years in diameter. How would you build a model of the Milky Way Galaxy? If you need help, refer to Making Models in the **Skill Handbook** on page 563.

Science Journal
Observe the stars in the night sky. In your Science Journal, draw the stars you observed. Now draw your own constellation based on those stars. Give your constellation a name. Why did you choose that name?

For a **preview** of this chapter, study this Reviewing Main Ideas before you read the chapter. After you have studied this chapter, you can use the Reviewing Main Ideas to **review** the chapter.

The Glencoe MindJogger, Audiocassettes, and CD-ROM provide additional opportunities for review.

Section 13-1 EARTH'S PLACE IN SPACE

The spinning of Earth on its axis is called **rotation.** This movement causes night and day. Earth also orbits around the sun in a regular, curved path. This movement is known as Earth's **revolution.** The moon moves, too, as it orbits Earth. The different positions of Earth, the sun, and the moon in space cause moon phases and **eclipses.** *Explain the difference between a lunar eclipse and a solar eclipse.*

Section 13-2 THE SOLAR SYSTEM

The solar system is made up of the nine planets and numerous other objects that orbit the sun. Planets are classified according to their distances from the sun. The inner planets— Mercury, Venus, Earth, and Mars—are closest to the sun. The outer planets—Jupiter, Saturn, Uranus, Neptune, and Pluto—are much farther away. Most of the outer planets are large, gas giants with rings and moons. *How is Pluto different from the other outer planets?*

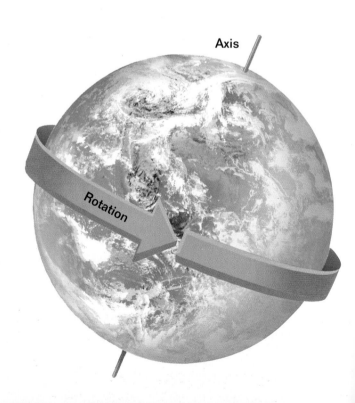

Axis

Rotation

Reading Check ✔

Use these words in sentences that do not relate to the sun, Earth, and moon: *rotation, revolution, waxing, waning, eclipse.*

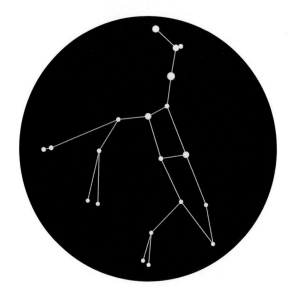

Section
13-3 STARS

Constellations are groups of stars that form patterns in the sky. They are named after animals, objects, or people—real or imaginary. Although stars may look the same from Earth, they differ greatly in temperature, size, and color. Our sun, for instance, is a medium-sized, yellow star. *What color are the hottest stars? The coolest?*

GALAXIES

Galaxies are groups of stars, gas, and dust held together by gravity. The three main types of galaxies are elliptical, spiral, and irregular. We live in the Milky Way, a spiral galaxy. Distances between galaxies are measured in light-years. A **light-year** is the distance light travels in a year—about 9.5 trillion km. *Why do we need special units of measurement for studying distances in space?*

Using Vocabulary

a. astronomical unit	**e.** light-year
b. constellation	**f.** revolution
c. eclipse	**g.** rotation
d. galaxy	**h.** solar system

Each phrase below describes a science term from the list. Write the term that matches the phrase describing it.

1. the shadow produced by the moon or Earth passing in front of the sun
2. the motion of Earth that produces day and night
3. a group of stars, gas, and dust held together by gravity
4. a group of stars that forms a pattern in the sky
5. the movement of Earth around the sun

Checking Concepts

Choose the word or phrase that best answers the question.

6. What causes seasons?
   A) equator   C) moon
   B) oceans   D) tilt of Earth's axis

7. When the moon is waning, it appears to be what?
   A) growing larger   C) a full moon
   B) growing smaller D) a new moon

8. An astronomical unit measures the distance from Earth to what?
   A) the moon
   B) the sun
   C) Mercury
   D) Pluto

9. Earth is which planet from the sun?
   A) first   C) third
   B) second   D) fourth

10. How many galaxies may be in the universe?
    A) 1 billion   C) 50 billion
    B) 10 billion   D) 100 billion

11. What does the spinning of Earth on its axis cause?
    A) night and day
    B) summer and winter
    C) moon phases
    D) solar eclipses

12. A light-year is used to measure distances between what?
    A) cities
    B) Earth and other planets
    C) galaxies
    D) oceans

13. How many planets are in the solar system?
    A) six
    B) seven
    C) eight
    D) nine

14. During a solar eclipse, the shadow of what object travels across part of Earth?
    A) the moon
    B) the sun
    C) Mars
    D) a comet

15. If the core of a neutron star is massive enough, what does it become?
    A) a galaxy
    B) a black hole
    C) a black dwarf
    D) a superstar

Thinking Critically

16. What conditions on Earth allow life to thrive?

17. Which of the planets in our solar system seems most like Earth? Which seems most different? Explain your answers, using facts about the planets.

18. How might a scientist predict the day and time of a solar eclipse?

19. Throughout history, different groups of people have viewed the constellations in different ways. Infer why this is true.

20. Which of the moon's motions are real? Which are apparent? Explain why each occurs.

Developing Skills

If you need help, refer to the Skill Handbook.

21. **Making and Using Tables:** Research the size, period of rotation, and period of revolution for each planet. Show this information in a table. How do tables help us to better understand information?

22. **Comparing and Contrasting:** Compare the inner planets with the outer planets. How are they alike? How are they different?

23. **Making a Model:** Based on what you have learned about the sun, the moon, and Earth, make a model of a lunar or a solar eclipse.

24. **Sequencing:** Sequence the following terms in order of smallest object to largest group: *galaxy, inner planets, solar system, universe, Earth.*

Solar System Information

Planet	Diameter (km)	Period of rotation	Period of revolution
Mercury	4878	59 d	87.97 d
Venus	12 104	243 d	224.70 d
Earth	12 756	24 h	365.26 d
Mars	6794	24.5 h	686.98 d
Jupiter	142 796	10 h	11.86 y
Saturn	120 660	10.4 h	29.46 y
Uranus	51 810	16.8 h	84.04 y
Neptune	49 528	16 h	164.79 y
Pluto	2290	7 d	248.53 y

THE PRINCETON REVIEW

Test-Taking Tip

Get to the Root of Things If you don't know a word's meaning, you can still get an idea of its meaning if you focus on its roots, prefixes, and suffixes. For instance, words that start with *non-, un-, dis-,* and *in-* generally reverse what the rest of the word means.

Test Practice

Use these questions to test your Science Proficiency.

1. As the moon revolves around Earth, it appears to change shape. What determines the moon shape you see on any given night?
   A) the speed of Earth's rotation
   B) the positions of the sun, the moon, and Earth in space
   C) the distance between the moon and the sun
   D) the tilt of Earth's axis

2. Stars begin their lives as huge clouds of gas and dust. Which statement **BEST** describes our sun?
   A) Our sun will become a supernova in 2 billion years.
   B) Our sun is cooler than the giant red star, Betelgeuse.
   C) Our sun is a medium-sized, yellow star.
   D) Our sun was formed when dust and gas came together and froze.

5

Interactions
in the
Physical
World

What's Happening Here?

In a warehouse in Salt Lake City, Utah, these table tennis players (left) are "wired for action." They are also equally matched. How so? Because they share a brain! The engineer on the right is directing all the action. Each of the engineer's movements is transferred electronically to the robot named Sarcos. In this unit, you will learn how compound machines, such as robots, are made from simple machines. You will also learn how electrical energy can accomplish such feats. You will explore another way energy moves in the form of electromagnetic waves, including radio, micro waves, and light. Telescopes, such as this one at Kitt Peak, Arizona (below), are used to collect light from distant objects. How do mirrors and lenses help magnify images, and how can scientists study light from the stars? These are a few of the questions you will explore in this unit.

*inter*NET CONNECTION

Explore the Glencoe Science Web Site at **www.glencoe.com/ sec/science/nc** to find out more about topics found in this unit.

Chapter Preview

Section 14-1
Structure of Matter

Section 14-2
Elements

Section 14-3
Compounds and Mixtures

Skills Preview

Skill Builders
- Interpret Data
- Compare and Contrast

Activities
- Make and Use a Table
- Form a Hypothesis

MiniLabs
- Make a Model
- Observe and Infer

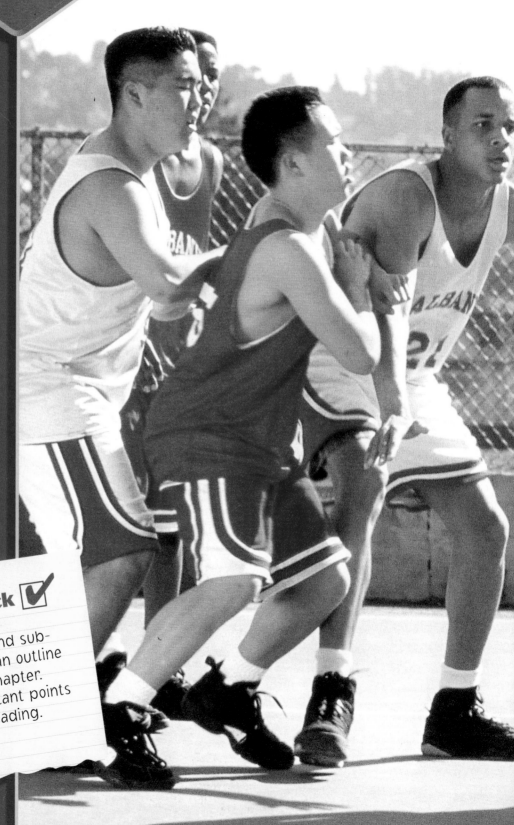

Reading Check ✔

Use the headings and sub-headings to make an outline as you read this chapter. Write a few important points under each subheading.

Explore Activity

You've just finished playing basketball. You're hot and thirsty. You reach for your bottle of water and, leaning back, squeeze out a long, thirst-quenching drink. Releasing your grip, you notice that the bottle is nearly empty. But, is the bottle really almost empty? According to the dictionary, empty means containing nothing. When you have finished all the water in the bottle, will it be empty? And, if it's full, what is it full of?

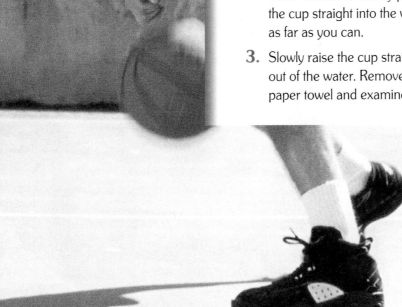

Observe Matter

1. Wad up a small piece of a dry paper towel or tissue paper and tape it to the bottom of the inside of a plastic drinking cup. When you turn the cup upside down, the towel or paper should remain inside the cup.

2. Fill a bowl or sink almost to the top with water. Hold the cup upside down over the water's surface. Slowly push the cup straight into the water as far as you can.

3. Slowly raise the cup straight out of the water. Remove the paper towel and examine it.

Science Journal

In your Science Journal, describe your experiment. Include a description of the paper after you removed it from the cup. Explain what you think happened. Was anything in the cup besides the paper? If so, what was it?

14·1 Structure of Matter

What You'll Learn

▶ What matter is
▶ What makes up matter
▶ The parts of an atom
▶ The models that are used for atoms

Vocabulary

matter
atom
law of conservation
    of matter
electron
nucleus
proton
neutron

Why It's Important

▶ Matter makes up your body, your environment, and the universe.

What is matter?

Did you decide that the bottle of water and the plastic cup in the Explore Activity were filled with air? Have you wondered what makes up the air around you? It's mostly nitrogen and oxygen. Nitrogen and oxygen are kinds of matter. Scientists define **matter** as anything that has mass and takes up space. So even if you can't see it or catch hold of it, air is matter.

What about the things you *can* see, taste, smell, and touch when you eat lunch in the cafeteria or walk around your neighborhood? These things are also made of matter. What about your own body? Yes, it's matter too. Through science, you will explore the many amazing kinds of matter that make up the universe—things as common as a flower or as spectacular as a supernova, both shown in **Figure 14-1.**

What isn't matter?

You can see the words on this page because of light. Does light have mass or take up space? What about the warmth from the sun or the heater in your classroom? Neither light nor heat take up any space. They don't have any mass either, so they are not forms of matter. Emotions, thoughts, and ideas also are not matter.

Figure 14-1 A flower in your backyard (A) and a supernova (a large exploding star) in a galaxy millions of light-years away (B) seem as different as night and day. But, the flower and supernova are the same in an important way—they're both matter. **How is matter defined?**

What makes up matter?

Suppose you cut a sheet of notebook paper into smaller and smaller pieces, as shown in **Figure 14-2.** Do the pieces seem to be made of the same matter as the large sheet you started with? If you could cut a small enough piece, would it still have the same properties as the large sheet of paper? Or, would it no longer be paper at all? People have asked questions like these—and wondered about what matter is made of—for centuries.

An Early Idea

Democritus, who lived from 460 to 370 B.C., was a Greek philosopher who thought the universe was made of empty space and tiny bits of stuff. He believed that the bits of stuff were so small they could no longer be divided into smaller pieces. He called these tiny pieces of stuff atoms. In fact, the term *atom* comes from a Greek word that means "cannot be divided." In science today, an **atom** is defined as a small particle that makes up most types of matter. Democritus thought that different types of atoms exist for every type of matter. His idea proved to be a small step in understanding the structure of matter that continues today.

Lavoisier's Contribution

Antoine Lavoisier (la VWAH see ay), a French chemist who lived about 2000 years after Democritus, was also curious about matter—especially when it changed from one form to another. Before Lavoisier, people thought matter could appear and disappear during changes such as burning and rusting. You might have thought the same thing—that matter can disappear—if you've ever watched wood burn to embers, then ashes in a fireplace. But, Lavoisier showed that wood and the oxygen it combines with during burning have the same mass as the ash, water, and

Figure 14-2 Paper is made up of carbon, hydrogen, and oxygen. So, if you could cut paper into small enough pieces, it wouldn't be paper at all. **What common type of matter is made up of only hydrogen and oxygen?**

Oxygen

+

Water vapor
and
carbon dioxide

+

Figure 14-3 When wood burns, matter is not lost. The total mass of the wood and the oxygen it combines with equals the total mass of the water vapor, carbon dioxide, and ashes produced. **When you burn wood in a fireplace, what is the source of the oxygen?**

carbon dioxide (KAR bun di AHK side) produced, as shown in **Figure 14-3.** In the same way, iron and oxygen have the same mass as the rust they form. From Lavoisier's work came the **law of conservation of matter.** This law states that matter is neither created nor destroyed, only changed in form.

Models of the Atom

Scientists often use models for things that are too small to be seen and observed easily, as well as things that are too complicated or too large to be understood easily. Throughout history, scientists have created and used models to help find out what atoms are made of and how they act.

One way to make a model is to make a small version of something larger. For example, if you wanted to design a new kind of sailboat, would you just come up with a design, build a full-sized boat, and hope it would float? It would be smarter—and safer—to first build and test a small model of your design. Then, if it doesn't float, you can change your design and build another model. You can keep trying until the model works. As with the model sailboat, scientists' models are changed as new information is gained.

Dalton's Atomic Model

In the early 1800s, an English schoolteacher and chemist named John Dalton studied the experiments of Lavoisier and many others. Dalton thought that an atomic model could explain the results of these experiments. He named his model *the atomic theory of matter.* Dalton's atomic model, like many scientific models, was a set of ideas—not an object. Dalton believed that matter was made of atoms that were too small to be seen by the human eye. He also thought that each type of matter was made of only one kind of atom. For example, gold atoms make up a gold nugget and give a gold ring its shininess, as well as its other properties.

Sizes of Atoms

Atoms are so small it would take about 1 million of them lined up in a row to equal the thickness of a human hair. To give you a better idea of how small atoms are, look at **Figure 14-4.** Imagine you are holding an orange in your hand. If you wanted to use only your eyes to see the individual atoms on the surface of the orange, the size of the orange would need to increase to the size of Earth. Then, imagine it is covered with billions and billions of marbles. Each marble would represent one of the atoms that make up the skin of the orange.

Figure 14-4 Imagining this orange is the size of Earth can help you visualize the size of an atom.

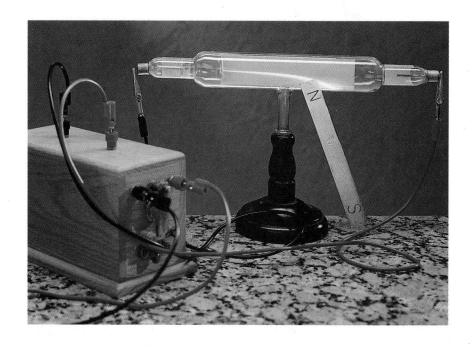

Figure 14-5 In this experiment, the magnet caused the cathode rays inside the tube to bend. **What do you think would happen to the cathode rays if the magnet were removed?**

Discovering the Electron

One of the many pioneers in the development of today's atomic model was J.J. Thomson, an Englishman. He conducted experiments using a vacuum tube, which is a glass tube that has all the air pumped out of it and then is sealed at both ends. Thomson's tube had metal plates at both ends. The plates were connected to a high-voltage electrical source that gave one of the plates, the *anode,* a positive charge and the other, the *cathode,* a negative charge. During his experiments, Thomson observed rays that traveled from the cathode to the anode. Because the rays came from the cathode, Thomson called them cathode rays. The rays were bent by a magnet, as seen in **Figure 14-5,** showing that the rays were made up of particles that had mass. The rays were bent by charged plates, also. Thomson knew that unlike charges attract each other and like charges repel each other. When he saw that the rays bent toward a positively charged plate, he concluded that the cathode rays were made up of negative particles. These invisible, negatively charged particles, which came from the metal atoms that made up the cathode, are called **electrons.** ✓

Mini Lab

Making a Model

Procedure 🥽

1. Your teacher will give you a sealed shoe box that contains one or more items.
2. Try to find out how many and what kinds of items are inside the box. You cannot look inside the box. The only observations you may make are by handling the box.

Analysis

1. How many items do you infer are in the box? Sketch the apparent shapes of the items and identify them if you can.
2. Compare your procedure with how scientists perform experiments and make models to find out more about the atom.

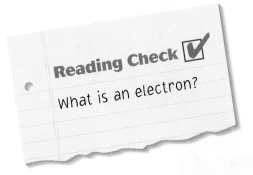

Reading Check ✓

What is an electron?

Imagine Thomson's excitement at this discovery. He had shown that atoms are not too tiny to divide after all. Rather, they are made up of even smaller subatomic particles. Other scientists soon built on Thomson's results and found that the electron had a small mass—in fact, 1/1837 the mass of the lightest atom, the hydrogen atom. In 1906, Thomson received the Nobel Prize in Physics for his discovery of the electron.

Matter that has equal numbers of positive and negative charges, and therefore has no *net* charge, is said to be neutral. Because most matter is neutral, Thomson knew that atoms had to contain both positive and negative charges. He pictured the atom as being made up of electrons embedded in a ball of positive charge. You might compare his model, shown in **Figure 14-6,** to something like tiny chocolate chips spread around in a ball of cookie dough. But, Thomson's model did not provide all the answers to the questions that puzzled scientists about atoms.

Rutherford—The Nucleus

If electrons are the negatively charged particles in atoms, what are the positively charged particles that also must be present? Also, how are the parts of the atom arranged? In 1909, a team of scientists led by Ernest Rutherford in England began to work on the mystery of atomic structure. They bombarded materials with alpha particles. Alpha particles are high-energy, positively charged particles. When the scientists beamed alpha particles at an extremely thin piece of gold foil, they were amazed at the results. Most of the particles passed straight through the foil as if it were not there at all. Other particles changed direction or even bounced back. Rutherford thought the result so remarkable that he later said, "It was almost as incredible as if you had fired a 15-inch shell at a piece of tissue paper, and it came back and hit you."

Rutherford and his team soon concluded that because so many of the alpha particles passed straight through the gold foil, its atoms must be mostly empty space.

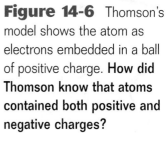

*inter*NET
CONNECTION

Visit the Glencoe Science Web Site at **www. glencoe.com/sec/ science/nc** for more information about electron energy levels in atoms.

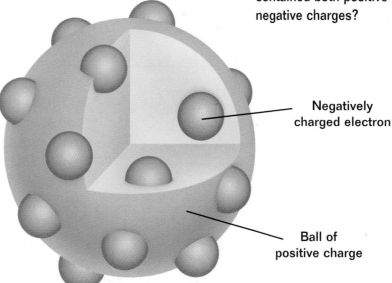

Figure 14-6 Thomson's model shows the atom as electrons embedded in a ball of positive charge. **How did Thomson know that atoms contained both positive and negative charges?**

Negatively charged electron

Ball of positive charge

Figure 14-7 Rutherford concluded that the atom must be mostly empty space in which electrons are scattered. He also thought the nucleus of the atom must be small and positively charged. **Where is most of the mass of the atom concentrated?**

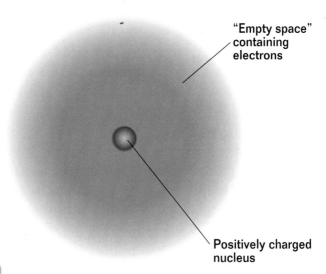

"Empty space" containing electrons

Positively charged nucleus

Inferring Atomic Structure

Procedure

1. Blow up a rubber balloon just enough to inflate it completely. Tie a knot in the balloon's opening to seal in the air.

2. Rub the balloon vigorously against a wool sweater or coat. Hold the balloon against a wall and then let go of it.

3. Take the balloon from the wall and tie a 30-cm length of string to the balloon's neck. Again, rub the balloon vigorously against a wool sweater or coat.

4. Have someone hold the string suspending the balloon. Run a rubber comb through your hair several times. Bring the comb close to the balloon.

Analysis

1. What did the balloon do when you held it against the wall and let go? Electrically charged objects are able to attract things around them that have either an opposite charge or are neutral. What happened to the balloon when it was rubbed against wool?

2. What happened when you brought the comb near the balloon? A rubber comb acquires a negative charge when rubbed through hair. What does that tell you about the charge acquired by the balloon when rubbed against wool?

However, because some of the alpha particles bounced off something that they hit, the gold atoms must contain small, massive, positively charged objects. Rutherford called the positively charged, central part of the atom the **nucleus** (NEW klee us). He named the positively charged particles in the nucleus **protons.** He also suggested that electrons were scattered in the mostly empty space around the nucleus, as shown in **Figure 14-7.**

Discovering the Neutron

Rutherford had been puzzled by one part of his experiments with alpha particles. Alpha particles seemed to be heavier than they should be. What could possibly cause the extra mass? James Chadwick, a student of Rutherford's, answered the question. Chadwick experimented with particles given off by atoms that had been bombarded with alpha particles. He found that, unlike electrons, the paths of these new particles were not affected by an electric field. To explain his observations, he said that these particles came from the nucleus and had no charge. Chadwick called these uncharged particles **neutrons.** His proton-neutron model of the atomic nucleus is still accepted today.

Today's Model of the Atom

Scientists in the early part of the twentieth century uncovered evidence that electrons in atoms were arranged in energy levels. The lowest energy level is closest to the nucleus and can hold only two electrons. Higher energy levels are farther from the nucleus and can contain more electrons. To explain these energy levels, some scientists thought that the electrons might orbit an atom's nucleus—something like how Earth and the other planets of our solar system orbit the sun.

The Electron Cloud Model

As a result of research that continues today, scientists now realize that because electrons are so small and move so fast, their energy levels are not neat, planetlike orbits around the nucleus. Rather, it seems most likely that the electrons move in what is called the atom's *electron cloud*, as shown in **Figure 14-8.** The electron cloud model helps explain what atoms do and what they don't do.

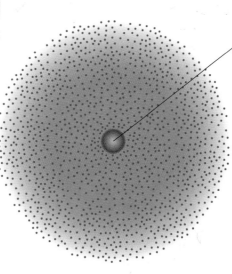

Nucleus

Figure 14-8 One model of the atom pictures the electrons moving around the nucleus in a region called an electron cloud. Dots represent places where electrons might be found. **What does the greater number of dots near the nucleus suggest?**

Section Assessment

1. List five things that are matter and five things that are not matter. Explain your answers.

2. Describe Dalton's contribution to today's understanding of matter.

3. Think of a rule that would help a fourth grader decide which things are matter and which things are not matter.

4. **Think Critically:** What made alpha particles heavier than Rutherford thought they should be?

5. **Skill Builder**
   Observing and Inferring Scientists inferred the structure of the atom based on their observations. Do the **Chapter 14 Skill Activity** on page 591 and practice observing and inferring.

Write a summary of what you learned about atoms. Include all of the vocabulary words listed in the Chapter Assessment in your summary.

14·2 Elements

Organizing the Elements

Have you watched television today? TV sets are common, yet each one is a complex device. The outer case is made mostly of plastic, and the screen is made of glass. Many of the parts that conduct electricity are metals or combinations of metals called alloys. Other parts in the interior of the set contain materials that barely conduct electricity. These different materials have one thing in common. Each is made up of even simpler materials. In fact, if you had the proper equipment, you could separate the plastics, glass, and metals into these simpler materials.

Eventually, though, you would reach a point where you couldn't separate the materials any further. What you would have is a collection of elements. An **element** is a material that cannot be broken down to simpler materials by ordinary means. At this time, 112 elements are known and 90 of them occur naturally on Earth. These elements make up gases in the air, minerals in rocks, and liquids such as water. Examples include oxygen and nitrogen in the air you breathe and the metals gold, silver, aluminum, and iron. The other 22 are known as synthetic elements. Synthetic elements have important uses in medical testing and in smoke detectors and heart pacemaker batteries. These elements, which may be found in stars, have been made in laboratories by machines like the one shown in **Figure 14-9.**

What You'll Learn

▶ What an element is
▶ The meaning of atomic mass and atomic number
▶ What an isotope is
▶ What metals, metalloids, and nonmetals are

Vocabulary
element
atomic number
atomic mass
isotope
mass number
metal
nonmetal
metalloid

Why It's Important

▶ Everything on Earth is made of the elements found on the periodic table.

Figure 14-9 This particle accelerator is at Fermilab, which is near Chicago, Illinois. The machine accelerates particles to extremely high speeds. When a particle hits and becomes part of an atom, a different element is formed.

Figure 14-10 When you look for a certain book in the library, a system of organization called the Dewey Decimal System helps you find the book quickly and efficiently. **Describe a system of organization that can help you find a pair of matching, black socks quickly in the morning.**

EARTH SCIENCE
INTEGRATION

Elements in Minerals
The mineral fluorite contains fluoride, a form of the element fluorine. Fluoride is added to water and is used in making toothpastes. It makes tooth enamel harder and helps fight tooth decay.

Suppose that you go to a library to look up information for a school assignment. Or, maybe you want to find a book that a friend told you about. When you go to the library, do you look on shelves at random as you walk up and down the rows? Probably not, unless you have lots of time or are just browsing. More likely, you depend on the library's system of organization to find the book you want quickly and efficiently, as shown in **Figure 14-10.**

The Periodic Table

When scientists need to look up information about an element or select one to use in the laboratory, they want to be quick and efficient, too. Chemists have created a chart called the periodic table of the elements to help them organize and display the elements. When you walk into a laboratory or science classroom, you often see this chart on the wall. Each element is represented by a chemical symbol that contains one to three letters. The symbols are a form of chemical shorthand that chemists use to save time and space—both on the periodic table and in written formulas. The symbols are an important part of an international system that is understood by scientists everywhere.

Using Math

Your body is made up primarily of five elements. By mass, the elements are:

oxygen	65%
carbon	18%
hydrogen	10%
nitrogen	3%
calcium	2%
other	2%

Make a circle graph that represents the elements in your body.

Atomic Number and Atomic Mass

Look up the element chlorine on the periodic table found inside the back cover of your textbook. Cl is the symbol for chlorine, as shown in **Figure 14-11,** but what are the two numbers? The top number, called the element's atomic number, is always a whole number. The **atomic number** tells you the number of protons in the nucleus of each atom of that element. Every atom of chlorine, for example, has 17 protons in its nucleus.

The number beneath the element's symbol is its atomic mass. An element's **atomic mass** tells you how heavy its atoms are compared with atoms of other elements. The unit scientists use for atomic mass is called the atomic mass unit, which is given the symbol u.

Isotopes and Mass Number

All the atoms of an element don't have to have the same mass. Some atoms of an element can have different numbers of neutrons in their nuclei than other atoms. Every chlorine atom contains 17 protons in its nucleus; however, some chlorine nuclei have 18 neutrons and others have 20. These two naturally occurring types of chlorine atoms are called isotopes. **Isotopes** (I suh tohps) are atoms of the same element that have different numbers of neutrons. You can tell someone exactly what type of chlorine atom you are referring to by using its mass number. An atom's **mass number** is the sum of its protons and neutrons [Mass number = number of protons + number of neutrons].

The atoms of chlorine that contain 17 protons and 18 neutrons have a mass number of 35 and are called chlorine-35. Those atoms that contain 17 protons and 20 neutrons are called chlorine-37. These two isotopes of chlorine are shown in **Figure 14-12.**

Figure 14-11 The periodic table block for chlorine shows its symbol, atomic number, and atomic mass. **Are chlorine atoms more or less massive than carbon atoms?**

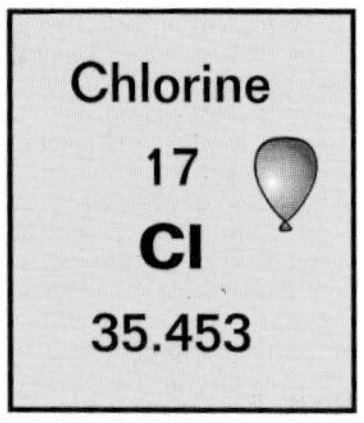

Chlorine

17

Cl

35.453

Figure 14-12 Chlorine is found naturally as two isotopes, chlorine-37 and chlorine-35. Chlorine-37 atoms are heavier than chlorine-35 atoms. The average mass of all chlorine atoms found naturally is 35.453 u. **Which type of chlorine atom is more numerous in nature?**

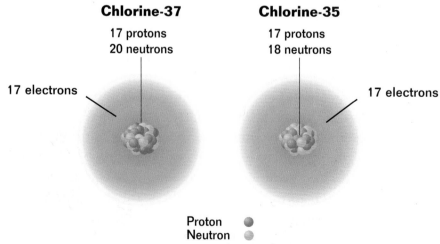

Chlorine-37
17 protons
20 neutrons
17 electrons

Chlorine-35
17 protons
18 neutrons
17 electrons

Proton
Neutron

Average Atomic Mass = 35.453 u

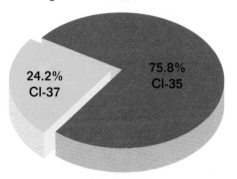

24.2%
Cl-37

75.8%
Cl-35

Figure 14-13 Chlorine-35 atoms make up 75.8 percent of chlorine. The remaining 24.2 percent of chlorine atoms are chlorine-37. If you have 1000 atoms of chlorine, 758 of the atoms are chlorine-35. The remaining 242 atoms are chlorine-37. The total mass of the 1000 atoms is 35 453 u, so the average mass of one chlorine atom is 35.453 u. **If an element has only one isotope, how does the mass of the isotope compare with the atomic mass of the element?**

Look at the periodic table block for chlorine, **Figure 14-11.** The element's atomic mass of 35.453 u can be misleading because not one chlorine atom has that mass. About 75 percent of chlorine atoms are chlorine-35 and 25 percent are chlorine-37, as shown in **Figure 14-13.** Therefore, 35.453 u is simply the average mass of chlorine atoms.

Classification of Elements

Elements fall into three general groups: metals, metalloids (MET ul oydz), and nonmetals. You use metals every day because they have many useful physical properties.

Metals generally have a shiny or metallic luster. Metals are good conductors of heat and electricity. For example, copper is often used in electrical circuits and cookware because it conducts heat and electricity well. All metals except mercury are solids at room temperature. Metals are malleable (MAL yuh bul), which means they can be bent and pounded into various shapes. Metals are also ductile, which means they can be drawn into wires without breaking, like the ones shown in **Figure 14-14.** If you look at the periodic table in the back of this textbook, you can see that most of the elements are metals.

Figure 14-14 Metals can be drawn into wires, a property called ductility. A wire's gauge is related to its thickness. A small number means that the wire is thicker.

Figure 14-15 Chlorine, bromine, and iodine are often used as disinfectants. **What nonmetals make up most of the air you breathe?**

Nonmetals are elements that are usually dull. Most are poor conductors of heat and electricity. Many are gases at room temperature, as shown in **Figure 14-15.** The solid nonmetals are generally brittle, meaning they cannot change shape easily without breaking. You can see that, except for hydrogen, the nonmetals are found on the right side of the periodic table.

Metalloids are elements such as silicon and germanium, which have characteristics of both metals and nonmetals. Some are shiny and many are conductors, but they are not as good at conducting heat and electricity as metals. All metalloids are solids at room temperature. Metalloids are found between the metals and nonmetals on the periodic table. ☑

Reading Check ☑

What is a metalloid?

Section Assessment

1. What are isotopes?

2. Explain some of the uses of metals.

3. **Think Critically:** Hector is new to your class today. He missed the lesson on how to use the periodic table to find information about the elements. Describe how you would help Hector find the atomic number for the element oxygen. Explain what this information tells him about oxygen.

4. **Skill Builder**
   Interpreting Data Look up the atomic mass of the element boron in the periodic table inside the back cover of this book. The naturally occurring isotopes of boron are boron-10 and boron-11. Which of the two isotopes is more abundant? Explain your reasoning. If you need help, refer to Interpreting Data in the **Skill Handbook** on page 560.

Using Math

An atom of niobium has a mass number of 91. How many neutrons are in the nucleus of the atom?

An isotope of phosphorus has 15 protons and 15 neutrons in the nucleus of each of its atoms. What is the mass number of the isotope?

Elements and the Periodic Table

Materials

- Large index cards
- Merck Index
- Encyclopedia
  * other reference materials
- Large bulletin board
- Paper (8½ × 14)
- Thumbtacks
  * pushpins

  * Alternate Materials

The periodic table organizes the elements. But, what do these elements look like, and what are they used for? In this activity, you'll examine some elements and share your findings with your classmates.

What You'll Investigate

What are some of the characteristics of the chemical elements, and what are they used for?

Goals

- **Classify** the chemical elements.
- **Make** your own periodic table that shows the classification of the elements.

Procedure

1. From the list provided by your teacher, select the number of elements you are assigned.

2. **Design** an index card for each of your selected elements. On each element's card, mark its atomic number in the upper left-hand corner and write its symbol and name in the upper right-hand corner.

3. Research each of the elements and write several sentences on the card about its appearance, its other properties, and its uses.

4. Based upon its properties, **decide** if each of your elements is likely a metal, a metalloid, or a nonmetal. Use the color of magic marker chosen by your teacher to write the appropriate word—*metal, metalloid,* or *nonmetal*—on each of your cards.

5. Work with your classmates to **make** a large periodic table. Use thumbtacks to attach your cards on a bulletin board in their proper positions on the table.

6. Draw your own periodic table on an 8½ × 14 sheet of paper. Put the elements' symbols and atomic numbers in the proper places on the table.

Conclude and Apply

1. **Interpret** the class data and **classify** the elements into the categories: metals, metalloids, and nonmetals. Highlight each of the three categories in a different color on your periodic table.

2. **Predict** the properties of a yet-undiscovered element located directly under francium on the periodic table.

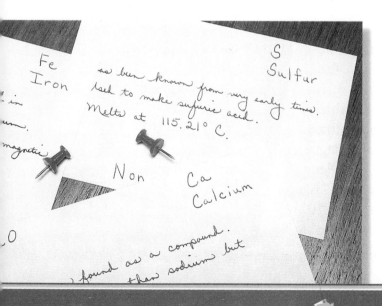

Development of the Periodic Table

Elements such as gold, silver, tin, copper, lead, and mercury have been known since ancient times. As more elements were discovered, people began to recognize patterns in their properties. Later, scientists used the patterns to develop ways of classifying the elements. For example, in 1817, Johann Döbereiner noticed that the atomic mass of strontium was halfway between the masses of calcium and barium, elements with similar chemical properties.

In the Cards

In the mid-nineteenth century, Dmitri Mendeleev published the first periodic table. Mendeleev recognized patterns in the properties and atomic masses of certain elements. In trying to extend the patterns, he created a card for each of the more than 60 elements known at the time. Each card contained the element's symbol, its atomic mass, and its characteristic chemical and physical properties. Mendeleev then arranged the cards on a table in order of increasing atomic mass, grouping elements of similar properties together. The resulting periodic table showed vertical, horizontal, and diagonal relationships. Mendeleev left blank spaces in his table for as-yet-undiscovered elements, and he predicted in detail what the chemical and physical properties of the missing elements would be when they were found.

New Discoveries

With the discovery of the atomic nucleus and isotopes in the early twentieth century, it became apparent that the properties of the elements vary periodically with their atomic numbers. Therefore, modern periodic tables arrange the elements according to atomic number rather than atomic mass. In the mid-1900s, the last major changes to the periodic table resulted from the work of Glenn Seaborg and his coworkers with the discovery of the transuranium elements from atomic number 94 to 102. Locate the element seaborgium on the periodic table. Scientists today continue to discover new elements.

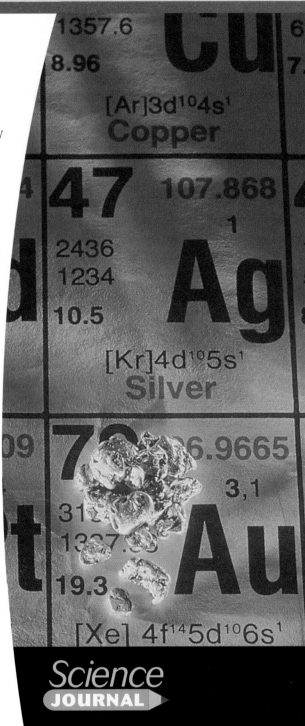

Science JOURNAL

What can you learn about an element from the periodic table? In your Science Journal, list the general information given for each element on the table.

Compounds and Mixtures

Substances

Scientists classify matter in several ways. For example, a sample of matter that has the same composition and properties throughout is called a **substance.** The chemical elements you learned about in Section 14-2 are pure substances. When elements combine with each other, different kinds of matter are formed.

Compounds

What do you call the colorless liquid that flows when you turn on the kitchen faucet? You probably call it water, but maybe you've seen it written H_2O and wondered what that meant. Hydrogen and oxygen occur both naturally as colorless gases, but H_2O tells you that these two elements can combine, as shown in **Figure 14-16,** to form a new, pure substance called a compound. A **compound** is a pure substance whose smallest unit is made up of atoms of more than one element. Millions of compounds can be made from combinations of elements, and the compounds almost always have properties that are different from the elements that make them up. Have you ever used hydrogen peroxide to disinfect a cut? Hydrogen peroxide is another compound made from the elements hydrogen and oxygen.

Figure 14-16 A space shuttle is powered by the reaction between liquid hydrogen and liquid oxygen. The reaction produces a large amount of energy and a single compound, water. **Why would a car that burns hydrogen rather than gasoline be friendly to the environment?**

What You'll Learn

► What a compound is
► The difference between types of mixtures

Vocabulary
substance
compound
law of definite proportions
mixture

Why It's Important

► Compounds and mixtures are part of your everyday life.

Compounds Need Formulas

What's the difference between water and hydrogen peroxide? H_2O is the chemical formula for water, and it tells you more than what elements make up the compound. Look at **Figure 14-17.** Water is made up of two atoms of hydrogen for every one atom of oxygen. H_2O_2 is the formula for hydrogen peroxide. The subscripts, numbers written below and to the right of the elements' symbols, mean that there are two atoms of hydrogen for every two atoms of oxygen in hydrogen peroxide. Carbon dioxide, CO_2, is another common compound. Carbon dioxide is made up of one atom of carbon for every two atoms of oxygen. Carbon and oxygen also can form the compound carbon monoxide, CO, a gas that is poisonous to all warm-blooded animals. As you can see, no subscript is used when one atom is present. The **law of definite proportions** states that a given compound is always made of the same elements in the same proportion by mass. For example, water always has two hydrogen atoms for every oxygen atom. ☑

Reading Check ☑

Propane has three atoms of carbon for every eight atoms of hydrogen. What is propane's chemical formula?

Figure 14-17 The elements hydrogen and oxygen can combine to form two compounds, water and hydrogen peroxide. Although both compounds are made up of the same elements, the ratios of hydrogen and oxygen atoms are different.

A H_2O_2, the formula for hydrogen peroxide, shows that it contains two hydrogen atoms for every two oxygen atoms.

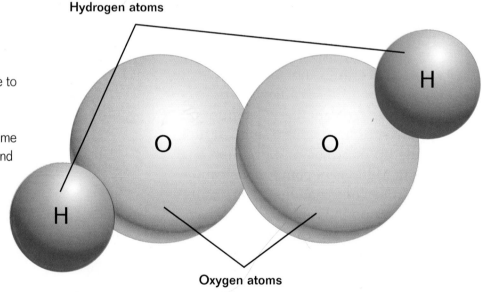

Hydrogen atoms

Oxygen atoms

B H_2O, the formula for water, shows that it contains two hydrogen atoms for each oxygen atom. **What is the ratio of hydrogen atoms to carbon atoms in methane, which has the formula CH_4?**

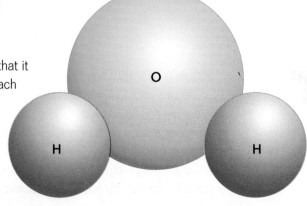

Mixtures

When two or more substances (elements or compounds) come together but don't combine to make a new, pure substance, a **mixture** results. Unlike compounds, the proportions of the substances in a mixture can be changed. For example, if you put some sand into a bucket of water, you have a mixture of sand and water. If you add more sand or more water, it's still a mixture of sand and water. The makeup of air, a mixture of nitrogen, oxygen, and other gases, can vary somewhat from place to place and time to time. Look around your classroom, home, or neighborhood. What other mixtures do you see? Did you know that your blood is a mixture made up of elements and compounds? It contains white blood cells, red blood cells, water, and a number of dissolved elements. The blood parts can be separated easily and used by different parts of your body.

You can often use a liquid to separate the parts of a mixture of solids. For example, you could add water to a mixture of sugar and sand. Only the sugar would dissolve in the water. The sand could then be separated from the sugar and water by pouring the mixture through a filter. Then, heating would dry off the water, leaving the sugar behind.

CONNECTION

Visit the Glencoe Science Web Site at **www. glencoe.com/sec/ science/nc** for more information about mixtures.

LIFE SCIENCE
◄ **INTEGRATION**

Problem Solving

Drinking Water from Salt Water

Suppose you are on a ship or live in a place that is near an ocean but does not have much freshwater for people to drink.

Can you use change in physical state to create a method for removing salt from ocean water? Distillation is the process of heating a mixture to separate its parts. Parts of the mixture boil at different temperatures. A more nearly pure substance results when the vapor from each part is cooled and condensed.

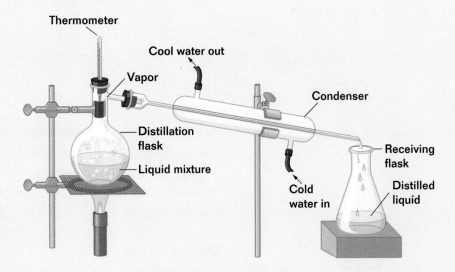

and condenses to a liquid. The liquid drips into the flask on the right.

A liquid mixture placed in the flask on the left is heated to boiling. As the vapor passes through the tube in the condenser in the middle, it is surrounded by cold water

Think Critically: Examine the distillation system in the photo. How could you use such a system to produce freshwater from ocean water?

Figure 14-18 Many commom materials are uniform mixtures.

A Sterling silver dinnerware is 92.5 percent silver and 7.5 percent copper.

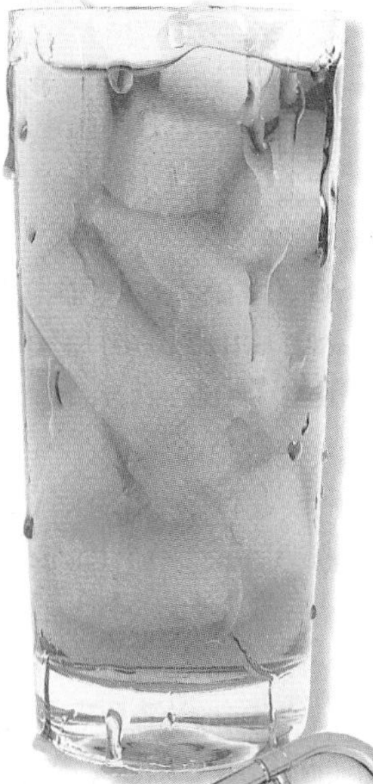

B The tea in this glass is a uniform mixture that is mostly water. **Is the mixture of ice and tea a uniform mixture?**

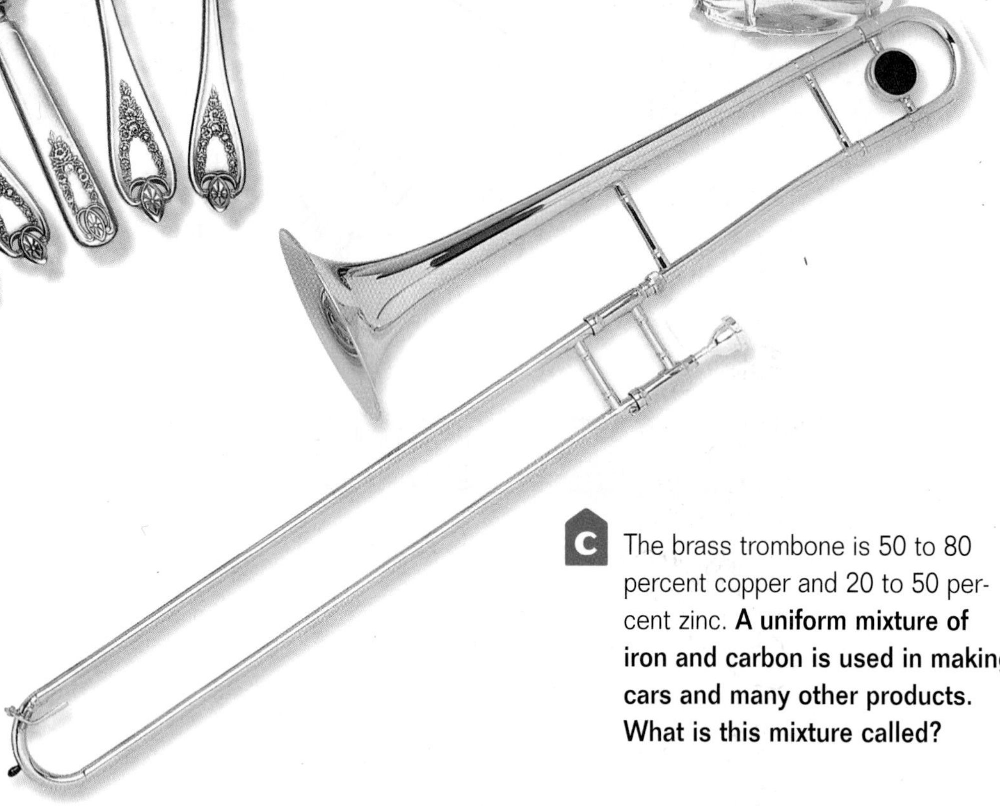

C The brass trombone is 50 to 80 percent copper and 20 to 50 percent zinc. **A uniform mixture of iron and carbon is used in making cars and many other products. What is this mixture called?**

Mixtures can be uniform or nonuniform. Uniform means the same throughout. Several uniform mixtures are shown in **Figure 14-18.** You can't see the different parts in this type of mixture. Air is a uniform mixture of gases. No matter how closely you look, you can't see the individual parts that make up air or the mixture called brass in the trombone shown in **Figure 14-18C.**

In a nonuniform mixture such as sand and water, you can see the different parts. A pepperoni and mushroom pizza is a tasty kind of nonuniform mixture. Other examples of this kind of mixture include tacos, a stew, a toy box full of toys, or your laundry basket at the end of the week. Several nonuniform mixtures are shown in **Figure 14-19.**

Figure 14-19 Nonuniform mixtures are part of your everyday life.

A You can see pieces of solid orange floating in liquid if you look at a glass of orange juice closely.

B Blood is a nonuniform mixture of many materials, including water, proteins, glucose, and fats. Some of these materials can be separated in the laboratory.

C Areas of different color in a rock show that it is made up of crystals of different materials. **A clear fruit drink is made up of many substances. Why is it a uniform mixture?**

Section Assessment

1. List three examples of compounds and three examples of mixtures.

2. The chemical formula for baking soda is $NaHCO_3$. Use the periodic table to write the names of the elements in baking soda. Which element's atoms are most numerous in baking soda?

3. How can you tell that a substance is a compound by looking at its formula?

4. **Think Critically:** Was your breakfast this morning a compound, a uniform mixture, or a nonuniform mixture? Review the definitions for a compound and a uniform mixture. Explain your answer based on these definitions.

5. **Skill Builder**
   Comparing and Contrasting
   Compare and contrast compounds and mixtures. If you need help, refer to Comparing and Contrasting in the **Skill Handbook** on page 556.

Using Computers

Database Use a computerized card catalog to find out about one element from the periodic table. Include information about the mixtures and/or compounds the element is found in. If you need help, refer to page 569.

Mystery Mixture

Materials

- Test tubes (3)
- Cornstarch
- Sugar
- Baking soda
- Mystery mixture
- Small scoops (3)
- Dropper bottles (2)
- Iodine solution
- White vinegar
- Candle
- Test-tube holder
- Small pie pan
- Matches

Cornstarch, baking powder, and powdered sugar are compounds that look alike. To avoid mistaking one for another, you may need to learn how to identify each one. You can learn chemical tests that identify these different compounds. For example, some compounds react with certain liquids to produce gases. Other combinations produce distinctive colors. Some compounds have high melting points. Others have low melting points.

What You'll Investigate

How can the compounds in an unknown mixture be identified by experimentation?

Goals

- **Test** for the presence of certain compounds.
- **Decide** which of these compounds are present in an unknown mixture.

Safety Precautions

Use caution when handling hot objects. Substances could stain or burn clothing. Be sure to point the test tube away from your face and your classmates while heating.

Procedure

1. **Copy** the data table into your Science Journal. **Record** your results for each of the following steps.

2. Place a small scoopful, or the amount indicated by your teacher, of cornstarch on the pie pan. Do the same for sugar and baking soda. Add a drop of vinegar to each. Wash and dry the pan after you have recorded your observations.

3. Place a small scoopful, or the amount indicated by your teacher, of cornstarch, sugar, and baking soda on the pie pan. Add a drop of iodine solution to each.

4. Place a small scoopful, or the amount indicated by your teacher, of each compound in a separate test tube. Hold the test tube with the test-tube holder. Gently heat the bottom of each test tube with the candle.

5. Now, use steps 2 to 4 to **test** your mystery mixture and find out which of these compounds it contains.

Conclude and Apply

1. Use your observations to form a hypothesis as to which compounds are in your mystery mixture. Describe how you arrived at your conclusion.

2. How would you be able to tell if all three compounds were not in your mystery mixture sample?

3. What would you conclude if you tested baking powder from your kitchen and found that it fizzed with vinegar, turned blue with iodine, and did not melt when heated?

Results of Tests			
To be tested	Vinegar fizzes	Iodine turns blue	Compound melts
Cornstarch			
Sugar			
Baking soda			
Mystery mix			

For a **preview** of this chapter, study this Reviewing Main Ideas before you read the chapter. After you have studied this chapter, you can use the Reviewing Main Ideas to **review** the chapter.

For a **preview** of this chapter, study this Reviewing Main Ideas before you read the chapter. After you have studied this chapter, you can use the Reviewing Main Ideas to **review** the chapter.

 The Glencoe MindJogger, Audiocassettes, and CD-ROM provide additional opportunities for review.

Section

14-1 STRUCTURE OF MATTER

Matter is anything that occupies space and has mass. It includes all the things that you can see, touch, taste, or smell. Matter does not include light, sound, or heat. *Can you think of anything else that is not matter?*

WHAT MAKES UP MATTER?

Matter is made up of atoms. **Atoms** are made of smaller parts called **protons, neutrons,** and **electrons.** Many models of atoms have been created as scientists try to discover and define the atom's internal structure. *What other models do you know about?*

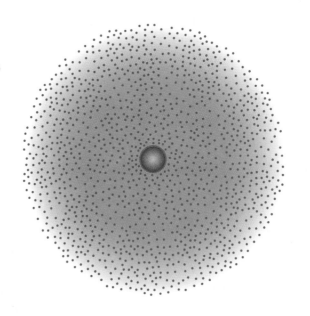

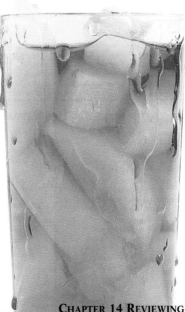

Section 14-2 ELEMENTS

Elements are the basic building blocks of matter. Each element has a unique set of properties and is generally classified as a metal, metalloid, or nonmetal. The chemical symbol for each element is understood by scientists everywhere. An element's **atomic number** tells how many protons its atoms contain, and its **atomic mass** tells how heavy its atoms are. **Isotopes** are two or more atoms of the same element that have different numbers of neutrons. *What element has the symbol Co?*

Chlorine
17
Cl
35.453

Reading Check ✓
Create a timeline of the important discoveries about atoms. Include the names of the scientists. Check other reference sources for dates when necessary.

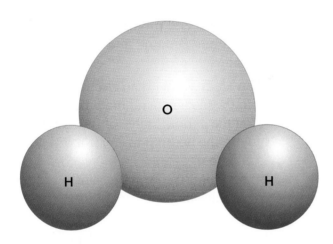

O

H   H

Section 14-3 COMPOUNDS

Compounds are pure substances produced when elements combine. Compounds contain specific proportions of the elements that make them up. A compound's properties are different from those of the elements from which it is formed. *Name five common compounds.*

MIXTURES

Mixtures are combinations of compounds and elements that have not formed new, pure substances. Uniform mixtures contain individual parts that cannot be seen. However, you can see the individual parts of nonuniform mixtures. *What are two mixtures of each type that you know about?*

Using Vocabulary

a. atom	**j.** mass number
b. atomic mass	**k.** matter
c. atomic number	**l.** metals
d. compound	**m.** metalloids
e. electron	**n.** mixtures
f. element	**o.** neutron
g. isotopes	**p.** nonmetals
h. law of conserva-	**q.** nucleus
tion of matter	**r.** proton
i. law of definite	**s.** substance
proportions	

Using the list above, replace the underlined words with the correct Vocabulary word.

1. The particle in the nucleus of the atom that carries a positive charge is the <u>neutron</u>.

2. The new substance formed when elements join is a <u>mixture</u>.

3. Anything that has mass and takes up space is <u>metal</u>.

4. The particles in the atom that account for most of the mass are protons and <u>electrons</u>.

5. Elements that are shiny, malleable, ductile, and good conductors of heat and electricity are <u>nonmetals</u>.

Checking Concepts

Choose the word or phrase that best answers the question.

6. What is a solution an example of?
   A) element   C) compound
   B) nonuniform   D) uniform
      mixture   mixture

7. The nucleus of one atom contains 12 protons and 12 neutrons, while the nucleus of another atom contains 12 protons and 16 neutrons. What are the atoms?
   A) chromium atoms
   B) two different elements
   C) isotopes of magnesium
   D) negatively charged

8. What is a compound?
   A) a mixture of compounds and elements
   B) a combination of two or more elements
   C) anything that has mass and occupies space
   D) the building block of matter

9. What does the atom consist of?
   A) electrons, protons, and alpha particles
   B) neutrons and protons
   C) electrons, protons, and neutrons
   D) elements, protons, and electrons

10. In an atom, where is an electron located?
    A) in the nucleus with the proton
    B) on the periodic table of the elements
    C) with the neutron to create a positive charge
    D) in a cloudlike formation surrounding the nucleus

11. How is matter defined?
    A) the negative charge in an atom
    B) anything that has mass and occupies space
    C) the mass of the nucleus
    D) sound, light, and energy

12. What are two atoms that have the same number of protons?
    A) metals   C) isotopes
    B) nonmetals   D) metalloids

13. What are the majority of the elements on the periodic table?
    A) metals   C) nonmetals
    B) metalloids   D) compounds

14. Which element is a metalloid?
    A) bromine   C) potassium
    B) silicon   D) iron

15. What are nonuniform mixtures?
   A) two kinds of mixtures
   B) the same throughout—the parts cannot be seen
   C) made of several different parts that can be seen
   D) like a soft drink

Thinking Critically

16. A chemical formula is written to indicate the makeup of a compound. What is the ratio of sulfur atoms to oxygen atoms in SO_2?

17. An atom contains seven electrons and seven protons. What element is this atom? Explain your answer.

18. What happens to an element when it becomes part of a compound?

19. Cobalt-60 and cobalt-59 are isotopes. How can they be the same element but have different mass numbers?

20. What did Rutherford's gold foil experiment tell scientists about atomic structure?

Developing Skills

If you need help, refer to the **Skill Handbook.**

21. **Interpreting Scientific Illustrations:** Look at the drawings of the two atoms below. Explain whether or not the atoms are isotopes.

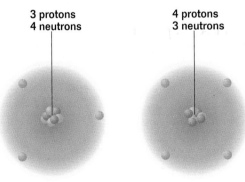

3 protons
4 neutrons

4 protons
3 neutrons

Proton
Neutron
Electron

THE
PRINCETON
REVIEW

Test-Taking Tip

What Does the Test Expect of Me? Find out what concepts, objectives, or standards are being tested well before the test. Keep these concepts in mind as you solve the questions.

Test Practice

Use these questions to test your Science Proficiency.

1. Which list of terms **BEST** describes the properties of metals?
   A) dull, brittle, nonconducting
   B) malleable, ductile, shiny, good conductors
   C) shiny, brittle, can conduct electricity
   D) gaseous, high density

2. Mixtures are divided into two categories. Which pair of examples **BEST** represents the two types of mixtures?
   A) a pizza and a tossed salad
   B) a baseball card collection and a CD collection
   C) a soft drink and a taco
   D) an iced soft drink and iced tea

3. What particles are found in the nucleus of a carbon-12 atom?
   A) 12 protons
   B) 12 neutrons and 12 protons
   C) 12 neutrons
   D) 6 protons and 6 neutrons

4. Which of these is **NOT** an element?
   A) water
   B) hydrogen
   C) chlorine
   D) oxygen

CHAPTER 15 Energy

Chapter Preview

Section 15-1
Energy Changes

Section 15-2
Temperature and
Thermal Energy

Section 15-3
Chemical Energy

Skills Preview

Skill Builders
- Make and Use a Graph
- Use Numbers

Activities
- Observe and Infer
- Interpret Data

MiniLabs
- Classify
- Compare and Contrast

Reading Check ✔

As you read this chapter about energy, list the cause-and-effect relationships you identify.

Explore Activity

Imagine yourself downhill skiing in the winter. You skillfully change the direction and speed of your skis by changing your body position. A surfboard rider feels the same sense of connection between his body position and the board's motion. So do a cyclist on a bike and a young child on a swing. All are aware of something changing—position, speed, or direction. Energy plays a part in all of these changes. Where else have you seen energy causing change?

Observe Energy

1. Obtain a new, wide rubber band.

2. As you hold the rubber band in both hands, touch it to your lower lip.

3. After moving it away from your face, quickly stretch the rubber band several times.

4. Touch the rubber band to your lip again. What differences do you observe?

5. Obtain additional materials from your teacher to observe more energy changes.

6. Throw away the rubber band after the activity.

Record your observations for each material in your Science Journal. Set up a table to help you compare your results.

15•1 Energy Changes

What You'll Learn

▶ What energy is and the forms it takes
▶ The difference between potential energy and kinetic energy

Vocabulary
energy
kinetic energy
potential energy
law of conservation of energy

Why It's Important

▶ The more you know about energy, the more efficiently you will use it.

Energy

Energy is a term you probably use every day. You may say that eating a plate of spaghetti gives you energy or that a gymnast has a lot of energy. But, do you know that a burning fire, a bouncing ball, and a tank of gasoline also have energy? Exactly what is energy?

What is energy?

The ancient Greek word for energy was *energos*, which means "active." Until the 1900s, people thought that energy was stored inside objects. Now we say that **energy** is the ability to cause change. Energy can change the temperature, shape, speed, or direction of an object. Energy can change the shape of modeling clay or the temperature of a cup of water. As you can see in **Figure 15-1,** you can use the energy of your muscles to change the speed of a bicycle by pedaling faster or slower, or by putting on the brakes. The person on a skateboard in **Figure 15-1** uses energy to the change the direction the skateboard takes.

Figure 15-1 The riders of the skateboard and bike use energy to change their speed and direction.

Energy Transformations

If you ask your friends what comes to mind when they think of energy, you will get many different answers. Some may mention the energy in a flame. Others may say energy is needed to run a race. These answers suggest that energy comes in different forms from a variety of sources. Is that true? A flame gives off energy in the form of heat and light. Eating a good breakfast gives your body the energy to move, think, and grow. Your body stores most of its energy in the form of fat. Nuclear power plants use energy from the center of the atom. It seems that energy comes in many forms. What other examples of energy can you think of?

Change Can Cause Change

Push down a bicycle pedal and the gears in the back wheel turn. The chemical energy in your muscles has been changed to mechanical energy. In the natural world, energy often changes from one form to another. Any change of energy from one form to another is called an energy transformation. Energy transformations take place all around you. When a car sits in the sun all day, the energy of light waves changes to a form of energy that warms the inside of the car. The energy in the chemicals used to make the fireworks in **Figure 15-2** changes to light, sound, and motion. In the Explore Activity, the energy you used to stretch and move the rubber band changed into energy that raised the temperature of the band.

During these and other types of energy transformations, the total amount of energy stays the same. No energy is ever lost or gained. Only the form of energy changes.

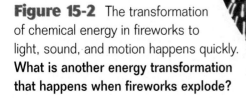

Figure 15-2 The transformation of chemical energy in fireworks to light, sound, and motion happens quickly. **What is another energy transformation that happens when fireworks explode?**

Figure 15-3 Glen Canyon Dam is located on the Colorado River in Arizona. Pipes lead water from the reservoir behind the dam to the hydroelectric generators in the power plant, which is located in front of the dam. The energy of the rushing water spins the generators' turbines, and kinetic energy is transformed into electricity. **What are some benefits of using water as a source of energy?**

Useful Changes

Since the earliest times, humans have experimented with different forms of energy. When early humans learned to make fires, they learned to use the chemical energy in wood to cook, stay warm, and light their way in the dark. Today, electrical energy is changed into thermal energy that warms your home. Also, electrical energy changes to light energy in a lightbulb when you flip on a switch. Chemical energy in fuel changes to the type of energy that runs the engine in the bus you take to school. The water heater in your home transforms energy in natural gas, or in electrical energy, to thermal energy that warms the water for a bath or shower. A hydroelectric plant, as shown in **Figure 15-3,** and a wind power plant transform the energy of moving water and wind into electrical energy.

Kinetic and Potential Energy

You've seen that energy can take many forms, such as light, heat, and motion. Two main types of energy are called kinetic energy and potential energy.

Kinetic Energy

If you were asked if a football thrown downfield has energy, you might say that it does because it is moving. Objects in motion have a type of energy called **kinetic** (kuh NET ihk) **energy.** A football thrown by a quarterback has kinetic energy. A skydiver falling toward Earth also has kinetic energy.

How much kinetic energy does it have?

Not all moving objects have the same amount of kinetic energy. Look at **Figure 15-4.** Which would have more kinetic energy, a train coming down the track or a girl in-line skating? The amount of kinetic energy an object has depends on the mass and speed of the object. If the train and the girl are traveling at the same speed, the train has more kinetic energy than the girl on skates because it has more mass. In this example, even if the train moves slowly and the girl skates as fast as she can, the train still has more kinetic energy because its mass is so much greater than the skater's mass. What would happen if two objects had the same mass? How would the kinetic energies of two trains heading toward the city compare if they had the same mass? The train that is traveling at the higher speed would have more kinetic energy than the slower one.

VISUALIZING
Kinetic Energy

Figure 15-4 When comparing the kinetic energies of any objects, you must consider both the masses and the speeds of the objects.

A Suppose this train and skater are moving at the same speed. **Which of them has more kinetic energy? Explain.**

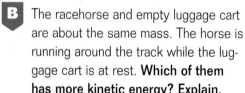

B The racehorse and empty luggage cart are about the same mass. The horse is running around the track while the luggage cart is at rest. **Which of them has more kinetic energy? Explain.**

Potential Energy

Suppose the ski lift in **Figure 15-5** takes a skier to the top of a hill and lets her rest there. Do you think the skier still has energy? She does. An object does not have to be moving to have energy. The skier has potential energy. A teacher may say that you have potential—the ability to do more work than you are doing right now. **Potential** (puh TEN chul) **energy** is not energy that comes from motion. It is energy that comes from position or condition. A skier at the top of a hill has potential energy. Even though she is not moving, she has the ability to move.

In general, whenever you raise an object above its original position, you give it the ability to fall. The energy the ski lift uses in taking a skier up a hill is changed. This energy becomes stored as potential energy in the skier. When more energy is used to raise her higher, there is more energy that has been transformed and stored in the skier as potential energy. This idea is similar to pouring water into a bottle and storing it to be used later during a basketball game. You can store potential energy to be used later when you need it. ☑

Potential Energy and Kinetic Energy Are Related

One of the easiest ways to see the difference between potential and kinetic energy is to work with a pendulum, as in **Figure 15-6**. A pendulum is a weight that swings back and forth from a single point.

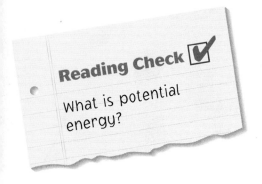

Reading Check ☑

What is potential energy?

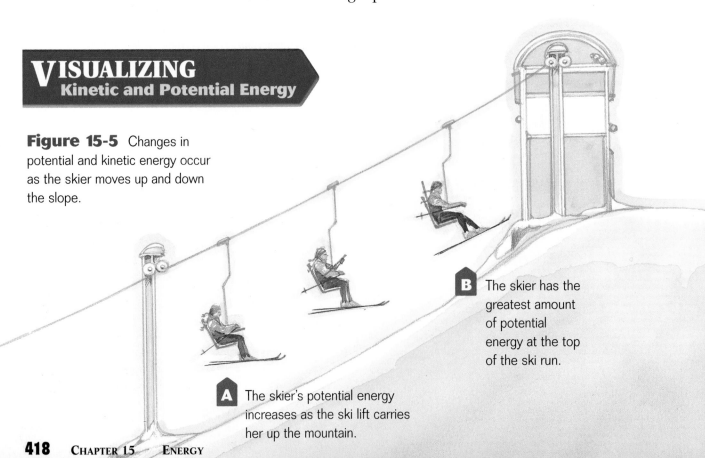

VISUALIZING
Kinetic and Potential Energy

Figure 15-5 Changes in potential and kinetic energy occur as the skier moves up and down the slope.

B The skier has the greatest amount of potential energy at the top of the ski run.

A The skier's potential energy increases as the ski lift carries her up the mountain.

A swing on a backyard swing set is a pendulum. The energy you use to pull back on a swing is changed and stored in the swing as potential energy. Similarly, potential energy can be stored in any pendulum by moving the weighted end to one side. When you let go of a pendulum, any stored potential energy in the pendulum is released. The pendulum swings down in a curved path, called an arc. The instant the pendulum moves, potential energy is transformed into kinetic energy.

There is a direct relationship between the amount of potential energy an object has and the amount of energy that can be transformed into kinetic energy. When a book is placed on a shelf, it has potential energy. That energy becomes kinetic energy if the book falls off the shelf. A book placed on a higher shelf has more potential energy—and more kinetic energy as it falls—than it would have on a lower shelf.

Transfer of Kinetic Energy

Kinetic energy can be transferred from one object to another when those objects collide. Think about the changes and transfer of energy during bowling. Success in bowling depends on the fact that energy can be transferred from one object to another. Even if the bowling ball does not touch all the pins, you can knock them all down with one roll of the ball. A transfer of kinetic energy also takes place when dominoes fall. You only need to give the first domino in the row a bit of kinetic energy by tapping it just enough to make it fall against the next

Figure 15-6 The people on this amusement park ride experience energy changes as the pendulum swings. **At what points would the potential energy be the greatest? The kinetic energy?**

C When the skier begins to ski down the slope, her potential energy starts to transform into kinetic energy.

D As the skier moves further down the mountain, more and more potential energy changes to kinetic energy. She has the least amount of potential energy just before reaching the bottom of the ski run.

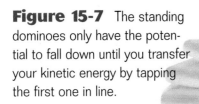

Figure 15-7 The standing dominoes only have the potential to fall down until you transfer your kinetic energy by tapping the first one in line.

Mini Lab

Classifying Types of Energy

Procedure

1. Examine the following list of activities.
2. Classify each activity as involving potential or kinetic energy. Hint: Ask yourself if the energy involved is stored (potential), moving (kinetic), or both.
   a. Eat an apple.
   b. Turn on a flashlight.
   c. Push a ball along the floor.
   d. Lift a weight.
   e. Burn a birthday candle.

Analysis

1. Make a table in your Science Journal with two columns.
2. Label the left column "potential" and the right column "kinetic."
3. List the type of activity you examined above in the correct column.
4. Compare your classifications with those of your lab partner.

domino. As the first domino falls into the next one, its kinetic energy is transferred to the second domino. This transfer of kinetic energy continues from domino to domino until the last one falls, as shown in **Figure 15-7.** It is important to know the difference between potential and kinetic energy. It is this difference that sometimes allows you to store energy for later use.

Conserving Energy

Following the trail of energy as it moves from source to source can be a challenge. In 1840, James Joule described the law of conservation of energy. According to the **law of conservation of energy,** energy cannot be created or destroyed. It only can be transformed from one form into another. This means the total amount of energy in the whole universe never changes. The universe doesn't make more energy. Energy doesn't just vanish into thin air either. The only change is the form in which energy may appear. Track the flow of energy in the case of a soccer ball. A soccer player has chemical energy in her muscles from the food she ate. The chemical energy is released as she swings her leg. Her leg now has kinetic energy.

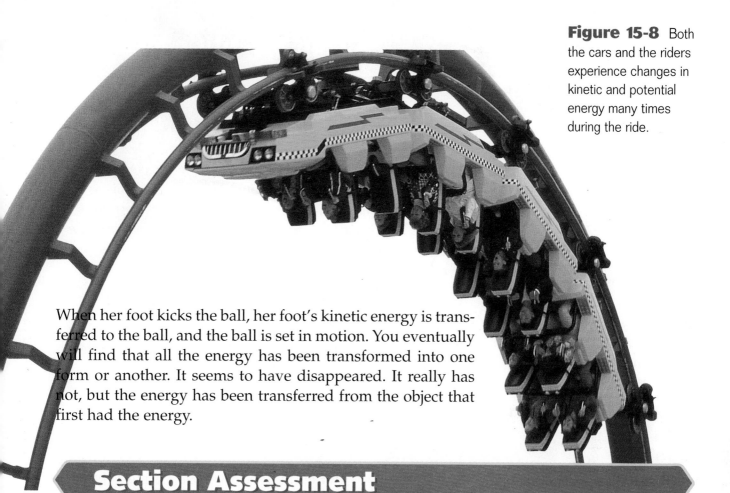

Figure 15-8 Both the cars and the riders experience changes in kinetic and potential energy many times during the ride.

When her foot kicks the ball, her foot's kinetic energy is transferred to the ball, and the ball is set in motion. You eventually will find that all the energy has been transformed into one form or another. It seems to have disappeared. It really has not, but the energy has been transferred from the object that first had the energy.

Section Assessment

1. If you are riding in a roller coaster as in **Figure 15-8,** how do you think your speed is related to your kinetic energy? Your potential energy?

2. As a roller coaster climbs to the top of the steepest hill on its track, when does the first car have the greatest potential energy? When does it have the greatest kinetic energy?

3. State the law of conservation of energy in your own words.

4. **Think Critically:** You get up in the morning, get dressed, eat breakfast, walk to the bus stop, and ride to school. List three different energy transformations that have taken place.

5. **Skill Builder**
   Making and Using Graphs A pendulum swings seven times per minute. If the string were half as long, the pendulum would swing ten times per minute. If the original length were twice as long, the pendulum would swing five times per minute. Make a bar graph that shows these data. Draw a conclusion from the results. If you need help, refer to Making and Using Graphs in the **Skill Handbook** on page 553.

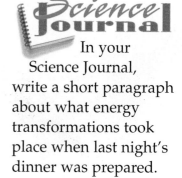

Science Journal In your Science Journal, write a short paragraph about what energy transformations took place when last night's dinner was prepared.

Where's the energy?

Did you know that several energy transfers occur during the process of making ice cream? At the beginning of this activity, you will transfer energy to the container of ingredients by rolling it back and forth across the desk. This will help the ingredients mix together. As the ingredients form small crystals, you also will observe another type of energy transfer as you make the ice cream.

What You'll Investigate

What are the various energy transfers that occur during the process of making ice cream?

Materials

- A desk
  *table
- Sugar (30 g)
- Whole milk (120 mL)
  *half & half (120 mL)
- Small, self-sealing freezer bag (1-quart or less)
- Ice
- Coffee can (large with lid)
- Rock salt (230 g)
- Thermometer
  *Alternate Materials

Goals

- **Observe** a transfer of energy.
- **Measure** a temperature change.

Safety Precautions

Do not taste, eat, or drink any materials used in the lab.

Procedure

1. **Put** the milk and sugar into the freezer bag.
2. **Take** the temperature of the mix and record it.
3. **Seal** the bag well and place the freezer bag inside the large coffee can.
4. **Pack** ice around and over the freezer bag.
5. **Pour** rock salt over the ice. Put the lid on the coffee can.
6. **Roll** the can across the desk at least 15 times.
7. **Let** the can stand for 15 minutes.
8. **Check** to see if the ice cream has frozen. If not, repeat steps 6 and 7.
9. **Take** the temperature of the ice cream and record it.

Conclude and Apply

1. What different types of energy can you **conclude** were involved in making the ice cream?
2. **Infer** what type of energy transferred out of the liquid mixture so it could become ice cream. How do you know?

Temperature and Thermal Energy

Temperature

What's today's temperature? If you looked at a thermometer, listened to a weather report on the radio, or saw a weather map on the news similar to the map in **Figure 15-9,** you probably used the air temperature to help you decide what to wear. Some days are so hot you don't need a jacket. Others are so cold you want to bundle up.

Hot and cold are terms that are used in everyday language to indicate temperature. They are not scientific words because they mean different things to different people. A summer day that seems hot to one person may seem just right to another. If you usually live in Florida but go swimming in the ocean off the coast of Maine while on vacation, you might find the water unbearably cold. Have you ever complained that a classroom was too cold when other students insisted that it was too warm?

Temperature Is an Average

What is temperature? Any material or object is made up of particles that are invisible to the naked eye. The particles that make up any object are constantly moving, even if the object appears to be perfectly still. Everything you can think of— your hand, the pencil on your desk, or even the desktop—is made up of moving particles. You learned that moving objects have kinetic energy. Because the particles that make up an object are in constant motion, they have kinetic energy. Faster-moving particles have more kinetic energy.

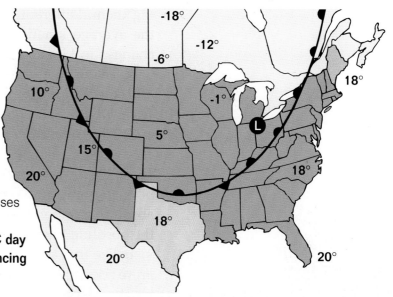

Figure 15-9 Each person senses temperature differently. **Would a person in Texas describe an 18°C day differently from a person experiencing an 18°C day in Maine? Why?**

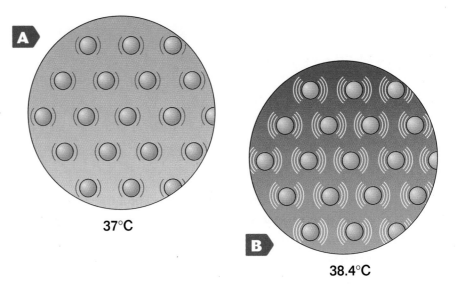

Figure 15-10 The temperature of the particles in B is higher than the temperature of the particles in A. **How does the motion of the particles differ in A and B? Why?**

37°C

38.4°C

If you could measure the kinetic energy of each particle in an object and average them, you would find the average kinetic energy of the particles. **Temperature** is a measure of the average kinetic energy of the particles in any object. The greater the average kinetic energy is, the higher an object's temperature is. For example, **Figure 15-10** shows particles at the normal human body temperature of 37°C. If a person has a body temperature of 38.4°C, the particles in the person's body have more kinetic energy than usual.

Temperature Scales

Because everyone experiences temperature differently, you cannot accurately measure temperature by how it feels to you. Recall that temperature is the average kinetic energy of all the particles. But, there is no easy method to measure the kinetic energy of each particle and then calculate an average. That is because the particles are extremely small. Even scientists using sensitive instruments have a difficult time observing them. Different temperature scales are used to measure the average kinetic energy of particles. These scales divide changes in kinetic energy of the particles into regular intervals. That is, the units are spaced apart evenly.

One scale you may use is the Fahrenheit (FAYR un hit) scale. On the Fahrenheit scale, water freezes at 32°F and boils at 212°F. A second temperature scale you will use in science class is the Celsius (SEL see us) scale. On the Celsius temperature scale, the freezing point of water is 0°C and water's boiling point is 100°C. Scientists often use the Kelvin, or absolute, temperature scale. It has this name because 0 K is the absolute lowest temperature an object can have. One can visualize that all particle motion stops at 0 K. As the temperature rises above 0 K, the particles begin to move with greater kinetic energy.

Thermal Energy

Hot soup will warm you because it has a large amount of thermal energy. **Thermal energy** is the total kinetic energy of the particles in a material. Because temperature is a measure of the average kinetic energy of an object's particles, it is also a measure of thermal energy. The amount of thermal energy in a bowl of soup is determined by the amount of soup in the bowl and the total amount of energy in the particles that make it up. Thermal energy flows from a warmer object to a cooler one. Thermal energy in the bowl of soup will transfer to your body and you will become warmer. ✔

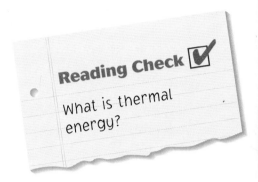

Reading Check ✔

What is thermal energy?

Heat and Thermal Energy

Thermal energy is what you may have been calling heat. It is important to note that heat and thermal energy are not the same. Look at **Figure 15-11.** Suppose you pick up a tall glass of iced tea. If you hold the glass for a long time, the drink warms up. Thermal energy from your hand transfers to the drink. A transfer of thermal energy from one object to another because of a difference in temperature is **heat.** Heat flows from warmer objects to cooler ones. Heat flows out of your hand and into the glass of iced tea. The thermal energy of the drink increases so it's temperature increases.

Heat also flows from warmer to cooler objects in a refrigerator. Your food is kept cold because thermal energy of the food is decreased by the flow of heat to the cold air inside the refrigerator. Refrigerators are designed to remove heat from the space inside where the food is stored.

How much heat?

When the same amount of heat is transferred to different materials, those materials may not experience the same increase in temperature. This difference is based on the chemical makeup and the amount of the material.

For example, water must absorb a large amount of heat before its temperature rises one degree. That is why water often is used as a coolant. The water in a car's radiator carries thermal energy away from the engine. How does the temperature of the water in a swimming pool compare to the air on a hot summer day? How do they compare at night when the air has cooled? The water is slower than its surroundings to change temperature. It takes longer for a large body of water to warm up or cool down

Figure 15-11 Heat flows from your hand to the glass of iced tea, making your hand feel cold. **Why do people wear gloves in cold weather?**

than it takes an equally large area of land or the surrounding air. As a result, air temperatures near a large lake or ocean remain fairly moderate year-round.

How do you feel heat?

Think about getting into a car that has been closed up on a sunny day. Do you prefer a car that has fabric-covered or vinyl-covered seats? Even though the masses of the seats are similar and the temperatures of the surroundings are the same, the vinyl material feels hotter on your skin than the fabric does. Your sense of touch responds to heat not to the actual temperature. Heat flows to your skin more easily from the vinyl than from the fabric. The greater the heat flow, the hotter the object feels to your skin. ✔

Transfer of Thermal Energy

A transfer of thermal energy into a material may cause a rise in the temperature of the material. The amount of thermal energy absorbed depends on the type of material. It also depends on the amount of material. The greater the amount of material there is, the more thermal energy it absorbs before its temperature rise can be measured. Suppose you transferred enough thermal energy to cause a small pot of water to boil. If you put the same amount of energy into a bathtub full of water, the temperature rise would be small, as shown in **Figure 15-12**. The heat absorbed must be shared by more particles of water in the bathtub. The average increase of thermal energy in each particle is quite small.

Reading Check ✔

Why do some materials feel hotter on your skin than others?

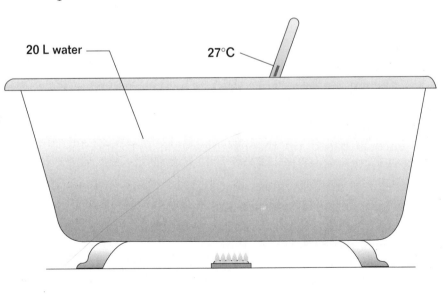

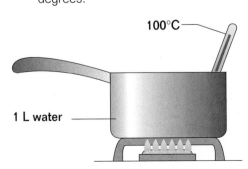

Figure 15-12 Applying an equal amount of thermal energy to the pan of water and the bathtub of water would not increase the water temperature the same number of degrees.

Thermal Energy on the Move

An overall transfer of energy occurs if there is a temperature difference between two areas or objects. Heat flows from warm places to cooler ones. Remember that temperature is a measure of thermal energy in an object. Heat flows from an area having greater thermal energy to an area that has less thermal energy. Thermal energy is transferred three ways: radiation, conduction, and convection. Conduction and convection transfer thermal energy through solids, liquids, or gases. Radiation however transfers thermal energy when little or no matter is present.

Radiation

Radiation is energy that travels by waves in all directions from its source. These waves may be visible light waves or types of energy waves that you cannot see. When these waves strike an object, their energy can be absorbed and the object's temperature rises. Radiation can travel through air and even through space where there is almost no material. The sun transfers energy to Earth through radiation. If you are out walking on a cool but sunny day, bend down to touch the sidewalk that is exposed to the sunlight. Perhaps you will notice that it feels warm. The pavement absorbs energy transferred from the sun by radiation. You take advantage of radiation when you warm yourself by a fire. The fire transfers its thermal energy to you. You become warmer. You also can use radiation to cook food. The microwave oven in your kitchen, such as the one shown in **Figure 15-13,** cooks food because of a transfer of energy by radiation.

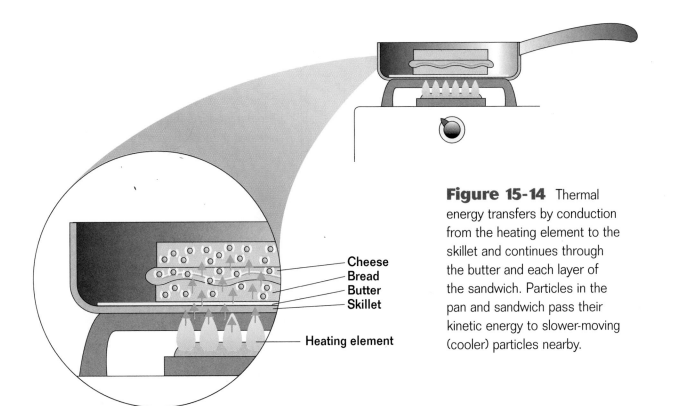

Figure 15-14 Thermal energy transfers by conduction from the heating element to the skillet and continues through the butter and each layer of the sandwich. Particles in the pan and sandwich pass their kinetic energy to slower-moving (cooler) particles nearby.

Cheese
Bread
Butter
Skillet

Heating element

Conduction

Have you ever picked up a silver spoon that was in a pot of boiling water and discovered that the spoon was now hotter than it was when you placed it there? Yeow! Quick! Where is the pot holder? The spoon handle became hot because of conduction. **Conduction** is the transfer of thermal energy from particle to particle through a material when there is a temperature difference. Conduction occurs because of the exchange of kinetic energy between the particles in a material, much the same way kinetic energy is transferred from a bowling ball to the pins. In the example of the spoon, kinetic energy continues to be transferred from the hotter end of the spoon to the cooler end because of the temperature difference.

Look at **Figure 15-14.** When you put a pan on the stove to make a grilled-cheese sandwich, the thermal energy from the stove transfers to the pan, making the particles within the pan move faster. Some of these particles bump into the particles in the bread and butter that are on the surface of the pan. Energy is transferred to the sandwich. This transferred energy causes the bread to toast and the cheese to melt. Even though conduction is a transfer of kinetic energy from particle to particle, the particles involved don't travel from one place to another. They simply move in place, bumping into each other and transferring energy from faster-moving particles to slower-moving ones. ☑

Reading Check ☑

What happens to the particles in a substance during conduction?

Conductors

Sometimes you want thermal energy to transfer rapidly, for example, as when you thaw frozen food. You could put a frozen hamburger on a metal tray to speed up the thawing process. Materials through which it is easy to transfer thermal energy are conductors. Most metals are good conductors of thermal energy. Metals such as gold, silver, and copper are superior conductors. That is why the silver spoon became so hot in the boiling water. Copper is widely available and less expensive than gold or silver. Copper can be attached to another metal, such as steel, to make a cooking pan. Many steel cooking pans have copper bottoms. A copper bottom conducts thermal energy more evenly. It helps spread heat across the bottom surface of the pan to prevent hot spots from forming. This allows food to cook evenly. ☑

Reading Check

What materials make good conductors?

Insulators

Materials that don't allow thermal energy to be conducted easily are insulators. You usually want your pizza to stay warm, so the best pizza places deliver it in an insulated box, as shown in **Figure 15-15.** The material used is one that will not transfer thermal energy. If you put a plastic spoon in boiling water, it's easy to hold it for a long time without burning your fingers because plastic transfers thermal energy poorly. Many cooking pans have plastic handles that won't melt instead of metal ones. These handles remain at a comfortable temperature while the pans are used for cooking. Other examples of insulators include wood and rubber. Ceramic tiles or several layers of cloth often are used as insulators.

Using Math

The yearly copper production average is 8 million metric tons. Most copper ores contain less than two percent copper. How many metric tons of copper ore are mined each year?

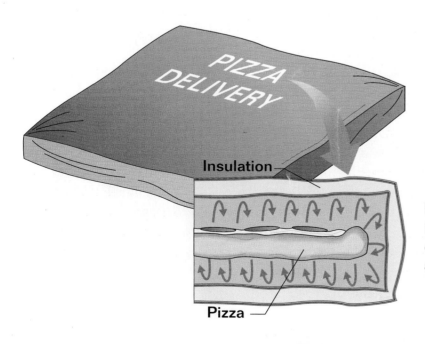

Insulation

Pizza

Figure 15-15 The material inside an insulated pizza carrier keeps the thermal energy from transferring out of the box and the carrier so your pizza stays warm.

Mini Lab

Comparing Energy Content

Procedure

1. Pour equal amounts of hot, cold, and room-temperature water into each of three transparent, labeled containers.
2. Measure and record the temperature of the water in each container.
3. Use a dropper to gently put a drop of food coloring in the center of each container.
4. After two minutes, observe each container.

Analysis

1. How are kinetic energy and temperature related?
2. In which container do the water particles have the most kinetic energy?
3. Based on the speed at which the food coloring spreads through the water, rank the containers from fastest to slowest. What can you infer about how water temperature affected the movement of the food coloring?

They protect a table surface from the hot bottoms of pans because these materials do not transfer thermal energy easily.

Convection

Some energy transfers involve particles that do not stay in place but move from one place to another. **Convection** transfers thermal energy when particles move from one place to another where there is a difference in temperature. This is most common in gases and liquids. Cool air sinks because it is more dense than warm air. Your home is heated by using the idea of convection. Look at **Figure 15-16.** Air is warmed in the furnace. The warm, less-dense air is then forced up through the air duct by the furnace's fan. The warm air circulates and rises through the room. As the air cools, it becomes more dense. The cool air sinks toward the floor, and it is then pulled through the air duct by the furnace's fan to be warmed again and recirculated. In the case of water, the warmer, less-dense water is forced up as the cooler, more-dense water sinks. Have you ever seen noodles cooking? The noodles are carried upward and downward as the hot water moves to the top, cools at the surface,

Figure 15-16 The furnace's fan helps circulate thermal energy through your home. Warmer air particles move upward while cooler air particles move downward.

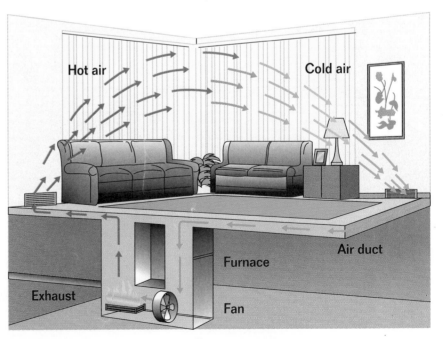

and then sinks. Convection causes warm and cool currents in the atmosphere, which produce Earth's weather.

The effects of warm and cool air currents are especially important to understanding how hurricanes and tornadoes form. Convection currents also are formed in oceans by cold water flowing from the poles and warm water flowing from tropical regions.

Have you ever seen an eagle or a hawk coasting high in the air? Look at the seagull in **Figure 15-17**. A bird can stay in the air without flapping its wings because it is held up by a thermal. A thermal is a column of warm air that is forced up as cold air around it sinks. It is a convection current in the air. A thermal is the same type of current used by people who are hang gliding. It helps keep them in the air as long as possible. You can see that thermal energy and its transfer affect you daily. How many uses of thermal energy can you see around you right now?

Figure 15-17 Moving air caused by convection helps lift this seagull so it does not need to flap its wings constantly.

Section Assessment

1. How is thermal energy transferred? List three ways and give an example for each from nature.

2. Popcorn can be cooked in a hot-air popper, in a microwave oven, or in a pan on the stove. Identify each method as convection, conduction, or radiation.

3. What condition must exist for transfer of thermal energy to occur?

4. **Think Critically:** How are temperature, thermal energy, and heat different?

5. 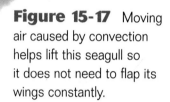 **Skill Builder**
   Using Numbers When selecting an energy source for heating a home, consumers try to think about cost. Do the **Chapter 15 Skill Activity** on page 592 and use proportions to determine the area of the solar collector needed to heat a home.

Using Math

To change a temperature from the Fahrenheit scale to the Celsius scale, you subtract 32 from the Fahrenheit temperature and multiply the difference by 5/9. If the temperature is 77°F, what is the Celsius temperature?

Activity 15·2

Materials

- Thermometers (−10°C to 110°C) (4)
- Self-sealing freezer bags (2)
- Water (100 mL)
- Ice cubes (2 to 3)
- Pancake syrup (100 mL)
  *corn syrup
- Beakers (4 large)
  *heat-safe glass containers
- Spoon
  *stirring rod
  *Alternate Materials

Can you observe a temperature change?

Different substances absorb thermal energy differently. You will heat two different materials. Then, by comparing the temperature of each material, you will infer which substance can absorb the most thermal energy before rising in temperature.

What You'll Investigate

Which material can absorb more thermal energy?

Goals

- **Measure** a temperature change.
- **Infer** a material's ability to absorb thermal energy.

Safety Precautions

- Use care when handling the heated bags and hot water.
- Do not taste, eat, or drink any materials used in the lab.

Procedure

1. **Design** two data tables in which to record your data of the temperature measurements of the hot- and cold-water beakers. Use the sample table to help you.

2. **Pour** 200 mL of hot tap water (about 90°C) into each of two large beakers.

3. **Pour** 200 mL of cool, tap water into each of two large beakers. Add two or three ice cubes and stir until the ice melts.

4. **Pour** 100 mL of room-temperature water into one bag and 100 mL of syrup into the other bag. Tightly seal both bags.

5. **Record** the starting water temperature of each hot beaker.

Place each bag into its own beaker of hot water.

6. **Record** the water temperature in each of the hot-water beakers every two minutes until the temperature does not change.

7. **Record** the starting water temperature of each cold beaker. If any ice cubes remain, **remove** them from the cold water.

8. Carefully **remove** the bags from the hot water and **put** each into its own beaker of cold water.

9. **Record** the water temperature in each of the cold-water beakers every two minutes until there is no change in temperature.

Water Temperatures—Hot Beaker			
Water–filled bag		Syrup–filled bag	
Time (min)	Temperature (°C)	Time (min)	Temperature (°C)
0		0	
2		2	
4		4	
6		6	
8		8	

Conclude and Apply

1. **Look** at your data. Which beaker of hot water reached a lower temperature—the beaker with the water-filled or syrup-filled bag?

2. In which beaker of cold water did you observe the greater temperature change after adding the bags?

3. Which material absorbed more heat? Which released more heat?

4. **Infer** which material conducts thermal energy better. Would either material make a good insulator? Explain.

15·3 Chemical Energy

Observing Chemical Energy

At dusk on a hot summer day, you may have seen fireflies glowing. Did you ever wonder how they make their eerie light? If you have seen light sticks at Halloween that glow for a short period of time, you have observed the same principle as behind the fireflies' glow. Energy in the form of light is released when a chemical reaction takes place inside the light stick. A campfire or a fire in an outdoor grill, such as the one in **Figure 15-18,** releases thermal energy and light energy because of a chemical reaction taking place. Whether or not you realize it, you experience and observe chemical energy in many reactions every day.

What is a chemical reaction?

In a chemical reaction, substances are either made or broken down. When particles of substances combine, bonds form between them. These bonds hold the particles together and a new product is formed. When a substance is broken down, the bonds between the particles are broken. This causes the particles to split apart.

What You'll Learn

- ▶ Where chemical energy is found
- ▶ How reaction rates are changed

  Vocabulary
  chemical energy

Why It's Important

- ▶ Chemical energy makes it possible for your body to move, grow, and stay warm.

Figure 15-18 The chemical energy stored in these charcoal briquettes is released and transformed into thermal energy and light energy.

Figure 15-19 The oxygen and hydrogen gases will not react unless energy is added.

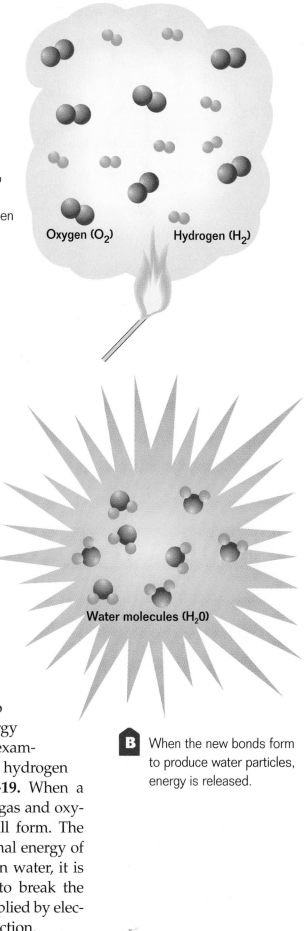

A The added energy from the flame causes the bonds to break in the oxygen particles and hydrogen particles.

Oxygen (O₂)   Hydrogen (H₂)

Water molecules (H₂O)

B When the new bonds form to produce water particles, energy is released.

Energy is stored in the bonds between particles in a substance. This stored (potential) energy within chemical bonds is called **chemical energy.** The potential energy stored in oil, gas, and coal is an important source of chemical energy. Food provides a source of chemical energy for our bodies. The muscles in our bodies transform some of this chemical energy into mechanical energy when they move. A weight lifter stores chemical energy in muscles in order to be able to lift heavier weights. Can you think of other examples of chemical reactions you participated in today?

Energy in Reactions

Changes in energy are a part of every chemical reaction. To break bonds, energy must be added. The reverse is also true. When bonds form, energy is released. Most reactions do not take place on their own. In some reactions, energy must be added before the reaction can begin. For example, energy is needed to start the reaction between hydrogen and oxygen to form water. Look at **Figure 15-19.** When a lighted match is placed in a mixture of hydrogen gas and oxygen gas, the mixture will explode and water will form. The energy to begin the reaction comes from the thermal energy of the flame. Once particles are bound together, as in water, it is difficult to split them apart. It requires energy to break the bonds. Energy to break chemical bonds can be supplied by electricity, heat, light, or motion, depending on the reaction.

Figure 15-20 Many processes take place in the preparation of food. The ingredients in moist, soft cookie dough use energy to change and become crispy, airy cookies.

Energy-Absorbing Reactions

Some chemical reactions need energy to keep going. A reaction that absorbs energy is called an endothermic (en duh THUR mihk) reaction. Endothermic chemical reactions take place in the preparation of food as shown in **Figure 15-20.** Thermal energy is absorbed by the food as it cooks. For example, an endothermic reaction takes place in some kinds of cookie dough. The baking soda absorbs energy and produces a gas that puffs up the cookies.

A process in nature that absorbs a lot of energy is photosynthesis. During photosynthesis, some cells in the leaves of green plants transform the energy from sunlight into chemical energy in the form of sugar. Once the plant is deprived of sunlight, the reaction stops. Photosynthesis is probably the most important endothermic process on Earth. Because of photosynthesis, plants provide us, and almost all other living things, with food and oxygen.

Problem Solving

Chemical Energy in Action

Lashawna twisted her ankle at track practice. To help ease the pain until she could have it checked, her coach suggested that she soak her ankle in a solution of Epsom salts.

Lashawna filled a small tub with lukewarm water. She then added half a box of Epsom salts to the water. As she was stirring the solution with her hand, the water became cool.

Lashawna didn't understand why the temperature of the water changed. Was she imagining things? How can you explain why the water became cold?

Think Critically: What kind of process takes place in the solution of Epsom salts, endothermic or exothermic? Explain.

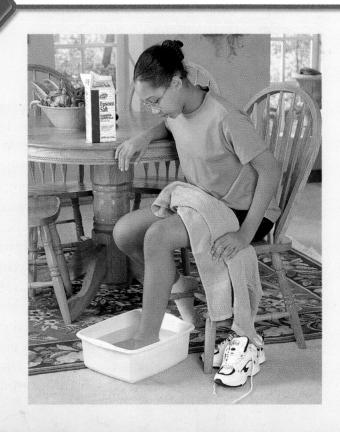

Figure 15-21 Demolition experts use the energy released by the reaction that causes the dynamite explosion to destroy this building in Hartford, Connecticut.

Energy-Releasing Reactions

Some chemical reactions are important because of their products. Other reactions are important because of the energy that is released. Exothermic (ek soh THUR mihk) reactions are reactions that give off energy. If you have used a chemical hand warmer on a cold day, then you felt the thermal energy released by the exothermic reaction taking place inside the hand warmer. The energy released from a dynamite explosion will demolish an old building as in **Figure 15-21.** Charcoal briquettes release a lot of energy as they react with oxygen, causing them to burn at a high temperature. Combustion, the burning of material in the presence of oxygen, is a familiar exothermic reaction. What other exothermic reactions can you think of?

Rate of Reaction

The rate of a chemical reaction can be sped up or slowed down by changing the temperature, stirring the mixture, or adding a catalyst. For example, will a spoonful of sugar dissolve faster in a glass of iced tea or in a cup of hot tea? If you have ever watched closely, you might have noticed that sugar dissolves faster in the hot tea. Dissolving sugar is a process that can be sped up by increasing the temperature.

What if you added sugar to your iced tea only to watch it sink and sit at the bottom of the glass? How would you get the sugar to dissolve? You would probably stir the iced tea to make the sugar dissolve faster. Even though the sugar dissolves on its own at the bottom of the glass, stirring it makes the dissolving process go more quickly.

A catalyst is a substance that changes the rate of a chemical reaction without any change to its own structure. Many cell processes in your body are sped up by the presence of catalysts. Catalysts in your body are substances called enzymes.

LIFE SCIENCE
◄ **INTEGRATION**

Figure 15-22

Salivary glands release saliva as you chew. The enzyme in saliva speeds up the chemical reaction that breaks down food as it travels to the stomach.

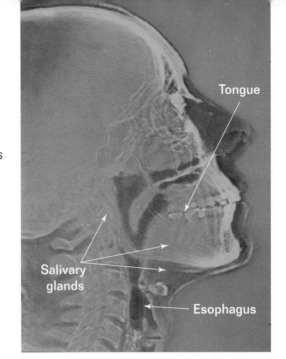

Tongue

Salivary glands

Esophagus

For example, when you chew a piece of bread, glands in your mouth, as shown in **Figure 15-22,** produce saliva that contains an enzyme. The enzyme in saliva acts as a catalyst to help break down starches more quickly into smaller molecules.

Many other chemical reactions depend on catalysts to help them work better. For example, the production of vegetable shortening, synthetic rubber, and high-octane gasoline are all chemical processes that succeed with the help of catalysts.

Section Assessment

1. Where is chemical energy found?

2. What happens to bonds when new products are made?

3. Name three ways to speed up a reaction.

4. **Think Critically:** How are exothermic and endothermic reactions different? How are they similar?

5. **Skill Builder**
   Classifying Divide the following list of reactions into two groups by classifying each reaction as endothermic or exothermic: burning wood, striking a match to light it, baking bread, and exploding dynamite. Explain why you placed each reaction into one group. If you need help, refer to Classifying in the **Skill Handbook** on page 549.

Using Computers

Word Processing Write one sentence that states, in your own words, the main idea of each major paragraph in this section about chemical energy. Use a word processor to type your summary of these important concepts. If you need help, refer to page 568.

Hot-Vent Inhabitants

Some Like It Hot

Deep below the ocean surface, where no sunlight can reach, Earth's crust moves apart and forms cracks in the seafloor called hydrothermal vents. Superheated, mineral-rich fluid as hot as 350°C flows out of the vents. In spite of the extreme temperatures, more than 300 species of organisms live in and around hydrothermal vents. Fish and giant tube worms (seen at left), giant clams, mussels, crabs, shrimp, microorganisms such as bacteria, and other life-forms live in this harsh, deep-ocean environment.

Extreme Environments

Microorganisms that live at these high temperatures are called thermophiles. Thermophiles living around hydrothermal vents have remarkable adaptations for surviving in such an environment. For example, some of these microorganisms use sulfur-containing compounds—rather than sunlight—as an energy source. Scientists once thought that life could not exist under extreme environmental conditions. Because life was discovered around hydrothermal vents, however, scientists theorize that microorganisms similar to those in hot-vent communities exist in other places long thought to be lifeless.

Europa, Jupiter's fourth-largest moon, is one place scientists are looking for signs of life. Although Europa's surface is solid ice, there may be a warm layer of liquid water underneath. If water and a geothermal energy source exist on Europa, life-forms also might be there and would give clues to early life-forms on Earth.

Future Uses

Research has shown that thermophilic bacteria have unique enzymes that help them survive brutal heat. Unlike more common enzymes, those of thermophiles do not stop functioning when exposed to high temperatures. Such enzymes may be useful in medicine and industry. For instance, medical researchers are investigating the use of these enzymes as anticancer and anti-AIDS agents.

inter NET CONNECTION

Visit the Glencoe Science Web Site at **www.glencoe.com/sec/science/nc** to find more information about deep-sea vents.

For a **preview** of this chapter, study this Reviewing Main Ideas before you read the chapter. After you have studied this chapter, you can use the Reviewing Main Ideas to **review** the chapter.

The Glencoe MindJogger, Audiocassettes, and CD-ROM provide additional opportunities for review.

Section
15-1 ENERGY CHANGES

Energy has the ability to cause change. It can change the temperature, shape, speed, or direction of an object. Some common types of energy forms are mechanical, chemical, thermal, light, nuclear, and electrical. *What are some examples of how energy changes form?*

KINETIC AND POTENTIAL ENERGY

Moving objects have **kinetic energy.** An object's mass and speed affect how much kinetic energy it has. Objects at rest can have stored energy in the form of **potential energy.** This energy comes from an object's position or condition—not from motion. *How are potential and kinetic energy related?*

CONSERVING ENERGY

Kinetic energy, as well as other forms of energy, can be transferred from one object to another. When energy is transferred or changes form, the total amount of energy stays the same. Energy cannot be created or destroyed. *After the last domino in the row falls, what happens to all the kinetic energy from the first domino?*

Reading Check ☑

List at least ten questions that a child might ask about energy and the changes it causes. Choose questions that are answered in the chapter.

Section

15-2 TEMPERATURE

Temperature measures the average kinetic energy of the particles in a material. Particles having more kinetic energy have higher temperatures than particles with less kinetic energy. The Fahrenheit, Celsius, and Kelvin scales are used to measure temperature. *Which would have more kinetic energy—the particles in an ice cube or a glass of water?*

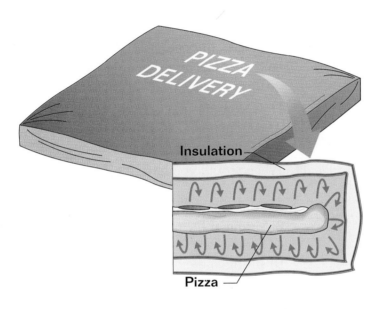

Insulation

Pizza

THERMAL ENERGY

Thermal energy is the total amount of kinetic energy of the particles in a material. The movement of thermal energy from a warmer object to a cooler one is called **heat.** The ability to absorb heat depends on the type of material and its quantity. Thermal energy moving by **radiation** travels by waves in all directions.

Conduction is the transfer of kinetic energy from particle to particle as they bump into each other.

Convection transfers energy by the movement of particles from one place to another. *What kind of energy transfer is involved in cooking a meal in a pan on the stove?*

Section

15-3 CHEMICAL ENERGY

The energy stored in chemical bonds is **chemical energy.** The energy stored in food and oil is an important source of chemical energy. Chemical reactions that release energy are exothermic reactions. Reactions that absorb energy are endothermic reactions. Raising the temperature, stirring, and adding catalysts can speed up chemical reactions. Reactions taking place in your body every day use enzymes as catalysts. Catalysts are used in making a number of commercial products. *How do catalysts affect chemical reactions?*

Chapter 15 Assessment

Using Vocabulary

a. chemical energy
b. conduction
c. convection
d. energy
e. heat
f. kinetic energy
g. law of conservation of energy
h. potential energy
i. radiation
j. temperature
k. thermal energy

Each of the following sentences is false. Make the sentence true by replacing the italicized word with a word from the above list.

1. Transfer of energy by direct contact is *radiation*.
2. Energy of motion is *potential energy*.
3. The movement of thermal energy from warm to cool objects is *temperature*.
4. A measure of the average kinetic energy of the molecules in a substance is called *heat*.
5. *Kinetic energy* is energy that is stored.

Checking Concepts

Choose the word or phrase that best answers each question.

6. Which of the following correctly describes energy?
   A) It can be created.
   B) It can be destroyed.
   C) It cannot change form.
   D) It can cause change.

7. What does a thermometer measure?
   A) heat
   B) total energy
   C) average kinetic energy
   D) chemical energy

8. What happens if two objects at different temperatures are touching?
   A) Thermal energy transfers from the warmer object.
   B) Thermal energy transfers from the cooler object.
   C) Thermal energy transfers to the warmer object.
   D) No thermal energy transfer takes place.

9. During an energy transfer, what happens to the total amount of energy?
   A) It increases.
   B) It decreases.
   C) It stays the same.
   D) It depends on the energy form being transferred.

10. How does the sun's energy reach us?
    A) conduction
    B) convection
    C) radiation
    D) insulation

11. When would you have the most potential energy?
    A) walking up the hill
    B) sitting at the top of the hill
    C) running up the hill
    D) sitting at the bottom of the hill

12. Which is **NOT** the name of a temperature scale?
    A) Joule
    B) Kelvin
    C) Celsius
    D) Fahrenheit

13. What is the name given to any material that transfers thermal energy easily?
    A) thermal
    B) insulator
    C) metal
    D) conductor

14. What also will increase as the speed of an object increases?
    A) kinetic energy
    B) mass
    C) weight
    D) potential energy

15. What type of energy transfer produces weather?
    A) radiation
    B) conduction
    C) convection
    D) atmospheric

Thinking Critically

16. Much discussion has focused on the need to drive more efficient cars and use less electricity. If the law of conservation of energy is true, why are people concerned about energy usage?

17. If heat flows in only one direction, how can both hot and cold liquids reach room temperature as they sit on a table?

18. Think about what happens to Jack and Jill in the nursery rhyme. What kinds of energy are used? How was each energy form used?

19. Compare the three temperature scales you learned about. How are they different? How are they similar?

20. Use what you know about the movement of thermal energy to explain why you would place a minor burn on your arm under cool, running water.

Developing Skills

If you need help, refer to the Skill Handbook.

21. Concept Mapping: Below is a concept map of the energy changes of a gymnast bouncing on a trampoline. Complete the map by indicating the type of energy—kinetic, potential, or both—the gymnast has at each of the following stages:
a) halfway up, **b)** the highest point,
c) halfway down, **d)** the lowest point, just before hitting the trampoline.

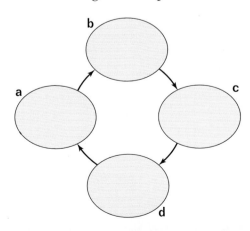

THE PRINCETON REVIEW

Test-Taking Tip

Make Yourself Comfortable When you take a test, try to make yourself as comfortable as possible. You will then be able to focus all your attention on the test.

Test Practice

Use these questions to test your Science Proficiency.

1. The sun is a source of thermal energy. Which description below **BEST** illustrates a change from thermal energy to potential chemical energy when solar energy strikes Earth?
A) ocean water warms
B) atmosphere cools
C) leaves of plants make food
D) icebergs melt

2. As you ski down a mountain, what type of energy transformation occurs?
A) Kinetic energy changes to potential energy.
B) Potential energy changes to kinetic energy.
C) Chemical energy changes to potential energy.
D) Mechanical energy changes to potential energy.

3. In an endothermic reaction, what happens to the energy?
A) Energy is released.
B) Energy is absorbed.
C) Energy is made.
D) There is no energy transfer.

Chapter Preview

Section 16-1
How does speed change?

Section 16-2
Why do things fall?

Section 16-3
How do things move?

Skills Preview

Skill Builders
- Cause and Effect

Activities
- Control Variables

MiniLabs
- Form a Definition

Reading Check ✔

Before you read the chapter, list the vocabulary terms. As you read, write the definitions in your own words.

Explore Activity

Skateboarders who can ride pipes make it look easy. They race down one side and up the other. They rise above the ledge and appear to float as they spin and return. They practice these tricks many times until they get them right. In this chapter, you'll learn how this complicated motion can be explained by forces such as gravity. With an understanding of forces and how they make things move, you will begin to unravel the secrets of these tricks.

The Marble Skateboard Model

1. Using the picture as a guide, use heavy paper to make a model of a half-pipe, the curved surface some skateboarders ride on. Use books to brace the edges. A marble will model the skateboard.

2. Release the marble from a point near the bottom of the curve. Observe the motion. How high does it go? When is its speed greatest?

3. Release the marble from a point near the top of the curve. Observe the motion. Compare this to the marble's motion in step 2.

Science Journal

In your Science Journal, describe your experiment and what you discovered. How did the different starting points affect how high the marble rolled up the side?

How does speed change?

Speed

Think of skateboarding down the side of a half-pipe for the first time. Your heart starts to pound as you move faster and faster. You feel the wind rush against your face. As you reach the bottom, you are going really fast and you feel excitement and fear. You flow through the change in direction as you start up the other side. Your speed decreases as you move higher up the wall. When you reach the top, you are at a near standstill. If you think fast, you can grab hold of the ledge and take a break. Otherwise, back down you go.

How fast were you going?

One way to describe motion is with numbers. To understand how to measure motion, think about the movement of the bicycles as they go down the hill in **Figure 16-1.** To know how fast one of the bicycles is traveling, you must know how far it has gone and how long it has been moving. These are measurements of distance and time.

To calculate any **average speed,** you divide the distance traveled by the time it takes to travel this distance.

$$\text{average speed} = \frac{\text{total distance traveled}}{\text{time}}$$

If the hill is 30 m long and it takes 15 s to travel this distance, then the equation is as follows.

$$\text{average speed} = \frac{30 \text{ m}}{15 \text{ s}} = 2 \text{ m/s}$$

This answer is read as "two meters per second." A **rate** is an expression, like 2 m/s, in which the denominator is time. Speed is the rate at which an object covers a distance. Speed is also called the rate of change of position.

Figure 16-1 To find each bikers's average speed, divide the distance down the hill by the time taken to cover that distance.

Average speed is useful if you don't care about the details of the motion. For example, suppose you went on a long road trip and traveled 640 km in 8 h. You would say you averaged 80 km/h, even though you may have stopped for red lights, got stuck in a traffic jam, or enjoyed a long stretch of high speed on a highway.

When you ride in a car, you can keep track of your speed by reading the speedometer, as shown in **Figure 16-2.** A speedometer allows you to know your speed at any time. How would you determine your speed at the bottom of the skateboard ramp?

Time to Accelerate

Average speed may not tell you everything you want to know. Sometimes, you want to know how motion is changing. **Acceleration** is the rate at which speed or direction changes. Some examples are given in **Figure 16-3.** If you know the change in speed, you can find your acceleration. If you know the acceleration, you can find your speed at any time.

At the top of the skateboard ramp, you are at rest. Your speed is 0 m/s. When you start down, you smoothly speed up, going faster and faster. If the angle of the ramp is made steeper, you will speed up at a greater rate.

Figure 16-2 The odometer in this car measures the distance traveled. The speedometer measures speed. **What units is speed measured in?**

Figure 16-3 Acceleration in the direction of motion speeds you up. If your speed doesn't change, acceleration is 0. Acceleration against the direction of motion slows you down.

Acceleration

→

Acceleration is zero

Acceleration

←

Calculating with Acceleration

Acceleration is found using the following formula.

$$\text{acceleration} = \frac{\text{change in speed}}{\text{time}}$$

$$a = \frac{\text{final speed} - \text{initial speed}}{t}$$

When an object starts from rest, the initial speed is 0. If an object starts at rest and accelerates smoothly to a final speed of 10 m/s in 2 s, the acceleration is found as follows.

$$a = \frac{10\ \text{m/s} - 0\ \text{m/s}}{2\ \text{s}} = 5\ \text{m/s}^2$$

If an object is slowing down, as a skateboard does when the rider brakes, it is accelerating opposite to the direction it is moving. It is losing speed. (Look back at **Figure 16-3.**) You may have heard this called deceleration. This book will use the term *negative acceleration* to describe slowing down because the speed is decreasing. If an object starts at 10 m/s and comes to rest in 2 s, the acceleration is negative. ☑

$$a = \frac{0\ \text{m/s} - 10\ \text{m/s}}{2\ \text{s}} = -5\ \text{m/s}^2$$

Reading Check ☑

What is negative acceleration?

Figure 16-4 As she accelerates at 1 m/s², the skateboarder's speed increases by 1 m/s each second. **What happens to her distance traveled each second?**

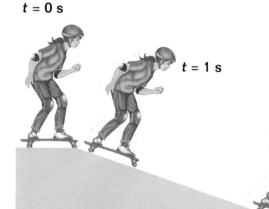

t = 0 s

t = 1 s

t = 2 s

t = 3 s

Table 16-1

Acceleration 1 m/s²		
Time (s)	Speed (m/s)	Distance (m)
0	0	0.0
1	1	0.5
2	2	2.0
3	3	4.5
4	4	8.0

You can calculate the skateboard's speed at a given time if you know its acceleration. This would be like having a speedometer attached directly to the board. You can find how fast you are going by using the formula below.

change in speed = acceleration × time

A skateboarder accelerating at 1 m/s² goes 1 m/s faster each second. **Table 16-1** in **Figure 16-4** shows the skateboarder's changing speed. For example, after 3 s the skateboarder is going 3 m/s.

In a car, an odometer measures distance traveled. How could you calculate the distance you travel on a skateboard? For constant acceleration, you can calculate the distance you travel in a given time if you start or end at rest.

$$\text{distance} = \frac{1}{2}(\text{acceleration})(\text{time})^2$$

$$d = \frac{1}{2}at^2$$

Using Math

Calculating with Negative Acceleration

Example Problem
You are skating at 4 m/s. You brake with an acceleration of −0.5 m/s². How long does it take you to come to a stop? How far do you travel?

Problem-Solving Steps
1. What is known? acceleration $a = -0.5$ m/s²; change in speed = 0 m/s − 4 m/s
2. What is unknown? time, t; distance, d
3. Use the equation change in speed = at to find t. Then, use $d = \frac{1}{2}at^2$ to find d.
4. Solution:

change in speed = at
   0 m/s − 4 m/s = $(-0.5$ m/s²$)t$
      −4 m/s = $(-0.5$ m/s²$)t$
         $t = 8$ s

$d = \frac{1}{2}at^2$

$d = \frac{1}{2}(0.5$ m/s²$)(8$ s$)^2$

$d = 16$ m

You come to a stop in 8 s, after traveling 16 m.

Practice Problem
A ball is thrown straight up with an initial speed of 25 m/s. The acceleration is −10 m/s². How long will it be until the ball comes to a stop? How high will it go?

Strategy Hint: Think about whether values should be positive or negative.

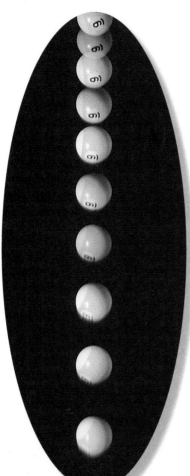

As your speed increases, you cover more and more distance in each second. **Figure 16-5** is a picture of a falling ball taken with a strobe light. The light flashes on and off at a steady rate, so the time between flashes remains the same. The picture lets you see how far the ball falls between flashes. Notice that the distance the ball travels between flashes increases. If the ball were not accelerating, it would move the same distance between each pair of flashes.

We have learned to use numbers to describe and predict motion. This ability has taken humankind to the depths of the oceans and to the moon. The same tools are used to predict the speed of a skateboard and the time for a spacecraft to reach Mars. The science of motion gives you the power to understand how things work and the ability to predict what will happen.

Figure 16-5 The longer an object accelerates, the farther it travels each second. **Falling at 9.8 m/s², how far has the object fallen after 5 s? After 6 s?**

Section Assessment

1. During rush-hour traffic in a big city, it can take 1.5 hours to travel 45 km. What is the average speed, in kilometers per hour, for this trip?

2. Suppose a car traveling 70 m/s brakes and takes 3 s to stop. What is the acceleration in m/s²? How far does the car travel before stopping?

3. A runner accelerates from 0 m/s to 3 m/s in 12 s. What is the acceleration?

4. **Think Critically:** Describe the motion of a skateboard as it accelerates down one side of a half-pipe and then up the other side. What would happen if the up side of the pipe were not as steep as the down side?

5. **Skill Builder**
   Using Numbers Do the **Chapter 16 Skill Activity** on page 593 to learn a problem solving strategy for using numbers in word problems.

Using Math

The space shuttle takes eight minutes to blast off and go into orbit. It accelerates at 30 m/s². How long is this time in seconds? How fast, in kilometers per second, is the shuttle going when it reaches its orbit? How far does it travel during this time?

Time Trials

Before a big car race, all the contestants must pass the time trials. Time trials are races against the clock instead of against other cars.

What You'll Investigate

Can time trials be used to predict the winner of a race?

Goals

- **Conduct** time trials.
- **Test** speed and distance predictions from the results of time trials.

Procedure 🥽 🧤

1. **Set up** a straightaway using two metersticks, as shown in the picture below. Use the tape to make a starting line at the beginning of the track.

2. **Test** the track with one car. If the car runs into the metersticks, move them further apart or devise some other remedy.

3. Wind up or push the first car, starting with the front of the car on zero of the meterstick. Time its trip to the end of the metersticks.

4. Repeat this at least three times for each car, and **record** your distance and time measurements in a table similar to the one shown.

5. **Calculate** the average time and distance.

Materials

- Metersticks (2)
- Stopwatch or watch that measures in seconds
- Toy cars
- Masking tape

6. **Calculate** the average speed using the averages for the time and distance.

Conclude and Apply

1. **Compare** the average speed of your car with those of your classmates.

2. **Predict** which car should win a 1-m race based on the time trials. Test your prediction.

3. **Predict** which car will travel farthest based on your measurements and observations. Test your prediction.

4. **Explain** whether time trials accurately predict which car will win the race. Were you able to predict which car would travel the furthest? **Explain** why or why not.

Time Trials Data		
Car _____	Time (s)	Distance (m)
Trial 1		
Trial 2		
Trial 3		
Average		

16·2 Why do things fall?

What You'll Learn

► How gravity pulls on everything

► What forces are and how they act

► The difference between weight and mass

Vocabulary

gravity   balanced
force   forces
weight   inertia
normal force   mass

Why It's Important

► You cannot escape the pull of gravity. It's the force that holds everything in the universe together.

Gravity

When the speed or direction of an object changes, it is accelerating. When you ride down a hill without pedaling your bicycle or jump out of a tree, you are accelerated downward. When you jump off a step, you immediately sense how Earth's gravity changes your speed and direction, although nothing actually grabs you and makes you move. A person who pushes or pulls you must touch you. The touch lets you know your motion is going to change. Earth, however, can pull you without touching you as shown in **Figure 16-6.**

Throughout history, people have tried to explain why things fall. The ancient Greeks were the first to use the word *gravity,* which means "heaviness." If an object fell to the ground, it had gravity. If it didn't fall but rose like smoke, the Greeks said it had *levity,* which means "lightness." The modern explanation of how gravity works was first given by Sir Isaac Newton, who lived in the 1600s. Legend says he developed his ideas about gravity when he observed a falling apple. He reasoned that Earth could pull on the moon in the same way that it pulls on an apple.

Figure 16-6 Gravity accelerates this diver toward Earth. **Does gravity act on the diver while she's standing on the diving board? Explain.**

Gravity is the attraction between all matter. *Newton's law of universal gravitation* states that all matter in the universe pulls on all other matter. A gravitational attraction exists between you and your desk, your book, and Alpha Centari. You don't notice this pull because gravity is weak for small or distant objects. Earth is so large and so close that its pull overwhelms these smaller pulls.

The gravitational pull of Earth gives the same acceleration to all the objects on its surface. Without air resistance, all objects fall with the same acceleration. Usually, air resistance is ignored for simple calculations. On Earth, the acceleration due to gravity is 9.8 m/s^2. If you move far away from Earth or are closer to a large body like the moon, this value changes, as shown in **Figure 16-7.** When a plane goes from 0 km/h to 200 km/h in 6 s, it's acceleration is approximately equal to the acceleration due to gravity on Earth. Fighter pilots who fly planes like the one in **Figure 16-8** can accelerate at more than eight times 9.8 m/s^2 when they make sudden turns. This acceleration is so high that it could make them pass out. To remain conscious, pilots wear pressurized suits.

Gravity Is a Force

You have learned that gravity pulls you straight down, and you know that if nothing is there to support you, you will fall. If you do fall, you will accelerate. Acceleration is the sign that a force is acting. A **force** is a push or a pull.

When you stand on the ground, Earth pulls you down and the ground pushes you up. There are many different types of forces. The downward force of gravity on you is called your **weight.**

Figure 16-7 The acceleration due to the moon's gravity is one-sixth the acceleration due to Earth's gravity. Astronauts had to find new ways to move in this weaker gravity.

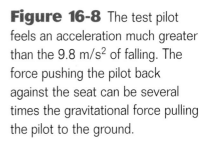

*inter*NET
CONNECTION

Visit the Glencoe Science Web Site at **www.glencoe.com/ sec/science/nc** for more information about gravity.

Figure 16-8 The test pilot feels an acceleration much greater than the 9.8 m/s^2 of falling. The force pushing the pilot back against the seat can be several times the gravitational force pulling the pilot to the ground.

Figure 16-9 The normal force is perpendicular to the surface. On a horizontal surface, the normal force is equal to the weight, but in the opposite direction, so the forces are balanced. **What happens if your weight is greater than the normal force of a stool you stand on?**

Reading Check ✓

What happens to an object acted on by balanced forces?

The upward force of the ground is called the **normal force** because it is normal (perpendicular) to the surface. When the forces acting on an object cancel each other, as in **Figure 16-9**, the forces are **balanced forces.** ✓

Measuring Force

A force is measured by the amount of acceleration it can give a mass. This is described by the following equation, also known as *Newton's second law of motion.*

$$\text{Force} = \text{mass} \times \text{acceleration}$$

$$F = ma$$

If a force can accelerate a 2-kg mass at 4 m/s², then the force is found as follows.

$$F = (2 \text{ kg})(4 \text{ m/s}^2)$$

$$= 8 \ \frac{\text{kg} \cdot \text{m}}{\text{s}^2}$$

$$= 8 \text{ N}$$

The force is 8 N. This answer introduces a unit called the newton, abbreviated N. It is named in honor of Sir Isaac Newton.

Forces are measured sometimes using springs. The more you stretch a spring, the harder it is to stretch it further. You may have tried pulling a rubber band. As you pull it back, it gets harder and harder to pull. If you measure how far you stretch it, you can use this to make a force measurement.

LIFE SCIENCE
INTEGRATION

Balanced Forces and Flight
A bird coasting with outspread wings uses balanced forces. The downward force of gravity is balanced by the upward force of air on the wings. What happens if the upward force is greater than the downward force?

Using Force to Calculate Acceleration

Example Problem

A 500-N net force is applied to a 4-kg object. What is the object's acceleration?

Problem-Solving Steps

1. What is known? force, F = 500 N; mass, m = 4 kg
2. What is unknown? acceleration, a
3. Use the equation $F = ma$.
4. Solution

$$F = ma$$
$$500 \text{ N} = (4 \text{ kg})a$$
$$a = 125 \text{ m/s}^2$$

The force provides an acceleration of 125 m/s².

Practice Problem

The same force is applied to a 100-kg object. What is the acceleration?

Strategy Hint: Check that units divide out properly, N/kg = m/s².

This is also how a spring scale, shown in **Figure 16-10,** works. When you measure using a spring scale, it is really the spring force you are reading.

Inertia and Mass

Have you ever noticed how hard it is to move a heavy object, even when it has wheels to help it move? If you try pushing someone much bigger than you who is wearing skates or standing on a skateboard, the person won't budge easily. This quality, **inertia** (ih NUR shah), is a measure of an object's ability to stay at rest or to keep moving. You also may have noticed that it is hard to stop someone who is much bigger than you are once that person is moving. If you think about it, the more matter an object has, the harder it will be to move. **Mass** measures the quantity of matter. Mass therefore describes an object's inertia.

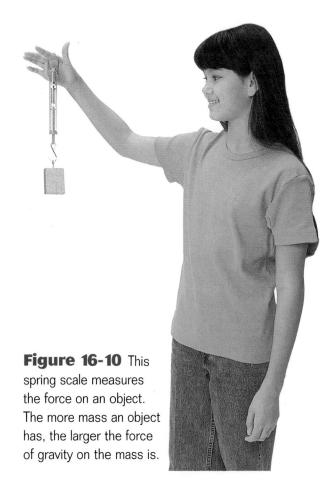

Figure 16-10 This spring scale measures the force on an object. The more mass an object has, the larger the force of gravity on the mass is.

Inferring Free Fall

Procedure 🤝 🥽 🧤

1. Attach a clothespin to either side of a rubber band. If the rubber band has bends, put the clothespins elsewhere on the band.

2. Hold one clothespin. Observe the shape of the band.

3. Drop the clothespin and observe the shape of the band as it falls.

Analysis

1. What did the rubber band look like as it fell? What does the shape mean?

2. Did the clothespins still have weight when they were falling? Why or why not?

Mass and Weight

Mass and weight are not the same thing, although both measure how much there is of something. Weight is a force due to Earth's gravitational pull. This means your weight changes if you move away from Earth. Mass measures the amount of matter in an object. It does not change. If you take an object to the moon, its weight is one-sixth its Earth weight. The amount of matter in the object, which is measured by its mass, remains the same on Earth or the moon.

You may have heard that the astronauts are weightless as they orbit Earth. This is not true. Earth's gravity holds the space shuttle in an orbit about 400 km above Earth's surface. At this distance, the astronauts weigh about nine-tenths their weight on Earth's surface. They seem to float, as in **Figure 16-11,** because the floor of the shuttle is also falling. There's nothing to stand up on. This is called free fall.

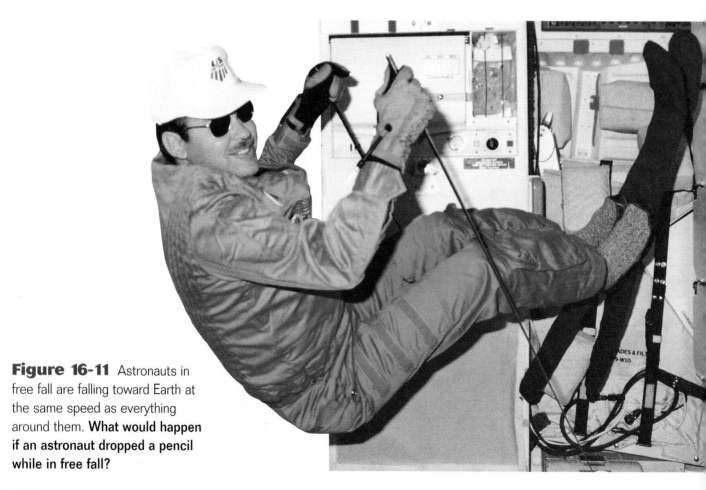

Figure 16-11 Astronauts in free fall are falling toward Earth at the same speed as everything around them. **What would happen if an astronaut dropped a pencil while in free fall?**

Measuring Weight

A familiar tool to measure force is a bathroom scale. It is used to measure weight. It has a small but stiff spring that is attached to a dial. As you step onto the scale, as shown in **Figure 16-12,** you compress the spring. As you compress the spring, you are actually falling. When the spring force and the force of gravity are balanced, the dial on the scale reads your weight.

Just as you have to push harder to move a big mass, Earth must exert more force on a heavy object. If you know an object's mass, you can calculate its weight using the formula $F = ma$.

$$\text{weight} = \text{mass} \times \text{acceleration due to gravity}$$
$$w = m(9.8 \text{ m/s}^2)$$

For example, if your mass is 50 kg, then your weight is found as follows.

$$w = m(9.8 \text{ m/s}^2)$$
$$= (50 \text{ kg})(9.8 \text{ m/s}^2)$$
$$= 490 \ \frac{\text{kg} \cdot \text{m}}{\text{s}^2}$$
$$= 490 \text{ N}$$

The floor exerts the same force, 490 N, to hold you up.

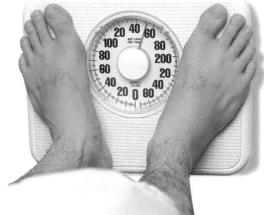

Figure 16-12 A bathroom scale measures the spring force that balances your weight.

Section Assessment

1. Suppose you traveled to a nearby planet and weighed your-self when you landed. If your mass is 50 kg and your portable bathroom scale reads 1240 N, what is the acceleration due to gravity on this planet? How does this compare with your weight on Earth? What planet do you think you are on?

2. Give an example of a force.

3. **Think Critically:** Look back at the Explore Activity at the beginning of the chapter. Now, suppose you roll a marble down the ramp that has twice the mass of the marble used in the Explore Activity. Would you expect the heavier marble to accelerate at a faster, slower, or the same rate as the lighter marble?

4.  **Skill Builder**
   Observing and Inferring When you begin riding up in an elevator, you feel heavier at first. Why? When do you feel lighter? Why? If you need help, refer to Observing and Inferring in the **Skill Handbook** on page 556.

Science Journal
    When the space shuttle astronauts orbit Earth, they feel like they have no weight, but they know they still have mass. Write about what it must be like to move around and work in free fall.

16·3 How do things move?

What You'll Learn

► How friction affects all motion
► How Newton's laws are used to understand motion

Vocabulary
Newton's laws of motion
friction

Why It's Important

► Newton's laws explain motions as simple as walking and as complicated as a rocket's launch.

Newton's Laws of Motion

In 1665, a deadly plague spread across Europe. People who lived in crowded cities were most affected. Sir Isaac Newton was in college at the time. The school closed down for two years because the disease was spreading rapidly. Newton, who was 23 years old, returned to his house in the country to wait for the plague to end. With no homework assigned, he spent his free time making up his own. He discovered many things about nature, including how gravity works and how light is made up of the colors of the rainbow. He also invented calculus, which is a branch of advanced mathematics. The most important of all his great discoveries was his understanding of how forces cause motion. He realized he could solve any problem of motion using rules now called **Newton's laws of motion,** shown in **Table 16-2.**

Table 16-2

Newton's Laws of Motion	
First Law	An object at rest will remain at rest or an object moving straight at constant speed will continue this motion until an unbalanced force acts on it.
Second Law	An object that has an unbalanced force acting on it will accelerate in the direction of the force.
Third Law	Forces always occur in equal but opposite pairs.

Newton's First Law

Newton's first law states, "An object at rest will remain at rest or an object moving straight at constant speed will continue this motion until an unbalanced force acts on it." For example, you wear a seat belt to hold you firmly in your automobile seat. If the car stops suddenly and you aren't wearing your seat belt, according to Newton's first law, you keep moving at the speed the car was traveling until your body hits something, such as the dashboard or window. Even if the car were moving at slow speed, this could lead to serious injury.

Have you ever been running fast and tried to come to a sudden stop? It's hard not to continue moving forward and fall. Newton's first law means that your body continues moving forward, even though your feet stop.

Friction

People are sometimes confused about Newton's first law because it seems that familiar objects in motion, like the sled in **Figure 16-13,** always come to rest. Remember that when an object slows down, it has a negative acceleration. Acceleration means an unbalanced force is acting on the object. Friction is one force that slows things down. **Friction** is a force that resists motion between two objects in contact. It always acts opposite to the direction of motion, as shown in **Figure 16-14.**

Speed

Friction

Figure 16-14 Friction between the wheels of the roller blades, the axles, and the ground acts against the direction of motion. This gives the person a negative acceleration, slowing him down.

Mini Lab

Measuring Friction

Procedure

1. Use your ring binder or a book for a slope.
2. Place a metal washer on the cover. Slowly lift the cover and stop when the washer just starts to move. Measure this angle with a protractor.
3. Repeat step 2 with a rubber washer.
4. Change the surface of your slope by taping a piece of plain paper, waxed paper, or sandpaper to it. Repeat steps 2 and 3.

Analysis

1. Which surface required the smallest angle to get the washer to move? What makes this combination different from the others?
2. What could you do to make the angle even smaller?
3. Compare and contrast the friction of the metal and rubber washers.

Reading Check

What type of surface provides little friction?

Have you ever tried to pull a sled or box across rough ground, like a parking lot? This is much harder than pulling it on smooth snow. The size of the friction force depends on the two surfaces involved. In general, the rougher the surface, the greater the friction. For example, if you push a hockey puck on an ice rink, it will go a great distance. If you try to push it with the same force on a smooth floor, it will stop sooner. If you push the puck on a rough carpet, it may barely move. ☑

Newton's Second Law

Remember the normal force from the previous section. When you stand on a flat surface, the downward force of your weight and the upward normal force are balanced. When you stand on a slight hill in skates, gravity pulls straight down on you. The normal force pushes straight out from the hill, as shown in **Figure 16-15.** The forces are not balanced, and you move downhill. The total of all the forces acting is the net force. An object that accelerates must be acted

interNET CONNECTION

Visit the Glencoe Science Web Site at **www.glencoe.com/ sec/science/nc** for more information about sports science.

Problem Solving

Illustrating Force

Sports equipment often is designed to increase friction. Good tread on tennis shoes helps you stay upright when running and changing direction. The handles of rackets and bats are designed to be easy to grip. Other sports require less friction. Skiers wax their skis to reduce friction with the trail. Windsurfers ride smooth boards.

Sporting goods companies have teams of scientists who analyze an athlete's movements and design equipment to maximize performance.

Draw an illustration of a rock climber's hand pulling down on a rock. Use arrows to indicate all the forces acting. Label the arrows. What happens when the net force on the climber is upward? Downward? When there is no net force?

Chalk increases friction. How does using chalk affect the net force on the climber?

Think Critically: Give another example of sports equipment that increases friction. How does increasing the friction help you play the sport?

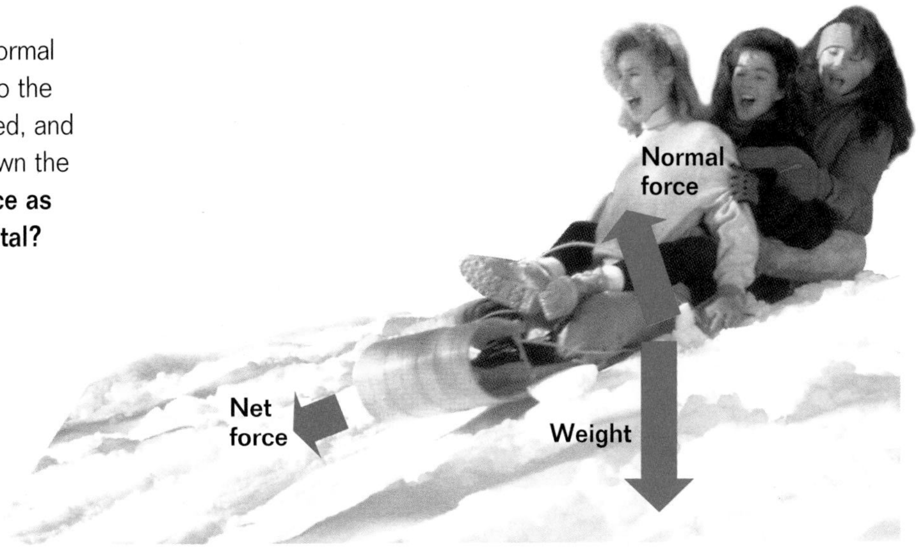

Figure 16-15 On a hill, the normal force is not opposite in direction to the weight. The forces are not balanced, and the net force accelerates you down the hill. **What happens to the net force as the slope becomes more horizontal?**

Normal force

Net force

Weight

on by a net force. If the hill were steeper, the net force would be greater, and you would accelerate more quickly. When the forces on an object are balanced, there is no acceleration and the net force is zero. (Look back at **Figure 16-9,** which shows balanced forces.) When the forces on an object are unbalanced, the net force is not zero, and the object accelerates.

As you sit reading this, two forces are acting on you: Earth's gravity downward and the chair's normal force upward. You are not accelerating because they are balanced. The net force is zero. If the leg of your chair suddenly broke, you would accelerate. Why?

Newton's second law describes how forces cause the motion of objects to change. It states, "An object that has an unbalanced force acting on it will accelerate in the direction of the force." Rearrange the $F = ma$ formula you learned.

$$\text{force} = \text{mass} \times \text{acceleration}$$

$$\text{acceleration} = \frac{\text{force}}{\text{mass}}$$

$$a = \frac{F_{net}}{m}$$

You use net force (F_{net}) because only the unbalanced part of a force causes acceleration, as shown in **Figure 16-15.**

According to Newton's second law, when an object feels a net force, its acceleration will depend on its mass. The more mass an object has, the harder it is to accelerate. Imagine using the same force to push an empty grocery cart and one full of heavy groceries. The full cart has much more inertia (mass). The more inertia an object has, the more force you must exert to move it. With the same force acting on the two carts, the full cart will have a much smaller acceleration compared to the empty cart. More mass means less acceleration if the force acting on the objects is the same.

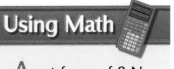

Using Math

A net force of 8 N acts on a 5-kg object. What acceleration does it give the object?

Newton's Third Law

Newton's third law says, "Forces always occur in equal but opposite pairs." If you apply a force to an object, the object will push back on you with an equal force. For example, when you walk, you push back on the sidewalk and the sidewalk pushes forward on you. When you push against the pool wall, as shown in **Figure 16-16,** the wall pushes back on you. How does anything ever move?

The equal but opposite forces in Newton's third law act on *different* objects. When you push on a door to open it, the door pushes back on you. Remember Newton's second law, $a = F_{net}/m$. The friction between your shoes and the floor provides a huge mass, you and the building, for the door's force to act on. You do not move because your acceleration is so small. Your force on the door produces more acceleration than the door's force on you. What would happen if you stood on skates and tried to push a large, heavy door?

Another familiar example is jumping off a boat. If you jump off a small boat, the boat moves back. You are pushing the boat back with your feet with the same force with which it pushes you forward. Because you are a lot heavier than the boat, it will accelerate more and move farther than you do. This situation is reversed when you jump off a big ferry. The force you exert on the boat provides a tiny acceleration to that large mass. You don't notice the ferry moving at all, but the force the boat exerts on you easily propels your smaller mass to the dock.

Figure 16-16 When the swimmer pushes against the pool wall, the wall returns an equal and opposite force. If the swimmer pushes a kickboard away, it pushes back with an equal and opposite force. **What happens if the swimmer and a friend push against each other while floating in the pool?**

A rocket blasting off illustrates Newton's third law, as shown in **Figure 16-17.** The force accelerating the gases downward is equal and opposite to the force accelerating the rocket upward. You can demonstrate this if you throw a heavy ball while standing on skates. You will roll in the direction opposite to your throw.

When you fall, Earth is pulling you down but you also are pulling Earth up. Because Earth has so much more mass than you do, Earth's movement is too small to detect. Astronomers have used Newton's third law to discover planets outside our solar system. A large planet pulls on the star it orbits just enough to cause a tiny motion of the star that astronomers on Earth can measure.

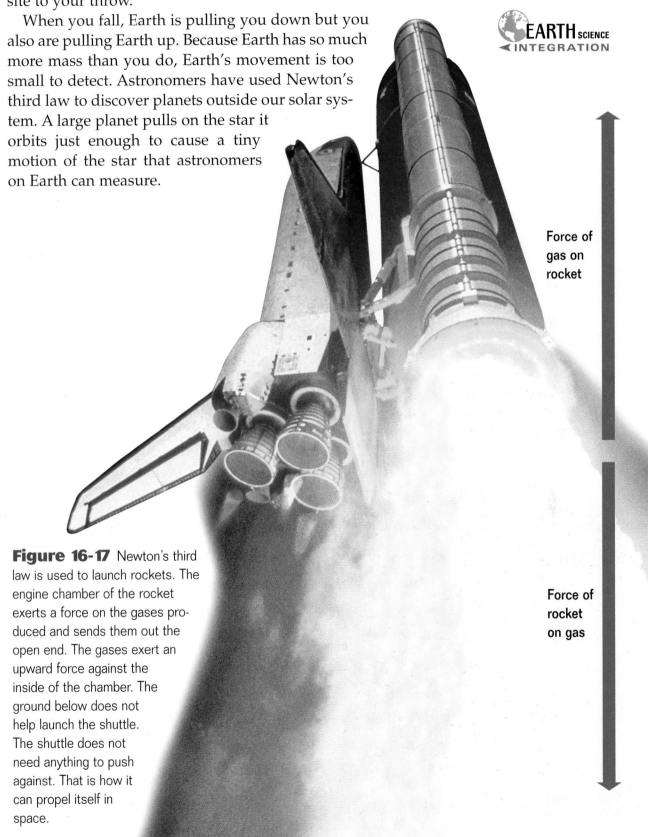

EARTH SCIENCE ◄INTEGRATION

Force of gas on rocket

Force of rocket on gas

Figure 16-17 Newton's third law is used to launch rockets. The engine chamber of the rocket exerts a force on the gases produced and sends them out the open end. The gases exert an upward force against the inside of the chamber. The ground below does not help launch the shuttle. The shuttle does not need anything to push against. That is how it can propel itself in space.

Figure 16-18 Newton's laws help you understand the forces involved when you shoot a basket.

C A net force, gravity, acts on the ball. According to Newton's second law, the ball accelerates in the direction of the force, so it slows down and turns after it is thrown.

D No force acts to counter the ball's forward motion, so it continues this motion according to Newton's first law.

B Newton's third law also explains the shot. The basketball is much smaller than the player, so the ball's acceleration up and forward is much greater than the player's corresponding acceleration back and down.

A This basketball player uses Newton's third law to jump. Her force down on the floor matches the floor's upward force on her.

Examples of Newton's Laws

As you begin to understand Newton's laws, you will see how they explain many motions you observe, as in **Figures 16-18** and **16-19.** When you ride a bicycle, it doesn't move until you start pedaling. An object at rest tends to stay at rest. This is Newton's first law at work. To go faster, you must pedal harder. You apply a force to move the pedal. This transmits a force to the wheels and the bike accelerates. This is Newton's second law. When you pedal at constant speed, the forward force exerted by the wheels and the backward forces of air resistance and friction are balanced. You keep moving at the same speed. This is Newton's first law again. If you are bicycling into a strong wind, you have to exert more force to go at that speed. If you have a tailwind pushing you, you can exert less force. If you coast on a flat surface, then air and friction act against your motion and slow you down. This is an example of Newton's second law—the net force causes negative acceleration and slows you down.

Whenever forces are acting, Newton's third law is also at work. For every force there has to be an equal but opposite force. When you push on the bicycle pedal, the pedal pushes back on you. Think about changing gears on a bike. Different gears make it easier or harder to pedal. When it is hard to pedal, you notice the force of the pedal against your foot.

Figure 16-19 Newton's laws describe what happens when these cyclists speed up, slow down, coast, or stop. **How do Newton's laws explain the motion of a bike coasting down a hill onto a level section of road?**

Figure 16-20 Newton's laws of motion are used to plan the launch, flight, and landing of space-craft. The *Mars Pathfinder* was placed on top of a Delta II launch vehicle to leave Earth. Air bags, parachutes, and rockets allowed *Pathfinder* to land on Mars. Once the rover *Sojourner* was released onto the surface, scientists sent signals from Earth to steer it around rocks and send it to points of interest to take samples.

You easily feel the force of air resistance against your body. Your body, in turn, exerts a force on the air. If you could see the air, you would see it bouncing off you as you plow through it. In every movement you make or see, you can spot Newton's three laws at work. They are used everywhere, as shown in **Figure 16-20.** These laws are the masters of motion.

Section Assessment

1. While you are skating, your friend pushes you from behind with a force of 50 N. If your mass is 45 kg, what is your acceleration?

2. Does friction provide negative acceleration or positive acceleration? Explain.

3. A skydiver falls at a constant speed when the upward force of air resistance balances the downward force of gravity. Is there a net force on the skydiver? Explain.

4. **Think Critically:** Give at least two examples of using inertia to your advantage.

5. **Skill Builder**
   Recognizing Cause and Effect
   Newton's third law is a good example of cause and effect. Explain why, using the example of a ball bouncing off a wall. If you need help, refer to Recognizing Cause and Effect in the **Skill Handbook** on page 557.

Using Computers

Spreadsheets Enter the formula $a = F_{net}/m$ in a spreadsheet. Find the acceleration given to various masses by a force of 100 N. Use masses 10 kg, 20 kg,. . . 100 kg. Also use your own mass, the mass of a car, and other familiar examples. If you need help, refer to page 574.

Building In Safety

The first cars hit the road without today's safety features, such as seat belts, windshields, or brake lights. Of course, there were few cars, and they traveled no faster than a horse and carriage. Today's cars travel at high speeds, and there are millions of cars on the road. As a result, car manufacturers are working to make cars safer, and police and legislatures are concerned with making driving safer.

Newton's laws of motion describe the behavior of an object such as a car or your body inside a car. Understanding Newton's laws is important in designing safe cars and developing safe driving habits.

Seat Belts, Air Bags, and Headrests

Newton's first law states that *an object in motion stays in motion until acted on by an unbalanced force.* When the car you are riding in comes to a sudden stop, your body keeps moving forward. Without a seat belt to hold you in place, you could be thrown against the windshield. An inflated air bag cushions your body, slowing your forward motion more gently than a seat belt alone can. At an auto show, left, a dummy is used to demonstrate the cushioning effect of an inflated air bag.

Newton's first law also indicates that an object at rest remains at rest until acted on by an unbalanced force. If you are sitting in a stopped car that is suddenly struck from behind, the seat presses you forward. A headrest makes sure your head also is pressed forward, preventing your neck from snapping backward painfully.

Braking

Newton's second law, *acceleration equals net force divided by mass,* explains why it takes longer for a heavier car to speed up and to come to a stop. If two vehicles have the same braking force, the heavier vehicle will accelerate more slowly and take longer to stop. A small sports car can brake at 10 m/s², a large sport utility vehicle at 7.5 m/s². At a speed of 100 km/h, the sports car can stop over a distance of about 32 m, while the sport utility vehicle will need roughly 53 m. A driver should allow more distance for braking in a heavier car.

Science JOURNAL

In a high-speed crash, your body might slow from 25 m/s to 0 m/s in 1 s. This is an acceleration of –25 m/s². Use $F = ma$ to calculate the force on your body during the crash. Compare this to the force of gravity, $F = m(9.8$ m/s²$)$. In your Science Journal, explain why states require that small children be strapped into a car seat rather than held in someone's lap.

Making a Paper Airplane

Materials

- Paper
- Measuring tape (50 m)
- Metric ruler
- Stopwatch
- Balance
- Tape
- Stapler
- Paper clips
- Scissors

When the Wright brothers set out to make the first powered airplane, they spent time researching flight and studying designs that had failed, as well as gliders that had been successful. They recognized the forces involved in flight, such as gravity, lift, thrust, and drag (a form of friction). If the lift is greater than gravity, then the plane will soar upward in the air. If the thrust is greater than the drag, then the plane will accelerate. Even today, these same forces must be considered when a new airplane is designed.

Recognize the Problem

How can a paper airplane that flies the longest time or the farthest distance be designed?

Form a Hypothesis

The design of the wing plays an important role in maximizing lift while reducing drag. An airfoil is the part of the wing responsible for controlling lift. The size, shape, angle, and cover material of the airfoil determine the lift and the drag that the wing will experience at a certain wind speed. **Form a hypothesis** about how your group can design a paper airplane that will either fly the longest period of time or go the farthest distance.

Goals

- **Research** paper airplane strategies.
- **Design** a paper airplane whose airfoil maximizes lift and minimizes drag.
- **Analyze** and **communicate** experimental results.

Safety Precautions

Data Sources

Visit the Glencoe Science Web Site at **www.glencoe.com/ sec/science/nc** to find more information, hints, and data from other students.

Test Your Hypothesis

Plan

1. You may use a single sheet of any type of paper. You also may cut, fold, tape, glue, or staple the paper to form your airplane.

2. **Design** one or more types of paper airplanes. What type of paper will you use? What will be the shape of the wing?

3. **Sketch** your design. **Organize** the data you expect to collect in a table similar to the one below.

4. The testing area should be flat and open. Where will you test your designs?

Do

1. Be sure your teacher approves your plan before you begin.

2. **Build** your design. Record its mass in your data table.

3. **Experiment** with different ways of flying your airplane. Record your observations in your data table.

4. **Modify** your design as you think necessary. Remember to change only one variable at a time.

5. Tell your teacher when you have finished the airplane that you think will fly as long and as far as possible.

6. Hold a class contest to determine three categories: greatest time in the air, greatest distance flown from starting point, and the greatest overall flight.

Draw Conclusions

1. **Compare and contrast** the designs your class came up with. What features did the winning planes have?

2. How did the planes that flew long distances differ from the planes that flew for a long time?

3. Which design minimized drag? Maximized lift?

4. Post your design at the Glencoe Science Web Site. How do your designs compare with the designs other classes have posted ?

Flight Data				
Trial	Mass (g)	Design change	Flight distance (m)	Flight time (s)

Chapter **16** Reviewing Main Ideas

For a **preview** of this chapter, study this Reviewing Main Ideas before you read the chapter. After you have studied this chapter, you can use the Reviewing Main Ideas to **review** the chapter.

The Glencoe MindJogger, Audiocassettes, and CD-ROM provide additional opportunities for review.

Section
16-1 SPEED AND ACCELERATION

All motion involves time and distance. Taken together, you get **average speed,** distance divided by time. This is used if the details of the motion aren't important. When speed changes, an object **accelerates.** It speeds up or slows down. It can also change direction. For constant accelerations, you can calculate your speed at any time using change in speed = at.

The distance traveled can be determined from the following equation.

$$d = \frac{1}{2}at^2$$

How does a ball move when it is thrown straight up into the air?

Section
16-2 GRAVITY

Gravity is a **force** that pulls on all objects that have mass. The acceleration due to gravity at Earth's surface is 9.8 m/s², as long as air resistance is minimal. **Mass** is the amount of matter in an object and is a property of the object. **Weight** is the force of gravity acting on the object's mass. Weight changes when gravity changes. *What is the difference between mass and weight?*

Reading Check ✓

List examples from your life that illustrate Newton's laws of motion. Exchange lists with a partner and check for accuracy.

Section
16-3 NEWTON'S FIRST LAW

Inertia and Newton's first law are often confused. **Inertia** is a measurement of how difficult it is to change an object's motion. Newton's first law says an object will remain at rest or moving at constant speed if no net force is acting on it. *Why does your drink slip off the dashboard when the car starts at a green light?*

NEWTON'S SECOND LAW

Newton's second law describes how unbalanced or net forces act on an object. The object will accelerate according to $F_{net} = ma$. Notice, for a certain amount of force, there is less acceleration for objects with more inertia (mass). *Which forces act on the shuttle when it launches? In what direction is the net force?*

NEWTON'S THIRD LAW

Newton's third law states that forces occur in equal but opposite pairs. *What are the forces between your shoes and the ground as you walk?*

Chapter 16 Assessment

Using Vocabulary

a. acceleration
b. average speed
c. balanced forces
d. force
e. friction
f. gravity
g. inertia
h. mass
i. Newton's laws of motion
j. normal force
k. rate
l. weight

For each set of Vocabulary terms below, explain the relationship that exists.

1. inertia, mass
2. average speed, rate
3. force, Newton's laws of motion
4. weight, normal force
5. mass, weight

Checking Concepts

Choose the word or phrase that best answers the question.

6. What is another name for inertia?
   A) weight
   B) gravity
   C) mass
   D) Newton's first law

7. What will an object acted upon by a net force do?
   A) accelerate
   B) remain at rest
   C) gain mass
   D) become balanced

8. Which of the following happens as you move away from Earth?
   A) Mass decreases and weight increases.
   B) Mass decreases and weight decreases.
   C) Mass stays the same and weight decreases.
   D) Mass stays the same and weight stays the same.

9. What does an object's weight depend on?
   A) shape
   B) mass
   C) speed
   D) volume

10. A car is driving at constant speed. Which of the following is **NOT** true?
    A) All the forces acting are balanced.
    B) A net force keeps it moving.
    C) Friction and air resistance are equal to the forward force of the engine.
    D) The car is not accelerating.

11. A large truck bumps a small car. Which of the following is true?
    A) The force of the truck on the car is greater.
    B) The force of the car on the truck is greater.
    C) The forces are the same.
    D) No force is involved.

12. What is the unit for acceleration?
    A) m/s^2
    B) $kg \cdot m/s^2$
    C) m/s
    D) N

13. What decreases friction?
    A) a rougher surface
    B) a smoother surface
    C) more speed
    D) more surface area

14. What would happen to a falling object if the air resistance acting on it became equal to the weight of the object?
    A) It would float.
    B) It would continue to accelerate.
    C) It would move at constant speed.
    D) It would start moving upward.

15. Which of the following is a force?
    A) inertia
    B) acceleration
    C) speed
    D) friction

Thinking Critically

16. You run 100 m in 25 s. If you then run the same distance in less time, does your average speed increase or decrease? Explain.

17. A cliff diver falling at $9.8 \ m/s^2$ takes 1.5 s to hit the water. How high is the cliff?

18. Using the information from the previous problem, at what speed does the diver hit the water?

19. Explain why a fast-moving freight train takes a few kilometers to stop.

20. What is the force of the rocket engines on a 2 million-kg space shuttle if it accelerates at 30 m/s²?

Developing Skills

If you need help, refer to the Skill Handbook.

21. **Making and Using Graphs:** Marion bicycles at an average speed of 10 km/h. Plot a distance-time graph of these data over six hours. How long does it take her to bike 25 km?

22. **Measuring in SI:** Which of the following speeds is the fastest: 20 m/s, 200 cm/s, or 0.2 km/s? HINT: Express all the speeds in meters per second and compare.

23. **Interpreting Data:** Use the following data of the acceleration of gravity on various planets and the maximum height a given person can jump.
    Which planet has the strongest gravity? Why would it be so hard to jump high on this planet? Where can you jump the highest? What do you think about the size and mass of this place?

Jump Height		
Planet	Gravity (m/s²)	Height (m)
Earth	9.8	0.75
Mars	3.7	2.0
Pluto	0.5	14.7
Jupiter	22.9	0.32

Test-Taking Tip

Get to the Root of Things If you don't know a word's meaning, you can still get an idea of its definition if you focus on its roots, suffixes, and prefixes. For example, words that start with *non-*, *un-*, *a-*, *dis-*, and *in-* generally reverse what the rest of the word means.

Test Practice

Use these questions to test your Science Proficiency.

1. Scientific laws cannot be proven true, only supported with the successful results of new experiments. Which of the following does **NOT** support Newton's laws of motion?
   A) An object cannot travel faster than the speed of light.
   B) The greater the mass of an object, the harder it is to move.
   C) An object accelerates in the direction of the net force.
   D) When an object feels a force, it returns the force in equal but opposite measure.

2. A man weighs 80 kg. About how much normal force does the floor exert to hold him up?
   A) 80 N
   B) 400 N
   C) 600 N
   D) 800 N

Chapter Preview

Section 17-1
What are waves?
Section 17-2
Wave Properties
Section 17-3
Wave Behavior

Skills Preview

Skill Builders
- Map Concepts
- Compare and Contrast

Activities
- Classify
- Measure in SI

MiniLabs
- Compare and Contrast
- Observe

Reading Check ✔

As you read, jot down ways your life would change if there were no waves. What would your life be like? Could you live at all?

Explore Activity

Think about a beautiful autumn day. You are sitting by a lake in a park. You hear music coming from a nearby school band practicing for a big game. A fish jumps out of the water and falls back making a splash. You see a circle of waves that move away from the fish's entry point. The circular waves pass by a floating leaf that fell from a tree nearby. How does the leaf move in response to the waves?

Observe Wave Behavior

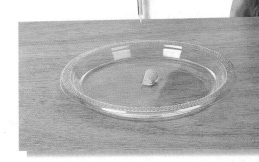

1. Set a large, clear, plastic plate (such as the ones carryout meals often come in) on your table.

2. Fill the plate with water to a depth of about 1 cm.

3. Fill a dropper with water.

4. Release a single drop of water onto the water's surface and observe what happens. Repeat as necessary.

5. Float a small cork or 1-cm piece of a soda straw on the surface of the water near the middle of the plate.

6. After the water becomes still again, release single drops at regular intervals from a height of about 10 cm and not directly above the floating object.

7. Repeat the procedure, but release the single drops from a height of about 20 cm.

Science **Journal**

In your Science Journal, record your observations and describe the movements of the floating object.

What You'll Learn

► Waves carry energy, not matter
► The difference between transverse waves and compressional waves

Vocabulary
wave
mechanical wave
electromagnetic wave
transverse wave
compressional wave

Why It's Important

► You can hear music because of waves.

Waves Carry Energy

In the Explore Activity, you saw that falling drops of water can move a floating object. You know that you can make something move by giving it a push or pull. But, the drops didn't hit the floating object. How did the energy from the falling drops travel through the water and move the object? Did you also notice that the ripples that moved in circles from the drop's entry point had peaks and valleys? These peaks and valleys make up water waves.

Waves are regular disturbances that carry energy through matter or space without carrying matter, as shown in **Figure 17-1A.** You also transfer energy when you throw a basketball or baseball to a friend. But, there is an important difference between a moving ball and a moving wave. As shown in **Figure 17-1B,** throwing a ball involves the transport of matter as well as energy.

Mechanical Waves

How does a wave carry energy but not matter? Here is one example you already know about. Sound travels as one type of wave motion. The sounds from a CD player reach your ears when the speakers vibrate back and forth and make sound waves.

Figure 17-1 The wave and the ball both carry energy.

A Waves on the water's surface carry energy from place to place, but the water itself moves mostly up and down.

B When you throw a ball to a friend, the ball carries both energy and matter. **What is another example of a moving object carrying both energy and matter?**

The sound waves transfer energy to anything in their path. When the waves reach your ears, they make your eardrums vibrate, as in **Figure 17-2.** If you've ever felt your house shake after a clap of thunder, you know that sound waves can carry large amounts of energy.

Waves that require matter to carry energy are called **mechanical waves.** The matter through which a mechanical wave travels is called a medium. A mechanical wave travels as energy is transferred from particle to particle in the medium. For example, a sound wave travels through the air because energy is transferred from gas molecule to gas molecule. Without a medium, you would not hear sounds. For example, sound waves can't travel in outer space. Imagine that you're standing on the moon. A person standing near you is telling you what she sees. But because there is no air on the moon to carry the sound, you won't hear a word she says—even if she yells at the top of her lungs.

Figure 17-2 When you hear a sound, it's because sound waves traveling through the air make your eardrums vibrate.

Water Waves

Water waves—like the ones you made in the Explore Activity—are also mechanical waves. Each falling water drop touched water molecules when it hit the water's surface. Thus, the droplet's energy was carried from molecule to molecule through the water. Remember that the molecules of water do not move forward along with the wave. Rather, the water's surface moves up and down. In this same way, the wave transfers energy to a boat or other floating object, as shown in **Figure 17-3.** Absorbing some of the energy, the object bobs up and down and moves slowly away from the source of the wave.

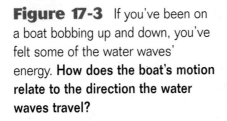
Figure 17-3 If you've been on a boat bobbing up and down, you've felt some of the water waves' energy. **How does the boat's motion relate to the direction the water waves travel?**

interNET
CONNECTION

Visit the Glencoe Science Web Site at **www. glencoe.com/sec/ science/nc** for more information about electromagnetic waves.

Reading Check

What are the highest points of transverse waves called?

Electromagnetic Waves

When you listen to the radio, watch TV, or use a microwave oven to cook, you use a different kind of wave—one that doesn't need matter as a medium.

Waves that do not require matter to carry energy are called **electromagnetic waves.** Electromagnetic waves can travel through air. They can even travel through the solid walls of your home. These are the kind of waves that bring you radio and TV programs. Electromagnetic waves also can travel through space to carry information to and from spacecraft. The X rays a doctor uses to see if you broke a bone and the light that carries the sun's energy to Earth are also electromagnetic waves.

Transverse Waves

In a mechanical **transverse wave,** matter moves back and forth at right angles to the direction the wave travels. All electromagnetic waves are transverse waves. You can make a model of a transverse wave. Tie one end of a rope to a doorknob. Hold the other end in your hand. Now, shake the end in your hand up and down. By adjusting the way you shake the rope, you can create a wave that seems to vibrate in place.

Does the rope appear to move toward the doorknob? It doesn't really move toward the door, because if it did, you also would be pulled in that direction. What you see is energy moving along the "rope" wave. You can see that the wave has peaks and valleys at regular intervals. As shown in **Figure 17-4,** the high points of transverse waves are called crests. The low points are called troughs. ✔

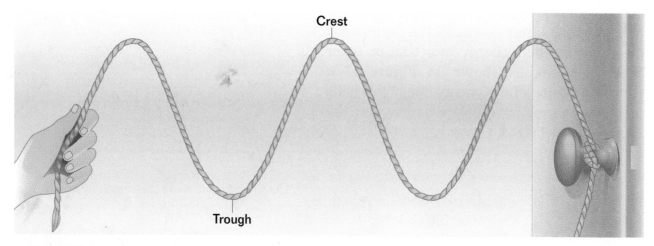

Crest

Trough

Figure 17-4 What does the vibrating rope carry from the hand to the door?

Figure 17-5 Sound waves are compressional waves.

 A This compressional wave carries energy along the spring, while the spring itself vibrates forward and backward.

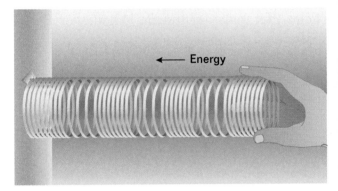

Energy ←

 B Vibrating strings make compressional waves that carry the harp's music to your ears. **What do you think vibrates to make compressional waves when a musician plays a trumpet?**

Compressional Waves

Mechanical waves can be either transverse or compressional. In a **compressional wave,** matter in the medium moves forward and backward in the same direction the wave travels. You can make a compressional wave by squeezing together and releasing several coils of a coiled spring toy, as shown in **Figure 17-5A.** When a compressional wave travels along a coiled spring, does the whole spring move along with the wave? If you tied a string around a single coil, you could watch that coil's movement as the wave passes. You would see that the coil moves forward and backward as the wave passes. So, like transverse waves, compressional waves carry only energy forward along the spring. The matter of the spring does not move along with the wave.

Sound Waves

Sound waves are compressional waves. How do you make sound waves when you talk or sing? If you hold your fingers against your throat while you hum, you can feel vibrations. These vibrations are actually the movements of your vocal cords. If you touch a stereo speaker while it's playing, you can feel the vibrations of the speaker, too. The sounds produced by the harp shown in **Figure 17-5B** are made when the strings of the instrument are made to vibrate.

Comparing Sounds

Procedure

1. Hold a wooden ruler firmly on the edge of your desk so that most of it extends off the edge of the desk.
2. Pluck the free end of the ruler so that it vibrates up and down. Pluck it easily at first, then with more energy.
3. Repeat step 2, moving the ruler about 1 cm further onto the desk. Continue until only about 5 cm extend off the edge.

Analysis

1. Compare the loudness of the sounds produced by using little energy with those using more energy.
2. Compare the pitches produced by the longer and shorter lengths of the object.

Making Sound Waves

How do vibrating vocal cords, strings, and other objects make sound waves? To find out, look at the drumhead stretched over the open end of the drum shown in **Figure 17-6.** When the drumhead moves upward, it touches some of the invisible particles that make up the air. When everything is quiet, the air particles are spaced about the same distance apart. But when the drumhead moves up, it pushes the air particles together. These groups of particles that are squeezed together are called a compression. When the drumhead moves downward, the air particles have more room and move away from each other. A place where particles are spaced far apart is called a rarefaction (rar uh FAK shun).

Figure 17-6 A vibrating drumhead makes compressions and rarefactions in the air. **How do your vocal cords make compressions and rarefactions in air?**

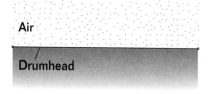

Air

Drumhead

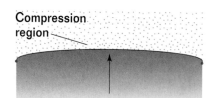

Compression region

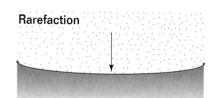

Rarefaction

Section Assessment

1. Give one example of a transverse wave and one example of a compressional wave.

2. Why can't a sound wave travel from a satellite to Earth?

3. Is light a mechanical wave or an electromagnetic wave? A transverse wave or a compressional wave?

4. **Think Critically:** How is it possible for a sound wave to transmit energy, but not matter?

5. **Skill Builder**

   Concept Mapping Create a concept map that shows the relationships between the following: *waves, mechanical waves, electromagnetic waves, compressional waves,* and *transverse waves.* If you need help, refer to Concept Mapping in the **Skill Handbook** on page 550.

Using Computers

Word Processing Use word-processing software to write short descriptions of the waves you encounter during a typical day. If you need help, refer to page 568.

Wave Properties

Amplitude

Waves have characteristics that you can see and measure. For example, you can describe a wave in a lake or ocean by how high it rises above, or falls below, the normal water level. This is called the wave's amplitude. The **amplitude** of a transverse wave is one-half the distance between a crest and a trough, as shown in **Figure 17-7A.** In a compressional wave, the amplitude is greater when the particles of the medium are squeezed closer together in each compression and spread farther apart in each rarefaction.

Amplitude and Energy

A wave's amplitude is important. It is a measure of the energy the wave carries. For example, the waves that make up bright light have greater amplitudes than the waves that make up dim light. Waves of bright light carry more energy than the waves that make up dim light. In a similar way, loud sound waves have greater amplitudes than soft sound waves. Loud sounds carry more energy than soft sounds.

If you've seen pictures of a hurricane that strikes a coastal area, you know that the waves caused by the hurricane can damage anything that stands in their path. Waves with large amplitudes carry more energy than waves with smaller amplitudes. The waves caused by the hurricane have much more energy than the small waves or ripples on a pond, as you can see in **Figure 17-7B.**

What **You'll Learn**

► What wave frequency and wavelength are
► Waves travel at different speeds

Vocabulary
amplitude
wavelength
frequency

Why **It's Important**

► A wave's energy depends on its amplitude.

Figure 17-7 A wave's amplitude is a measure of how much energy it carries.

A The higher the crests (and the lower the troughs) of a wave, the greater the wave's amplitude is.

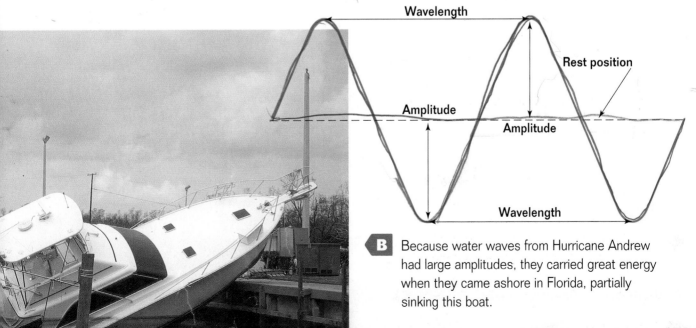

B Because water waves from Hurricane Andrew had large amplitudes, they carried great energy when they came ashore in Florida, partially sinking this boat.

Tsunamis are huge sea waves that are caused by underwater earthquakes or volcanic eruptions. Because of their large amplitudes, tsunamis carry tremendous amounts of energy. They cause great damage when they move ashore.

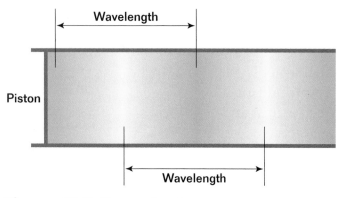

Figure 17-8 The wavelength of a compressional wave is measured from one compression or rarefaction to the next. **When the piston moves to the right, does it make a compression or a rarefaction?**

Figure 17-9 The wavelengths and frequencies of electromagnetic waves vary greatly. **Which waves have longer wavelengths, radio waves or visible light waves?**

Wavelength

Another way to describe a wave is by its wavelength. **Wavelength** is the distance between a point on one wave and an identical point on the next wave—from a crest to a crest or from a trough to a trough, as shown in **Figure 17-7A**. For a compressional wave, the wavelength is the distance between adjacent compressions or rarefactions, as shown in **Figure 17-8**.

Wavelength is an important characteristic of a wave. For example, the difference between red light and green light is that they have different wavelengths. Like all electromagnetic waves, light is a transverse wave. The wavelength of visible light determines its color. In this example, the wavelength of red light is longer than the wavelength of green light. Some electromagnetic waves, like X rays, have short wavelengths. Others, like microwaves in an oven, have longer wavelengths. The range of wavelengths of electromagnetic waves is shown in **Figure 17-9**.

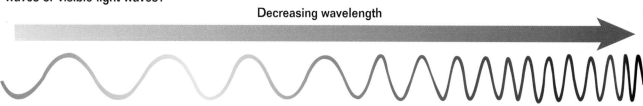

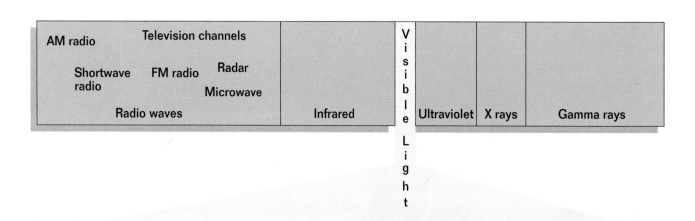

Frequency

The **frequency** of a wave is the number of waves that pass a given point in 1 s. Frequency is measured in waves per second, or hertz (Hz). For a given speed, waves with longer wavelengths have lower frequencies. Fewer long waves pass a given point in 1 s. Waves with shorter wavelengths have higher frequencies because more waves pass a given point in 1 s. Frequency is illustrated in **Figure 17-10A** and **B.**

The wavelength of an electromagnetic light wave determines the color of the light. In a sound wave, the frequency (associated with its wavelength) determines the pitch. Pitch is the highness or lowness of a sound. A flute makes musical notes with a high pitch. A tuba produces notes with a low pitch. When you sing "do re mi fa so la ti do," both the pitch and frequency increase from note to note. In other words, high-pitched sound waves have high frequencies. Low-pitched sound waves have low frequencies. ✔

Global Positioning Systems
Maybe you've used a global positioning system (GPS) receiver to determine your location while driving, boating, or hiking. Earth-orbiting satellites send out electromagnetic radio waves that give the satellites' exact locations and times of transmission. The GPS receiver calculates the distance to each satellite and displays your location to within about 16 m.

Wave Speed

You've probably watched a distant thunderstorm approach on a hot summer day. You see a bolt of lightning flash between a dark cloud and the ground. Do the sound waves, or thunder, produced by the lightning bolt reach your ears at the same instant you see the lightning? If the thunderstorm is many kilometers away, several seconds may pass between the time you see the lightning and you hear the thunder. This happens because light travels much faster in air than sound does. Light is an electromagnetic wave that travels through air at about 300 million m/s. Sound is a mechanical wave that travels through air at about 340 m/s.

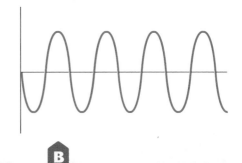

Reading Check ✔
What determines the pitch of a sound?

Figure 17-10 Wave A has a longer wavelength and a lower frequency than wave B. **Why does a wave with a long wavelength have a low frequency?**

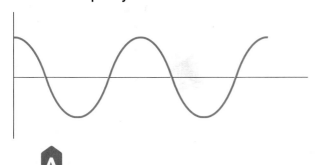

A   B

Determining Wave Speed

You can calculate the speed of a wave by multiplying its frequency by its wavelength. For example, suppose you know that a sound wave has a frequency of 266 Hz and a wavelength of 1.29 m. (Remember that 266 Hz means that 266 sound waves pass a given point in 1 s.) The wave's speed is given by the following calculation.

wave frequency × wavelength = wave speed
266 Hz × 1.29 m = 343 m/s

The speed of the wave is 343 m/s.

Light waves don't always travel at the same speed. For example, the speed of light waves is slightly higher in empty space than in air. And, light waves travel only about 200 million m/s in glass. You can see that this is much slower than the speed light travels in air. The speed of sound waves varies, too. Have you ever heard sounds while swimming underwater? Have you ever put your ear against a wall or on the ground to hear something more clearly? If you have, you may have noticed something interesting. Sound travels faster in liquids and solids than in gases like air.

Using Math

You can calculate the speed of a wave in meters per second (m/s) by multiplying the wave's frequency in hertz (Hz) by its wavelength in meters (m). This calculation is possible because 1 Hz = 1/s. For example, 266 Hz × 1.29 m = 266 1/s × 1.29 m = 343 m/s.

Section Assessment

1. Why is the statement "The speed of light is 300 million m/s" not always correct?

2. How does the frequency of a wave change as its wavelength changes?

3. In what part of a compressional wave are the particles spaced farthest apart?

4. Why is a sound wave with a large amplitude more likely to damage your hearing than one with a small amplitude?

5. **Think Critically:** Explain the differences between the waves that make up bright green light and dim red light.

6. **Skill Builder**
   Interpreting Scientific Diagrams
   Scientific diagrams can help you understand wave properties. Do the **Chapter 17 Skill Activity** on page 594 to learn about a compressional wave, its parts, and its wavelength.

Using Math

If a sound wave traveling through water has a speed of 1470 m/s and a frequency of 2340 Hz, what is its wavelength?

Waves on a Spring

Waves are rhythmic disturbances that carry energy through matter or space. Studying waves can help you understand how the sun's energy reaches Earth and sounds travel through the air.

What You'll Investigate

In this activity, you will create transverse and compressional waves on a coiled spring and investigate some of their properties.

Goals

- **Create** transverse and compressional waves on a coiled spring.
- **Investigate** wave properties such as speed and amplitude.

Procedure

1. **Prepare a data table** such as the one shown.
2. Work in pairs or groups and clear a place on an uncarpeted floor about 6 m long and 2 m wide.
3. While one team member grasps one end of the coiled spring toy with one hand, another team member should stretch it to the length suggested by the teacher. **Measure** the length of the coiled spring toy. **CAUTION:** *Coiled springs can be damaged permanently by overstretching or tangling. Be careful to follow the teacher's instructions.*
4. **Create** a wave by having one team member make a quick sideways snap of the wrist. Time several waves as they travel from one end of the coiled spring toy to the other. Record the average time in your data table.
5. Repeat step 4 using waves that have slightly larger amplitudes.
6. Use one hand to squeeze together about 20 of the coils near you. **Observe** what happens to the unsqueezed coils. Release the coils and **observe** what happens.

Materials

- Long, coiled spring toy
- Meterstick
- Stopwatch
- Piece of colored yarn (5 cm)

7. Quickly push one end of the coiled spring toward your partner, then pull it back to its original position.
8. Tie the piece of colored yarn to a coil near the middle of the coiled spring toy. Repeat step 7, **observing** what happens to the string.

Wave Data	
Length of stretched spring toy	
Average time for a wave to travel from end to end—step 4	
Average time for a wave to travel from end to end—step 5	

Conclude and Apply

1. **Classify** the wave pulses you created in steps 4 and 5 and those you created in steps 6 to 8 as compressional or transverse.
2. **Calculate** and **compare** the speeds of the waves in steps 4 and 5.
3. **Classify** the unsqueezed coils in step 6 as a compression or a rarefaction.
4. **Compare and contrast** the motion of the yarn in step 8 with the motion of the wave. Did the coil that had the yarn attached to it move along the coiled spring toy or did the wave's energy pass through that coil?

17•3 Wave Behavior

Reflection

What You'll Learn

► Waves can reflect from some surfaces
► How waves usually change direction when they move from one material into another
► Waves are able to bend around barriers

Vocabulary

reflection   diffraction
refraction   interference

Why It's Important

► Without wave reflection, you couldn't read the words on this page.

You've probably yelled to a friend across a gymnasium or down a long hallway. When you did this, you might have heard an echo of your voice. What property of sound caused the echo?

When you look in a mirror, what property of light lets you see your face? Both the echo of your voice and the face you see in the mirror are caused by wave reflection. **Reflection** occurs when a wave strikes an object or surface and bounces off. An echo is reflected sound. Sound reflects from all surfaces. Your echo bounced off the walls, floor, ceiling, furniture, and people. In old western movies, light reflected off a mirror was often used to send a message over long distances. When you see your face in a mirror, as shown in **Figure 17-11A,** reflection occurs. Light from your face hits the mirror and reflects back to your eyes.

A mirror is smooth and even. However, when light reflects from an uneven or rough surface, you can't see an image because the reflected light scatters in many different directions, as shown in **Figure 17-11B.**

Figure 17-11

A If light didn't reflect from you and the mirror, you wouldn't be able to see yourself in the mirror.

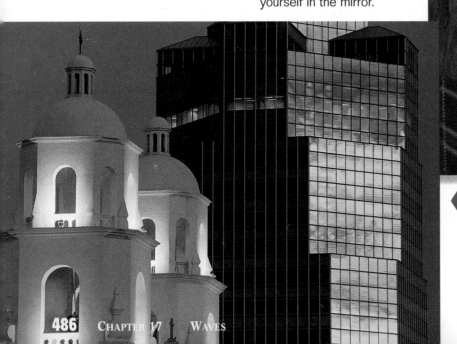

B The building at the far left has a rough surface that scatters light in different directions. Its surface is not smooth and shiny like the building on the right, which is mirror-like. **Why should a mirror's reflective surface be made as smooth as possible?**

Refraction

You've already seen that a wave changes direction when it reflects from a surface. Can a wave change its direction at other times? Perhaps you've used a magnifying glass to examine your skin, an insect, a coin, or a stamp. An object appears larger when viewed through a magnifying glass. This happens because the light rays from the object change direction when they pass from the air into the glass. They change direction again when they pass from the glass into the air. The bending of a wave as it moves from one medium into another is called **refraction.**

Refraction and Wave Speed

The speed of a wave is different in different substances. For example, light waves move slower in water than in air. Refraction occurs when the speed of a wave changes as it passes from one substance to another. As shown in **Figure 17-12A** and **B,** a line has been drawn perpendicular to the water's surface. This line is called the normal.

Try at Home

Mini Lab

Observing How Light Refracts

Procedure

1. Fill a large, opaque drinking glass or cup nearly to the brim with water.
2. Place a white soda straw in the water at an angle, with approximately one-third of its length extending out of the water.
3. Looking directly down into the cup from above, observe the straw where it meets the water.
4. Placing yourself so that the straw angles to your left or right, slowly back away about 1 m. If necessary, lower your head until you eliminate any unwanted glare from the water's surface. Observe the straw as it appears above, at, and below the surface of the water.

Analysis

1. Describe the straw's appearance as you looked directly down on it.
2. Compare the straw's appearance above and below the water's surface when you looked at it from the side. Draw a diagram and explain the apparent effect.

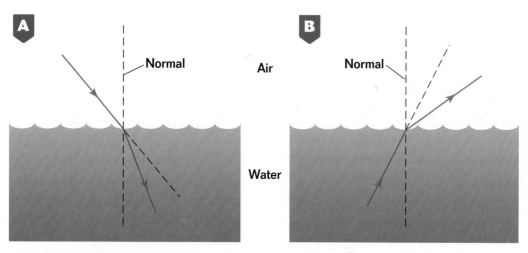

Figure 17-12 As the light ray in A passes from air into water, it refracts toward the normal. As the light ray in B passes from water into air, it refracts away from the normal.

When a light ray passes from air into water, it slows down and bends toward the normal. The more the light ray slows, the more its direction changes. When the ray passes from water into air, it speeds up and bends away from the normal.

You notice refraction when you look at an angle into a lake or pond and spot a fish near the bottom. Refraction makes the fish appear to be closer to the surface and farther away from you than it really is, as shown in **Figure 17-13.** Refraction also gives diamonds and other gems their wonderful sparkle. **Figure 17-14** illustrates how refraction and reflection produce a rainbow when light waves from the sun pass into and out of water droplets in the air. ✔

Reading Check ✔

What produces a rainbow?

Diffraction

It's time for lunch. You're walking down the hallway to the cafeteria. As you near the open door, you can hear people talking and the clink and clank of tableware. But how do the sound waves reach your ears before you get to the door? The sound waves must be able to bend around the corners of the door, as shown in **Figure 17-15A. Diffraction** is the bending of waves around a barrier.

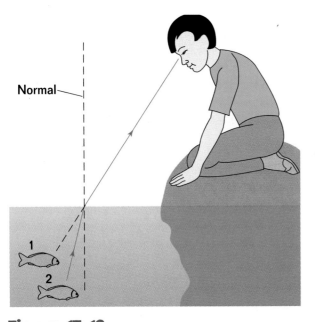

Figure 17-13
Refraction makes the fish at location 2 appear to be at location 1.

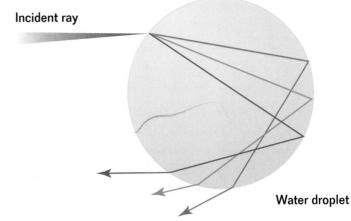

Incident ray

Sunlight

Water droplet

Figure 17-14 Light rays refract when they enter and leave a raindrop, and they reflect from the far side of the drop. Because different colors refract at different angles, they leave the drop separated into the colors of the spectrum. (Ray angles have been shown larger than they actually are for clarity.) **Which color of light shown on the diagram refracts most?**

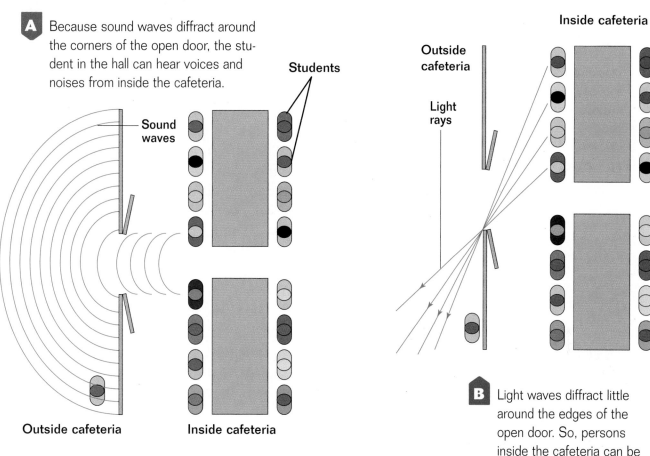

Figure 17-15 Sound waves and light waves diffract differently through an open door.

A Because sound waves diffract around the corners of the open door, the student in the hall can hear voices and noises from inside the cafeteria.

Students

Sound waves

Outside cafeteria

Inside cafeteria

Inside cafeteria

Outside cafeteria

Light rays

B Light waves diffract little around the edges of the open door. So, persons inside the cafeteria can be seen only when the student in the hall meets light rays streaming through the door. **How does diffraction explain why a boat inside a harbor rocks slightly from water waves outside the harbor?**

Diffraction of Light

Can light waves diffract, too? You can't see your friends in the cafeteria until you reach the open door, so the light waves must not diffract as much as the sound waves, as shown in **Figure 17-15.**

Are light waves able to diffract at all? As a matter of fact, light waves do bend around the edges of an open door. You can see some effects of light diffraction when you view a bright light through a small slit such as the one between two pencils held close together. However, the amount the light bends is extremely small. As a result, the diffraction of light is far too small to allow you to see around the corner into the cafeteria. The reason that light waves don't diffract much when they pass through an open door is that the wavelengths of visible light are much smaller than the width of the door. Sound waves that you can hear have much longer wavelengths. They bend more readily around the corners of an open door. Waves diffract best when the wavelength of the wave is similar in size to the barrier or opening.

Interference

Imagine a marching band that has only one of each kind of instrument. When this band performs on a football field, will it fill the stadium with sound? Having several of each instrument play the same notes at the same times produces much louder and more spectacular music. For example, the sound waves of many trumpets combine to make sound waves with larger amplitudes. The sound produced by many trumpets is therefore louder than the sound from a single trumpet. The ability of two or more waves to combine and form a new wave when they overlap is called **interference** (ihn tur FEER uns).

Constructive interference occurs when waves meet, for example, crest to crest and trough to trough. The amplitudes of these combining waves add together to make a larger wave, as shown in **Figure 17-16A, B,** and **C.** Destructive interference occurs, for example, when the crest of one wave meets the trough of another wave. In destructive interference, the amplitudes of the combining waves make a smaller wave. Sometimes, they produce no wave at all, as shown in **Figure 17-16D, E,** and **F** on the next page.

Reflected light waves sometimes produce interesting interference patterns. The colorful interference patterns that result from the microscopic pits in compact discs are one example.

inter NET
C O N N E C T I O N

Visit the Glencoe Science Web Site at **www. glencoe.com/sec/ science/nc** for more information about wave interference.

Problem Solving

Scattering Light

Why is the sky blue and the sunset red? Surprisingly, both effects have the same cause. Sunlight contains all colors of the visible spectrum. When sunlight passes through Earth's atmosphere, particles in the air scatter some colors more than others. Shorter-wavelength violet and blue light waves are scattered most, green and yellow waves a little, and longer-wavelength orange and red light waves even less.

The sky appears blue during the day because the scattered blue light waves reflect to your eyes from dust particles and water droplets in the air. However, at sunrise and sunset, the sky appears red because light waves from the sun pass through more of the atmosphere before reaching Earth's surface. With so much of the blue and violet light scattered away, only the orange and red waves reach your eyes.

Think Critically: You've seen the beautiful array of colors in a rainbow on a day that has both sunshine and water droplets in the air. You've viewed the colorful light pattern from a compact disc. What do the blue color of the daytime sky, the red color of a sunset, a multicolored rainbow, and the light pattern from a compact disc have in common? How are they different?

Figure 17-16

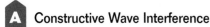

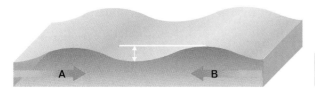 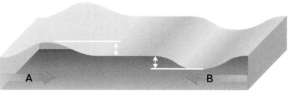

A Constructive Wave Interference
Crests of waves A and B approach each other from different directions. The waves have equal amplitudes.

D Destructive Wave Interference
A crest of wave A and trough of wave B approach each other from different directions. The amplitude of A equals the amplitude of B.

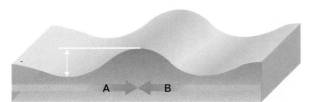 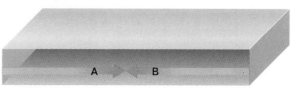

B When crests A and B meet, they briefly form a new wave, A + B, which has an amplitude equal to the sum of the amplitudes of the two waves.

E When the waves meet, they briefly form a new wave, A + B, which has an amplitude of zero for an instant.

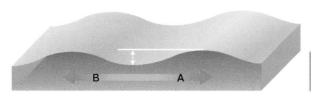 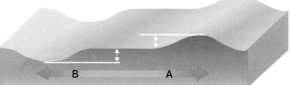

C The waves have passed through each other unchanged.

F The waves have passed through each other unchanged. **Compare and contrast constructive and destructive interference.**

Useful Interference

You may have seen someone cut grass with a power lawn mower or cut wood with a chain saw. In the past, many people who've performed these tasks have damaged their hearing because of the loud noises produced by these machines. Today, ear protectors can reflect and absorb some of the noise from lawn mowers and chain saws. The ear protectors lower the amplitudes of the harmful waves. The smaller-amplitude waves that reach the ears no longer damage eardrums.

Pilots of small planes have had an interesting problem. They couldn't shut out all the noise of the plane's motor. If they did, they wouldn't be able to hear instructions from air-traffic controllers. Engineers invented special earphones that contain electronic circuits. These circuits produce sound frequencies that destructively interfere with engine noise that might be harmful.

However, the sound frequencies produced do not interfere with human voices, allowing the pilot to hear and understand normal conversation. In these examples, destructive interference can be a benefit, as shown in **Figure 17-17.**

Figure 17-17 Some airplane pilots use ear protectors that muffle engine noise but don't block human voices. People who operate chain saws need ear protectors that greatly reduce the engine noise that could be harmful.

Section Assessment

1. White objects reflect light. Why don't you see your reflection when you look at a building made of rough, white stone?

2. If you're standing on one side of a building, how are you able to hear the siren of an ambulance on the other side of the building?

3. What behavior of light enables magnifying glasses and contact lenses to bend light rays and help people see more clearly?

4. **Think Critically:** Why don't light rays that stream through an open window into a darkened room spread evenly through the entire room?

5.  **Skill Builder**
   Comparing and Contrasting When light rays pass from water into a certain type of glass, the rays refract toward the normal. Compare and contrast the speed of light in water and in the glass. If you need help, refer to Comparing and Contrasting in the **Skill Handbook** on page 556.

Science **Journal**
Look and listen carefully as you travel home from school or walk down the street where you live. What examples of wave reflection and refraction do you notice? Describe each of these in your Science Journal, and explain whether it's an example of reflection or refraction.

Graphing Waves

Constructive and Destructive Interference

Waves have special characteristics. The wavelength is the horizontal distance between a point on one wave and an identical point on the next wave. The amplitude is the vertical distance from the crest (or trough) of a wave to a position halfway between crest and trough.

When two waves meet in such a way that a new wave with greater amplitude is formed, it is called constructive interference. If the new wave formed has a smaller amplitude than either original wave or an amplitude of zero, it is called destructive interference.

Problem

Draw a graph for the new wave formed by combining Waves A and B.

Solution

Notice that nine points on each wave are labeled with red dots and numbers. These points will be used to graph the new wave.

To graph the new wave formed by combining Waves A and B, find nine points for the new graph by adding the "height" of Waves A and B at each labeled point.

Point 1 (new): height of Wave A point 1 + height of Wave B point 1 = 0 + 0 = 0.

Point 2 (new): height of Wave A point 2 + height of Wave B point 2 = 2 + 4 = 6.

Point 3 (new): height of Wave A point 3 + height of Wave B point 3 = 4 + 8 = 12.

Continuing the process, you'll find that the remaining points have heights 6, 0, 6, 12, 6, and 0. A graph for the new wave looks like this:

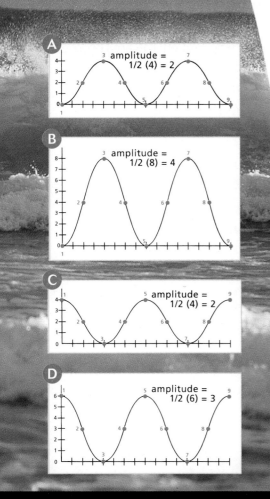

To find a wave's amplitude, count the vertical units between the lowest and highest points on the graph and divide by 2. Because the new wave has greater amplitude (6) than either Wave A (2) or B (4), this problem is an example of constructive interference.

Practice
PROBLEMS

In the following problems, draw the graph and determine whether each is a case of constructive or destructive interference.

1. Draw a graph for the new wave formed by combining Waves B and D.

2. Draw a graph representing the combination of Waves C and D.

3. Draw a graph representing the combination of Waves A and C.

4. Draw graphs for two waves of your choice. Show the new wave formed by combining the two.

Activity 17·2

On The Internet

Doing the Wave

When an earthquake occurs, the waves of energy are recorded at points all over the world by instruments called seismographs. By comparing the data that they collected from their seismographs, scientists discovered that the interior of Earth must be made of layers of different materials. How did the seismographs tell them that Earth is not the same medium all the way through?

Materials

- Coiled spring toy
- Stopwatch
  * clock with a second hand
- Meterstick
- Tape

  * Alternate Materials

Recognize the Problem

Can the speed of a wave be used to identify the medium through which it travels?

Form a Hypothesis

Think about what you know about the relationship between the frequency, wavelength, and speed of a wave in a medium. **Make a hypothesis** about how you can measure the speed of a wave within a medium and use that information to identify an unknown medium.

Goals

- **Measure** the speed of a wave within a coiled spring toy.
- **Predict** whether the speed you measured will be different in other types of coiled spring toys.

Data Sources

Go to the Glencoe Science Web Site at **www.glencoe.com/sec/ science/nc** for more information, hints, and data collected by other students.

Wave Data						
Trial	Length spring was stretched (m)	Number of crests	Wavelength (m)	Number of vibrations timed	Number of seconds vibrations were timed (s)	Wave speed (m/s)
1						
2						
3						

Test Your Hypothesis

Plan 👓

1. **Make a data table** in your Science Journal like the one shown.

2. **Write** a detailed description of the coiled spring toy you are going to use. Be sure to include its mass and diameter, the width of a coil, and what it is made of.

3. **Decide as a group** how you will **measure** the frequency and length of waves in the spring toy. What are your variables? Which variables must be controlled? What variable do you want to measure?

4. Repeat your experiment three times.

Do

1. Make sure your teacher approves your plan before you begin.

2. Carry out the experiment as you have planned.

3. While you are doing the experiment, **record** your observations and measurements in your data table.

Analyze Your Data

1. **Calculate** the frequency of the waves by dividing the number of vibrations you timed by the number of seconds you timed them. Record your results in your data table.

2. Use the following formula to **calculate** the speed of a wave in each trial.

   wavelength $\times$ wave frequency = wave speed

3. **Average** the wave speeds from your trials to determine the speed of a wave in your coiled spring toy.

Draw Conclusions

1. **Post** the description of your coiled spring toy and your results on the Glencoe Science Web Site.

2. **Compare and contrast** your results with the results of other students.

3. How does the type of coiled spring toy and the length it was stretched affect the wave speed? Was your hypothesis supported?

4. Would it make a difference if an earthquake wave were transmitted through Earth's solid mantle or the molten outer core?

For a **preview** of this chapter, study this Reviewing Main Ideas before you read the chapter. After you have studied this chapter, you can use the Reviewing Main Ideas to **review** the chapter.

The Glencoe MindJogger, Audiocassettes, and CD-ROM provide additional opportunities for review.

Section
17-1 WAVES CARRY ENERGY

Waves are rhythmic disturbances that carry energy but not matter. **Mechanical waves** can travel only through matter. Other waves, called **electromagnetic waves,** can travel through space. *What kind of waves carry the sun's energy to Earth? An earthquake's energy through Earth?*

TRANSVERSE AND COMPRESSIONAL WAVES

In a mechanical **transverse wave,** matter in the medium the wave travels through moves back and forth at right angles to the direction the wave travels. In a **compressional wave,** matter in the medium moves forward and backward in the same direction as the wave. *Why doesn't a sound wave travel through space?*

Section
17-2 AMPLITUDE, FREQUENCY, AND WAVELENGTH

Waves can be described by their characteristics. The **amplitude** of a transverse wave is one half the distance between a crest and a trough. **Wavelength** is the distance between a point on one wave and an identical point on the next wave. The **frequency** of a wave is the number of waves that pass a given point in 1 s. *How is the amplitude of a wave related to the amount of energy it carries?*

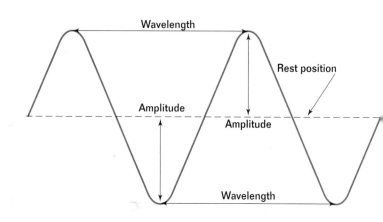

Reading Check ✔

Construct a chart that compares and contrasts reflection, refraction, diffraction, and interference.

Section 17-3 REFLECTION

Reflection occurs when a wave strikes an object or surface and bounces off. You can see your image in a mirror because of reflection. *How does wave reflection explain echoes in a large canyon?*

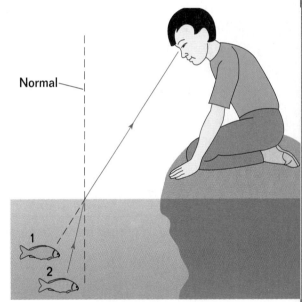

Normal

REFRACTION

The bending of a wave as it moves from one medium into another is called **refraction.** A wave changes direction, or refracts, when its speed changes. *In what situation does a wave not change its direction when it passes from one medium into another?*

DIFFRACTION AND INTERFERENCE

The bending of waves around a barrier is called **diffraction.** The ability of two or more waves to combine and form a new wave when they overlap is called **interference.** *What kind of interference produces waves with the largest amplitudes?*

Chapter 17 Assessment

Using Vocabulary

a. amplitude
b. compressional wave
c. diffraction
d. electromagnetic wave
e. frequency
f. interference
g. mechanical wave
h. reflection
i. refraction
j. transverse wave
k. wave
l. wavelength

Using the list above, replace the underlined words with the correct Vocabulary words.

1. <u>Diffraction</u> is the change in direction of a wave.
2. The type of wave that has rarefactions is a <u>transverse wave</u>.
3. The distance between two adjacent crests of a transverse wave is the <u>frequency</u>.
4. The greater the <u>wavelength</u> of a wave, the more energy the wave carries.
5. A <u>mechanical wave</u> can travel through space.

Checking Concepts

Choose the word or phrase that best answers the question.

6. What is the material through which mechanical waves travel?
   A) charged particles
   B) space
   C) a vacuum
   D) a medium
7. What is carried from particle to particle in a water wave?
   A) speed   C) energy
   B) amplitude D) matter
8. What are the lowest points on a transverse wave called?
   A) crests   C) compressions
   B) troughs   D) rarefactions

9. What determines the pitch of a sound wave?
   A) amplitude   C) speed
   B) frequency   D) refraction
10. What is the distance between adjacent wave compressions?
    A) one wavelength C) 1 m/s
    B) 1 km   D) 1 Hz
11. What occurs when a wave strikes an object or surface and bounces off?
    A) diffraction   C) a change in speed
    B) refraction   D) reflection
12. What is the name for a change in the direction of a wave when it passes from one medium into another?
    A) refraction   C) reflection
    B) interference D) diffraction
13. What type of wave is a sound wave?
    A) transverse
    B) electromagnetic
    C) compressional
    D) refracted
14. When two waves overlap and interfere destructively, what does the resulting wave have?
    A) a greater amplitude
    B) more energy
    C) a change in frequency
    D) a lower amplitude
15. What is the difference between blue light and green light?
    A) They have different wavelengths.
    B) One is a transverse wave and the other is not.
    C) They travel at different speeds.
    D) One is mechanical and the other is not.

Thinking Critically

16. Explain what kind of wave, transverse or compressional, is produced when an engine bumps into a string of coupled railroad cars on a track.

17. Is it possible for an electromagnetic wave to travel through a vacuum? Through matter? Explain your answers.
18. Why does the frequency of a wave decrease as the wavelength increases?
19. Why don't you see your reflected image when you look at a white, rough surface?
20. If a cannon fires at a great distance from you, why do you see the flash before you hear the sound?

Developing Skills

If you need help, refer to the **Skill Handbook**.

21. **Using Numbers:** A microwave travels at the speed of light and has a wavelength of 0.022 m. What is its frequency?
22. **Forming a Hypothesis:** Form a hypothesis that can explain this observation. Waves A and B travel away from Earth through Earth's atmosphere. Wave A continues on into space, but wave B does not.
23. **Recognizing Cause and Effect:** Explain how the object shown below causes compressions and rarefactions as it vibrates in air.

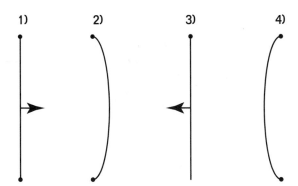

24. **Comparing and Contrasting:** AM radio waves have wavelengths between about 200 m and 600 m, while FM radio waves have wavelengths of about 3 m. Why can AM radio signals often be heard behind buildings and mountains while FM radio signals cannot?

THE PRINCETON REVIEW

Test-Taking Tip

Don't Cram If you don't know the material by the week before the test, you're less likely to do well. Set up a time line for your practice and preparation so that you're not rushed. Then, you will have time to deal with any problem areas.

Test Practice

Use these questions to test your Science Proficiency.

1. Two sounds have the same pitch, but one is louder than the other. What is different about the two sounds?
   A) their amplitudes
   B) their frequencies
   C) their wavelengths
   D) their speeds

2. What produces the colors seen when light reflects from CDs?
   A) wavelength
   B) interference
   C) refraction
   D) compression

3. The speed of a light ray increases as it passes at an angle from one medium into another. What happens to the ray?
   A) Its direction does not change.
   B) It travels along the normal.
   C) It bends toward the normal.
   D) It bends away from the normal.

4. What kind of waves requires a medium?
   A) all transverse waves
   B) only some compressional waves
   C) all electromagnetic waves
   D) all mechanical waves

Chapter Preview

Section 18-1
Properties of Light

Section 18-2
Reflection and Mirrors

Section 18-3
Refraction and Lenses

Section 18-4
Microscopes, Telescopes, and Cameras

Skills Preview

Skill Builders
- Form a Hypothésis
- Compare and Contrast

Activities
- Observe and Infer
- Use Scientific Methods

MiniLabs
- Observe and Infer
- Form a Hypothesis

Reading Check ✔

As you read this chapter, list vocabulary terms that are also used in other subject areas, such as *medium* and *frequency*. Explain the meaning of these terms.

Explore Activity

What do you see when you look around you? Everything you see results from light waves that enter your eye. These light waves are emitted by objects like the sun or light-bulbs and are reflected by objects such as trees, books, people, and furniture. Laser beams like the ones shown here are also made of light waves. Lenses and mirrors can cause light waves to change direction and make objects seem larger or smaller. What happens to light as it passes from one material to another?

Observe Light Bending

1. Place two paper cups next to each other and put a penny in the bottom of each cup.

2. Stand so you can look straight down into both cups.

3. Fill one of the cups with water and observe what happens to the penny in that cup.

4. Slide the cup with no water away from you just until you can no longer see the penny.

5. Have your partner pour water into this cup and observe what seems to happen to the penny.

Science Journal

In your Science Journal, record your observations. Did adding water make the cup look deeper or shallower?

18·1 Properties of Light

What is light?

Have you ever dropped a rock on the smooth surface of a pond and watched the ripples spread outward, as shown in **Figure 18-1?** You produced a wave. The wave was all the ripples made by the rock striking the water. The impact of the rock added energy to the water. As the ripples spread out, they carried some of that energy.

Light also carries energy. A source of light like the sun or a lightbulb gives off light waves, just as the rock hitting the pond caused ripples to spread out from the point of impact. The ripples spread out only on the surface of the pond, but light waves spread out in all directions from the light source as shown in **Figure 18-2.**

Sometimes, it is easier to talk about just one narrow beam of light traveling in a straight line, which is called a **light ray.** You can think of a source of light as emitting light rays that are traveling away from the source in all directions.

However, light waves are different from ripples on a pond. If the pond dried up and there was no water, there could be no ripples. Waves on a pond need a material in which to travel—water. Any material in which a wave travels is called a **medium.** Light is a special type of wave called an electromagnetic wave. An **electromagnetic wave** is a wave that does not need a medium in which to travel. Electromagnetic waves can travel in a vacuum, as well as in materials such as air, water, and glass.

What You'll Learn

► The wave nature of light
► How light interacts with materials
► Why objects appear colored

Vocabulary
light ray
medium
electromagnetic wave
reflection
wavelength
frequency

Why It's Important

► Most of what you know about your surroundings comes from information carried by light waves.

Figure 18-1 Ripples on the surface of a pond are produced by an object hitting the water. As the ripples spread out from the point of impact, they carry energy.

Figure 18-2 A source of light, such as a lightbulb, emits light rays in all directions. **Why does a flashlight emit only a narrow beam of light?**

Light and Matter

Have you ever been in a closed room with no windows? You can see nothing until you turn on a light or open a door and let in light from outside. Unlike a candle flame, a lightbulb, or the sun, most objects do not give off light on their own. These objects can be seen only if light waves from another source bounce off the object and into your eyes, as shown in **Figure 18-3.** The process of light striking an object and bouncing off is called **reflection.** Right now, you can see these words because light is reflecting from the page and into your eyes. ☑

Reading Check ☑

What must happen for you to see an object?

Figure 18-3 Light waves are given off by the lightbulb. Some of these light waves hit the page and are reflected. The student sees the page when some of these reflected waves enter the student's eyes.

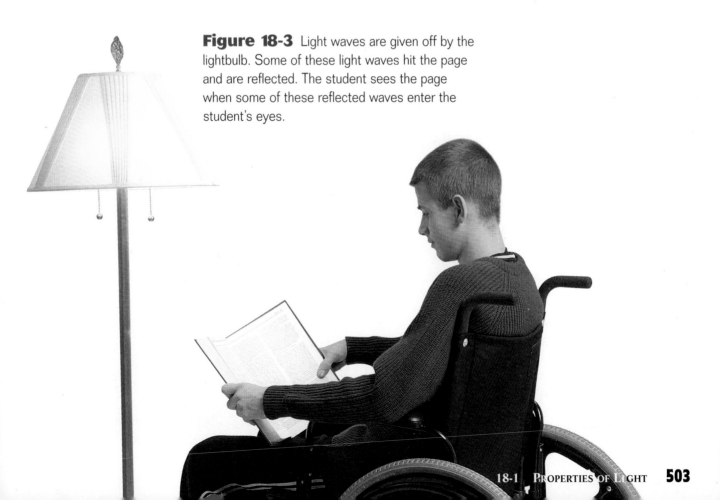

A An opaque object allows no light to pass through it.

B A translucent object allows some light to pass through it.

C A transparent object allows almost all light to pass through it.

Figure 18-4 Materials are opaque, translucent, or transparent depending on how much light passes through them.

Opaque, Translucent, and Transparent

When light waves strike an object, some of the light can be absorbed by the object, some of the light is reflected, and some of the light may pass through the object. How much light is absorbed, reflected, and passes through the object depends on what the object is made of.

Materials that let no light pass through them are *opaque* (oh PAYK). You cannot see other objects through opaque objects. Materials, such as glass, that allow nearly all the light to pass through are *transparent*. You can clearly see other objects through transparent materials. Other materials allow only some light to pass through so objects behind them cannot be seen clearly. These materials, such as waxed paper or frosted glass, are *translucent* (trans LEW sent). Examples of opaque, translucent, and transparent objects are shown in **Figure 18-4.**

Figure 18-5 Like all waves, ripples on a water surface have a wavelength.

A The wavelength is the distance between ripples.

B A cross section of the water surface is shown. The energy added by the impact of the rock causes water to pile up at each ripple.

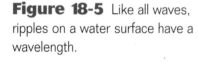
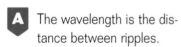
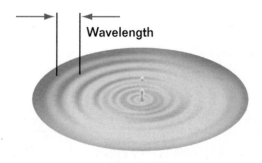

Wavelength

Wavelength

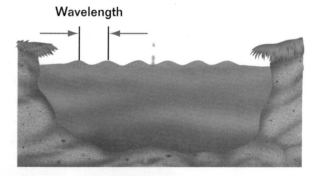

The Electromagnetic Spectrum

Light waves, like all waves, have a property called wavelength. Look at **Figure 18-5.** For ripples on a pond, the **wavelength** is the distance between the tops of two adjacent ripples. The number of wavelengths that pass a point in one second is the **frequency** of the wave. For waves that travel at the same speed, frequency and wavelength are related. As the wavelength decreases, the frequency increases.

The electromagnetic waves you see as light are part of the electromagnetic spectrum. **Figure 18-6** shows how electromagnetic waves are classified according to their wavelengths. All electromagnetic waves travel with a speed of about 300 million m/s in a vacuum. Electromagnetic waves also carry energy, just like the ripples in the pond. The energy carried by an electromagnetic wave increases as the wavelength decreases and the frequency increases.

Of all the electromagnetic waves, radio waves carry the least energy. They have wavelengths longer than about 1 cm. Television signals, as well as AM and FM radio signals, are types of radio waves. You can't see these waves with your eyes, nor can you sense them in any other way, but they are being absorbed, reflected, and transmitted by your body even as you read this! The highest-energy radio waves are called microwaves.

EARTH SCIENCE
INTEGRATION

Earth's Ozone Layer
Ozone is formed high in Earth's atmosphere by sunlight striking oxygen molecules. However, chemical compounds called CFCs, which are used in air conditioners and refrigerators, can remove ozone from the ozone layer. To prevent this, the use of CFCs is being phased out. Visit the Glencoe Science Web Site at www.glencoe.com/sec/science/nc for more information about the effects of CFCs on the ozone layer.

Figure 18-6 Electromagnetic waves are classified according to their wavelengths and frequencies. Visible light is only a small section of the electromagnetic spectrum.

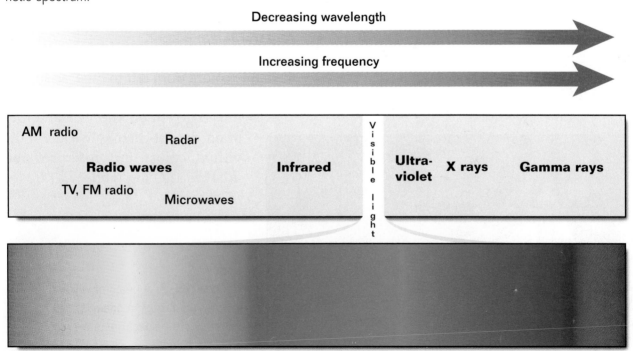

Decreasing wavelength

Increasing frequency

AM radio

Radar

Radio waves   Infrared   Visible light   Ultra-violet   X rays   Gamma rays

TV, FM radio

Microwaves

Mini Lab

Viewing Colors Through Color Filters

Procedure

1. Obtain sheets of red, green, and blue construction paper.
2. Obtain a piece of red cellophane and green cellophane.
3. Look at each sheet of paper through the red cellophane and record the color of each sheet.
4. Look at each sheet of colored paper through the green cellophane and record the color of each sheet.
5. Hold both pieces of cellophane together and look at each sheet of colored paper. Record the color of each sheet.

Analyze

Explain why the sheets of paper changed color when you looked at them through the pieces of cellophane.

Electromagnetic waves with wavelengths less than radio waves, but greater than visible light, are called infrared waves. You can't see these waves either, but they are emitted by the sun and make your skin feel warm.

The sun also emits ultraviolet waves that carry enough energy to damage living cells. Earth's atmosphere contains a layer of a compound called ozone that blocks most of the sun's ultraviolet waves from reaching Earth's surface. Still, exposure to those ultraviolet waves that do get through can cause sunburn. Exposure to these waves over a long period of time can lead to early aging of the skin and possibly skin cancer.

Visible light is the narrow range of the electromagnetic spectrum that we can detect with our eyes. What we see as different colors are electromagnetic waves of different wavelengths. Red light has the longest wavelength (lowest frequency), and blue light has the shortest wavelength (highest frequency).

Color

Why does grass look green or a rose look red? The answer has to do with the way objects absorb and reflect light. The light from the sun or a lightbulb may look white, but it is actually a mixture of light waves of all visible colors from red to blue, as shown in **Figure 18-7.** When all these colors are mixed together, the eye and the brain do not distinguish the individual colors but interpret the mixture as being white.

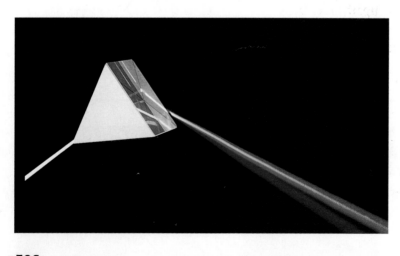

Figure 18-7 A beam of white light passing through a prism is separated into a spectrum of all the visible colors.

Figure 18-8

A Examine the pair of gym shoes and socks as seen under white light. **Why do the socks appear blue under white light?**

B The same shoes and socks were photographed through a red filter. **Why do the blue socks appear black when viewed under red light?**

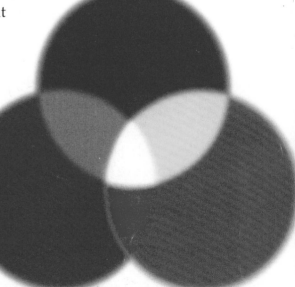

When this mixture of waves strikes an object that is not transparent, the object absorbs some of the light energy. Some of the light waves that are not absorbed are reflected. If the object reflects the red waves and absorbs all the others, the object appears red. Similarly, objects that look blue reflect only the blue waves. Some objects reflect all the colors in the visible spectrum. These objects appear white, while objects that absorb all visible light appear black. **Figure 18-8** shows gym shoes and socks as seen under white light and as seen when viewed through a red filter, which allows only red light to pass through.

The Primary Colors

How many colors are there? Often, the visible spectrum is said to be made up of red, orange, yellow, green, blue, indigo, and violet light. But, this is usually done for convenience. In reality, humans can distinguish thousands of colors, including many such as brown, pink, and purple that are not found in the spectrum.

Light of almost any color can be made by mixing different amounts of red light, green light, and blue light. Red, green, and blue are called the primary colors. Look at **Figure 18-9.** White light is produced where beams of red, green, and blue light overlap. Yellow light is produced where red and green light overlap. However, even though the light looks yellow, it still consists of light waves of two different wavelengths. You see the color yellow because of the way your brain interprets the combination of the red and green light striking your eye.

Figure 18-9 By mixing together light from the three primary colors—red, blue, and green—all the visible colors can be made.

Color Pigments

If you have ever painted a picture, you may have mixed together paints of different colors to make a new color. Materials like paint that are used to change the color of other objects, like the walls of a room or an artist's canvas, are called *pigments*. If you've ever tried mixing red and green paint together, you've probably realized that mixing piments forms colors in a different way than mixing colored lights.

Like all colored materials, pigments absorb some colors and reflect others. When you mix pigments, the colors that reach your eye are the colors that are not absorbed by the mixture. The primary pigment colors are not red, blue, and green, but instead are yellow, magenta, and cyan. You can make any colored pigment by mixing different amounts of these primary pigment colors, as shown in **Figure 18-10.**

The primary pigment colors are related to the primary light colors. A yellow pigment absorbs blue light and reflects red and green. A magenta pigment absorbs green light and reflects red and blue. A cyan pigment absorbs red light and reflects blue and green. Thus each of the primary pigment colors is white light with one of the primary light colors removed.

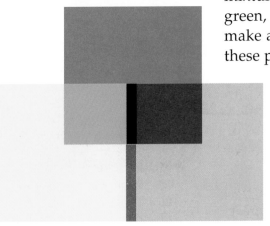

Figure 18-10 The three primary color pigments—yellow, magenta, and cyan—can form all the visible colors when mixed together in various amounts.

Section Assessment

1. Which has a higher frequency, red light or blue light?
2. What is the difference between an opaque object and a transparent object?
3. What colors are reflected by an object that appears black? Explain.
4. **Think Critically:** Why is it cooler to wear light-colored clothes on a hot day than dark clothes?
5. **Skill Builder**
   Observing and Inferring A white plastic bowl and a black plastic bowl have been sitting in sunlight. You observe that the black bowl feels warmer than the white bowl. From this information, infer which bowl absorbs and which bowl reflects more sunlight. If you need help, refer to Observing and Inferring in the **Skill Handbook** on page 556.

Science Journal Read an article about the greenhouse effect and draw a diagram in your Science Journal explaining how the greenhouse effect works.

Reflection and Mirrors

The Law of Reflection

Have you ever noticed your image in a pool or lake? If the surface of the water is smooth, you can see your image clearly. If the surface is wavy, your image seems to be distorted. The image you see is the result of light reflecting from the surface and traveling to your eye.

When a light ray strikes a surface and is reflected, the reflected ray obeys the law of reflection. **Figure 18-11** shows a light ray striking a surface and being reflected. Imagine a line drawn perpendicular to the surface where the light ray strikes the surface. This line is called the normal to the surface. The incoming ray and the normal form an angle called the angle of incidence. The reflected light ray also forms an angle with the normal called the angle of reflection. The **law of reflection** states that the angle of incidence is equal to the angle of reflection. This is true for any surface, no matter what material it is made of.

Reflection from Surfaces

Why can you see your reflection in some surfaces such as mirrors, and not see any reflection from a surface such as a piece of paper? The answer is related to difference in smoothness of the two surfaces.

What You'll Learn

► How light is reflected from rough and smooth surfaces
► How a plane mirror forms an image
► How concave and convex mirrors form an image

Vocabulary
law of reflection
focal point
focal length

Why It's Important

► Mirrors can change the direction of light waves and enable you to see images, such as your own face, that normally would not be in view.

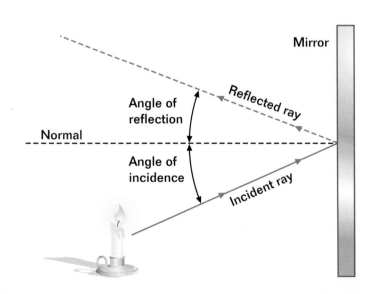

Figure 18-11 A light ray strikes a surface and is reflected. The angle of incidence is always equal to the angle of reflection. This is the law of reflection.

Figure 18-12 A highly magnified view of the surface of a paper towel shows that the surface is made of many cellulose wood fibers that make it rough and uneven.

Magnification: 35×

The surface of the paper is not as smooth as the surface of a mirror. Even though the paper may look smooth, **Figure 18-12** shows that under a microscope, its surface looks rough. The uneven surface of the paper causes light rays to be reflected in many directions as shown in **Figure 18-13.** The reflection of light waves from a rough surface is diffuse reflection. The mirrorlike reflection from a smooth surface that produces a sharp image of an object is called regular reflection. ✔

A piece of foil is smooth enough to act like a mirror and produce a regular reflection. If you crumple the foil, its surface no longer acts like one mirror. Now it acts like many tiny mirrors. Each of these tiny mirrors produces a regular reflection, but the reflections go in many different directions.

Reading Check ✔

Why does a rough surface cause a diffuse reflection?

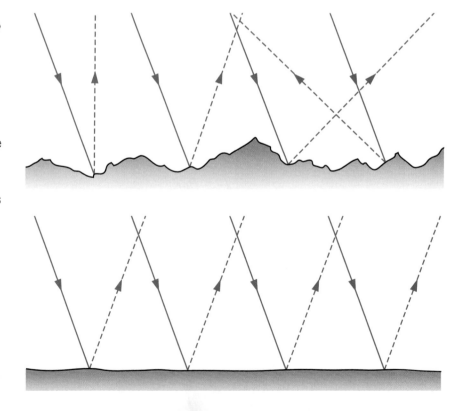

Figure 18-13 A rough surface (A) causes parallel light rays to be reflected in many different directions. A smooth surface (B) causes parallel light rays to be reflected in a single direction.

Reflection by Plane Mirrors

Did you glance in the mirror before leaving for school this morning? If you did, you probably saw your reflection in a plane mirror. A plane mirror is a mirror with a flat reflecting surface. The mirror produced an image of you that seemed to be coming from behind the mirror. The image in the mirror also had your left and right sides reversed. How was that image formed?

Figure 18-14A shows a person looking into a plane mirror. Light waves from the sun or a source of artificial light strike each part of the person. These light rays bounce off the person according to the law of reflection, and some of these rays strike the mirror. The rays that strike the mirror also are reflected according to the law of reflection. **Figure 18-14A** shows the path traveled by some of the rays that have bounced off the person and have been reflected by the mirror into the person's eye.

Why does the image seem to be behind the mirror? Your brain processes the light rays that enter your eyes and creates the sensation of seeing. Your brain interprets the light rays that have bounced off the mirror as having followed the path shown by the dashed lines in **Figure 18-14B.** The resulting image looks as though it is behind the mirror, even though there is nothing there. The image appears to be the same distance behind the mirror as the person is in front of the mirror.

Figure 18-14 A plane mirror forms an image by changing the direction of light rays.

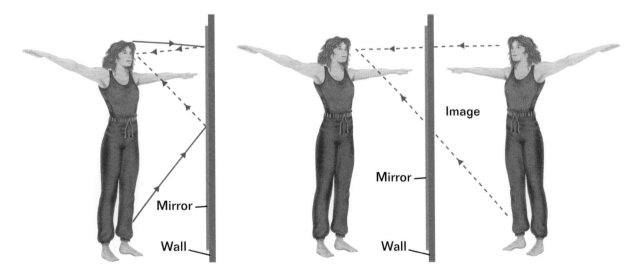

A Light rays that bounce off a person strike the mirror. Some of these light rays are reflected into the person's eye. As examples, the figure shows a light ray from the person's head and a ray from the leg.

B The light rays shown entering the person's eye in **Figure 18-14A** seem to be coming from a person behind the mirror.

Concave and Convex Mirrors

Some mirrors are not flat. A concave mirror has a surface that is curved inward, like the inside of a spoon. Unlike plane mirrors, concave mirrors cause light rays to come together, or converge. This difference causes the two types of mirrors to form different types of images.

A straight line drawn perpendicular to the center of a concave or convex mirror is called the optical axis. Look at **Figure 18-15A.** For a concave mirror, light rays that travel parallel to the optical axis and strike the mirror are reflected so that they pass through a single point on the optical axis called the **focal point.** The distance along the optical axis from the center of the mirror to the focal point is called the **focal length.**

VISUALIZING
Images Formed by Concave Mirrors

Figure 18-15 The image formed by a concave mirror depends on the location of the object.

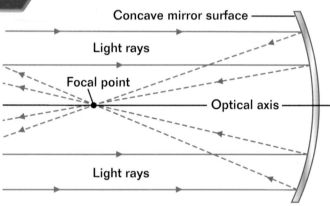

A A concave mirror reflects all light rays traveling parallel to the optical axis so that they pass through the focal point.

B If the object is farther from the mirror than the focal length, the mirror forms an image that is inverted.

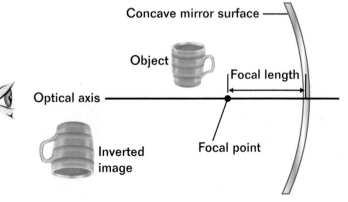

C This photograph shows the image formed by a concave mirror when the object is more than one focal length from the mirror.

The image formed by a concave mirror depends on the position of the object relative to the focal point of the mirror. **Figure 18-15B** shows how the image is formed if the object is farther from the mirror than the focal point, and **Figure 18-15C** is a photograph of such an image. The image is upside down, or inverted, and the size of the image decreases as the object is moved farther away from the mirror.

Light rays from an object placed at the focal point strike the mirror and are reflected so they travel parallel to the optical axis. If a light source is placed at the focal point, a beam of light will be produced. For example, in a flashlight the bulb is placed at the focal point of a concave reflector.

However, if the object is closer to the mirror than the focal point, **Figures 18-15D** and **18-15E** show that the image formed is upright. The image gets larger as the object moves closer to the mirror.

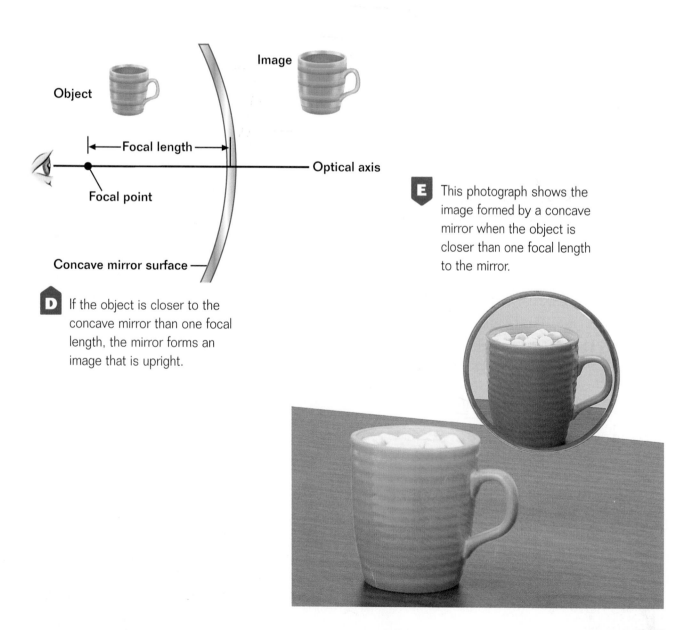

Object

Image

Focal length

Optical axis

Focal point

Concave mirror surface

D If the object is closer to the concave mirror than one focal length, the mirror forms an image that is upright.

E This photograph shows the image formed by a concave mirror when the object is closer than one focal length to the mirror.

Figure 18-16 A convex mirror forms an image.

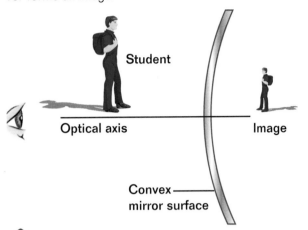

Student

Optical axis

Image

Convex mirror surface

A No matter how far the object is from a convex mirror, the image is always upright and smaller than the object.

B A convex mirror causes incoming light rays that are traveling parallel to the optical axis to spread apart after they are reflected.

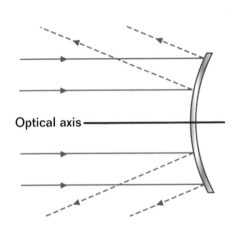

Optical axis

A convex mirror has surface that curves outward, like the outside of a spoon. **Figure 18-16A** shows how a convex mirror causes light rays to spread apart, or diverge. **Figure 18-16B** shows that the image formed by a convex mirror seems to be behind the mirror, like the image formed by a plane mirror. Like a plane mirror, the image formed by a convex mirror is always upright. But unlike a plane mirror, the image formed by a convex mirror is always smaller than the object.

Convex mirrors are used as security mirrors mounted above the aisles in stores and as outside rearview mirrors on cars and trucks. When used in this way on cars and trucks, objects seem smaller and farther away than they really are. As a result, these mirrors sometimes carry a warning that objects viewed in the mirror are closer than they seem.

Section Assessment

1. As you walk toward a large, vertical plane mirror, describe what happens to your image.

2. If the surface of a concave mirror is made more curved, what happens to its focal length?

3. **Think Critically:** The surface of a car is covered with dust and looks dull. After the car is washed and waxed, you can see your image reflected in the car's surface. Explain.

4. **Skill Builder**
   Forming a Hypothesis When you look at a window at night, you can sometimes see two images of yourself. Make a hypothesis to explain why two images are seen. If you need help, refer to Forming a Hypothesis in the **Skill Handbook** on page 558.

Using Computers

Spreadsheet Design a table using spreadsheet software to compare the images formed by plane, concave, and convex mirrors. Include in your table how the images depend on the distance of the object from the mirror. If you need help, refer to page 574.

Reflection from a Plane Mirror

Materials
- Flashlight
- Small plane mirror, at least 10 cm on a side
- Protractor
- Metric ruler
- Scissors
- Black construction paper
- Tape
- Modeling clay

A light ray strikes the surface of a plane mirror and is reflected. Is there a relationship between the direction of the incoming light ray and the direction of the reflected light ray?

What You'll Investigate
How does the angle of incidence compare with the angle of reflection for a plane mirror?

Goals
- **Measure** the angle of incidence and the angle of reflection for a light ray incident on a plane mirror.

Procedure

1. With the scissors, **cut** a slit in the construction paper and **tape** it over the flashlight lens. Make sure the slit is centered on the lens.

2. **Place** the mirror at one end of the unlined paper. Push the mirror into the lump of clay so it stands vertically, and tilt the mirror so it leans slightly toward the table.

3. **Measure** with the ruler to find the center of the bottom edge of the mirror and mark it. Then, use the protractor and the ruler to **draw** a line on the paper perpendicular to the mirror from the mark. Label this line P.

4. Using the protractor and the ruler, **draw** lines on the paper outward from the mark at the center of the mirror at angles of 30°, 45°, and 60° to line P.

5. Turn on the flashlight and place it so the beam is along the 60° line. This is the angle of incidence. **Locate** the reflected beam on the paper, and **measure** the angle the reflected beam makes with line P. **Record** this angle in your data table. This is the angle of reflection. If you cannot see the reflected beam, slightly increase the tilt of the mirror.

6. Repeat step 5 for the 30°, 45°, and P lines.

Conclude and Apply

1. What happened to the beam of light when it was shined along line P?

2. What can you **infer** about the relationship between the angle of incidence and the angle of reflection?

18·3 Refraction and Lenses

What You'll Learn

▶ Why light rays refract
▶ How convex and concave lenses form images

Vocabulary
refraction   convex lens
lens   concave lens

Why It's Important

▶ Many of the images you see every day in photographs, on TV, and in movies are made by using lenses.

Refraction

If you have ever looked at a glass of water that had a pencil in it, you may have noticed that the pencil appeared bent, as in **Figure 18-17.** You may have noticed in the Explore Activity that the penny under water seemed closer than the other penny. These images are due to the bending of light rays as they pass from one material to another. What causes light rays to change direction?

The Speeds of Light

The speed of light in empty space is about 300 million m/s. Light passing through a medium such as air, water, or glass travels slower than the speed of light in empty space. This is because the atoms that make up the medium interact with the light wave and slow it down. **Figure 18-18** shows how slowly light moves in some materials.

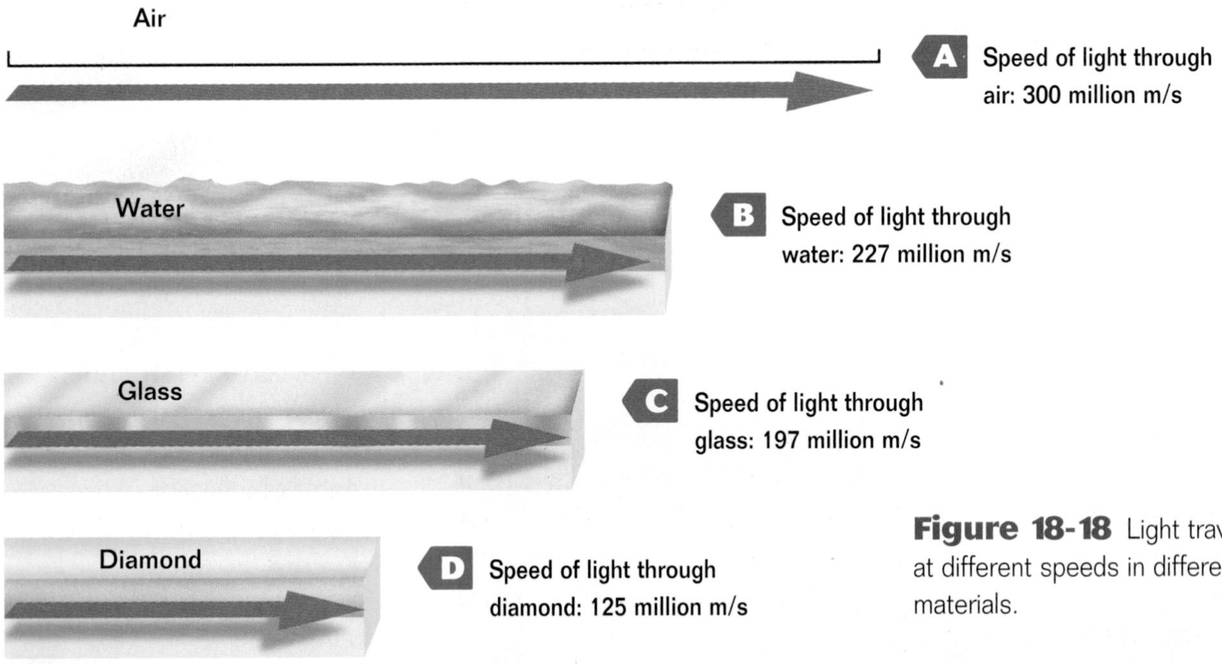

Figure 18-17 A pencil in a glass of water looks as if it has been broken at the water line.

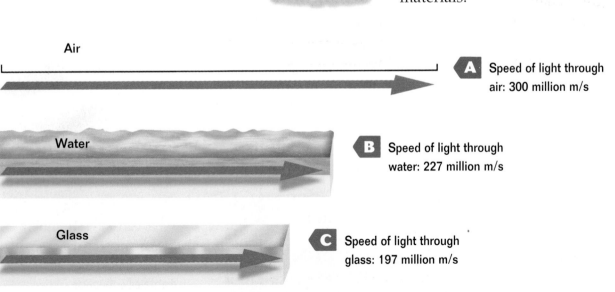

A Speed of light through air: 300 million m/s

B Speed of light through water: 227 million m/s

C Speed of light through glass: 197 million m/s

D Speed of light through diamond: 125 million m/s

Figure 18-18 Light travels at different speeds in different materials.

Figure 18-19 A light ray is bent as it travels from air into glass. **In which medium does light travel more slowly?**

The Refraction of Light Waves

What happens when light waves travel from air into water where the speed of light is different? If the wave is traveling at an angle to the boundary between two materials, it changes direction. The bending of a light wave due to a change in speed when the wave moves from one medium to another is called **refraction. Figure 18-19** shows an example of refraction. The larger the change in speed, the more the light wave is refracted. ☑

Why does a change in speed cause the light wave to bend? Imagine a set of wheels on a car that travels from pavement to mud. The wheel that enters the mud first is slowed, while the other wheel continues at the original speed. This causes the wheel axle to turn as shown in **Figure 18-20,** and the wheels change direction.

Light behaves in a similar manner. Imagine again a light wave traveling from air into water. The first part of the wave to enter the water is slowed, just as the wheel that first hits the mud is slowed. Then, the rest of the wave is slowed down as it enters the water so the whole wave is turned, just like the axle.

Reading Check

What causes light to bend?

Convex and Concave Lenses

Do you like snapping pictures of your friends and family with a camera? Have you ever watched a bird through binoculars or peered at something tiny through a magnifying glass? All of these involve the use of lenses. A **lens** is a transparent object with at least one curved side that causes light to bend. The amount of bending can be controlled by making the sides more or less curved. The more curved the sides, the more a ray of light entering the lens is bent.

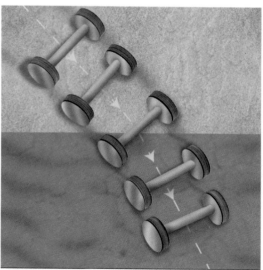

Figure 18-20 An axle turns as the wheels cross the boundary between pavement and mud. **How would the axle turn if the wheels were going from mud to pavement?**

Convex Lenses

A lens that is thicker in the center than at the edges is a **convex lens.** Convex lenses are also called converging lenses. Light rays traveling parallel to the optical axis are bent so they meet at the focal point, as shown in **Figure 18-21A.** If the surface is highly curved, the focal point is close to the lens and the focal length is short.

The image formed by a convex lens is similar to the image formed by a concave mirror. For both, the type of image depends on how far the object is from the focal point. Look at **Figure 18-21B.** If the object is farther than two focal lengths from the lens, the image is inverted and smaller than the object.

If the object is closer to the lens than one focal length, then the rays coming from points on the object diverge after passing through the lens, as shown in **Figure 18-21C.** The image formed is right-side up and larger than the object. Have you ever

Figure 18-21 A convex lens forms an image that depends on the distance from the object to the lens.

A Light rays parallel to the optical axis are bent so that they pass through the focal point.

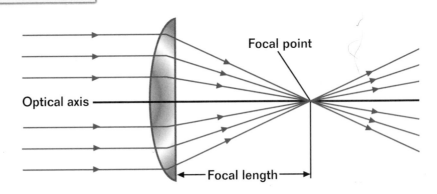

C If the object is closer to the lens than one focal length, the image formed is enlarged and upright.

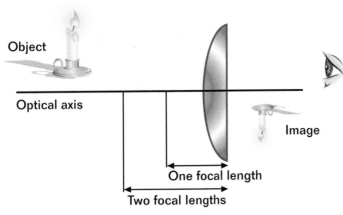

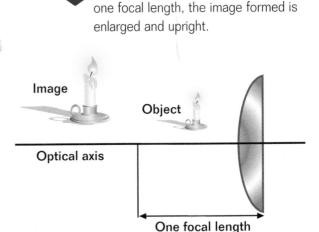

B If the object is far from the lens, the image formed is smaller than the object and inverted.

used a magnifying glass? The image formed was right-side up and larger than the object. The image continues to get larger as the magnifying glass is brought closer to the object.

Concave Lens

A lens that is thicker at the edges than in the middle is a **concave lens.** A concave lens is also called a diverging lens. **Figure 18-22** shows how light rays traveling parallel to the optical axis are bent after passing through a concave lens.

A concave lens causes light rays to diverge, and the light rays are not brought to a focus. The type of image formed by a concave lens is similar to that formed by a convex mirror. The image is upright and smaller than the object. Concave lenses are used in eyeglasses to correct problems people sometimes have in seeing objects that are far away.

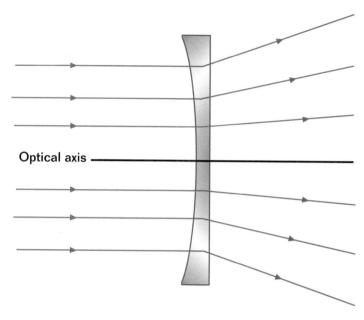

Optical axis

Figure 18-22 A concave lens causes light rays traveling parallel to the optical axis to diverge.

Section Assessment

1. How is the image formed by a concave lens similar to the image formed by a convex mirror?

2. To magnify an object, would you use a convex lens or a concave lens?

3. Describe two ways, using convex and concave lenses, to form an image that is smaller than the object.

4. **Think Critically:** A light wave is bent more as it travels from air to glass than in traveling from air to water. Is the speed of light greater in water or glass? Explain.

5. **Skill Builder**
   Predicting Air that is cool is more dense than air that is warm. Look at **Figure 18-18** and predict whether the speed of light is faster in warm air or cool air. If you need help, refer to Predicting in the **Skill Handbook** on page 566.

Skill Handbook on page 566.

Using Math

Earth is about 150 000 000 km from the sun. Use the formula *distance = speed × time* to calculate how many seconds it takes a beam of light to travel from Earth to the sun. About how many minutes does it take?

Materials

- Convex lens
- Modeling clay
- Meterstick
- Flashlight
- Masking tape
- Cardboard with white sur-face, about 20-cm square

Image Formation by a Convex Lens

The type of image formed by a convex lens, also called a converging lens, is related to the distance of the object from the lens. This distance is called the object distance. The location of the image is also related to the distance of the object from the lens. The distance from the lens to the image is called the image distance. What happens to the position of the image as the object gets nearer or farther from the lens?

What You'll Investigate

How are the image distance and object distance related for a convex lens?

Goals

- **Measure** the image distance as the object distance changes.
- **Observe** the type of image formed as the object distance changes.

Safety Precautions

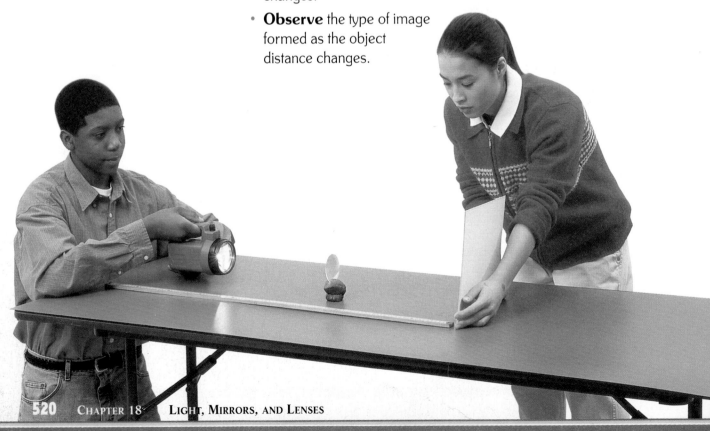

Procedure

1. **Design** a data table in which to record your data. You will need three columns in your table. One column will be for the object distance, another will be for the image distance, and the third will be for the type of image.

2. **Use** the modeling clay to make the lens stand vertically upright on the lab table.

3. **Form** the letter F on the glass surface of the flashlight with masking tape.

4. Turn on the flashlight and place it 1 m from the lens. **Position** the flashlight so the flashlight beam is shining through the lens.

5. **Record** the distance from the flashlight to the lens in the object distance column in your data table.

6. Hold the cardboard vertically upright on the other side of the lens, and move it back and forth

Convex Lens Data		
Object Distance	**Image Distance**	**Image Type**

until a sharp image of the letter F is obtained.

7. **Measure** the distance of the card from the lens using the meterstick, and **record** this distance in the image distance column in your data table.

8. **Record** in the third column of your data table whether the image is upright or inverted, and smaller or larger.

9. Repeat steps 6–9 for object distances of 50 cm and 25 cm.

Conclude and Apply

1. How did the image distance change as the object distance decreased?

2. How did the image change as the object distance decreased?

3. What would happen to the size of the image if the flashlight were much farther away than 1 m?

18·4 Microscopes, Telescopes, and Cameras

What You'll Learn

▶ How microscopes magnify objects
▶ How telescopes make distant objects visible
▶ How cameras work

Why It's Important

▶ Microscopes and telescopes are used to view parts of the universe that can't be seen with the eye alone. Cameras record images of the world around you.

Microscopes

Lenses have been used since the early 1600s to produce images of objects too small to be seen with the eye alone. Today, a compound microscope like the one in **Figure 18-23A** uses a combination of lenses to magnify objects by as much as 2500 times.

Figure 18-23B shows how a microscope forms an image. An object, such as a drop of water from a pond, is placed close to a convex lens called the objective lens. This lens produces an enlarged image inside the microscope tube. The light rays from that image then pass through a second convex lens called the eyepiece, or ocular, lens. This lens further magnifies the image formed by the objective lens. This results in a much larger image than a single lens can produce.

Figure 18-23 A compound microscope uses lenses to magnify objects.

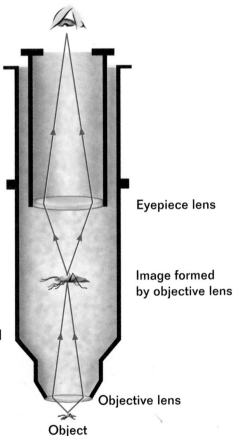

A A compound microscope often has more than one objective lens, each giving a different magnification. A light underneath the objective lens makes the image bright enough to see clearly.

B The objective lens in a compound microscope forms an enlarged image, which is then magnified by the eyepiece lens. **How would the image be affected if the eyepiece lens were a concave lens?**

Eyepiece lens

Image formed by objective lens

Objective lens

Object

Telescopes

While microscopes are used to magnify very small objects, telescopes are used to examine objects that may be quite large but are far away. The first telescopes also were invented in the early 1600s, at about the same time as the first microscopes. Much of what we know about the distant universe has come from images and other information gathered by telescopes.

Refracting Telescopes

The simplest refracting telescopes use two convex lenses to form an image of a distant object. Just as in a compound microscope, light passes through an objective lens that forms an image. That image is then magnified by an eyepiece lens, as shown in **Figure 18-24.**

An important difference between a telescope and a microscope is the size of the objective lens. More light from a faraway object can enter a large objective lens than a small one. This makes images appear brighter and more detailed when they are magnified by the eyepiece. Increasing the size of the objective lens makes it possible to see stars and galaxies that are too far away to see with a telescope that has a small objective lens. Thus, the main purpose of a telescope is not to magnify the image, but to gather as much light as possible from distant objects. In **Figure 18-25**, the largest refracting telescope ever made is shown. ☑

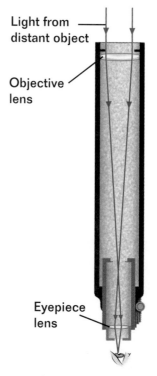

Figure 18-24 A refracting telescope is made from an objective lens and an eyepiece lens. The objective lens forms an image that is magnified by the eyepiece lens.

Reading Check ☑

How does a telescope objective lens enable distant objects to be seen?

Figure 18-25 The refracting telescope at the Yerkes Observatory in Wisconsin has the largest objective lens in the world. It has a diameter of 1 m.

Reflecting Telescopes

There are limits to how big a refracting telescope can be. One problem is that its objective lens can be supported only around its edges. If the lens is extremely large, it cannot be supported enough to keep it from sagging slightly under its own weight. This causes the image it forms to become distorted.

Reflecting telescopes can be made much larger than refracting telescopes. This is because they use a concave mirror instead of an objective lens to gather light from a distant object, as shown in **Figure 18-26B.** A small plane mirror called a secondary mirror is used to reflect the image toward the side of the telescope tube, where it is magnified by an eyepiece.

Because only the one reflecting surface on the mirror needs to be carefully made, telescope mirrors are less expensive to make than lenses of a similar size. Also, mirrors can be supported more rigidly on their back side so they can be made much larger without sagging under their own weight. The Keck Telescope in Hawaii is the largest reflecting telescope in the world with a mirror 10 m in diameter. **Figure 18-26A** shows another one of the largest telescopes in the world, the reflecting telescope at Mount Palomar in southern California.

Figure 18-26 Reflecting telescopes gather light by using a concave mirror.

A The Hale telescope at the Mount Palomar observatory in southern California has a concave mirror that is 5.1 m in diameter.

B Light entering the telescope tube is reflected by a concave mirror onto the secondary mirror. An eyepiece lens is used to magnify the image formed by the concave mirror. The secondary mirror in the largest telescopes usually reflects the rays through a hole in the concave mirror, instead of the side of the tube.

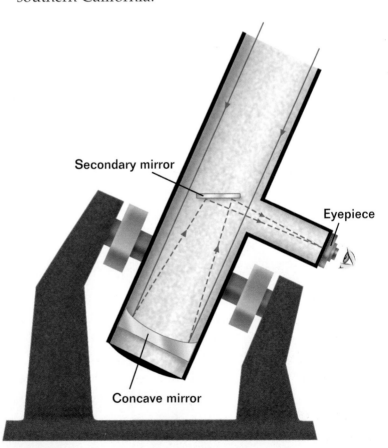

Secondary mirror

Eyepiece

Concave mirror

Cameras

You may have seen a number of photographs today in books, magazines, and newspapers. And, you may have used a camera yourself to take photographs. A typical camera has a convex lens that forms an image on a section of film. Remember that a convex lens forms an image that is reduced and inverted if the object is more than two focal lengths away. A camera lens is a convex lens used in this way. Look at the camera shown in **Figure 18-27.** When the shutter is open, the convex lens forms an image on a piece of film that is sensitive to light. The film contains chemicals that undergo chemical reactions when struck by light. This causes light areas and dark areas in the image to be recorded. If the film is sensitive to color, the colors of the object also are recorded.

An image that is too bright may overexpose the film. If there is too little light that reaches the film, the image may be too dark. To control the amount of light reaching the film, a camera also contains a device called the diaphragm.

Figure 18-27 A camera uses a convex lens to form an image on a piece of light-sensitive film. The image formed by a camera lens is smaller than the object. The amount of light striking the film is controlled by the diaphragm.

Problem Solving

Radio Telescopes

On a clear night, you may be able to see the visible light from hundreds of stars. But, stars and galaxies emit radio waves, as well as visible light. Unlike light waves, radio waves from space are not affected by turbulence in Earth's atmosphere. These radio waves can be detected even on cloudy or stormy nights when no stars can be seen. By studying these radio waves, scientists can learn about the birth and death of stars and galaxies.

Just as reflecting and refracting telescopes collect light from distant stars and galaxies, radio telescopes collect radio waves. The photograph shows the radio telescope at Green Banks, West Virginia. The collector of a radio telescope is usually called the *dish*, and the device supported above the center of the dish is the *detector*. The detector contains electronic instruments that help to amplify and record the radio waves.

Solve the Problem

1. Examine the photograph carefully. Is a radio telescope a reflecting telescope or a refracting telescope? Explain.

2. How are the position of the detector and the focal point of the radio telescope related?

Think Critically: Do you think the information gathered by radio telescopes could be improved if a radio telescope were placed into orbit above Earth's atmosphere? Why or why not?

The diaphragm is opened to let more light onto the film and closed to reduce the amount of light striking the film.

Camera Lenses

The image on the film depends on the camera lens used. Suppose you wished to photograph a friend. The size of your friend's image on the film depends on the focal length of the lens. The shorter the focal length, the smaller the image. To focus the image sharply, the lens must be moved closer to the film as the focal length is made smaller.

If you wanted the photograph to include your friend and the surrounding scenery, you would use a wide-angle lens. This lens has a short focal length and is positioned close to the film. If, instead, you wished to photograph only your friend's face, you might use a telephoto lens. This lens has a long focal length and must be positioned far from the film.

With a zoom lens, you can control the size of your friend's image in a photograph. The focal length of a zoom lens can be adjusted by moving the lens closer or farther from the film. A zoom lens is useful because it can be used as both a telephoto and a wide-angle lens.

Section Assessment

1. How is a compound microscope different from a magnifying glass?
2. Why are reflecting telescopes the biggest telescopes and not refracting telescopes?
3. Why is the objective lens of a refracting telescope bigger than the objective lens of a microscope?
4. **Think Critically:** If you could buy only one lens for your camera, what type of lens would you buy? Why?
5. **Skill Builder**
   Communicating Scientists need to clearly explain to others the results of their experiments, as well as their hypotheses and ideas. They do this by carefully writing research papers. Do the **Chapter 18 Skill Activity** on page 595 to learn how to write a research paper.

Using Math

The size of an image is related to the magnification of an optical instrument by the following formula:

Image size = magnification × object size

A blood cell has a diameter of about 0.001 cm. How large is the image formed by a microscope with a magnification of 1000?

Scientific Notation

A microscope allows us to see extremely small organisms. A cell that measures only 0.0007 cm in diameter can be seen clearly with a powerful microscope. A telescope can be used to see far-away objects, such as the galaxy, left. By using a telescope, we can see a galaxy as far as 2.2 million light-years away.

Scientists and mathematicians have devised a short way to write extremely small or large numbers. This is known as scientific notation. In scientific notation, a number is written as a number that is at least 1 but less than 10 multiplied by a power of 10.

How to Determine Scientific Notations

1. To write 2 200 000 in scientific notation, you first need a number that is at least 1 but less than 10. The number 2.2 is related to 2 200 000 and is at least 1 but less than 10. If you divide 2 200 000 by 2.2, you get 1 000 000. So, 2 200 000 = 2.2 × 1 000 000. Numbers such as 1 000 000 can be written as a power of ten.

$$10 = 10^1$$
$$100 = 10 \times 10 = 10^2$$
$$1000 = 10 \times 10 \times 10 = 10^3$$
$$10\ 000 = 10 \times 10 \times 10 \times 10 = 10^4$$
$$100\ 000 = 10 \times 10 \times 10 \times 10 \times 10 = 10^5$$
$$1\ 000\ 000 = 10 \times 10 \times 10 \times 10 \times 10 \times 10 = 10^6$$

2.2 × 1 000 000 in scientific notation is 2.2×10^6.

2. To write 0.0007 in scientific notation, you first need a number that is at least 1 but less than 10. You can see that 7 is related to 0.0007 and is at least 1 but less than 10. If you divide 0.0007 by 7, you get 0.0001. So, 0.0007 = 7 × 0.0001. Numbers such as 0.0001 can be written as a power of ten using a negative number.

$$0.1 = \frac{1}{10} = 10^{-1}$$

$$0.01 = \frac{1}{100} = 10^{-2}$$

$$0.001 = \frac{1}{1000} = 10^{-3}$$

7 × 0.0001 in scientific notation is 7×10^{-4}.

Practice
PROBLEMS

1. One type of bacteria measures 0.000 015 cm in length. Write this number in scientific notation.
2. Pluto is 5.92 billion km from the sun. Write this number in scientific notation.
3. A light-year is the distance that light travels in one year. Light travels at about 300 million m/s. How many kilometers are in a light-year? Write your answer in scientific notation.

Chapter 18 Reviewing Main Ideas

For a **preview** of this chapter, study this Reviewing Main Ideas before you read the chapter. After you have studied this chapter, you can use the Reviewing Main Ideas to **review** the chapter.

The Glencoe MindJogger, Audiocassettes, and CD-ROM provide additional opportunities for review.

18-1 PROPERTIES OF LIGHT

Light is an **electromagnetic wave** and can travel in a vacuum. The energy carried by a light wave increases as the **frequency** gets larger. When a light wave strikes an object, some of the light wave's energy may be reflected, some may be absorbed, and some may be transmitted through the object. The color of a light wave depends on its wavelength. The color of an object depends on which wavelengths of light are reflected by the object. Light of almost any color can be made by mixing different amounts of red, green, and blue light. Mixing pigments such as paints makes colors by subtracting colors from the light that strikes the pigments. *How does the wavelength of a light wave change as its frequency increases?*

18-2 REFLECTION OF LIGHT

Light reflected from the surface of an object obeys the **law of reflection:** the angle of incidence equals the angle of reflection. Diffuse reflection occurs when a surface is rough, while regular reflection occurs from very smooth surfaces and produces a clear, mirrorlike image. The image seen in a plane mirror seems to come from behind the mirror and is the same size as the object. The image formed by a concave mirror depends on the position of the object relative to the **focal point** of the mirror. Convex mirrors cause light waves to diverge and produce upright images smaller than the object. *Why doesn't diffuse reflection produce sharp, clear images?*

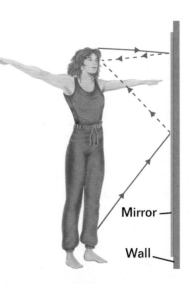

Mirror

Wall

Reading Check ✓

• Describe **Figure 18-15** so that a student in the third or fourth grade could understand the ideas shown.

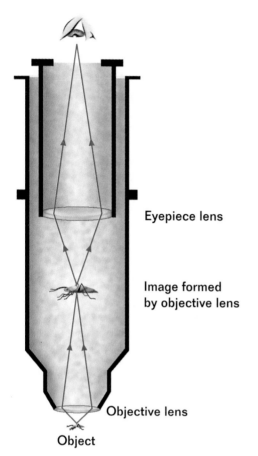

Eyepiece lens

Image formed by objective lens

Objective lens

Object

Section 18-3 REFRACTION OF LIGHT

Light waves tend to travel in straight lines, unless they change speed when they travel into another medium. Then, the waves change direction at the boundary between the two media. This change in direction is called **refraction.** A **convex lens** causes light waves to converge. The type of image formed by a convex lens depends on the location of the object relative to the focal point. A **concave lens** causes light waves to diverge. *How close must an object be to a convex lens to form an enlarged image?*

Section 18-4 MICROSCOPES, TELESCOPES, AND CAMERAS

A compound microscope is used to enlarge small objects. A convex objective lens forms an enlarged image that is further enlarged by an eyepiece lens. Most telescopes today are reflecting telescopes that use a concave mirror to form a real image that is enlarged by an eyepiece. The larger the mirror, the more light it can gather and the better the image formed by the tele- scope. Cameras use a lens to form an image on a light-sen- sitive piece of film. *Do the lenses used in micro- scopes, telescopes, and cameras cause light rays to converge or diverge?*

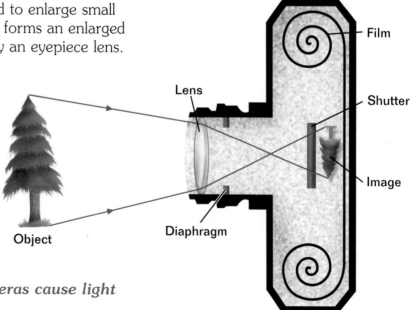

Film

Lens

Shutter

Object

Diaphragm

Image

Chapter 18 Assessment

Using Vocabulary

a. concave lens
b. convex lens
c. electromagnetic wave
d. focal length
e. focal point
f. frequency
g. law of reflection
h. lens
i. light ray
j. medium
k. reflection
l. refraction
m. wavelength

Match each phrase with the correct term from the list of Vocabulary words.

1. the bending of light when it changes speed in passing from one material to another
2. a part of a light wave traveling in a single direction
3. the number of wavelengths that pass a point in 1 s
4. the distance of the focal point from the center of the lens or mirror
5. the material in which a light wave travels

Checking Concepts

Choose the word or phrase that completes the sentence or answers the question.

6. What type of image does a plane mirror form?
   A) upright
   B) inverted
   C) magnified
   D) all of the above

7. How are light waves different than radio waves?
   A) Light waves have a higher frequency.
   B) Light waves have a longer wavelength.
   C) Light waves have a longer focal length.
   D) Radio waves are sound waves.

8. Which of the following types of electromagnetic waves is the most energetic?
   A) visible
   B) X rays
   C) infrared
   D) ultraviolet

9. The lowest-frequency visible light waves have what color?
   A) blue
   B) red
   C) infrared
   D) ultraviolet

10. Which of the following is true about an object that looks red?
    A) It absorbs only red light.
    B) It transmits only red light.
    C) It can be seen only in red light.
    D) None of the above.

11. In reflection, how is the angle of incidence related to the angle of reflection?
    A) It is always the same.
    B) It is always greater.
    C) It is twice as large.
    D) It depends on the change in the speed of light.

12. Why does a camera have a diaphragm?
    A) to control the amount of light striking the film
    B) to move the lens closer to the film
    C) to change the focal length of the lens
    D) to close the shutter

13. Which of the following can be used to magnify objects?
    A) a concave lens
    B) a convex lens
    C) a convex mirror
    D) all of the above

14. What is an object that reflects some light and transmits some light called?
    A) colored
    B) diffuse
    C) opaque
    D) translucent

15. How do the sides of a convex lens change as its focal length decreases?
    A) They become flatter.
    B) They become concave.
    C) They become more curved.
    D) They become regular reflectors.

Thinking Critically

16. Do all light rays that strike a convex lens pass through the focal point?

17. Does a plane mirror focus light rays? Why or why not?

18. Explain why a rough surface, such as a road, is a better reflector when it is wet.

19. If the speed of light were the same in all materials, could lenses be used to magnify objects? Why or why not?

20. A singer is wearing a blue outfit. What color spotlights would make the outfit appear black? Explain.

Developing Skills

If you need help, refer to the Skill Handbook.

21. Using Graphs: The graph below shows how the distance of an image from a convex lens is related to the distance of the object from the lens.

A) How does the image move as the object gets closer to the lens?

B) The magnification of the image is given by:

$$magnification = \frac{image\ distance}{object\ distance}$$

How does the magnification change as the object gets closer to the lens?

C) What is the magnification when the object is 20 cm from the lens?

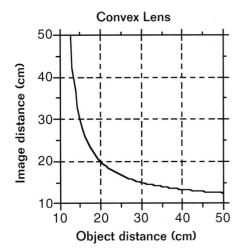

Test-Taking Tip

Practice, Practice, Practice Practice to improve *your* performance. Don't compare yourself with anyone else.

Test Practice

Use these questions to test your Science Proficiency.

1. Two vases are identical except one is glass and the other is made of black plastic. If they are side by side in a well-lit room, which vase absorbs more light energy?
A) The black vase absorbs more.
B) The glass vase absorbs more.
C) They absorb the same amount.
D) They both absorb no light energy.

2. In glass, blue light travels slightly slower than red light. If a beam of white light passes through a glass convex lens, which statement describes what happens?
A) The blue light is brought to a focus closer to the lens than the red light.
B) The red light is focused closer to the lens than the blue light.
C) All colors are focused at the same point, regardless of how slowly they move in the glass lens.
D) Not enough information has been given.

Appendices

Appendix A 533
Safety in the Science Classroom

Appendix B 534
SI/Metric to English Conversions

Appendix C 535
SI Units of Measurement

Appendix D 536
Care and Use of a Microscope

Appendix E 537
Diversity of Life: Classification of Living Organisms

Appendix F 541
Minerals

Appendix G 543
Rocks

Appendix H 544
Topographic Map Symbols

Appendix I 545
Weather Map Symbols

Appendix J 546
Star Charts

Safety in the Science Classroom

1. Always obtain your teacher's permission to begin an investigation.

2. Study the procedure. If you have questions, ask your teacher. Be sure you understand any safety symbols shown on the page.

3. Use the safety equipment provided for you. Goggles and a safety apron should be worn during an investigation.

4. Always slant test tubes away from yourself and others when heating them.

5. Never eat or drink in the lab, and never use lab glassware as food or drink containers. Never inhale chemicals. Do not taste any substances or draw any material into a tube with your mouth.

6. If you spill any chemical, wash it off immediately with water. Report the spill immediately to your teacher.

7. Know the location and proper use of the fire extinguisher, safety shower, fire blanket, first aid kit, and fire alarm.

8. Keep all materials away from open flames. Tie back long hair and loose clothing.

9. If a fire should break out in the classroom, or if your clothing should catch fire, smother it with the fire blanket or a coat, or get under a safety shower. NEVER RUN.

10. Report any accident or injury, no matter how small, to your teacher.

Follow these procedures as you clean up your work area.

1. Turn off the water and gas. Disconnect electrical devices.

2. Return all materials to their proper places.

3. Dispose of chemicals and other materials as directed by your teacher. Place broken glass and solid substances in the proper containers. Never discard materials in the sink.

4. Clean your work area.

5. Wash your hands thoroughly after working in the laboratory.

Table A-1

First Aid	
Injury	**Safe Response**
Burns	Apply cold water. Call your teacher immediately.
Cuts and bruises	Stop any bleeding by applying direct pressure. Cover cuts with a clean dressing. Apply cold compresses to bruises. Call your teacher immediately.
Fainting	Leave the person lying down. Loosen any tight clothing and keep crowds away. Call your teacher immediately.
Foreign matter in eye	Flush with plenty of water. Use eyewash bottle or fountain.
Poisoning	Note the suspected poisoning agent and call your teacher immediately.
Any spills on skin	Flush with large amounts of water or use safety shower. Call your teacher immediately.

Appendix
B

SI/Metric to English Conversions

	When you want to convert:	To:	Multiply by:
Length	inches	centimeters	2.54
	centimeters	inches	0.39
	feet	meters	0.30
	meters	feet	3.28
	yards	meters	0.91
	meters	yards	1.09
	miles	kilometers	1.61
	kilometers	miles	0.62
Mass and Weight*	ounces	grams	28.35
	grams	ounces	0.04
	pounds	kilograms	0.45
	kilograms	pounds	2.2
	tons (short)	tonnes (metric tons)	0.91
	tonnes (metric tons)	tons (short)	1.10
	pounds	newtons	4.45
	newtons	pounds	0.23
Volume	cubic inches	cubic centimeters	16.39
	cubic centimeters	cubic inches	0.06
	cubic feet	cubic meters	0.03
	cubic meters	cubic feet	35.30
	liters	quarts	1.06
	liters	gallons	0.26
	gallons	liters	3.78
Area	square inches	square centimeters	6.45
	square centimeters	square inches	0.16
	square feet	square meters	0.09
	square meters	square feet	10.76
	square miles	square kilometers	2.59
	square kilometers	square miles	0.39
	hectares	acres	2.47
	acres	hectares	0.40
Temperature	Fahrenheit	5/9 (°F − 32) =	Celsius
	Celsius	9/5 (°C) + 32 =	Fahrenheit

*Weight as measured in standard Earth gravity

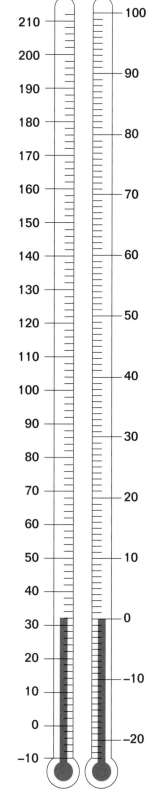

Appendix C

SI Units of Measurement

Table C-1

SI Base Units					
Measurement	**Unit**	**Symbol**	**Measurement**	**Unit**	**Symbol**
length	meter	m	temperature	kelvin	K
mass	kilogram	kg	amount of substance	mole	mol
time	second	s			

Table C-2

Units Derived from SI Base Units		
Measurement	**Unit**	**Symbol**
energy	joule	J
force	newton	N
frequency	hertz	Hz
potential difference	volt	V
power	watt	W
pressure	pascal	Pa

Table C-3

Common SI Prefixes					
Prefix	**Symbol**	**Multiplier**	**Prefix**	**Symbol**	**Multiplier**
Greater than 1			Less than 1		
mega-	M	1 000 000	*deci-*	d	0.1
kilo-	k	1 000	*centi-*	c	0.01
hecto-	h	100	*milli-*	m	0.001
deca-	da	10	*micro-*	μ	0.000 001

Appendix D

Care and Use of a Microscope

Eyepiece Contains a magnifying lens you look through

Body tube Connects the eyepiece to the revolving nosepiece

Arm Supports the body tube

Revolving nosepiece Holds and turns the objectives into viewing position

Low-power objective Contains the lens with low-power magnification

High-power objective Contains the lens with the highest magnification

Stage clips Hold the microscope slide in place

Stage Supports the microscope slide

Coarse adjustment Focuses the image under low power

Light source Allows light to reflect upward through the diaphragm, the specimen, and the lenses

Fine adjustment Sharpens the image under high and low magnification

Base Provides support for the microscope

Care of a Microscope

1. Always carry the microscope holding the arm with one hand and supporting the base with the other hand.

2. Don't touch the lenses with your fingers.

3. Never lower the coarse adjustment knob when looking through the eyepiece lens.

4. Always focus first with the low-power objective.

5. Don't use the coarse adjustment knob when the high-power objective is in place.

6. Store the microscope covered.

Using a Microscope

1. Place the microscope on a flat surface that is clear of objects. The arm should be toward you.

2. Look through the eyepiece. Adjust the diaphragm so that light comes through the opening in the stage.

3. Place a slide on the stage so that the specimen is in the field of view. Hold it firmly in place by using the stage clips.

4. Always focus first with the coarse adjustment and the low-power objective lens. Once the object is in focus on low power, turn the nosepiece until the high-power objective is in place. Use ONLY the fine adjustment to focus with the high-power objective lens.

Making a Wet-Mount Slide

1. Carefully place the item you want to look at in the center of a clean, glass slide. Make sure the sample is thin enough for light to pass through.

2. Use a dropper to place one or two drops of water on the sample.

3. Hold a clean coverslip by the edges and place it at one edge of the drop of water. Slowly lower the coverslip onto the drop of water until it lies flat.

4. If you have too much water or a lot of air bubbles, touch the edge of a paper towel to the edge of the coverslip to draw off extra water and force out air.

Appendix
E

Diversity of Life: Classification of Living Organisms

Scientists use a six-kingdom system of classification of organisms. In this system, there are two kingdoms of organisms, Kingdoms Archaebacteria and Eubacteria, which contain organisms that do not have a nucleus and lack membrane-bound structures in the cytoplasm of their cells. The members of the other four kingdoms have cells which contain a nucleus and structures in the cytoplasm that are surrounded by membranes. These kingdoms are Kingdom Protista, Kingdom Fungi, the Kingdom Plantae, and the Kingdom Animalia.

Kingdom Archaebacteria

One-celled prokaryotes; absorb food from surroundings or make their own food by chemosynthesis; found in extremely harsh environments including salt ponds, hot springs, swamps, and deep-sea hydrothermal vents.

Kingdom Eubacteria

Cyanobacteria one-celled prokaryotes; make their own food; contain chlorophyll; some species form colonies; most are blue-green

Bacteria one-celled prokaryotes; most absorb food from their surroundings; some are photosynthetic; many are parasites; round, spiral, or rod-shaped

Kingdom Protista

Phylum Euglenophyta one-celled; can photosynthesize or take in food; most have one flagellum; euglenoids

Phylum Bacillariophyta one-celled; make their own food through photosynthesis; have unique double shells made of silica; diatoms

Phylum Dinoflagellata one-celled; make their own food through photosynthesis; contain red pigments; have two flagella; dinoflagellates

Phylum Chlorophyta one-celled, many-celled, or colonies; contain chlorophyll; make their own food; live on land, in fresh water, or salt water; green algae

Phylum Rhodophyta most are many-celled; photosynthetic; contain red pigments; most live in deep saltwater environments; red algae

Phylum Phaeophyta most are many-celled; photosynthetic; contain brown pigments; most live in saltwater environments; brown algae

Phylum Foraminifera many-celled; take in food; primarily marine; shells constructed of calcium carbonate, or made from grains of sand; forams

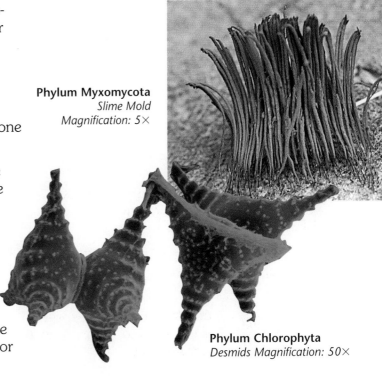

Phylum Myxomycota
Slime Mold
Magnification: 5×

Phylum Chlorophyta
Desmids Magnification: 50×

Appendix
E

Phylum Rhizopoda one-celled; take in food; move by means of pseudopods; free-living or parasitic; amoebas

Phylum Zoomastigina one-celled; take in food; have one or more flagella; free-living or parasitic; zoomastigotes

Phylum Ciliophora one-celled; take in food; have large numbers of cilia; ciliates

Phylum Sporozoa one-celled; take in food; no means of movement; parasites in animals; sporozoans

Phylum Myxomycota and Acrasiomycota: one- or many-celled; absorb food; change form during life cycle; cellular and plasmodial slime molds

Phylum Oomycota many-celled; live in fresh or salt water; are either parasites or decomposers; water molds, rusts and downy mildews

Kingdom Fungi

Phylum Zygomycota many-celled; absorb food; spores are produced in sporangia; zygote fungi; bread mold

Phylum Ascomycota one- and many-celled; absorb food; spores produced in asci; sac fungi; yeast

Phylum Basidiomycota many-celled; absorb food; spores produced in basidia; club fungi; mushrooms

Phylum Deuteromycota: members with unknown reproductive structures; imperfect fungi; penicillin

Lichens organisms formed by symbiotic relationship between an ascomycote or a basidiomycote and green alga or cyanobacterium

Kingdom Plantae
Non-seed Plants

Division Bryophyta nonvascular plants; reproduce by spores produced in capsules; many-celled; green; grow in moist land environments; mosses and liverworts

Division Lycophyta many-celled vascular plants; spores produced in conelike structures; live on land; are photosynthetic; club mosses

Division Sphenophyta vascular plants; ribbed and jointed stems; scalelike leaves; spores produced in conelike structures; horsetails

Division Pterophyta vascular plants; leaves called fronds; spores produced in clusters of sporangia called sori; live on land or in water; ferns

Division Bryophyta
Liverwort

Lichens
British soldier lichen
Magnification: 3×

Appendix E

Seed Plants

Division Ginkgophyta: deciduous gymnosperms; only one living species; fan-shaped leaves with branching veins; reproduces with seeds; ginkgos

Division Cycadophyta: palmlike gymnosperms; large featherlike leaves; produce seeds in cones; cycads

Division Coniferophyta: deciduous or evergreen gymnosperms; trees or shrubs; needlelike or scalelike leaves; seeds produced in cones; conifers

Division Gnetophyta: shrubs or woody vines; seeds produced in cones; division contains only three genera; gnetum

Division Anthophyta: dominant group of plants; ovules protected in an ovary; sperm carried to ovules by pollen tube; produce flowers and seeds in fruits; flowering plants

Kingdom Animalia

Phylum Porifera: aquatic organisms that lack true tissues and organs; they are asymmetrical and sessile; sponges

Phylum Cnidaria: radially symmetrical organisms; have a digestive cavity with one opening; most have tentacles armed with stinging cells; live in aquatic environments singly or in colonies; includes jellyfish, corals, hydra, and sea anemones

Phylum Platyhelminthes: bilaterally symmetrical worms; have flattened bodies; digestive system has one opening; parasitic and free-living species; flatworms

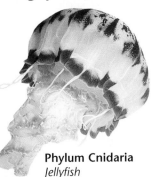

Phylum Cnidaria
Jellyfish

Phylum Arthopoda
Orb Weaver Spider

Division Coniferophyta
Pine cone

Division Anthophyta
Strawberry Blossoms

Phylum Arthropoda
Hermit Crab

Phylum Mollusca
Florida Fighting Conch

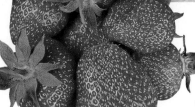

Division Anthophyta
Strawberries

Phylum Annelida
Sabellid Worms Feather Duster

Appendix E

Phylum Nematoda: round, bilaterally symmetrical body; digestive system with two openings; many parasitic forms but mostly free-living; roundworms

Phylum Mollusca: soft-bodied animals, many with a hard shell; a mantle covers the soft body; aquatic and terrestrial species; includes clams, snails, squid, and octopuses

Phylum Annelida: bilaterally symmetrical worms; have round, segmented bodies; terrestrial and aquatic species; includes earthworms, leeches, and marine polychaetes

Phylum Arthropoda: largest phylum of organisms; have segmented bodies; pairs of jointed appendages; have hard exoskeletons; terrestrial and aquatic species; includes insects, crustaceans, spiders, and horseshoe crabs

Phylum Echinodermata: marine organisms; have spiny or leathery skin; water-vascular system with tube feet; radial symmetry; includes sea stars, sand dollars, and sea urchins

Phylum Chordata: organisms with internal skeletons; specialized body systems; paired appendages; all at some time have a notochord, dorsal nerve cord, gill slits, and a tail; include fish, amphibians, reptiles, birds, and mammals

Phylum Arthropoda
Giant Swallowtail Butterfly

Phylum Echinodermata
Blood Sea Star and Red Sea Urchin

Phylum Chordata
Eastern Box Turtle

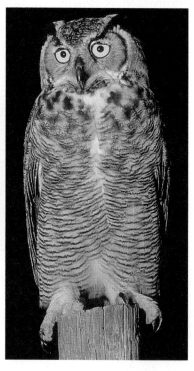

Phylum Chordata
Lemon Butterfly fish

Phylum Chordata
Great Horned Owl

Minerals

Mineral (formula)	Color	Streak	Hardness	Breakage pattern	Uses and other properties
graphite (C)	black to gray	black to gray	1–1.5	basal cleavage (scales)	pencil lead, lubricants for locks, rods to control some small nuclear reactions, battery poles
galena (PbS)	gray	gray to black	2.5	cubic cleavage perfect	source of lead, used in pipes, shields for X rays, fishing equipment sinkers
hematite (Fe_2O_3)	black or reddish brown	reddish brown	5.5–6.5	irregular fracture	source of iron; converted to "pig" iron, made into steel
magnetite (Fe_3O_4)	black	black	6	conchoidal fracture	source of iron, naturally magnetic, called lodestone
pyrite (FeS_2)	light, brassy, yellow	greenish black	6–6.5	uneven fracture	source of iron, "fool's gold"
talc ($Mg_3Si_4O_{10}(OH)_2$)	white greenish	white	1	cleavage in one direction	used for talcum powder, sculptures, paper, and tabletops
gypsum ($CaSO_4 \cdot 2H_2O$)	colorless, gray, white brown	white	2	basal cleavage	used in plaster of paris and dry wall for building construction
sphalerite (ZnS)	brown, reddish brown, greenish	light to dark brown	3.5–4	cleavage in six directions	main ore of zinc; used in paints, dyes and medicine
muscovite ($KAl_3Si_3O_{10}(OH)_2$)	white, light gray, yellow, rose, green	colorless	2–2.5	basal cleavage	occurs in large flexible plates; used as an insulator in electrical equipment, lubricant
biotite ($K(Mg, Fe)_3(AlSi_3O_{10})(OH)_2$)	black to dark brown	colorless	2.5–3	basal cleavage	occurs in large flexible plates
halite (NaCl)	colorless, red, white, blue	colorless	2.5	cubic cleavage	salt; soluble in water; a preservative

Appendix F

Minerals

Mineral (formula)	Color	Streak	Hardness	Breakage pattern	Uses and other properties
calcite ($CaCO_3$)	colorless, white, pale blue	colorless, white	3	cleavage in three directions	fizzes when HCl is added; used in cements and other building materials
dolomite ($CaMg(CO_3)_2$)	colorless, white, pink green, gray black	white	3.5–4	cleavage in three directions	concrete and cement; used as an ornamental building stone
fluorite (CaF_2)	colorless, white, blue green, red yellow, purple	colorless	4	cleavage in four directions	used in the manufacture of optical equipment; glows under ultraviolet light
hornblende ($(CaNa)_{2-3}(Mg, Al,Fe)_5(Al,Si)_2 Si_6O_{22}(OH)_2$)	green to black	gray to white	5–6	cleavage in two directions	will transmit light on thin edges; 6-sided cross section
feldspar ($KAlSi_3O_8$) ($NaAlSi_3O_8$) ($CaAl_2Si_2O_8$)	colorless, white to gray, green	colorless	6	two cleavage planes meet at ~90° angle	used in the manufacture of ceramics
augite ($(Ca, Na)(Mg, Fe, Al)(Al, Si)_2O_6$)	black	colorless	6	cleavage in two directions	square or 8-sided cross section
olivine ($(Mg, Fe)_2 SiO_4$)	olive, green	none	6.5–7	conchoidal fracture	gemstones, refractory sand
quartz (SiO_2)	colorless, various colors	none	7	conchoidal fracture	used in glass manufacture, electronic equipment, radios, computers, watches, gemstones

Appendix G

Rocks

Rock Type	Rock Name	Characteristics
Igneous (intrusive)	Granite	Large mineral grains of quartz, feldspar, hornblende, and mica. Usually light in color.
	Diorite	Large mineral grains of feldspar, hornblende, mica. Less quartz than granite. Intermediate in color.
	Gabbro	Large mineral grains of feldspar, hornblende, augite, olivine, and mica. No quartz. Dark in color.
Igneous (extrusive)	Rhyolite	Small mineral grains of quartz, feldspar, hornblende, and mica or no visible grains. Light in color.
	Andesite	Small mineral grains of feldspar, hornblende, mica or no visible grains. Less quartz than rhyolite. Intermediate in color.
	Basalt	Small mineral grains of feldspar, hornblende, augite, olivine, mica or no visible grains. No quartz. Dark in color.
	Obsidian	Glassy texture. No visible grains. Volcanic glass. Fracture looks like broken glass.
	Pumice	Frothy texture. Floats. Usually light in color.
Sedimentary (detrital)	Conglomerate	Coarse-grained. Gravel or pebble-sized grains.
	Sandstone	Sand-sized grains 1/16 to 2 mm in size.
	Siltstone	Grains are smaller than sand but larger than clay.
	Shale	Smallest grains. Usually dark in color.
Sedimentary (chemical or biochemical)	Limestone	Major mineral is calcite. Usually forms in oceans, lakes, rivers, and caves. Often contains fossils.
	Coal	Occurs in swampy, low-lying areas. Compacted layers of organic material, mainly plant remains.
Sedimentary (chemical)	Rock Salt	Commonly forms by the evaporation of seawater.
Metamorphic (foliated)	Gneiss	Well-developed banding because of alternating layers of different minerals, usually of different colors. Common parent rock is granite.
	Schist	Well-defined parallel arrangement of flat, sheet-like minerals, mainly micas. Common parent rocks are shale, phyllite.
	Phyllite	Shiny or silky appearance. May look wrinkled. Common parent rocks are shale, slate.
	Slate	Harder, denser, and shinier than shale. Common parent rock is shale.
Metamorphic (non-foliated)	Marble	Interlocking calcite or dolomite crystals. Common parent rock is limestone.
	Soapstone	Composed mainly of the mineral talc. Soft with a greasy feel.
	Quartzite	Hard and well cemented with interlocking quartz crystals. Common parent rock is sandstone.

Topographic Map Symbols

Primary highway, hard surface	
Secondary highway, hard surface	
Light-duty road, hard or Improved surface	
Unimproved road	
Railroad: single track and multiple track	
Railroads in juxtaposition	
Buildings	
Schools, church, and cemetery	cem
Buildings (barn, warehouse, etc)	
Wells other than water (labeled as to type)	o oil o gas
	water
Tanks: oil, water, etc. (labeled only if water)	
Located or landmark object; windmill	
Open pit, mine, or quarry; prospect	
Marsh (swamp)	
Wooded marsh	
Woods or brushwood	
Vineyard Land subject to controlled inundation	
Submerged marsh	
Mangrove	
Orchard	
Scrub	
Urban area	
Spot elevation	×7369
Water elevation	670

Index contour	
Supplementary contour	
Intermediate contour	
Depression contours	
Boundaries: National	
State	
County, parish, municipal	
Civil township, precinct, town, barrio	
Incorporated city, village, town, hamlet	
Reservation, National or State	
Small park, cemetery, airport, etc.	
Land grant	
Township or range line, United States land survey	
Township or range line, approximate location	
Perennial streams	
Elevated aqueduct	
Water well and spring	
Small rapids	
Large rapids	
Intermittent lake	
Intermittent streams Aqueduct tunnel	
Glacier Small falls	
Large falls	
Dry lake bed	

Appendix

I

Weather Map Symbols

Sample Plotted Report at Each Station

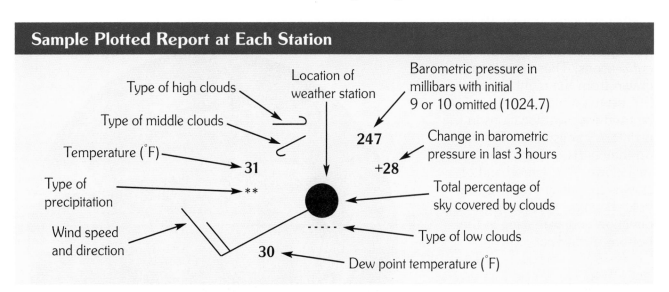

Sample Plotted Report at Each Station

Precipitation	Wind speed and direction		Sky coverage		Some types of high clouds	
≡ Fog	○	0 knots; calm	○	No cover	⌐⊃	Scattered cirrus
★ Snow	╱	1–2 knots	◐	1/10 or less		
● Rain	⋎	3–7 knots	◕	2/10 to 3/10	⌐⊃⊃	Dense cirrus in patches
⊤₹ Thunder-storm	⋎	8–12 knots	◑	4/10	⌐⌐	Veil of cirrus covering entire sky
	⋎	13–17 knots	◐	1/2		
	⋎	18–22 knots	◓	6/10		
, Drizzle	⋎	23–27 knots	◕	7/10	⌐	Cirrus not covering entire sky
▽ Showers	⋎	48–52 knots	◑	Overcast with openings		
	1 knot = 1.852 km/h		●	Complete overcast		

Some types of middle clouds		Some types of low clouds		Fronts and pressure systems	
╱	Thin altostratus layer	⌒	Cumulus of fair weather	(H) or High	Center of high-or
╱╱	Thick altostratus layer	⌣	Stratocumulus	(L) or Low	low-pressure system
╱	Thin altostratus in patches	-----	Fractocumulus of bad weather	▲▲▲▲	Cold front
				●●●●	Warm Front
⌒	Thin altostratus in bands	—	Stratus of fair weather	▲●▲●	Occluded front
				●⌣●⌣	Stationary front

Appendix
J

Star Charts

Shown here are star charts for viewing stars in the northern hemisphere during the four different seasons. These charts are drawn from the night sky at about 35° north latitude, but they can be used for most locations in the northern hemisphere. The lines on the charts outline major constellations. The dense band of stars is the Milky Way. To use, hold the chart vertically, with the direction you are facing at the bottom of the map.

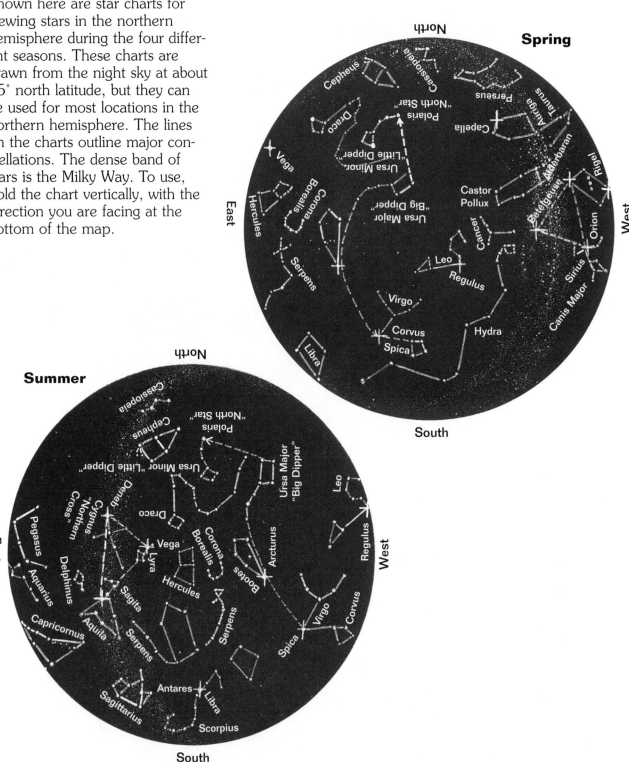

Appendix

J

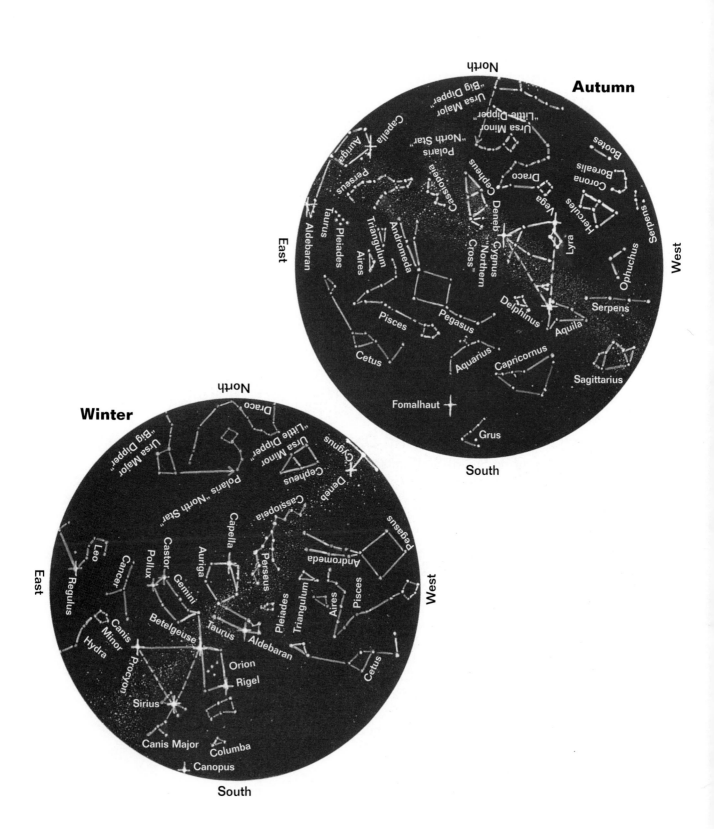

Autumn

North

Ursa Major "Big Dipper"
Ursa Minor "Little Dipper"
Polaris "North Star"
Bootes
Capella
Auriga
Cassiopeia
Corona Borealis
Perseus
Cepheus
Draco
Hercules
Serpens
Taurus
Andromeda
Triangulum
Deneb Cygnus "Northern Cross"
Vega
Lyra
Ophuchus
Aldebaran
Aires
West
Pleiades
East
Pisces
Pegasus
Delphinus
Serpens
Aquila
Cetus
Aquarius
Capricornus
Sagittarius
Fomalhaut
Grus

South

Winter

North

Draco
Ursa Major "Big Dipper"
Ursa Minor "Little Dipper"
Cygnus
Polaris "North Star"
Cepheus
Deneb
Cassiopeia
Capella
Pegasus
Leo
Castor
Pollux
Auriga
Perseus
Andromeda
East
Regulus
Cancer
Gemini
West
Canis Minor
Betelgeuse
Taurus
Aldebaran
Pleiades
Triangulum
Aires
Pisces
Hydra
Procyon
Orion
Rigel
Cetus
Sirius
Canis Major
Columba
Canopus

South

Skill Handbook

Table of Contents

Science Skill Handbook

Organizing Information
Communicating 549
Classifying... 549
Sequencing 550
Concept Mapping....................................... 550
Making and Using Tables 552
Making and Using Graphs 553

Thinking Critically
Observing and Inferring 554
Comparing and Contrasting............................... 556
Recognizing Cause and Effect 557

Practicing Scientific Processes
Forming Operational Definitions........................... 558
Forming a Hypothesis.................................... 558
Designing an Experiment to Test a Hypothesis 559
Separating and Controlling Variables 560
Interpreting Data................................ 560

Representing and Applying Data
Interpreting Scientific Illustrations......... 562
Making Models 563
Measuring in SI 564
Predicting 566
Using Numbers 567

Technology Skill Handbook

Software
Using a Word Processor................ 568
Using a Database...................... 569
Using Graphics Software................ 570
Using a Computerized Card Catalog 571
Developing Multimedia Presentations 572
Using E-mail 573
Using an Electronic Spreadsheet 574

Hardware
Using a CD-ROM 575
Using Probeware...................... 575
Using a Graphing Calculator 576

Science Skill Handbook

Organizing Information

Communicating

The communication of ideas is an important part of our everyday lives. Whether reading a book, writing a letter, or watching a television program, people everywhere are expressing opinions and sharing information with one another. Writing in your Science Journal allows you to express your opinions and demonstrate your knowledge of the information presented on a subject. When writing, keep in mind the purpose of the assignment and the audience with which you are communicating.

Examples Science Journal assignments vary greatly. They may ask you to take a viewpoint other than your own; perhaps you will be a scientist, a TV reporter, or a committee member of a local environmental group. Maybe you will be expressing your opinions to a member of Congress, a doctor, or to the editor of your local newspaper, as shown in **Figure 1.** Sometimes, Science Journal writing may allow you to summarize information in the form of an outline, a letter, or in a paragraph.

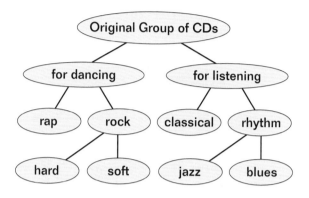

Figure 2 Classifying CDs

Classifying

You may not realize it, but you make things orderly in the world around you. If you hang your shirts together in the closet or if your favorite CDs are stacked together, you have used the skill of classifying.

Classifying is the process of sorting objects or events into groups based on common features. When classifying, first observe the objects or events to be classified. Then, select one feature that is shared by some members in the group, but not by all. Place those members that share that feature into a subgroup. You can classify members into smaller and smaller subgroups based on characteristics.

Remember, when you classify, you are grouping objects or events for a purpose. Keep your purpose in mind as you select the features to form groups and subgroups.

Example How would you classify a collection of CDs? As shown in **Figure 2,** you might classify those you like to dance to in one subgroup and CDs you like to listen to in the next subgroup. The CDs you like to dance to could be subdivided

Figure 1 A Science Journal entry

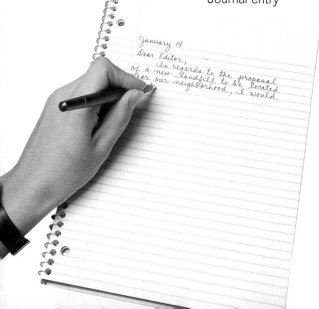

into a rap subgroup and a rock subgroup. Note that for each feature selected, each CD fits into only one subgroup. You would keep selecting features until all the CDs are classified. **Figure 2** shows one possible classification.

Figure 3 A recipe for bread contains sequenced instructions

Sequencing

A sequence is an arrangement of things or events in a particular order. When you are asked to sequence objects or events within a group, figure out what comes first, then think about what should come second. Continue to choose objects or events until all of the objects you started out with are in order. Then, go back over the sequence to make sure each thing or event in your sequence logically leads to the next.

Example A sequence with which you are most familiar is the use of alphabetical order. Another example of sequence would be the steps in a recipe, as shown in **Figure 3.** Think about baking bread. Steps in the recipe have to be followed in order for the bread to turn out right.

Concept Mapping

If you were taking an automobile trip, you would probably take along a road map. The road map shows your location, your destination, and other places along the way. By looking at the map and finding where you are, you can begin to understand where you are in relation to other locations on the map.

A concept map is similar to a road map. But, a concept map shows relationships among ideas (or concepts) rather than places. A concept map is a diagram that visually shows how concepts are related. Because the concept map shows relationships among ideas, it can make the meanings of ideas and terms clear, and help you understand better what you are studying.

There is usually not one correct way to create a concept map. As you construct one type of map, you may discover other ways to construct the map that show the

Figure 4 Network tree describing U.S. currency

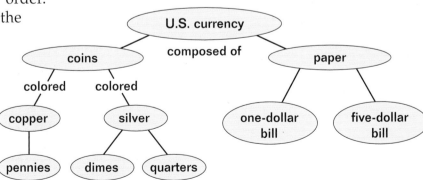

relationships between concepts in a better way. If you do discover what you think is a better way to create a concept map, go ahead and use the new one. Overall, concept maps are useful for breaking a big concept down into smaller parts, making learning easier.

Examples

Network Tree Look at the concept map about U.S. currency in **Figure 4.** This is called a network tree. Notice how some words are in ovals while others are written across connecting lines. The words inside the ovals are science concepts. The lines in the map show related concepts. The words written on the lines describe the relationships between concepts.

When you are asked to construct a network tree, write down the topic and list the major concepts related to that topic on a piece of paper. Then look at your list and begin to put them in order from general to specific. Branch the related concepts from the major concept and describe the relationships on the lines. Continue to write the more specific concepts. Write the relationships between the concepts on the lines until all concepts are mapped. Examine the concept map for relationships that cross branches, and add them to the concept map.

Events Chain An events chain is another type of concept map. An events chain map, such as the one describing a typical morning routine in **Figure 5,** is used to describe ideas in order. In science, an events chain can be used to describe a sequence of events, the steps in a procedure, or the stages of a process.

When making an events chain, first find the one event that starts the chain. This

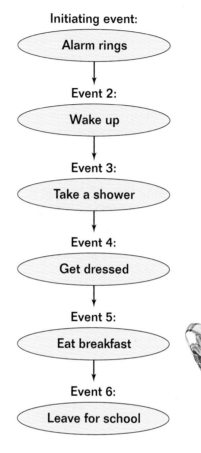

Initiating event:

Alarm rings

Event 2:

Wake up

Event 3:

Take a shower

Event 4:

Get dressed

Event 5:

Eat breakfast

Event 6:

Leave for school

Figure 5 Events chain of a typical morning routine

event is called the initiating event. Then, find the next event in the chain and continue until you reach an outcome. Suppose you are asked to describe what happens when your alarm rings. An events chain map describing the steps might look like **Figure 5.** Notice that connecting words are not necessary in an events chain.

Cycle Map A cycle concept map is a special type of events chain map. In a cycle concept map, the series of events does not produce a final outcome. Instead, the last event in the chain relates back to the initiating event.

As in the events chain map, you first decide on an initiating event and then list each event in order. Because there is no outcome and the last event relates back to the initiating event, the cycle repeats itself. Look at the cycle map describing the relationship between day and night in **Figure 6.**

Figure 6 Cycle map of day and night.

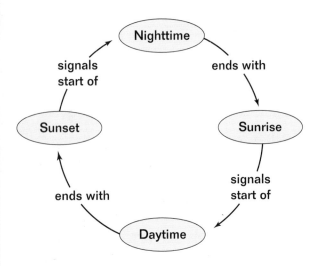

Spider Map A fourth type of concept map is the spider map. This is a map that you can use for brainstorming. Once you have a central idea, you may find you have a jumble of ideas that relate to it, but are not necessarily clearly related to each other. As illustrated by the homework spider map in **Figure 7,** by writing these ideas outside the main concept, you may begin to separate and group unrelated terms so that they become more useful.

Figure 7 Spider map about homework.

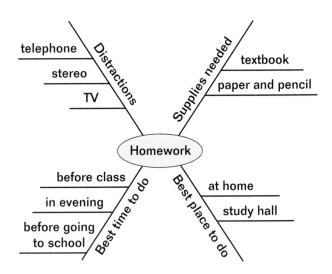

Making and Using Tables

Browse through your textbook and you will notice tables in the text and in the activities. In a table, data or information are arranged in a way that makes it easier for you to understand. Activity tables help organize the data you collect during an activity so that results can be interpreted.

Example Most tables have a title. At a glance, the title tells you what the table is about. A table is divided into columns and rows. The first column lists the items to be compared. In **Figure 8,** the collection of recyclable materials is being compared in a table. The row across the top lists the specific characteristics being compared. Within the grid of the table, the collected data are recorded.

What is the title of the table in **Figure 8?** The title is "Recycled Materials." What is being compared? The different materials being recycled and on which days they are recycled.

Making Tables To make a table, list the items to be compared down in columns and the characteristics to be compared across in rows. The table in

Science Skill Handbook

Figure 8 Table of recycled materials

Recycled Materials			
Day of Week	Paper (kg)	Aluminum (kg)	Plastic (kg)
Mon.	4.0	2.0	0.5
Wed.	3.5	1.5	0.5
Fri.	3.0	1.0	1.5

Figure 8 compares the mass of recycled materials collected by a class. On Monday, students turned in 4.0 kg of paper, 2.0 kg of aluminum, and 0.5 kg of plastic. On Wednesday, they turned in 3.5 kg of paper, 1.5 kg of aluminum, and 0.5 kg of plastic. On Friday, the totals were 3.0 kg of paper, 1.0 kg of aluminum, and 1.5 kg of plastic.

Using Tables How much plastic, in kilograms, is being recycled on Wednesday? Locate the column labeled "Plastic (kg)" and the row "Wed." The data in the box where the column and row intersect is the answer. Did you answer "0.5"? How much aluminum, in kilograms, is being recycled on Friday? If you answered "1.0," you understand how to use the parts of the table.

Making and Using Graphs

After scientists organize data in tables, they may display the data in a graph. A graph is a diagram that shows the relationship of one variable to another. A graph makes interpretation and analysis of data easier. There are three basic types of graphs used in science—the line graph, the bar graph, and the circle graph.

Examples

Line Graphs A line graph is used to show the relationship between two variables. The variables being compared go on two axes of the graph. The independent variable always goes on the horizontal axis, called the x-axis. The dependent variable always goes on the vertical axis, called the y-axis.

Suppose your class started to record the amount of materials they collected in one week for their school to recycle. The collected information is shown in **Figure 9.**

You could make a graph of the materials collected over the three days of the school week. The three weekdays are the independent variables and are placed on the x-axis of your graph. The amount of materials collected is the dependent variable and would go on the y-axis.

After drawing your axes, label each with a scale. The x-axis lists the three weekdays. To make a scale of the amount of materials collected on the y-axis, look at the data values. Because the lowest amount collected was 1.0 and the highest was 5.0, you will have to start numbering at least at 1.0 and go through 5.0. You decide to start numbering at 0 and number by ones through 6.0, as shown in **Figure 10.**

Next, plot the data points for collected paper. The first pair of data you want to plot is Monday and 5.0 kg of paper.

Figure 9 Amount of recyclable materials collected during one week

Materials Collected During Week		
Day of Week	Paper (kg)	Aluminum (kg)
Mon.	5.0	4.0
Wed.	4.0	1.0
Fri.	2.5	2.0

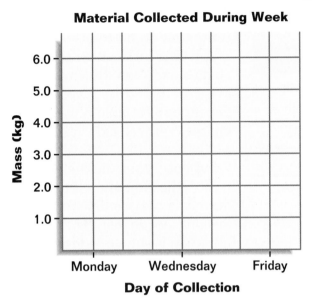

Figure 10 Graph outline for material collected during week

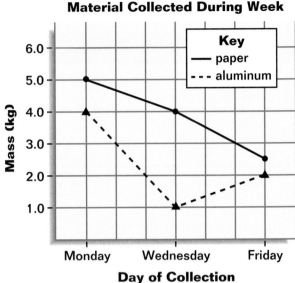

Figure 11 Line graph of materials collected during week

Locate "Monday" on the *x*-axis and locate "5.0" on the *y*-axis. Where an imaginary vertical line from the *x*-axis and an imaginary horizontal line from the *y*-axis would meet, place the first data point. Place the other data points the same way. After all the points are plotted, connect them with the best smooth curve. Repeat this procedure for the data points for aluminum. Use continuous and dashed lines to distinguish the two line graphs. The resulting graph should look like **Figure 11.**

Bar Graphs   Bar graphs are similar to line graphs. They compare data that do not continuously change. In a bar graph, vertical bars show the relationships among data.

To make a bar graph, set up the *x*-axis and *y*-axis as you did for the line graph. The data is plotted by drawing vertical bars from the *x*-axis up to a point where the *y*-axis would meet the bar if it were extended.

Look at the bar graph in **Figure 12** comparing the mass of aluminum collected

over three weekdays. The *x*-axis is the days on which the aluminum was collected. The *y*-axis is the mass of aluminum collected, in kilograms.

Circle Graphs   A circle graph uses a circle divided into sections to display data. Each section represents part of the whole. All the sections together equal 100 percent.

Suppose you wanted to make a circle graph to show the number of seeds that germinated in a package. You would count the total number of seeds. You find that there are 143 seeds in the package. This represents 100 percent, the whole circle.

You plant the seeds, and 129 seeds germinate. The seeds that germinated will make up one section of the circle graph, and the seeds that did not germinate will make up the remaining section.

To find out how much of the circle each section should take, divide the number of seeds in each section by the total number of seeds. Then, multiply your answer by 360, the number of degrees in a circle, and round to the nearest whole number. The

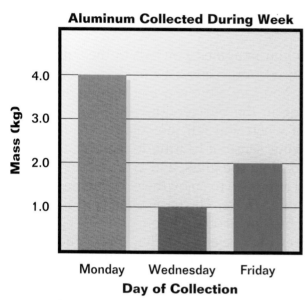

Figure 12 Bar graph of aluminum collected during week

section of the circle graph in degrees that represents the seeds germinated is figured below.

$$\frac{129}{143} \times 360 = 324.75 \text{ or } 325 \text{ degrees (or } 325°)$$

Plot this group on the circle graph using a compass and a protractor. Use the compass to draw a circle. It will be easier to

measure the part of the circle representing the non-germinating seeds, so subtract 325° from 360° to get 35°. Draw a straight line from the center to the edge of the circle. Place your protractor on this line and use it to mark a point at 325°. Use this point to draw a straight line from the center of the circle to the edge. This is the section for the group of seeds that did not germinate. The other section represents the group of 129 seeds that did germinate. Label the sections of your graph and title the graph as shown in **Figure 13.**

Figure 13 Circle graph of germinated seeds

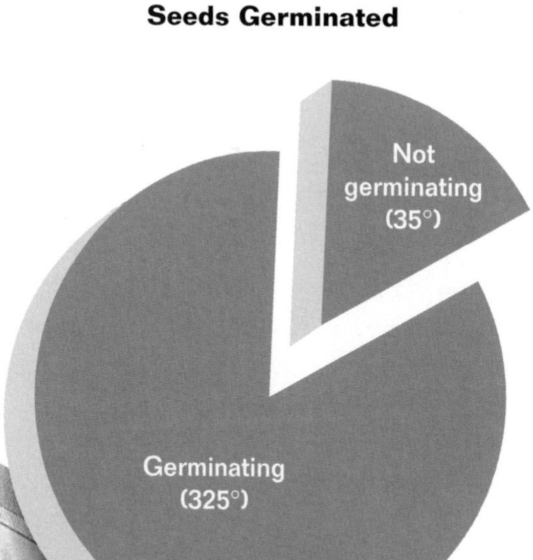

Seeds Germinated

Not germinating (35°)

Germinating (325°)

Science Skill Handbook

Thinking Critically

Observing and Inferring

Observing Scientists try to make careful and accurate observations. When possible, they use instruments such as microscopes, thermometers, and balances to make observations. Measurements with a balance or thermometer provide numerical data that can be checked and repeated.

When you make observations in science, you'll find it helpful to examine the entire object or situation first. Then, look carefully for details. Write down everything you observe.

Example Imagine that you have just finished a volleyball game. At home, you open the refrigerator and see a jug of orange juice on the back of the top shelf. The jug, shown in **Figure 14,** feels cold as you grasp it. Then, you drink the juice, smell the oranges, and enjoy the tart taste in your mouth.

Figure 14 Why is this jug of orange juice cold?

As you imagined yourself in the story, you used your senses to make observations. You used your sense of sight to find the jug in the refrigerator, your sense of touch when you felt the coldness of the jug, your sense of hearing to listen as the liquid filled the glass, and your senses of smell and taste to enjoy the odor and tartness of the juice. The basis of all scientific investigation is observation.

Inferring Scientists often make inferences based on their observations. An inference is an attempt to explain or interpret observations or to say what caused what you observed.

When making an inference, be certain to use accurate data and observations. Analyze all of the data that you've collected. Then, based on everything you know, explain or interpret what you've observed.

Example When you drank a glass of orange juice after the volleyball game, you observed that the orange juice was cold as well as refreshing. You might infer that the juice was cold because it had been made much earlier in the day and had been kept in the refrigerator, or you might infer that it had just been made, using both cold water and ice. The only way to be sure which inference is correct is to investigate further.

Comparing and Contrasting

Observations can be analyzed by noting the similarities and differences between two or more objects or events that you observe. When you look at objects or events to see how they are similar, you are comparing them. Contrasting is looking for differences in similar objects or events.

Science Skill Handbook

Figure 15 Table comparing the nutritional value of *Cereal A* and *Cereal B*

Nutritional Value		
	Cereal A	Cereal B
Serving size	103 g	105 g
Calories	220	160
Total Fat	10 g	10 g
Protein	2.5 g	2.6 g
Total Carbohydrate	30 g	15 g

Example Suppose you were asked to compare and contrast the nutritional value of two kinds of cereal, *Cereal A* and *Cereal B*. You would start by looking at what is known about these cereals. Arrange this information in a table, like the one in **Figure 15.**

Similarities you might point out are that both cereals have similar serving sizes, amounts of total fat, and protein. Differences include *Cereal A* having a higher calorie value and containing more total carbohydrates than *Cereal B.*

Recognizing Cause and Effect

Have you ever watched something happen and then made suggestions about why it happened? If so, you have observed an effect and inferred a cause. The event is an effect, and the reason for the event is the cause.

Example Suppose that every time your teacher fed the fish in a classroom aquarium, she or he tapped the food container on the edge of the aquarium. Then, one day your teacher just happened to tap the edge of the aquarium with a pencil while making a point. You observed the fish swim to the surface of the aquarium to feed, as shown in **Figure 16.** What is the effect, and what would you infer to be the cause? The effect is the fish swimming to the surface of the aquarium. You might infer the cause to be the teacher tapping on the edge of the aquarium. In determining cause and effect, you have made a logical inference based on your observations.

Perhaps the fish swam to the surface because they reacted to the teacher's waving hand or for some other reason. When scientists are unsure of the cause of a certain event, they design controlled experiments to determine what causes the event. Although you have made a logical conclusion about the behavior of the fish, you would have to perform an experiment to be certain that it was the tapping that caused the effect you observed.

Figure 16 What cause-and-effect situations are occurring in this aquarium?

Science Skill Handbook

Practicing Scientific Processes

You might say that the work of a scientist is to solve problems. But when you decide how to dress on a particular day, you are doing problem solving, too. You may observe what the weather looks like through a window. You may go outside and see whether what you are wearing is heavy or light enough.

Scientists use an orderly approach to learn new information and to solve problems. The methods scientists may use include observing to form a hypothesis, designing an experiment to test a hypothesis, separating and controlling variables, and interpreting data.

Forming Operational Definitions

Operational definitions define an object by showing how it functions, works, or behaves. Such definitions are written in terms of how an object works or how it can be used; that is, what is its job or purpose?

Figure 17 What observations can be made about this dog?

Example Some operational definitions explain how an object can be used.
- A ruler is a tool that measures the size of an object.
- An automobile can move things from one place to another.

Or such a definition may explain how an object works.
- A ruler contains a series of marks that can be used as a standard when measuring.
- An automobile is a vehicle that can move from place to place.

Forming a Hypothesis

Observations You observe all the time. Scientists try to observe as much as possible about the things and events they study so they know that what they say about their observations is reliable.

Some observations describe something using only words. These observations are called qualitative observations. Other observations describe how much of something there is. These are quantitative observations and use numbers, as well as words, in the description. Tools or equipment are used to measure the characteristic being described.

Example If you were making qualitative observations of the dog in **Figure 17,** you might use words such as *furry, yellow,* and *short-haired.* Quantitative observations of this dog might include a mass of 14 kg, a height of 46 cm, ear length of 10 cm, and an age of 150 days.

Hypotheses Hypotheses are tested to help explain observations that have been made. They are often stated as *if* and *then* statements.

Examples Suppose you want to make a perfect score on a spelling test. Begin by thinking of several ways to accomplish this. Base these possibilities on past observations. If you put each of these possibilities into sentence form, using the words *if* and *then,* you can form a hypothesis. All of the following are hypotheses you might consider to explain how you could score 100 percent on your test:

If the test is easy, then I will get a perfect score.

If I am intelligent, then I will get a perfect score.

If I study hard, then I will get a perfect score.

Perhaps a scientist has observed that plants that receive fertilizer grow taller than plants that do not. A scientist may form a hypothesis that says: If plants are fertilized, then their growth will increase.

Designing an Experiment to Test a Hypothesis

In order to test a hypothesis, it's best to write out a procedure. A procedure is the plan that you follow in your experiment. A procedure tells you what materials to use and how to use them. After following the procedure, data are generated. From this generated data, you can then draw a conclusion and make a statement about your results.

If the conclusion you draw from the data supports your hypothesis, then you can say that your hypothesis is reliable. *Reliable* means that you can trust your conclusion. If it did not support your hypothesis, then you would have to make new observations and state a new hypothesis—just make sure that it is one that you can test.

Example Super premium gasoline costs more than regular gasoline. Does super premium gasoline increase the efficiency or fuel mileage of your family car? Let's figure out how to conduct an experiment to test the hypothesis, "*if* premium gas is more efficient, *then* it should increase the fuel mileage of our family car." Then a procedure similar to **Figure 18** must be written to generate data presented in **Figure 19** on the next page.

These data show that premium gasoline is less efficient than regular gasoline. It took more gasoline to travel one mile (0.064) using premium gasoline than it does to travel one mile using regular gasoline (0.059). This conclusion does not support the original hypothesis made.

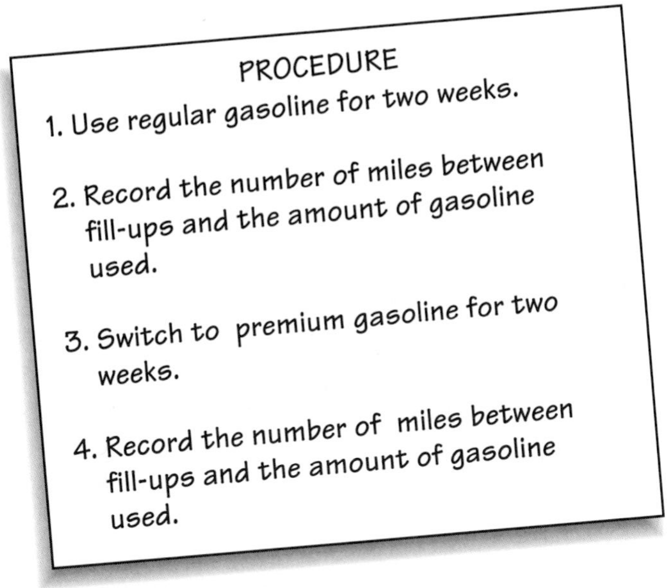

PROCEDURE

1. Use regular gasoline for two weeks.

2. Record the number of miles between fill-ups and the amount of gasoline used.

3. Switch to premium gasoline for two weeks.

4. Record the number of miles between fill-ups and the amount of gasoline used.

Figure 18 Possible procedural steps

Figure 19 Data generated from procedure steps

Gasoline Data			
	Miles traveled	Gallons used	Gallons per mile
Regular gasoline	762	45.34	0.059
Premium gasoline	661	42.30	0.064

Separating and Controlling Variables

In any experiment, it is important to keep everything the same except for the item you are testing. The one factor that you change is called the *independent variable*. The factor that changes as a result of the independent variable is called the *dependent variable*. Always make sure that there is only one independent variable. If you allow more than one, you will not know what causes the changes you observe in the independent variable. Many experiments have *controls*—a treatment or an experiment that you can compare with the results of your test groups.

Example In the experiment with the gasoline, you made everything the same except the type of gasoline being used. The driver, the type of automobile, and the weather conditions should remain the same throughout. The gasoline should also be purchased from the same service station. By doing so, you made sure that at the end of the experiment, any differences were the result of the type of fuel being used—regular or premium. The type of gasoline was the *independent factor* and the gas mileage achieved was the *dependent factor*. The use of regular gasoline was the *control*.

Interpreting Data

The word *interpret* means "to explain the meaning of something." Look at the problem originally being explored in the gasoline experiment and find out what the data show. Identify the control group and the test group so you can see whether or not the variable has had an effect. Then, you need to check differences between the control and test groups.

Figure 20 Which gasoline type is most efficient?

Science Skill Handbook

These differences may be qualitative or quantitative. A qualitative difference would be a difference that you could observe and describe, while a quantitative difference would be a difference you can measure using numbers. If there are differences, the variable being tested may have had an effect. If there is no difference between the control and the test groups, the variable being tested apparently has had no effect.

Example Perhaps you are looking at a table from an experiment designed to test the hypothesis: If premium gas is more efficient, then it should increase the fuel mileage of our family car. Look back at **Figure 19** showing the results of this experiment. In this example, the use of regular gasoline in the family car was the control, while the car being fueled by premium gasoline was the test group.

Data showed a quantitative difference in efficiency for gasoline consumption. It took 0.059 gallons of regular gasoline to travel one mile, while it took 0.064 gallons of the premium gasoline to travel the same distance. The regular gasoline was more efficient; it increased the fuel mileage of the family car.

What are data? In the experiment described on these pages, measurements were taken so that at the end of the experiment, you had something concrete to interpret. You had numbers to work with. Not every experiment that you do will give you data in the form of numbers. Sometimes, data will be in the form of a description. At the end of a chemistry experiment, you might have noted that

Figure 21

one solution turned yellow when treated with a particular chemical, and another remained colorless, as water, when treated with the same chemical. Data, therefore, are stated in different forms for different types of scientific experiments.

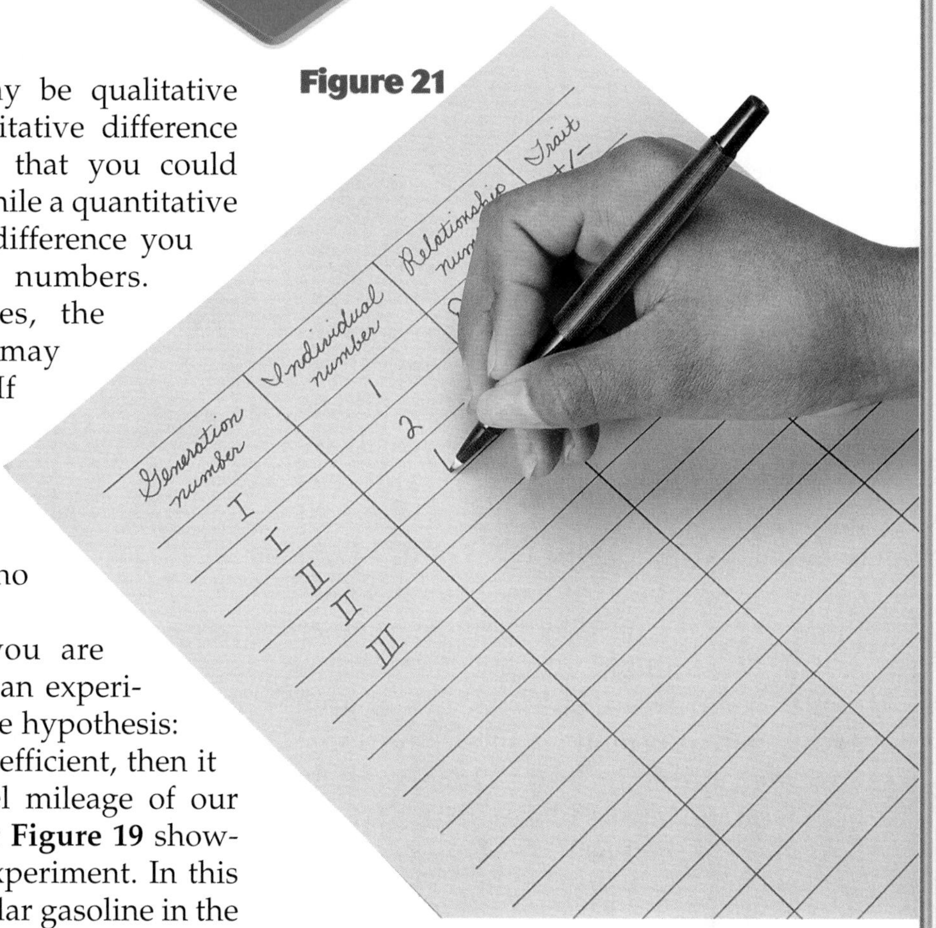

Are all experiments alike? Keep in mind as you perform experiments in science that not every experiment makes use of all of the parts that have been described on these pages. For some, it may be difficult to design an experiment that will always have a control. Other experiments are complex enough that it may be hard to have only one dependent variable. Real scientists encounter many variations in the methods that they use when they perform experiments. The skills in this handbook are here for you to use and practice. In real situations, their uses will vary.

Science Skill Handbook

Representing and Applying Data

Interpreting Scientific Illustrations

As you read a science textbook, you will see many drawings, diagrams, and photographs. Illustrations help you to understand what you read. Some illustrations are included to help you understand an idea that you can't see easily by yourself. For instance, we can't see atoms, but we can look at a diagram of an atom and that helps us to understand some things about atoms. Seeing something often helps you remember more easily. Illustrations also provide examples that clarify difficult concepts or give additional information about the topic you are studying. Maps, for example, help you to locate places that may be described in the text.

Examples

Captions and Labels Most illustrations have captions. A caption is a comment that identifies or explains the illustration. Diagrams, such as **Figure 22,** often have

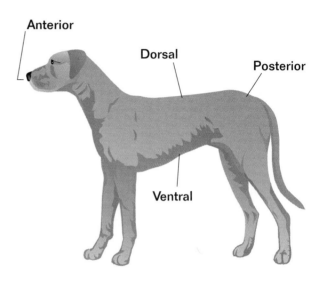

Figure 23 The orientation of a dog is shown here.

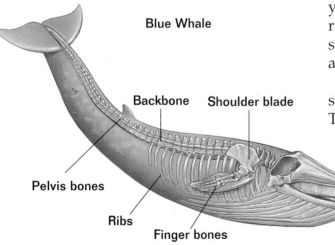

Figure 22 A labeled diagram of a blue whale

labels that identify parts of the organism or the order of steps in a process.

Learning with Illustrations An illustration of an organism shows that organism from a particular view or orientation. In order to understand the illustration, you may need to identify the front (anterior) end, tail (posterior) end, the underside (ventral), and the back (dorsal) side, as shown in **Figure 23.**

You might also check for symmetry. A shark in **Figure 24** has bilateral symmetry. This means that drawing an imaginary line through the center of the animal from the anterior to posterior end forms two mirror images.

Radial symmetry is the arrangement of similar parts around a central point. An object or organism, such as a hydra, can be divided anywhere through the center into similar parts.

Some organisms and objects cannot be divided into two similar parts. If an

Science Skill Handbook

Figure 24 A shark (A) illustrating bilateral symmetry and a pear (B) illustrating a longitudinal section and a cross section

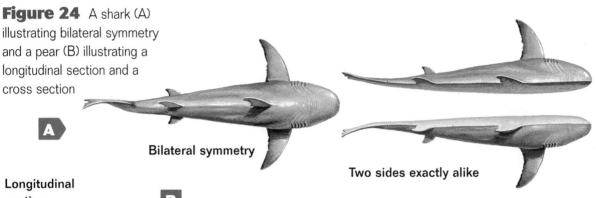

A

Bilateral symmetry

Two sides exactly alike

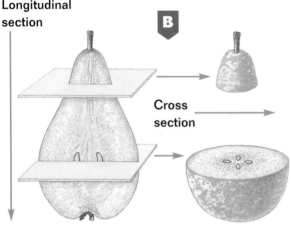

Longitudinal section

B

Cross section

organism or object cannot be divided, it is asymmetrical. Regardless of how you try to divide a natural sponge, you cannot divide it into two parts that look alike.

Some illustrations enable you to see the inside of an organism or object. These illustrations are called sections. **Figure 24** also illustrates some common sections.

Look at all illustrations carefully. Read captions and labels so that you understand exactly what the illustration is showing you.

Making Models

Have you ever worked on a model car, plane, or rocket? These models look, and sometimes work, much like the real thing, but they are often on a different scale than the real thing. In science, models are used to help simplify large or small processes or structures that otherwise would be dif-

ficult to see and understand. Your understanding of a structure or process is enhanced when you work with materials to make a model that shows the basic features of the structure or process.

Example In order to make a model, you first have to get a basic idea about the structure or process involved. You decide to make a model to show the differences in size of arteries, veins, and capillaries. First, read about these structures. All three are hollow tubes. Arteries are round and thick. Veins are flat and have thinner walls than arteries. Capillaries are small.

Now, decide what you can use for your model. Common materials are often most useful and cheapest to work with when making models. As illustrated in **Figure 25** on the next page, different kinds and sizes of pasta might work for these models. Different sizes of rubber tubing might do just as well. Cut and glue the different noodles or tubing onto thick paper so the openings can be seen. Then label each. Now you have a simple, easy-to-understand model showing the differences in size of arteries, veins, and capillaries.

What other scientific ideas might a model help you to understand? A model of a molecule can be made from balls of modeling clay (using different colors for the different elements present) and toothpicks (to show different chemical bonds).

Science Skill Handbook

Figure 25 Different types of pasta may be used to model blood vessels

A working model of a volcano can be made from clay, a small amount of baking soda, vinegar, and a bottle cap. Other models can be devised on a computer. Some models are mathematical and are represented by equations.

Measuring in SI

The metric system is a system of measurement developed by a group of scientists in 1795. It helps scientists avoid problems by providing standard measurements that all scientists around the world can understand. A modern form of the metric system, called the International System, or SI, was adopted for worldwide use in 1960.

The metric system is convenient because unit sizes vary by multiples of 10. When changing from smaller units to larger units, divide by 10. When changing from larger units to smaller, multiply by 10. For example, to convert millimeters to centimeters, divide the millimeters by 10. To convert 30 millimeters to centimeters, divide 30 by 10 (30 millimeters equal 3 centimeters).

Prefixes are used to name units. Look at **Figure 26** for some common metric prefixes and their meanings. Do you see how the prefix *kilo-* attached to the unit *gram* is *kilogram*, or 1000 grams? The prefix *deci-* attached to the unit *meter* is *decimeter*, or one-tenth (0.1) of a meter.

Examples

Length You have probably measured lengths or distances many times. The meter is the SI unit used to measure length. A baseball bat is about one meter long. When measuring smaller lengths, the meter is divided into smaller units called centimeters and millimeters. A centimeter is one-hundredth (0.01) of a meter, which is about the size of the width of the fingernail on your ring finger. A millimeter is one-thousandth of a meter (0.001), about the thickness of a dime.

Most metric rulers have lines indicating centimeters and millimeters, as shown in

Figure 26 Common metric prefixes

Metric Prefixes			
Prefix	Symbol	Meaning	
kilo-	k	1000	thousand
hecto-	h	200	hundred
deca-	da	10	ten
deci-	d	0.1	tenth
centi-	c	0.01	hundredth
milli-	m	0.001	thousandth

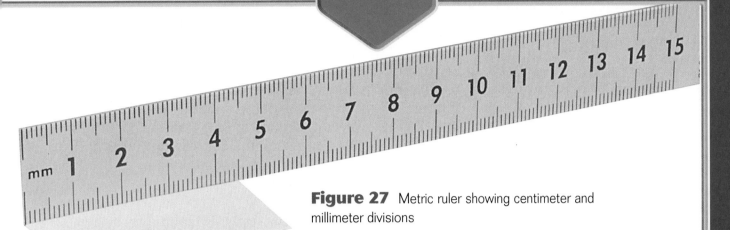

Figure 27 Metric ruler showing centimeter and millimeter divisions

Figure 27. The centimeter lines are the longer, numbered lines; the shorter lines are millimeter lines. When using a metric ruler, line up the 0-centimeter mark with the end of the object being measured, and read the number of the unit where the object ends, in this instance 4.5 cm.

Surface Area Units of length are also used to measure surface area. The standard unit of area is the square meter (m^2). A square that's one meter long on each side has a surface area of one square meter. Similarly, a square centimeter, (cm^2), shown in **Figure 28,** is one centimeter long on each side. The surface area of an object is determined by multiplying the length times the width.

Volume The volume of a rectangular solid is also calculated using units of length. The cubic meter (m^3) is the standard SI unit of volume. A cubic meter is a cube one meter on each side. You can determine the volume of rectangular solids by multiplying length times width times height.

Liquid Volume During science activities, you will measure liquids using beakers and graduated cylinders marked in milliliters, as illustrated in **Figure 29.** A graduated cylinder is a cylindrical container marked with lines from bottom to top.

Liquid volume is measured using a unit called a liter. A liter has the volume of 1000 cubic centimeters. Because the prefix *milli-* means thousandth (0.001), a milliliter equals one cubic centimeter. One milliliter of liquid would completely fill a cube measuring one centimeter on each side.

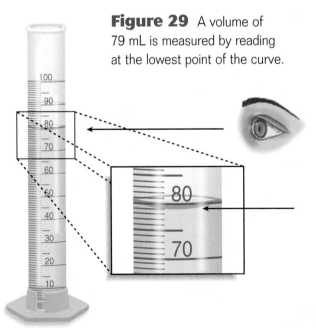

Figure 29 A volume of 79 mL is measured by reading at the lowest point of the curve.

Figure 28 A square centimeter

1 cm

1 cm

Mass Scientists use balances to find the mass of objects in grams. You might use a beam balance similar to **Figure 30.** Notice that on one side of the balance is a pan and on the other side is a set of beams. Each beam has an object of a known mass called a *rider* that slides on the beam.

Before you find the mass of an object, set the balance to zero by sliding all the riders back to the zero point. Check the pointer on the right to make sure it swings an equal distance above and below the zero point on the scale. If the swing is unequal, find and turn the adjusting screw until you have an equal swing.

Place an object on the pan. Slide the rider with the largest mass along its beam until the pointer drops below zero. Then move it back one notch. Repeat the process on each beam until the pointer swings an equal distance above and below the zero point. Add the masses on each beam to find the mass of the object.

You should never place a hot object or pour chemicals directly onto the pan. Instead, find the mass of a clean beaker or a glass jar. Place the dry or liquid chemicals in the container. Then find the combined mass of the container and the chemicals. Calculate the mass of the chemicals by subtracting the mass of the empty container from the combined mass.

Predicting

When you apply a hypothesis, or general explanation, to a specific situation, you predict something about that situation. First, you must identify which hypothesis fits the situation you are considering.

Examples People use prediction to make everyday decisions. Based on previous observations and experiences, you may form a hypothesis that if it is wintertime, then temperatures will be lower. From past experience in your area, temperatures are lowest in February. You may then use this hypothesis to predict specific temperatures and weather for the month of February in advance. Someone could use these predictions to plan to set aside more money for heating bills during that month.

Figure 30 A beam balance is used to measure mass.

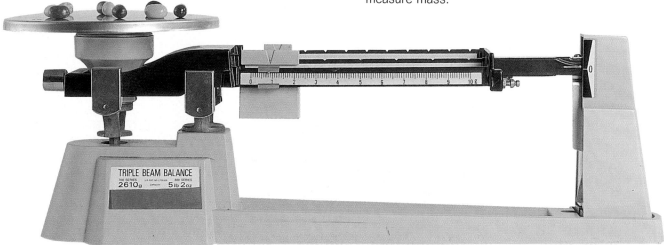

Science Skill Handbook

Using Numbers

When working with large populations of organisms, scientists usually cannot observe or study every organism in the population. Instead, they use a sample or a portion of the population. To sample is to take a small representative portion of organisms of a population for research. By making careful observations or manipulating variables within a portion of a group, information is discovered and conclusions are drawn that might then be applied to the whole population.

Scientific work also involves estimating. To estimate is to make a judgment about the size of something or the number of something without actually measuring or counting every member of a population.

Examples Suppose you are trying to determine the effect of a specific nutrient on the growth of black-eyed Susans. It would be impossible to test the entire population of black-eyed Susans, so you would select part of the population for your experiment. Through careful experimentation and observation on a sample of the population, you could generalize the effect of the chemical on the entire population.

Here is a more familiar example. Have you ever tried to guess how many beans were in a sealed jar? If you did, you were estimating. What if you knew the jar of beans held one liter (1000 mL)? If you knew that 30 beans would fit in a 100-milliliter jar, how many beans would you estimate to be in the one-liter jar? If you said about 300 beans, your estimate would be close to the actual number of beans. Can you estimate how many jelly beans are on the cookie sheet in **Figure 31?**

Scientists use a similar process to estimate populations of organisms from bacteria to buffalo. Scientists count the actual number of organisms in a small sample and then estimate the number of organisms in a larger area. For example, if a scientist wanted to count the number of bacterial colonies in a petri dish, a microscope could be used to count the number of organisms in a one-square-centimeter sample. To determine the total population of the culture, the number of organisms in the square-centimeter sample is multiplied by the total number of square centimeters in the culture.

Figure 31

Sampling a group of jelly beans allows for an estimation of the total number of jelly beans in the group.

Technology Skill Handbook

Using a Word Processor

Suppose your teacher has assigned you to write a report. After you've done your research and decided how you want to write the information, you need to put all that information on paper. The easiest way to do this is with a word processor.

A word processor is a computer program in which you can write your information, change it as many times as you need to, and then print it out so that it looks neat and clean. You can also use a word processor to create tables and columns, add bullets or cartoon art, include page numbers, and even check your spelling.

Example Last week in Science class, your teacher assigned a report on the history of the atom. It has to be double spaced and include at least one table. You've collected all the facts, and you're ready to write your report. Sitting down at your computer, you decide you want to begin by explaining early scientific ideas about the atom and then talk about what scientists think about the atom now.

After you've written the two parts of your report, you decide to put a heading or subtitle above each part and add a title to the paper. To make each of these look different from the rest of your report, you can use a word processor to make the words bigger and bolder. The word processor also can double space your entire report, so that you don't have to add an extra space between each line.

You decide to include a table that lists each scientist that contributed to the theory of the atom along with his or her contribution. Using your word processor, you can create a table with as many rows and columns as you need. And, if you forget to include a scientist in the middle, you can go back and insert a row in the middle of your table without redoing the entire table.

When you've finished with your report, you can tell the word processor to check your spelling. If it finds misspelled words, it often will suggest a word you can use to replace the misspelled word. But, remember that the word processor may not know how to spell all the words in your report. Scan your report and double check your spelling with a dictionary if you're not sure if a word is spelled correctly.

After you've made sure that your report looks just the way you want it on the screen, the word processor will print your report on a printer. With a word processor, your report can look like it was written by a real scientist.

Helpful Hints

- If you aren't sure how to do something using your word processor, look under the help menu. You can look up how to do something, and the word processor will tell you how to do it. Just follow the instructions that the word processor puts on your screen.

- Just because you've spelled checked your report doesn't mean that the spelling is perfect. The spell check can't catch misspelled words that look like other words. So, if you've accidentally typed *mind* instead of *mine*, the spell checker won't know the difference. Always reread your report to make sure you didn't miss any mistakes.

Technology Skill Handbook

Using a Database

Imagine you're in the middle of research project. You are busily gathering facts and information. But, soon you realize that its becoming harder and harder to organize and keep track of all the information. The tool to solve "information overload" is a database. A database is exactly what it sounds like—a base on which to organize data. Similar to how a file cabinet organizes records, a database also organizes records. However, a database is more powerful than a simple file cabinet because at the click of a mouse, the entire contents can be reshuffled and reorganized. At computer-quick speeds, databases can sort information by any characteristic and filter data into multiple categories. Once you use a database, you will be amazed at how quickly all those facts and bits of information become manageable.

Example For the past few weeks, you have been gathering information on living and extinct primates. A database would be ideal to organize your information. An entry for gorillas might contain fields (categories) for fossil locations, brain size, average height, earliest fossil, and so on. Later on, if you wanted to know which primates have been found in Asia, you could quickly filter all entries using Asia in the field that listed locations. The database will scan all the entries and select the entries containing Asia. If you wanted to rank all the primates by arm length, you would sort all the entries by arm length. By using different combinations of sorting and filtering, you can discover relationships between the data that otherwise might remain hidden.

Helpful Hints

- Before setting up your own database, it's easier to learn the features of your database software by practicing with an established database.
- Entering the data into a database can be time consuming. Learn shortcuts such as tabbing between entry fields and automatic formatting of data that your software may provide.
- Get in the habit of periodically saving your database as you are entering data. That way, if something happens and your computer locks up or the power goes out, you won't lose all of your work.

Most databases have specific words you can use to narrow your search.

- AND: If you place an AND between two words in your search, the database will look for any entries that have both the words. For example, "blood AND cell" would give you information about both blood and cells.
- OR: If you place an OR between two words, the database will show entries that have at least one of the words. For example, "bird OR fish" would show you information on either birds or fish.
- NOT: If you place a NOT between two words, the database will look for entries that have the first word but do not have the second word. For example, "reproduction NOT plant" would show you information about reproduction but not about plant reproduction.

Technology Skill Handbook

Using Graphics Software

Having trouble finding that exact piece of art you're looking for? Do you have a picture in your mind of what you want but can't seem to find the right graphic to represent your ideas? To solve these problems, you can use graphics software. Graphics software allows you to change and create images and diagrams in almost unlimited ways. Typical uses for graphics software include arranging clip-art, changing scanned images, and constructing pictures from scratch. Most graphics-software applications work in similar ways. They use the same basic tools and functions. Once you master one graphics application, you can use any other graphics application relatively easily.

Example For your report on bird adaptations, you want to make a poster displaying a variety of beak and foot types. You have acquired many photos of birds, scanned from magazines and downloaded off the Internet. Using graphics software, you separate the beaks and feet from the birds and enlarge them. Then, you use arrows and text to diagram the particular features that you want to highlight. You also highlight the key features in color, keeping the rest of the graphic in black and white. With graphics software, the possibilities are endless. For the final layout, you place the picture of the bird next to enlarged graphics of the feet and beak. Graphics software allows you to integrate text into your diagrams, which makes your bird poster look clean and professional.

Helpful Hints

- As with any method of drawing, the more you practice using the graphic software, the better your results.

- Start by using the software to manipulate existing drawings. Once you master this, making your own illustrations will be easier.
- Clip art is available on CD-ROMs, and on the Internet. With these resources, finding a piece of clip art to suit your purposes is simple.
- As you work on a drawing, save it often.
- Often you can learn a lot from studying other people's art. Look at other computer illustrations and try to figure out how the artist created it.

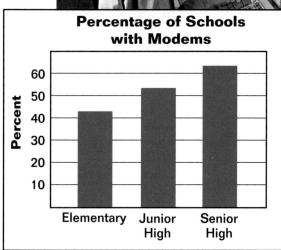

Percentage of Schools with Modems

Technology Skill Handbook

Using a Computerized Card Catalog

When you have a report or paper to research, you go to the library. To find the information, skill is needed in using a computerized card catalog. You use the computerized card catalog by typing in a subject, the title of a book, or an author's name. The computer will list on the screen all the holdings the library has on the subject, title, or author requested.

A library's holdings include books, magazines, databases, videos, and audio materials. When you have chosen something from this list, the computer will show whether an item is available and where in the library to find it.

Example You have a report due on dinosaurs, and you need to find three books on the subject. In the library, follow the instructions on the computer screen to select the "Subject" heading. You could start by typing in the word *dinosaurs*. This will give you a list of books on that subject. Now you need to narrow your search to the kind of dinosaur you are interested in, for example, *Tyrannosaurus rex*. You can type in *Tyrannosaurus rex* or just look through the list to find titles that you think would have information you need. Once you have selected a short list of books, click on each selection to find out if the library has the books. Then, check on where they are located in the library.

Helpful Hints

- Remember that you can use the computer to search by subject, author, or title. If you know a book's author, but not the title, you can search for all the books the library has by that author.
- When searching by subject, it's often most helpful to narrow your search by using specific search terms. If you don't find enough, you can then broaden your search.
- Pay attention to the type of materials found in your search. If you need a book, you can eliminate any videos or other resources that come up in your search.
- Knowing how your library is arranged can save a lot of time. The librarian will show you where certain types of material are kept and how to find something.

Developing Multimedia Presentations

It's your turn—you have to present your science report to the entire class. How do you do it? You can use many different sources of information to get the class excited about your presentation. Posters, videos, photographs, sound, computers, and the Internet can help show our ideas. First, decide the most important points you want your presentation to make. Then, sketch out what materials and types of media would be best to illustrate those points. Maybe you could start with an outline on an overhead projector, then show a video, followed by something from the Internet or a slide show accompanied by music or recorded voices. Make sure you don't make the presentation too complicated, or you will confuse yourself and the class. Practice your presentation a few times for your parents or brothers and sisters before you present it to the class.

Example Your assignment is to give a presentation on bird-watching. You could have a poster that shows what features you use to identify birds, with a sketch of your favorite bird. A tape of the calls of your favorite bird or a video of birds in your area would work well with the poster. If possible, include an Internet site with illustrations of birds that the class can look at.

Helpful Hints

- Carefully consider what media will best communicate the point you are trying to make.
- Keep your topic and your presentation simple.
- Make sure you learn how to use any equipment you will be using in your presentation.
- Practice the presentation several times.
- If possible, set up all of the equipment ahead of time. Make sure everything is working correctly.

Technology Skill Handbook

Using E-mail

It's science fair time and you want to ask a scientist a question about your project, but he or she lives far away. You could write a letter or make a phone call. But you can also use the computer to communicate. You can do this using electronic mail (E-mail). You will need a computer that is connected to an E-mail network. The computer is usually hooked up to the network by a device called a *modem*. A modem works through the telephone lines. Finally, you need an address for the person you want to talk with. The E-mail address works just like a street address to send mail to that person.

Example There are just a few steps needed to send a message to a friend on an E-mail network. First, select Message from the E-mail software menu. Then, enter the E-mail address of your friend. Next, type your message. Make sure you check it for spelling and other errors. Finally, click the Send button to mail your message and off it goes! You will get a reply back in your electronic mailbox. To read your reply, just click on the message and the reply will appear on the screen.

Helpful Hints

- Make sure that you have entered the correct address of the person you're sending the message to.
- Reread your message to make sure it says what you want to say, and check for spelling and grammar.
- If you receive an E-mail message, respond to it as soon as possible.
- If you receive frequent E-mail messages, keep them organized by either deleting them or saving them in folders according to the subject or sender.

Technology Skill Handbook

Using an Electronic Spreadsheet

Your science fair experiment has produced lots of numbers. How do you keep track of all the data, and how can you easily work out all the calculations needed? You can use a computer program called a *spreadsheet* to keep track of data that involve numbers. A spreadsheet is an electronic worksheet. Type in your data in rows and columns, just as in a data table on a sheet of paper. A spreadsheet uses some simple math to do calculations on the data. For example, you could add, subtract, divide, or multiply any of the values in the spreadsheet by another number. Or you can set up a series of math steps you want to apply to the data. If you want to add 12 to all the numbers and then multiply all the numbers by 10, the computer does all the calculations for you in the spreadsheet. Below is an example of a spreadsheet that is a schedule.

Example Let's say that to complete your project, you need to calculate the speed of the model cars in your experiment. Enter the distance traveled by each car in the rows of the spreadsheet. Then enter the time you recorded for each car to travel the measured distance in the column across from each car. To make the formula, just type in the equation you want the computer to calculate; in this case, *speed = distance ÷ time.* You must make sure the computer knows what data are in the rows and what data are in the columns so the calculation will be correct. Once all the distance and time data and the formula have been entered into the spreadsheet program, the computer will calculate the speed for all the trials you ran. You can even make graphs of the results.

	A	B	C	D
1	Test Runs	Time	Distance	Speed
2	Car 1	5 mins.	5 miles	60 mph
3	Car 2	10 mins.	4 miles	24 mph
4	Car 3	6 mins.	3 miles	30 mph

Test Run Data

Helpful Hints

- Before you set up the spreadsheet, sketch out how you want to organize the data. Include any formulas you will need to use.
- Make sure you have entered the correct data into the correct rows and columns.
- As you experiment with your particular spreadsheet program you will learn more of its features.
- You can also display your results in a graph. Pick the style of graph that best represents the data you are working with.

Technology Skill Handbook

Using a CD-ROM

What's your favorite music? You probably listen to your favorite music on compact discs (CDs). But, there is another use for compact discs, called CD-ROM. CD-ROM means Compact Disc-Read Only Memory. CD-ROMs hold information. Whole encyclopedias and dictionaries can be stored on CD-ROM discs. This kind of CD-ROM and others are used to research information for reports and papers. The information is accessed by putting the disc in your computer's CD-ROM drive and following the computer's installation instructions. The CD-ROM will have words, pictures, photographs, and maybe even sound and video on a range of topics.

Example Load the CD-ROM into the computer. Find the topic you are interested in by clicking on the Search button. If there is no Search button, try the Help button. Most CD-ROMs are easy to use, but refer to the Help instructions if you have problems. Use the arrow keys to move down through the list of titles on your topic. When you double-click on a title, the article will appear on the screen. You can print the article by clicking on the Print button. Each CD-ROM is different. Click the Help menu to see how to find what you want.

Helpful Hints

- Always open and close the CD-ROM drive on your computer by pushing the button next to the drive. Pushing on the tray to close it will stress the opening mechanism over time.
- Place the disc in the tray so the side with no printing is facing down.
- Read through the installation instructions that come with the CD-ROM.
- Remember to remove the CD-ROM before you shut your computer down.

Using Probeware

Data collecting in an experiment sometimes requires that you take the same measurement over and over again. With probeware, you can hook a probe directly to a computer and have the computer collect the data about temperature, pressure, motion, or pH. Probeware is a combination sensor and software that makes the process of collecting data easier. With probes hooked to computers, you can make many measurements quickly, and you can collect data over a long period of time without needing to be present. Not only will the software record the data, most software will graph the data.

Example Suppose you want to monitor the health of an enclosed ecosystem. You might use an oxygen and a carbon dioxide sensor to monitor the gas concentrations or humidity or temperature. If the gas concentrations remain stable, you could predict that the ecosystem is healthy. After all the data is collected, you can use the software to graph the data and analyze it. With probeware, experimenting is made efficient and precise.

Helpful Hints

- Find out how to properly use each probe before using it.
- Make sure all cables are solidly connected. A loose cable can interrupt the data collection and give you inaccurate results.
- Because probeware makes data collection so easy, do as many trials as possible to strengthen your data.

Technology Skill Handbook

Using a Graphing Calculator

Science can be thought of as a means to predict the future and explain the past. In other language, if x happens, can we predict y? Can we explain the reason y happened? Simply, is there a relationship between x and y? In nature, a relationship between two events or two quantities, x and y, often occurs. However, the relationship is often complicated and can only be readily seen by making a graph. To analyze a graph, there is no quicker tool than a graphing calculator. The graphing calculator shows the mathematical relationship between two quantities.

Example If you have collected data on the position and time for a migrating whale, you can use the calculator to graph the data. Using the linear regression function on the calculator, you can determine the average migration speed of the whale. The more you use the graphing calculator to solve problems, the more you will discover its power and efficiency.

Graphing calculators have some keys that other calculators do not have. The keys on the bottom half of the calculator are those found on all scientific calculators. The keys located just below the screen are the graphing keys. You will also notice the up, down, left, and right arrow keys. These allow you to move the cursor around on the screen, to "trace" graphs that have been plotted, and to choose items from the menus. The other keys located on the top of the calculator access the special features such as statistical computations and programming features.

A few of the keystrokes that can save you time when using the graphing calculator are listed below.

- The commands above the calculator keys are accessed with the [2nd] or [ALPHA] key. The [2nd] key and its commands are yellow and the [ALPHA] and its commands are green.
- [2nd] [ENTRY] copies the previous calculation so you can edit and use it again.
- Pressing [ON] while the calculator is graphing stops the calculator from completing the graph.
- [2nd] [QUIT] will return you to the home (or text) screen.
- [2nd] [A-LOCK] locks the [ALPHA] key, which is like pressing "shift lock" or "caps lock" on a typewriter or computer. The result is that all letters will be typed and you do not have to repeatedly press the [ALPHA] key. (This is handy for programming.) Stop typing letters by pressing [ALPHA] again.
- [2nd] [OFF] turns the calculator off.

Helpful Hints

- Mastering the graphing calculator takes practice. Don't expect to learn it all in an afternoon.
- Programming a graphing calculator takes a plan. Write out all of the steps before entering them.
- It's easiest to learn how to program the calculator by first using programs that have already been written. As you enter them, figure out what each step is telling the calculator to do.

Skill Activities

Table of Contents

Chapter 1 Separating and Controlling Variables 578
Chapter 2 Using Numbers. 579
Chapter 3 Making Models. 580
Chapter 4 Interpreting Tables 581
Chapter 5 Observing and Inferring 582
Chapter 6 Concept Mapping. 583
Chapter 7 Communicating 584
Chapter 8 Classifying 585
Chapter 9 Observing and Inferring 586
Chapter 10 Predicting 587
Chapter 11 Recognizing Cause and Effect. 588
Chapter 12 Making and Using Graphs 589
Chapter 13 Inferring 590
Chapter 14 Observing and Inferring 591
Chapter 15 Using Numbers. 592
Chapter 16 Using Numbers. 593
Chapter 17 Interpreting Scientific Illustrations 594
Chapter 18 Communicating 595

Separating and Controlling Variables

Background

Scientists often will conduct experiments to answer questions, test hypotheses, or solve problems. In any experiment, it is important to keep all factors the same except for the one you are testing. The factor you change is called the independent variable. If you change more than one variable in an experiment, you will not know which factor caused the effects you observe in the experiment.

Identify the independent variable in the following experiment.

Suppose a scientist has the job of studying the factors that affect the growth rate of marigolds. She sets up four plants to test her experiment. Descriptions of the plants are listed below.

Procedure

Study the experiment descriptions and identify the independent variable. You may wish to make a table to organize the information.

Plant 1—soil mix A, 12 hours of light per day, no fertilizer, 22°C, water every other day.

Plant 2—soil mix A, 12 hours of light per day, no fertilizer, 22°C, water once a week.

Plant 3—soil mix A, 12 hours of light per day, no fertilizer, 22°C, water every day.

Plant 4—soil mix A, 12 hours of light per day, no fertilizer, 22°C, no water.

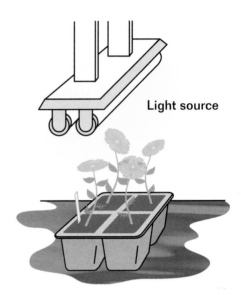

Light source

Practicing the SKILL

1. What variable is being tested in this experiment?
2. Name three other variables in this experiment.
3. Plant 2 grew taller than Plant 3. Infer what caused this effect.
4. Write a hypothesis that would be appropriate for this experimental design.
5. How might the experiment change if the scientist wanted to study the effect of sunlight on the growth rate of marigolds? Write a hypothesis for this experiment.

For more skill practice, do the

GLENCOE TECHNOLOGY

Chapter 1 Interactive Exploration on the **Science Voyages Grade 6 CD-ROM.**

Using Numbers

Background

Data can be reported in a variety of ways. Sometimes, data presented as percentages are more useful than data presented as a list of numbers. For example, if you learned that your city experienced 91 days that had a high temperature of over 20°C last year, you might think that the weather was quite warm for most of the year. But, what if you learned that the temperature rose above 20°C only 25 percent of the year? Would you interpret those results differently than the first results? The data presented as a percentage can provide a meaningful description.

However, you need to make sure you know exactly what the percentage represents. Sometimes, data results can be misleading. If 70 percent of the people polled before an election said they planned to vote for candidate A and 30 percent said they planned to vote for candidate B, would you think that candidate A would be the winner? Before you make a decision based on data, you should find out if the research method is biased, or slanted toward one particular view.

Percentages provide a useful means of summarizing and reporting data. How would you go about presenting information as a percentage?

Procedure

1 Results of a class survey show the different types of transportation that 35 students use to get to school every day. Look at the data in the table.

2 To calculate the percentage of the class that walks to school, use the following formula:

$$\frac{\text{number of students who walk}}{\text{total number of students surveyed}} \times 100$$

$$\frac{10}{35} \times 100 = 29\%$$

About 29 percent of the class walks to school.

Transportation to School	
Method of Transportation	**Number of Students**
Walk	10
Ride a bus	14
Ride a bike	4
Ride in a car	7

Practicing the SKILL

1 Use the data in the table to calculate the percentage of students who use each method of transportation.

2 There are 30 students in a class. If 65 percent of the class reports that cheese pizza is their favorite lunch, how many students is that?

For more skill practice, do the Chapter 2 Interactive Exploration on the **Science Voyages Grade 6 CD-ROM.**

GLENCOE TECHNOLOGY

Making Models

Background

Architects, builders, and designers often use detailed drawings as they plan their work. These are known as floorplans and represent a type of scale drawing. A scale drawing is a 2-dimensional model where an object's size and location are kept in the same proportions as in the actual object. For example, suppose a floorplan has a scale of 1 cm = 1 m. A room shown on this plan measures 10 cm × 15 cm. The actual room is 10 m × 15 m. A 1 m × 2 m desk in that room would be drawn as a rectangle 1 cm × 2 cm. The procedure below will help you make a scale drawing of your classroom.

Procedure

1. Measure the length and width of your classroom and decide on a scale to use that will allow your plan to cover most of your piece of paper. For example, if your paper is 25 cm × 36 cm and your room is 12 m × 15 m you could use a scale of 1 cm = 0.5 m. This would create a drawing of the classroom that measures 24 cm × 30 cm, which would fit on the paper.

2. Convert the dimensions of the room to your floorplan scale. Use a pencil and ruler to neatly draw the outline of the room on your paper.

3. Measure the width of the doorway and where it is located. Convert these measurements to your floorplan scale and draw the doorway on your plan.

4. Measure your teacher's desk and how far it is located from the walls. Use these measurements to accurately draw the desk in its proper position on your floorplan.

5. Repeat the procedure for any windows and other furniture in the classroom.

6. Title your classroom map and be sure to include your scale in the map key.

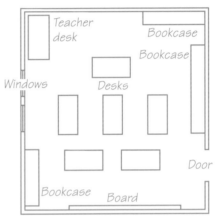

Classroom floor plan (scale: 1 cm = 2 m)

Practicing the SKILL

Imagine that your teacher has received two new computer workstations. Each station has a desk that measures 1 m × 2 m. Use your scale drawing to determine where these workstations might fit in the classroom. You may need to "move" some furniture on your map. Draw the workstations on your classroom floorplan.

For more skill practice, do the Chapter 3 Interactive Exploration on the **Science Voyages Grade 6 CD-ROM**.

GLENCOE TECHNOLOGY

Interpreting Tables

Background

To organize data in a more understandable form, scientists often use data tables. The ability to use data tables is a useful skill. In this activity, you will practice interpreting information in a table. You also will learn to retrieve data from a table that answer specific questions.

Procedure

1. Study the Mineral Characteristics table below. Each row contains information about a specific mineral and each column compares a single mineral characteristic.

2. What characteristic could you use to distinguish between pyrite and graphite?

3. If you had a mineral with a glassy luster and a colorless streak, which of the minerals in the table could it be? What characteristic could you use to narrow the identification to a single mineral?

Practicing the SKILL

1. The minerals in the table are arranged in order according to one of the four characteristics. Which characteristic is it? Explain your answer.

2. Which mineral in the table has the greatest hardness?

For more skill practice, do the Chapter 4 Interactive Exploration on the **Science Voyages Grade 6 CD-ROM.**

GLENCOE TECHNOLOGY

Mineral Characteristics				
Mineral	**Streak**	**Hardness**	**Specific gravity**	**Luster**
graphite	black	1–1.5	2.3	metallic
talc	colorless	1.0	2.7–2.8	pearly
fluorite	colorless	4.0	3.18	glassy
topaz	colorless	8.0	3.4–3.6	glassy
sphalerite	light brown	3.5–4	3.9–4.1	resinous*
pyrite	black	6–6.5	5.0	metallic

*Resinous luster means having the luster of resin, a yellowish-brown substance secreted by plants.

Observing and Inferring

Background

You have learned that mechanical weathering occurs when rocks break apart without changing their chemical composition. Two common mechanisms of mechanical weathering are ice wedging and growing plants.

Mechanical weathering from plants can cause problems with human-made structures such as sidewalks, driveways, walls, and house foundations. These structures usually are made of concrete, a rocklike material made of sand, crushed rock, and cement. People often plant trees near sidewalks, driveways, and houses, or there may be preexisting trees in the area. Tree roots will grow beneath the concrete slabs. As the roots grow in diameter, they generate a force that is often great enough to lift and crack the concrete. A broken sidewalk is a relatively minor problem to replace, but if tree roots lift and break a house foundation, it can lead to expensive repairs.

Procedure

1. Carefully observe the outside environment where you live. Look for evidence of mechanical weathering caused by plant roots. Some good places to look might be sidewalks, driveways, and walls near large trees. In addition, you might also look for areas where plant roots have cracked large rocks.

2. Once you have found a good example, write a description and draw a sketch of the mechanical weathering you observe.

3. Use a ruler to measure in centimeters how wide a crack is, or how much the structure has been lifted by the plant. This is called displacement. Note this distance in your written description.

4. Do some research to find out when the sidewalk, driveway, or wall was built or when the tree was planted. Use this information to determine the age of the crack.

Practicing the SKILL

1. Share your observations with the class. How many different examples of mechanical weathering were observed?

2. What was the greatest amount of displacement that was observed?

3. If you were able to determine how old your structure is, divide the displacement by the age to calculate how many centimeters per year the crack moves.

For more skill practice, do the

Chapter 5 Interactive Exploration on the **Science Voyages Grade 6 CD-ROM.**

Concept Mapping

Background

You have learned that erosion is the process by which surface materials are transported between locations by the agents of gravity, wind, water, and glaciers. Erosional agents can be divided into two main groups: erosion caused by moving or flowing water, such as rivers and ocean waves; and erosion caused by other agents like glaciers, gravity, and wind. All of these erosional forces have similarities and differences. A concept map of erosional forces can help you understand these relationships.

Procedure

A list of terms related to erosion by glaciers, gravity, and wind is written above. Study the list and create separate tree concept maps for these three agents of erosion. Select terms for each specific tree from the list. Some of the terms may not be used. Wind has been done for you.

Erosion Terms	
gravity	glacial deposits
glaciers	slow movement
mass movement	glacial erosion features
till	fast movement
moraine	creep
outwash plains	rock slide
leaning trees and telephone poles	material moved by ice
mudflow	piles of broken rock
curved scars	thick mix of sediment and water
cirque	slump
arête	U-shaped valleys

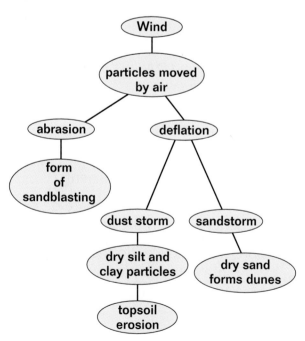

Practicing the SKILL

1. Describe two characteristics that glaciers, gravity, and wind, as erosional agents, have in common.

2. For each erosional agent, describe one characteristic that is not shared by the other two agents.

3. How do concept maps help you learn about erosional forces?

For more skill practice, do the Chapter 6 Interactive Exploration on the **Science Voyages Grade 6 CD-ROM.**

GLENCOE TECHNOLOGY

Communicating

Background

Not all of the information that we read is presented honestly or accurately. In order to make informed decisions, you must be able to evaluate critically the information you read to make sure that the information is not only accurate but also that it is not biased or slanted to one particular view. Use the following guidelines to determine if the scientific information you read is reliable.

Procedure

(1) Check the background of the author. Most articles written in journals or magazines give a brief biographical sketch of the author. Is the author a professional in the field about which he or she is writing, or is the author trained in another, unrelated field? Has the author earned awards in that field or awards from any of the major scientific societies?

(2) Check the source of the article. Has the article been written for a scientific journal or has the article appeared in a popular magazine or local newspaper?

(3) Evaluate the emotional level of the information. Scientific information is generally written in a straightforward style. When you read an article, consider the question: Does the headline or title make you angry, sad, or happy?

(4) Read the article for how the content is presented. Check to see that concepts are clearly explained and supported by research. Be wary if many conclusions are drawn from only one, limited experiment. Also watch for overuse of such comments as "I think," or "In my opinion."

(5) Determine whether the information has been taken out of context. Is the scientist writing the article or has someone reinterpreted the scientist's comments? Is it possible that only parts of the quoted comments are reported?

Practicing the SKILL

(1) Read the following headlines. Which one do you think would contain more reliable information?

- **Strange Fish Kill Has Public Upset**
- **Scientists Investigate the Death of Fish in Plum River**

(2) Which of the following three periodicals would be the best source of information for the situations below?

- *An environmental periodical*
- *A consumer periodical*
- *An encyclopedia*

a. Which detergent will clean your clothes the best?

b. What new compounds are being used in making detergents?

c. What effect do phosphate detergents have on the environment?

For more skill practice, do the Chapter 7 Interactive Exploration on the **Science Voyages Grade 6 CD-ROM.**

GLENCOE TECHNOLOGY

Classifying

Background

Keys are used to identify things that are already classified.

In this Skill Activity, you will learn about some trees and how they have been classified. For this activity you need to know that needlelike leaves are shaped like needles and scalelike leaves are like the scales on a fish or a lizard. You also need to collect a variety of gymnosperm leaves.

Procedure

① Look at illustrations or actual examples of gymnosperm leaves.

② Make a data table and record the number of each sample in the first column.

③ Use the key below to identify the leaves. There may be differences among the leaves. Choose the statement that describes most of the leaves on the branch. By following the key, the numbered steps will lead you to the name of the plant.

Key to Classifying Leaves

1. All leaves are needlelike.
   a. yes, go to 2
   b. no, go to 8

2. Needles are in clusters.
   a. yes, go to 3
   b. no, go to 4

3. Clusters contain 2, 3, or 5 needles.
   a. yes, pine
   b. no, cedar

4. Needles grow on all sides of the stem.
   a. yes, go to 5
   b. no, go to 7

5. Needles grow from a woody peg.
   a. yes, spruce
   b. no, go to 6

6. Needles appear to grow from the branch.
   a. yes, Douglas fir
   b. no, hemlock

7. Most of the needles grow upward.
   a. yes, fir
   b. no, redwood

8. All needles are scalelike but not prickly.
   a. yes, arborvitae
   b. no, juniper

Practicing the SKILL

① What trait was used to separate the gymnosperm leaves into two groups?

② What are two traits of a hemlock?

③ What gymnosperms have scalelike leaves?

④ Describe a spruce leaf.

⑤ How are pine and cedar leaves alike?

For more skill practice, do the Chapter 8 Interactive Exploration on the **Science Voyages Grade 6 CD-ROM.**

GLENCOE TECHNOLOGY

Observing and Inferring

Background

One of the best tools for learning science is having good observation skills. You can learn by simply watching things happen. This was the main tool that Aristotle used when he made many of his discoveries. He kept detailed records of his observations. Over time, he collected much information about the living things in his surroundings. He made many inferences from his observations. Some have been proven to be true, but others have been shown not to be true. Other scientists used many of his recorded observations for further study.

Procedure

1. Your teacher will tape to your back a card with the name of a plant, flower, fruit, or vegetable written on it.

2. For thirty minutes, move around the classroom and have other students act out clues to the name on your card. No one should speak during the observation time.

3. Keep a list of the clues then make an inference about the name written on your card.

Practicing the SKILL

1. Were you able to infer the correct name on your card?

2. How many clues did you observe before you knew the name on your card?

3. How many of your classmates correctly inferred the names on their cards?

For more skill practice, do the Chapter 15 Interactive Exploration on the **Science Voyages Grade 6 CD-ROM.**

GLENCOE TECHNOLOGY

Predicting

Background

Large populations of organisms need to be counted to determine the overall health of the species. However, counting each individual in a population can be time consuming and confusing. Therefore, scientists have developed methods for estimating the number of individuals in a population in order to save time. In this activity, you will predict the number of beetles by estimating the total number.

Ladybird Numbers		
Predicted number _____ Time _____		
Number in top left square ×	Total number of squares =	Estimated total number
_____	_____	_____
Actual number _____ Time _____		

Procedure

(1) Estimate the number of ladybird beetles in the figure to the right and record the number in a table like the one shown.

(2) Place tracing paper over the diagram. Make a population count by placing a checkmark next to each ladybird beetle. Record the actual number of beetles in the table. Next to this number, record the amount of time it took to make the count.

(3) Count the ladybird beetle population a second time by sampling. A sample is made by selecting and counting only a portion of the population. Count the number of ladybird beetles in the top left square and record this number in the table.

(4) Enter the total number of squares in the table. Multiply the number of ladybird beetles in the top left square by the total number of squares. Record this estimated total number in the table.

(5) At the top of the table, record the amount of time it took to make the sample count.

Practicing the SKILL

(1) How many ladybird beetles did you estimate were shown?

(2) Which way was faster—making an actual count or sampling?

(3) Were the results exactly the same?

For more skill practice, do the Chapter 10 Interactive Exploration on the **Science Voyages Grade 6 CD-ROM.**

Recognizing Cause and Effect

Background

Have you ever wondered why something happened? Scientists often wonder "why." They carefully observe an event and then try to determine why it occurred. This relationship between an event and why it occurred is the *effect*. The reason it happened is the *cause*. One effect often may have more than one possible cause. It is often difficult to identify the specific cause, or causes, of a given event. For example, your grade on a test is an effect. The reasons you got that grade are the causes. These could include your study habits, attendance, attention in class, and your physical condition. Analyzing the causes of events can help change an effect if it was undesirable, or re-create it if it was good.

Procedure

Make a copy of the Cause-and-Effect Data table in your Science Journal, and fill in the appropriate cause or effect.

Cause-and-Effect Data	
Cause	**Effect**
1.	1. Desert animals rest during the day.
2. A population is separated from individuals of its own group and no longer can mate with them.	2.
3.	3. Ducks are able to migrate over long distances.
4. A sudden change occurs in the climate and environment.	4.

Practicing the SKILL

Look for possible cause-and-effect relationships in the figure at the left.
For more skill practice, do the Chapter 11 Interactive Exploration on the **Science Voyages Grade 6 CD-ROM.**

GLENCOE TECHNOLOGY

Making and Using Graphs

Background

The length of time it takes for a satellite to complete one orbit is called the orbital period. The greater the altitude of a satellite, the longer its orbital period. Satellites that stay above the same spot on Earth's surface are called geostationary satellites. The orbital period of a geostationary satellite equals 24 h. Communication systems for telephone and television use geostationary satellites.

What is the altitude of a geostationary orbit? Try the following procedure to determine the altitude of a geostationary orbit.

Orbital Data			
Altitude of orbit (km)	Orbital velocity (km/hr)	Orbital circumference (km)	Orbital period (hr)
10 000	26 470	46 400	
20 000	17 770	103 000	
30 000	11 920	229 000	
40 000	10 560	292 000	
50 000	9575	354 000	

Procedure

① The Orbital Data table lists the altitude, speed, and circumference of six different orbits. The orbital period can be calculated by dividing the circumference by the speed. Calculate the orbital periods for each altitude and record the data.

② Make a line graph that compares the altitude and orbital period.

Orbital Periods of Earth Satellites

Orbital Period (h): 0, 10, 20, 30, 40
Orbital Altitude (km): 10 000, 30 000, 50 000

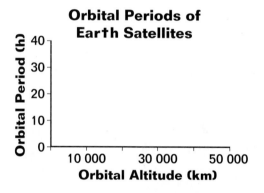

Practicing the SKILL

① What is the relationship between the altitude and the orbital speed?

② What is the approximate altitude of a satellite in a geostationary orbit?

For more skill practice, do the Chapter 12 Interactive Exploration on the **Science Voyages Grade 6 CD-ROM.**

GLENCOE TECHNOLOGY

Inferring

Background

The surfaces of Earth's moon, Mercury, and other planetary bodies are often covered with craters. Scientists usually are unable to determine the exact age of the craters because they do not have actual rock samples. However, photographs taken by satellites help scientists determine the rough ages of the craters. For example, if two craters overlap, the crater that appears to be underneath is the older of the two.

Procedure

The figure below is a diagram showing an area containing several craters. Each crater is labeled by a letter in its center. Study the relationships between the craters and determine their relative ages.

Practicing the SKILL

1. Which crater appeared first, crater A or crater C?

2. Can the approximate age of crater J be determined? Why or why not?

3. What is the approximate diameter of crater D?

4. List craters A through I in order of increasing age (youngest crater first).

For more skill practice, do the Chapter 13 Interactive Exploration on the **Science Voyages Grade 6 CD-ROM.**

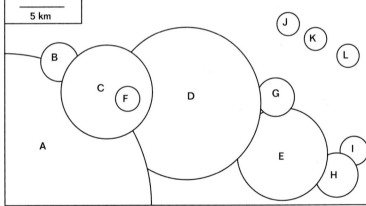

Observing and Inferring

Background

Suppose you smell a cinnamon-like scent. You might suspect someone nearby is baking cinnamon rolls. However, you might be wrong. The scent might be from candy or a kind of air freshener. You cannot be sure unless you actually see the source of the scent. Whenever you use your senses, you are making *observations* about the world around you. When you make a conclusion based on what you observe, you are making an *inference*. When you smell a scent and conclude that the scent is from a cinnamon roll, you are *inferring*.

Scientists use their senses to make observations. Based on what they observe, they make inferences. The inferences help them solve problems and predict future events. You can make observations and inferences about almost anything. Try improving your observing skills by looking carefully at an object. A visual observation should be made in an orderly way. First, look at the entire object. Then, look at its parts.

Procedure

① Observe **Figure A** carefully. Write down your observations on a separate paper.

② Did you notice (1) the color of the candle, (2) the blackened wick, (3) the melted wax on the candle and in the holder, and (4) the color of the holder?

③ Now, try making inferences based on what you observed in **Figure A.** You can base your observations on your own experience with candles. You might infer (1) how long the candle was lit (based on the amount of melted wax), (2) how much of the candle has melted, or

(3) why the candle is not burning now. Inferences are based on incomplete information. Therefore, they may be incorrect. The flame may have been lit for only a short time, for example.

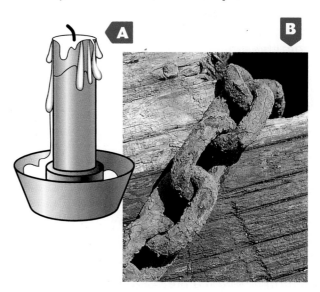

Practicing the SKILL

① Look carefully at **Figure B.** On a separate sheet of paper, write down what you observe.

② Write down what you can infer from your observations. Explain how you made each inference and, if possible, how it may be incorrect.

For more skill practice, do the

Chapter 14 Interactive Exploration on the **Science Voyages Grade 6 CD-ROM.**

Using Numbers

Background

Consumers who are energy conscious and who live in sunny climates look to solar-energy technicians to help them utilize energy from the sun.

One type of solar-energy system that a solar-heating technician can suggest collects the sun's energy, transforms that energy into thermal energy, stores thermal energy in bins of rocks, and then distributes heated air to various parts of the house by means of duct work.

The diagram below shows the solar-collector component of a solar-energy system on the roof of a house.

A solar-heating technician calculates the area of a home and the area of the solar collectors in square feet (ft^2), instead of using a metric unit, such as the square meter (m^2). In the United States, the use of English units, such as feet and yards, is still a common practice in many industries. For example, fabric stores sell material by the yard, and gas companies calculate how much natural gas homes use by the cubic foot (ft^3).

The technician can use the fact that a home owner will need 1 ft^2 of solar-collector area for every 2.5 to 4 ft^2 of living space.

Suppose you are a home owner who wants to heat 1200 ft^2 of living space by using a solar-heating system. You contact a solar-heating technician and ask to have 400 ft^2 of solar collector installed. Is your request reasonable?

Procedure

(1) You can test your request by using the following proportion.

$$\frac{\text{collector area}}{\text{living space}}$$

(2) Solve the proportion.

$$\frac{\text{collector area}}{\text{living space}} = \frac{400 \text{ ft}^2}{1200 \text{ ft}^2} = \frac{1}{3}$$

(3) Compare the calculated proportion you requested against the technician's given guidelines about area of solar collector per area of living space. Because 1 ft^2 of solar collector per 3 ft^2 of living space is between 1 ft^2 of collector per 2.5 ft^2 and 1 ft^2 of collector per 4 ft^2 of living space, the request is reasonable.

Practicing the SKILL

Determine whether each estimate of collector space is reasonable. Explain each answer.

(1) 300 ft^2 of collector per 1200 ft^2 of living space

(2) 300 ft^2 of collector per 1500 ft^2 of living space

For more skill practice, do the Chapter 15 Interactive Exploration on the **Science Voyages Grade 6 CD-ROM.**

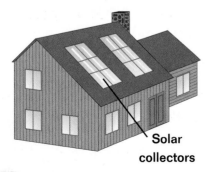

Solar collectors

Using Numbers

Background

The ability to analyze a problem and to reason through a solution is an important skill in science. It often involves forming a mental picture of the problem. Making a quick sketch or drawing of the problem also can help you get a better sense of the problem. Your ability to "see" the problem will strengthen as you practice solving word problems.

Read the strategy below that provides a logical plan for attacking word problems. Pay attention to how each step is used in solving sample problems.

Problem Solving Strategy

(1) Read the problem carefully. Be sure you understand all the terms used. Restate the problem in your own words.

(2) Identify the quantities that are given in the problem.

(3) Identify the quantity that is unknown.

(4) Examine the problem carefully to find a relationship between what is given and what you are asked to find. Identify the equation that contains these quantities.

(5) If necessary, solve the equation for the unknown quantity.

(6) Substitute the given values into the equation, along with their proper units.

(7) Check to see if the answer will be in the proper units.

(8) Solve the equation.

(9) Check your answer to see if it is reasonable.

Now, use the problem solving strategy to solve the following problem.

Procedure

(1) Carefully read and understand the problem.

> A hiker walked for 2.0 h at a speed of 6.5 km/h. How far did the hiker walk?

(2) **Given:** time, $t = 2.0$ h
speed, $v = 6.5$ km/h

(3) **Unknown:** distance, d

(4) **Basic Equation:** $v = d/t$

(5) **Solution:** $d = vt$

(6) $\qquad d = (6.5 \text{ km/h})(2.0 \text{ h})$

(7) $\qquad d = (\text{km/h})(\text{h}) = \text{km}$

(8) $\qquad d = (6.5 \text{ km/h})(2.0 \text{ h}) = 13 \text{ km}$

(9) It is reasonable for a hiker to cover 13 km in 2 hours.

Practicing the SKILL

(1) An ant moves 30 mm in 72 s. How fast is it moving?

(2) A car goes 25 km in 0.60 h and then travels 39 km in the next 1.5 h. What is the average speed for the entire trip?

For more skill practice, do the Chapter 16 Interactive Exploration on the **Science Voyages Grade 6 CD-ROM.**

GLENCOE TECHNOLOGY

Interpreting Scientific Illustrations

Background

You may have heard the saying "A picture is worth a thousand words." A good scientific diagram often can explain an idea better than several paragraphs of words. In order to get the most from diagrams, do the following.

- Study the entire diagram. Review the part of the text that the diagram illustrates.

- If there is a caption, read it carefully.

- Read all the labels and identify the parts.

- Visualize the dimensions. Arrows often indicate distances and direction. Distances often are indicated between arrows. The heads of the arrows show where the measurements start and end.

Use these guidelines to interpret the diagram at right.

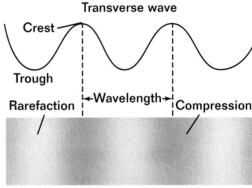

Procedure

1. What is the purpose of this diagram?

2. Identify the text in Chapter 17 to which the diagram relates. Locate the discussions about types of waves.

3. What does the crest of a transverse wave correspond to on a compressional wave?

4. What does the trough of a transverse wave correspond to on a compressional wave?

5. What is another way you can diagram the wavelength of a transverse wave?

Practicing the SKILL

1. What do the darker areas of the compressional wave represent?

2. What are the white areas?

3. How would you measure one wavelength of a compressional wave?

For more skill practice, do the Chapter 17 Interactive Exploration on the **Science Voyages Grade 6 CD-ROM.**

GLENCOE TECHNOLOGY

Communicating

Background

Have you ever wanted to learn more about a topic? Writing a report is one way you can explore new topics. You can learn about anything from the galaxy Andromeda to the element zirconium.

Scientists also write reports. Their reports give them the chance to communicate their work to other scientists in their field and to exchange ideas.

Procedure

1. Select a topic for your paper that interests you.

2. Once you have chosen a topic, go to the library to find information. Start with *The Reader's Guide to Periodical Literature*. It lists magazine articles by subject. To find books on your topic, look in the card catalog. Using technology also can help you find good sources of information.

3. Write down the author and title of each reference. For books, record the publisher and date of publication. For magazine articles, include the name and date of the magazine, the volume, and the issue number. Also indicate the page numbers where the reference is located.

4. As you read your references, decide what is important. In your own words, write down the information and where you found it. Keep your notes brief.

5. After you have read all your material, pick out the main ideas and the subtopics. Use them to make a detailed outline. Once this is done, you are ready to write. At the end of the paper, list the references you used.

Practicing the SKILL

1. Research the Hubble Space Telescope.

2. Communicate the information you find by writing a report.

For more skill practice, do the Chapter 3 Interactive Exploration on the **Science Voyages Grade 6 CD-ROM.**

GLENCOE TECHNOLOGY

English Glossary

This glossary defines each key term that appears in **bold type** in the text. It also shows the page number where you can find the word used.

A

abiotic factors: all the nonliving, physical features of the environment, including light, soil, water, and temperature, and that help determine which species can survive in an area. (ch. 10, p. 269)

abrasion: erosion that occurs when wind-blown sediments strike rock, scraping the surface and wearing it away. (ch. 6, p. 167)

acceleration: rate at which speed or direction changes; can be found by dividing the change in speed by the given time. (ch. 16, p. 447)

adaptation: any structure or behavior that helps an organism survive in its environment; develops in a population over a long period of time. (ch. 11, p. 298)

amplitude: measure of the energy a wave carries; one-half the distance between a crest and a trough of a transverse wave. (ch. 17, p. 481)

angiosperms (AN jee uh spurmz): vascular plants that flower, have their seeds contained in a fruit, and are the most common form of plant life on Earth. (ch. 8, p. 233)

astronomical (as truh NAHM uh kul) **unit:** average distance from Earth to the sun (150 million km), which is used to measure vast distances in space. (ch. 13, p. 363)

atom: small particle that makes up most types of matter and is made up of smaller parts called protons, neutrons, and electrons. (ch. 14, p. 387)

atomic mass: number that tells how heavy an element's atoms are compared with atoms of other elements. (ch. 14, p. 396)

atomic number: whole number that tells how many protons are in the nucleus of each atom of an element. (ch. 14, p. 396)

auxin: type of plant hormone that can cause plants to show positive phototropism. (ch. 9, p. 255)

average speed: distance traveled divided by the time it takes to travel this distance. (ch. 16, p. 446)

B

balanced forces: describes forces acting on an object that cancel each other. (ch. 16, p. 454)

bar graph: tool that uses bars to show the relationships between variables; can be horizontal or vertical and can display any numerical data. (ch. 2, p. 46)

biodiversity (bi oh duh VUR suh tee): measure of the number of different species in an area. (ch. 11, p. 297)

biosphere (BI uh sfihr): part of Earth that supports organisms, is the highest level of biological organization, and is made up of all Earth's ecosystems. (ch. 10, p. 268)

biotic factors: living or once-living organisms in the environment. (ch. 10, p. 271)

C

cambium (KAM bee um): vascular plant tissue that produces new xylem and phloem cells. (ch. 8, p. 229)

carrying capacity: largest number of individuals an environment can support and maintain over a long period of time. (ch. 7, p. 182; ch. 10, p. 276)

cellulose (SEL yuh lohs): organic compound made of long chains of glucose molecules; forms the rigid cell walls of plants. (ch. 8, p. 216)

chemical energy: energy stored within chemical bonds. (ch. 15, p. 435)

chemical weathering: type of weathering that occurs when air, water, and other substances react with minerals in rocks. (ch. 5, p. 127)

circle graph: tool used to show the parts of a whole. (ch. 2, p. 46)

climate: pattern of weather that occurs in a particular area over many years. (ch. 5, p. 128)

common ancestor (AN ses tur): shared ancestor of different species that all arose from one population. (ch. 11, p. 307)

community: consists of groups of populations that interact with each other in a given area and depend on each other for food, shelter, and for other needs. (ch. 10, p. 272)

composting: piling yard wastes where they can gradually decompose. (ch. 7, p. 196)

compound: pure substance produced when elements combine and whose properties are different from those of the elements from which it is formed. (ch. 14, p. 401)

compressional wave: wave in which matter in the medium moves forward and backward in the same direction the wave travels. (ch. 17, p. 479)

concave lens: lens whose edges are thicker than its middle; causes light waves to diverge. (ch. 18, p. 519)

conduction: transfer of thermal energy from particle to particle through a material when there is a temperature difference (ch. 15, p. 428).

conic projection: map projection that is accurate for small areas of Earth and is made by projecting points and lines from a globe onto a cone. (ch. 3, p. 75)

conservation: careful use of resources to reduce damage to the environment by means such as reducing our use of materials, reusing items, and recycling materials. (ch. 7, p. 195)

constant: factor in an experiment that doesn't change. (ch. 1, p. 19)

constellation (kahn stuh LAY shun): group of stars that forms a pattern in the sky and is named after a real or imaginary animal, person, or object. (ch. 13, p. 372)

contour interval: difference in elevation between two side-by-side contour lines. (ch. 3, p. 77)

contour line: line on a map that connects points of equal elevation. (ch. 3, p. 77)

control: standard used for comparison in an experiment. (ch. 1, p. 19)

convex lens: lens whose center is thicker than its edges; causes light waves to converge. (ch. 18, p. 518)

convection: transfer of thermal energy that happens when particles move from one place to another where there is a temperature difference (ch. 15, p. 430).

creep: mass movement that occurs when sediments slowly inch their way down a hill and that is common in areas of freezing and thawing. (ch. 6, p. 153)

crystal: solid material that has an orderly arrangement of atoms; mineral crystals have smooth surfaces, sharp edges, and points. (ch. 4, p. 94)

cuticle (KYEWT ih kul): waxy, protective layer covering the stems, leaves, and flowers of some land plants; is secreted by the plant's cell walls and slows the evaporation of water. (ch. 8, p. 217)

D

day-neutral plant: plant that does not have a specific photoperiod and whose flowering process can begin over a wide range of hours of darkness. (ch. 9, p. 258)

deflation: erosion caused by wind blowing across loose sediments, eroding only fine-grained particles such as clay and sand, and leaving behind coarse sediments. (ch. 6, p. 167)

dependent variable: factor being measured in an experiment. (ch. 1, p. 19)

deposition: dropping of sediments that occurs when an agent of erosion loses its energy of motion and is no longer able to carry its load. (ch. 6, p. 151)

dicot: class of angiosperm that has two seed leaves inside its seeds, vascular bundles that occur in rings, and flower parts in multiples of four or five. (ch. 8, p. 234)

diffraction: bending of waves around a barrier. (ch. 17, p. 488)

E

eclipse (ee KLIHPS): event that happens when the moon passes between the sun and Earth (a solar eclipse) or Earth passes between the sun and the moon (lunar eclipse). (ch. 13, p. 359)

ecological pyramid: model used to describe the transfer of energy from the producers of an ecosystem through successive levels of organisms in the food chain. (ch. 10, p. 284)

ecology: study of the interactions that take place among organisms and between organisms and the physical features of the environment. (ch. 10, p. 269)

ecosystem: consists of a biotic community and the abiotic factors that affect it. (ch. 10, p. 272)

electromagnetic spectrum: arrangement of electromagnetic radiation according to wavelength. (ch. 12, p. 329)

electromagnetic wave: waves that do not need matter to carry energy; can travel through air, through solid walls, and through space and have wavelengths and frequencies that vary greatly. (ch. 18, p. 502); type of wave, such as a light wave or a radio wave, that can travel in a vacuum as well as in various materials. (ch. 18, p. 502)

electron: negatively charged particle found in a cloudlike formation surrounding an atom's nucleus. (ch. 14, p. 390)

element: naturally occurring or synthetic material that cannot be broken down to simpler materials by ordinary means, has a unique set of properties, and that is generally classified as a metal, a metalloid, or a nonmetal. (ch. 14, p. 394)

energy: ability to cause change; can affect the temperature, speed, shape, or direction of an object. (ch. 15, p. 414)

equator: imaginary line at 0° latitude that circles Earth halfway between the north and south poles and divides Earth into two equal halves. (ch. 3, p. 70)

erosion: process that wears away surface materials and moves them from one place to another by agents such as gravity, glaciers, wind, and water. (ch. 6, p. 150)

estimation: method of making a rough measurement. (ch. 2, p. 31)

extrusive: type of igneous rock that forms when magma cools quickly on Earth's surface, few or no visible mineral crystals, and usually a smooth, sometimes glassy appearance. (ch. 4, p. 104)

F

fault-block mountains: sharp, jagged mountains that are made of huge, tilted blocks of rocks that are separated from surrounding rock by faults. (ch. 3, p. 68)

focal length: distance of the focal point from the center of the mirror or lens. (ch. 18, p. 510)

focal point: single point on the optical axis of a mirror or lens. (ch. 18, p. 510)

folded mountains: mountains that are created when rock layers are squeezed from opposite sides and the layers buckle and fold. (ch. 3, p. 66)

foliated (FOH lee ay tud): type of metamorphic rock with bands of minerals that have been heated and squeezed into parallel layers. (ch. 4, p. 114)

food chain: model that describes the feeding relationships in a community, usually has three or four links, and shows how energy in the form of food passes from one organism to another. (ch. 10, p. 283)

food web: model used to describe a series of overlapping food chains and that shows the many organisms that feed on more than one level in an ecosystem. (ch. 10, p. 284)

force: a push or a pull; can be measured by the amount of acceleration it can give a mass. (ch. 16, p. 219)

fossil: traces or remains of ancient life. (ch. 11, p. 308)

fossil record: all the fossils that scientists have recovered from the ground; gives scientists strong evidence that life has changed over time. (ch. 11, p. 314)

frequency: number of waves that pass a given point in one second; measured in waves per second, or hertz (Hz). (ch. 17, p. 483; ch. 18, p. 505)

friction: force that resists motion between two objects in contact and that always acts opposite to the direction of motion. (ch. 16, p. 459)

G

galaxy (GAL uk see): group of stars, gas, and dust held together by gravity. (ch. 13, p. 375)

gems: valuable minerals, such as diamonds, that can be cut and polished, are clear with no blemishes, and have beautiful luster or color. (ch. 4, p. 98)

geologic time scale: record of life on Earth put together by scientists that is divided into eras and periods and lists major evolutionary events. (ch. 18, p. 315)

glaciers: moving masses of ice and snow that are responsible for creating many landforms on Earth through erosion and deposition. (ch. 6, p. 158)

graph: tool used to collect, organize, and summarize data in a visual way so that it is easy to use and understand. (ch. 2, p. 45)

gravity: attraction between all matter; a force that pulls on all objects that have mass. (ch. 16, p. 453)

guard cells: in a plant leaf, the cells that surround the stomata and that open and close them. (ch. 8, p. 231)

gymnosperms (JIHM nuh spurmz): vascular plants that produce seeds on the surface of the female reproductive structures, do not have flowers, and generally have needlelike or scalelike leaves. (ch. 8, p. 232)

H

habitat: physical location where an organism lives. (ch. 10, p. 279)

hazardous wastes: poisonous, cancer-causing, or radioactive wastes that are dangerous to living things. (ch. 7, p. 191)

heat: energy transfer that causes a change in temperature. (ch. 15, p. 425)

horizon: a soil layer in the soil profile; most areas have three—the A horizon (top soil layer), the B horizon (middle layer), and the C horizon (bottom layer). (ch. 5, p. 134)

humus (HYEW mus): dark-colored, decayed organic matter in soil that serves as a nutrient source for plants, promotes good soil structure, and helps soil hold water. (ch. 5, p. 133)

hypothesis: statement that can be tested; based on observations, research, and prior knowledge of a problem. (ch. 1, p. 18)

I

ice wedging: mechanical weathering process that occurs when water freezes in the cracks of rocks and expands, breaking the rock apart. (ch. 5, p. 126)

igneous (IHG nee us) **rock:** rock formed when magma from inside Earth cools and hardens on Earth's surface or under Earth's surface; can be extrusive or intrusive. (ch. 4, p. 103)

independent variable: the one factor changed by the person doing the experiment. (ch. 1, p. 19)

inertia (ih NUR shah): measure of an object's ability to remain at rest or to keep moving. (ch. 16, p. 455)

inference: conclusion based on an observation. (ch. 1, p. 18)

interference: ability of two or more waves to combine and form a new wave when they overlap; can be constructive, forming a larger wave, or destructive, forming a smaller wave. (ch. 17, p. 490)

International Date Line: transition line for calendar days, located at the 180° meridian. (ch. 3, p. 72)

intrusive: type of igneous rock produced when magma cools slowly below Earth's surface and that has large, easily seen crystals. (ch. 4, p. 105)

isotopes (I suh tohps): two or more atoms of the same element that have different numbers of neutrons. (ch. 14, p. 396)

K

Kelvin: scale that measures temperature in SI; begins at zero kelvin, which is the coldest temperature possible in nature. (ch. 2, p. 41)

kilogram (kg): SI unit for mass. (ch. 2, p. 40)

kinetic (kuh NET ihk) **energy:** energy of motion; is influenced by an object's mass and speed and can be transferred from one object to another when objects collide. (ch. 15, p. 416)

L

landfill: area where waste is deposited; the majority of U.S. garbage goes into landfills. (ch. 7, p. 191)

latitude: distance in degrees either north or south of the equator. (ch. 3, p. 70)

law of conservation of energy: states that energy cannot be created or destroyed but only transformed from one form to another. (ch. 15, p. 420)

law of conservation of matter: states that matter is neither created nor destroyed, only changed in form. (ch. 14, p. 388)

law of definite proportions: states that a given compound is always made of the same elements in the same proportion by mass. (ch. 14, p. 402)

law of reflection: states that the angle of incidence is equal to the angle of reflection. (ch. 18, p. 509)

leaching: removal of minerals that have been dissolved in water. (ch. 5, p. 135)

lens: transparent object that has at least one curved side that causes light to bend. (ch. 18, p. 517)

light ray: narrow beam of light traveling in a straight line. (ch. 18, p. 502)

light-year: distance light travels in a year (about 9.5 trillion km), which is used

photoperiodi... number of h... ness it receive...

photosynthesis: fo... takes place in the... cells, where carbon... water in the soil, and ... form glucose and oxyg...

pioneer species: first pla... new or disturbed environ... change environmental cond... other plant species can grow ... 8, p. 221)

plain: landform that is a large, f... interior and coastal plains make ... percent of all land areas in the U... States. (ch. 3, p. 62)

plateau (pla TOH): landform that is a fla... raised area made of nearly horizontal rocks that have been uplifted by forces within Earth. (ch. 3, p. 64)

plucking: process that adds boulders, gravel, and sand to a glacier's bottom and sides as water freezes and thaws and breaks off pieces of surrounding rocks. (ch. 6, p. 160)

population: all the individuals of one species that live in the same area at the same time and compete with each other for food, water, mates, and space. (ch, 7, p. 183; ch. 10, p. 272)

population density: size of a population that occupies an area of limited size. (ch. 10, p. 275)

population explosion: rapidly increasing number of humans on Earth due to factors such as modern medicine, better sanitation, better nutrition, and more people surviving to the age when they can have children. (ch. 7, p. 183)

potential (puh TEN chul) **energy:** energy that is stored and that comes from an object's position or condition. (ch. 15, p. 418)

prime meridian: imaginary line represent-

measure distances between ... (ch. 13, p. 377)

limiting factor: any biotic or ab... that restricts the number of ... in a population. (ch. 10, p. ...

line graph: tool used to sho... ship between two variabl...

litter: leaves, twigs, and ot... ter in the A horizon ... humus when it is expo... ing organisms. (ch. 5, ...

loess (LUSS): wind ... grained, tightly ... (ch. 6, p. 171)

long-day plant: pl... ten to twelve h... the flowering...

longitude: dist... of the prim...

...itude; runs from the north of ... Greenwich, England, to the ... (ch. 3, p. 159)

... final stage in the U.S. effort ... moon—on July 20, 1969, ...g was the first human to ... lunar surface. (ch. 12, p. ...

...cond stage in the U.S. ... the moon, in which a ...ts met and connected ...cecraft while in orbit.

...st step in the U.S. effort ...n, in which a piloted ...fully orbited around ...d safely. (ch. 12, p. 340)

...e nucleus of an atom ...sitive charge. (ch. 14,

map le... symb... **map** ... **map** ... ta... m... m...

radia... all a... p. 427)

radio teles... a large, cu... radio wave... that can be ... night and dur... p. 331)

...ravels by waves in ...ts source (ch. 15,

...lescope that uses ...ollect and record ...ugh space and ...the day or at ...her. (ch. 12,

rate: fraction in whi... denominator have ... 16, p. 446)

...ator and ...ts. (ch.

rate: ratio of two measu... ferent units—for examp... sured in kilometers per ... (ch. 2, p. 41)

...dif-

recyclable: any item that can be ... and used again in order to cons... ural resources and reduce soli... (ch. 7, p. 197)

reflecting telescope: optical telescope

uses a mirror (or mirrors) to focus light and produce an image at the focal point. (ch. 12, p. 330)

reflection: occurs when a wave strikes an object or surface and bounces off. (ch. 17, p. 486; ch. 18, p. 503)

refracting telescope: optical telescope that uses a double convex lens to focus light and form an image at the focal point. (ch. 12, p. 330)

refraction: bending of a light wave when it changes speed in moving from one material to another. (ch. 17, p. 487; ch. 18, p. 517)

remote sensing: way of collecting information about Earth from a distance—for example, by satellites and sonar. (ch. 3, p. 80)

respiration: series of chemical reactions by which all living cells break down food to release energy. (ch. 9, p. 250)

revolution (rev oh LEW shun): movement of Earth around the sun, which takes one year to do once. (ch. 13, p. 357)

rhizoids: threadlike roots that are only a few cells in length and that anchor liverworts and mosses in place. (ch. 8, p. 220)

Robinson projection: map projection that has accurate continent shapes and accurate land areas; has parallel latitude lines and curved longitude lines. (ch. 3, p. 75)

rock: solid material that is usually made of two or more minerals and that can be metamorphic, igneous, or sedimentary. (ch. 4, p. 92)

rock cycle: diagram that shows how rocks are constantly changed from one kind of rock to another. (ch. 4, p. 115)

rotation (roh TAY shun): spinning of Earth on its axis, which occurs once every 24 hours and causes night and day. (ch. 13, p. 356)

S

satellite: any object that revolves around another object; can be natural (Earth's moon) or artificial (*Sputnik I*). (ch. 12, p. 336)

science: process of trying to understand the world around us. (ch. 1, p. 7)

scientific methods: step-by-step procedures of scientific problem solving; can include recognizing the problem, forming a hypothesis, testing the hypothesis, analyzing the data, and drawing conclusions. (ch. 1, p. 14)

sedimentary (sed uh MENT uh ree) **rock:** rock formed when pieces of other rocks, plant and animal matter, or dissolved minerals collect to form rock layers. (ch. 4, p. 106)

short-day plant: plant that needs twelve or more hours of darkness to begin the flowering process. (ch. 9, p. 257)

SI: International System of Units, which was designed to give a worldwide standard of physical measurement for science, industry, and commerce and uses units such as the meter, cubic meter, kilogram, and kelvin. (ch. 2, p. 37)

slump: mass movement that happens when loose materials or rock layers slip down a slope, and a curved scar is left where the slumped materials originally rested. (ch. 6, p. 152)

soil: material that supports vegetation and is a mixture of weathered rock, mineral fragments, organic matter, water, and air; may take thousands of years to form. (ch. 5, p. 132)

soil profile: vertical section of soil layers. (ch. 5, p. 134)

solar system: nine planets and other objects that orbit the sun. (ch. 13, p. 362)

space probe: instrument that travels out into the solar system to gather information and sends the data back to Earth. (ch. 12, p. 337)

space shuttle: reusable spacecraft that carries astronauts, satellites, and other materials to and from space. (ch. 12, p. 344)

space station: large artificial satellite that provides support systems, living quarters, and equipment so that humans can live and work in space and conduct research not possible on Earth. (ch. 12, p. 345)

stomata: openings on leaf surfaces or leaflike structures through which gases like carbon dioxide and water vapor may enter and leave a plant. (ch. 9, p. 244)

stomata: small pores in the leaf surfaces surrounded by guard cells; allow carbon dioxide, oxygen, and water to enter and leave a leaf. (ch. 8, p. 231)

substance: sample of matter that has the same composition and properties throughout. (ch. 14, p. 401)

symbiosis (sihm bee OH sus): any close relationship between two or more different species. (ch. 10, p. 277)

T

table: tool used to display information in rows and columns so that it is easier to read and understand. (ch. 2, p. 45)

technology: use of knowledge gained through scientific thinking and problem solving to make products or tools people can use. (ch. 1, p. 9)

temperature: measure of the average kinetic energy of the particles in any object; the greater the average kinetic energy, the higher an object's temperature. (ch. 15, p. 424)

thermal energy: total amount of kinetic energy of the particles in a material. (ch. 15, p. 425)

till: mixture of different-sized sediments dropped from the base of a slowing glacier and that can cover huge areas of land. (ch. 6, p. 162)

topographic map: shows the changes in elevation of Earth's surface and shows natural features such as mountains and rivers and cultural features such as roads and cities. (ch. 3, p. 76)

transpiration: loss of water vapor through the stomata of a leaf. (ch. 9, p. 245)

transverse wave: wave in which matter moves back and forth at right angles to the direction the wave travels. (ch. 17, p. 478)

tropism: response of a plant to an outside stimulus such as gravity or light. (ch. 9, p. 254)

U

upwarped mountains: mountains that are formed when crust is pushed up by forces inside Earth, and the material on top of the crust is eroded to form sharp peaks and ridges. (ch. 3, p. 67)

V

vascular plant: plant with vascular tissue, a "pipeline" that moves water, food, and dissolved substances to cells throughout the plant. (ch. 8, p. 218)

volcanic mountains: mountains that form when molten material reaches Earth's surface through a weak area of crust, piles up in layers, and forms a cone-shaped structure. (ch. 3, p. 68)

W

water cycle: constant journey of water molecules on Earth as they rise into the atmosphere, fall to land or the ocean as rain or snow, and flow into rivers and oceans through the processes of evaporation, condensation, and precipitation. (ch. 10, p. 286)

wavelength: distance between a point on one wave and an identical point on the next wave, measured from crest to crest or trough to trough; in compressional waves, is measured from one compression or rarefaction to the next. (ch. 17, p. 482;ch. 18, p. 505)

waves: regular disturbances that carry energy through matter or space without carrying matter; can have different amplitudes, frequencies, wavelengths, and speeds (ch. 17, p. 476).

weathering: mechanical or chemical process that breaks down rocks into smaller and smaller fragments. (ch. 5, p. 124)

weight: downward pull of gravity on an object. (ch. 16, p. 453)

xylem (ZI lum): vascular plant tissue made up of tubular vessels that transport water and dissolved substances up from the roots throughout the plant. (ch. 8, p. 229)

Glossary/Glosario

Este glossario define cada término clave que aparece en **negrillas** en el texto. También muestra el número de página donde se usa dicho término.

A

abiotic factors / factores abióticos: Características físicas inanimadas que a menudo determinan los organismos que pueden sobrevivir en cierto ambiente. (Cap. 10, pág. 269)

abrasion / abrasión: Tipo de erosión que ocurre cuando los sedimentos arrastrados por el viento golpean las rocas. (Cap. 6, pág. 167)

acceleration / aceleración: Razón a la cual cambia la rapidez o la dirección. (Cap. 16, pág. 447)

adaptation / adaptación: Cualquier forma corporal, proceso corporal o comportamiento que le ayuda a un organismo a sobrevivir en su ambiente y a llevar a cabo sus procesos vitales. (Cap. 11, pág. 298)

amplitude / amplitud: La mitad de la distancia entre una cresta y un valle de una onda transversal; una medida de la energía que transporta una onda. (Cap. 17, pág. 481)

angiosperms / angiospermas: Plantas vasculares que florecen y producen frutos que contienen semillas. Son la forma de vida vegetal más común sobre la Tierra. (Cap. 8, pág. 233)

astronomical unit/unidad astronómica: Distancia promedio de la Tierra al sol (150 millones km), la cual se usa para medir las vastas distancias en el espacio. (Cap. 13, pág. 363)

atom / átomo: La partícula más pequeña que compone la mayoría de los tipos de materia. (Cap. 14, pág. 387)

atomic mass / masa atómica: Indica el peso de los átomos de un elemento en comparación con los átomos de otros elementos. (Cap. 14, pág. 396)

atomic number / número atómico: Indica el número de protones en el núcleo de cada átomo de un elemento. (Cap. 14, pág. 396)

auxin / auxina: Tipo de hormona vegetal. (Cap. 9, pág. 255)

average speed / rapidez promedio: La distancia viajada entre el tiempo que llevó viajar dicha distancia. (Cap. 16, pág. 446)

B

balanced forces / fuerzas equilibradas: Ocurren cuando las fuerzas que actúan sobre un objeto se cancelan entre sí. (Cap. 16, pág. 454)

bar graph / gráfica de barras: La que usa barras para mostrar relaciones entre variables. (Cap. 2, pág. 46)

biodiversity / biodiversidad: Medida del número de diferentes especies en un área. (Cap. 11, pág. 297)

biosphere / biosfera: La parte de la Tierra que sostiene organismos vivos. (Cap. 10, pág. 268)

biotic factors / factores bióticos: Cualquier organismo vivo o que alguna vez estuvo vivo, en un ambiente. (Cap. 10, pág. 271)

C

cambium / cambium: Tejido que produce nuevas células de xilema y de floema. (Cap. 8, pág. 229)

carrying capacity / capacidad de carga: El mayor número de individuos, de una especie en particular, que el planeta puede soportar y mantener durante un largo período de tiempo. (Cap. 7, pág. 182; Cap. 10, pág. 276)

cellulose / celulosa: Compuesto orgánico hecho de cadenas largas de moléculas de glucosa, del cual están formadas las paredes celulares de las plantas. (Cap. 8, pág. 216)

chemical energy / energía química: Energía almacenada (potencial) en los enlaces químicos de las partículas de una sustancia. (Cap. 15, pág. 435)

chemical weathering / meteorización química: Meteorización que ocurre cuando el agua, el aire y otras sustancias reaccionan con los minerales presentes en las rocas. (Cap. 5, pág. 127)

circle graph / gráfica circular: Gráfica que muestra las partes de un todo mediante un círculo. (Cap. 2, pág. 46)

climate / clima: Patrón de tiempo que ocurre en una región en particular, a lo largo de muchos años. (Cap. 5, pág. 128)

common ancestor / antepasado común: Antepasado que comparten especies diferentes, las cuales todas se originaron de una población. (Cap. 11, pág. 307)

community / comunidad: Grupo de poblaciones que interactúan entre sí en un área determinada. (Cap. 10, pág. 272)

composting / abono orgánico: Desechos vegetales que se apilan para que se descompongan paulatinamente. (Cap. 7, pág. 196)

compound / compuesto: Sustancia pura cuya unidad constitutiva está compuesta por átomos de más de un elemento. (Cap. 14, pág. 401)

compressional wave / onda de compresión: Onda en la cual la materia en el medio se mueve de un lado para otro en la misma dirección en que viaja la onda. (Cap. 17, pág. 479)

concave lens / lente cóncava: Lente que es más gruesa en las orillas que en el centro y que desvía las ondas luminosas. (Cap. 18, pág. 519)

conduction / conducción: Transferencia de energía térmica de una partícula a otra a través de un material, cuando existe una diferencia de temperaturas. (Cap. 15, pág. 428)

conic projection / proyección cónica: Se usa para producir mapas de áreas pequeñas proyectando puntos y líneas desde un globo a un cono. (Cap. 3, pág. 75)

conservation / conservación: Uso cuidadoso de los recursos, lo cual disminuye el daño al ambiente. (Cap. 7, pág.195)

constant / constante: Factor que permanece igual en un experimento. (Cap. 1, pág. 19)

constellation / constelación: Grupo de estrellas que forman un patrón en el firmamento y el cual ha recibido su nombre de personajes reales o imaginarios como animales, personas u objetos. (Cap. 13, pág. 372)

contour interval / intervalo entre curvas de nivel: Diferencia en elevación entre dos curvas de nivel consecutivas. (Cap. 3, pág. 77)

contour line / curva de nivel: Línea en un mapa que conecta puntos de igual elevación. (Cap. 3, pág. 77)

control / control: Un estándar que se usa para comparar. (Cap. 1, pág. 19)

convection / convección: Transferencia de energía térmica que ocurre cuando las partículas se mueven de un lugar a otro donde existe una diferencia de temperaturas. (Cap. 15, pág. 430)

convex lens / lente convexa: Lente que es más gruesa en el centro que

en las orillas; hace que las ondas luminosas converjan. (Cap. 18, pág. 518)

creep / corrimiento: Movimiento que recibe su nombre por la manera en que los sedimentos lentamente se deslizan cuesta abajo, pulgada a pulgada. Es común en áreas que se congelan y descongelan. (Cap. 6, pág. 153)

crystal / cristal: Material sólido cuyos átomos están arreglados en patrones repetitivos; se puede formar cuando el magma se enfría y cuando los líquidos que contienen minerales disueltos se evaporan. (Cap. 4, pág. 94)

cuticle / cutícula: Capa cerosa protectora que cubre los tallos, hojas y flores de algunas plantas terrestres; es secretada por las paredes celulares de la planta y disminuye la evaporación de agua. (Cap. 8, pág. 217)

D

day-neutral plant / planta de día neutro: Planta que no requiere un fotoperíodo específico y en la cual el proceso de floración puede comenzar dentro de una gama de horas de oscuridad. (Cap. 9, pág. 258)

deflation / deflacción: Erosión causada cuando el viento sopla los sedimentos sueltos, extrayendo pequeñas partículas tales como la arcilla, el cieno y la arena, y dejando atrás materiales más gruesos. (Cap. 6, pág. 167)

dependent variable / variable dependiente: Es el factor que se mide en un experimento. (Cap. 1, pág. 19)

deposition / depositación: Etapa final del proceso de erosión. Ocurre cuando los agentes erosivos disminuyen su energía erosiva y depositan los sedimentos y las rocas que transportaban. (Cap. 6, pág. 151)

dicot / dicotiledónea: Tipo de angiosperma que contiene dos cotiledones dentro de sus semillas. (Cap. 8, pág. 234)

diffraction / difracción: Doblamiento de una onda alrededor de una barrera. (Cap. 17, pág. 488)

E

eclipse / eclipse: Evento que sucede cuando la luna pasa entre el sol y la Tierra (eclipse solar) o la Tierra pasa entre el sol y la luna (eclipse lunar). (Cap. 13, pág. 359)

ecological pyramid / pirámide ecológica: Modelo que representa la transferencia de energía en la biosfera. (Cap. 10, pág. 284)

ecology / ecología: Ciencia que estudia las interacciones entre los organismos y entre los organismos y los rasgos físicos del ambiente. (Cap. 10, pág. 269)

ecosystem / ecosistema: Consiste en una comunidad biótica y de los factores abióticos que la afectan. (Cap. 10, pág. 272)

electromagnetic spectrum / espectro electromagnético: Arreglo de radiación electromagnética, de acuerdo con sus longitudes de onda. (Cap. 12, pág. 329)

electromagnetic wave / onda electromagnética: Tipo de onda, como las ondas luminosas o las radiales, que puede viajar en el vacío y también en otros materiales (Cap. 18, pág. 502); ondas que no requieren materia para transportar energía y que pueden viajar a través del aire. (Cap. 17, pág. 478)

electron / electrón: Partícula con carga negativa. (Cap. 14, pág. 390)

element / elemento: Material que no se puede descomponer en materiales más simples por medios comunes. (Cap. 14, pág. 394)

energy / energía: Capacidad de causar cambio; puede afectar la rapidez, forma o dirección de un objeto. (Cap. 15, pág. 414)

equator / ecuador: Línea imaginaria que circunda la Tierra exactamente equidistante entre los polos norte y sur. El ecuador separa la Tierra en dos mitades iguales llamadas hemisferio norte y hemisferio sur. (Cap. 3, pág. 70)

erosion / erosión: Proceso que desgasta los materiales de la superficie y los transporta de un lugar a otro. Los principales agentes de la erosión son la gravedad, los glaciares, el viento y el agua. (Cap. 6, pág. 150)

estimation / estimación: Valoración bruta de la medida de un objeto, haciendo una conjetura basada en la experiencia. (Cap. 2, pág. 31)

extrusive / extrusiva: Roca ígnea que se forma cuando la lava se enfría sobre la superficie terrestre; posee pocos cristales minerales pequeños o no posee ningún cristal mineral; por lo general presenta una apariencia vidriosa y lisa. (Cap. 4, pág. 104)

F

fault-block mountains / montañas de bloques de falla: Montañas formadas por inmensos bloques rocosos inclinados y separados de rocas circundantes por fallas. (Cap. 3, pág. 68)

focal length / longitud focal: Distancia desde el centro del espejo o lente hasta el punto focal. (Cap. 18, pág. 512)

focal point / punto focal: Punto único del eje óptico de un espejo o lente. (Cap. 18, pág. 512)

folded mountains / montañas plegadas: Tipo de montañas que se forman cuando las capas rocosas son apretadas desde lados opuestos, haciendo que se doblen y plieguen. (Cap. 3, pág. 66)

foliated / foliada: Tipo de roca que presenta bandas de minerales que han sido calentados y compactados formando capas paralelas; por ejemplo, la pizarra, el gneiss, la filita y el esquisto. (Cap. 4, pág. 114)

food chain / cadena alimenticia: Manera simple de mostrar cómo la energía de los alimentos pasa de un organismo a otro. (Cap. 10, pág. 283)

food web / red alimenticia: Serie de cadenas alimenticias sobrepuestas. (Cap. 10, pág. 284)

force / fuerza: Cualquier empuje o atracción. (Cap. 16, pág. 453)

fossil / fósil: Restos o huellas de vida antigua. (Cap. 11, pág. 308)

fossil record / récord fósil: Todos los fósiles que los científicos han recobrado del suelo. Los fósiles de casi cada grupo principal de plantas o animales forman parte del récord fósil. (Cap. 11, pág. 314)

frequency / frecuencia: Número de ondas que pasan por un punto fijo en un segundo. Se mide en ondas por segundo o hertz (Hz). (Cap. 17, pág. 483; Cap. 18, pág. 505)

friction / fricción: Fuerza que resiste el movimiento entre dos objetos en contacto. (Cap. 16, pág. 459)

G

galaxy / galaxia: Grupo de estrellas, gas y polvo que se mantienen juntos debido a la gravedad. (Cap. 13, pág. 375)

gems / gemas: Minerales raros que se pueden cortar y pulir dándoles una apariencia bella. Son ideales para la joyería. (Cap. 4, pág. 98)

geologic time scale / escala del tiempo geológico: Especie de diario del récord fósil de la vida sobre la

Tierra que han recopilado los científicos. (Cap. 11, pág. 315)

glaciers / glaciares: Masas móviles de hielo y nieve. (Cap. 6, pág. 158)

graph / gráfica: Representación gráfica que se usa para recoger, organizar y resumir datos de manera visual. (Cap. 2, pág. 45)

gravity / gravedad: Atracción que existe entre toda la materia. (Cap. 16, pág. 453)

guard cells / células guardianas: Células alrededor del estoma que lo abren y lo cierran. Junto con la cutícula y los estomas, son adaptaciones que ayudan a las plantas a sobrevivir sobre tierra. (Cap. 8, pág. 231)

gymnosperms / gimnospermas: Plantas vasculares que producen semillas en la superficie de las estructuras reproductoras femeninas. (Cap. 8, pág. 232)

H

habitat / hábitat: Ubicación física en donde vive un organismo (Cap. 10, pág. 279)

hazardous wastes / desechos peligrosos: Desechos venenosos, cancerígenos o radiactivos que causan daño a los seres vivos. (Cap. 7, pág. 191)

heat / calor: Transferencia de energía que ocasiona un cambio de temperatura. (Cap. 15, pág. 425)

horizon / horizonte: Nombre que recibe cada capa del perfil del suelo. (Cap. 5, pág. 134)

humus / humus: Materia de color oscuro que se forma de la descomposición de la materia orgánica, como las plantas. (Cap. 5, pág. 133)

hypothesis / hipótesis: Enunciado que se puede probar y el cual está basado en observación, investigación y conocimiento previo del problema bajo estudio. (Cap. 1, pág. 18)

I

ice wedging / grietas debido al hielo: Proceso de meteorización mecánica que ocurre cuando el agua se congela en las grietas de las rocas y se expande, rompiendo la roca en pedazos. (Cap. 5, pág. 126)

igneous rock / roca ígnea: Se forma cuando el material derretido, llamado magma, que se halla en las profundidades de la Tierra se enfría y se solidifica; puede ser intrusiva o extrusiva. (Cap. 4, pág. 103)

independent variable / variable independiente: Es el factor que puedes cambiar en un experimento. (Cap. 1, pág. 19)

inertia / inercia: Medida de la capacidad de un objeto de permanecer en reposo o de continuar moviéndose. (Cap. 16, pág. 455)

inference / inferencia: Conclusión basada en una observación. (Cap. 1, pág. 18)

interference / interferencia: La capacidad de dos o más ondas de combinarse y formar una nueva onda cuando se sobreponen una sobre la otra. (Cap. 17, pág. 490)

International Date Line / Línea Internacional de cambio de fecha: Es la línea de transición para los días del calendario. (Cap. 3, pág. 72)

intrusive / intrusiva: Roca ígnea que se forma cuando el magma se enfría dentro de la corteza terrestre. Las rocas ígneas intrusivas, por lo general, poseen granos minerales grandes. (Cap. 4, pág. 105)

isotopes / isótopos: Átomos del mismo elemento que poseen diferentes números de neutrones. (Cap. 14, pág. 396)

K

Kelvin / Kelvin: Escala para medir la temperatura en el SI; comienza en cero Kelvin, la temperatura más fría posible en la naturaleza. (Cap. 2, pág. 41)

kilogram / kilogramo: Unidad de masa del SI. (Cap. 2, pág. 40)

kinetic energy / energía cinética: Energía que poseen los objetos en movimiento. (Cap. 15, pág. 416)

L

landfill / vertedero controlado: Área en donde se depositan los residuos. (Cap. 7, pág. 191)

latitude / latitud: Distancia, en grados, ya sea al norte o al sur del ecuador. (Cap. 3, pág. 70)

law of conservation of energy / ley de conservación de la energía: Ley que enuncia que la energía no puede ser creada ni destruida, solo puede ser transformada de una forma a otra. (Cap. 15, pág. 420)

law of conservation of matter / ley de conservación de la materia: Enuncia que la materia no puede ser creada ni destruida, sino que solo cambia de forma. (Cap. 14, pág. 388)

law of definite proportions / ley de proporciones definidas: Ley que enuncia que un compuesto dado siempre está formado por los mismos elementos en la misma proporción por masa. (Cap. 14, pág. 402)

law of reflection / ley de reflexión: Ley que enuncia que el ángulo de incidencia es igual al ángulo de reflexión. Esto es cierto para cualquier superficie sea cual sea el material de que esté hecha. (Cap. 18, pág. 509)

leaching / lixiviación: Extracción de materiales, al ser disueltos en agua. (Cap. 5, pág. 135)

lens / lente: Objeto transparente con por lo menos un lado encorvado que hace que la luz se doble. (Cap. 18, pág. 517)

light ray / rayo de luz: Trayectoria muy estrecha de luz que viaja en línea recta. (Cap. 18, pág. 502)

light-year / año-luz: Distancia que la luz viaja en un año (aproximadamente 9.5 trillones de km), la cual se usa para medir las distancias entre las galaxias. (Cap. 13, pág. 377)

limiting factor / factor limitante: Cualquier factor biótico o abiótico que limita el número de individuos en una población. (Cap. 10, pág. 275)

line graph / gráfica lineal: Representación gráfica que muestra la relación entre dos variables y en la cual ambas variables deben ser numéricas. (Cap. 2, pág. 45)

litter / lecho superficial: Capa compuesta de hojas, ramas y otros materiales orgánicos, la cual se convierte en humus. (Cap. 5, pág. 135)

loess / loes: Depósitos de grano fino arrastrados por el viento. (Cap. 6, pág. 171)

long-day plant / planta de día largo: Planta que necesita, generalmente, menos de diez a doce horas de oscuridad para comenzar el proceso de floración. (Cap. 9, pág. 257)

longitude / longitud: Se refiere a la distancia, en grados, al este o al oeste del primer meridiano. (Cap. 3, pág. 71)

M

map legend / leyenda de un mapa: Explica el significado de los símbolos que se usan en un mapa. (Cap. 3, pág. 78)

map scale / escala de un mapa: Relación entre las distancias en el mapa y las distancias verdaderas en la superficie terrestre. (Cap. 3, pág. 78)

mass / masa: Unidad que se usa para medir la cantidad de materia en un objeto (Cap. 2, pág. 40); cantidad de materia que posee un objeto. (Cap. 16, pág. 455)

mass extinction / extinción en masa: La desaparición en gran escala de muchas especies en un lapso corto de tiempo. (Cap. 11, pág. 317)

mass movement / movimiento de masa: Movimiento de materiales cuesta abajo debido solo a la gravedad. Algunos movimientos de masa pueden ocurrir lentamente, pero otros sin embargo ocurren rápidamente. (Cap. 6, pág. 152)

mass number / número de masa: Equivale a la suma de los protones y neutrones de un átomo. (Cap. 14, pág. 396)

matter / materia: Cualquier cosa que posee masa y que ocupa espacio. (Cap. 14, pág. 386)

measurement / medida: Una manera de describir el mundo haciendo uso de los números. (Cap. 2, pág. 30)

mechanical waves / ondas mecánicas: Ondas que solo pueden viajar a través de un medio: la materia. (Cap. 17, pág. 477)

mechanical weathering / meteorización mecánica: Proceso que parte las rocas, pero sin cambiar su composición química. (Cap. 5, pág. 125)

medium / medio: Cualquier material por el cual viaja una onda. (Cap. 18, pág. 502)

Mercator projection / proyección de Mercator: Tipo de mapa que muestra las formas correctas de los continentes, pero sus áreas están distorsionadas. (Cap. 3, pág. 75)

metalloids / metaloides: Elementos que poseen características tanto de los metales como de los no metales y que son por lo general quebradizos y opacos; no son buenos conductores de calor y de electricidad como los metales. (Cap. 14, pág. 398)

metals / metales: Elementos que generalmente tienen lustre metálico o brillante, son buenos conductores de calor y electricidad, son maleables y dúctiles. Todos los metales, excepto el mercurio, son sólidos a temperatura ambiente. (Cap. 14, pág. 397)

metamorphic rock / roca metamórfica: Roca que se forma cuando las rocas más antiguas se calientan o se compactan; la palabra metamórfica significa "que cambia de forma". (Cap. 4, pág. 113)

meter (m) / metro (m): Unidad de longitud del SI. (Cap. 2, pág. 38)

minerals / minerals: Materiales sólidos inorgánicos que ocurren en forma natural y que poseen una composición definida y un arreglo ordenado de átomos. (Cap. 4, pág. 92)

mixtures / mezclas: Combinaciones de dos o más sustancias que no se han combinado para formar nuevas sustancias puras; pueden ser uniformes: en las que no se pueden ver las partes individuales, o no uniformes: en las que se pueden ver las partes individuales. (Cap. 14, pág. 403)

monocot / monocotiledónea: Tipo de angiosperma que contiene un cotiledón dentro de sus semillas. (Cap. 8, pág. 234)

moraine / morena frontal o terminal: Tipo de depósito parecido a un cerro que se forma de tierra y piedras arrastradas por un glaciar. Este tipo de depósito no cubre un área muy amplia de terreno. (Cap. 6, pág. 162)

N

natural selection / selección natural: Proceso en que los organismos cuyas características los hacen más aptos para sus ambientes sobreviven, se reproducen y pasan esas características a su progenie. (Cap. 11, pág. 304)

neutron / neutrón: Partícula que no posee ninguna carga eléctrica. (Cap. 14, pág. 392)

Newton's laws of motion / leyes de movimiento de Newton: Leyes descubiertas por Sir Isaac Newton para resolver cualquier problema de movimiento. (Cap. 16, pág. 458)

niche / nicho: Papel de un organismo en el ecosistema. (Cap. 10, pág. 279)

nitrogen cycle / ciclo del nitrógeno: Transferencia de nitrógeno de la atmósfera a las plantas y de regreso a la atmósfera o directamente a las plantas de nuevo. (Cap. 10, pág. 288)

non-foliated / no foliada: Tipo de roca que no presenta capas o bandas distintivas; por ejemplo, la cuarcita, el mármol y la esteatita. (Cap. 4, pág. 114)

nonmetals / no metales: Elementos que por lo general son opacos y malos conductores de calor y electricidad. (Cap. 14, pág. 398)

nonvascular plant / planta no vascular: Planta que carece de tejido vascular y que usa otros medios para mover agua y sustancias a través de la planta. (Cap. 8, pág. 218)

normal force / fuerza normal: La fuerza ascendente que ejerce la tierra sobre cualquier objeto, la cual es perpendicular a la superficie. (Cap. 16, pág. 454)

nucleus / núcleo: Centro con carga positiva del átomo. (Cap. 14, pág. 392)

O

observations / observaciones: Información que recoges usando tus sentidos, principalmente los sentidos de la visión y la audición, pero también el tacto, el gusto y el olfato. (Cap. 1, pág. 18)

observatory / observatorio: Edificio que alberga la mayoría de los telescopios ópticos usados por astrónomos profesionales. (Cap. 12, pág. 330)

orbit / órbita: Trayectoria curva que sigue un objeto a medida que gira alrededor de otro objeto en el espacio. Por ejemplo, los planetas giran, en órbitas, alrededor del Sol. (Cap. 12, pág. 336)

ore / mena: Mineral o roca que contiene algo útil que puede minarse para obtener una ganancia; por ejemplo el hierro se extrae del mineral hematita. (Cap. 4, pág. 99)

oxidation / oxidación: Ocurre cuando un material, como el hierro, se expone al oxígeno y al agua. La oxidación causa la herrumbre. (Cap. 5, pág. 128)

P

phloem / floema: Tejido vegetal compuesto de células tubulares. Transporta alimentos desde el lugar en donde se fabrican hasta otras partes de la planta, en donde es usado o almacenado. (Cap. 8, pág. 229)

photoperiodism / fotoperiodismo: Respuesta de una planta al número de horas de luz y oscuridad que recibe diariamente. (Cap. 9, pág. 257)

photosynthesis / fotosíntesis: Proceso mediante el cual las plantas utilizan la energía luminosa para producir alimento. (Cap. 9, pág. 247)

pioneer species / especie pionera: Organismos que son los primeros en crecer en áreas nuevas o que han sido alteradas. (Cap. 8, pág. 221)

plain / llanura: Extensa superficie de terreno relativamente llano. (Cap. 3, pág. 62)

plateau / meseta: Área llana situada en partes elevadas de terreno. (Cap. 3, pág. 64)

plucking / ablación: Proceso en que un glaciar rompe las rocas mediante la acción del agrietamiento debido al hielo; resulta en piedras grandes, grava y arena. (Cap. 6, pág. 160)

population / población: Organismos individuales de la misma especie que viven en el mismo lugar y que pueden producir crías. (Cap. 7, pág. 183; Cap. 10, pág. 272)

population density / densidad demográfica: El tamaño de una población que ocupa un área de tamaño limitado. (Cap. 10, pág. 275)

population explosion / explosión demográfica: Rápido crecimiento de la población humana. (Cap. 7, pág. 183)

potential energy / energía potencial: Energía almacenada que no proviene del movimiento, sino de la posición o condición de un objeto.

(Cap. 15, pág. 418)

prime meridian / primer meridiano: Punto de referencia para distancias de este a oeste, el cual representa longitud 0°. (Cap. 3, pág. 159)

Project Apollo / Proyecto Apolo: Etapa final del programa americano de viajar a la luna. (Cap. 12, pág. 341)

Project Gemini / Proyecto Gemini: Segunda etapa en la meta de viajar a la luna. (Cap. 12, pág. 340)

Project Mercury / Proyecto Mercurio: Proyecto que inició el programa americano de viajar a la luna. (Cap. 12, pág. 340)

proton / protón: Partícula que posee una carga eléctrica positiva en el núcleo. (Cap. 14, pág. 392)

R

radiation / radiación: Energía que viaja en forma de ondas, desde su fuente, en todas direcciones. (Cap. 15, pág. 427)

radio telescope / radiotelescopio: Tipo de telescopio que se usa para estudiar ondas radiales que viajan a través del espacio. (Cap. 12, pág. 331)

rate / razón: Fracción en la cual el numerador y el denominador se expresan en diferentes unidades. (Cap. 16, pág. 446)

rate / tasa: Una razón de dos medidas que usan diferentes unidades. (Cap. 2, pág. 41)

recyclable / reciclable: Cualquier artículo que se puede procesar y volver a usar, para así conservar los recursos naturales y disminuir los desechos sólidos. (Cap. 7, pág. 197)

reflecting telescope / telescopio reflector: Telescopio que usa un espejo como objetivo para enfocar la luz del objeto bajo observación. (Cap. 12, pág. 330)

reflection / reflexión: Ocurre cuando una onda choca contra un objeto o superficie y luego rebota. (Cap. 17, pág. 486; Cap. 18, pág. 503)

refracting telescope / telescopio refractor: Telescopio en que la luz del objeto pasa a través de una lente convexa doble, en donde la luz se dobla formando una imagen sobre el punto focal; luego el ocular magnifica la imagen. (Cap. 12, pág. 330)

refraction / refracción: Cambio en la dirección de propagación de una onda luminosa debido a un cambio en velocidad, al moverse la onda de un medio a otro. (Cap. 17, pág. 487; Cap. 18, pág. 517)

remote sensing / teledetección remota: Manera de recopilar información, desde el espacio, acerca de la Tierra, mediante el uso de satélites y sonar, por ejemplo. (Cap. 3, pág. 80)

respiration / respiración: Serie de reacciones químicas que llevan a cabo todos los organismos para descomponer el alimento y liberar energía. (Cap. 9, pág. 250)

revolution / revolución: Movimiento de la Tierra alrededor del sol, el cual dura un año. (Cap. 13, pág. 357)

rhizoids / rizoides: Raíces filamentosas con solo unas cuantas células de grosor que anclan las hepáticas y los musgos en su lugar. (Cap. 8, pág. 220)

Robinson projection / proyección de Robinson: Mapa que muestra las formas correctas de los continentes y extensiones territoriales precisas. (Cap. 3, pág. 75)

rock / roca: Material compuesto por lo general de dos o más minerales; como por ejemplo, el basalto. (Cap. 4, pág. 92)

rock cycle / ciclo de las rocas: Proceso de cambio en el cual un tipo de roca se convierte en otro tipo de roca. (Cap. 4, pág. 115)

rotation / rotación: Movimiento de la Tierra sobre su eje, el cual ocurre cada 24 horas y ocasiona los días y las noches. (Cap. 13, pág. 356)

S

satellite / satélite: Cualquier objeto que gira alrededor de otro objeto. (Cap. 12, pág. 336)

science / ciencia: Es el proceso de tratar de entender el mundo. (Cap. 1, pág. 7)

scientific methods / métodos científicos: Procedimientos paso a paso que se usan para resolver problemas científicos y que involucran varios pasos. (Cap. 1, pág. 14)

sedimentary rock / roca sedimentaria: Tipo de roca que se forma cuando los pedazos de rocas, plantas y animales o minerales disueltos se acumulan formando capas rocosas. (Cap. 4, pág. 106)

short-day plant /planta de día corto: Planta que necesita doce o más horas de oscuridad para comenzar el proceso de floración. (Cap. 9, pág. 257)

SI / SI: Sistema Internacional de medidas establecido en 1960 y diseñado para proveer un estándar mundial de medidas físicas para la ciencia, la industria y el comercio. (Cap. 2, pág. 37)

slump / derrumbe: Movimiento de masa que ocurre cuando materiales sueltos o capas rocosas se deslizan cuesta abajo. (Cap. 6, pág. 152)

soil / suelo: Mezcla de roca meteorizada, materia orgánica, fragmentos minerales, agua y aire. (Cap. 5, pág. 132)

soil profile / perfil del suelo: Capas diferentes de suelo. (Cap. 5, pág. 134)

solar system / sistema solar: Los nueve planetas y otros objetos que giran alrededor del sol. (Cap. 13, pág. 362)

space probe / sonda espacial: Instrumento que viaja por el sistema solar, reúne información y la envía a la Tierra. (Cap. 12, pág. 337)

space shuttle / transbordador espa- **cial:** Nave espacial reutilizable que transporta a astronautas, satélites y otros materiales hacia el espacio y desde el mismo. (Cap. 12, pág. 344)

space station / estación espacial: Estación en el espacio que posee viviendas, áreas de trabajo y de ejercicio, y todo el equipo y sistemas auxiliares que necesitan los seres humanos para vivir y trabajar en el espacio. (Cap. 12, pág. 345)

stomata / estomas: Aberturas en la superficie de las hojas de las plantas, o en la superficie de estructuras que parecen hojas, las cuales permiten que el dióxido de carbono, el agua y el oxígeno entren y salgan de la planta. (Cap. 8, pág. 231; Cap. 9, pág. 244)

substance / sustancia: Muestra de materia que tiene la misma composición y propiedades en toda su extensión. (Cap. 14, pág. 401)

symbiosis / simbiosis: Cualquier relación estrecha entre dos o más especies diferentes. (Cap. 10, pág. 277)

T

table / tabla: Representación gráfica de información en hileras y columnas para facilitar la lectura y entendimiento de los datos representados. (Cap. 2, pág. 45)

technology / tecnología: Aplicación del conocimiento adquirido a través de la ciencia para elaborar productos o herramientas que la gente pueda usar. (Cap. 1, pág. 9)

temperature / temperatura: Es una medida de la energía cinética promedio de las partículas de cualquier objeto. Entre más alta sea la energía cinética promedio de un objeto, mayor será su temperatura. (Cap. 15, pág. 424)

thermal energy / energía térmica: La energía cinética total de las partículas de un material. (Cap. 15, pág. 425)

till / morena: Mezcla de sedimentos de diferentes tamaños: piedras grandes, arena, arcilla y cieno que deposita la base un glaciar, cuando este disminuye su velocidad. Este tipo de depósito puede cubrir grandes extensiones de terreno. (Cap. 6, pág. 162)

topographic map / mapa topográfico: Mapa que muestra los cambios en elevación del relieve terrestre. (Cap. 3, pág. 76)

transpiration / transpiración: Pérdida de agua a través de los estomas de la hoja. (Cap. 9, pág. 245)

transverse wave / onda transversal: Tipo de onda mecánica en la cual la materia se mueve de un lado a otro formando ángulos rectos con la dirección en que viaja la onda. (Cap. 17, pág. 478)

tropism / tropismo: Respuesta de una planta a un estímulo exterior. Puede ser positivo o negativo. (Cap. 9, pág. 254)

upwarped mountains / montañas plegadas anticlinales: Montañas que se forman cuando la corteza terrestre es empujada hacia arriba por fuerzas del interior de la Tierra. (Cap. 3, pág. 67)

vascular plant / planta vascular: Planta con tejidos que forman un sistema que transporta agua, nutrientes y otras sustancias a lo largo de la planta. (Cap. 8, pág. 218)

volcanic mountains / montañas volcánicas: Montañas que comienzan a formarse cuando el material derretido llega hasta la superficie terrestre a través de un área debilitada de la corteza y forma una estructura en forma de cono. (Cap. 3, pág. 68)

W

water cycle / ciclo del agua: Involucra los procesos de evaporación, condensación y precipitación. (Cap. 10, pág. 286)

wavelength / longitud de onda: Distancia entre un punto de una onda y otro punto idéntico en la siguiente onda, como por ejemplo, de una cresta a la siguiente o de un valle al siguiente. (Cap. 17, pág. 482; (Cap. 18, pág. 505)

waves / ondas: Perturbaciones regulares que transportan energía a través de la materia o del espacio, sin transportar materia; pueden tener diferentes amplitudes, frecuencias, longitudes de onda y velocidades. (Cap. 17, pág. 476)

weathering / meteorización: Proceso que rompe las rocas en fragmentos más y más pequeños. (Cap. 5, pág. 124)

weight / peso: La fuerza descendiente que ejerce la gravedad. (Cap. 16, pág. 453)

xylem / xilema: Tejido compuesto de vasos tubulares que transportan agua y sustancias disueltas desde las raíces a través de toda la planta. (Cap. 8, pág. 229)

Index

The index for *Science Voyages* will help you locate major topics in the book quickly and easily. Each entry in the index is followed by the numbers of the pages on which the entry is discussed. A page number given in **boldface type** indicates the page on which that entry is defined. A page number given in *italic type* indicates a page on which the entry is used in an illustration or photograph. The abbreviation *act.* indicates a page on which the entry is used in an activity.

A

Abiotic factors, **269**–270, *269*, 290
Abrasion, **167**–168, *168*, 177
Acceleration, **447**–449, 470
  due to gravity, 453, 470
Accuracy, *31*, 33–35, *33*, 54
Acid, chemical weathering and, 127
Active optics, 332
Adaptation(s), **298**
  behavioral, *299*, 320
  diversity and, 298–301, *298*, *299*, *300*, *301*, 320
  of plants to land, 216, *216*, *217*
  through natural selection, 304–305, *304–305*, *act.* 312–313, 321
Aerial photography, 84, *84*
Aerobic respiration, 250–252. *See also* Respiration
Agriculture. *See* Farming
Airfoil, 468
Algae, 270, 278, *282*
  green, 215, 216, *216*
Alpha particles, 393
  thermal energy, 441, *441*
  hydroelectric power, 416, *416*
Amethyst, *94*
Amplitude, **481**–482, *481*, 493, *493*, 496, *496*

Ancestors
  anatomy and, 310–311, *310*, *311*, 321
  common, **307**, 311
Angiosperms, *219*, 228, **233**–234, *233*, *234*, 236, *236*, 239
Angle of incidence, 509
Angle of reflection, 509
Animals
  adaptation of, 298–301, *298*, *299*, *300*, *301*, 320
  grazing, 189
Anode, 390
Antarctica, 159
Anthophyta, *219*
Apollo, Project, **341**
Appalachian Mountains, *63*, 64, 66, *66*
Aquifers, 194
Archaeologist, 7, *7*
Archaeology, *act.* 5, 7–11, *act.* 12–13, 24
Archaeopteryx, 311
Arctic National Park, *164*
Arctic, animals in, 299–301, *300*, *301*
Arête (horn), 161, *161*
Asteroid belt, 366, 379
Astronauts, *326*, 340–341, *340*, *341*, 345, 346
Astronomical unit (AU), **363**
Athabaska Glacier, *163*
Atlantic Coastal Plain, 63, *63*
Atlantis space shuttle, 346

Atmosphere
  of planets, 190
Atom(s), **387**, 408
  in minerals, 92
  model of, 388–393, 391, *391*, *392*, *393*, 408, *408*
  nucleus of, 391–392, *392*
  size of, 389, *389*
  structure of, 388, *391*, *393*, *393*
Atomic mass, **396**, 411
Atomic number, **396**, 411
Atomic theory of matter, 389
Augite, 98
Auxin, **255**, 263
Average speed, **446**–447, 470
Axis, of Earth, *356*, *357*, 357, 378, *378*

B

Bacteria, 278, *283*
Balanced forces, **454**
Barbary (McIntyre), 369
Basalt, *act.* 91, 92
Bees, 211, *211*
Behavioral adaptations, *299*, 320
Betelgeuse, *373*
Big Dipper, 372, *372*
Biochemical sedimentary rocks, 108, *108–109*
Biodiversity, **297**, *297*, 318,

318, 320

Biological organization, levels of, 271–272, *271*
  deserts, 169
  tropical rain forests, *140*, *297*, 297, 318, *320*

Biosphere, **268**–269, *268*, 290

Biotic factors, **271,** 290

Biotic potential, 276

Birds
  adaptation of, *299*
  ancestors of, *311*
  in forests, 297, *297*
  migration of, *299*
  as predators, 276
  similarities among, 303, *303*
  variation among, 303, *303*

Black hole, 374

Body
  composition of, 395
  energy in, 415
  enzymes in, 437–439, 441

Bog, 224–225, 227, *227*

Boiling flask, *52*

Boiling point, 41, *41*

Brachiosaurus, 316, *316*

Brass, 403, *403*

Bromine, *398*

Bryophytes, *219*, 220–221, *220*, *221*, 224, 238

Burning (combustion), 387, 388, *388*, 437

C

Cactus, 299, *299*

Caladium plant, 298, *298*

Calcite, *95*, 97, 98, 127

Calendar dates, 72, 73

Camarasaurus, *109*

Cambium, **229,** *229*

Cameras, 525--526, 529

Car design and safety, 467

Carbon cycle, 287, *287*

Carbon dioxide
  in atmospheres of planets, 190
  in burning, 387–388, *388*
  formula for, 402
  in photosynthesis, 244–249, *247*, 262
  in respiration, 251, *251*, 252, 263

Carbon monoxide, 404

Carbonic acid, 127

Carboniferous period, 224, *225*

Caretonoids, 215

Carnivores, *282*, *283*

Carnivorous plants, 259

Carrots, 230

Carrying capacity, **182,** 183, **276,** *276*

Cartography, 79, *79*, 84, *84*

Cassini space probe, 349

Catalysts, 437–438, 441

Cathedral Rocks (Arizona), *106–107*

Cathode rays, 390, *390*

Cathode, 390

Caves, 127, *127*, *144*

Cellulose, **216**

Cell walls, 214, 216

Celsius scale, 41, 424, 431, 441

Centimeter, 32, 38

Chadwick, James, 392

Chalk, 108, *109*, *act.* 130–131

Charon (moon of Pluto), 365

Cheetah, *249*

Chemical energy, 416, 434–438, *434*, **435,** *435*, *436*, *437*, *438*, 441

Chemical formula, 402

Chemical reactions, 434–438, *434*, *435*, *436*, *437*, *438*, 441

Chemical sedimentary rocks, 107

Chemical weathering, **127**–128, *127*, *128*, 137,

144, *144*

Chewing, 438, *438*

Chlorine, 396–397, *396*, *397*, *398*

Chlorophyll, 214, 215, 246, *246*, 247, *247*

Chloroplast, 231, 249, 262

Cirque, 161, *161*

Cities, 194, *194*, *207*

Clamp, *51*

Classification
  of elements, 397, *397*
  of minerals, 97
  of plants, 218–219, *219*
  of types of energy, 420

Clay, 127

Cleavage, 95, *95*

Climate, **128**
  soil types and, 137–138, *138*, *139*
  weathering and, 128–129, *129*

Club mosses, *219*, 238

Coal, 108

Coastal plains, 62–63, *63*, 64

Color, 506–508, 528
  of minerals, 95

Colorado Plateau, *64–65*, 65

Combustion *See also* Burning

Comets, 364, *364*

Commensalism, *278*, 279

Common ancestor, **307,** 311

Communication satellites, 337. *See also* Satellites

Communities, 271, **272,** 290
  interactions in, 276–279, *278*, *279*, 290

Competition, 275

Composting, 143, *143*, **196**

Compounds, **401**-402, *401*, *403*, 409

Compression, 480, *480*

Compressional waves, **479**–480, *479*, *480*, 482, *482*, *act.* 485, 496

Concave lenses, 517, **519,** 529

Concave mirrors, 512–514, 528

Conclusion, 21

Conduction, **428**-429, *428*, 441

Conductor, 429, *429*

Cone-bearing plants, 215, 217, 232, *232–233*

Conglomerate, *106*, 107

Conic projection, **75**, *75*, 87

Conifer(s), *219*, 232, *232*

Conservation, **195**
of resources, 195–196

Constants, **19**, 25

Constellations, **372**, *372*, 373, 379

Constructive interference, 490, 491–492, *491*, *492*, 493

Consumers, 282–283, *283*

Continental glaciers, 158–159, *158*, *159*

Contour plowing, *189*

Controls, **19**, 25

Convection, **430**-431, *430*, *431*, 441

Convection currents, 430–431, *431*

Convex lenses, 517, **518**, 529
image formation with, *act.* 520–521

Convex mirrors, 512–514, 528

Cooperation, international
in space exploration, 346–348, *346–347*, 351

Copper, *95*, 99, 100, *100*, *101*, 397, 429, *429*

Coral reef, *108*, 272

Corrosion (rust), 128, *128*, 144, 389, 390

Cosmonauts, 340, 346–347

Creep, *152*, **153**, 176

Crest, wave, 478, *478*, *481*, 493

Cretaceous period, 215, *316–317*

Crop production, and soil,

136, *136*, 141

Crustaceans, *282*

Crystal(s), 93, *93*, **94,** *94, act.* 110–111

Cubic centimeter, 39

Cubic meter, 37, 39, *39*

Currents
convection, 430–431, *431*

Cuticle, **217,** *217*

Cuyabeno Wildlife Reserve (Ecuador), *140*

Cyanobacteria, 278

Cycad(s), *219*, 232

Cycles, 285–288
carbon, 287, *287*
nitrogen, 287–**288**, *288*
rock, **115**, *115*, 119

Cytoplasm, 250, *251*, 263

D

Dalton, John, 389

Dates, 72, *73*

Day-neutral plants, **258**, *258*

Deceleration. *see* Negative Acceleration

Deciduous trees, *246*

Decomposers, *283*

Deer, 275, *275*

Definite proportions, law of, **402**

Deflation, **167**, *167*, 177

Democritus, 387

Density, population, 184, *274*, *274*, **275**, *275*

Dependent variables, **19**, 25

Deposition, **151**
erosion and, 150–157, *150*, *151*, *152*, *153*, *154*, *155*
glacial, 162–164, *162*, *163*, *164*, 177
gravity and, 151–155, *152*, *153*, *154*, 176
by wind, 171–173, *171*, *172*, *173*, 177

Desalination, 403, *403*

Desert(s), 169

soils, *138*, 140

Desertification, 140

Destructive interference, 490, 491–492, *491*, *492*, 493

Detrital sedimentary rocks, 106–107

Dewey Decimal System, *395*

Diamonds, 98, 99, *99*

Diaphragm, 525

Dicots, **234,** *235, act.* 237, 239

Diffraction, **488**–489, *489*, 497

Diffuse reflection, 510, 528

Digits, and precision, 35

Dinosaurs
extinction of, 316, *316–317*, 317
fossils of, 308, *311*, 314, *314*, *321*
size of, *act.* 319

Diorite, *104*

Discovery space shuttle, 331, *331*, 344–345

Diseases, plants and, 218

Distances
calculation of, 449, 450
measuring, 39, *39*, 362–363, 364, 377, 378
observing, 359
in space, 362–363, 364, 377, 378

Distillation, 403

Diversity
adaptation and, 298–301, *298*, *299*, *300*, *301*, 320
biodiversity, **297,** *297*, 318, *318*, 320
of life, *act.* 295, 296–301, *296*, *297*, *298*, *299*, *300*, *301*

DNA, 307, 309, *309*, 321

Dobsonian reflector, *330*

Dogs, *309*

Drag, 468

Drawing
scale, *act.* 42
scientific, 44, *44*

Dropper, *52*

Ducks, *303*

Ductility, 397, *397*

Dunes, *170*, 171–173, *172, 173*, 177

Dust Bowl, 166, *166, 169*

Dust storms, 168–169, *169*

Döbereiner, Johann, 400

E

Earth, 356–360, 367, *367*, 378
  distance from sun, 364
  equator of, 70, *70*
  gravity of, 336
  location in solar system, *363*
  latitude on, 70–71, *70, 71*, 86, *86*
  longitude on, 71, *71*, 86, *86*
  model of, *act.* 82–83
  revolution of, 357, *357*
  rotation of, 356, *356*
  tilt on axis, *356*, 357, *357*, 378
  time on, 72, *72, 73*
  views of, *act.* 61, 80–81, *80, 81*. *See also* Map(s)
Earth materials, 90–119, *act.* 91
  igneous rocks, 103–105, *103, 104–105, act.* 110–111, *115*, 118
  metamorphic rocks, 113–114, *113, 114, act.* 117, 119
  minerals, 92–101, *92, 93, 94, 95, 96, 98, 99, 100, 101*, 118
  sedimentary rocks, 106–109, *106–107, 108, 109, 115*, 116, 119
Earthquake, tsunamis caused by, 482
Earthquake faults. *See* Fault(s), earthquake

Earthworms, 279, *279*
Eclipse, **359**
  lunar, 359, *360*
  solar, 359, *359*
Ecological pyramids, **284**
Ecologist, *268*
Ecology, **269,** 290
Ecosystems, *271*, **272,** *272, 279*, 290
  energy flow through, 282–288, *282–283, 284, 285, 286, 287*, 291
Electricity
  hydroelectric power, 418, *418*
  wind power, 418
Electromagnetic radiation, 328–329, *328, 329*
Electromagnetic spectrum, *328–329*, **329,** 350, 482, *482*, 505–506
Electromagnetic waves, 328–329, *328, 329*, 350, **478,** *478*, 482, *482*, 496, **502,** 528
Electron, **390,** *391*, 408
Electron cloud, 393, *393*
Elements, **394,** 409
  classification of, 397, *397*
  isotopes of, 396–397, *396*, 409
  organizing, 394–398, *396*
  periodic table of, 395–398, *396, act.* 399, 400, *400*
  synthetic, 394
Elevation, 63
Elliptical galaxy, *375*, 376
Emerald, 98
Endothermic reaction, 436, *436*, 441
Energy, 412–441, **414**
  amplitude and, 481, *481*
  chemical, 415, 436–440, *434*, **435,** *435, 436, 437, 438*, 441
  in chemical reactions, 435–438, *435, 436, 437,*

438, 441
  classifying types of, 420
  comparing energy content, 430
  conduction of, 428–429, *428*, 441
  conservation of, 420–421, *421*, 440
  convection of, 430–431, *430, 431*, 441
  flow through ecosystems, 282–288, *282–283, 284, 285, 286, 287*, 291
  geothermal, 439, *439*
  in human body, 415
  kinetic, **416,** *417*, 418–421, *418–419, 420, 421*, 440
  mechanical, 415
  nuclear, 415
  observing, *act.* 413
  potential, **418**-419, *418–419, 421*, 435, 441
  radiation of, 427, *427*, 441
  temperature and, 423–426, *423, 424, 425, 426*
  thermal. *See* Thermal energy
  transfer of, 419–420, *420, act.* 422, 426–431, *426, 427, 428, 429, 430, 431*
  transformations in, 415–416, *415, 416*, 440
Energy-absorbing reaction, 436, *436*
Energy-releasing reaction, 437, *437*
Energy pyramid, 284–285, *285*, 291
Environment, 180–207
Environment(s)
  adaptation to, 298–301, *298, 299, 300, 301*, 320
  carrying capacity of, 182, 183, 276, *276, 277*
  conservation and, 195–196

impact of population on, 184–185, *184, 185*

limiting factors of, 275, *275, 277,* act. 280–281, 290

living, 268–269, *268,* 271–272, *271, 272,* 290

nonliving, 269–270, *269, 270,* 290

phytoremediation and, 192–193, *192*

population growth and, *act.* 181, 182–185, *182, 183,* 206

waste disposal and, *180–181,* 191–192, *191,* 193
See also Land use

Enzymes, 437–438, 441

Epidermis, in plants, 231, *231*

Epsom salt, 436

Equator, **70,** *70*

Eras, 315, 321

Erosion
farming and, 189
by water, 189

Erosion, 148–179, *148–149,* act. 149, **150**
deposition and, 150–157, *150, 151, 152, 153, 154, 155*
glacial, 158, 160–162, *160–161,* 177
gravity and, 151–157, *152, 153, 154, 155,* 176
reducing, 139–141, *141,* 170–171, *170,* 176
of soil, 139, 170–171, *170*
by surface water, 150–151, *150*
by wind, 167–171, *167, 168, 169, 170, 171, act.* 174–175, 177

Esker, 163, *163*

Estimation, **31**–32, *31,* 54

Ethylene (ethene), 256, *256,* 263

Etna, Mount, *103*

Eukaryotic cells, 250, *251,* 263

Europa (moon of Jupiter), 339, *339*

Evolution
of plants, 215–218, *215, 216, 217*

Evaporation, 93, 286, *286*

Excavations, *6,* 10–11, *10,* 24
models of, *act.* 5, *act.* 12–13

Exothermic reaction, 437, *437,* 441

Extinction, 316–317
mass, *316–317,* **317**

Extrusive igneous rock, 103, **104,** *104, 105, act.* 110–111, 118

Fahrenheit scale, 41, 424, 431, 441

Farming
composting and, 143, *143*
erosion in, 189
land use for, 188–189, *188, 189*
no-till, 141, *141,* 189
organic, 188–189, *188*
soil loss and, 139–140, *140,* 141, *141*
soil quality and, 136, *136,* 141
terraced, 156, *156*

Fault-block mountains, **68,** *68*

Feldspar, 98

Ferns, *219,* 222, *222,* 224, *224,* 238, *238*

Fertilizers, 136, 188, 207

Fireflies, 434, *434*

Fish, 30, *30,* 279, 283, *283,* 310, *310,* 439, *439*

Fissures, 104

Flight, balanced forces, 454

Flooding, 194

Flowering plants, 215, 217, 218, 233–234, *233, 234,* 239

Forest(s)
cutting, 190, *190,* 196
rain, *190*

Fluorite, *93*

Focal length, **512**

Focal point, **512,** 528

Folded mountains, **66,** *66*

Foliated metamorphic rocks, **114,** *114*

Food chain, *282–283,* **283**–284, 291

Food web, **284,** *284,* 285, *285*

Force, **453,** 453–454
balanced, **454**
measuring, 454–455
net, 460–461
normal, **454,** 460

Forests,
rain, *140,* 297, *297,* 318, *320*
sunlight in, 270, *270*

Formula, chemical, 402

Fossil record, 215, *215,* 222, **314**

Fossil(s), 5, *30,* 108, *109,* **308,** *308, 311,* 314, *314,* 321, *321*

Fracture, 95, *95*

Free fall, 456, *456*

Freezing point, 41, *41*

Frequency, **483,** *483,* 496
of a wave, 505

Friction, **459**

Frogs, *282*

Fruits, 228, 256, *256*

Fuel formation of, 224–225

Fungi, 278, *283*

Funnel, *52*

Galaxies, **375**–377, *375, 376, 377,* 379

Galena, *96*, 99
Galilei, Galileo, 332
Gamma rays, 328, 329, *329*
Gas(es)
  exchange in plants,
  244–245, *244, 245*, 262
Gemini, Project, **340**
Gems, **98**–99, *99*
Geologic time scale, **315,**
  315, 321
Geothermal energy, 439, *439*
Ginkgoes, *219*, 232, *233*
Glacial grooving, *act.* 165
Glacier(s), **158**–165, 177, *177*
  continental, 158–159, *158,*
  159
  deposition by, 162–164,
  162, 163, 164, 177
  erosion by, 158, 160–162,
  160–161, 177
  valley, 159, *159*, 161–162,
  161, 164, act. 165
Global Positioning System
  (GPS), 36, *36*, 80, 483
Globe, *act.* 61
Glucose
  in photosynthesis, 247,
  247, 248, 262
  in respiration, *251, 252*
Gneiss, 114, *114, act.* 117
Gnetophytes, *219*, 232, *233*
Gold foil experiment
  (Rutherford), 393
GPS *See* Global Positioning
  System
Grain, 136, *136*, 236
Gram, 40
Grand Canyon, 65
Grand Tetons, *124*
Granite, *act.* 91, 92, *105*, 127
Graph(s), **45,** 55
  bar, **46,** *46*
  circle, **46,** *46*
  line, **45,** *45*
  making and using, 47, *act.*
  48–49, 57, 175, 281, 293
  misleading, 47, *47*

Graphite, *93*
Gravitational attraction, 453
Gravity, 452–454, **453,** 470
  and acceleration on
  Earth, 453
  deposition and, 151–155,
  152, 153, 154, 176
  effects of, 346
  erosion and, 151–157, *152,*
  153, 154, 155, 176
  orbits and, 336
Great Plains, 63, 64
Great Red Spot (Jupiter),
  366
Green algae, 215, 216, *216*
Greenland, 159
Ground penetrating radar
  (GPR), 23
Ground pines, 222, 223
Groundwater, 194
Guard cells, **231,** *231,*
  244–245, *244*, 262
Gulf Coastal Plain, 63, *63,*
  64
Guthrie, Woody, 166, *166*
Gymnosperms, 228, **232,**
  232–233, 235, *235*, 239
Gypsum, *92*, 98, *98*

Habitat, **279,** 290
Hadrosaur fossil, *314*
Halite (rock salt), 94, *94*, 97,
  107
Hand, as unit of
  measurement, *act.* 29
Hardness, 96–97
Hawaii, volcanoes in, 68, 69
Hawks, 276
Hazardous waste, **191**–192,
  207
Heat, **427,** 443
  thermal energy and,
  427–428, *427*
Hematite, *93*, 98, 99
Herbaceous stems, 230

Herbicides, 188
Herbivore, *282*
Hertz (Hz), 483
Horizon A, soil, **134**–136,
  134, 135, 138, 145
Horizon B, soil, 135
Horizon C, soil, 136
Hormones, plant, 255–256,
  256, 263
Horn (arête), 161, *161*
Hornblende, 98
Horsetails, *219*, 222, *222,*
  223–224, *223*, 238
Horticulturalists, 143
Hot-vent inhabitants, 439,
  439
Hubble Space Telescope, 331,
  331, 350
Humus, **133,** 139, 145
Hurricanes, 481, *481*
Hydroelectric power, 416,
  416
Hydrogen
  liquid, 401
  on moon, 349
  reaction with oxygen, *435*
  in water, 401, *402*
Hydrogen peroxide,
  401–402, *402*
Hypothesis, **18**–19, 25
  forming, 18
  testing, 19

Ice wedging, **126,** *126*
Igneous rock, **103**–105, *103,*
  104–105, act. 110–111, *115,*
  118
Image, 511
Independent variables, **19,**
  25
Inertia, **455,** 461
Inference, **18,** 20, 22
Infrared radiation, *328–329,*
  329
Insecticides, 188

Infrared waves, 506

Inner planets, 367–368, *367, 368*, 378

Insects
diversity of, 296, *296*
in food chain, 283
See also individual insects

Insulator, 431, *431*

Interactions
in communities, 276–279, *278, 279*, 290
among living organisms, 274–279, *274, 275, 276, 277, 278, 279*, 290

Interference, wave, **490**–492, *490, 491, 492, 493, 493*, 497

Interior plains, *62, 63*, 64

International Date Line, **72, *73***

International Space Station (ISS), *346, 347*–348, 351, 369

International System of Units (SI), **37**–41, 55, 353

Intrusive igneous rock, 103, *104*, **105**, *105*, act. 110–111

Io (moon of Jupiter), 366

Iron, 99, 128

Irregular galaxy, *375*, 376

Isotopes, **396**-397, *396*, 409

Jasper National Park, *163*

Jupiter, *362*, 366, *366*
distance from sun, 364
exploration of, 338, *338, 339, 339*, 350
moons of, 366, 339, *339*

Kangaroo rats, 298

Kaolinite clay, 127

Keck telescopes (Hawaii), *332*

Kelvin scale, **41**, *41*, 426, 441

Kilogram, 37, **40**

Kilometer, 39, *39*

Kimberlite magma, 99, *99*

Kinetic energy, **416**, *417*, 440
potential energy and, 418–419, *418–419, 421*
transfer of, 419–420, *420*

Knightia fish, 30, *30*

Laboratory equipment, 50–53, *50–53*

Land use, 188–196, 207
conservation and, 155–157, *156, 157*, 195–196
erosion from, 188–189, *188, 189 See* Erosion
for grazing livestock, 189
hazardous wastes and, 191–192, 207
for human-built structures, 193–194, *194*, 207
for natural reserves, 195, *195*
phytoremediation and, 192–193, *192*
for waste disposal, *180–181*, 191, *191*
as wood source, 190, *190*

Landfill, *180–181*, **191**, *191*, 196, act. 200, 207

Landforms, 62–69, 86
mountains. *See* Mountains
plains, 62–64, *62, 63*, 86
plateaus, 64–65, *64–65*, 86
of United States, *63*

Landslide, *157*

Latitude, **70**–71, *70, 71*, 86

Lava, 104, *104–105*, 116, *116*

Lavoisier, Antoine, 387

Law(s)
of conservation of energy, 420-421, *421*, 440
of conservation of matter, **388**
of definite proportions, **402**
of motion. *See* Newton's laws of motion
of reflection, **509**

Leaching, **135**, *135*

Leaves, 230–231, *231*, 244–245, 246, *246*, act. 253, *254*, 262

Legend, map, **78**, *78*

Length, measurement of, 32, 37, 38–39, *38, 39*, 53, *53*

Lenses, 516, **517**–519

Lens
objective, 522, *522*

Levity, 452

Lichens, 278

Life
diversity of, act. 295, 296–301, *296, 297, 298, 299, 300, 301*
history of, 314–318, *314, 315–316, 317, 318*
unity of, 303–311, *303, 304–305, 306, 307, 308, 309, 310, 311*

Lift, 468

Light, 502, 528
as abiotic factor, *269*, 270, *270*
bending, 329
diffraction of, 489, *489*, 497
electromagnetic spectrum of, *328–329*, **329**, 350
and matter, 503
observing, act. 327, 330–333, *330, 332, 333*, act. 334
reflection of, 486, *486*, 490, 497
refraction of, 487–488, *487*, 497
speed of, 329, 516
visible, 329

waves of, 482, *482,* 483–484, 486, *486,* 487–488, *487,* 489, *489,* 490

white, *act.* 327, 507

Light-gathering power in photosynthesis, *246,* 247, *247,* 262

plant responses to, 255, *255,* 257–258, *258,* 263

of telescopes, 331

Light pollution, 340

Light ray, **502**

Light-year, **377,** 379

Limestone, 108, *108, 109,* 127, *127*

Limiting factors, **275,** *275, 277, act.* 280–281, 290

Line graph, **45**

Liquid(s), 53, 403

Liter, 39

Litter, **135**

Living environment, 268–269, *268,* 271–272, *271, 272,* 290

Liverwort, *215,* 220, *220, 221,* 225, 238

Lizards, 306–307, *306–307*

Loess, **171,** *171,* 177

Long-day plants, **257,** *257*

Longitude, **71,** *71,* 86

Lunar eclipse, 359, *360*

Lunar Prospector spacecraft, 349

Lunar Rover Vehicle, *341, 350*

Luster, 96, *96*

M

Magma, 93, 99, 103, 105, *105*

Magnesium, 99

Magnetism, 97

Magnetite, *93,* 97

Malaria, 218

Magnifying power of telescopes, 331, 333

Mammoths, 318

Map(s), 74–81, 87

contour lines on, 77

improvements in, 84

latitude on, 70–71, *70, 71,* 86

longitude on, 70, 71, *71,* 86

projections on, 74–75, *74, 75,* 87

remote sensing and, 79, 80–81, 87

three-dimensional, 78

topographic, **76**–79, *76, 78, 79, act.* 85, 87

uses of, 78–79

of world, *act.* 61

Mapmaking, 13, 79, *79,* 84, *84*

Map legend, **78,** *78*

Map scale, **78**

Marble, 114, *114*

Marble/skateboard model, 445

Mars, *363,* 367, *367*

distance from sun, 364

exploration of, 338, 348

Mass, **40, 455,** 456, 470

atomic, **396,** 409

measurement of, 37, 40, *40,* 53

Mastodons, 5, 318, *318*

Mass extinction, *316–317,* **317**

Mass movements, **152**–155, *152, 153, 154, 155, 157*

Mass number, **396**

Matter, *act.* 385, **386**-405

atomic theory of, 389

cycles of, 285–288, *286, 287, 288*

law of conservation of, 390

and light, 503

structure of, 386–393, *386, 387, 388,* 391, *391, 392, 393,* 408

McIntyre, Vonda N., 369

Measurement, 28–55, *act.* 29, **30,** *30, 31, 32,* 53

accuracy of, *31,* 33–35, *33,* 54

of distance, 39, *39,* 362–363, 364, 377, 378

estimation and, 31–32, *31,* 54

of frequency, 483

of length, 32, 37, 38–39, *38, 39,* 53, *53*

of mass, 37, 40, *40,* 53

precision of, *32,* 33–35, *33,* 54

rounding and, 34

in SI, 37–41, 55

of space, *act.* 267, 362–363, 364, 377, 378

of temperature, 37, 41, *41,* 53, 424, *426,* 431, 441

of time, 37

units of, 37–41

of volume, 37, 39, *39,* 53, *53*

of water absorption by moss, 221

of weight, 40, *40*

Measuring cup, *32*

Mechanical energy, 417

Mechanical waves, 476–**477,** *477,* 496

Mechanical weathering, **125**–126, *125, 126,* 144, *144*

Medicine, plants in, 218, *218*

Medium, **502**

Mendeleev, Dmitri, 400

Meniscus, 53

Mercator projection, *74,* **75,** 87

Mercury, *363,* 364, 368, *368*

Mercury Project, **340**

Metal, **397,** *397,* 409

extracting from soil, 192, *192*

Metallic minerals, 96

Metalloids, **398,** 409

Metamorphic rocks, **113**–114, *113, 114, act.* 117, 119

Meteorites, 368

Meter, 32, **38**

Mica, *95,* 98, *98*

Micrometer, 37, 38, *38*

Microscopes, 522, *522,* 529

Microwave oven, 427, *427,* 482

Microwaves, *328, 329,* 505

Migration, *299,* 320

Milky Way galaxy, 376, *376*

Millimeter, 32, 38

Minerals, **92**–101, *92, 93, 98, 99,* 118

  classifying, 97

  cleavage of, 95, *95*

  color of, 95

  common, 98–101, *99, 100, 101*

  crystals, 93, *93,* 94, *94, act.* 110–111

  fracture of, 95, *95*

  gems, 98–99, *99*

  hardness of, 96–97

  identifying origin of, 98

  luster of, 96, *96*

  magnetism in, 97

  metallic, 96

  mining of, 99, *100*

  nonmetallic, 96, *96*

  ores, *93,* 99–101, *100, 101*

  properties of, 94–97, *94, 95, 96*

  as resource, *80*

  streak of, 95–96, *96*

Mining, 99, *100*

Mir space station, 346–347, 351

Mirrors, 486, *486,* 510–514

Mitochondria, 250, 251, *251,* 263

Mixtures, **403**-405, *act.* 406–407, 409

  nonuniform, 404, *405,* 409

  uniform, 404, *404,* 409

Models

  of atom, 388–393, *391, 392, 393,* 408, *408*

  of constellations, 373

  of Earth, *act.* 82–83

  of effects of gravity, 346

  of excavation, *act.* 5, *act.* 12–13

  of population growth, *act.* 181

  of run-off, 194

Mohs, Friedrich, 96

Mohs scale, 96–97

Monocots, **234,** *234, act.* 237, 239

Moon(s)

  eclipse of, 359, *360*

  exploration of, *326–327,* 340–341, *341,* 349

  of Jupiter, 339, *339*

  orbit of, 337

  of other planets, *338, 339, 339, 349, 349,* 365, 366

  phases of, 358, *358, act.* 361

  of Saturn, *338, 349, 349*

  sun and, 358

  water on, 349

Moraine, **162,** *163*

Mosses, *215, 219,* 220–221, *220, 221, 222, 223, 223,* 225, 227, *227,* 238

Moths, *278*

Mountains, *62, 63,* 65–69, 86, *86*

  fault-block, **68,** *68*

  folded, **66,** *66*

  upwarped, **67,** *67*

  volcanic, **68**-69, *69*

  weathering and, *124*

Mudflows, 154–155, *155*

Music, *479,* 479–480, *480,*

  of the Dust Bowl, 166, *166,* 483,

Musk oxen, *301*

Mustard plant, 201, *201*

Mutualism, 278

N

Nanometer, 38

NASA (National Aeronautics and Space Administration), 337, 344, 347, 348, 349

Native Americans, 102, *102*

Natural preserves, 195, *195*

Natural selection, **304**–305, *304–305, act.* 312–313, 321

Naturalist, 145, *145*

Navajo sand painting, 102, *102*

Nebula, *374, 377*

Negative acceleration, *447*

  calculation of, 449

Neptune, *338, 339, 362,* 364, 365, *365*

Net force, 460–461, *461*

Neutron, **392,** 408, 409

Neutron star, 374, *374*

Never Cry Wolf (Mowat), 289

Newton, 454

Newton, Sir Isaac, 452

Newton's laws

  and car design, 467

  first law of motion, 458–460, 471

  of motion, **458**–463, *464,* 471

  of motion, examples of, 465–466

  second law of motion, 454, 460–461, 471

  third law of motion, 462–463, *463,* 471

  of universal gravitation, 453

Niche, **279,** 290

Nitrogen cycle, 287–**288,** *288*

No-till farming, 189

Noise, 491–492, *492*

Non-foliated metamorphic rocks, **114,** *114*

Nonliving environment, 269–270, *269, 270,* 290
Nonmetal, **398,** *398,* 409
Nonmetallic minerals, 96, *96*
Nonuniform mixtures, 404, *405,* 409
Nonvascular plants, **218,** 220–221, *220, 221,* 238
Normal, 487–488, *487*
Normal force, **454,** 460
Nova, *See* Supernova
Nuclear energy, 417
Nucleus, 391-**392,** *392*

Observation, **18**
Observatory, **330**
Obsidian, *95*
Odometer, *447*
Opaque, 504
Optical axis, 512
Optical telescopes, 330–331, *330, 332, act.* 334, 350, *350*
Optics, 332
Orbits, **336,** *336,* 350
of moon, 337
Orchids, *278*
Ores, *93,* **99**–101, *100, 101*
Organic contaminants, 193
Organic farming, 188–189, *188*
Organisms, 271
interactions among, 274–279, *274, 275, 276, 277, 278, 279,* 290
symbiosis between, 277–279, *278,* 290
Orion Nebula, *377*
Ornitholestes, 311
Outer planets, 365–366, *365, 366,* 378
Outwash, 163, *163,* 177
Owls, 276
Oxidation, **128**

in burning, 387, *388*
chemical weathering and, 128, *128*
liquid, 401
reaction with hydrogen, *435*
in water, 401–402, *402*
Oxygen
in photosynthesis, *247,* 248, 249, 262
in respiration, 250, 263
Ozone
layer, 505
and ultraviolet waves, 506

Paleozoic era, 215, 222, 224
Palisade layer, 231, *231*
Pan balance, 40, *40*
Paper, *387*
Parasitism, 279
Peat bogs, 225, 227, *227*
Pebbles, 107
Pendulum, *421*
Period(s), geologic, 315, 321
Periodic table, 395–398, *396, 396, act.* 399, 400, *400*
Pesticides, 188, 207
Petri dish, *52*
Phases, of moon, 358, *358, act.* 361
Phloem, **229,** *229*
Photoperiodism, **257**–258, *258*
Photosynthesis, 246–249, **247,** 262, 436
food-making process in, 247–248, *247*
importance of, 249
in plants, 218, 229, 190, *245,* 246–249, *246,* 262
respiration vs., 250
Phototropism, 255, *255*
Phyllite, 114

Phytoplankton, *282, 283,* 285
Phytoremediation, 192–193, *192*
Pigments and color, 508
Pioneer species, **221,** 238
Pitch, 483
Plains, **62**-64, 86
coastal, 62–63, *63,* 64
interior, *62, 63,* 64
Plane mirrors, 528
reflection by, 510–511, reflection from, *act.* 515
Planets
atmospheres of, 190
distances from sun, 364
exploration of, *338,* 348, 349, *349*
inner, 367–368, *367, 368,* 378
locations in solar system, *362–363*
outer, 365–366, *365, 366,* 378
space colonies on, *act.* 370–371
See also Space exploration; *names of individual planets*
Plant(s), 212–263, *212–213*
adaptations of, 216, *216, 217,* 298–301, *298, 299*
carnivorous, 259
characteristics of, 214–215, *214,* 238, *238*
classification of, 218–219, *219*
cone-bearing, 215, 217, 232, *232*
day-neutral, **258,** *258*
edible, *act.* 213
fertilizers and, 188, 207
flowering, 215, 217, 218, 233–234, *233, 234,* 239
flowers of, *388*
gas exchange in, 244–245, *244, 245,* 262

hormones of, 255–256, *256*, 263

leaves of, 230–231, *231*, 244–245, *246*, *act.* 253, *254*, 262

light and, 255, *255*, 257–258, *258*, 263

long-day, **257**, *257*

mechanical weathering and, 125–126, *125*, *126*, 144, *144*

in medicine, 218, *218*

nonvascular, **218**, 220–221, *220*, *221*, 238

origin and evolution of, 215–218, *215*, *216*, *217*

photoperiods of, 257–258, *258*

photosynthesis in, 190, 218, 229, *245*, 246–249, *246*, 262

phytoremediation by, 192–193, *192*

pollution-absorbing, 201, *201*

in rain forests, 297, *297*

reproduction by, 217

respiration of, 249–252, *249*, *251*, *252*, 263

responses of, 254–258, *254*, *255*, *256*, *257*, *act.* 260–261, 263

roots of, 139, 170–171, *170*, 230, *230*

seasons and, 246, *246*, 257, 258

seed, 228–236, *228*, *229*, *230*, *231*, *232*, *233*, *234*, *235*, *236*, *act.* 237, 239, *239*

seedless, 220–226, *220*, *221*, *222*, *223*, *224*, *225*, *act.* 226, 238, *238*

short-day, **257**, *257*

sizes of, 214, 224

soil erosion and, 139, 170–171, *170*

stems of, 229–230

stomata of, 231, *231*,

244–245, *244*, *245*, *act.* 253, 262

symbiotic relationships of, 278, *278*

tropisms and, 254–255, *254*, *255*, *act.* 260–261, 263

vascular, **218**, 222–225, *222*, *223*, *224*, *225*, 229, *229*, 238, 239, *239*

water and, 229, *act.* 243, 244–245, *244*, *245*, 247, 248, 262, 263

Plateaus, **64**–65, *64–65*, 86

Plowing and soil loss, 139–140, *140*, 141, *141*

Plucking, **160**, 177

Pluto, *339*, 364, 365, *365*

Polar bears, 300, *300*

Pollution

by hazardous wastes, 191–192, 207

light, 340

reducing with plants, 201, *201*

Population(s), **183**, *271*, **272**, 290

biotic potential of, 276

calculating growth of, 277

carrying capacity and, 276, *276*

characteristics of, 274–276, *274*, *275*, *276*

density of, 184, 274, *274*, **275**, *275*

explosion, *182*, **183**-184, *183*, *act.* 186–187, 196, 206

growth of, *act.* 181, 182–184, *182*, *183*, *act.* 186–187, 196, 206

impact on environment, 184–187, *184*, *185*

limiting factors and, 275, *275*, *act.* 280–281, 290

spacing in, 274, *274*

Potential energy, **418**-419, *418–419*, *421*, 435, 440

Prairie soils, *138*

soil types and, 137, *138*

Precision, *32*, 33, *33*, 54

Predation, 276, 278

Primary colors, 507

Prime meridian, *70*, **71**

Primroses, *257*

Prism, 329, *506*

Problem recognition, 15–18, *15*, 25

Producers, 282, *282*

Project Apollo, **341**

Project Gemini, **340**

Project Mercury, **340**

Projections, map, 74–75, *74*, *75*, 87

Prokaryotic cells, 250, 263

Protons, **392**, 408

Pyrite, 96

Quail, 298

Quartz, *92*, *94*, 98

Quartzite, 114

Radar, 23, *23*

Radiation, **427**

electromagnetic, 328–329, *328–329*, 350

of energy, *427*, 441

infrared, *328–329*, 329

observing, *act.* 327, 329–334, *330*, *332*, *333*, *act.* 334

from space, 328–333, 350

ultraviolet, 329, *329*, 367

Radio telescope, **333**, 350, 525

Radio waves, *328*, 329, 333, 505, *505*

Rain forests, *140*, 190, 297, *297*, 318, *320*

Rarefaction, 480, *480*

Rate of reaction, 439–440
Rate, **41, 446**
Ray
  incident, 509, *509*
  reflected, 509, *509*
Reaction
  chemical, 434–438, *434,*
  435, 436, 437, 448, 441
  endothermic, 436, *436,*
  441
  energy-absorbing, 436,
  436
  energy-releasing, 437, *437*
  exothermic, 437, *437,* 441
  rate of, 437–438
Recyclable objects, **197**
Recycling, 195, 197–199,
  197, 198, 202–205, 207
Reducing, 195, 207
Redwood trees, *210–211,*
  211
Reef, *108,* 272
Reflecting telescope, **330,**
  330, act. 334, 350, 524
Reflection, **486,** *486,* 490,
  497, **503,** 509, 509–511, 528
  from a plane mirror, *act.*
  515
Refracting telescope, **330,**
  330, act. 334, 350, 523
Refraction, **487**–488, *487,*
  488, 497, 516–519, **517,**
  529
Regular reflection, 510, 528
Remote sensing, 79, **80**–81,
  80, 81, 87
Remotely operated vehicles
  (ROVs), *341,* 350
Reproduction of plants, 217
Reserves, natural, 195, *195*
Resin, 235, *235, 239*
Resources, conservation of,
  195–196
Respiration, **250**
  photosynthesis vs., 250
  of plants, 249–252, *249,*
  251, 252, 263
  in yeast, 250

Reusing, 195, 198, 207
Revolution, **357,** *357*
Rhizoids, **220,** 221
Rhyolite, *105*
Rings, of Saturn, 366
Robinson projection, **75,** *75,*
  87
Robot rovers, *341,* 348, *350*
Robots, *9*
Rock(s), *act.* 91, **92,** 103–119
  biochemical, 108, *108–109*
  chemical, 107
  detrital, 106–107
  foliated, **114,** *114*
  formation from fossils,
  108, *109*
  igneous, **103**–105, *103,*
  104–105, act. 110–111, *115,*
  118
  metamorphic, **113**–114,
  113, 114, act. 117, 119
  non-foliated, **114,** *114*
  sedimentary, **106**–109,
  106–107, 108, 109, 115,
  116, 119
  soil formation and, 132,
  132, 144
  visualizing, *104–105,*
  106–107
  volcanic, 103–105, *103,*
  104–105
Rock cycle, **115,** *115,* 119
Rock salt (halite), 94, *94,* 97,
  107
Rocket, 337, 463
Rockslides, 153–154, *153,*
  154
Rocky Mountains, *63,* 64,
  67, 67
Roots, 170–171, *170,* 230,
  230
Rotation, **356,** *356*
Rounding, 34
ROVs (remotely operated
  vehicles), *341, 350*
Runoff, 194
Rust (corrosion), 128, *128,*
  144, 387, 388

Rutherford, Ernest, 391

S

Safety
  in laboratory, 51
  symbols for, 50
Salicylates, 218
Saliva, 438, *438*
Salt
  in oceans, 403
  rock (halite), 94, *94,* 97,
  107
Sandstone, 106, *106,* 107
Sandstorms, 168
Sand dunes, *170,* 171–173,
  172, 173, 177
Sand painting, 102, *102*
Sanitary landfill, **191,** *191*
Satellite(s), 87, **336**–337, *336,*
  344, 345, 350
  for Global Positioning
  System, 36
  Topex-Poseidon, 80, *80*
Saturn, *362,* 366, *366*
  distance from sun, 364
  exploration of, *338,* 349,
  349
  moons of, *338,* 349, *349*
  rings of, 366
Scale
  drawing, *act.* 42
  geologic time, **315,** *315,*
  321
  map, **78**
  for measurement, *34,* 40,
  40
  of mineral hardness
  (Mohs scale), 96–97
  temperature, 41, *41,* 426,
  433, 443
Schist, 114, *114*
Science, **7,** 24
  nature of, 4–25
Science fair, *21,* 25
Scientific methods, **14**
Scientific notation, 527

Scientific problem solving, 14–21, 25

Scouring rush (horsetails), *219*, 222, *222*, 223–224, *223*, 238

Sea anemones, 279

Sea Beam, 80–81, *81*

Sea otters, 300

Seaborg, Glenn, 400

Seals, 300

Season(s), 246, *246*, 257, 258, 357, *357*

Sediment, 106

Sedimentary rocks, **106**–109, *106–107, 108, 109, 115,* 116, 119

Seed, 228

Seed plants, 228–237, *228*
  angiosperms, *219*, 228, 233–234, *233, 234*, 236, *236*, 239
  dicots, 234, *235, act.* 237, 239
  gymnosperms, 228, 232, *232–233, 235, 235*, 239
  importance of, 234–236
  leaves of, 230–231, *231*
  monocots, 234, *234, act.* 237, 239
  roots of, 230, *230*
  stems of, 229–230
  vascular tissue of, 229, *229*, 239, *239*

Seedless plants, 220–226, 238, *238*
  comparing, *act.* 226
  nonvascular, 220–221, *220, 221*, 238
  vascular, 222–225, *222, 223, 224, 225*, 238

Shale, 107, *107*

Shaw, Amanda, 25

Sheep, *43*

Short-day plants, **257,** *257*

SI (International System of Units), **37**–41, 55

Sickle-cell anemia, *370*

Siltstone, 107, *107*

Silver, *404*

Size, observing, 359

Skylab space station, 345, 351

Slate, 114, *114*

Slope
  erosion and, 155–156, *156, 157*
  soil profiles and, 138

Slump, **152,** *152,* 176

Smelting, 100, *100*

Snails, *282–283*

Soapstone, 114, *114*

Soil, **132**–142
  as abiotic factor, *269*, 270
  characteristics of, *act.* 142
  composition of, 133, 134, 145, *act.* 273
  erosion of, 139–141, 170–171, *170, 189*
  extracting metals from, 192, *192*
  formation of, 124, 132, *132–133, 138,* 145
  loss of, 139–140, *140,* 141, *141*
  as resource, 138–139
  topsoil, 135
  types of, 137–138, *138, 139*

Soil profile, **134**–136, *134, 135,* 138

Sojourner robot rover, 348, *350*

Solar cooker, 427

Solar eclipse, 359, *359*

Solar system, 354–371, **362,** *362–363,* 378–379
  asteroid belt in, 366
  comets in, 364, *364*
  Earth and moon in, 356–361, *356, 357, 358, 359, 360, act.* 361, 378
  inner planets in, 367–368, *367, 368,* 378
  outer planets in, 365–366, *365, 366,* 378

Sonar, 80–81, *81,* 87

Sound waves, 329, 476–477, *477,* 479–480, *479, 480, 481,* 483–484, 488, 489, *489,* 490

Sound(s)
  comparing, 479
  pitch of, 483
  speed of, 483–484

Space
  measurement of, *act.* 267, 362–363, 364, 377, 379
  radiation from, 328–333, 350

Space colony, *act.* 370–371

Space exploration, 326–351, *act.* 327
  international cooperation in, 346–348, *346–347,* 351
  of moon, *326–327,* 340–341, *341,* 349
  of planets, *338–339,* 348, 349, *349*
  satellites in, 336–337, *336,* 344, 345, 350
  space probes in, 337–339, *337, 338–339,* 340, 348, 349, *349,* 350
  space shuttles in, 331, *331,* 344–345, *344–345,* 346, 348, 351, *351*
  space stations in, 345–346, *346–347,* 347–348, 351, *351*
  telescopes in, 329–334, *330, 332, 333, act.* 334, 350, *350*

Space probes, **337**–339, *337, 338–339,* 340, 348, 349, *349,* 350

Space shuttles, 331, *331,* **344**–345, *344–345,* 346, 348, 351, *351, 403*

Space stations, **345**–346,

346–347, 347–348, 351, 351, 369, 369
Spacing, of populations, 274, *274*
Species, pioneer, **221,** 238
Spectrum
electromagnetic, *328–329,* **329,** 350, 482, *482*
Speed, 329, 446–447, 470
average, **446**
calculation of, 450
of light, 360, 516
of sound, 483–484
of waves, 483–484, 487–488, 496
Speedometer, *447, 449*
Sphagnum moss, 227
Spike moss, *222, 223, 223*
Spiral galaxy, 376, *376*
Spongy layer, 231, *231*
Spore, 220, 221, 223, *223, 224,* 238
Sporophyte, *220*
Spreadsheets, computer, 368
Spring scale, 40, *40, 455*
Sputnik I, 336, 337, 340
Squirrels, 304, *304–305*
Star(s), 372–374, 379
colors of, 373, 379
comparing, *373*
constellations of, 372, *372, 373,* 379
lives of, 373–374, *374, 375*
neutron, 374, *374*
number of, *act.* 355
sighting of, *act.* 342–343
supergiant, 374, *374*
temperatures of, 373, 379
See also Sun
Stems, 229–230
Stomata, **231,** *231,* **244**–245, *244, 245, act.* 253, 262
Streak, 95–96, *96*
Structures, human-built, 193–194, *194,* 207
electromagnetic radiation from, 329

Subscripts, 402
Substance, **401**
Sun
Betelgeuse compared to, *373*
distances of planets from, 364
life stages of, 374
moon and, 358
Supergiants, 374, *374*
Supernova, 374, *375,* 377, *386, 408*
Surface smoothness and reflection, 509–510
Swamp, 224, *225*
Symbiosis, **277**-279, *278,* 290
Symbols
safety, 50
on topographic maps, *78*
Synthetic elements, 394

Tables, **45,** *45*
Talc, *96*
Tapeworms, *278,* 279
Taurus constellation, 372
Technology, **9,** 24
aerial photography, 84, *84*
in exploration of moon, *341, 350*
Global Positioning System (GPS), 36, *36,* 80, 483
Hubble Space Telescope, 331, *331,* 350
International Space Station, *346–347, 347–348,* 351, *369, 369*
Lunar Rover Vehicle, *341, 350*
microwave oven, 427, *427,* 482
nuclear power, 415
radar, 23, *23*

remote sensing, 79, 80–81, *80, 81,* 87
remotely operated vehicles (ROVs), *341, 350*
robots, *9*
robot rover, *341,* 348, *350*
satellites, 36, 80, *80,* 336–337, *336,* 344, 345, 350
solar cooker, 427
space probes, 337–339, *337, 338–339,* 340, 348, 349, *349,* 350
space shuttles, 331, *331,* 344–345, *344–345,* 346, 348, 351, *351,* 403
space stations, 345–346, *346–347, 347–348,* 351, *351*
telescopes, 329–334, *330, 332, 333, act.* 334, 350, *350*
Telescopes, 329–334, *333, 375,* 523–524, 529
Hubble, 331, *331, 332,* 350
interpreting data about, 331
Keck, 332, *332*
light-gathering power of, 331
magnifying power of, 331, 333
optical, 330–331, *330, 332, act.* 334, 350, *350*
radio, **333,** 350
reflecting, **330,** *330, act.* 334, 350
refracting, **330,** *330, act.* 334, 350
Temperate soils, *138*
Temperature, **424,** 441
as abiotic factor, *269,* 270
energy and, 423–426, *423, 424, 425, 426*
hot-vent inhabitants, 439, *441*
measurement of, 37, 41, *41,* 53, 424, *426,* 431, 441

observing changes in, *act.* 432–433
of stars, 373, 379
on Venus, 367
Temperature scales, 41, *41*, 424, 431, 441
Terraces, 156, *156*
Theories, 18
atomic theory of matter, 389
Thermal energy, **425**–433, 441
absorption during cooking, 436
conduction of, 428–429, *428*, 441
convection of, 430–431, *430*, *431*, 441
heat and, 425–426, *425*
observing changes in, *act.* 432–433
radiation of, 427, *427*, 441
transfer of, 426–431, *426*, *427*, *428*, *429*, *430*, *431*
Thermal, 431, *431*
Thermometer, *51*, *53*, 426
Thermophiles, 439, *439*
Thigmotropism, 254–255, *254*
Thomson, J.J., 390–391
Three-dimensional maps, 78
Thrust, 468
Thunderstorms, 483
Till, **162**, *162*, 177
Time
geologic, 315, *315*, 321
measurement of, 37
rate and, 41
Time zones, 72, *72*, *73*
Titan (moon of Saturn), *338*, 349, *349*
Tobago Rain Forest (Caribbean), *140*
Topex-Poseidon Satellite, 80, *80*
Topographic maps, **76**–79, *76*, *78*, *79*, *act.* 85, 87

Topsoil, 135, 189
Translucent, 504
Transparent, 504
Transpiration, **245**
Transverse waves, **478**, *478*, 482, *act.* 485, 496
Trash disposal, *180–181*, 191, *191*, 193
Trees
cutting, 190, *190*, 196
deciduous, *246*
gymnosperms, 232, *232–233*, 235, *235*, 239
mechanical weathering and, 125–126, *125*, *126*, 144, *144*
pollution-absorbing, 201
redwood, *210–211*, 211
stems of, 229–230
symbiotic relationships of, *278*
vascular tissue of, *229*, *239*
Trilobites, 308, *308*
Tropical rain forests, *140*, 297, *297*, 318, *320*
Tropics, 140, *140*
Tropisms, **254**–255, *254*, *255*, *act.* 260–261, 263
Trough, wave, 478, *478*, *481*, 493
Tsunami, 482
Tube worms, 439, *439*
Turtles, *283*
Tyrannosaurus rex, 316, *316*

Ultraviolet radiation, 329, *329*, 367
Ultraviolet waves, 506
Uniform mixtures, 404, *404*, 409
Unit analysis, 38
United States

landforms of, *63*
profile of, 64
Unity of life, 303–311, *303*, *304–305*, *306–307*, *308*, *309*, *310*, *311*
Universe, 377
Upwarped mountains, **67**, *67*
Uranus, *338*, *339*, *362*, 364, 365, *365*
Ursa Major, 372, *372*

Valley glaciers, 159, *159*, 161–162, *161*, *164*, *act.* 165
Variables
dependent, **19**, 25
independent, **19**, 25
Vascular plants, **218**
seed, 229, *229*, 239, *239*
seedless, 222–225, *222*, *223*, *224*, *225*, 238
Vent, 441, *441*
Venus, *363*, 367, *367*
distance from sun, 364
surface temperatures on, 367
Vinegar, 97
Visible light, 506
Volcanic mountains, **68**–69, *69*
Volcano(es), 221
eruptions of, 99, *103*
rocks from, 103–105, *103*, *104–105*
Volume, measurement of, 37, 39, *39*, 53, *53*

Waning moon, *358*
Waste
hazardous, **191**–192, 207

Waste disposal, *180–181,* 191–192, *191,* 193

Water vapor

Water
  as abiotic factor, *269,* 270
  algae and, 216, *216*
  boiling point of, 41, *41*
  chemical weathering and, 127, *127, 128,* 137
  elements in, 401, *402*
  erosion by, 150–151, *150*
  formation of, 435, *435*
  freezing point of, 41, *41*
  groundwater, 194
  hydroelectric power from, 418, *418*
  on moon, 349
  moss, 221
  ocean waves, *476,* 477
  plants and, *act.* 243, 229, 244–245, *244, 245,* 247, 248, 262, 263

Water cycle, **286**–287, *286*
  atmosphere and, 286–287, *286*

Water vapor
  in burning, 387–388, *388*
  See also Climate

Wave(s), 474–497, **476,** *476, act.* 494–495
  amplitude of, 481–482, *481,* 493, *493,* 496
  behavior of, *act.* 475, 486–492, *486, 487, 488, 489, 490, 491, 492*
  compressional, **479**–480, *479, 480,* 482, *482, act.* 485, 496
  crest of, 478, *478, 481,* 493
  diffraction of, 488–489, *489,* 497
  electromagnetic, 328–329, *328–329,* **478,** *478,* 482, *482,* 496
  frequency of, 483, *483,* 496

interference and, 490–492, *490, 491, 492, 493, 493,* 497
  light, 482, *482,* 483–484, 486, *486,* 487–488, *487, 489, 489,* 490
  mechanical, 476–**477,** *477,* 496
  microwaves, *328,* 329
  properties of, 481–484, *481, 482, 483,* 496
  radio, *328,* 329
  reflection of, 486, *486,* 490, 497
  refraction of, 487–488, *487, 488,* 497
  sound, 329, 476–477, *477,* 479–480, *479, 480,* 481, 483–484, 488, 489, *489,* 490
  speed of, 483–484, 487–488
  transverse, **478,** *478,* 482, *act.* 485, 496
  trough of, 478, *478, 481,* 493
  water, 477

Wavelength, **482,** *482, 483,* 496, **505,** 528
  hurricanes, 481, *481*
  thunderstorms, 483
  See also Climate

Waxing moon, *358*

Waxy cuticles, 217, *217*

Weather satellites, 337

Weathering, **124**–131
  of chalk, *act.* 130–131
  chemical, **127**–128, *127, 128,* 137, 144, *144*
  climate and, 128–129, *129*
  evidence of, 124, *124*
  mechanical, **125**–126, *125, 126,* 144, *144*
  observing, *act.* 123
  soil types and, 137

Weight, **453,** 456, 470
  measuring, 40, 457

Weightless, 456

Weightlessness, effects of, 346, *348*

Whales, 285, *285*

White Cliffs of Dover, *109*

White light, observing, *act.* 327

Wind, 167–175
  deposition by, 171–173, *171, 172, 173,* 177
  erosion by, 167–171, *167, 168, 169, 170, 171, act.* 174–175, 177

Wind power, 418

Windbreaks, 170, *170*

Wolves, *309*

Wood harvests, 190, *190*

Woodpeckers, 302, *302*

Woody stems, 230

World map, *act.* 61

Worms, *133,* 279, *279,* 441, *441*

X ray, 329, *329, 438,* 478, 482

Xylem, **229,** *229*

Yeast, 250

Yellowstone National Park, *164*

Yucca moth, *278*

Yucca plant, *278*

Zinnias, *257*

Art Credits

Photo Credits

Cover - (tl)Steve Gettle/ENP Images, (tr)Mendola/Jeff Lynch/The Stock Market, (b)Schafer & Hill/Tony Stone Images.

UNIT 1

Chapter 1 - 4-5 Jim Richardson/Corbis Los Angeles; **5** Matt Meadows; **6** Wendell Metzen/Bruce Coleman Inc.; **7** (t)Coco McCoy/Rainbow, (b)Mark Burnett/Photo Researchers; **9** (l)KS Studio, (r)Ted Horowitz/The Stock Market; **10** (l)Latent Image, (r)Morton & White; **11** Bob Daemmrich/Stock Boston; **12** KS Studio; **13** StudiOhio; **15** Geoff Butler; **16** (t)Matthew Borkoski/Stock Boston, (b)Matt Meadows; **19** Morrison Photography; **21** Brent Turner/BLT Productions; **23** (t)Lynn Weinstein/Woodfin Camp & Assoc., (b)Hank Morgan/Rainbow; **24** (t)Coco McCoy/Rainbow, (b)Wendell Metzen/Bruce Coleman Inc.; **24-25** courtesy Amanda Shaw and Focus One.

Chapter 2 - 28-29 Al Bello/Allsport; **29** Matt Meadows; **30** David M. Dennis; **31** (t)Duomo/William R. Sallaz, (b)Scott Cunningham; **32** (l)Doug Martin, (r)StudiOhio; **34** Timothy Fuller; **36** (l)Rockwell/TSADO/Tom Stack & Assoc., (r)courtesy Magellan Corporation; **37** Nicholas DeVore/Tony Stone Images; **38** Biophoto Assoc./Photo Researchers; **39** Fred Bavendam/Tony Stone Images; **40** (tl)Matt Meadows, (bl)NASA/FPG, (r)file photo; **42** Doug Martin; **43** (r)Duomo/Chris Cole, (others)Paul McCormick/The Image Bank; **44** Doug Martin; **45** (t)F. D'Elbee/The Image Bank, (b)Bill Ross/Corbis Los Angeles; **46** (t)Oliver Benn/Tony Stone Images; (b)Lynn M. Stone; **47** Duomo/William Sallaz; **48** KS Studio; **50 51 52** Matt Meadows; **53** (t)Matt Meadows, (b)Doug Martin; **54** David M. Dennis.

UNIT 2

384-385 Photo by Randy Montoya/Sandia National Laboratories; **385** Tony Arruza/Bruce Coleman Inc.

Chapter 3 - 60-61 NASA; **61** StudiOhio; **65** Stephen J. Krasemannn/DRK Photo; **66** Peter French/DRK Photo; **67** Phil Lauro/Profiles West; **68** Daniel D. Lamoreux/Visuals Unlimited; **69** Paul Chesley/Tony Stone Images; **72** Doug Martin; **76** Jeff Gnass; **79** Geographix, Inc.; **83** Matt Meadows; **84** Bob Sacha with Chip Calvin; **85** Matt Meadows; **86** Peter French/DRK Photo; **87** (t)Jeff Gnass, (b)Geographix, Inc.

Chapter 4 - 90-91 Galen Rowell/Mountain Light; **91** Matt Meadows; **92** Morrison Photography; **93** (t)Charles D. Winters/Photo Researchers, (b)Morrison Photography; **94** (t)Morrison Photography, (bl)John Sohlden/Visuals Unlimited, (br)Matt Meadows; **95** (tr)Biophoto Assoc./Photo Researchers, (others)Morrison Photography; **96** Morrison Photography; **98** (t)E.R. Degginger/Bruce Coleman Inc., (b)E.R. Degginger/Color-Pic; **99** Bill Bachman/Photo Researchers; **100** (t)Harvey Lloyd/Peter Arnold Inc., (b)John Cancalosi/Peter Arnold Inc.; **101** (tr)Tim Courlas, (l)Ken Frick, (c)Matt Meadows, (cr)Pictures Unlimited; **102** Adam Woolfitt/Woodfin Camp & Associates; **103** Otto Hahn/Peter Arnold Inc.; **104** (l)E.R. Degginger/Color-Pic, (r)Morrison Photography; **105** (l)Morrison Photography, (r)Breck P. Kent/Earth Scenes; **106** Morrison Photography; **106-107** Jim Corwin/Photo Researchers; **107** (t)Kevin Schafer/Peter Arnold Inc., (bl,br)Morrison Photography; **108** (l)Fred Bavendam/Minden Pictures, (r)Mark Burnett/Photo Researchers; **109** (tl)Alan D. Carey/Photo Researchers, (tr)Mark Burnett/Photo Researchers, (bl)Morrison Photography, (br) E.R. Degginger/Color-Pic; **110 111** Matt Meadows; **112** Darek Karp/Earth Scenes; **113** (l)A.J. Copely/Visuals Unlimited, (r)Phil Degginger/Color-Pic; **114** (tl)Fred Bruemmer/Peter Arnold Inc., (tr)Jerome Wyckoff/Earth Scenes, (c)E.R. Degginger/Color-Pic, (bl)M. Bruce/Color-Pic, (br)Peter Arnold/Peter Arnold Inc.; **115** (l)Al Giddings, (tr)E.R. Degginger/Color-Pic, (br)Jerome Wyckoff/Earth Scenes; **116** Magrath Photography/SPL/Photo Researchers; **117** Matt Meadows; **118** (tr)Studiohio, (others)Morrison Photography; **119** (t)E.R. Degginger/Color-Pic, (c)A.J. Copley/Visuals Unlimited,

(b)Darek Karp/Earth Scenes.

Chapter 5 - 122-123 Henry Georgi/Comstock; **123** Matt Meadows; **124** (l)Larry Roberts, (r)William Silliker/Earth Scenes; **125** StudiOhio; **126** Chuck Wise/Earth Scenes; **127** Tom Bean/DRK Photo; **128** Carr Clifton/Minden Pictures; **129** (l)Henley & Savage/The Stock Market, (r)Tom Stack & Assoc.; **130** Matt Meadows; **134** Rich Buzzelli/Tom Stack & Assoc.; **135** William E. Ferguson; **136** H.R. Bramaz/Peter Arnold Inc.; **137** USDA; **140** (t)Lee Battaglia/Colorific!, (bl)Dr. Morely Read/Science Photo Library/Photo Researchers, (br) S. Michael Bisceglie/Earth Scenes; **141** Larry Lefever from Grant Heilman; **142** Matt Meadows; **143** (l)Bianca Lavies, (r)Paintings by William H. Bond, National Geographic Art Division; **144** Tom Bean/DRK Photo; **145** (t)William E. Ferguson, (b)courtesy Susan Colclazer.

UNIT 3

Chapter 6 - 148-149 Henry Georgi/Comstock; **149** Matt Meadows; **150** Rod Plank/Photo Researchers; **151** Jack Stein Grove/Profiles West; **152** (t)Thomas G. Rampton from Grant Heilman, (b)E.R. Degginger/Color-Pic; **153** Chris Cox; **154** Stephan C. Porter; **155** Tim Crosby/Liaison International; **156** Nigel J.H. Smith/Earth Scenes; **157** A. Ramey/Stock Boston; **159** (t)Wolfgang Kaehler, (b)Cliff Leight; **160** (l)Phil Schermeister/National Geographic Image Collection, (r) Mark Burnett; **161** Cliff Leight; **162** E.R. Degginger/Color-Pic; **163** Grant Heilman Photography; **164** (l)Tom Till, (r)Tom Bean/DRK Photo; **165** Matt Meadows; **166** (l)Science VU/Visuals Unlimited, (r)courtesy the National Archives/Photo-Assist, Inc.; **167** Debbie Dean; **168** (t)Floyd Holdman/The Stock Market, (b)Runk/Schoenberger from Grant Heilman; **170** Mark Boulton/Photo Researchers; **171** Grant Heilman Photography; **172** Jeff Gnass; **174 175** Matt Meadows; **176** A. Ramey/Stock Boston; **177** (t)Cliff Leight, (b)M.J. Cole/Earth Scenes.

Chapter 7 - 180-181 Ray Pfortner/Peter Arnold, Inc.; **181** Mark Burnett; **182** Jon Feingersh/The Stock Market; **184** Matt Meadows; **185** Richard Hutchings; **186** Matt Meadows; **188** (l)Roy Morsch/The Stock Market, (r)Michael Ableman; **189** (t)Jim Wark/Peter Arnold, Inc., (b)Larry Lefever from Grant Heilman; **190** Frans Lanting/Minden Pictures; **193** Mark Burnett; **194** Rick Iwasaki/Tony Stone Images; **195** Jack Dykinga; **198** (l,r)Kenji Kerins, (c)file photo; **200** Matt Meadows; **201** (l)ARS-Banuelos, (r)Nigel Cattlin/Holt Studios International/Photo Researchers; **202** KS Studio; **202-205** file photo; **203** file photos; **204** (tl)Telegraph Colour Library/FPG International, (tr)Hank Morgan/Science Source/Photo Researchers, (bl)file photo, (br)Jose Fuste Raga/The Stock Market; **205** (tl)Mark Burnett, (tr, bl, br)file photos; **206** (l)Jon Feingersh/The Stock Market, (r)Richard Hutchings; **207** (t)Rick Isasaki/Tony Stone Images, (b)Kenji Kerins.

Chapter 8 - 212-213 Aaron Haupt; **213** file photo; **214** Michael P. Gadomski/Photo Researchers; **215** (t)Jan Hirsch/Science Photo Library/Photo Researchers,(b)Doug Sokell/Visuals Unlimited, (l)Pat O'Hara/DRK Photo, (r)John Shaw/Tom Stack & Associates; **217** (l)Runk/Schoenberger from Grant Heilman, (c)Harold Hofman/Photo Researchers, (r)Kevin Schafer/Peter Arnold, Inc.; **218** David Cavagnaro/DRK Photo; **220** (l)John Kaprielian/Photo Researchers, (r)Barry L. Runk from Grant Heilman; **221** Kevin Schafer/Peter Arnold, Inc.; **222** (tr)Jane Grushow from Grant Heilman, (c)Stephen J. Krasemann/Photo Researchers, (l)Rod Planck/Photo Researchers, (br)David S. Addison/Visuals Unlimited; **223** (t)Runk/Schoenberger from Grant Heilman, (c)Sydney Karp/Photos/NATS, (b)Richard L. Carton/Photo Researchers; **224** Walter H. Hodge/Peter Arnold, Inc.; **225** Ludek Pesek/Science Photo Library/Photo Researchers; **226** Aaron Haupt; **227** (l)John D. Cunningham/Visuals Unlimited, (r)Ira Block, Courtesy Silkeborg Museum, Denmark; **228** Jeff Greenberg/Visuals Unlimited; **230** Runk Schoenberger from Grant Heilman; **232** (l)Richard Shiel/Earth Scenes, (r)Kenneth W.

PERIODIC TABLE OF THE ELEMENTS

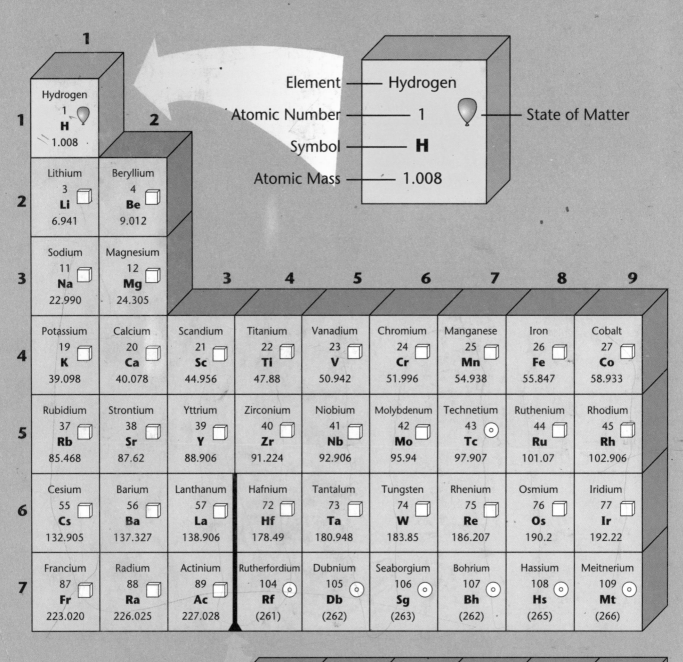

Element — Hydrogen

Atomic Number — 1 — State of Matter

Symbol — **H**

Atomic Mass — 1.008